BENCHMARK Series

MICROSOFT®
EXCEL 2000

CORE AND EXPERT CERTIFICATION

NITA RUTKOSKY
Pierce College at Puyallup
Puyallup, Washington

MEREDITH FLYNN
Bowling Green State University
Bowling Green, Ohio

MICROSOFT OFFICE
Microsoft®
OFFICE
USER SPECIALIST

APPROVED COURSEWARE

EMCParadigm

Senior Editor	Sonja M. Brown
Developmental Editor	Tom Modl
Cover Designer	Chris Vern Johnson
Art Director	Joan D'Onofrio
Text Designer	Jennifer Wreisner
Desktop Production Specialists	Leslie Anderson, Michelle Lewis, Julie Hansen, Desktop Solutions
Tester	Nancy Sauro
Indexer	Tina Trettin

Publishing Team—George Provol, Publisher; Janice Johnson, Director of Product Development; Lori Landwer, Marketing Manager; Shelley Clubb, Electronic Design and Production Manager.

Registered Trademarks—Microsoft, Windows, PowerPoint, Outlook, and the MOUS icon are registered trademarks of Microsoft Corporation in the United States and other countries. IBM is a registered trademark of IBM Corporation.

Acknowledgments—The author and publisher wish to thank the following reviewers for their technical and academic assistance: Debra Griggs, Bellevue Community College, Bellevue, Washington; Debra Mecham Moore, Cuesta Community College, San Luis Obispo, California; and Janet Sheppard, Collin County Community College, Plano, Texas.

We also wish to thank Denise Senguin, Fanshawe College, London, Ontario, for adapting portions of this text.

Library of Congress Cataloging-in-Publication Data
Rutkosky, Nita Hewitt.
    Microsoft Excel 2000 / Nita Rutkosky, Meredith Flynn.
        p.   cm.
    Includes index.
    ISBN 0-7638-0236-0 (text + CD-ROM)
    1. Microsoft Excel for Windows. 2. Business—Computer programs.
3. Electronic spreadsheets.   I. Title.
HF5548.4.M523R88   1999
005.369—dc21   99-32091
                                                CIP

Text + CD: ISBN 0-7638-0236-0
Order Number 04332

© 2000 by Paradigm Publishing Inc.
    Published by **EMC**Paradigm
    875 Montreal Way
    St. Paul, MN 55102
    (800) 535-6865
    E-mail: **educate@emcp.com**
    Web Site: www.emcp.com

Printed in the United States of America

10   9   8   7   6   5   4

Contents

Excel 2000
Expert Level   Expert E-1

Page numbers include "Expert E" to denote Microsoft Office User Specialist (MOUS) Expert Certification for Excel 2000 throughout this section.

Introduction

Most new personal computers in the marketplace today are preloaded with the Microsoft®
Windows® operating system or with Windows-based applications such as Microsoft Office 2000.
This popular suite of programs includes Word, Excel, Access, PowerPoint, and additional
applications in certain editions.

In this textbook, students build upon their basic knowledge of Excel 2000. They learn the
basic, intermediate, and advanced features of Excel, as well as ways in which this program interacts
with Windows and the Internet.

Students need some prior computer experience and familiarity with using Windows in order to
use this textbook. Additionally, knowledge of basic high school freshman mathematics is required.

Approved Courseware for the Microsoft Office User Specialist (MOUS) Program

The logo on the cover of this text means that Microsoft has approved this text as courseware that
teaches all of the skills that students need to master to pass the Core Certification exam and/or
Expert Certification exam in Excel 2000. These skills and the corresponding page numbers of
related instruction in the text are listed on the page that precedes chapter 1 of each level.

The MOUS program is used to test and validate a student's skills and thereby supply objective
proof to an employer or prospective employer that the student knows how to use a program efficiently
and productively. For more information on the MOUS program and where to take the certification
exam, visit Microsoft's Web site at *www.microsoft.com* or the specific MOUS site at *www.mous.net*.

Focus on Certification

The Excel 2000 Core Level covers how to present, manipulate, and calculate numerical data in
Excel worksheets. They will also learn how to present the data more visually by charting it.
Integrated topics include inserting clip art images in Word documents and Excel worksheets, and
creating maps with Excel data.

The Excel 2000 Expert Level covers formatting worksheets with advanced techniques; working with
templates and workbooks; using advanced spreadsheet functions; working with lists and analysis
tools in Excel; managing and auditing worksheets; and collaborating with workgroups. The
integrated topic involves combining Word and Excel files for the Internet.

Chapter Structure
Each chapter contains the following sections:

- Performance Objectives that identify the specific learning goals of the chapter.
- Introductory material that provides an overview of new concepts and features.
- Step-by-step exercises at the computer, which allow students to practice using the
  features(s) presented in the chapter.
- Chapter Summary.
- Commands Review.
- Thinking Offline, a short-answer, knowledge self-check.
- Working Hands-On, skill assessments that require students to complete
  exercises without step-by-step instructions; this section includes an
  exercise that requires use of the Help feature as indicated by an icon.

Additional simulation exercises called Performance Assessments at the end of each level require students to make decisions about document preparation and formatting. These applied exercises provide ample opportunity to practice new features as well as previously learned features. The Writing Activities offer students the opportunity to write and format business documents. In addition, there is an Internet Activity in which students explore the Internet and use Excel or another Office application to report on the information that they discover. In this section, students demonstrate problem-solving, critical-thinking, and creative-thinking abilities as well as hands-on computer skills.

Completing Computer Exercises

Some computer exercises in the chapters require the student to access and use an existing file. Exercise files are available on the CD-ROM that accompanies this textbook. The files for each chapter are saved in individual folders named for the chapters in which they are used, as indicated by a CD icon and chapter folder name on the first page of each chapter. The folders are grouped into two larger folders: Excel Core Student Files and Excel Expert Student Files.

Chapter 01E

Before beginning a chapter, the student should copy the folder from the CD-ROM to a preformatted data disk. After completing the exercises in a chapter, the student should delete the chapter folder to ensure adequate storage space for the next chapter's files. Students should check with the instructor first, however. The inside back cover provides detailed instructions on how to copy and delete folders.

Industry Standards from the SCANS Commission

This textbook covers the important goals of the Secretary's Commission on Achieving Necessary Skills (SCANS), a joint commission from the Department of Education and Labor. The overall goal of the commission was to establish interdisciplinary standards that should be required for all students. SCANS skill standards emphasize the integration of competencies from the areas of information gathering and research, technology, basic skills, and thinking skills.

In addition, all educators agree that curricula can be strengthened by classroom work that is authentic and relevant to learners, i.e., classroom work that connects context to content. Teaching in context helps students move away from a subject-specific orientation to an integrative learning that includes decision making, problem solving, and critical thinking. The concepts and applications material in each level of this book is designed to reflect an interdisciplinary emphasis, as well as implement the SCANS standards. SCANS places heavy emphasis on communication skills as well as on activity planning and follow-through, each of which is part of chapter and level exercises wherever appropriate.

Examples of context-relative and SCANS-related work are found in the chapter skill assessments called Working Hands-On, which reinforce acquired technical skills while providing practice in decision making and problem solving. Other examples, in the Performance Assessments sections, offer simulations that require students to demonstrate their understanding of the major skills and technical features within a framework of critical and creative thinking. The Writing Activities toward the end of each level make it clear that students are not just producers, but editors and writers as well.

Emphasis on Visual Learning

Microsoft Office programs such as Excel operate within the Windows operating system, a graphical user interface (GUI) that provides a visually oriented environment by using icons to represent program features. This textbook also emphasizes a graphical environment with icons that represent specific learning components. For example, figures that illustrate numerous steps done at the computer are labeled with "bubble" callouts corresponding to the steps. The student can easily follow the steps by seeing the exact spot on the computer screen where a certain action is required on their part.

Icons offer additional visual learning cues. A computer icon 🐾 appears next to Performance Assessments, a hands-on-keyboard icon 🖮 identifies the Writing Activities at the end of each level, and a globe icon 🌐 displays next to the Internet Activity at the end of each level.

Upon completion of the course, students will have mastered the basic and intermediate features (Core Level MOUS skills) and/or advanced features (Expert Level MOUS skills) of Excel 2000. They also will have practiced some basic skills in using Windows and acquired a solid foundation in the problem-solving and communication competencies so important in the contemporary workplace.

Learning Components that Accompany This Text

The following products for instructors and students correspond to this text and enhance its teaching possibilities. These products may be ordered by contacting an EMC/Paradigm Publishing Customer Care representative by phone at (800) 535-6865 or via E-mail at *educate@emcp.com* and supplying the order number as follows:

Textbook Web site at *www.emcp.com*. Watch for updates, tips, and instructional activities for students and instructors at the text's Resource Center link.

Microsoft® Excel 2000 Instructor's Guide with CD-ROM, Order Number 02332. The Instructor's Guide contains a suggested course syllabi, grade sheets, and assignment sheets for Core and Expert Levels; comprehensive Excel tests and answers to use as final exams; Supplemental Performance Assessments; and a list of PowerPoint slides available on the CD. For each chapter, the Instructor's Guide also provides a summary of chapter contents, Teaching Hints, Thinking Offline answers, and Working Hands-On model answers for all exercises. The Instructor's CD-ROM contains everything found in the print Instructor's Guide plus model answer files for all exercises and PowerPoint slides for classroom use.

Microsoft® Excel 2000 Test Generator, Order Number 59332. The Paradigm Test Generator is a full featured test-creation program that offers instructors a wide variety of options for generating and editing tests. Instructors can create custom tests that include questions from the existing test banks or insert new questions. The test bank provided on this disk offers more than 1,300 questions that range in difficulty and discrimination levels. All of the standard question types plus graphic and procedure-oriented items are included.

onCourse Excel 2000 Web Site. onCourse is a program that allows instructors to create a personalized Web site for the course easily and quickly. Available on a CD-ROM, the onCourse program offers self-study quizzes for students, lecture notes, study aids, Internet links, and a discussion forum tool. To facilitate instructor's Web site development, course information is already included. Instructors can easily add information or change any of the information on the template to directly match the exact needs for a particular course.

Excel

CORE LEVEL

MICROSOFT® EXCEL 2000

CORE LEVEL MOUS SKILLS

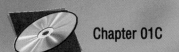 Chapter 01C

Preparing and Formatting an Excel Worksheet

PERFORMANCE OBJECTIVES

Upon successful completion of chapter 1, you will be able to:

- Identify the various elements of an Excel worksheet.
- Create, save, and print a worksheet.
- Enter data in a worksheet.
- Edit data in a worksheet.
- Select cells in a worksheet.
- Apply formatting to data in cells.
- Change column widths and row heights.
- Format numbers in a worksheet.
- Add borders, shading, and patterns to cells in a worksheet.
- Apply an autoformat to selected cells in a worksheet.
- Use the Help feature.

Many companies use a spreadsheet for numerical and financial data and to analyze and evaluate information. An Excel spreadsheet can be used for activities such as creating financial statements, preparing budgets, managing inventory, and analyzing cash flow. In addition, numbers and values can be easily manipulated to create "what if" situations. For example, using a spreadsheet, a person in a company can ask questions such as "What if the value in this category is decreased?" "How would that change affect the department budget?" Questions like these can be easily answered in an Excel spreadsheet. Change the value in a category and Excel will recalculate formulas for the other values. In this way, a spreadsheet can be used not only for creating financial statements or budgets but also as a planning tool.

Creating a Worksheet

Open Excel by clicking the Start button at the left side of the Taskbar, pointing to Programs, and then clicking *Microsoft Excel*. When Excel is opened, you are presented with a blank worksheet in a screen like the one shown in figure 1.1. The elements of a blank Excel worksheet are described in figure 1.2.

On your screen, the Standard and Formatting toolbars may display side by side with only a portion of the buttons visible. If this is the case, move the Formatting toolbar below the Standard toolbar by completing the following steps:

1. Click Tools and then Customize.
2. At the Customize dialog box, click the Options tab. (Skip this step if the Options tab is already selected.)
3. Click the Standard and Formatting toolbars share one row option. (This removes the check mark.)
4. Click the Close button to close the dialog box.

The display of the Standard and Formatting toolbars (as well as other toolbars) can be turned on or off. To do this, position the mouse pointer anywhere on a toolbar, and then click the *right* mouse button. At the drop-down menu that displays, click the toolbar name you want turned on or off. You can also turn on or off the display of a toolbar by clicking View on the Menu bar, pointing to Toolbars, and then clicking the toolbar name.

figure 1.1

Blank Excel Worksheet

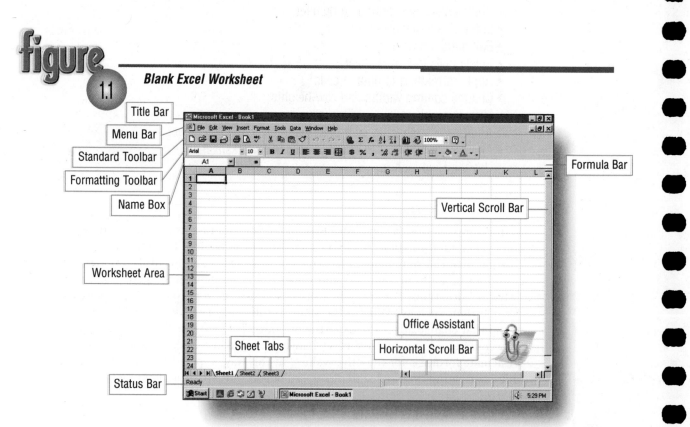

figure 1.2

Elements of an Excel Worksheet

Title bar:	The Title bar displays the name of the program along with the name of a workbook. The buttons at the far right side of the Title bar can be used to minimize, restore, or close Excel.
Menu bar:	Excel commands are grouped into related functions and placed on the Menu bar. For example, options for formatting cells, rows, or columns are grouped in the Format option on the Menu bar.
Standard toolbar:	Icons for the most common commands in Excel are placed on the Standard toolbar.
Formatting toolbar:	Functions that are used to format elements of a worksheet are placed on buttons on the Formatting toolbar.
Name box:	The cell address, also called the cell reference, displays in the Name box and includes the column letter and row number.
Formula bar:	The Formula bar provides information about the active cell. Formulas can be entered and edited in the Formula bar.
Sheet tabs:	The sheet tabs identify the current worksheet. The tab for the active worksheet displays with a white background while the inactive worksheets display with a gray background (the background color may vary depending on the Windows color scheme).
Scroll bars:	A vertical scroll bar displays at the right side of the worksheet, and a horizontal scroll bar displays at the bottom of the Worksheet. These scroll bars are used to navigate within a worksheet.
Status bar:	The Status bar is located below the horizontal scroll bar and displays information about the worksheet and the currently active cell.
Worksheet area:	The worksheet area is a collection of cells where information such as labels, values, or formulas is entered. A cell is an intersection between a row and a column.

A document created in Excel is referred to as a *workbook*. An Excel workbook consists of individual worksheets (or *sheets*) like the sheets of paper in a notebook. Notice the tabs located toward the bottom of the Excel window that are named *Sheet1*, *Sheet2*, and so on. The area containing the gridlines in the Excel window is called the *worksheet area*. Figure 1.3 identifies the elements of the worksheet area. Create a worksheet in the worksheet area that will be saved as part of a workbook. Columns in a worksheet are labeled with letters of the alphabet, and rows are numbered.

figure
1.3

Elements of a Worksheet Area

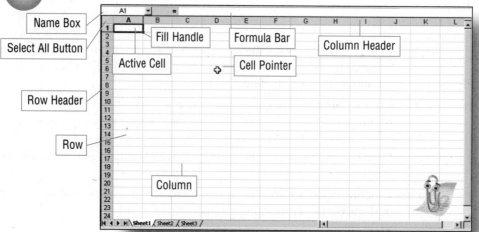

The gray vertical and horizontal lines that define the cells in the worksheet area are called *gridlines*. When the insertion point (which displays as a thick white plus sign) is positioned in a cell, the *cell address*, also called the *cell reference*, displays at the left side of the Formula bar in what is called the *Name box*. The cell reference includes the column letter and row number. For example, if the insertion point is positioned in the first cell of the worksheet, the cell reference *A1* displays in the Name box located at the left side of the Formula bar. In a worksheet, the cell containing the insertion point is considered the *active cell*. The active cell is surrounded by a thick black border.

To make a cell active, position the cell pointer in the cell, and then click the left mouse button.

Entering Data in a Cell

Enter data such as a heading, number, or value, in a cell. To enter data in a cell, make the desired cell active, and then key the data. To move the insertion point to the next cell in the worksheet, press the Tab key. Other commands for moving the insertion point within a worksheet are displayed in figure 1.4.

figure
1.4

Commands for Moving Insertion Point in a Worksheet

To move the insertion point here	Press
Down to the next cell	Enter
Up to the next cell	Shift + Enter
Next cell	Tab
Previous cell	Shift + Tab
Cell at beginning of row	Home
Next cell in the direction of the arrow	Up, down, left, or right arrow keys
Last cell in worksheet	Ctrl + End

First cell in worksheet	Ctrl + Home
Cell in next window (approximately 16-24 rows)	Page Down
Cell in previous window (approximately 16-24 rows)	Page Up
Cell in window to right (approximately 8-11 columns)	Alt + Page Down
Cell in window to left (approximately 8-11 columns)	Alt + Page Up

Another method for moving the insertion point to a specific cell is to use the Go To feature. To use this feature, click Edit and then Go To. At the Go To dialog box, key the cell reference in the Reference text box, and then click OK.

When you are ready to key data into the active cell, check the Status bar. The word *Ready* should display at the left side. As data is being keyed in the cell, the word *Ready* changes to *Enter*. Data being keyed in a cell displays in the cell as well as in the Formula bar. If the data being keyed is longer than the cell can accommodate, the data overlaps the next cell to the right (it does not become a part of the next cell—it simply overlaps it). You will learn how to change column widths to accommodate data later in this chapter.

If the data you enter in a cell consists of text and the text does not fit into the cell, it overlaps the next cell. If, however, you enter a number in a cell, specify it as a number (rather than text) and the number is too long to fit in the cell, Excel changes the display in the cell to number symbols *(###)*. This is because Excel does not want you to be misled by a number when you see only a portion of it in the cell.

In addition to moving the insertion point with the keyboard, you can also move it using the mouse. To make a specific cell active with the mouse, position the mouse pointer, which displays as a white plus sign (called the *cell pointer*), on the desired cell, and then click the left mouse button. The cell pointer displays as a white plus sign when positioned in a cell in the worksheet and displays as an arrow pointer when positioned on other elements of the Excel window such as toolbars or scroll bars.

Scroll through a worksheet using the vertical and/or horizontal scroll bars. Scrolling shifts the display of cells in the worksheet area but does not change the active cell. Scroll through a worksheet until the desired cell is visible and then click the desired cell.

Using Automatic Entering Features

Excel contains several features that help you enter data into cells quickly and efficiently. These features include *AutoComplete*, which automatically inserts data in a cell that begins the same as a previous entry; *AutoCorrect*, which automatically corrects many common typographical errors; and *AutoFill*, which will automatically insert words, numbers, or formulas in a series.

Use the Go To dialog box to move to a specific cell.

If a cell entry displays as ##### or as a scientific notation (such as 2.35E+08), the column width is too narrow to display the entire entry.

Drag the vertical scroll box in a worksheet and row numbers display in a yellow box. Drag the horizontal scroll box and column letters display.

The AutoComplete feature will automatically insert data in a cell that begins the same as a previous entry. For example, in exercise 1, you will key the name *Roger Bellamy* in a cell. Later you will key the name *Robert Jorgenson* in a cell. As you key the *R* in *Robert*, the AutoComplete feature will automatically insert *Roger Bellamy*. Since this is not the data you want in the cell, simply continue keying the correct name and it will take the place of the data inserted by AutoComplete. This feature can be very useful in a worksheet that contains repetitive data entries. For example, consider a worksheet that repeats the word *Payroll*. The second and subsequent times this word is to be inserted in a cell, simply keying the letter *P* will cause AutoComplete to insert the entire word.

The AutoCorrect feature automatically corrects many common typing (keying) errors. To see what symbols and words are in the AutoCorrect feature, click <u>T</u>ools and then <u>A</u>utoCorrect. This displays the AutoCorrect dialog box shown in figure 1.5 with a list box containing the replacement data.

figure
1.5

AutoCorrect Dialog Box

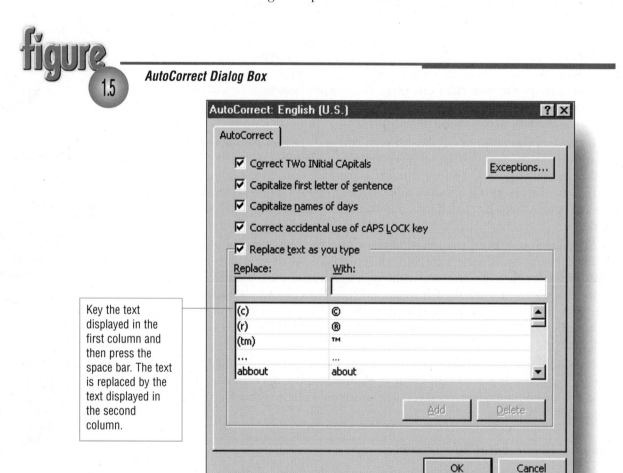

Key the text displayed in the first column and then press the space bar. The text is replaced by the text displayed in the second column.

At the AutoCorrect dialog box, key the text shown in the first column in the list box, and the text in the second column is inserted in the cell. Along with symbols, the AutoCorrect dialog box contains commonly misspelled words and common typographical errors. The AutoCorrect feature is a helpful tool when entering text in cells.

When a cell is active, it is surrounded by a thick, black border. A small, black square is located at the bottom right side of this border. This black square is called the AutoFill *fill handle* (see figure 1.3). With the fill handle, you can quickly fill a range of cells with the same data or with consecutive data. For example, suppose you need to insert the year 2000 in consecutive cells. To do this quickly, key 2000 in the first cell, position the mouse pointer on the fill handle, hold down the left mouse button, drag across the cells where you want the year inserted, and then release the mouse button.

You can also use the AutoFill fill handle to insert a series in consecutive cells. For example, suppose you are creating a worksheet with data for all the months in the year. Key **January** in the first cell, position the mouse pointer on the fill handle, hold down the left mouse button, drag down or across to 11 more cells, and then release the mouse button. Excel automatically inserts the other eleven months in the year in the proper order. When using the fill handle, the cells must be adjacent. Figure 1.6 identifies the sequence inserted in cells by Excel when specific data is entered.

AutoFill Fill Handle Series

Enter this data	And the AutoFill fill handle will insert this sequence in adjacent cells
(Commas represent data in separate cells.)	
January	February, March, April, etc...
Jan	Feb, Mar, Apr, etc...
Jan 98, Jan 99	Jan-98, Jan-99, Jan-00, Jan-01, etc...
Monday	Tuesday, Wednesday, Thursday, etc...
Product 1	Product 2, Product 3, Product 4, etc...
Qtr 1	Qtr 2, Qtr 3, Qtr 4
2, 4	6, 8, 10, etc...

Certain sequences, such as *2, 4* and *Jan 98, Jan 99* require that both cells be selected before using the fill handle. If only the cell containing *2* is active, the fill handle will insert *2*s in the selected cells. The list in figure 1.6 is only a sampling of what the AutoFill fill handle can do. You may find a variety of other sequences that can be inserted in a worksheet using the AutoFill fill handle.

If you do not want a series to increment, hold down the Ctrl key while dragging the fill handle.

Editing Data in a Cell

Edit data being keyed in a cell by pressing the Backspace key to delete the character left of the insertion point or pressing the Delete key to delete the character to the right of the insertion point. To change the data in a cell, click the cell once to make it active, and then key the new data. When a cell containing data is active, anything keyed will take the place of the existing data. If you want to edit only a portion of the data in a cell, double-click the cell. This makes the cell active, moves the insertion point inside the cell, and displays the word *Edit* at the left side of the Status bar. Move the insertion point using the arrow keys or the mouse and then make the needed corrections. If you are using the keyboard, you can press the Home key to move the insertion point to the first character in the cell or Formula bar, or press the End key to move the insertion point to the last character.

When you are done editing the data in the cell, be sure to change out of the *Edit* mode. To do this, make another cell active. You can do this by pressing Enter, Tab, or Shift + Tab. You can also change out of the *Edit* mode and return to the *Ready* mode by clicking another cell or the Enter button on the Formula bar.

If the active cell does not contain data, the Formula bar displays only the cell reference (by column letter and row number). As data is being keyed in a cell, the two buttons shown in figure 1.7 display on the Formula bar to the right of the name box. Click the Cancel button to delete the current cell entry. You can also delete the cell entry by pressing the Esc key. Click the Enter button to indicate that you are done keying or editing the cell entry. When you click the Enter button on the Formula bar, the word *Enter* (or *Edit*) located at the left side of the Status bar changes to *Ready*.

Enter

Cancel

1.7

Buttons on the Formula Bar

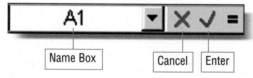

Name Box   Cancel   Enter

Saving a Workbook

Save

Ctrl + S is the keyboard command to display the Save As dialog box.

Save an Excel workbook, which may consist of a worksheet or several worksheets, by clicking the Save button on the Standard toolbar or clicking <u>F</u>ile and then <u>S</u>ave. At the Save As dialog box, key a name for the workbook in the File <u>n</u>ame list box, and then press Enter or click <u>S</u>ave. A workbook file name can contain up to 255 characters, including drive letter and any folder names, and can include spaces. Some symbols cannot be used in a file name.

Filenames cannot include any of the following characters:

forward slash (/)	question mark (?)
backslash (\)	quotation mark (")
greater than sign (>)	colon (:)
less than sign (<)	semicolon (;)
asterisk (*)	pipe symbol (|)

To save an Excel workbook onto a disk, change to drive A (or the drive where the disk is located) before saving the workbook. You can do this at the Save As dialog box by clicking the down-pointing triangle at the right side of the Save <u>i</u>n text box and then clicking *3½ Floppy (A:)* at the drop-down menu.

Saving an Excel Workbook as a Web Page

An Excel workbook can be saved in HTML format and made available for publishing on the Internet or on an intranet. The advantage to saving an Excel workbook as a Web page is that users can have access to the workbook data without having Excel installed. All a user needs to view the Excel Web page is a Web browser and access to the Internet or an intranet.

To save an Excel workbook as a Web page, open the desired workbook, then click File, and then Save as Web Page. At the Save As dialog box, key a name for the Excel Web page and then press Enter or click Save.

Open

Ctrl + O is the keyboard command to display the Open dialog box.

Opening a Workbook

Open an Excel workbook by displaying the Open dialog box and then double-clicking the desired workbook name. Display the Open dialog box by clicking the Open button on the Standard toolbar or by clicking File and then Open.

Printing a Workbook

To print an Excel workbook, open the workbook you want printed, and then click the Print button on the Standard toolbar. This prints the active worksheet in the workbook. If you want more control over printing, click File and then Print to display the Print dialog box shown in figure 1.8.

Print

Ctrl + P is the keyboard command to display the Print dialog box.

Print Dialog Box

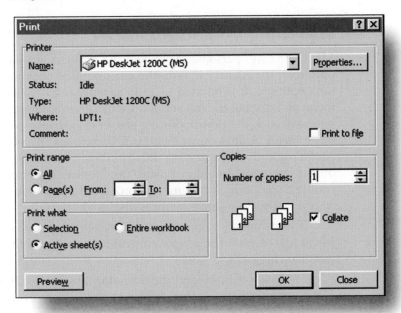

At the Print dialog box, the currently selected printer name displays in the Name text box. If other printers are installed, click the down-pointing triangle at the right side of the Name text box to display a list of printers.

The Active sheet(s) option in the Print what section is selected by default. At this setting, the currently active worksheet will print. If you want to print an entire workbook that contains several worksheets, click Entire workbook in the Print what section. Click the Selection option in the Print what section to print the currently selected cells.

If you want more than one copy of a worksheet or workbook printed, change to the desired number of copies with the Number of copies option in the Copies section. If you want the copies printed collated, make sure there is a check mark in the Collate check box in the Copies section.

A worksheet within a workbook can contain more than one page. If you want to print specific pages of a worksheet within a workbook, click Page(s) in the Print range section, and then specify the desired page numbers in the From and To text boxes.

If you want to preview the worksheet before printing, click the Preview button that displays at the bottom left corner of the dialog box. This displays the worksheet as it will appear on the printed page. After viewing the worksheet, click the Close button that displays toward the top of the Preview screen.

Closing a Workbook and Exiting Excel

Close

To close an Excel workbook, click the Close button that displays at the right side of the Menu bar (the second Close button from the top) or click File and then Close. To exit Excel, click the Close button that displays at the right side of the Title bar (the first Close button from the top) or click File and then Exit. You can also exit Excel by double-clicking the Excel icon that displays at the left side of the Menu bar.

Expanding Drop-Down Menus

Microsoft Excel personalizes menus and toolbars as you work. When you click an option on the Menu bar, only the most popular options display (considered first-rank options). It is referred to as an *adaptive menu*. To expand the drop-down menu and display the full set of options (first-rank options as well as second-rank options), click the down-pointing arrows that display at the bottom of the drop-down menu. A drop-down menu will also expand if you click an option on the Menu bar and then pause on the menu for a few seconds. Second-rank options on the expanded drop-down menu display with a lighter gray background. If you choose a second-rank option, it is promoted and becomes a first-rank option the next time the drop-down menu is displayed.

If you want all menu options displayed when you click an option on the Menu bar, turn off the adaptive menu feature. To do this, you would complete the following steps:

1. Click Tools, expand the drop-down menu by clicking the down-pointing arrows that display at the bottom of the menu, and then click Customize.
2. At the Customize dialog box, click the Options tab.

3. At the Customize dialog box with the Options tab selected, click in the Menus show recently used commands first check box to remove the check mark.
4. Click the Close button to close the dialog box.

In this textbook, you will not be instructed to expand the drop-down menu. If you do not see a specified option, click the down-pointing arrow that display at the bottom of the menu to expand it. Or, consider turning off the adaptive menu feature to display all menu options.

Completing Computer Exercises

At the end of sections within chapters and at the end of chapters, you will be completing hands-on exercises at the computer. These exercises will provide you with the opportunity to practice the presented functions and commands. The skill assessment exercises at the end of each chapter include general directions. If you do not remember how to perform a particular function, refer to the text in the chapter.

Copying Data Documents

In several exercises in each chapter, you will be opening documents provided with this textbook. Before beginning each chapter, copy the chapter folder from the CD that accompanies this textbook to a floppy disk (or other folder). Steps on how to copy a folder from the CD to your floppy disk are printed on the back cover of this textbook.

Changing the Default Folder

At the end of this and the remaining chapters in the textbook, you will be saving documents. More than likely, you will want to save documents onto a disk. You will also be opening documents that have been saved on your disk.

To save documents on and open documents from your disk, you will need to specify the drive where your disk is located as the default folder. Once you specify the drive where your disk is located, Excel uses it as the default folder until you exit the Excel program. The next time you open Excel, you will again need to specify the drive where your disk is located. You only need to change the default folder once each time you enter the Excel program.

You can change the default folder at the Open dialog box or the Save As dialog box. To change the folder to the *Chapter 01C* folder on the disk in drive A at the Open dialog box, you would complete the following steps:

1. Click the Open button on the Standard toolbar (the second button from the left); or click File and then Open.
2. At the Open dialog box, click the down-pointing triangle at the right side of the Look in: text box.
3. From the drop-down list that displays, click *3½ Floppy (A:)*.
4. Double-click Chapter 01C that displays in the list box.
5. Click the Cancel button in the lower right corner of the dialog box.

If you want to change the default folder permanently, make the change at the Options dialog box with the General tab selected. To permanently change the default folder to drive A:, you would complete these steps:

1. Click Tools and then Options.
2. At the Options dialog box, click the General tab.
3. At the Options dialog box with the General tab selected, select the current text in the Default file location text box, and then key **A:**.
4. Click the OK button.

Creating a Worksheet

1. Open Excel by completing the following steps:
   a. At the Windows desktop, click the Start button that displays at the left side of the Taskbar.
   b. At the pop-up menu that displays, point to Programs.
   c. At the next pop-up menu that displays, click *Microsoft Excel*.
2. At the Excel worksheet that displays, create the worksheet shown in figure 1.9 by completing the following steps:
   a. With cell A1 the active cell (displays with a thick black border), key **Name**.
   b. Press the Tab key (to make cell B1 the active cell).
   c. Key **Hours** and then press the Tab key. (This makes cell C1 the active cell).
   d. Key **Rate** and then press Enter to move the insertion point to cell A2.
   e. With A2 the active cell, key the name **Avery**.
   f. Continue keying the data shown in figure 1.9. Key the dollar signs as shown in the figure. Use the Tab key to move to the next cell in the row, press Shift + Tab to move to the previous cell in the row, or press the Enter key to move down a row to the cell at the left margin. (For other commands for moving the insertion point, refer to figure 1.4.)
3. After keying the data shown in the cells in figure 1.9, save the worksheet by completing the following steps:
   a. Click the Save button on the Standard toolbar.
   b. At the Save As dialog box, make the drive where your disk is located the active drive, and the *Chapter 01C* folder the active folder, and then key **Excel C1, Ex 01** in the File name text box.
   c. Press Enter or click the Save button.
4. Print Excel C1, Ex 01 by clicking the Print button on the Standard toolbar. (The gridlines will not print.)
5. Close Excel C1, Ex 01.

Exercise 1

	A	B	C	D
1	Name	Hours	Rate	
2	Avery	45	$19.50	
3	Connors	35	$18.75	
4	Estrada	24	$15.00	
5	Juergens	24	$17.50	
6	Mikulich	20	$15.25	
7	Talbot	15	$10.00	
8				

Selecting Cells

Cells within a worksheet can be formatted in a variety of ways. For example, the alignment of data in cells or rows can be changed or character formatting can be added. To identify the cells that are to be affected by the formatting, the specific cells need to be selected.

Selecting Cells Using the Mouse

Select specific cells in a worksheet using the mouse or select columns or rows. Methods for selecting cells using the mouse display in figure 1.10.

Selecting with the Mouse

To select this	Do this
Column	Position the cell pointer on the column header (a letter) and then click the left mouse button.
Row	Position the cell pointer on the row header (a number) and then click the left mouse button.
Adjacent cells	Drag with mouse to select specific cells.
Nonadjacent cells	Hold down the Ctrl key while clicking column header, row header, or specific cells.
All cells in worksheet	Click the Select All button (refer to figure 1.3).

Selected cells, except the active cell, display with a light blue background (this may vary) rather than a white background. The active cell is the first cell in the selection block and displays in the normal manner (white background with black data). Selected cells remain selected until you click a cell with the mouse or press an arrow key on the keyboard.

Selecting Cells Using the Keyboard

The keyboard can be used to select specific cells within a worksheet. Figure 1.11 displays the commands for selecting specific cells.

figure

1.11

Selecting Cells Using the Keyboard

To select	Press
Cells in direction of arrow key	Shift + arrow key
To beginning of row	Shift + Home
To beginning of worksheet	Shift + Ctrl + Home
To last cell in worksheet containing data	Shift + Ctrl + End
An entire column	Ctrl + spacebar
An entire row	Shift + spacebar
Entire worksheet	Ctrl + A or Ctrl + Shift + spacebar

Selecting Data within Cells

The selection commands presented select the entire cell. You can also select specific characters within a cell. To do this with the mouse, position the cell pointer in the desired cell, and then double-click the left mouse button. Drag with the I-beam pointer through the data you want selected. If you are using the keyboard, hold down the Shift key, and then press the arrow key that moves the insertion point in the desired direction. Data the insertion point passes through will be selected. You can also press F8 to turn on the Extend mode, move the insertion point in the desired direction to select the data, and then press F8 to turn off the Extend mode.

Applying Formatting with Buttons on the Formatting Toolbar

A variety of formatting can be applied to cells in a worksheet using buttons on the Formatting toolbar. With buttons on the Formatting toolbar shown in figure 1.12, you can change the font and font size and bold, italicize, and underline data in cells. To apply bold to a cell or selected cells, click the Bold button on the Formatting toolbar; click the Italic button to apply italics; and click the Underline button to apply underlining formatting.

With other buttons on the Formatting toolbar, you can change the alignment of text within cells, increase or decrease the number of digits after a decimal point, increase or decrease indents, change the cell border, add fill color to a cell, and change text color.

B
Bold

I
Italic

<u>U</u>
Underline

figure 1.12

Formatting Toolbar

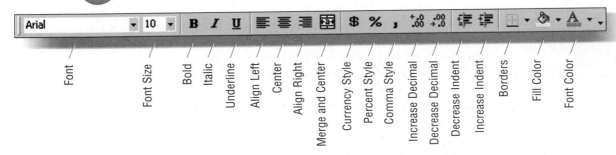

Previewing a Worksheet

Before printing a worksheet, consider previewing it to see how it will appear when printed. To preview a worksheet, click the Preview button in the Print dialog box; click the Print Preview button on the Standard toolbar; or click File and then Print Preview. This causes the document to display on the screen as it will appear when printed. Figure 1.13 displays the worksheet named Excel Worksheet 01 in Print Preview. Notice that the gridlines in the worksheet will not print.

Print Preview

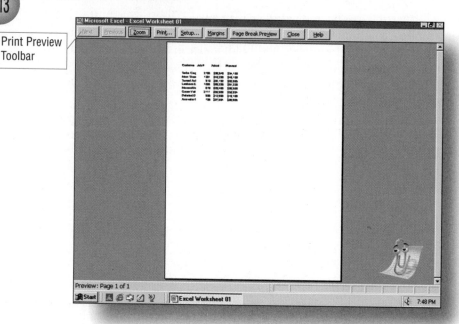

figure
1.13
Worksheet in Print Preview

Print Preview Toolbar

To zoom in on the worksheet and make the display bigger, click the Zoom button on the Print Preview toolbar. This toolbar displays at the top of the screen immediately below the Title bar. Click the Print button on the Print Preview toolbar to send the worksheet to the printer. Click the Setup button and the Page Setup dialog box displays where you can specify the orientation of the page and the paper size. Clicking the Margins button causes margin boundary lines to display on the worksheet. Clicking this button again removes the margin boundary lines. (You will learn more about these options in chapter 2.) After viewing the worksheet, click the Close button to remove Print Preview and return to the worksheet.

In Print Preview with the Margins button active, change worksheet margins by dragging margin borders.

Hint

Changing the Zoom Setting

In Print Preview, you can zoom in on the worksheet and make the display bigger. You can also change the size of the display at the worksheet (not in Print Preview) with the options on the Zoom button. To change the percentage of display, click the down-pointing triangle at the right side of the Zoom button on the Standard toolbar and then click the desired percentage at the drop-down list. You can also click in the Zoom button to select the current percentage measurement, key a new percentage, and then press Enter.

exercise 2

Selecting and Applying Character Formatting to Cells

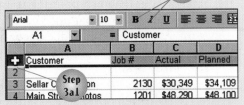

1. Open Excel Worksheet 01.
2. Save the worksheet with Save As and name it Excel C1, Ex 02.
3. Apply character formatting to data within cells by completing the following steps:
   a. Select and then bold and italicize the first row by completing the following steps:
      1) Position the cell pointer on the row 1 header and then click the left mouse button. (This is the number 1 that displays at the left side of the screen, immediately left of *Customer*.)
      2) Click the Bold button and then click the Italic button on the Formatting toolbar.
   b. Select and then bold the data in cells A3 through A10 by completing the following steps:
      1) Position the cell pointer in cell A3, hold down the left mouse button, drag the cell pointer to cell A10, and then release the mouse button.
      2) Click the Bold button on the Formatting toolbar.
   c. Select and then italicize the data in cells B3 through D10 by completing the following steps:
      1) Position the cell pointer in cell B3, hold down the left mouse button, drag the cell pointer to cell D10, and then release the mouse button.
      2) Click the Italic button on the Formatting toolbar.
4. Make the following changes to data within cells in the worksheet:
   a. Double-click cell A5 (contains *Sunset Automotive*).
   b. Delete the word *Automotive* and then key **Transport**. (When completed, the company name should be *Sunset Transport*.)
   c. Click once in cell A9 (contains *Detailed Designs*) and then key **Mustang Supply**. (Clicking only once allows you to key over the existing data.)
   d. Click once in cell B6 (contains *1009*) and then key **885**.
   e. Edit cell D10 by completing the following steps:
      1) Click Edit and then Go To.
      2) At the Go To dialog box, key **D10** in the Reference text box, and then click OK.
      3) Key **75225** (over *$86,905*).
   f. Click once in any other cell.

5. Preview the worksheet by completing the following steps:
   a. Click the Print Preview button on the Standard toolbar.
   b. At the print preview screen, click the Zoom button. (This alternately increases and decreases the display of the worksheet cells.)
   c. Click the Zoom button again, then close Print Preview.
6. Change the zoom display in Ready mode by completing the following steps:
   a. Click the down-pointing triangle at the right side of the Zoom button on the Standard toolbar and then click *200%* at the drop-down list.
   b. After viewing the document at 200% display, click in the Zoom button (this selects *200%*), key **150**, and then press Enter. (This changes the zoom percentage to 150%.)
   c. Change the zoom back to 100% by clicking the down-pointing triangle at the right side of the Zoom button and then clicking *100%* at the drop-down list.
   d. After viewing the worksheet, click the Close button.
7. Save the document again with the same name (Excel C1, Ex 02).
8. Print and then close Excel C1, Ex 02. (The gridlines will not print.)

exercise  3

Changing the Font and Font Color for Data in a Worksheet

1. Open Excel Worksheet 01.
2. Save the worksheet with Save As and name it Excel C1, Ex 03.
3. Make the following changes to the worksheet:
   a. Select the entire worksheet and then change the font and font color by completing the following steps:
      1) Click the Select All button. (This is the gray button that displays immediately left of column header A and immediately above row header 1.)
      2) Click the down-pointing triangle at the right side of the Font button on the Formatting toolbar.
      3) At the drop-down menu that displays, scroll down the list and then click *Garamond*. (If Garamond is not available, choose another serif typeface such as Century Schoolbook.)
      4) Click the down-pointing triangle at the right side of the Font Size button on the Formatting toolbar and then click *11* at the drop-down menu.
      5) Click the down-pointing triangle at the right side of the Font Color button (this is the last button on the Formatting toolbar). At the palette of color choices, click the blue color that is the sixth color from the left in the second row.

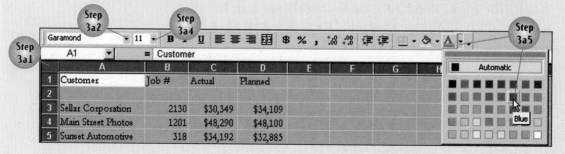

    b. Click once in cell A6 and then change *Linstrom Enterprises* to *Jefferson, Inc.*

    c. Double-click in cell A7 and then change *Morcos Media* to *Morcos Corp.*

    d. Click once in cell C6 and then change *$63,293* to *$59,578.*

    e. Double-click in cell C10 and then change the second number from a *7* to an *8.*

    f. Click once in any other cell.

4. Preview the worksheet by completing the following steps:

    a. Click the Print Preview button on the Standard toolbar.

    b. At the print preview screen, increase the size of the display by clicking the <u>Z</u>oom button. (Skip this step if the size is already increased.)

    c. After viewing the worksheet, click the <u>C</u>lose button.

5. Save the document again with the same name (Excel C1, Ex 03).

6. Print Excel C1, Ex 03. (The gridlines will not print. If you are not printing on a color printer, the data will print in black rather than blue.)

7. Print selected cells by completing the following steps:

    a) Select cells A1 through C10.

    b) Click <u>F</u>ile and then <u>P</u>rint.

    c) At the Print dialog box, click Selection in the Print what section.

    d) Click OK.

8. Click outside the selected area to deselect the cells and then close Excel C1, Ex 03.

Changing Column Width and Row Height

Columns in a worksheet are the same width by default, and rows are the same height. In some worksheets you may want to change column widths or row heights to accommodate more or less data. Changes to column widths or row heights can be made using the mouse on column or row boundaries or at a dialog box.

Changing Column Width

The width of one column or selected columns can be changed using the mouse on column boundaries or at the Column Width dialog box.

Changing Column Width with Column Boundaries

The mouse can be used to change the width of a column or selected columns. For example, to increase the size of column B, you would position the mouse pointer on the black boundary line between columns B and C in the column header until the mouse pointer turns into a double-headed arrow pointing left and right. With the double-headed arrow displayed, you would hold down the left mouse button, drag the boundary to the right to increase the size of column B, and then release the mouse button when the column is the desired width.

The width of selected columns that are adjacent can be changed at the same time. To do this, select the columns and then drag one of the column boundaries within the selected columns. As the boundary is being dragged, the column width changes for all selected columns.

As a column boundary is being dragged, the column width displays in a yellow box above the mouse pointer. The column width number that displays represents the average number of characters in the standard font that can fit in a cell.

exercise 4

Changing Column Width Using a Column Boundary

1. At a blank Excel worksheet, create the worksheet shown in figure 1.14 by completing the following steps:

    a. Change the width of column A by completing the following steps:

        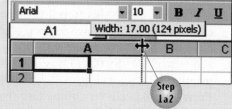

        1) Position the mouse pointer on the column boundary in the column header between columns A and B until it turns into a double-headed arrow pointing left and right.

        2) Hold down the left mouse button, drag the column boundary to the right until *Width: 17.00 (124 pixels)* displays in the yellow box, and then release the mouse button.

    b. Change the width of columns B, C, and D by completing the following steps:

        1) Select columns B, C, and D. To do this, position the cell pointer on the letter B in the column header, hold down the left mouse button, drag the cell pointer to the letter D in the column header, and then release the mouse button.

        2) Position the cell pointer on the column boundary between columns B and C until it turns into a double-headed arrow pointing left and right.

        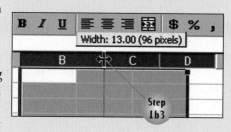

        3) Hold down the left mouse button, drag the column boundary to the right until *Width: 13.00 (96 pixels)* displays in the yellow box, and then release the mouse button.

    c. Key the data in the cells as shown in figure 1.14. Key the dollar signs and decimal points as shown. Use the Tab key to move to the next cell and press Shift + Tab to move to the previous cell. For other commands for moving the insertion point, refer to figure 1.4. (Consider using the AutoFill fill handle for the months. To do this, key **October** in cell B1, position the mouse pointer on the fill

        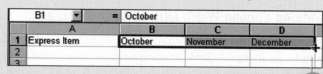

        handle, hold down the left mouse button, drag to cell D1, and then release the mouse button.)

    d. After keying the data in the cells, make the following formatting changes:

        1) Select the entire worksheet and then change the font to 12-point Tahoma (or a similar sans serif typeface).

        2) Select row 1 and then apply bold and italic formatting.

2. Save the worksheet and name it Excel C1, Ex 04.
3. Preview the worksheet.
4. Print and then close Excel C1, Ex 04.

Exercise 4

	A	B	C	D	E
1	Expense Item	October	November	December	
2	Salaries	$25,450.50	$26,090.65	$26,445.00	
3	Lease	$5,650.00	$5,650.00	$5,560.00	
4	Insurance	$5,209.65	$5,335.55	$5,621.45	
5	Utilities	$2,100.50	$2,249.75	$2,441.35	
6	Maintenance	$1,430.00	$1,119.67	$1,450.50	
7					

A column width in an existing worksheet can be adjusted to fit the longest entry in the column. To automatically adjust a column width to the longest entry, position the cell pointer on the column boundary at the right side of the column, and then double-click the left mouse button.

exercise 5

Changing Column Width Automatically in an Existing Worksheet

1. Open Excel Worksheet 01.
2. Save the worksheet with Save As and name it Excel C1, Ex 05.
3. Select the entire worksheet and then change the font to 14-point Times New Roman.
4. Adjust the width of the first column to accommodate the longest entry in the column by completing the following steps:
   a. Position the cell pointer on the column boundary between columns A and B until it turns into a double-headed arrow pointing left and right.
   b. Double-click the left mouse button.

5. Select row 1 and then click the Bold button on the Formatting toolbar.
6. Save the document again with the same name (Excel C1, Ex 05).
7. Preview the worksheet.
8. Print and then close Excel C1, Ex 05.

Changing Column Width at the Column Width Dialog Box

At the Column Width dialog box shown in figure 1.15, you can specify a column width number. The column width number represents the average number of characters in the standard font that will fit in a cell. Increase the column width number to make the column wider or decrease the column width number to make the column narrower.

To display the Column Width dialog box, click Format, point to Column, and then click Width. At the Column Width dialog box, key the number representing the average number of characters in the standard font that you want to fit in the column, and then press Enter or click OK.

CORE

figure
1.15
Column Width Dialog Box

exercise 6

Changing Column Width at the Column Width Dialog Box

1. At a blank Excel worksheet, create the worksheet shown in figure 1.16 by completing the following steps:
   a. Change the width of column A by completing the following steps:
      1) Make sure any cell in column A is active.
      2) Click Format, point to Column, and then click Width.
      3) At the Column Width dialog box, key **10** in the Column width text box.
      4) Press Enter or click OK to close the dialog box.

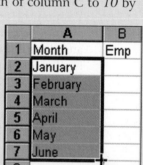

   b. Make any cell in column B active and then change the width of column B to *5* by completing steps similar to those in step 1a.
   c. Make any cell in column C active and then change the width of column C to *10* by completing steps similar to those in step 1a.
   d. Make any cell in column D active and then change the width of column D to *10* by completing steps similar to those in step 1a.
   e. Key the data in the cells as shown in figure 1.16. Use the fill handle to insert the months.
   f. After keying the data in the cells, make the following formatting changes:
      1) Select the entire worksheet and then change the font to 12-point Garamond (or a similar serif typeface).
      2) Select row 1 and then apply bold formatting.
2. Save the worksheet and name it Excel C1, Ex 06.
3. Preview the worksheet.
4. Print and then close Excel C1, Ex 06.

	A	B
1	Month	Emp
2	January	
3	February	
4	March	
5	April	
6	May	
7	June	

Step 1e

Exercise 6

	A	B	C	D	E
1	Month	Emp	Actual	Budget	
2	January	320	$3,121.50	$3,005.60	
3	February	197	$3,450.78	$3,500.20	
4	March	763	$2,109.45	$2,229.67	
5	April	804	$4,312.50	$4,110.30	
6	May	334	$5,110.40	$4,995.00	
7	June	105	$1,894.35	$1,995.15	
8					

Changing Row Height

Row height can be changed in much the same manner as column width. For example, you can change the row height using the mouse on a row boundary, or at the Row Height dialog box.

Changing Row Height with Row Boundaries

Change row height using a row boundary in the same manner as you learned to change column width. To do this, position the cell pointer on the boundary between rows in the row header until it turns into a double-headed arrow pointing up and down, hold down the left mouse button, drag up or down until the row is the desired height, and then release the mouse button.

The height of selected rows that are adjacent can be changed at the same time. (The height of nonadjacent rows will not all change at the same time.) To do this, select the rows, and then drag one of the row boundaries within the selected rows. As the boundary is being dragged, the row height changes for all selected rows.

As a row boundary is being dragged, the row height displays in a yellow box above the mouse pointer. The row height number that displays represents a point measurement. There are approximately 72 points in a vertical inch. Increase the point size to increase the row height; decrease the point size to decrease the row height.

Changing Row Height Using a Row Boundary

1. Open Excel Worksheet 05.
2. Save the worksheet with Save As and name it Excel C1, Ex 07.
3. Make the following changes to the worksheet:
   a. Change the font size of January to 14 by completing the following steps:
      1) Make cell A1 the active cell.
      2) Click the down-pointing triangle at the right of the Font Size button on the Formatting toolbar.
      3) From the drop-down menu that displays, click *14*.

b. Change the height of row 1 by completing the following steps:
   1) Position the cell pointer on the row boundary between rows 1 and 2 until it turns into a double-headed arrow pointing up and down.
   2) Hold down the left mouse button, drag the row boundary down until *Height: 27.00 (36 pixels)* displays in the yellow box, and then release the mouse button.

c. Change the height of rows 2 through 8 by completing the following steps:
   1) Select rows 2 through 8. To do this, position the cell pointer on the number 2 in the row header, hold down the left mouse button, drag the cell pointer to the number 8 in the row header, and then release the mouse button.
   2) Position the cell pointer on the row boundary between rows 2 and 3 until it turns into a double-headed arrow pointing up and down.
   3) Hold down the left mouse button, drag the row boundary down until *Height: 21.00 (28 pixels)* displays in the yellow box, and then release the mouse button.

4. Save the worksheet again with the same name (Excel C1, Ex 07).
5. Preview the worksheet.
6. Print and then close Excel C1, Ex 07.

Changing Row Height at the Row Height Dialog Box

At the Row Height dialog box shown in figure 1.17, you can specify a row height number. To display the Row Height dialog box, click F**o**rmat, point to **R**ow, and then click H**e**ight.

Row Height Dialog Box

1.17

Row Height	? X
Row height:	12.75
OK	Cancel

exercise 8

Changing Row Height at the Row Height Dialog Box

1. Open Excel Worksheet 07.
2. Save the worksheet with Save As and name it Excel C1, Ex 08.
3. Make the following changes to the worksheet:
   a. Change the font size of *REAL PHOTOGRAPHY* to 14 and turn on bold.
   b. Change the height of row 1 by completing the following steps:
      1) Make any cell in row 1 active.
      2) Click Format, point to Row, and then click Height.
      3) At the Row Height dialog box, key **30** in the Row height text box, and then press Enter or click OK.
   c. Change the height of rows 2 through 10 by completing the following steps:
      1) Select rows 2 through 10.
      2) Click Format, point to Row, and then click Height.
      3) At the Row Height dialog box, key **20** in the Row height text box, and then press Enter or click OK.
4. Save the worksheet again with the same name (Excel C1, Ex 08).
5. Preview the worksheet.
6. Print and then close Excel C1, Ex 08.

Row Height	? X
Row height:	30
OK	Cancel

Step 3b3

Formatting Data in Cells

An Excel worksheet contains default formatting. For example, by default, letters and words are aligned at the left of a cell, numbers are aligned at the right, and data is set in a 10-point sans serif typeface such as Arial. Depending on the data you are entering in cells, you may want to change some of these default settings.

> Use the Format Painter button on the Standard toolbar to copy formatting from one range of cells to another.

Formatting Numbers

Numbers in a cell, by default, are aligned at the right and decimals and commas are not displayed unless they are keyed in the cell. Also, numbers display in a 10-point sans serif typeface such as Arial. Depending on the type of numbers used in a worksheet, you may want to change these default settings. You can format numbers using a *format symbol*, or change number formatting with buttons on the Formatting toolbar or with options at the Format Cells dialog box.

Format symbols you can use to format numbers include a percent sign (%), a comma (,), and a dollar sign ($). For example, if you key the number *$45.50* in a cell, Excel automatically applies Currency formatting to the number. If you key *45%*, Excel automatically applies the Percent formatting to the number.

Five buttons on the Formatting toolbar can be used to format numbers in cells. The five buttons are shown and described in figure 1.18.

Number Formatting Buttons on Formatting Toolbar

Click this button	Named	To do this
$	Currency Style	Add a dollar sign, any necessary commas, and a decimal point followed by two decimal digits, if none are keyed; right align number in cell
%	Percent Style	Multiply cell value by 100 and display result with a percent symbol; right align number in cell
,	Comma Style	Add any necessary commas and a decimal point followed by two decimal digits, if none are keyed; right align number in cell
.00	Increase Decimal	Increase number of decimal places displayed after decimal point in selected cells
.00	Decrease Decimal	Decrease number of decimal places displayed after decimal point in selected cells

(*Note: Before entering percent numbers in a cell, check to make sure automatic percent entry is enabled. To do this, click* Tools *and then* Options. *At the Options dialog box, click the Edit tab. Make sure there is a check mark in the* Enable automatic percent *entry* option *and then click OK.*)

Increase Decimal

.00

Decrease Decimal

Specify the formatting for numbers in cells in a worksheet before keying the numbers, or format existing numbers in a worksheet. The Increase Decimal and Decrease Decimal buttons on the Formatting toolbar will change decimal places for existing numbers only.

Formatting Numbers with Buttons on the Formatting Toolbar

1. At a blank Excel worksheet, create the worksheet shown in figure 1.19 by completing the following steps:
   a. Change the width of column A to 13.00.
   b. Select columns B, C, and D, and then change the column width to 10.00.
   c. Change the width of column E to 8.00.
   d. Key the data in the cells as shown in figure 1.19.
   e. After keying the data in the cells, make the following number formatting changes:

1) Select cells B3 through D12.
2) Click the Currency Style button on the Formatting toolbar.
3) Click twice the Decrease Decimal button on the Formatting toolbar. (There should now be no decimal places in the numbers in the selected cells.)
4) Select cells E3 through E12.
5) Click the Percent Style button on the Formatting toolbar.
6) Click twice the Increase Decimal button on the Formatting toolbar. (There should now be two decimal places in the percent numbers in the selected cells.)

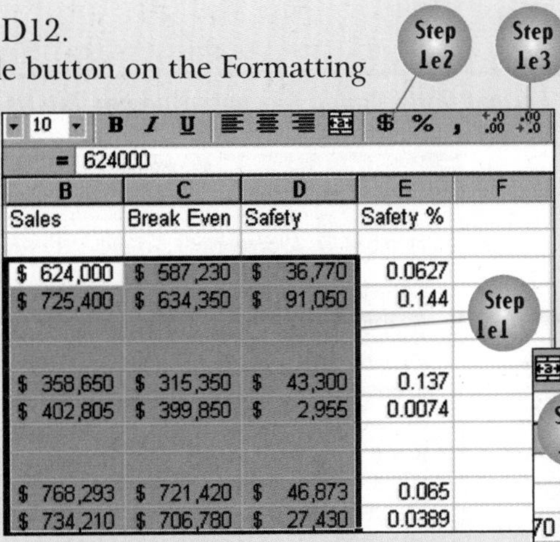

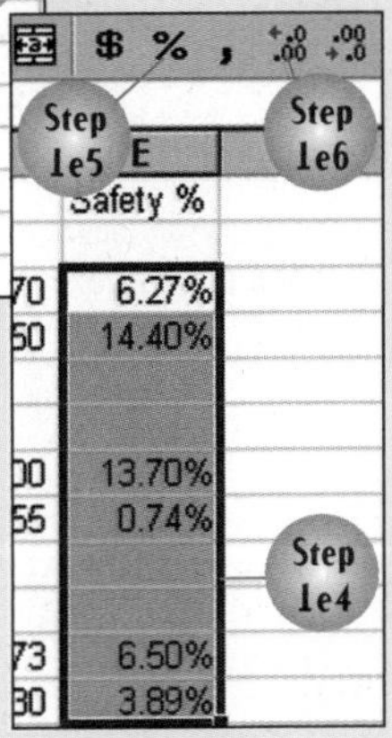

   f. Select and then bold column A.
   g. Select and then bold row 1.
2. Save the worksheet and name it Excel C1, Ex 09.
3. Preview the worksheet.
4. Print and then close Excel C1, Ex 09.

		B	C	D	E	F
		Sales	Break Even	Safety	Safety %	
		$ 624,000	$ 587,230	$ 36,770	0.0627	
		$ 725,400	$ 634,350	$ 91,050	0.144	
		$ 358,650	$ 315,350	$ 43,300	0.137	
		$ 402,805	$ 399,850	$ 2,955	0.0074	
		$ 768,293	$ 721,420	$ 46,873	0.065	
		$ 734,210	$ 706,780	$ 27,430	0.0389	

= 624000

Step 1e2 Step 1e3 Step 1e1 Step 1e5 Step 1e6 Step 1e4

Safety %
6.27%
14.40%
13.70%
0.74%
6.50%
3.89%

figure 1.19

Exercise 9

	A	B	C	D	E	F
1		Sales	Break Even	Safety	Safety %	
2	Product A					
3	Budget	624000	587230	36770	0.0627	
4	Actual	725400	634350	91050	0.144	
5						
6	Product B					
7	Budget	358650	315350	43300	0.137	
8	Actual	402805	399850	2955	0.0074	
9						
10	Product C					
11	Budget	768293	721420	46873	0.065	
12	Actual	734210	706780	27430	0.0389	
13						

Numbers in cells can also be formatted with options at the Format Cells dialog box with the Number tab selected as shown in figure 1.20. Display this dialog box by clicking Format and then Cells.

figure 1.20

Format Cells Dialog Box with Number Tab Selected

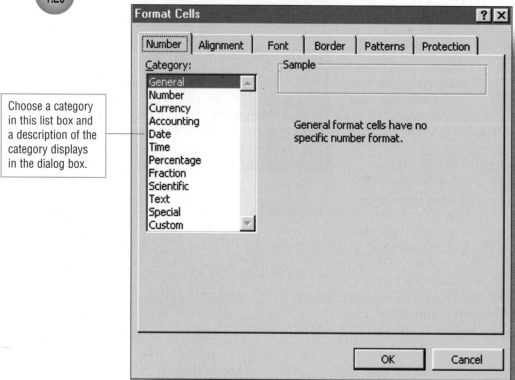

Choose a category
in this list box and
a description of the
category displays
in the dialog box.

The left side of the dialog box displays number categories. The default category is *General*. At this setting no specific formatting is applied to numbers except right aligning numbers in cells. The other number categories are described in figure 1.21.

figure 1.21

Number Categories at the Format Cells Dialog Box

Click this category	To apply this number formatting
Number	Specify number of decimal places and whether or not a thousand separator should be used; choose the display of negative numbers; right align numbers in cell
Currency	Apply general monetary values; dollar sign is added as well as commas and decimal points, if needed; right align numbers in cell
Accounting	Line up the currency symbol and decimal points in a column; add dollar sign and two digits after a decimal point; right align numbers in cell
Date	Display date as date value; specify the type of formatting desired by clicking an option in the Type list box; right align date in cell

Time	Display time as time value; specify the type of formatting desired by clicking an option in the <u>T</u>ype list box; right align time in cell
Percentage	Multiply cell value by 100 and display result with a percent symbol; add decimal point followed by two digits by default; number of digits can be changed with the <u>D</u>ecimal places option; right align number in cell
Fraction	Specify how fraction displays in cell by clicking an option in the <u>T</u>ype list box; right align fraction in cell
Scientific	Use for very large or very small numbers. Use the letter E to tell Excel to move a decimal point a specified number of positions
Text	Treat number in cell as text; number is displayed in cell exactly as keyed
Special	Choose a number type, such as Zip Code, Phone Number, or Social Security Number in the <u>T</u>ype option list box; useful for tracking list and database values
Custom	Specify a numbering type by choosing an option in the <u>T</u>ype list box

Formatting Numbers at the Format Cells Dialog Box

1. Open Excel Worksheet 02.
2. Save the worksheet with Save As and name it Excel C1, Ex 10.
3. Make the following changes to the worksheet:
    a. Change the number formatting by completing the following steps:
        1) Select cells B2 through D8.
        2) Click Format and then Cells.
        3) At the Format Cells dialog box with the Number tab selected, click *Currency* in the <u>C</u>ategory section.
        4) Click the down-pointing triangle at the right of the <u>D</u>ecimal places option until *0* displays in the <u>D</u>ecimal places text box.
        5) Click OK to close the dialog box.
    b. Select and then bold and italicize row 1.
4. Save the worksheet again with the same name (Excel C1, Ex 10).
5. Print Excel C1, Ex 10.
6. With Excel C1, Ex 10 still open, change the display of negative numbers by completing the following steps:
    a. Select cells D2 through D8.
    b. Click Format and then Cells.

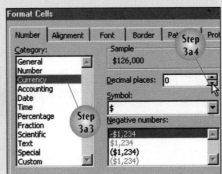

c. At the Format Cells dialog box, click the fourth option displayed in the <u>N</u>egative numbers list box (displays as *($1,234)*).

d. Click OK to close the dialog box.

7. Save the worksheet again with the same name (Excel C1, Ex 10).

8. Preview the worksheet.

9. Print and then close Excel C1, Ex 10.

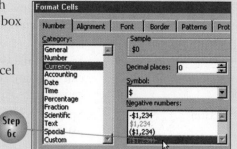

Alignment, Indenting, and Rotating Data in Cells

Align Left

Center

Align Right

Merge and Center

The alignment of data in cells depends on the type of data entered. For example, words or text combined with numbers entered in a cell are aligned at the left edge of the cell while numbers are aligned at the right. Alignment of data can be controlled with buttons on the Formatting toolbar or options at the Format Cells dialog box with the Alignment tab selected.

Four buttons on the Formatting toolbar, shown in figure 1.22, can be used to control the alignment of data in a cell or selected cells. Click the Align Left button to align data at the left side of a cell, click the Center button to align data between the left and right side of a cell, and click Align Right to align data at the right side of a cell. Click the Merge and Center button to merge selected cells and center data within the merged cells.

Indent text within a cell or selected cells by clicking the Increase Indent button or the Decrease Indent button on the Formatting toolbar. These buttons are identified in figure 1.22. The Increase Indent button will move text within the cell or selected cells to the right while the Decrease Indent button will move text to the left.

figure

1.22

Alignment and Indent Buttons on the Formatting Toolbar

Data aligning and indenting can also be controlled at the Format Cells dialog box with the Alignment tab selected as shown in figure 1.23.

figure 1.23

Format Cells Dialog Box with Alignment Tab Selected

Click this down-pointing triangle to choose a horizontal alignment.

Enter an Indent increment in this box.

Click this down-pointing triangle to choose a vertical alignment.

Control how text fits in a cell with options in the Text control section.

Rotate text in a cell by clicking a point on this arc, or key a rotation degree in the Degrees text box.

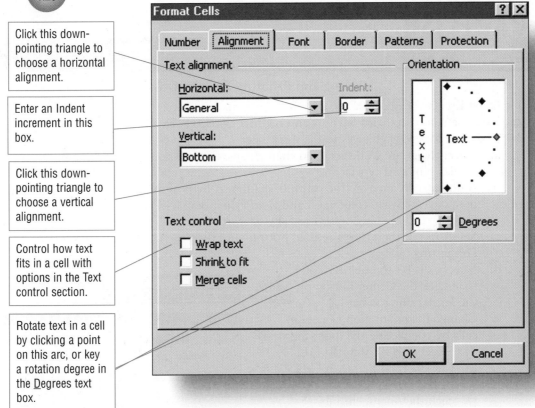

Click the down-pointing triangle at the right of the Horizontal option box and a list of alignment options displays. This list includes Left (Indent), Center, Right, Fill, Justify, and Center Across Selection. Choose the desired horizontal alignment from this list.

By default, data in a cell is aligned at the bottom of the cell. This alignment can be changed to top, center, or justify with choices from the Vertical drop-down list. To display this list, click the down-pointing triangle at the right side of the Vertical option.

Use the Indent box to indent cell contents from the left side of the cell. Each increment entered in the Indent box is equivalent to the width of one character.

In the Orientation section of the Format Cells dialog box with the Alignment tab selected, you can choose to rotate data. A portion of the Orientation section shows points on an arc. Click a point on the arc to rotate the text along that point. You can also key a rotation degree in the Degrees text box. Key a positive number to rotate selected text from the lower left to the upper right of the cell. Key a negative number to rotate selected text from the upper left to the lower right of the cell.

As you learned earlier, if data keyed in a cell is longer than the cell, it overlaps the next cell to the right. If you want data to remain in a cell and wrap to the next line within the same cell, click the Wrap text option in the Text control section of the dialog box. Click the Shrink to fit option to reduce the size of the text font so all selected data fits within the column. Use the Merge cells option to combine two or more selected cells into a single cell. If you want to enter data on more than one line within a cell, enter the data on the first line and then press Alt + Enter. Pressing Alt + Enter moves the insertion point to the next line within the same cell.

exercise 11

Aligning and Rotating Data in Cells

1. Open Excel Worksheet 01.
2. Save the worksheet with Save As and name it Excel C1, Ex 11.
3. Make the following changes to the worksheet:
   a. Select the entire worksheet and then change the font to 12-point Tahoma (or a similar sans serif typeface).
   b. Automatically increase the width of column A by positioning the cell pointer on the boundary between columns A and B and then double-clicking the left mouse button.
   c. Select row 1, then click the Bold button, and then the Center button on the Formatting toolbar.
   d. Select cells B3 through B10 and then click the Center button on the Formatting toolbar.
   e. Change the orientation of data in cells by completing the following steps:
      1) Select cells B1 through D1.
      2) Click Format and then Cells.
      3) At the Format Cells dialog box, click the Alignment tab.
      4) Select the 0 in the Degrees text box and then key **45**.
      5) Click OK to close the dialog box.

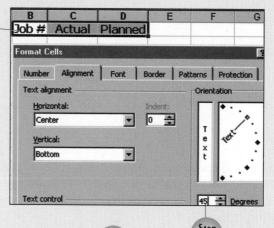

4. Merge and center data in a cell by completing the following steps:
   a. Select cells A12 through D12.
   b. Click the Merge and Center button on the Formatting toolbar.
   c. Turn on bold, key **YEARLY JOB REPORT**, and then press Enter.
5. Save the worksheet again with the same name (Excel C1, Ex 11).
6. Preview the worksheet.
7. Print and then close Excel C1, Ex 11.

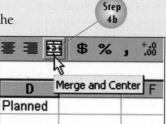

Changing the Font at the Format Cells Dialog Box

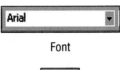

Font

Font Size

As you learned earlier in this chapter, the font for data can be changed with the Font button on the Formatting toolbar and the font size can be changed with the Font Size button. The font for data in selected cells can also be changed at the Format Cells dialog box with the Font tab selected as shown in figure 1.24.

figure
1.24

Format Cells Dialog Box with Font Tab Selected

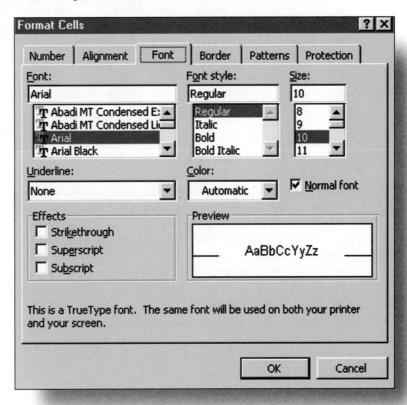

At the Format Cells dialog box with the Font tab selected, you can change the font, font style, font size, and font color. You can also change the underlining method and add effects such as superscript and subscript.

Changing the Font and Font Color of Data in Cells

1. Open Excel Worksheet 02.
2. Save the worksheet with Save As and name it Excel C1, Ex 12.
3. Make the following changes to the worksheet:
   a. Change the font and font color by completing the following steps:
      1) Select the entire worksheet.
      2) Click Format and then Cells.
      3) At the Format Cells dialog box, click the Font tab.

4) At the Format Cells dialog box with the Font tab selected, click *Garamond* in the Font list box (you will need to scroll down the list to make this font visible).

5) Click *12* in the Size list box (you will need to scroll down the list to make this size visible).

6) Click the down-pointing triangle at the right of the Color text box (contains the word *Automatic*).

7) At the palette of color choices that displays, click the Blue color.

8) Click OK to close the dialog box.

b. Change the font color for the cells in row 1 by completing the following steps:

1) Select row 1.
2) Click Format and then Cells.
3) At the Format Cells dialog box, make sure the Font tab is selected.
4) Click the down-pointing triangle at the right side of the Color text box.
5) At the palette of color choices, click a red color (you choose the red).
6) Click OK to close the dialog box.

c. Select cells B2 through D8 and then change the number formatting to *Currency* with zero decimal places.

d. Select cells A2 through A8 and then click twice on the Increase Indent button on the Formatting toolbar. (This indents the text from the left side of the cells.)

e. Automatically adjust the width of columns A, B, C, and D.

4. Save the worksheet again with the same name (Excel C1, Ex 12).

5. Preview the worksheet.

6. Print and then close Excel C1, Ex 12.

Borders

Formatting Cells

Formatting can be applied to cells in a worksheet. For example, borders can be added to cells as well as patterns and shading. Excel also offers a feature called *AutoFormat* that applies predesigned formatting to a worksheet.

Adding Borders to Cells

The gridlines that display in a worksheet do not print. Borders that will print can, however, be added to cells. Borders can be added by clicking the Borders button on the Formatting toolbar or with options from the Format Cells dialog box with the Border tab selected.

One method for applying borders is to select the cell or range of cells, click the down-pointing triangle at the right of the Borders button, and then click a border.

Hint

To add a border to a cell or selected cells, make the desired cell active or select the desired cells, and then click the Borders button on the Formatting toolbar. By default, a single line border is added to the bottom of the active cell or the selected cells. To change the style of border, click the down-pointing triangle at the right of the Borders button. This causes a palette of border style choices to display. Click the choice that represents the type of border desired for the cell or selected cells. Clicking the desired border style removes the palette and also applies that border style to the active cell or the selected cells.

exercise 13

Adding Borders to Cells Using the Borders Button

1. Open Excel Worksheet 01.
2. Save the worksheet with Save As and name it Excel C1, Ex 13.
3. Make the following changes to the worksheet:
   a. Select the entire worksheet and then change the font size to 11 points.
   b. Automatically adjust the width of column A.
   c. Select row 1 and then turn on bold and change the alignment to center.
   d. Select cells B3 through B10 and then change the alignment to center.
   e. Add a border to all cells in the worksheet (that contain data) by completing the following steps:
      1) Select cells A1 through D10 (this includes all the cells containing data in the worksheet).
      2) Click the down-pointing triangle at the right of the Borders button on the Formatting toolbar.
      3) At the palette of border style choices that displays, click the All Borders option (second option from the left in the bottom row).
   f. Add a double-line border to the bottom of selected cells by completing the following steps:
      1) Select cells A1 through D1.
      2) Click the down-pointing triangle at the right of the Borders button on the Formatting toolbar.
      3) At the palette of border style choices that displays, click the Bottom Double Border option (first option from the left in the middle row).

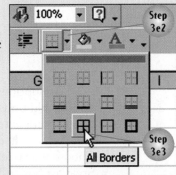

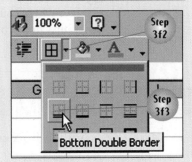

4. Save the worksheet again with the same name (Excel C1, Ex 13).
5. Preview the worksheet.
6. Print and then close Excel C1, Ex 13.

Borders can also be added to the active cell or selected cells with options at the Format Cells dialog box with the Border tab selected as shown in figure 1.25.

Format Cells Dialog Box with Border Tab Selected

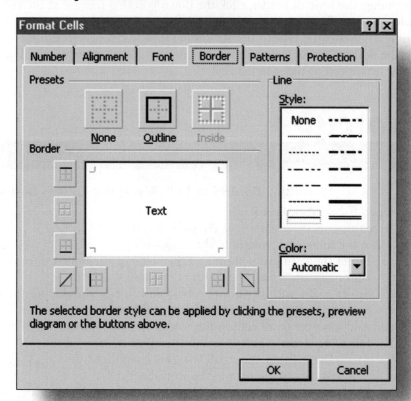

With options in the Presets section, you can remove borders with the <u>N</u>one option, add only outside borders with the <u>O</u>utline option, or click the <u>I</u>nside option to add borders to the inside of selected cells. In the Border section of the dialog box, specify the side of the cell or selected cells to which you want to apply a border. Choose the style of line desired for the border with the options that display in the <u>S</u>tyle list box. Add color to border lines with choices from the color palette that displays when you click the down-pointing triangle located at the right side of the <u>C</u>olor text box (contains the word *Automatic*).

exercise 14

Adding Borders to Cells at the Format Cells Dialog Box

1. Open Excel Worksheet 02.
2. Save the worksheet with Save As and name it Excel C1, Ex 14.
3. Make the following changes to the worksheet:
   a. Select the entire worksheet, display the Format Cells dialog box with the Font tab selected, change the font to 12-point Century Schoolbook (or a similar serif typeface), change the color to green (you determine the green), and then close the dialog box.

b. Select row 1 and then turn on bold and change the alignment to center.
c. Select cells B2 through D8, display the Format Cells dialog box with the Number tab selected, change the Category option to *Currency* with zero decimal places, and then close the dialog box.
d. Automatically adjust the width of columns A, B, C, and D.
e. Add a green outline border to the worksheet by completing the following steps:

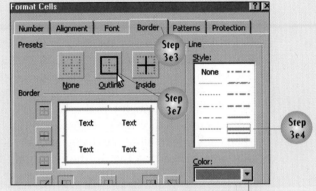

1) Select cells A1 through D8 (all cells containing data).
2) Click Format and then Cells.
3) At the Format Cells dialog box, click the Border tab.
4) Click the sixth option from the top in the second column in the Style list box.
5) Click the down-pointing triangle located at the right side of the Color text box (contains the word *Automatic*).
6) At the palette of color choices, click the same green color that you chose for the font.
7) Click the Outline option in the Presets section of the dialog box.
8) Click OK to close the dialog box.

4. Save the worksheet again with the same name (Excel C1, Ex 14).
5. Preview the worksheet.
6. Print and then close Excel C1, Ex 14.

Adding Shading and a Pattern to Cells

To enhance the visual display of cells and data within cells, consider adding shading and/or a pattern to cells. Color shading can be added to cells in a worksheet by clicking the Fill Color button on the Formatting toolbar. Color shading and/or a pattern can be added to cells in a worksheet with options at the Format Cells dialog box with the Patterns tab selected.

    To add color shading using the Fill Color button on the Formatting toolbar, make the desired cell active or select the desired cells, and then click the Fill Color button. By default, the color yellow is added to the cell or selected cells. To add a shading of a different color, click the down-pointing triangle at the right of the Fill Color button, and then click the desired color at the palette that displays.

Fill Color

Apply shading and patterns to cells at the Format Cells dialog box with the Patterns tab selected.

Hint

exercise 15

Adding Borders and Shading to Cells

1. Open Excel Worksheet 02.
2. Save the worksheet with Save As and name it Excel C1, Ex 15.
3. Make the following changes to the worksheet:
   a. Select the entire worksheet, display the Format Cells dialog box with the Font tab selected, change the font to 12-point Arial and the color to blue (sixth color from the left in the second row), and then close the dialog box.
   b. Select row 1 and then turn on bold and change the alignment to center.
   c. Select cells B2 through D8, display the Format Cells dialog box with the Number tab selected, change the Category option to *Currency* with zero decimal places, and then click OK to close the dialog box.
   d. Automatically adjust the width of columns A through D.
   e. Add a border to all cells in the worksheet that contain data by completing the following steps:
      1) Select cells A1 through D8 (this includes all the cells containing data in the worksheet).
      2) Click the down-pointing triangle at the right of the Borders button on the Formatting toolbar.
      3) At the palette of border style choices that displays, click the All Borders option (second option from the left in the bottom row).
   f. Add light turquoise shading to the cells in the worksheet containing data by completing the following steps:
      1) Select cells A1 through D8. (Skip this step if the cells are already selected.)
      2) Click the down-pointing triangle at the right of the Fill Color button on the Formatting toolbar.
      3) At the palette of shading color choices that displays, click the light turquoise color that is the fifth option from the left in the bottom row.

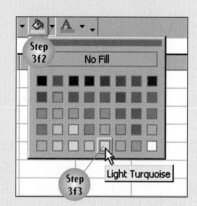

4. Save the worksheet again with the same name (Excel C1, Ex 15).
5. Preview the worksheet.
6. Print and then close Excel C1, Ex 15.

Color shading as well as a pattern can be added to the active cell or selected cells with options at the Format Cells dialog box with the Patterns tab selected as shown in figure 1.26.

figure 1.26 Format Cells Dialog Box with Patterns Tab Selected

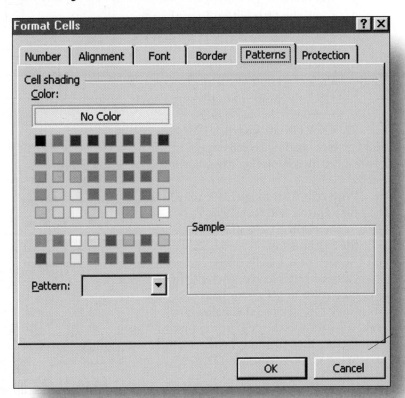

Choose a color shading for a cell or selected cells by clicking a color choice in the Color palette. To add a pattern to a cell or selected cells, click the down-pointing triangle at the right of the Pattern text box, and then click the desired pattern. When you click a pattern, that pattern displays in the Sample box in the dialog box. The Sample box also displays any color shading that has been chosen.

exercise 16

Adding Shading and a Pattern to Cells

1. Open Excel Worksheet 01.
2. Save the worksheet with Save As and name it Excel C1, Ex 16.
3. Make the following changes to the worksheet:
   a. Select the entire worksheet and then change the font to 12-point Garamond (or a similar serif typeface).
   b. Automatically adjust the width of columns A through D.
   c. Select row 1 and then turn on bold and change the alignment to center.
   d. Select cells B3 through B10 and then change the alignment to center.
   e. Add a border to cells A1 through D10 in the worksheet by completing the following steps:

1) Select cells A1 through D10.
2) Click Format and then Cells.
3) At the Format Cells dialog box, click the Border tab.
4) Click the fifth option from the top in the second column in the Style list box.
5) Click the Outline button in the Presets section of the dialog box.
6) Click the Inside button in the Presets section of the dialog box.
7) Click OK to close the dialog box.

4. Add a color shading to cells in the worksheet by completing the following steps:

   a. With cells A1 through D10 still selected, click Format and then Cells.
   b. At the Format Cells dialog box, click the Patterns tab.
   c. At the Format Cells dialog box with the Patterns tab selected, click the light blue color in the Color palette.
   d. Click OK to close the dialog box.

5. Add a pattern to the cells in the first row by completing the following steps:

   a. Select cells A1 through D1.
   b. Click Format and then Cells.
   c. At the Format Cells dialog box, make sure the Patterns tab is selected.
   d. Click the down-pointing triangle at the right side of the Pattern text box.
   e. From the palette of pattern choices that displays, click the fourth pattern choice in the top row.
   f. Click OK to close the dialog box.

6. Save the worksheet again with the same name (Excel C1, Ex 16).
7. Preview the worksheet.
8. Print and then close Excel C1, Ex 16.

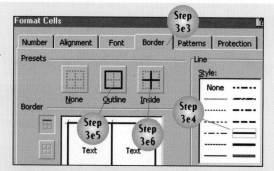

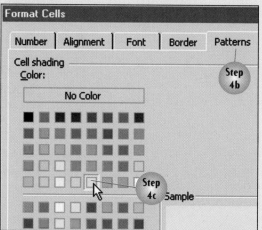

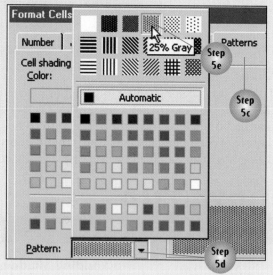

Formatting with AutoFormat

Excel includes an AutoFormat feature that automatically applies formatting to a worksheet. To display the AutoFormat dialog box, click Format and then AutoFormat. At the AutoFormat dialog box, shown in figure 1.27, predesigned autoformats display along with the name for the format.

figure
1.27

AutoFormat Dialog Box

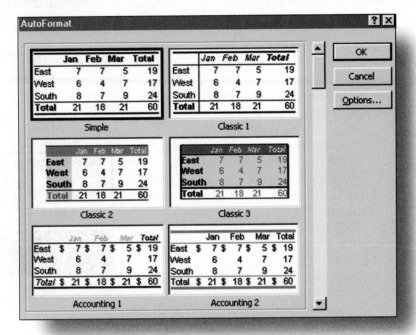

To automatically format a worksheet, select the cells that make up the worksheet, and then click Format and then AutoFormat. (Do not click the Select All button—this selects the entire worksheet, even the empty cells. If you apply an autoformat to all cells, it may lock up your computer.) At the AutoFormat dialog box, click the desired worksheet format, and then click OK; or, double-click the desired worksheet format. Not all formats display at one time. Use the vertical scroll bar at the right side of the list box to view additional formats.

You can make some changes to the predesigned autoformat. To do this, click the Options button that displays at the right side of the AutoFormat dialog box. This causes a number of check box options to display at the bottom of the dialog box. Remove the check mark from options that you do not want applied to the worksheet. For example, suppose you like a predesigned format except the font. To change back to the default font, select the format in the list box, click the Options button, and then click Font. This removes the check mark from the Font check box and also changes the font in the sample worksheet.

If you want to apply the special formatting only to specific portions of the worksheet, select the portions of the worksheet to which you want the formatting applied, and then display the AutoFormat dialog box.

exercise 17

Formatting a Worksheet with AutoFormat

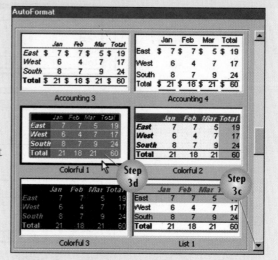

1. Open Excel Worksheet 01.
2. Save the worksheet with Save As and name it Excel C1, Ex 17.
3. Apply autoformatting to the worksheet by completing the following steps:
   a. Select cells A1 through D10.
   b. Click Format and then AutoFormat.
   c. At the AutoFormat dialog box, click the down scroll arrow on the vertical scroll bar until the *Colorful 1* sample worksheet displays.
   d. Double-click *Colorful 1*.
4. Save the document again with the same name (Excel C1, Ex 17).
5. Print and then close Excel C1, Ex 17.

Using Help

Excel's Help feature is an on-screen reference manual containing information about Excel features and commands. Excel's Help feature is similar to the Windows Help and the Help features in Word, PowerPoint, and Access. Get help using the Office Assistant or turn off the Assistant and get help from the Help Topics dialog box.

Getting Help from the Office Assistant

The Office Assistant will provide information about specific topics. To get help using the Office Assistant, click the Office Assistant or click Help and then Microsoft Excel Help. This causes a box to display above the Office Assistant. Key a question in the box about a specific Excel feature and then click the Search button. The Office Assistant displays a list of topics related to the question. At this list, click the desired topic, and information will display in a Microsoft Excel Help dialog box. After reading the information, click the Close button located in the upper right corner of the dialog box (contains an X).

Hiding/Turning Off the Office Assistant

To hide the Office Assistant, click Help and then Hide the Office Assistant. Redisplay the Office Assistant by clicking the Microsoft Excel Help button on the Standard toolbar or by clicking Help and then Show the Office Assistant.

The Office Assistant can also be turned off for the entire session. To do this, click the Office Assistant and then click the Options button that displays in the yellow box. At the Office Assistant dialog box that displays, click the Use the Office Assistant option to remove the check mark, and then click OK as shown in figure 1.28.

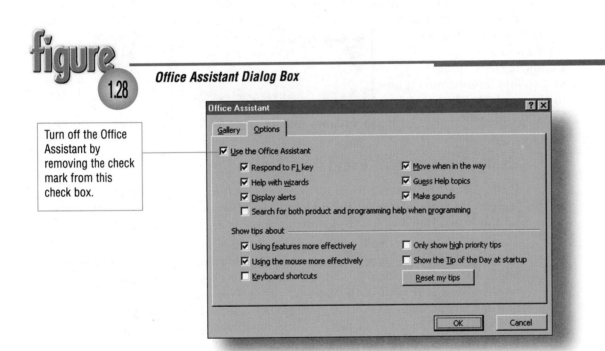

figure
1.28

Office Assistant Dialog Box

Turn off the Office Assistant by removing the check mark from this check box.

Getting Help from the Office Assistant

1. At a clear Excel worksheet, make sure the Office Assistant is visible. (If it is not, click Help and then Show the Office Assistant.)
2. Find information on changing column width by completing the following steps:
   a. Click the Office Assistant.

b. Key **How do I change column width?** in the box that displays near the Office Assistant.
c. Click the <u>S</u>earch button.
d. When the list of related topics displays in the box, click Change column width.
e. Read the information that displays in the Microsoft Excel Help dialog box.
f. Print the information by clicking the Print button on the Help toolbar.
g. Close the Microsoft Excel Help dialog box by clicking the Close button located in the upper right corner of the dialog box (contains an X).
3. Complete steps similar to those in 2 to find information on how to change the height of rows.
4. Close the worksheet.

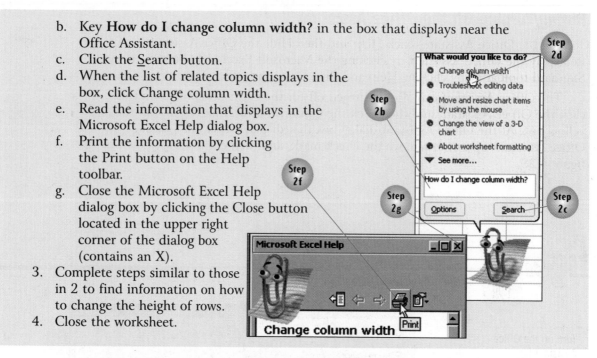

Using the Microsoft Excel Help Dialog Box

If the Office Assistant is turned off you can search for information on Excel features using the Microsoft Excel Help Dialog Box shown in figure 1.29. Three tabs display in the dialog box—<u>C</u>ontents, <u>A</u>nswer Wizard, and <u>I</u>ndex.

In the <u>C</u>ontents tab a list of categories displays preceded by an icon of a closed book. Most of these categories contain additional categories. To display the additional categories, double-click the category or click the small plus sign in the box displayed at the left of the category name. This causes the closed book icon to display as an open book icon. Double-click a topic below the category name to further expand the list or display the help topic associated for the item at the right side of the dialog box.

Click the <u>A</u>nswer Wizard tab and a text box displays preceded by the question "<u>W</u>hat would you like to do?" Key your question in the text box and then click the <u>S</u>earch button to display a list of categories in the Select <u>t</u>opic to display list box. Click a topic in the list box and information about the topic displays at the right side of the dialog box.

With the <u>I</u>ndex tab selected, enter a keyword in the <u>T</u>ype keywords list box, and then click the <u>S</u>earch button. Topics related to the keyword display in the <u>C</u>hoose a topic list box. Click a topic in this list box and information about the topic displays at the right side of the dialog box. You can also scroll through the alphabetical Or choose <u>k</u>eywords list box to display the desired topic.

While you are browsing through the Microsoft Excel Help dialog box you will notice words or terms that are underlined and displayed in blue. These words or terms are hyperlinks. Click the blue underlined text to jump to the help text for the term. After reading the hyperlink help text, return to the previous screen by clicking the Back button at the top of the dialog box. When you return to the previous help page, the hyperlink you just returned from will be displayed in a different color to indicate you have read that item.

Click the Print button at the top of the Microsoft Excel Help dialog box to print the current help topic.

figure **1.29**

Microsoft Excel Help Dialog Box with Contents Tab Selected

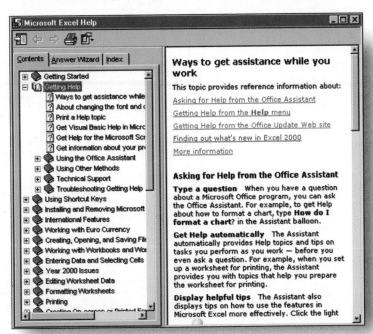

exercise 19

Turning Off the Office Assistant and Using the Help Dialog Box

1. At a clear Excel worksheet, turn off the Office Assistant by completing the following steps (if the Office Assistant is already turned off, skip this step):

   a. Click the Office Assistant.

   b. Click the Options button in the yellow box.

   c. At the Office Assistant dialog box, click the Use the Office Assistant check box (this removes the check mark).

   d. Click OK to close the dialog box.

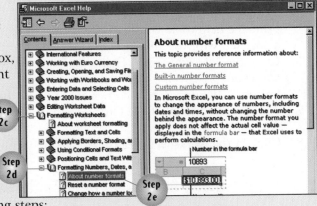

2. Use the Help feature with the Contents tab selected to find information on formatting numbers by completing the following steps:

   a. Click Help on the Menu bar and then click Microsoft Excel <u>H</u>elp.

   b. If necessary, click the <u>C</u>ontents tab in the Microsoft Excel Help dialog box.

   c. Double-click *Formatting Worksheets* in the Contents list box.

   d. Double-click *Formatting Numbers, Dates, and Times* to expand the list of subtopics.

   e. Click the *About number formats* subtopic that displays below Formatting Numbers, Dates, and Times.

f. Read the information displayed at the right side of the dialog box, then click one of the blue underlined terms to jump to the help topic associated with the term.

g. Return to the previous help page by clicking the Back button.

3. Use the Help feature with the Answer Wizard tab selected to find information on borders by completing the following steps:

a. Click the Answer Wizard tab.

b. Key **How do I apply a border to a cell?** in the What would you like to do? text box and then click the Search button.

c. Read the information on applying borders at the right side of the dialog box.

d. Print the help topic.

4. Use the Help feature with the Index tab selected to find information on editing a cell entry by completing the following steps:

a. Click the Index tab.

b. Key **edit** in the Type keywords text box and then click the Search button.

c. Click the topic *Edit cell contents* that displays in the Choose a topic list box.

d. Read the information on editing that displays at the right side of the dialog box.

e. Print the help topic.

5. Use the Contents tab, Answer Wizard tab, or the Index tab to find information on moving and scrolling through a worksheet. Print the help topic you find associated with this item.

6. Close the Microsoft Excel Help dialog box by clicking the close button at the upper right corner of the dialog box (contains an X).

7. Turn on the display of the Office Assistant by clicking Help and then Show the Office Assistant.

8. Click in the worksheet area to remove the yellow box near the Office Assistant.

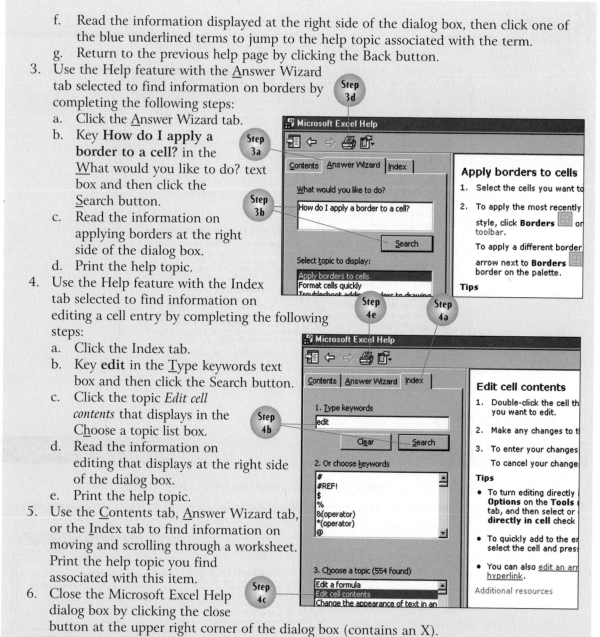

Using Additional Help Features

Click the Help option on the Menu bar, and a variety of methods to obtain help are displayed. Choose the What's This option to point to a specific item and display information about the item. For example, to display information about a button on a toolbar, click Help, and then click What's This. This causes the mouse pointer to display with a question mark attached to it. Click the button on the toolbar that you would like information on and a yellow box will display with some help text associated for the button.

Click Office on the <u>W</u>eb from the <u>H</u>elp drop-down menu and you are connected to the Microsoft Office Update web site. From this site, you can get answers to most frequently asked questions about Excel. You can also get up-to-date tips, templates, clip art, and Help files.

If you have·been a Lotus 1-2-3 user and would like information on how to carry out a Lotus command you are familiar with in Excel, click <u>H</u>elp, then click <u>L</u>otus 1-2-3 Help.

Excel contains a self-repairing feature that will fix errors in Excel. To run this feature, click <u>H</u>elp, and then click Detect and <u>R</u>epair. This displays the Detect and Repair dialog box with a message telling you that during the process you may be asked to provide the installation source and/or exit open applications. Click the <u>S</u>tart button to begin the detect and repair process.

The last option on the <u>H</u>elp drop-down menu, <u>A</u>bout Microsoft Excel, displays information such as the release date, license number, and system information. You can also display information about Microsoft's technical support.

Using What's This

1. At a clear Excel worksheet, use the What's This feature by completing the following steps:
   a. Click <u>H</u>elp and then click What's <u>T</u>his. (This causes the mouse pointer to display with a question mark attached to it.)
   b. Click the E-mail button on the Standard toolbar (fourth button from the left).
   c. Read the information displayed in the yellow box and then click in the worksheet screen outside the yellow box to remove it.
   d. Click Help and then click What's <u>T</u>his.
   e. Click the Merge and Center button on the Formatting toolbar.
   f. Read the information displayed in the yellow box and then click in the worksheet screen outside the yellow box to remove it.
   g. Click <u>H</u>elp and then click What's <u>T</u>his.
   h. Click a button on either the Standard or Formatting toolbar that you would like to know about.
   i. After reading the information displayed in the yellow box, click in the worksheet screen outside the yellow box to remove it.

Using ScreenTips

Excel includes a ScreenTips feature that is available in every dialog box and displays as a button containing a question mark. It is located just to the left of the close button in each dialog box. To use the ScreenTips feature, click the ScreenTips button, and then click an item in the dialog box. Excel will display a brief explanation about the option.

exercise 21

Using ScreenTips

1. At a clear Excel worksheet, display information about items in the Print dialog box by completing the following steps:
   a. Display the Print dialog box.
   b. Click the ScreenTips button. (This button is located in the upper right corner of the dialog box just left of the close button and displays as a question mark.)
   c. Click the Collate option.
   d. Read the information on collating and then click in a blank area inside the dialog box to clear the yellow box.
   e. Click the ScreenTips button.
   f. Click the Properties button in the Printer section of the Print dialog box.
   g. Read the information on properties and then click in a blank area inside the dialog box to clear the yellow box.
2. Close the Print dialog box.

chapter summary

➤ Use an Excel spreadsheet to create financial statements, prepare budgets, manage inventory, and analyze cash flow. Numbers and values can be easily manipulated in an Excel spreadsheet to answer "what if" questions.

➤ A document created in Excel is called a workbook. A workbook consists of individual worksheets. The intersection of columns and rows in a worksheet are referred to as cells.

➤ An Excel window contains the following elements: Title bar, Menu bar, Standard toolbar, Formatting toolbar, Formula bar, worksheet area, sheet tabs, scroll bars, and Status bar.

➤ The gray vertical and horizontal lines that define cells in the worksheet area are called gridlines.

➤ When the insertion point is positioned in a cell, the cell reference displays in the Name box located at the left side of the Formula bar. The cell reference includes the column letter and row number.

➤ To enter data in a cell, make the cell active, and then key the data. To move the insertion point to the next cell, press the Tab key. To move the insertion point to the previous cell, press Shift + Tab. For other insertion point movement commands, refer to figure 1.4.

➤ Data being entered in a cell displays in the cell as well as in the Formula bar.

➤ The AutoComplete feature will automatically insert a previous entry if the character or characters being keyed in a cell match a previous entry.

➤ Use the AutoFill fill handle to fill a range of cells with the same or consecutive data.

➤ If data entered in a cell consists of text (letters) and the text does not fit into the cell, it overlaps the cell to the right. However, if the data being entered are numbers and do not fit in the cell, the numbers are changed to number symbols (###).

➤ To replace data in a cell, click the cell once, and then key the new data. To edit data within a cell, double-click the cell, and then make necessary changes.

➤ Select all cells in a column by clicking the column header. Select all cells in a row by clicking the row header. Select all cells in a worksheet by clicking the Select All button located immediately to the left of the column headers.

- To select cells with the keyboard, refer to figure 1.11.
- Preview a worksheet by clicking the Preview button in the Print dialog box; clicking the Print Preview button on the Standard toolbar; or clicking File and then Print Preview.
- Change the size of the worksheet display with options on the Zoom button on the Standard toolbar.
- Apply character formatting to selected cells with buttons on the Formatting toolbar such as Font, Font Size, Bold, Italic, Underline, and Font Color.
- Change column width by dragging the column header boundary with the mouse. As a column header boundary is being dragged, the column width displays in a yellow box above the mouse pointer. This number represents the average number of characters in the standard font that will fit in a cell.
- To automatically adjust a column to accommodate the longest entry in the column, double-click the column header boundary on the right.
- Column width can be changed at the Column Width dialog box.
- Format numbers in cells with the Currency Style, Percent Style, Comma Style, Increase Decimal, and Decrease Decimal buttons on the Formatting toolbar.
- Numbers in cells can also be formatted at the Format Cells dialog box with the Number tab selected.
- Change alignment of data within cells with these buttons on the Formatting toolbar: Align Left, Center, Align Right, and Merge and Center.
- Alignment of data within cells can also be changed at the Format Cells dialog box with the Alignment tab selected.
- Indent text in a cell or selected cells by clicking the Increase Indent button on the Formatting toolbar. Decrease the indent of text in a cell or selected cells by clicking the Decrease Indent button.
- The font type, font size, font style, and font color for data in a cell or selected cells can be changed with options at the Format Cells dialog box with the Font tab selected.
- Add borders to a cell or selected cells with the Borders button on the Formatting toolbar or options at the Format Cells dialog box with the Border tab selected.
- Color shading can be added to a cell or selected cells with the Color button on the Formatting toolbar. Shading as well as a pattern can be added to a cell or selected cells with options at the Format Cells dialog box with the Patterns tab selected.
- Apply automatic formatting to selected cells in a worksheet with autoformats available at the AutoFormat dialog box.
- Excel's Help feature is an on-screen reference manual containing information about Excel features and commands.
- To get help from the Office Assistant, click the Assistant, key a question, and then click the Search button.
- The Office Assistant can be turned off using the Options button in the Office Assistant yellow box.
- When the Office Assistant has been turned off, use the Help, Microsoft Excel Help to search for information using the Contents, Answer Wizard, or Index.
- Use What's This from the Help drop-down menu to view information about a screen element.
- Use the ScreenTips button in a dialog box to view a brief explanation about the option.

commands review

	Mouse/Keyboard
Display Save As dialog box	Click File and then Save As
Display Open dialog box	Click Open button on Standard toolbar; or click File and then Open
Display Print dialog box	Click File and then Print
Close a worksheet	Click File and then Close
Display worksheet in Print Preview	Click Preview button in Print dialog box; click Print Preview button on Standard toolbar; or click File and then Print Preview
Change Zoom display	Click down-pointing triangle at right side of Zoom button on Standard toolbar
Display Column Width dialog box	Click Format, point to Column, and then click Width
Display Row Height dialog box	Click Format, point to Row, and then click Height
Display Format Cells dialog box	Click Format and then Cells
Display AutoFormat dialog box	Click Format and then AutoFormat

thinking offline

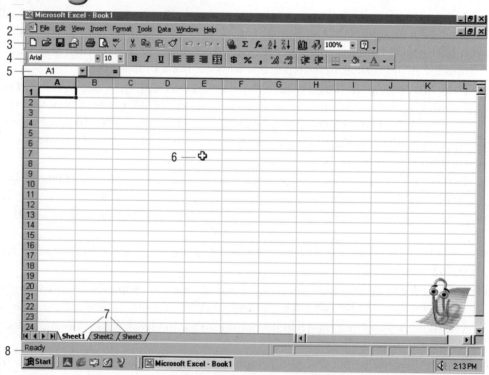

Identifying: Look at the Excel screen shown above. This screen contains numbers with lines pointing to specific items. Write the name of the item after the number below that corresponds with the number in the Excel screen.

1. _____   5. _____
2. _____   6. _____
3. _____   7. _____
4. _____   8. _____

Completion: In the space provided at the right, indicate the correct term or command.

1. Press this key on the keyboard to move the insertion point to the next cell. _____

2. Press these keys on the keyboard to move the insertion point to the previous cell. _____

3. Columns in a worksheet are labeled with this. _____

4. Rows in a worksheet are labeled with this. _____

5. Click this button in the worksheet area to select all cells in the table. _____

6. The gray vertical and horizontal lines that define the cells in a worksheet area are referred to as this. _____

7. If a number entered in a cell is too long to fit inside the cell, the number is changed to this. _____

8. Data being keyed in a cell displays in the cell as well as here. _____

9. This is the name of the small, black square that displays in the bottom right corner of the active cell. _____

10. To select nonadjacent columns using the mouse, hold down this key on the keyboard while clicking the column headers. _____

11. This toolbar contains buttons for applying character formatting to data within selected cells. _____

12. To automatically adjust a column width to accommodate the longest entry in the cell, do this with the mouse on the column header boundary. _____

13. As a column boundary is being dragged, the column width displays in this. _____

14. Click this button on the Formatting toolbar to multiply the value of numbers in selected cells by 100 and display the result followed by a percent symbol. _____

15. Click this button on the Formatting toolbar to add a dollar sign, any necessary commas, and a decimal point followed by two decimal digits to numbers in selected cells. _____

16. Click this button on the Formatting toolbar to merge selected cells and center any data within the cells. _____

17. Add color shading to selected cells in a document with options at the Format Cells dialog box with this tab selected. _____

18. Automatically apply formatting to selected cells in a worksheet with formats available at this dialog box. _____

19. Use this tab in the Microsoft Excel Help dialog box to search for information by typing a keyword. _____

20. This help feature is available in all dialog boxes and can be used to view a brief explanation of an option. _____

working hands-on

Assessment 1

1. Create the worksheet shown in figure 1.30 by completing the following steps:
   a. Select the entire worksheet and then change the font to 12-point Garamond (or a similar serif typeface).
   b. Select column headers A, B, and C and then change the column width to 14.00.
   c. Select row 1 and then turn on bold and change the alignment to center.
   d. Key the data shown in figure 1.30.
   e. After keying the data, select cells B2 through C6, and then change the number formatting to *Currency* with zero decimal places.
2. Save the worksheet and name it Excel C1, SA 01.
3. Print and then close Excel C1, SA 01.

figure

1.30 **Assessment 1**

	A	B	C	D
1	**Expense**	**Original**	**Current**	
2	Labor	97000	98500	
3	Material	129000	153000	
4	Subcontracts	20450	21600	
5	Permits	1200	1350	
6	Tax	1950	2145	
7				

Assessment 2

1. Open Excel Worksheet 03.
2. Save the worksheet with Save As and name it Excel C1, SA 02.
3. Make the following changes to the worksheet:
   a. Select the entire worksheet and then change the font to 11-point Tahoma (or a similar sans serif typeface).
   b. Select row 1 and then turn on bold.
   c. Select row 2 and then turn on bold and italics and change the alignment to center.
   d. Select cells A1 through D1 and then click the Merge and Center button on the Formatting toolbar.
   e. Select cells B3 through D8 and then click the Percent Style button on the Formatting toolbar.
   f. Select rows 1 through 8 and then change the row height to 18.00.
   g. Automatically adjust the widths of columns A through D.
4. Save the worksheet again with the same name (Excel C1, SA 02).
5. Print and then close Excel C1, SA 02.

Assessment 3

1. Open Excel C1, SA 01.
2. Save the worksheet with Save As and name it Excel C1, SA 03.
3. Make the following changes to the worksheet:
   a. Change the font for the entire worksheet to 14-point Arial and change the font color to violet.
   b. Change the font color to dark blue for the cells in row 1.
   c. Automatically adjust the widths of columns A, B, and C.
   d. Add a single-line outside border to cells A1 through C6.
4. Save the worksheet again with the same name (Excel C1, SA 03).
5. Print and then close Excel C1, SA 03.

Assessment 4

1. Open Excel C1, SA 02.
2. Save the worksheet with Save As and name it Excel C1, SA 04.
3. Make the following changes to the worksheet:
   a. Change the font for the entire worksheet to 12-point Garamond (or a similar serif typeface) and the font color to violet.
   b. Select row 2, turn off bold and italics, and then change the font color to dark blue.
   c. Select row 1 and then change the font color to dark blue.
   d. Select cells A1 through D8 and then add an outside border with a line style of your choosing.
4. Save the worksheet again with the same name (Excel C1, SA 04).
5. Print and then close Excel C1, SA 04.

Assessment 5

1. Open Excel C1, SA 01.
2. Save the worksheet with Save As and name it Excel C1, SA 05.
3. Add the following formatting to the worksheet:
   a. Select the cells that create the worksheet and then add a border around all cells (you choose the border line style).
   b. With the worksheet cells still selected, add light yellow shading to all cells.
   c. Select cells A1 through C1 and then add a pattern of your choosing to the cells.
4. Save the worksheet again with the same name (Excel C1, SA 05).
5. Print and then close Excel C1, SA 05.

Assessment 6

1. Create an Excel worksheet with the information shown in figure 1.31. You determine the following:
   a. Font
   b. Width of columns
   c. Number formatting
2. Add the following enhancements to the worksheet:
   a. Add a border to all cells in the worksheet containing data.
   b. Add a color shading to all cells in the worksheet containing data.

c. Add a pattern to column headings (the cells containing *Project, Projected,* and *Actual*).

3. Save the completed worksheet and name it Excel C1, SA 06.
4. Print and then save Excel C1, SA 06.

Assessment 6

CAPITAL PROJECT SUMMARY

Project	Projected	Actual
Rail siding installation	$43,300	$41,200
Cement slabs	$12,000	$13,980
Silos	$28,420	$29,600
Conveying system	$56,700	$58,200
Modulators	$8,210	$8,100
Winder	$6,400	$7,100

Assessment 7

1. Open Excel Worksheet 02.
2. Save the worksheet with Save As and name it Excel C1, SA 07.
3. Select cells A1 through D8 and then apply an autoformat. (Choose an autoformat that properly displays the numbers in the worksheet.)
4. Save the worksheet again with the same name (Excel C1, SA 07).
5. Print and then close Excel C1, SA 07.

Assessment 8

1. Use the Office Assistant to learn more about how to move and scroll within an Excel worksheet.

2. After reading and printing the information, create a worksheet containing the information. Set this up as a worksheet with two columns (cells will contain only text—not numbers). Create the worksheet with the following features:
   a. Create a title for the worksheet.
   b. Set the text in cells in a serif typeface and change the text color.
   c. Add borders to the cells (you determine the border style).
   d. Add a color shading to cells (you determine the color—make it complementary to the text color).
3. Save the completed worksheet and name it Excel C1, SA 08.
4. Print and then close Excel C1, SA 08.

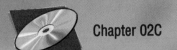

Chapter 02C

Maintaining and Enhancing a Worksheet

2

PERFORMANCE OBJECTIVES

Upon successful completion of chapter 2, you will be able to:
- Insert rows and columns in a worksheet.
- Delete rows and columns in a worksheet.
- Clear data in cells.
- Change worksheet margins.
- Center a worksheet horizontally and vertically on the page.
- Insert a page break in a worksheet.
- Print gridlines and row and column headings.
- Hide and unhide a worksheet, column, or row.
- Set and clear a print area.
- Specify more than one print area in Page Break Preview.
- Change the print quality.
- Complete a spelling check on a worksheet.
- Find and replace data in a worksheet.
- Sort data in cells in ascending and descending order.

Some worksheets, once created, may require maintenance. This maintenance might include adding or deleting data and changing existing data. In this chapter, you will learn to add and delete rows and columns in a worksheet. You will also learn to control the formatting of a worksheet page. For example, you will learn to change worksheet margins, create headers and footers, print column and row titles, print gridlines, and center a worksheet horizontally and vertically on the page.

Inserting/Deleting Rows and Columns

New data may need to be included in an existing worksheet. For example, a row or several rows of new data may need to be inserted into a worksheet; or, data may need to be removed from a worksheet.

Inserting Rows

At the Insert dialog box, specify the direction in which cells should move.

After a worksheet has been created, rows can be added to (inserted into) the worksheet. Insert a row with options from the Insert drop-down menu or with options at the Insert dialog box. By default, a row is inserted above the row containing the active cell. To insert a row in a worksheet, make a cell active in the row below where the row is to be inserted, then click Insert and then Rows. If you want to insert more than one row, select the number of rows in the worksheet that you want inserted, then click Insert and then Rows.

A row can also be inserted by making a cell active in the row below where the row is to be inserted, clicking Insert, and then clicking Cells. This causes the Insert dialog box to display as shown in figure 2.1. At the Insert dialog box, click Entire row. This inserts an entire row above the active cell.

(Before completing computer exercises, delete the Chapter 01C *folder on your disk. Next, copy the* Chapter 02C *folder from the CD that accompanies this textbook to your disk and then make* Chapter 02C *the active folder.)*

figure 2.1

Insert Dialog Box

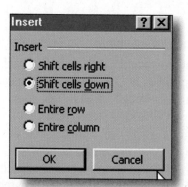

exercise 1

Inserting Rows in a Worksheet

1. Open Excel Worksheet 01.
2. Save the worksheet with Save As and name it Excel C2, Ex 01.
3. Make the following changes to the worksheet:
   a. Add two rows and enter data in the new cells by completing the following steps:
      1) Select rows 7 and 8 in the worksheet.
      2) Click Insert and then Rows.
      3) Key the following data in the specified cells (you do not need to key the dollar sign or the comma in cells containing money amounts):

A7	=	Summit Clinic
B7	=	570
C7	=	$33,056
D7	=	$32,500
A8	=	Franklin Center
B8	=	690
C8	=	$19,745
D8	=	$19,250

    b. Select cells A1 through D12 and then apply an autoformat of your choosing. (Make sure the numbers display properly.)

4. Save the document again with the same name (Excel C2, Ex 01).

5. Print and then close Excel C2, Ex 01.

Inserting Columns

Columns can be inserted in a worksheet in much the same way as rows. Insert a column with options from the Insert drop-down menu or with options at the Insert dialog box. By default, a column is inserted immediately to the left of the column containing the active cell. To insert a column in a worksheet, make a cell active in the column immediately to the right of where the new column is to be inserted, then click Insert and then Columns. If you want to insert more than one column, select the number of columns in the worksheet that you want inserted, then click Insert and then Columns.

    A column can also be inserted by making a cell active in the column immediately to the right of where the new column is to be inserted, then clicking Insert and then Cells. This causes the Insert dialog box shown in figure 2.1 to display. At the Insert dialog box, click Entire column. This inserts an entire column immediately to the left of the active cell.

Inserting a Column in a Worksheet

1. Open Excel Worksheet 03.
2. Save the document with Save As and name it Excel C2, Ex 02.
3. Make the following changes to the worksheet:
    a. Add a column to the worksheet and enter data in the new cells by completing the following steps:
      1) Click in any cell in column D.
      2) Click Insert and then Columns.
      3) Key the following data in the specified cell:

D2	=	2001
D3	=	0.55
D4	=	0.4
D5	=	1.12
D6	=	1.85
D7	=	0.22
D8	=	0.055

b. Change the contents of cell E2 from *Prior Year* to *2000*.
c. Select cells B3 through E8 and then click the Percent Style button on the Formatting toolbar.
d. Select cells A1 through E8 and then apply an autoformat of your choosing.
4. Save the worksheet again with the same name (Excel C2, Ex 02).
5. Print and then close Excel C2, Ex 02.

Deleting Cells, Rows, or Columns

Specific cells in a worksheet or rows or columns in a worksheet can be deleted. To delete a specific cell, make the cell active, and then press the Delete key. You can also select the cells to be deleted and then press the Delete key. If you use the Delete key to delete cell(s), only the cell text is deleted. The empty cell(s) remain(s) in the worksheet.

If you want to delete the cell(s) as well as the cell text, make the specific cell active or select cells, then click Edit and then Delete. At the Delete dialog box shown in figure 2.2, choose what you wanted deleted, and then click OK.

Delete Dialog Box

At the Delete dialog box, the Shift cells left option is selected by default. At this setting, cells will shift left after the selected cell (or cells) is deleted. Click Shift cells up and cells will shift up after the selected cell (or cells) is deleted. Click Entire row to delete the row containing the active cell or click Entire column to delete the column containing the active cell.

The Delete dialog box can also be displayed by positioning the cell pointer in the worksheet, clicking the *right* mouse button, and then clicking Delete on the shortcut menu. To delete several rows of cells, select the rows, then click Edit and then Delete. To delete several columns of cells, select the columns, then click Edit and then Delete.

Clearing Data in Cells

With the Clear option from the Edit drop-down menu, the contents of selected cells can be cleared. This is useful in a situation where the cells are to remain but the contents need to be changed. To clear cell contents, select the cells, click Edit, point to Clear, and then click <u>A</u>ll. This deletes the cell contents and the cell formatting. Click <u>F</u>ormats to remove formatting from selected cells while leaving the data. Click <u>C</u>ontents to remove the contents of the cell, leaving any formatting. You can also press the Delete key to clear the contents of the selected cells.

One method for clearing the contents of a cell is to right-click the cell and then click Clear Contents at the shortcut menu.

Deleting Columns and Deleting and Clearing Rows in a Worksheet

1. Open Excel Worksheet 02.
2. Save the worksheet with Save As and name it Excel C2, Ex 03.
3. Make the following changes to the worksheet:
   a. Delete column D in the worksheet by completing the following steps:
      1) Click in any cell in column D.
      2) Click <u>E</u>dit and then <u>D</u>elete.
      3) At the Delete dialog box, click Entire <u>c</u>olumn.
      4) Click OK or press Enter.
   b. Delete row 5 by completing the following steps:
      1) Select row 5.
      2) Click <u>E</u>dit and then <u>D</u>elete.
   c. Clear row contents by completing the following steps:
      1) Select rows 5 and 6.
      2) Click <u>E</u>dit, point to Cle<u>a</u>r, and then click <u>C</u>ontents.
   d. Key the following data in the specified cell:

A5	=	**Lodging**
B5	=	**4535**
C5	=	**5100**
A6	=	**Entertainment**
B6	=	**3210**
C6	=	**3000**

   e. Select cells A1 through C7 and then apply the *Accounting 1* autoformat.
   f. Clear cell formatting and then apply different formatting by completing the following steps:
      1) Select cells A1 through C1.
      2) Click <u>E</u>dit, point to Cle<u>a</u>r, and then click <u>F</u>ormats.
      3) With cells A1 through C1 still selected, click the Bold button on the Formatting toolbar and then click the Center button.
4. Save the worksheet again with the same name (Excel C2, Ex 03).
5. Print and then close Excel C2, Ex 03.

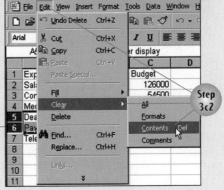

Formatting a Worksheet Page

The worksheets you have been creating and printing have fit on one sheet of paper. The worksheet has been printed in what is referred to as *portrait* orientation with default top and bottom margins of 1 inch and left and right margins of 0.75 inches. These settings can be changed with options at the Page Setup dialog box. The Page Setup dialog box contains several tabs for controlling the appearance of the worksheet page.

Controlling the Page Layout

Print Preview

The Page Setup dialog box with the Page tab selected as shown in figure 2.3 provides options for controlling the layout of the worksheet on the page. To display this dialog box, click File and then Page Setup. You can also display the Page Setup dialog box while in Print Preview. To do this, click the Print Preview button on the Standard toolbar. At the Print Preview screen, click the Setup button. At the Page Setup dialog box, make sure the Page tab is selected.

Page Setup Dialog Box with Page Tab Selected

Control how information is printed on the page with choices in the Orientation section of the Page Setup dialog box. The two choices in the Orientation section are represented by sample pages. A sample page that is taller than it is wide shows how the default orientation (Portrait) prints data on the page. The other choice, Landscape, will rotate the data and print it on a page that is wider than it is tall. The Landscape orientation might be useful in a worksheet that contains more columns than rows.

With options in the Scaling section of the Page Setup dialog box, you can adjust the size of the data in the worksheet by percentage. You can also specify on how many pages you want the data to fit. For example, if a worksheet contains too many columns to print on one page, choosing Fit to and leaving *1* as the number of pages will cause the display percentage to be decreased until the columns all fit on one page.

By default, an Excel worksheet is printed on standard paper, which is 8.5 inches wide and 11 inches long. This paper size can be changed with options from the Paper size drop-down menu. Some paper size options include *Legal 8 1/2 x 14 in* and *Executive 7 1/4 x 10 1/2*. (Your paper size names may vary.) Paper size choices will vary depending on the selected printer. To view the list of paper sizes, click the down-pointing triangle at the right of the Paper size text box.

Depending on the printer you are using, you may or may not have choices for setting the print quality. The numbers that display in the Print quality text box will vary depending on the selected printer. To view a list of print quality choices, click the down-pointing triangle at the right side of the Print quality text box. Choose a higher *dpi* (dots per inch) number to improve the quality of the print.

The worksheets you have printed so far have not been numbered. If you turn page numbering on (discussed in the next section), the first worksheet page is numbered 1 and any additional pages are incrementally numbered. With the First page number option, you can specify a different beginning page number. To do this, select *Auto* in the First page number text box, and then key the new starting number.

Turning On Page Numbering

By default, worksheet pages are not numbered. Page numbering can be applied to a workbook with options at the Page Setup dialog box with the Header/Footer tab selected as shown in figure 2.4. To display this dialog box, click File and then Page Setup. At the Page Setup dialog box, click the Header/Footer tab.

figure
2.4

Page Setup Dialog Box with Header/Footer Tab Selected

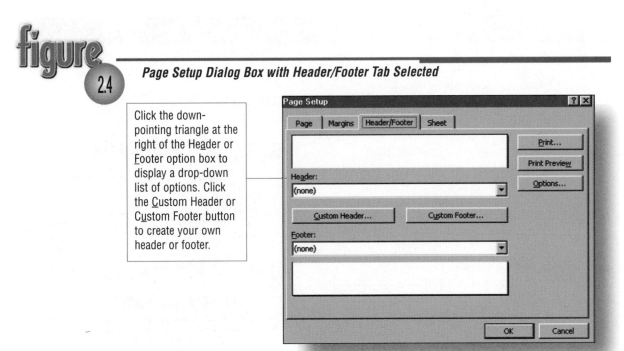

Click the down-pointing triangle at the right of the Header or Footer option box to display a drop-down list of options. Click the Custom Header or Custom Footer button to create your own header or footer.

To insert page numbering at the top of every page, click the Custom Header button on the Page Setup dialog box. Click the Custom Footer button to insert page numbering at the bottom of every page. If you click the Custom Footer button, the Footer dialog box shown in figure 2.5 displays. (The Header dialog box will display in a similar manner.) At the Footer dialog box, page numbering can be inserted at the Left section, Center section, or Right section of the page. Click in the text box below the desired location. Insert page numbering by clicking the Page Number button. (The buttons are identified in figure 2.5). Click OK to close the Footer dialog box and then click OK to close the Page Setup dialog box.

Page Number

figure
2.5

Footer Dialog Box

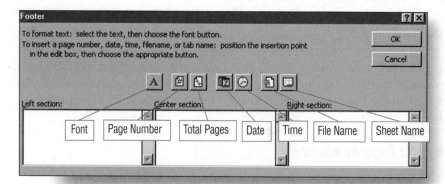

exercise 4

Changing Page Orientation and Inserting Page Numbering

1. Open Excel Worksheet 06.
2. Save the worksheet with Save As and name it Excel C2, Ex 04.
3. Change the orientation of the worksheet and insert page numbering by completing the following steps:
   a. Click File and then Page Setup.
   b. At the Page Setup dialog box, click the Page tab.
   c. Click the Landscape option.
   d. Click twice on the up-pointing triangle at the right side of the Adjust to text box. (This inserts *110%* in the text box.)
   e. Click the Header/Footer tab.
   f. At the Page Setup dialog box with the Header/Footer tab selected, click the Custom Footer button.
   g. At the Footer dialog box, click in the text box below Center section.
   h. Click the Page Number button (second button from the left).
   i. Click OK to close the Footer dialog box.
   j. Click OK to close the Page Setup dialog box.
4. Save the worksheet again with the same name (Excel C2, Ex 04).
5. Preview the worksheet by clicking the Print Preview button on the Standard toolbar. After viewing the worksheet in Print Preview, click the Close button.
6. Print Excel C2, Ex 04. (Before printing this worksheet, check with your instructor to determine if your printer can print in landscape orientation.)

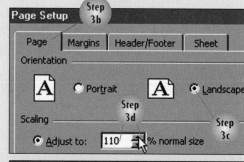

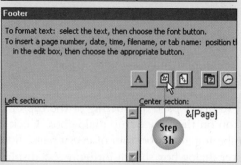

7. With Excel C2, Ex 04 still open, change the page orientation, scale the size of the worksheet so it fits on one page, and change the beginning page number to 3 by completing the following steps:

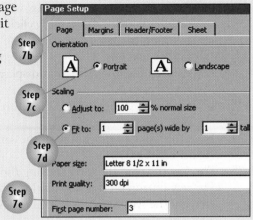

a. Click File and then Page Setup.
b. At the Page Setup dialog box, click the Page tab.
c. Click the Portrait option.
d. Click the Fit to option.
e. Select *Auto* that displays in the First page number text box and then key **3**.
f. Click OK to close the dialog box.

8. Save the worksheet again with the same name (Excel C2, Ex 04).
9. Preview the worksheet and then print and close Excel C2, Ex 04.

Inserting Headers/Footers

In the previous section, you learned how to insert page numbers in a header or footer. You can also create a header or footer containing text you want to print on every page. If you want specific text to print at the top of each page of the worksheet, create a header. Create a footer for text you want to print at the bottom of each page.

At the Page Setup dialog box with the Header/Footer tab selected (see figure 2.4), Excel offers a variety of header and footer text options. Click the down-pointing triangle after the Header text box and a drop-down list displays with options for inserting the user's name, document name, current date, and page number. The same list will display if you click the down-pointing triangle at the right of the Footer text box.

Creating a Header and Footer

1. Open Excel Worksheet 06.
2. Save the worksheet with Save As and name it Excel C2, Ex 05.
3. Insert a header and footer in the worksheet by completing the following steps:
   a. Click File and then Page Setup.
   b. At the Page Setup dialog box, click the Header/Footer tab.
   c. At the Page Setup dialog box with the Header/Footer tab selected, click the Custom Header button.
   d. At the Header dialog box, click in the text box below Center section.
   e. Key **Microcomputer Applications**.
   f. Click OK to close the Header dialog box.

g. At the Page Setup dialog box with the Header/Footer tab selected, click the down-pointing triangle at the right side of the Footer text box.

h. At the drop-down list that displays, click *Page 1 of ?*.

i. Click OK to close the Page Setup dialog box.

4. Save the worksheet again with the same name (Excel C2, Ex 05).

5. Preview the worksheet by clicking the Print Preview button on the Standard toolbar. After viewing the worksheet in Print Preview, click the Close button.

6. Print and then close Excel C2, Ex 05.

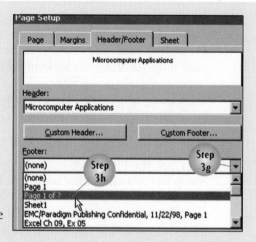

Changing Worksheet Margins

Excel uses 1-inch top and bottom margins for a worksheet and 0.75-inch left and right margins. These default margins can be changed at the Page Setup dialog box with the Margins tab selected as shown in figure 2.6.

Page Setup Dialog Box with Margins Tab Selected

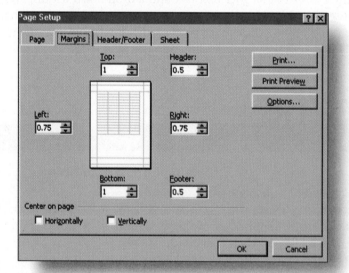

The Preview section of the dialog box displays the worksheet page showing the cells and margins. As you increase or decrease the Top, Bottom, Left, or Right margin measurements, the sample worksheet page reflects the change. You can also increase or decrease the measurement from the top of the page to the header with the Header option or the measurement from the footer to the bottom of the page with the Footer option.

Changing Worksheet Margins

1. Open Excel Worksheet 02.
2. Save the worksheet with Save As and name it Excel C2, Ex 06.
3. Select cells A1 through D8 and then apply the *Accounting 2* autoformat.
4. Change the orientation of the worksheet and change the worksheet margins by completing the following steps:
   a. Click File and then Page Setup.
   b. At the Page Setup dialog box, click the Page tab.
   c. Click the Landscape option.
   d. Click the Margins tab.
   e. At the Page Setup dialog box with the Margins tab selected, click the up-pointing triangle at the right of the Top text box until *3.5* displays.
   f. Click the up-pointing triangle at the right of the Left text box until *3.5* displays.
   g. Click OK to close the dialog box.
5. Save the worksheet again with the same name (Excel C2, Ex 06).
6. Preview the worksheet by clicking the Print Preview button on the Standard toolbar. After viewing the worksheet in Print Preview, click the Close button.
7. Print and then close Excel C2, Ex 06.

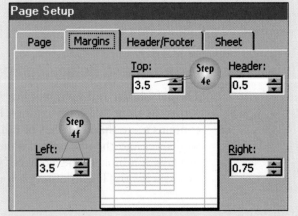

Centering a Worksheet Horizontally and/or Vertically

Many of the worksheets you have printed have been short and printed in the upper left corner of the page. A worksheet can be better centered on a page by changing the margins. But an easier method for centering a worksheet is to use the Horizontally and/or Vertically options that display at the bottom of the Page Setup dialog box with the Margins tab selected. If you choose one or both of these options, the worksheet page in the Preview section displays how the worksheet will print on the page.

exercise 7

Horizontally and Vertically Centering a Worksheet

1. Open Excel Worksheet 03.
2. Save the worksheet with Save As and name it Excel C2, Ex 07.
3. Select cells B3 through D8 and then click the Percent Style button on the Formatting toolbar.

4. Select cells A1 through D8 and then apply the *Colorful 2* autoformat.
5. Horizontally and vertically center the worksheet by completing the following steps:
   a. Click <u>F</u>ile and then Page Set<u>u</u>p.
   b. At the Page Setup dialog box, click the Margins tab.
   c. Click the Hori<u>z</u>ontally option.
   d. Click the <u>V</u>ertically option.
   e. Click OK to close the dialog box.
6. Save the worksheet again with the same name (Excel C2, Ex 07).
7. Preview the worksheet by clicking the Print Preview button on the Standard toolbar. After viewing the worksheet in Print Preview, click the <u>C</u>lose button.
8. Print and then close Excel C2, Ex 07.

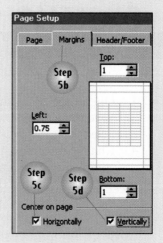

Inserting and Removing Page Breaks

The default left and right margins of 0.75 inches allow a total of 7 inches of cells across the page (8.5 inches minus 1.5 inches equals 7 inches). If a worksheet contains more than 7 inches of cells across the page, a page break is inserted in the worksheet and the remaining columns are moved to the next page. A page break displays as a broken line along cell borders. Figure 2.7 shows the page break in Excel Worksheet 06. (The location of your page break may vary.)

Page Break

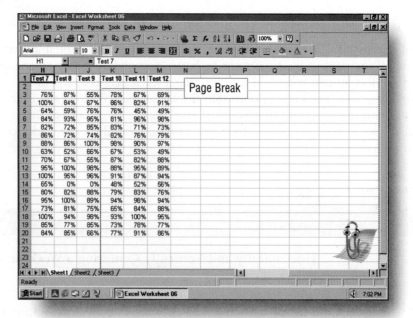

A page break also displays horizontally in a worksheet. By default, a worksheet can contain approximately 9 inches of cells vertically down the page. This is because the paper size is set by default at 11 inches. With the default top and bottom margins of 1 inch, this allows 9 inches of cells to print on one page.

Excel automatically inserts a page break in a worksheet. You can, however, insert your own if you would like more control over what cells print on a page. To insert your own page break, select the column or row, click Insert and then Page Break. A page break is inserted immediately left of the selected column or immediately above the selected row. If you want to insert both a vertical and horizontal page break at the same time, make a cell active, click Insert and then Page Break. This causes a vertical page break to be inserted at the left side of the active column and a horizontal page break to be inserted immediately above the active cell. To remove a page break, select the column or row or make the desired cell active, click Insert and then Remove Page Break.

The page break automatically inserted by Excel may not be visible initially in a worksheet. One way to display the page break is to preview the worksheet. When you close the Print Preview screen, the page break will display in the worksheet. In Print Preview, click the Next button on the Preview bar to display the next page in the worksheet. Click the Previous button to display the previous page in the worksheet.

Excel provides a page break view that will display worksheet pages and page breaks. To display this view, click View and then Page Break Preview. This causes the worksheet to display similar to the worksheet shown in figure 2.8. The word *Page* along with the page number is displayed in gray behind the cells in the worksheet. A blue line displays indicating the page break. You can move the page break by positioning the arrow pointer on the blue line, holding down the left mouse button, dragging the line to the desired location, and then releasing the mouse button. (If the Office Assistant is displaying a yellow box welcoming you to the page break preview, you must click OK before you can move the blue line.) To return to the normal view, click View and then Normal.

To display a page break in a worksheet, you may need to display the worksheet in Print Preview and then close Print Preview.

figure
2.8

Worksheet in Page Break Preview

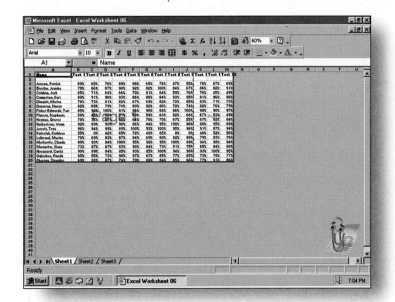

exercise 8

Inserting a Page Break in a Worksheet

1. Open Excel Worksheet 06.
2. Save the worksheet with Save As and name it Excel C2, Ex 08.
3. View the default page break inserted automatically by Excel by completing the following steps:
    a. Click the Print Preview button on the Standard toolbar.
    b. After previewing the worksheet, click the Close button.
    c. At the worksheet, click the right scroll triangle at the right side of the horizontal scroll bar until columns J and K are visible. The default page break should display between columns J and K. (The default page break displays as a dashed line. The location of the page break may vary slightly.)
4. Make the following formatting changes:
    a. Select the entire table and then change the font to 12-point Century Schoolbook (or a similar serif typeface such as Garamond).
    b. If necessary, automatically adjust the width of column A.
    c. Select columns B through M and then drag one of the selected column boundaries to the right until the column width displays as *9.00* in the yellow box.
    d. Insert a page break between columns F and G by completing the following steps:
        1) Select column G.
        2) Click Insert and then Page Break.
        3) Click once in any cell in column F.
5. View the worksheet in Page Break Preview by completing the following steps:
    a. Click View and then Page Break Preview. (If a "Welcome to Page Break Preview" message box displays, click OK.)
    b. View the pages and page breaks in the worksheet.
    c. Click View and then Normal to return to the normal view.
6. Horizontally and vertically center the worksheet by completing the following steps:
    a. Click File and then Page Setup.
    b. At the Page Setup dialog box, click the Margins tab.
    c. Click the Horizontally option.
    d. Click the Vertically option.
    e. Click OK to close the dialog box.
7. Save the worksheet again with the same name (Excel C2, Ex 08).
8. Preview the worksheet by clicking the Print Preview button on the Standard toolbar. After viewing the worksheet in Print Preview, click the Close button.
9. Print and then close Excel C2, Ex 08.

Printing Column and Row Titles on Multiple Pages

Columns and rows in a worksheet are usually titled. For example, in Excel Worksheet 06, column titles include *Name, Test 1, Test 2, Test 3*, etc. Row titles include the names of the people who have taken the tests. If a worksheet prints on more than one page, having column and/or row titles printing on each page can be useful. For example, when you printed Excel C2, Ex 08, the names of the people did not print on the second page. This makes matching test scores with names difficult.

Column and/or row titles can be printed on each page of a worksheet. To do this, click File and then Page Setup. At the Page Setup dialog box, click the Sheet tab. This displays the dialog box as shown in figure 2.9.

figure
2.9

Page Setup Dialog Box with Sheet Tab Selected

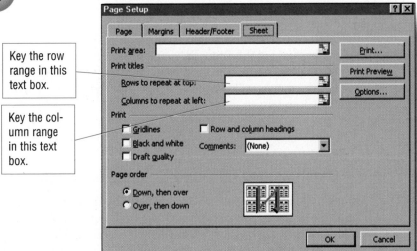

Key the row range in this text box.

Key the column range in this text box.

At the Page Setup dialog box with the Sheet tab selected, specify the range of row cells you want to print on every page in the Rows to repeat at top text box. Key a cell range using a colon. For example, if you want cells A1 through J1 to print on every page, you would key **A1:J1** in the Rows to repeat at top text box. Key the range of column cells you want to print on every page in the Columns to repeat at left text box.

Printing Column Titles on Each Page of a Worksheet

1. Open Excel Worksheet 06.
2. Save the worksheet with Save As and name it Excel C2, Ex 09.
3. Make the following formatting changes to the worksheet:
   a. Select the entire table and then change the font to 12-point Garamond (or a similar serif typeface).
   b. If necessary, automatically adjust the width of column A.
   c. Select columns B through M and then drag one of the selected column boundaries to the right until the column width displays as *8.00* in the yellow box above the mouse pointer. (This will change the width of columns B through M to 8.00.)
   d. Select row 1 and then change the alignment to center.

4. Specify that you want column titles to print on each page by completing the following steps:
   a. Click File and then Page Setup.
   b. At the Page Setup dialog box, click the Sheet tab.
   c. At the Page Setup dialog box with the Sheet tab selected, click in the Columns to repeat at left text box.
   d. Key **A1:A20**.
   e. Click OK to close the dialog box.

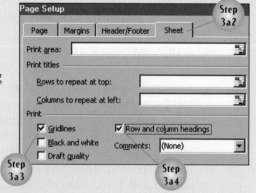

5. Save the worksheet again with the same name (Excel C2, Ex 09).
6. Preview the worksheet by clicking the Print Preview button on the Standard toolbar. At the Print Preview screen, click the Next button to display the second page of the worksheet. Notice that the names will print on page 2. After viewing the worksheet in Print Preview, click the Close button.
7. Print and then close Excel C2, Ex 09.

Printing Gridlines and Row and Column Headings

By default, gridlines do not print. Print gridlines by inserting a check mark in the Gridlines option at the Page Setup dialog box with the Sheet tab selected.

The gridlines that create the cells in a worksheet, by default, do not print. If you would like these gridlines to print, display the Page Setup dialog box with the Sheet tab selected, and then click Gridlines in the Print section. This inserts a check mark in the check box. At the Page Setup dialog box with the Sheet tab selected, you can also click Row and column headings and the row numbers and column letters will print with the worksheet.

If you are printing with a color printer, you can print the worksheet in black and white. To do this, display the Page Setup dialog box with the Sheet tab selected, and then click Black and white. This option is located in the Print section of the dialog box.

Printing Gridlines and Row and Column Headings

1. Open Excel Worksheet 05.
2. Save the worksheet with Save As and name it Excel C2, Ex 10.
3. Make the following changes to the worksheet:
   a. Specify that the gridlines and row and column headings are to print by completing the following steps:
      1) Click File and then Page Setup.
      2) At the Page Setup dialog box, click the Sheet tab.
      3) Click the Gridlines check box in the Print section to insert a check mark.
      4) Click the Row and column headings check box in the Print section to insert a check mark.

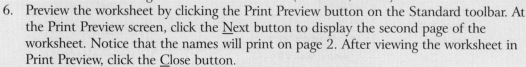

> b. With the Page Setup dialog box still displayed, click the Margins tab.
> c. At the Page Setup dialog box with the Margins tab selected, click the Horizontally option and then click the Vertically option.
> d. Click OK to close the dialog box.
> 4. Save the worksheet again with the same name (Excel C2, Ex 10).
> 5. Preview the worksheet by clicking the Print Preview button on the Standard toolbar. After viewing the worksheet in Print Preview, click the Close button.
> 6. Print and then close Excel C2, Ex 10.

Customizing Print Jobs

A variety of options are available for customizing print jobs. You can hide columns and/or rows before printing a worksheet, specify a printing area in a worksheet, and specify a print quality.

Hiding and Unhiding Workbook Elements

Various elements in a workbook, such as worksheets, columns, and rows, can be hidden. You may want to hide a worksheet that contains sensitive information, hide rows and/or columns that you are not using or do not want others to view, or hide elements in a workbook in order to use as much of the screen as possible to display specific worksheet data.

To hide a worksheet, display the worksheet, then click Format, point to Sheet, and then click Hide. To hide columns in a worksheet, select the columns to be hidden, click Format, point to Column, and then click Hide. To hide selected rows, click Format, point to Row, and then click Hide.

To make a hidden worksheet visible, click Format, point to Sheet, and then click Unhide. At the Unhide dialog box that displays, double-click the name of the hidden worksheet you want to display. To make a hidden column visible, select the column to the left and the column to the right of the hidden column, and then click Format, point to Columns, and then click Unhide. To make a hidden row visible, select the row above and the row below the hidden row, then click Format, point to Rows, and then click Unhide.

If the first row or column is hidden, use the Go To feature to make the row or column visible. To do this, click Edit and then Go To. At the Go To dialog box, key **A1** in the Reference text box, and then click OK. At the worksheet, click Format, point to Column or point to Row, and then click Unhide.

Printing a Specific Area of a Worksheet

Use the Print Area feature to select and print specific areas in a worksheet. To use this feature, select the cells you want to print, then click File, point to Print Area, and then click Set Print Area. This inserts a border around the selected cells. Click the Print button on the Standard toolbar and the cells within the border are printed.

You can specify more than one print area in a worksheet in Page Break Preview. To do this, display the worksheet in Page Break Preview. Select the first group of cells, then click File, point to Print Area, and then click Set Print Area. Select the next group of cells, right-click in the selected cells, and then click Add to Print Area at the shortcut menu. Clear a print area by selecting the area, clicking File, pointing to Print Area, and then clicking Clear Print Area.

Each area specified as a print area will print on a separate page. If you want nonadjacent print areas to print on the same page, consider hiding columns and/or rows in the worksheet to bring the areas together.

Changing Print Quality

Most printers have more than one level of print quality. The print quality choices vary with printers and may include options such as *Quality, Faster, Custom, Best, Normal,* and/or *Econofast.* To display information about currently selected printer, display the Print dialog box and the click the Properties button. This displays a properties dialog box with choices and tabs specific to the selected printer. You should be able to find printing quality options at this dialog box. You may need to click on different tabs to find the print quality options.

Customizing a Printing Job

1. Open Excel Worksheet 06.
2. Specify a print area by completing the following steps:
   a. Select cells A1 through B20.
   b. Click File, point to Print Area, and then click Set Print Area.
   c. With the border surrounding the cells A1 through B20, click the Print button on the Standard toolbar.
   d. Clear the print area by making sure cells A1 through B20 are selected and then clicking File, pointing to Print Area, and then clicking Clear Print Area.
3. Suppose you want to print all the student names and just the percentages for Test 6 and you want the information to print on one page. To do this, hide columns B through F and select the print area by completing the following steps:
   a. Select columns B through F.
   b. Click Format, point to Column, and then click Hide.
   c. Select cells A1 through G20. (Columns A and G are now adjacent.)
   d. Click File, point to Print Area, and then click Set Print Area.
   e. Change the print quality and print the specified print area by completing the following steps:
      1) Click File and then Print.
      2) At the Print dialog box, click the Properties button.
      3) At the printer properties dialog box, look for a printing quality option. (You may need to click on various tabs to find this option.)
      4) Click the faster printing quality and then click OK to close the dialog box. (If there is no faster printing quality option, choose a printing quality other than the default.)
      5) At the Print dialog box, click OK.
   f. Clear the print area by making sure cells A1 through G20 are selected and then clicking File, pointing to Print Area, and then clicking Clear Print Area.
   g. Make the hidden columns visible by selecting columns A and G and then clicking Format, pointing to Columns, and then clicking Unhide.
4. Close Excel Worksheet 06 without saving the changes.

Completing a Spelling Check

To spell check text in a worksheet using Excel's spell checking feature, make the first cell in the worksheet active, then click the Spelling button on the Standard toolbar or click Tools and then Spelling. Figure 2.10 displays the Spelling dialog box. At this dialog box, you can click a button to tell Excel to ignore a word or you can replace a misspelled word with a word from the Suggestions list box.

Spelling

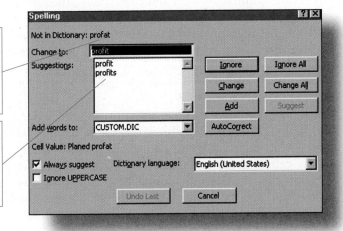

figure
2.10

Excel Spelling Dialog Box

The word in the worksheet not found in the spell check dictionary displays here.

Suggested spellings display in the Suggestions list box.

Using Undo and Redo

Excel includes an Undo button on the Standard toolbar that will reverse certain commands or delete the last data keyed in a cell. For example, if you apply an autoformat to selected cells in a worksheet and then decide you want the autoformatting removed, click the Undo button on the Standard toolbar. If you decide you want the autoformatting back again, click the Redo button on the Standard toolbar.

Undo

Redo

In addition to using the Undo and Redo buttons on the Standard toolbar, you can select options from the Edit drop-down menu to undo or repeat actions. The first two options at the Edit drop-down menu will vary depending on the last action completed. For example, if you just clicked the Currency Style button on the Formatting toolbar, and then displayed the Edit drop-down menu, the first option displays as Undo Style and the second option displays as Repeat Style. If you decide you do not want the currency style applied, click Edit and then Undo Style. You can also just click the Undo button on the Standard toolbar.

exercise 12

Spell Checking and Formatting a Worksheet

1. Open Excel Worksheet 04.
2. Save the worksheet with Save As and name it Excel C2, Ex 12.
3. Complete a spelling check on the worksheet by completing the following steps:
   a. Make sure cell A1 is the active cell.
   b. Click the Spelling button on the Standard toolbar.
   c. Click Change as needed to correct misspelled words in the worksheet.
   d. At the message telling you the spelling check is completed, click OK.
4. Make the following formatting changes to the document:
   a. Select the entire worksheet and then change the font to 11-point Univers (or a similar sans serif typeface such as Tahoma).
   b. Select cells A1 through B12 and then apply the *Accounting 4* autoformat.
   c. Select cells B3 through B12 and then click the Currency Style button on the Formatting toolbar.
   d. With cells B3 through B12 still selected, click twice on the Decrease Decimal button on the Formatting toolbar.
   e. Make cell B4 active and then add a single-line border at the bottom of the cell. (To do this, click the down-pointing triangle at the right side of the Borders button on the Formatting toolbar and then click the Bottom Border option.)
   f. Make cell B5 active and then add a double-line border at the bottom of the cell. (To do this, click the down-pointing triangle at the right side of the Borders button on the Formatting toolbar and then click the Bottom Double Border option.)
   g. Make cell B10 active and then add a single-line border at the bottom of the cell.
   h. Make cell B12 active and then add a double-line border at the bottom of the cell.
   i. Select row 1 and then turn on bold.
   j. Select cells A1 through B12 and then add a pale blue color shading.
   k. After looking at the worksheet with the light blue color shading, you decide you want to remove it. To do this, click the Undo button on the Standard toolbar.
5. Save the worksheet again with the same name (Excel C2, Ex 12).
6. Print and then close Excel C2, Ex 12.

Finding and Replacing Data in a Worksheet

Excel provides a find feature you can use to look for specific data and either replace it with nothing or replace it with other data. This feature is particularly helpful in a large worksheet with data you want to find quickly. Excel also includes a find and replace feature. Use this to look for specific data in a worksheet and replace it with other data.

To find specific data in a worksheet, click Edit and then Find. This displays the Find dialog box shown in figure 2.11. Key the data you want to find in the Find what text box and then click the Find Next button. Continue clicking the Find Next button to move to the next occurrence of the data.

Ctrl + F is the keyboard command to display the Find dialog box.

Hint

Find Dialog Box

To find specific data in a worksheet and replace it with other data, click Edit and then Replace. This displays the Replace dialog box shown in figure 2.12. Enter the data for which you are looking in the Find what text box. Press the Tab key or click in the Replace with text box and then enter the data that is to replace the data in the Find what text box.

Ctrl + H is the keyboard command to display the Replace dialog box.

Replace Dialog Box

The Replace dialog box contains four command buttons at the right side. Click the Find Next button to tell Excel to find the next occurrence of the data. Click the Replace button to replace the data and find the next occurrence. If you know that you want all occurrences of the data in the Find what text box replaced with the data in the Replace with text box, click the Replace All button. Click the Close button to close the Replace dialog box.

By default, Excel will look for any data that contains the same characters as the data in the Find what text box, without concern for the characters before or after the entered data. For example, in exercise 13, you will be looking for test scores of 0%. If you do not specify to Excel that you want to find cells that contain just 0%, Excel will stop at any cell containing a 0%. In this example, Excel would stop at a cell containing 90% or a cell containing 100%. To specify that the only data that should be contained in the cell is what is entered in the Find what text box, insert a check mark in the Find entire cells only check box.

If the Find dialog box or the Replace dialog box obstructs your view of the worksheet, move the box by clicking and dragging the title bar.

If the Match case option at the Replace dialog box is active (contains a check mark), Excel will look for only that data that exactly matches the case of the data entered in the Find what text box. Remove the check mark from this check box if you do not want Excel to find exact case matches. Excel, by default, searches by rows in a worksheet. This can be changed to *By Columns* with the Search option.

Finding and Replacing Data

1. Open Excel Worksheet 06.
2. Save the worksheet with Save As and name it Excel C2, Ex 13.
3. Find all occurrences of 0% in the worksheet and replace with 70% by completing the following steps:
   a. Click Edit and then Replace.
   b. At the Replace dialog box, key **0%** in the Find what text box.
   c. Press the Tab key (this moves the insertion point to the Replace with text box).
   d. Key **70%**.
   e. Click Find entire cells only.
   f. Click the Replace All button.
4. Select the entire worksheet and then change the font to 10-point Century Schoolbook (or a similar serif typeface).
5. Automatically adjust the width of columns A through M.
6. Save the worksheet again with the same name (Excel C2, Ex 13).
7. Display the Page Setup dialog box with the Page tab selected, click the Landscape option, and then close the dialog box.
8. Print and then close Excel C2, Ex 13.

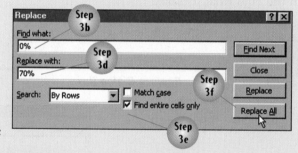

Excel's Find feature is very similar to the Find and Replace feature. The difference is that Find will only find data and will not replace it. To use Find, click Edit and then Find. This causes the Find dialog box to display. This dialog box contains many of the same options as the Find and Replace dialog box. Use Find if you are looking for specific data in a worksheet.

Sort Ascending

Sort Descending

Sorting Data

Excel is primarily a spreadsheet program, but it also includes some basic database functions. With a database program, you can alphabetize information or arrange numbers numerically. Data can be sorted by columns in a worksheet. By default, Excel will sort special symbols such as *, @, and # first, numbers second, and letters third. Sort data in a worksheet using the Sort Ascending or Sort Descending buttons on the Standard toolbar or at the Sort dialog box.

Sorting Data Using Buttons on the Standard Toolbar

To sort data in a worksheet using the buttons on the Standard toolbar, open the worksheet, select the cells containing data you want to sort, and then click the Sort Ascending button (sorts text A through Z; sorts numbers lowest to highest) or Sort Descending button (sorts text Z through A; sorts numbers highest to lowest). If you select more than one column in a worksheet, Excel will sort the data in the first selected column.

exercise 14

Sorting Data Using the Sort Ascending and Sort Descending Buttons

1. Open Excel Worksheet 03.
2. Save the worksheet with Save As and name it Excel C2, Ex 14.
3. Make the following formatting changes to the worksheet:
   a. Merge and center the data in cell A1 across cells A1 through D1.
   b. Bold the data in cell A1.
   c. Bold the data in cells B2 through D2.
   d. Automatically adjust the width of columns A through D.
   e. Select cells B3 through D8 and then click the Percent Style button on the Formatting toolbar.
4. Sort the data in the first column alphabetically in ascending order by completing the following steps:
   a. Select cells A3 through D8.
   b. Click the Sort Ascending button on the Standard toolbar.

5. Save the worksheet again with the same name (Excel C2, Ex 14).
6. Print Excel C2, Ex 14. (Do not close the worksheet.)
7. Sort the data in the first column alphabetically in descending order by completing steps similar to those in step 4 except click the Sort Descending button on the Standard toolbar.
8. Save the worksheet again with the same name (Excel C2, Ex 14).
9. Print and then close Excel C2, Ex 14.

Sorting Data at the Sort Dialog Box

If you want to sort data in a column other than the first selected column, use the Sort dialog box. If you select just one column in a worksheet and then click the Sort Ascending or Sort Descending button on the Standard toolbar, only the data in that column is sorted. If this data was related to data to the left or right of the data in the column, that relationship is broken. For example, if you sort cells B3 through B8 in Excel C2, Ex 14, the percentages for *Bondholder's equity ratio* are now *23%, 39%,* and *41%,* when they should be *45%, 39%,* and *41%.*

Use the Sort dialog box to sort data and maintain the relationship of all cells. To sort using the Sort dialog box, select the cells you want sorted, then click <u>D</u>ata and then <u>S</u>ort. This displays the Sort dialog box shown in figure 2.13.

Sort Dialog Box

The data displayed in the <u>S</u>ort by text box will vary depending on what you have selected. Generally, the data that displays is the title of the first column of selected cells. If the selected cells do not have a title, the data may display as *Column A*. Use this option to specify what column you want sorted. Using the Sort dialog box to sort data in a column maintains the relationship of the data.

exercise 15

Sorting Data Using the Sort Dialog Box

1. Open Excel C2, Ex 14.
2. Save the worksheet with Save As and name it Excel C2, Ex 15.
3. Sort the percentages in cells B3 through B8 in ascending order and maintain the relationship to the other data by completing the following steps:
   a. Select cells A3 through D8.
   b. Click <u>D</u>ata and then <u>S</u>ort.
   c. At the Sort dialog box, click the down-pointing triangle at the right of the Sort by text box, and then click *Actual* from the drop-down list.
   d. Make sure <u>A</u>scending is selected in the Sort by section of the dialog box. If not, click <u>A</u>scending.
   e. Click OK to close the dialog box.

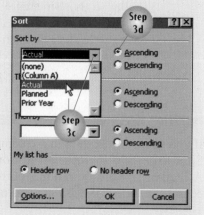

4. Save the worksheet again with the same name (Excel C2, Ex 15).
5. Print Excel C2, Ex 15.
6. Sort the percentages in cells B3 through B8 in *descending* order and maintain the relationship of the data by completing steps similar to those in step 3.
7. Save the worksheet again with the same name (Excel C2, Ex 15).
8. Print and then close Excel C2, Ex 15.

Sorting More than One Column

When sorting data in cells, you can sort on more than one column. For example, in exercise 16, you will be sorting the average test scores in ascending order and then sorting the names of the students alphabetically. In this sort, the test averages are sorted first and then students with the same average are sorted alphabetically within that average. For example, there are several average scores of 76%. Students within that average—not all students—are sorted alphabetically.

To sort on more than one column, select all columns in the worksheet that need to remain relative, and then display the Sort dialog box. At the Sort dialog box, specify the first column you want sorted in the Sort by text box, and then specify the second column in the first Then by text box. In Excel, you can sort on up to three columns. If you want to sort the data in a third column, you would specify that in the second Then by text box.

> If you are not satisfied with the results of a sort, immediately click the Undo button on the Standard toolbar.
>
> Hint

exercise 16

Sorting Data in Two Columns

1. Open Excel Worksheet 06.
2. Save the worksheet with Save As and name it Excel C2, Ex 16.
3. Select and then delete row 2.
4. Sort the Test 1 percentages in cells B2 through B19 in ascending order and then sort alphabetically by the names in the first column by completing the following steps:
   a. Select cells A2 through M19.
   b. Click Data and then Sort.
   c. At the Sort dialog box, click the down-pointing triangle at the right side of the Sort by text box, and then click *Test 1* from the drop-down list.
   d. Make sure Ascending is selected in the Sort by section of the dialog box. If not, click Ascending.
   e. Click the down-pointing triangle at the right of the first Then by text box and then click *Name* in the drop-down list.
   f. Make sure Ascending is selected in the first Then by section.
   g. Click OK to close the dialog box.
5. Save the worksheet again with the same name (Excel C2, Ex 16).

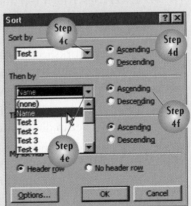

6. Display the Page Setup dialog box with the Page tab selected, click the Landscape option, and then close the dialog box.
7. Print the worksheet. (Notice how the names of the students with the same Test 1 percentages are alphabetized.)
8. Close Excel C2, Ex 16.

chapter summary

➤ Insert a row in a worksheet by clicking Insert and then Rows. To insert more than one row, select the number of rows you want inserted, and then click Insert and then Rows. A row can also be inserted at the Insert dialog box.

➤ Insert a column in a worksheet by clicking Insert and then Columns. To insert more than one column, select the number of columns you want inserted, and then click Insert and then Columns. A column can also be inserted at the Insert dialog box.

➤ Delete a specific cell by clicking Edit and then Delete. This displays the Delete dialog box where you can specify if you want to delete just the cell or an entire row or column.

➤ Contents of a cell can be removed with the Clear option from the Edit drop-down menu or by pressing the Delete key.

➤ By default, a worksheet prints on the page in portrait orientation. This can be changed to landscape orientation at the Page Setup dialog box with the Page tab selected.

➤ The percentage size of data in a worksheet can be adjusted with options in the Scaling section of the Page Setup dialog box with the Page tab selected.

➤ The paper size can be changed with the Paper size option at the Page Setup dialog box with the Page tab selected.

➤ Create a header and/or footer for worksheet pages with options at the Page Setup dialog box with the Header/Footer tab selected.

➤ The beginning page number in a worksheet can be changed with the First page number option at the Page Setup dialog box with the Page tab selected.

➤ Excel uses 1-inch top and bottom margins and 0.75-inch left and right margins for a worksheet. These default margins can be changed at the Page Setup dialog box with the Margins tab selected.

➤ Center a worksheet horizontally and/or vertically on a page with options at the Page Setup dialog box with the Margins tab selected.

➤ Insert a page break in a worksheet with Insert and then Page Break.

➤ Print column and row titles on every page of a multiple-paged worksheet with options at the Page Setup dialog box with the Sheet tab selected.

➤ Gridlines, column letters, and row numbers can be printed with options at the Page Setup dialog box with the Sheet tab selected.

➤ You can hide and unhide a worksheet in a workbook or columns or rows in a worksheet.

➤ Use the Print Area feature to select and print specific areas in a worksheet. Specify more than one print area in Page Break Preview.

➤ The print quality for most printers can be changed with options at the properties dialog box. Display the dialog box by clicking the Properties button at the Print dialog box.

➤ Complete a spelling check on a worksheet by clicking the Spelling button on the Standard toolbar or clicking Tools and then Spelling.

➤ Click the Undo button to reverse certain commands or delete the last data keyed in a cell. Click the Redo button to repeat the last command or action, if possible.

➤ Find data with options at the Find dialog box and find and replace data in a worksheet with options at the Replace dialog box.

➤ Sort the first column of selected cells with the Sort Ascending or Sort Descending buttons on the Standard toolbar.

➤ Use the Sort dialog box to sort on a column other than the first column, to maintain the relationship of the data, or to sort on more than one column.

commands review

	Mouse/Keyboard
Insert a row	Click Insert, Rows
Insert a column	Click Insert, Columns
Display Insert dialog box	Click Insert, Cells
Display Delete dialog box	Click Edit, Delete
Clear cell	Click Edit, Clear or press the Delete key
Display Page Setup dialog box	Click File and then Page Setup
Insert a page break	Click Insert, Page Break
Hide columns	Select columns, click Format, point to Column, then click Hide
Hide rows	Select rows, click Format, point to Row, then click Hide
Unhide columns	Select column to left and right, then click Format, point to Column, then click Unhide
Unhide rows	Select row above and below, then click Format, point to Row, then click Unhide
Set a print area	Select cells, then click File, point to Print Area, then click Set Print Area
Clear a print area	Select cells, then click File, point to Print Area, then click Clear Print Area
Display Spelling dialog box	Click Spelling button on Standard toolbar or click Tools, Spelling
Display Find dialog box	Click Edit, Find
Display Replace dialog box	Click Edit, Replace
Sort first selected column in ascending order	Click Sort Ascending button on Standard toolbar
Sort first selected column in descending order	Click Sort Descending button on Standard toolbar
Display Sort dialog box	Click Data, Sort

thinking offline

Completion: In the space provided at the right, indicate the correct term, command, or number.

1. By default, a row is inserted in this direction from the row containing the active cell.

2. By default, a column is inserted in this direction from the column containing the active cell.

3. By default, a worksheet prints in this orientation on a page.

4. Change the page orientation at the Page Setup dialog box with this tab selected.

5. This is the default paper size.

6. This is the worksheet default top and bottom margin measurement.

7. This is the worksheet default left and right margin measurement.

8. A worksheet can be horizontally and/or vertically centered with options at the Page Setup dialog box with this tab selected.

9. Click this menu sequence to insert a page break in a worksheet.

10. Specify to print gridlines at the Page Setup dialog box with this tab selected.

11. To make a hidden column visible, select these columns and then click Format, point to Column, and then click Unhide.

12. Use this feature to print specific areas in a worksheet.

13. To complete a spelling check on a worksheet, click this button on the Standard toolbar.

14. To display the Sort dialog box, click Sort from this drop-down menu.

15. List the steps you would complete to print column titles in a multiple-paged worksheet.

16. List the steps you would complete to find all occurrences of *January* in a worksheet and replace with *July*.

17. List the steps you would complete to sort the second column of data in ascending order in the worksheet displayed below.

	A	B	C	D
1	SALES BY GEOGRAPHIC TERRITORY			
2	Territory	Actual	Budget	
3	Northwest	$ 459,309	$ 465,000	
4	Northeast	$ 794,209	$ 820,000	
5	Southwest	$ 351,309	$ 350,000	
6	Southeast	$ 408,123	$ 400,000	
7				

working hands-on

Assessment 1

1. Open Excel Worksheet 07.
2. Save the worksheet with Save As and name it Excel C2, SA 01.
3. Make the following changes to the worksheet:
   a. Delete column E.
   b. Bold the data in cell A1.
   c. Bold the data in row 2.
   d. Select columns B through D and then change the width of the columns to 13.00.
   e. Create a column between columns C and D (when the column is inserted, the data in column D moves over to column E).
   f. Select cells D3 through D10 and then change the number formatting to *General*. (Do this at the Format Cells dialog box with the Number tab selected.)
   g. Key the following data in the specified cells:
      D2 = **Periods**
      D3 = 2 (*Hint: Use the fill handle to copy the 2s.*)
      D4 = 2
      D5 = 2
      D6 = 2
      D7 = 2
      D8 = 2
      D9 = 2
      D10 = 2
   h. Select and then center the data in cells D3 through D10.
   i. Add a row above row 6 and then key the following data in the specified cells:

$$A6 = \text{Facsimile}$$
$$B6 = 670.00$$
$$C6 = 150.00$$
$$D6 = 2$$
$$E6 = 4$$

    j. Select cells A1 through E11 and then apply the *Colorful 1* autoformat.
    k. Select cells D3 through E11 and then change the alignment to center.
4. Save the worksheet again with the same name (Excel C2, SA 01).
5. Print and then close Excel C2, SA 01.

Assessment 2

1. Open Excel Worksheet 01.
2. Save the worksheet with Save As and name it Excel C2, SA 02.
3. Make the following changes to the worksheet:
    a. Select the worksheet and then change the font to 10-point Century Schoolbook (or a similar serif typeface).
    b. Automatically adjust the width of column A.
    c. Bold and center the data in row 1.
    d. Delete row 2.
    e. Select cells B2 through B9 and then change the alignment to center.
4. Change the worksheet top margin to 2 inches and the left margin to 2.25 inches and then print the worksheet.
5. Save the worksheet again with the same name (Excel C2, SA 02).
6. Close Excel C2, SA 02.

Assessment 3

1. Open Excel Worksheet 06.
2. Save the worksheet with Save As and name it Excel C2, SA 03.
3. Make the following changes to the worksheet:
    a. Select the worksheet and then change the font to 11-point Garamond (or a similar serif typeface).
    b. If necessary, automatically adjust the width of column A.
    c. If necessary, adjust slightly columns K, L, and M so the title (such as *Test 10, Test 11*, and so on) fits in the cell.
    d. Delete row 2 and then delete rows 8 and 9.
    e. Create the header *Excel Test Scores* that prints at the right margin on both pages.
    f. Create a footer that prints *Page x* (where *x* represents the correct page number) at the bottom center of the page.
4. Save the worksheet again with the same name (Excel C2, SA 03).
5. Print the worksheet so the column titles (names) print on both pages.
6. Print the worksheet again in landscape orientation.
7. Close Excel C2, SA 03.

Assessment 4

1. Open Excel Worksheet 02.
2. Save the worksheet with Save As and name it Excel C2, SA 04.
3. Make the following changes to the worksheet:
    a. Select the entire worksheet and then change the font to 12-point Tahoma (or a similar sans serif typeface).

    b.   Select row 1 and then bold and center the data.
    c.   Select cells B2 through D8 and then click the Currency Style button on the Formatting toolbar.
    d.   With cells B2 through D8 still selected, click twice the Decrease Decimal button on the Formatting toolbar.
    e.   Select columns A through D and then automatically adjust the size of the columns to accommodate the amounts.
4. Save the worksheet again with the same name (Excel C2, SA 04).
5. Print the worksheet, including gridlines and the row and column headings.
6. Close Excel C2, SA 04.

Assessment 5

1. Open Excel C2, SA 01.
2. Save the worksheet with Save As and name it Excel C2, SA 05.
3. Make the following changes to the worksheet:
    a.   Find all occurrences of cells containing only the number *2* and then replace it with the number *1*.
    b.   Find all occurrences of cells containing only the number *6* and then replace it with the number *5*.
    c.   Delete row 10.
4. Save the worksheet again with the same name (Excel C2, SA 05).
5. Print the worksheet horizontally and vertically centered on the page.
6. Close Excel C2, SA 05.

Assessment 6

1. Open Excel C2, SA 01.
2. Save the worksheet with Save As and name it Excel C2, SA 06.
3. Select cells A3 through E11 and then click the Sort Ascending button on the Standard toolbar.
4. Print the worksheet horizontally and vertically centered on the page.
5. With the worksheet still open, select cells A3 through E11, and then sort the numbers in column B in ascending order (do this at the Sort dialog box).
6. Print the worksheet horizontally and vertically centered on the page.
7. With the worksheet still open, select cells A3 through E11, and then sort by the numbers in the *Life of Asset* column in ascending order and then by *Equipment* in ascending order. (This is one sort.)
8. Save the worksheet again with the same name (Excel C2, SA 06).
9. Print the worksheet horizontally and vertically centered on the page.
10. Close Excel C2, SA 06.

Assessment 7

1. Open Excel Worksheet 06.
2. Save the worksheet with Save As and name it Excel C2, SA 07.
3. Make the following changes to the worksheet:
    a.   Delete columns J through M.
    b.   Delete row 2 and then delete row 13.
    c.   Select cells A2 through I18 and then sort by names in descending order.

d. Select cells A1 through I18 and then apply an autoformat of your choosing.
4. Save the worksheet again with the same name (Excel C2, SA 07).
5. Print the worksheet horizontally and vertically centered on the page and insert page numbering at the bottom center of the page.
6. Close Excel C2, SA 07.

Assessment 8

1. Open Excel Worksheet 06.
2. Print student names and scores for Test 12 on one page by completing the following steps:
   a. Hide columns B through L.
   b. Specify A1 through M20 as a print area.
   c. Print the print area. (Make sure the cells print on one page.)
   d. Clear the print area.
   e. Make columns B through L visible.
3. Close Excel Worksheet 06 without saving the changes.

Assessment 9

1. Use Excel's Office Assistant and ask the question "What is Excel's default sorting order?"
2. Display information on default sort orders. After reading and printing the information presented by the Office Assistant, create a worksheet containing a summary of the information. Create the worksheet with the following features:
   a. Create a title for the worksheet.
   b. Set the data in cells in a serif typeface and change the data color.
   c. Add borders to the cells (you determine the border style).
   d. Add a color shading to cells (you determine the color—make it complementary to the data color).
3. Save the completed worksheet and name it Excel C2, SA 09.
4. Print and then close Excel C2, SA 09.

 Chapter 03C

Maintaining Workbooks and Creating Web Pages

Once you have been working with Excel 2000 for a period of time you will have accumulated several workbook files. Workbooks should be organized into folders to facilitate fast retrieval of information. Occasionally you should perform file maintenance activities such as copying, moving, renaming, and deleting files to ensure the file list in your various folders is manageable.

A workbook can be saved as a web page and hyperlinks included to post information on the company intranet or globally through the Internet. Another method to distribute a workbook electronically is by e-mailing it.

Maintaining Workbooks

Many file management tasks can be completed at the Open and Save As dialog boxes. These tasks can include copying, moving, printing, and renaming workbooks; opening multiple workbooks; and creating a new folder. To display the

Open dialog box, shown in figure 3.1, click the Open button on the Standard toolbar or click File and then Open. To display the Save As dialog box, click File and then Save As.

figure 3.1

Open Dialog Box

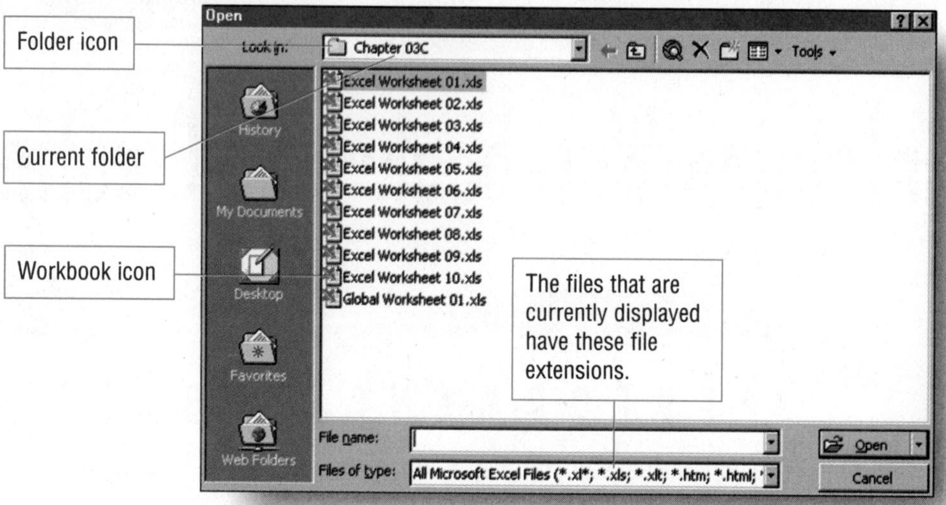

Folder icon

Current folder

Workbook icon

The files that are currently displayed have these file extensions.

Some document maintenance tasks such as creating a folder and deleting documents are performed by using buttons on the Open dialog box or Save As dialog box toolbar. Figure 3.2 displays the Open dialog box toolbar buttons.

figure 3.2

Open Dialog Box Toolbar Buttons

Back

Up One Level

Search the Web

Delete

Create New Folder

Views

Tools

Creating a Folder

In Excel, workbooks should be grouped logically and stored in folders. For example, all workbooks related to one department could be stored in one folder with the department name as the folder name. A folder can be created within a folder. If you create workbooks for a department by individual, each individual could have a folder name within the department folder. The main folder on a disk or drive is called the root folder. Additional folders are created as a branch of this root folder.

At the Open or Save As dialog boxes, workbook file names display in the list box preceded by a workbook icon; a folder name is preceded by a folder icon. The folder and workbook icons are displayed in figure 3.1.

Create a new folder by clicking the Create New Folder button located on the dialog box toolbar at the Open dialog box or Save As dialog box. At the New Folder dialog box shown in figure 3.3, key a name for the folder in the Name text box, and then click OK or press Enter. The new folder becomes the active folder.

figure
3.3

New Folder Dialog Box

New Folder | ? X
Current Folder:
A:\
Name: |

OK
Cancel

If you want to make the previous folder the active folder, click the Up One Level button on the dialog box toolbar. Clicking this button changes to the folder that was up one level from the current folder. After clicking the Up One Level button, the Back button becomes active. Click this button and the previously active folder becomes active again.

A folder name can contain a maximum of 255 characters. Numbers, spaces, and symbols can be used in the folder name, except those symbols explained in chapter 1 in the Saving a Workbook section.

(Before completing computer exercises, delete the Chapter 02C *folder on your disk. Next, copy the* Chapter 03C *folder from the CD that accompanies this textbook to your disk.)*

exercise

Creating a Folder

1. Create a folder named *Finance* on your disk by completing the following steps:
   a. Display the Open dialog box and then double-click the *Chapter 03C* folder name to make it the active folder.
   b. Click the Create New Folder button (located on the dialog box toolbar).
   c. At the New Folder dialog box, key Finance.
   d. Click OK or press Enter. (The Finance folder is now the active folder.)
   e. Change back to the *Chapter 03C* folder by clicking the Up One Level button on the dialog box toolbar.
2. Click the Cancel or Close button to close the Open dialog box.

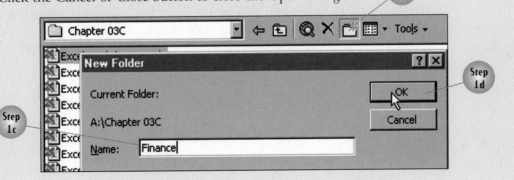

Selecting Documents

Workbook management tasks can be completed on one workbook or more than one selected workbook. For example, you can move one workbook to a different folder, or you can select several workbooks and move them all in one operation. Selected workbooks can be opened, deleted, copied, moved, or printed.

To select one workbook, display the Open dialog box, and then click the desired workbook in the file list. To select several adjacent workbooks (workbooks displayed next to each other), using the mouse, you would complete the following steps:

1. Display the Open dialog box.
2. Click the first workbook to select it.
3. Position the arrow pointer on the last workbook to be selected, hold down the Shift key, and then click the left mouse button.

You can also select workbooks that are not adjacent in the Open dialog box. To do this with the mouse, you would complete the following steps:

1. Display the Open dialog box.
2. Click the first workbook you want selected.
3. Hold down the Ctrl key.
4. Click each additional workbook you want selected.
5. When all desired workbooks are selected, release the Ctrl key.

When the Open dialog box is displayed, the first workbook in the Look in list box is automatically selected. Before selecting documents, deselect the first workbook (unless this first workbook is to be included with the other selected workbooks). To deselect the first workbook, position the arrow pointer anywhere in a clear portion of the Look in list box (not on a workbook name), and then click the left mouse button.

Deleting Workbooks and Folders

At some point, you may want to delete certain workbooks from your data disk or any other disk or folder in which you may be working. If you use Excel on a regular basis, you should establish a periodic system for deleting workbooks that are no longer used. The system you choose depends on the work you are doing and the amount of folder or disk space available. To delete a workbook, display the Open or Save As dialog box, select the workbook, and then click the Delete button on the dialog box toolbar. At the dialog box asking you to confirm the deletion, click Yes.

You can also delete a workbook by displaying the Open dialog box, selecting the workbook to be deleted, clicking the Tools button on the dialog box toolbar, and then clicking Delete at the drop-down menu. Another method for deleting a document is to display the Open dialog box, right-click the document to be deleted, and then click Delete at the shortcut menu.

Deleting a Workbook

1. Delete a workbook by completing the following steps:
   a. Display the Open dialog box with *Chapter 03C* as the active folder.
   b. Click Excel Worksheet 05 to select it.
   c. Click the Delete button on the dialog box toolbar.
   d. At the Confirm File Delete dialog box asking if you are sure you want to delete the item, click Yes.
2. Close the Open dialog box.

Deleting Selected Workbooks

1. Delete selected workbooks by completing the following steps:
   a. Display the Open dialog box with *Chapter 03C* as the active folder.
   b. Click Excel Worksheet 02.
   c. Hold down the Shift key and then click Excel Worksheet 04.
   d. Click the Tools button on the dialog box toolbar.
   e. At the drop-down menu that displays, click Delete.

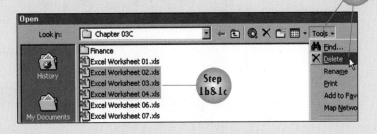

   f. At the Confirm File Delete dialog box asking if you are sure you want to delete these 3 items, click Yes.
   g. At the second Confirm File Delete dialog box telling you that Excel Worksheet 02 is a read-only file and asking if you are sure you want to delete it, click the Yes to All button.
2. Close the Open dialog box.

A folder and all its contents can be deleted at the Open or Save As dialog box. Delete a folder and its contents in the same manner as deleting a workbook or selected workbooks.

Deleting to the Recycle Bin

Workbooks deleted from your data disk are deleted permanently. (There are recovery programs, however, that will help you recover deleted text. If you accidentally delete a workbook(s) from a disk, do not do anything more with the disk until you can run a recovery program.) Workbooks deleted from the hard drive are automatically sent to the Windows Recycle Bin. If you accidentally delete a workbook to the Recycle Bin, it can be easily restored. To free space on the hard drive, empty the Recycle Bin on a periodic basis. Restoring a workbook from or emptying the contents of the Recycle Bin is done at the Windows desktop (not in Excel). To empty the Recycle Bin, you would complete the following steps:

1. Display the Windows desktop. (If you are currently working in Excel, click the Minimize button at the right side of the Title bar. [The Minimize button contains the single underline symbol (_)]. Be sure to click the Minimize button on the Title bar and not the one just below it on the Menu bar.)
2. At the Windows desktop, double-click the Recycle Bin icon (usually located at the left side of the desktop).
3. At the Recycle Bin dialog box, shown in figure 3.4, click File and then Empty Recycle Bin.
4. At the Confirm Multiple File Delete dialog box asking if you are sure you want to delete these items, click Yes.

Recycle Bin Dialog Box

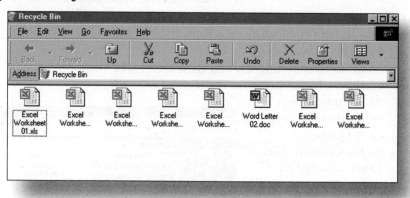

If you want to empty only specific files from the Recycle Bin, hold down the Ctrl key while clicking the files to be emptied. Position the arrow pointer on one of the selected files, click the right mouse button, and then click the left mouse button on Delete. At the Confirm Multiple File Delete dialog box asking if you want to delete the selected items, click Yes.

A file or selected files can also be restored from the Recycle Bin. To do this, you would complete the following steps:

1. At the Windows desktop, double-click the Recycle Bin icon.
2. At the Recycle Bin dialog box, click the file to be restored. (If you are restoring more than one file, hold down the Ctrl key while clicking the desired files.)
3. Click File and then Restore.

At the Recycle Bin dialog box, you can also restore a file by positioning the arrow pointer on the file to be restored, clicking the right mouse button, and then clicking the left mouse button on Restore.

If you minimized the Excel application by clicking the Minimize button, you can maximize (display the Excel screen) the Excel program at the desktop by clicking the Microsoft Excel button located on the Taskbar (at the bottom of the screen).

Copying Files

In previous chapters, you opened a workbook from the data disk and saved it with a new name on the same disk. This process makes an exact copy of the workbook, leaving the original on the disk. You copied workbooks and saved the new workbook in the same folder as the original. You can also copy a workbook into another folder and use the workbook's original name or give it a different name, or select workbooks at the Open dialog box and copy them to the same folder or into a different folder. To copy a workbook into another folder, you would complete the following steps:

1. Open the workbook you want to copy.
2. Display the Save As dialog box.
3. At the Save As dialog box, change to the desired folder. To do this, click the down-pointing triangle to the right of the Save in text box, and then click the desired folder at the drop-down menu.
4. Click the Save button in the lower right corner of the dialog box.

The Open and Save As dialog boxes contain an Up One Level button (located on the dialog box toolbar—see figure 3.2). Use this button if you want to change to the folder that is up one level from the current folder.

Saving a Copy of an Open Workbook

1. Open Excel Worksheet 10.
2. Save the workbook with Save As and name it Quota&Bonus. (Make sure *Chapter 03C* is the active folder.)
3. Save a copy of the Quota&Bonus workbook in the *Finance* folder created in exercise 1 by completing the following steps: (If you did not complete exercise 1, check with your instructor before continuing.)
   a. With Quota&Bonus still open, display the Save As dialog box.
   b. At the Save As dialog box, change to the *Finance* folder. To do this, double-click *Finance* at the beginning of the list box (folders are listed before documents).
   c. Click the Save button located in the lower right corner of the dialog box.
4. Close Quota&Bonus.
5. Change back to the *Chapter 03C* folder by completing the following steps:
   a. Display the Open dialog box.
   b. Click the Up One Level button located on the dialog box toolbar.
   c. Click Cancel or Close to close the Open dialog box.

A workbook can be copied to another folder without opening the workbook first. To do this, use the <u>C</u>opy and <u>P</u>aste options from a shortcut menu at the Open (or Save As) dialog box.

Copying a Workbook at the Open Dialog Box

1. Copy Excel Worksheet 07 to the *Finance* folder by completing the following steps:
   a. Display the Open dialog box with *Chapter 03C* as the active folder.
   b. Position the arrow pointer on Excel Worksheet 07, click the right mouse button, and then click <u>C</u>opy at the shortcut menu.
   c. Change to the Finance folder by double-clicking Finance at the beginning of the list box.
   d. Position the arrow pointer in any white area (not on a workbook name) in the list box, click the right mouse button, and then click <u>P</u>aste at the shortcut menu.
2. Change back to the *Chapter 03C* folder by clicking the Up One Level button located on the dialog box toolbar.
3. Close the Open dialog box.

A workbook or selected workbooks can be copied into the same folder. When you do this, Excel names the duplicated document(s) "Copy of xxx" (where xxx is the current workbook name). You can copy one workbook or selected workbooks into the same folder.

Copying Selected Workbooks within the Same Folder

1. Copy workbooks into the same folder by completing the following steps:
   a. Display the Open dialog box with *Chapter 03C* the active folder.
   b. Select Excel Worksheet 01, Excel Worksheet 07, and Excel Worksheet 09. (To do this, hold down the Ctrl key while clicking each workbook name.)
   c. Position the arrow pointer on one of the selected workbooks, click the right mouse button, and then click <u>C</u>opy at the shortcut menu.

d. Position the arrow pointer in any white area in the list box, click the left mouse button to deselect the three workbook names, click the right mouse button, and then click <u>P</u>aste at the shortcut menu. (In a few seconds, Excel will redisplay the Open dialog box with the following workbooks added: Copy of Excel Worksheet 01, Copy of Excel Worksheet 07, and Copy of Excel Worksheet 09.)

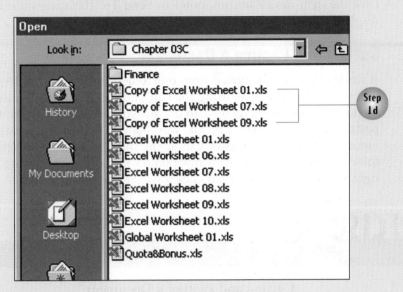

2. Close the Open dialog box.

exercise 7

Copying Selected Workbooks into a Different Folder

1. Copy selected workbooks to the *Finance* folder by completing the following steps:
   a. Display the Open dialog box with *Chapter 03C* as the active folder.
   b. Select Excel Worksheet 06, Excel Worksheet 08, and Excel Worksheet 10.
   c. Position the arrow pointer on one of the selected documents, click the right mouse button, and then click <u>C</u>opy at the shortcut menu.
   d. Double-click the *Finance* folder.
   e. When the *Finance* folder displays, position the arrow pointer in any white area in the list box, click the right mouse button, and then click <u>P</u>aste at the shortcut menu.

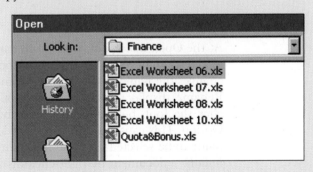

   f. Click the Up One Level button to change back to the *Chapter 03C* folder.
2. Close the Open dialog box.

Sending Workbooks to a Different Drive or Folder

With the Copy and Paste options from the shortcut menu at the Open or Save As dialog box, you can copy workbooks to another folder or drive. With the Send To option, you can quickly send a copy of a workbook to another drive or folder. To use this option, position the arrow pointer on the workbook you want copied, click the right mouse button, point to Send To (this causes a side menu to display), and then click the desired drive or folder.

Cutting and Pasting a Document

A workbook can be removed from one folder or disk and inserted in another folder or on another disk using the Cut and Paste options from the shortcut menu at the Open dialog box. To do this you would display the Open dialog box, position the arrow pointer on the workbook to be removed (cut), click the right mouse button, and then click Cut at the shortcut menu. Change to the desired folder or drive, position the arrow pointer in a white area in the list box, click the right mouse button, and then click Paste at the shortcut menu.

Cutting and Pasting a Document

1. Move a workbook to a different folder by completing the following steps:
   a. Display the Open dialog box with *Chapter 03C* as the active folder.
   b. Position the arrow pointer on Excel Worksheet 09, click the right mouse button, and then click Cut at the shortcut menu.
   c. Double-click *Finance* to make it the active folder.
   d. Position the arrow pointer in the white area in the list box, click the right mouse button, and then click Paste at the shortcut menu.
   e. At the Confirm File Move dialog box asking if you are sure you want to move the file, click Yes. (This dialog box usually does not appear when you cut and paste. Because the files you copied from your student CD-ROM are read-only files, this warning message appears.)
   f. Click the Up One Level button to make the *Chapter 03C* folder the active folder.
2. Close the Open dialog box.

Renaming Workbooks

At the Open dialog box, use the Rename option from the Tools drop-down menu or the shortcut menu to give a workbook a different name. The Rename option changes the name of the workbook and keeps it in the same folder. To use Rename, display the Open dialog box, click once on the document to be renamed, click the Tools button on the dialog box toolbar and then click the Rename Option. This causes a thin black border to surround the workbook name and the name to be selected. Key the new name and then press Enter. You can also rename a document by right-clicking the workbook name at the Open dialog box and then clicking Rename at the shortcut menu. Key the new name for the workbook and then press the Enter key.

Renaming a Document

1. Rename a workbook located in the *Finance* folder by completing the following steps:
   a. Display the Open dialog box with *Chapter 03C* as the active folder.
   b. Double-click *Finance* to make it the active folder.
   c. Click once on Excel Worksheet 07 to select it.
   d. Click the Tools button on the dialog box toolbar.
   e. At the drop-down menu that displays, click Rename.
   f. Key Equipment.xls and then press the Enter key.
   g. At the message asking if you are sure you want to change the name of the read-only file, click Yes.
   h. Complete steps similar to those in 1c through 1g to rename Excel Worksheet 09 to Equipment-Usage.xls.
   i. Click the Up One Level button.
2. Close the Open dialog box.

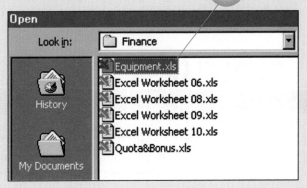

Deleting a Folder and Its Contents

As you learned earlier in this chapter, a workbook or selected workbooks can be deleted. In addition to workbooks, a folder (and all its contents) can be deleted. Delete a folder in the same manner as a document is deleted.

Deleting a Folder and Its Contents

1. Delete the Finance folder and its contents by completing the following steps:
   a. Display the Open dialog box with *Chapter 03C* as the active folder.
   b. Click once on the *Finance* folder to select it.
   c. Click the Delete button on the dialog box toolbar.
   d. At the Confirm Folder Delete dialog box asking if you want to remove the folder and all its contents, click Yes.
   e. At the Confirm File Delete dialog box telling you that Equipment-Usage.xls is a read-only file and asking if you are sure you want to delete it, click the Yes to All button.
2. Close the Open dialog box.

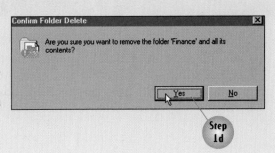

Opening Multiple Workbooks

A workbook or selected workbooks can be opened all at once at the Open dialog box. To open one workbook, display the Open dialog box, position the arrow pointer on the desired workbook, click the right mouse button, and then click <u>O</u>pen at the shortcut menu. To open more than one workbook, select the workbooks in the Open dialog box, position the arrow pointer on one of the selected workbooks, click the right mouse button, and then click Open at the shortcut menu.

Closing Workbooks

If more than one workbook is open, all open workbooks can be closed at the same time. To do this, hold down the Shift key, click <u>F</u>ile and then Close All. Holding down the Shift key before clicking <u>F</u>ile causes the <u>C</u>lose option to change to <u>C</u>lose All.

Opening and Closing Several Workbooks

1. Open several workbooks by completing the following steps:
   a. Display the Open dialog box with *Chapter 03C* as the active folder.
   b. Select Excel Worksheet 01, Excel Worksheet 06, Excel Worksheet 08, and Excel Worksheet 10.
   c. Position the arrow pointer on one of the selected workbooks, click the right mouse button, and then click the left mouse button on <u>O</u>pen.
2. Close the open workbooks by completing the following steps:
   a. Hold down the Shift key.
   b. Click <u>F</u>ile and then <u>C</u>lose All.

Printing Documents

Up to this point, you have opened a workbook and then printed it. With the <u>P</u>rint option from the Too<u>l</u>s drop-down menu or the <u>P</u>rint option from the shortcut menu at the Open dialog box, you can print a workbook or several workbooks without opening them.

Printing Documents

1. Display the Open dialog box with *Chapter 03C* as the active folder.
2. Select Excel Worksheet 01 and Excel Worksheet 08.
3. Click the Too<u>l</u>s button on the dialog box toolbar.
4. At the drop-down menu that displays, click <u>P</u>rint.

Managing Worksheets

Individual worksheets within a workbook can be moved or copied within the same workbook or to another existing workbook. Exercise caution when moving sheets because calculations or charts based on data on a worksheet might become inaccurate if you move the worksheet.

Copy a Worksheet to Another Workbook

To copy a worksheet to another existing workbook, open both the source and the destination workbook files. Activate the sheet you want to copy in the source workbook, click Edit, and then Move or Copy Sheet, or right-click the sheet tab located at the bottom of the screen just above the status bar and select Move or Copy from the shortcut menu. At the Move or Copy dialog box shown in figure 3.5, select the destination workbook name from the To book drop-down list, select the worksheet that you want the copied worksheet placed before in the Before Sheet list box, click the Create a copy check box, and then click OK.

figure
3.5

Move or Copy Dialog Box

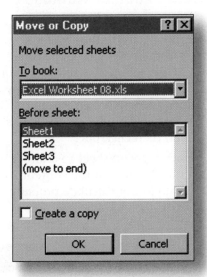

Copying a Worksheet to Another Workbook

1. Open Excel Worksheet 08 and Copy of Excel Worksheet 09.
2. Copy the Equipment Usage Report Worksheet from the workbook named Copy of Excel Worksheet 09 to the Excel Worksheet 08 workbook by completing the following steps:
   a. Click the button on the Taskbar for the workbook named Copy of Excel Worksheet 09 to activate the workbook.

b. Right-click the Sheet1 tab located at the bottom left of the screen just above the status bar, and then select <u>M</u>ove or Copy from the shortcut menu.

c. Click the down-pointing triangle next to the <u>T</u>o book text box, then select Excel Worksheet 08 from the drop-down list.

d. Click *Sheet2* in the <u>B</u>efore Sheet list box.

e. Click the <u>C</u>reate a copy check box.

f. Click OK.

g. Excel switches to the workbook Excel Worksheet 08 and inserts the copied sheet with the sheet name *Sheet 1 (2)*.

3. Save Excel Worksheet 08 using Save As and name it Excel C3, Ex 13.

4. Print the entire Excel C3, Ex 13 workbook by completing the following steps:

a. Click <u>F</u>ile, and then select <u>P</u>rint.

b. Click <u>E</u>ntire workbook in the Print what section.

c. Click OK.

5. Close Excel C3, Ex 13.

6. Close Copy of Excel Worksheet 09.

Move a Worksheet to Another Workbook

To move a worksheet to another existing workbook, open both the source and the destination workbook files. Activate the sheet you want to move in the source workbook, click <u>E</u>dit, and then <u>M</u>ove or Copy Sheet, or right-click the sheet tab located at the bottom of the screen just above the status bar and select <u>M</u>ove or Copy from the shortcut menu. At the Move or Copy dialog box shown in figure 3.5, select the destination workbook name from the <u>T</u>o book drop-down list, select the worksheet that you want the copied worksheet placed before in the <u>B</u>efore Sheet list box, and then click OK.

Be careful when moving a worksheet to another workbook file. If formulas exist in the workbook that depend on the contents of the cells in the worksheet that is moved, they will no longer calculate properly.

Moving a Worksheet to Another Workbook

1. Open Excel Worksheet 01.

2. Save the workbook with Save As and name it Excel C3, Ex 14 W01.

3. Open Excel Worksheet 10.

4. Save the workbook with Save As and name it Excel C3, Ex 14 W02.

5. Move Sheet1 from Excel C3, Ex 14 W02 to Excel C3, Ex 14 W01 by completing the following steps:

a. Click the button on the Taskbar for the workbook named Excel C3, Ex 14 W02 to activate the workbook.

b. Click <u>E</u>dit and then select <u>M</u>ove or Copy Sheet.

   c. Click the down-pointing triangle next to the <u>T</u>o book text box, then select Excel C3, Ex 14 W01 from the drop-down list.

   d. Click *Sheet2* in the <u>B</u>efore Sheet list box.

   e. Click OK.

   f. Excel switches to the workbook Excel C3, Ex 14 W01 and inserts the moved sheet with the sheet name *Sheet 1 (2)*.

6. Save the worksheet using the same name (Excel C3, Ex 14 W01).

7. Print the entire Excel C3, Ex 14 W01 workbook by completing the following steps:

   a. Click <u>F</u>ile, and then select <u>P</u>rint.

   b. Click <u>E</u>ntire workbook in the Print what section.

   c. Click OK.

8. Close Excel C3, Ex 14 W01.

9. Close Excel C3, Ex 14 W02 *without saving changes*.

Rename a Worksheet

The worksheets in exercises 13 and 14 that were moved or copied were assigned the name *Sheet 1 (2)* in the destination workbooks. This name, or for that matter, *Sheet1*, is not a very descriptive reference of what is contained in the worksheet. When you are working with multiple worksheets in a workbook, it is useful to change the name of the worksheets to help identify the location of data.

If a company was storing payroll for 12 months of the year in one workbook file with each month's payroll stored in an individual worksheet, the worksheets could be renamed January, February, March, and so on.

To rename a worksheet, right-click the sheet tab at the bottom left of the screen, then select <u>R</u>ename from the shortcut menu. The existing name will be selected. Key the new worksheet name and then press Enter. Another method that can be used to rename the worksheet is to double-click the existing sheet name, key the new name, and then press Enter.

Rename a Worksheet

1. Open Excel C3, Ex 14 W01.

2. Save the workbook with Save As and name it Excel C3, Ex 15.

3. Change the name of the two worksheets by completing the following steps:

   a. Right-click the sheet tab named *Sheet 1 (2)*, and then select <u>R</u>ename from the shortcut menu.

   b. Key **Sales by Salesperson** and then press Enter.

   c. Click the Sheet1 tab to activate the Sheet1 worksheet.

   d. Double-click the sheet tab *Sheet1*.

   e. Key **Sales by Customer** and then press Enter.

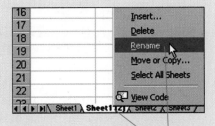

Step 3a

4. Save the revised worbook using the same name (Excel C3, Ex 15).

5. Close Excel C3, Ex 15.

Company Intranets

Computers within a company can be connected by a private network referred to as an "intranet." An intranet uses Internet technology to distribute *internal* company information to the employees within the organization. Think of an intranet as a company's private Internet—the web site is only accessible within the company. Intranets are gaining popularity among corporations looking to reduce costs in information distribution, workgroup collaboration, and training. With the widespread use of the Internet, most employees would need little training on how to make use of the intranet.

Sending a Workbook By E-mail

You may have an Excel workbook that you want to send to another individual with an e-mail account. Sending a workbook by e-mail has the advantage that the recipient can open the workbook and make changes to it if desired. This is one method of collaborating on a workbook within an organization. Individuals can make changes to the contents of the worksheets and e-mail the workbook back and forth. The recipient of the e-mail must have Microsoft Excel installed on their system to be able to open the file. The e-mail feature in Excel works with Microsoft Outlook to send the message with the workbook attached to it. System configurations can be quite varied and you may find that your screen does not exactly match what you see in the figure in this section. Steps in exercise 16 may need to be modified to accommodate your system.

To send a workbook by e-mail, open the workbook, and then click the E-mail button on the Standard toolbar. This displays the e-mail header below the Formatting toolbar as shown in figure 3.6. When the e-mail header displays, Outlook is automatically opened.

figure
3.6

E-Mail Header

E-mail Header

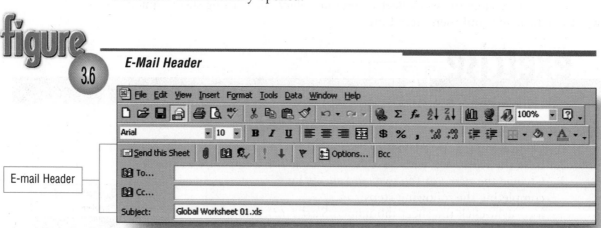

At the e-mail header, fill in the recipient information and then click the Send this Sheet button. Excel sends a copy of the workbook to the recipient and closes the e-mail header. The original workbook remains open for editing. When the workbook is saved, the e-mail information is saved with the document.

The e-mail header contains buttons you can use to customize the e-mail message. Buttons are available for sending a copy of a document, selecting a name from an address book, establishing a priority level, and specifying delivery options.

Sending a Workbook by E-mail

(Note: Before completing this exercise, check with your instructor in case your system configuration requires changes to the steps. If you cannot send e-mail, consider completing all the steps in the exercise except step 3e.)

1. Open Excel C3, Ex 15.
2. Save the workbook with Save As and name it Excel C3, Ex 16.
3. Send Excel C3, Ex 16 by e-mail to your instructor by completing the following steps:
   a. Click the E-mail button on the Standard toolbar.
   b. At the E-mail dialog box, click *Send the current sheet as the message body* and then click OK.
   c. At the e-mail header, key your instructor's name or e-mail account in the To: text box. (Check with your instructor for specific instructions at this step.)
   d. Click the Importance: High button in the E-mail header. This is the button with the red exclamation point in it.
   e. Click the Send this Sheet button.

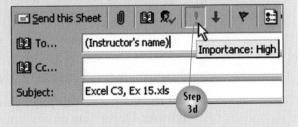

4. Save the workbook again with the same name (Excel C3, Ex 16).
5. Close Excel C3, Ex 16.

Creating a Web Page

An Excel workbook can be saved as a Web page. The Web page can be viewed in the default Web browser software, and hyperlinks can be inserted in the Web page to jump to other workbooks or sites on the Internet with additional information pertaining to the workbook content. In an organization, an Excel workbook may be saved as a web page and posted on the company intranet as a timely method of distributing the workbook to the company employees.

Saving a Workbook as a Web Page

Save a workbook as a Web page by opening the workbook and then clicking File and then Save as Web Page. At the Save As dialog box shown in figure 3.7, key a name for the Web page in the File name text box if you want to save the web page with a name that is different from the one provided, and then click the Save button.

Save As Dialog Box

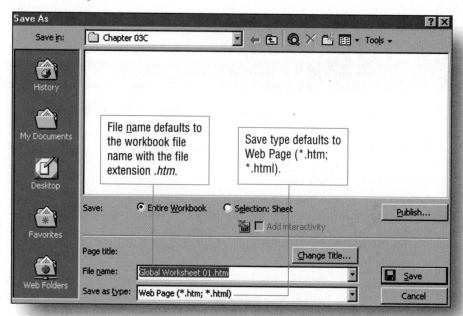

Previewing a Workbook in Web Page Preview

When creating a Web page, you may want to preview it in your default Web browser. Depending on the browser you are using, some of the formatting in a workbook may not display in the browser. To preview a workbook in your default Web browser, click File and then click Web Page Preview. This displays the currently open worksheet in the default Web browser and displays formatting supported by the browser.

Close the web browser window when you are finished previewing the page to return to Microsoft Excel.

Creating Hyperlinks

A hyperlink is text in a web page that has been attached to a file name or Uniform Resource Locator (URL is the method used to uniquely identify each location on the Internet), which causes the user to jump to the other file or Internet location when the hyperlinked text is clicked. Hyperlinked text in a web page is usually displayed underlined and in a different color (usually blue). You can insert a hyperlink in a Web page or any Excel worksheet. To do this, select the text you want specified as the hyperlink, and then click the Insert Hyperlink button on the Standard toolbar. At the Insert Hyperlink dialog box shown in figure 3.8, key the Web site URL in the Type the file or Web page name text box, and then click OK.

Another method for creating a hyperlink is to key the URL in an Excel worksheet. When you key the complete URL, Excel automatically converts the URL to a hyperlink and changes the color of the URL.

figure
3.8

Insert Hyperlink Dialog Box

Key the URL or file name you want to link to in this text box.

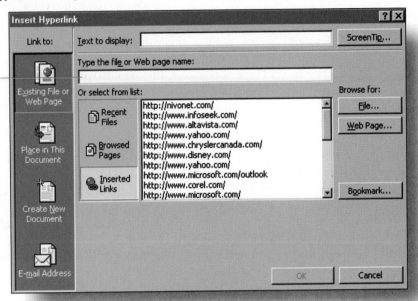

exercise 17

Creating a Folder, Saving a Workbook as a Web Page, Previewing the Web Page, and Creating Hyperlinks

1. Create a folder named *Web Pages* within the *Chapter 03C* folder on your disk.
2. Open Global Worksheet 01.
3. Save the worksheet as a Web page in the *Web Pages* folder by completing the following steps:
   a. Click File and then Save as Web Page.
   b. At the Save As dialog box, double-click *Web Pages* in the list box.
   c. Select the text in the File name text box and then key Global Web Page.
   d. Click the Save button.
4. Preview the document in Web Page Preview by completing the following steps:
   a. Click File and then click Web Page Preview.

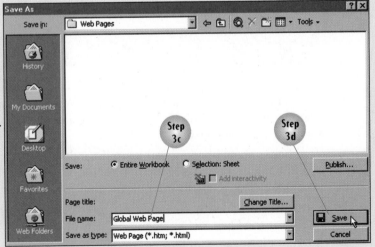

b. If the viewing area in the browser is limited, click the Maximize button located in the upper right corner of the browser window.

c. After viewing the worksheet in the Web browser, click File and then Close.

5. Create a hyperlink so that clicking *TWA* displays the TWA Web page by completing the following steps:

a. Click cell G8 (this is the cell containing *TWA*).

b. Click the Insert Hyperlink button on the Standard toolbar.

c. At the Insert Hyperlink dialog box, key **http://www.twa.com** in the Type the file or Web page name text box.

d. Click OK. (This changes the color of the *TWA* text and also adds underlining to the text.)

e. Repeat steps 5b to 5d in cell G11.

6. Complete steps similar to those in step 5 to create a hyperlink from *NorthWest* to the URL *http://www.nwa.com* in cells G9 and G10.

7. Complete steps similar to those in step 5 to create a hyperlink from *Air Canada* to the URL **http://www.aircanada.ca** in cell G12.

8. Click the Save button on the Standard toolbar to save the Web page with the hyperlinks added.

9. Jump to the hyperlinked sites by completing the following steps:

a. Make sure you are connected to the Internet.

b. Click one of the *TWA* hyperlinks.

c. When the TWA Web page displays, scroll through the page, and then click on a hyperlink that interests you.

d. After looking at this next page, click File and then Close.

e. At the Global Web Page document, click the *Air Canada* hyperlink.

f. At the Air Canada Web page, click the hyperlink to see their site displayed in English.

g. After viewing the Air Canada page, click File and then Close.

h. At the Global Web Page document, click one of the *NorthWest* hyperlinks.

i. At the NorthWest Web page, click a link that interests you.

j. After viewing the NorthWest page, click File and then Close.

10. Print and then close Global Web Page.

chapter summary

➤ File management tasks such as copying, moving, printing, and renaming workbooks; opening multiple workbooks; and creating a new folder can be performed at the Open and Save As dialog boxes.

➤ Workbooks should be grouped logically and stored in folders. A folder can be created within a folder. The main folder on a disk or drive is called the root folder. Additional folders are created as a branch of this root folder.

➤ Create a new folder by clicking the Create New Folder button located on the dialog box toolbar at the Open dialog box or Save as dialog box.

➤ A folder name can contain a maximum of 255 characters.

➤ Use the Shift key while selecting workbooks to select multiple workbooks that are adjacent.

➤ Use the Ctrl key while selecting workbooks to select multiple workbooks that are not adjacent.

➤ To delete a workbook, select the workbook, and then click the Delete button on the dialog box toolbar; click Tools, and then click Delete at the drop-down menu; or right-click the document to be deleted, and then click Delete at the shortcut menu.

➤ Workbooks deleted from your data disk are deleted permanently.

➤ Workbooks and/or folders deleted from the hard drive are automatically sent to the Windows Recycle Bin where they can be restored or permanently deleted.

➤ A copy of an existing workbook can be created by opening the workbook and then using the Save As command to assign the workbook a different file name.

➤ Use the Copy and Paste options from the shortcut menu at the Open (or Save As) dialog box to copy a workbook from one folder to another folder or drive.

➤ When you copy a workbook into the same folder it originates from, Excel names the duplicated document(s) "Copy of xxx" (where xxx is the original workbook name).

➤ With the Send To option from the shortcut menu, you can quickly send a copy of a workbook to another drive or folder.

➤ A workbook can be removed from a folder or disk and inserted in another folder or on another disk using the Cut and Paste options from the shortcut menu.

➤ Use the Rename option from the Tools drop-down menu or the shortcut menu to give a workbook a different name.

➤ Multiple workbooks can be opened, closed, or printed.

➤ To move or copy a worksheet to another existing workbook, open both the source and the destination workbook files and then open the Move or Copy Sheet dialog box.

➤ Change the name of worksheets to help identify the data contained in them.

➤ An intranet uses Internet technology to distribute company information to the employees within the organization.

➤ To send a workbook by e-mail, open the workbook, click the E-mail button on the Standard toolbar, enter the recipient information, and then click Send this Sheet.

➤ Save a workbook as a Web page by opening the workbook, clicking File, and then Save as Web Page. Key the name of the web page in the Save As dialog box and then click Save.

➤ To preview a workbook in your default Web browser, click File and then click Web Page Preview.

➤ To create a hyperlink in a workbook, select the text you want to attach a hyperlink to, click the Insert Hyperlink button on the Standard toolbar, and then key the file name or Web site URL in the Type the file or Web page name text box.

commands review

	Mouse/Keyboard
Open dialog box	Click File, then Open; or click Open button on the Standard toolbar
Save As dialog box	Click File, then Save As
Recycle Bin dialog box	Minimize Excel and then click Recycle Bin icon on the Windows desktop
Move or Copy Sheet dialog box	Click Edit, then click Move or Copy Sheet; or right-click sheet tab and then click Move or Copy
Close All	Hold Shift and click File, and then select Close All
Send a workbook by E-mail	Open workbook and then click the E-mail button on the Standard toolbar
Save a workbook as a Web page	Click File, then select Save As Web Page
Web Page Preview	Click File, then select WebPage Preview
Create a hyperlink	Select text, then click Insert Hyperlink button on Standard toolbar; or click Insert, then select Hyperlink

thinking offline

Completion: In the space provided at the right, indicate the correct term, command, or number.

1. File management tasks such as copying workbooks, moving workbooks, or deleting workbooks can be performed at the Open dialog box or this dialog box.

2. Select multiple nonadjacent workbooks by holding down this key while clicking each workbook name.

3. Do this action with the mouse to open the shortcut menu for a workbook at the Open dialog box.

4. To move a file from one folder to another folder or drive, use these options from the shortcut menu.

5. Workbooks and/or folders deleted from Excel can be restored by opening this feature in Windows.

6. Rename a workbook by selecting it and then clicking this button on the dialog box toolbar.

7. To send a workbook by e-mail click the E-mail button located on this toolbar.

8. When you select Save As Web Page from the File menu, Excel changes the file extension for the current workbook from .xls to this.

9. Selecting We<u>b</u> Page Preview opens this application. _____

10. To create a hyperlink to an Internet location, you need to enter this at the Insert Hyperlink dialog box. _____

working hands-on

Assessment 1

1. Display the Open dialog box with *Chapter 03C* as the active folder.
2. Create a new folder named *Sales* in the *Chapter 03C* folder.
3. Copy Excel Worksheet 01 and Excel Worksheet 10 to the *Sales* folder.
4. Rename Excel Worksheet 01 to *Sales by Job* in the *Sales* folder.
5. Rename Excel Worksheet 10 to *Sales by Salesperson* in the *Sales* folder.
6. Change the active folder back to *Chapter 03C*.
7. Close the Open dialog box.

Assessment 2

1. Display the Open dialog dialog box.
2. Delete all of the workbooks in the *Chapter 03C* folder that begin with *Copy of*.
3. Move all of the workbooks that begin with *Excel Worksheet* to the Sales folder.
4. Change the active folder back to *Chapter 03C*.
5. Close the Open dialog box.

Assessment 3

1. Display the Open dialog box.
2. Open all of the workbooks that begin with *Excel C3, Ex*.
3. Make Excel C3, Ex 15 the active window.
4. Close Excel C3, Ex 15.
5. Make Excel C3, Ex 14 W01 the active window.
6. Close all of the open Excel Workbooks.

Assessment 4

1. Display the Open dialog box and make *Sales* the active folder.
2. Open Excel Worksheet 07 and Excel Worksheet 08.
3. Copy *Sheet1* from Excel Worksheet 07 and position it before *Sheet2* in Excel Worksheet 08.
4. With Excel Worksheet 08 as the active workbook, rename *Sheet1* to *Conway Construction*.
5. With Excel Worksheet 08 as the active workbook, rename *Sheet1 (2)* to *Real Photography*.
6. Save Excel Worksheet 08 with Save As and name it Excel C3, SA 04.
7. E-mail Excel C3, SA 04 to your instructor.
8. Close Excel Worksheet 07 and Excel C3, SA 04.

Assessment 5

1. Display the Open dialog box with Chapter 03C as the active folder.
2. Open Books Galore Worksheet 01.

3. Save Books Galore Worksheet 01 as a Web page in the *Web Pages* folder on your disk and name it *Books Galore Web Page*.
4. Preview the web page in the default browser.
5. Close the browser application window.
6. Print and then close Books Galore Web Page.

Assessment 6

1. Open Books Galore Web Page.
2. Select E12 and hyperlink it to http://www.microsoft.com.
3. Select E13 and hyperlink it to http://www.symantec.com.
4. Select E14 and hyperlink it to http://www.nasa.gov.
5. Select E15 and hyperlink it to http://www.cnn.com.
6. Save the revised web page using the same name (Books Galore Web Page).
7. Print and then close Books Galore Web Page.

Assessment 7

1. Open Books Galore Web Page.
2. Make sure you are connected to the Internet and then click the hyperlink to NASA.
3. Jump to a link from the NASA Web page that interests you.
4. Print the page you viewed from NASA and then close the browser application window.
5. Jump to each of the remaining links in the Web page. At each Web page jump to a link that interests you and print the page you viewed and then close the browser application window.
6. Close Books Galore Web Page.

Assessment 8

1. Display the Open dialog box with *Chapter 03C* as the active folder.
2. Delete the *Web Pages* folder and its contents.
3. Delete the *Sales* folder and its contents.
4. Close the Open dialog box.

Assessment 9

1. Assume you work for XYZ Corporation in the Sales and Marketing Department. You prepare Excel workbook files daily for three divisions in XYZ Corporation: European Division, North American Division, and Asian Division. Generally, the type of work you are creating in Excel is either confidential sales targets for each division manager, or routine price quotations for the individual representatives.
2. Use Microsoft Excel Help to find out how to change the Save options to automatically create a backup copy of a workbook and assign a password to open the file.
3. Prepare a memo to your instructor in Word that outlines your file management plan. Include the following details.
   a. How would you organize the folders?
   b. When would you choose to use the automatic backup feature?
   c. When would you assign a password to a workbook file?
   d. How often should workbook files be archived to a floppy disk and the corresponding copy on the hard drive deleted?
4. Save the memo and name it Word C3, SA 09
5. Print and then close Word C3, SA 09

 Chapter 04C

Moving Data within and between Workbooks

4

Moving and pasting or copying and pasting selected cells in different locations in a worksheet can be useful for rearranging data in a worksheet or for saving time. Up to this point, the workbooks you have been working in have consisted of only one worksheet. In this chapter, you will learn to create a workbook with several worksheets and complete tasks such as copying and pasting data within and between worksheets. You will also work with multiple workbooks and complete tasks such as sizing, moving, and arranging workbooks, and opening and closing multiple workbooks.

Formatting in a large workbook containing multiple worksheets can be automated with styles. A style is a predefined set of formatting attributes. In this chapter, you will learn to define, apply, modify, remove, delete, and copy styles.

Moving, Copying, and Pasting Cells

Situations may arise where you need to move cells to a different location within a worksheet; or, you may need to copy repetitive data in a worksheet. You can perform these actions by selecting cells and then using the Move, Copy, and/or Paste buttons on the Standard toolbar. You can also perform these actions with the mouse or with options from the Edit drop-down menu.

Moving Selected Cells

Cut

Paste

Selected cells and cell contents can be moved in a worksheet and between worksheets. Selected cells can be moved with the Cut and Paste buttons on the Standard toolbar, by dragging with the mouse, or with options on the Edit drop-down menu.

To move selected cells with buttons on the Standard toolbar, select the cells, and then click the Cut button. This causes a moving dashed line to display around the selected cells. Click the cell where you want the first selected cell to be inserted and then click the Paste button on the Standard toolbar. If you change your mind and do not want to move the selected cells, press the Esc key to remove the moving dashed line or double-click in any cell.

Ctrl + X is the keyboard command to cut selected data.

To move selected cells with the mouse, select the cells, and then position the mouse pointer on any border of the selected cells until it turns into an arrow pointer. Hold down the left mouse button, drag the outline of the selected cells to the desired location, and then release the mouse button.

Selected cells can also be moved by selecting the cells and then clicking Edit and then Cut. This causes a moving dashed line to display around the selected cells. Click the cell where you want the first selected cell to be inserted and then click Edit and then Paste.

Ctrl + V is the keyboard command to paste data.

(Before completing computer exercises, delete the Chapter 03C folder on your disk. Next, copy the Chapter 04C folder from the CD that accompanies this textbook to your disk and make Chapter 04C the active folder.)

exercise

Moving Selected Cells in a Worksheet

1. Open Excel Worksheet 02.
2. Save the worksheet with Save As and name it Excel C4, Ex 01.
3. Make the following changes to the worksheet:
   a. Move cells in column D to column E by completing the following steps:
      1) Select cells D1 through D8.
      2) Click the Cut button on the Standard toolbar.
      3) Click cell E1 to make it active.
      4) Click the Paste button on the Standard toolbar.
   b. Move cells in column B to column D by completing the following steps:
      1) Select cells B1 through B8.
      2) Position the mouse pointer on any boundary of the selected cells until it turns into an arrow pointer.
      3) Hold down the left mouse button, drag the outline of the selected cells to column D, and then release the mouse button. (After the cells are moved, they should occupy cells D1 through D8.)

	A	B	C	D	E
1	Expense	Actual	Budget		Variance
2	Salaries	126000	126000		0
3	Commissions	58000	54500		-500
4	Media space	8250	10100	D1:D8	1850
5	Travel expenses	6350	6000		-350
6	Dealer display	4140	4500		360
7	Payroll taxes	2430	2200		-230
8	Telephone	1450	1500		50

Step 3b1

Step 3b3

c. Delete column B.

d. Select cells A1 through D8 and then apply the Accounting 2 autoformat.

e. Select row 1 and then turn on Bold and change the alignment to center.

4. Save the worksheet again with the same name (Excel C4, Ex 01).

5. Print and then close Excel C4, Ex 01.

Copying Selected Cells

Copying selected cells can be useful in worksheets that contain repetitive data. To copy cells, select the cells, and then click the Copy button on the Standard toolbar. Click the cell where you want the first selected cell to be copied and then click the Paste button on the Standard toolbar.

Copy

Selected cells can also be copied using the mouse and the Ctrl key. To do this, select the cells to be copied, and then position the mouse pointer on any border around the selected cells until it turns into an arrow pointer. Hold down the Ctrl key and the left mouse button, drag the outline of the selected cells to the desired location, and then release the left mouse button and then the Ctrl key. The mouse pointer displays with a plus (+) symbol attached to it when you drag the selected cells while holding Ctrl to indicate copying as opposed to moving.

Ctrl + C is the keyboard command to copy selected data.

The Copy and Paste options from the Edit drop-down menu can also be used to copy selected cells in a worksheet. To do this, select the cells, and then click Edit and then Copy. Click the cell where you want the first selected cell to be copied and then click Edit and then Paste.

Collecting and Pasting Multiple Items

In Office 2000 there is a new feature called *collecting and pasting*. With this feature, you can collect up to 12 different items and then paste them in various locations. Display the Clipboard toolbar when you want to collect and paste items. Display this toolbar by right-clicking an existing toolbar and then clicking Clipboard. Select text or an object you want to copy and then click the Copy button on the Clipboard toolbar. Continue selecting text or items and clicking the Copy button. To insert an item, position the insertion point in the desired location and then click the Clipboard button representing the item. Position the insertion point on a button and a ScreenTip displays with information on the item. If the item is text, the first 50 characters display. When all desired items are inserted, click the Clear Clipboard button to remove any remaining items.

When you click the Copy button on the Standard toolbar, selected cells display surrounded by a moving border.

exercise 2

Collecting and Pasting Cells

1. Open Excel Worksheet 06.

2. Save the worksheet with Save As and name it Excel C4, Ex 02.

3. Make cell A22 the active cell, turn on bold, and then key **Top Performers**.

4. Display the Clipboard toolbar by right-clicking an existing toolbar and then clicking Clipboard at the drop-down list.

5. Collect several rows of cells and then paste them by completing the following steps:

a. Click the row header for row 9 (this selects the entire row).

b. Click the Copy button on the Clipboard toolbar.
c. Click the row header for row 13 and then click the Copy button on the Clipboard toolbar.
d. Click the row header for row 16 and then click the Copy button on the Clipboard toolbar.

6. Paste the copied cells by completing the following steps:
a. Make cell A23 active.
b. Click the button on the Clipboard toolbar representing row 13. (To find this button, position the arrow pointer on a button on the Clipboard toolbar until the ScreenTip displays. Look for the ScreenTip that begins *Jewett, Troy 98% 94%...*).
c. Make cell A24 active.
d. Click the button on the Clipboard toolbar representing row 16 (look for the ScreenTip that begins *Markovits, Claude 89% 93%...*).
e. Make cell A25 active.
f. Click the button on the Clipboard toolbar representing row 9 (look for the ScreenTip that begins *Fisher-Edwards, Teri 89% 93%...*).

7. Click the Clear Clipboard button on the Clipboard toolbar.
8. Close the Clipboard toolbar.
9. Save the worksheet again with the same name (Excel C4, Ex 02).
10. Print and then close Excel C4, Ex 02.

Creating a Workbook with Multiple Worksheets

Up to this point, each workbook you have been creating has contained one worksheet. As you learned in chapter 1, a workbook can contain several worksheets. You can create a variety of worksheets within a workbook for related data. For example, a workbook may contain a worksheet for the expenses for each salesperson in a company and another worksheet for the monthly payroll for each department within the company. Another example is recording sales statistics for each quarter in individual worksheets within a workbook.

The copy and paste features can be useful in creating more than one worksheet within a workbook. These features are helpful if there is some consistency in data within each worksheet. For example, you can create a worksheet containing information on a product and then this information can be copied to another worksheet where you would change data in specific cells. By default, a workbook contains three worksheets. To insert an additional worksheet in a workbook, click Insert and then Worksheet.

To copy selected cells to a new worksheet, select the cells, click the Copy button on the Standard toolbar, click the worksheet tab (displayed immediately above the Status bar) representing the desired worksheet, and then click the Paste button.

Printing a Workbook Containing Multiple Worksheets

You can print specific worksheets in a workbook by selecting the tabs of the desired worksheets.

In exercise 3, you will create a workbook that contains four worksheets. When printing this workbook, by default, Excel will print only the worksheet currently displayed. If you want to print all worksheets in a workbook, display the Print dialog box by clicking File and then Print. At the Print dialog box, click Entire workbook in the Print what section, and then click OK.

Another method for printing specific worksheets within a workbook is to select the tabs of the worksheets you want to print. To do this, open the desired workbook, hold down the Ctrl key, and then click the desired tabs. (If the tabs are adjacent, you can use the Shift key.)

exercise 3

Copying Cells to Different Worksheets

1. Open Excel Worksheet 02.
2. Save the worksheet with Save As and name it Excel C4, Ex 03.
3. Add a fourth worksheet by clicking Insert and then Worksheet. (This adds a *Sheet4* tab before the *Sheet1* tab.)
4. Click the *Sheet1* tab to make worksheet 1 active and then make the following changes to the worksheet:
   a. With any cell in row 1 active, add a row. (This adds a row at the beginning of the worksheet.)
   b. Key **First Quarter** in cell A1.
   c. Select cells A1 through D9 and then apply the Accounting 1 autoformat.
   d. Select cells A1 through D1 and then click the Merge and Center button on the Formatting toolbar.
   e. Select cells B3 through D9 and then decrease the decimal places to none.
   f. Copy cells and paste them into worksheets 2, 3, and 4 by completing the following steps:
      1) Click the Select All button that displays immediately to the left of the column A header and immediately above the row 1 header.
      2) Click the Copy button on the Standard toolbar.
      3) Click the *Sheet2* tab that displays immediately above the Status bar.
      4) At worksheet 2, make sure cell A1 is the active cell, and then click the Paste button.
      5) Click the *Sheet3* tab that displays immediately above the Status bar.
      6) At worksheet 3, make sure cell A1 is the active cell, and then click the Paste button.
      7) Click the *Sheet4* tab.
      8) At worksheet 4, make sure cell A1 is the active cell, and then click the Paste button.
   g. Click the *Sheet2* tab and then make the following changes to cell entries in worksheet 2:
      A1: From *First Quarter* to *Second Quarter*
      B4: From *58,000* to *60500*
      C4: From *54,500* to *58500*
      D4: From *(3,500)* to *-2000*
      B8: From *2,430* to *2510*
      C8: From *2,200* to *2350*
      D8: From *(230)* to *-160*
   h. Click the *Sheet3* tab and then make the following changes to cell entries in worksheet 3:
      A1: From *First Quarter* to *Third Quarter*
      B4: From *58,000* to *60200*
      C4: From *54,500* to *60500*
      D4: From *(3,500)* to *300*
      B8: From *2,430* to *2500*
      C8: From *2,200* to *2550*
      D8: From *(230)* to *50*

i. Click the *Sheet4* tab and then make the following changes to cell entries in worksheet 4:

A1: From *First Quarter* to *Fourth Quarter*
B4: From *58,000* to *61000*
C4: From *54,500* to *60500*
D4: From *(3,500)* to *-500*
B8: From *2,430* to *2550*
C8: From *2,200* to *2500*
D8: From *(230)* to *-50*

5. Save the workbook again with the same name (Excel C4, Ex 03).
6. Print all the worksheets in the workbook by completing the following steps:
   a. Make sure there are no selected cells (just an active cell).
   b. Click <u>F</u>ile and then <u>P</u>rint.
   c. At the Print dialog box, click <u>E</u>ntire workbook in the Print what section.
   d. Click OK. (Each worksheet will print on a separate piece of paper.)
7. Close Excel C4, Ex 03.

Managing Worksheets

Right-click a sheet tab and a shortcut menu displays with the options <u>I</u>nsert, <u>D</u>elete, <u>R</u>ename, <u>M</u>ove or Copy, and <u>S</u>elect All Sheets. Use these options to manage worksheets in a workbook. For example, remove a worksheet by clicking the <u>D</u>elete option. Move or copy a worksheet by clicking the Move or Copy option. Clicking this option causes a Move or Copy dialog box to display where you specify before what sheet you want to move or copy the selected sheet. By default, Excel names worksheets in a workbook *Sheet1, Sheet2, Sheet3,* and so on. To rename a worksheet, click the <u>R</u>ename option (this selects the default sheet name), and then key the desired name.

You can manage more than one worksheet at a time by selecting the worksheets first. If the tabs are adjacent, click the first tab, hold down the Shift key, and then click the last tab. If the tabs are nonadjacent, click the first tab, hold down the Ctrl key, and then click any other tabs you want selected.

Deleting Selected Worksheets

1. Open Excel C4, Ex 03.
2. Save the workbook with Save As and name it Excel C4, Ex 04.
3. Delete worksheets 3 and 4 by completing the following steps:
   a. Click the left mouse button on *Sheet3* that displays at the bottom of the workbook window.
   b. Hold down the Ctrl key, click *Sheet4*, and then release the Ctrl key.
   c. Position the arrow pointer on the *Sheet4* tab and then click the *right* mouse button.
   d. At the pop-up menu that displays, click the left mouse button on <u>D</u>elete.
   e. At the message telling you that the selected sheets will be permanently deleted, click OK.

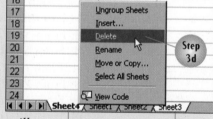

4. Rename worksheets 1 and 2 by completing the following steps:
   a. Right-click the *Sheet1* tab, click <u>R</u>ename at the shortcut menu, and then key **First Quarter**.
   b. Right-click the *Sheet2* tab, click <u>R</u>ename at the shortcut menu, and then key **Second Quarter**.
5. Move the Second Quarter sheet tab by completing the following steps:
   a. Right-click the Second Quarter sheet tab and then click <u>M</u>ove or Copy at the shortcut menu.
   b. At the Move or Copy dialog box, make sure *First Quarter* is selected in the <u>B</u>efore sheet list box, and then click OK.
6. Save the workbook again with the same name (Excel C4, Ex 04).
7. Print the entire workbook (two worksheets).
8. Close Excel C4, Ex 04.

Splitting a Worksheet into Windows and Freezing and Unfreezing Panes

In some worksheets, not all cells display at one time in the worksheet area (such as Excel Worksheet 06). When working in worksheets with more cells than can display at one time, you may find splitting the worksheet window into panes helpful. Split the worksheet window into panes with the <u>S</u>plit option from the <u>W</u>indow drop-down menu or using the split bars that display at the top of the vertical scroll bar and at the right side of the horizontal scroll bar. These split bars are identified in figure 4.1.

Split Bars

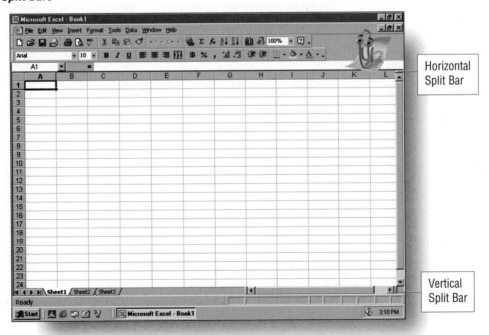

Horizontal Split Bar

Vertical Split Bar

To split a window with the split bar located at the top of the vertical scroll bar, position the mouse pointer on the split bar until it turns into a double-headed arrow with a short double line in the middle. Hold down the left mouse button, drag down the thick gray line that displays until the pane is the desired size, and then release the mouse button. Split the window vertically with the split bar at the right side of the horizontal scroll bar.

To split a worksheet window with the <u>W</u>indow drop-down menu, click <u>W</u>indow and then <u>S</u>plit. This causes the worksheet to be split into four window panes as shown in figure 4.2. The windows are split by thick gray lines (with a three-dimensional look).

4.2

Split Window with Four Panes

<table>
<tr><td></td><td>A</td><td>B</td><td>C</td><td>D</td><td>E</td><td>F</td><td>G</td><td>H</td><td>I</td><td>J</td><td>K</td><td>L</td><td>M</td></tr>
<tr><td>1</td><td>Name</td><td>Test 1</td><td>Test 2</td><td>Test 3</td><td>Test 4</td><td>Test 5</td><td>Test 6</td><td>Test 7</td><td>Test 8</td><td>Test 9</td><td>Test 10</td><td>Test 11</td><td>Test 12</td></tr>
<tr><td>2</td><td></td><td></td><td></td><td></td><td></td><td></td><td></td><td></td><td></td><td></td><td></td><td></td><td></td></tr>
<tr><td>3</td><td>Arnson, Patrick</td><td>89%</td><td>65%</td><td>76%</td><td>89%</td><td>98%</td><td>65%</td><td>76%</td><td>87%</td><td>55%</td><td>78%</td><td>67%</td><td>69%</td></tr>
<tr><td>4</td><td>Barclay, Jeanine</td><td>78%</td><td>66%</td><td>87%</td><td>90%</td><td>92%</td><td>82%</td><td>100%</td><td>84%</td><td>67%</td><td>86%</td><td>82%</td><td>91%</td></tr>
<tr><td>5</td><td>Calahan, Jack</td><td>65%</td><td>71%</td><td>64%</td><td>66%</td><td>70%</td><td>81%</td><td>64%</td><td>59%</td><td>76%</td><td>76%</td><td>45%</td><td>49%</td></tr>
<tr><td>6</td><td>Cumpston, Kurt</td><td>89%</td><td>91%</td><td>90%</td><td>93%</td><td>86%</td><td>80%</td><td>84%</td><td>93%</td><td>95%</td><td>81%</td><td>96%</td><td>98%</td></tr>
<tr><td>7</td><td>Dimmitt, Marian</td><td>78%</td><td>73%</td><td>81%</td><td>82%</td><td>67%</td><td>69%</td><td>82%</td><td>72%</td><td>85%</td><td>83%</td><td>71%</td><td>73%</td></tr>
<tr><td>8</td><td>Donovan, Nancy</td><td>82%</td><td>89%</td><td>79%</td><td>74%</td><td>80%</td><td>82%</td><td>86%</td><td>72%</td><td>74%</td><td>82%</td><td>76%</td><td>79%</td></tr>
<tr><td>9</td><td>Fisher-Edwards, Teri</td><td>89%</td><td>93%</td><td>100%</td><td>91%</td><td>86%</td><td>90%</td><td>88%</td><td>86%</td><td>100%</td><td>98%</td><td>90%</td><td>97%</td></tr>
<tr><td>10</td><td>Flanery, Stephanie</td><td>58%</td><td>45%</td><td>63%</td><td>51%</td><td>60%</td><td>59%</td><td>63%</td><td>52%</td><td>66%</td><td>67%</td><td>53%</td><td>49%</td></tr>
<tr><td>11</td><td>Heyman, Grover</td><td>78%</td><td>75%</td><td>87%</td><td>88%</td><td>64%</td><td>76%</td><td>70%</td><td>67%</td><td>55%</td><td>87%</td><td>82%</td><td>88%</td></tr>
<tr><td>12</td><td>Herbertson, Wynn</td><td>92%</td><td>80%</td><td>93%</td><td>90%</td><td>86%</td><td>84%</td><td>95%</td><td>100%</td><td>98%</td><td>88%</td><td>95%</td><td>89%</td></tr>
<tr><td>13</td><td>Jewett, Troy</td><td>98%</td><td>94%</td><td>99%</td><td>89%</td><td>100%</td><td>93%</td><td>100%</td><td>95%</td><td>96%</td><td>91%</td><td>87%</td><td>94%</td></tr>
<tr><td>14</td><td>Kwieciak, Kathleen</td><td>55%</td><td>0%</td><td>42%</td><td>65%</td><td>72%</td><td>40%</td><td>65%</td><td>0%</td><td>0%</td><td>48%</td><td>52%</td><td>56%</td></tr>
<tr><td>15</td><td>Leibrand, Maxine</td><td>78%</td><td>69%</td><td>83%</td><td>87%</td><td>84%</td><td>69%</td><td>80%</td><td>82%</td><td>88%</td><td>79%</td><td>83%</td><td>76%</td></tr>
<tr><td>16</td><td>Markovits, Claude</td><td>89%</td><td>93%</td><td>84%</td><td>100%</td><td>95%</td><td>92%</td><td>95%</td><td>100%</td><td>89%</td><td>94%</td><td>98%</td><td>94%</td></tr>
<tr><td>17</td><td>Moonstar, Siana</td><td>73%</td><td>87%</td><td>67%</td><td>83%</td><td>90%</td><td>84%</td><td>73%</td><td>81%</td><td>75%</td><td>65%</td><td>84%</td><td>88%</td></tr>
<tr><td>18</td><td>Nyegaard, Curtis</td><td>90%</td><td>89%</td><td>84%</td><td>85%</td><td>93%</td><td>85%</td><td>100%</td><td>94%</td><td>98%</td><td>93%</td><td>100%</td><td>95%</td></tr>
<tr><td>19</td><td>Oglesbee, Randy</td><td>65%</td><td>55%</td><td>73%</td><td>90%</td><td>87%</td><td>67%</td><td>85%</td><td>77%</td><td>85%</td><td>73%</td><td>78%</td><td>77%</td></tr>
<tr><td>20</td><td>Pherson, Douglas</td><td>69%</td><td>82%</td><td>87%</td><td>74%</td><td>70%</td><td>82%</td><td>84%</td><td>85%</td><td>66%</td><td>77%</td><td>91%</td><td>86%</td></tr>
</table>

A window pane will display the active cell. As the insertion point is moved through the pane, another active cell with a blue background may display. This additional active cell displays when the insertion point passes over one of the gray lines that creates the pane. As you move through a worksheet, you may see both active cells—one with a normal background and one with a blue background. If you make a change to the active cell, the change is made in both. If you want only one active cell to display, freeze the window panes by clicking <u>W</u>indow and then <u>F</u>reeze Panes. With panes frozen, only the display of the pane with the active cell will change. To unfreeze panes, click <u>W</u>indow and the Un<u>f</u>reeze Panes.

The thick gray lines that divide the window into panes can be moved using the mouse. To do this, position the mouse pointer on the line until it turns into a double-headed arrow with a double line in the middle. Hold down the left mouse button, drag the outline of the gray line until it is positioned in the desired location, and then release the mouse button. If you want to move both the horizontal and vertical lines at the same time, position the mouse pointer on the intersection of the thick gray lines until it turns into a four-headed arrow. Hold down the left mouse button, drag the thick gray lines in the desired direction, and then release the mouse button.

By splitting a worksheet into windows, you can maintain the display of column headings while editing or keying text in cells. You can do the same for row headings. You will be doing this with a worksheet in exercise 5.

exercise 5

Splitting Windows and Editing Cells

1. Open Excel Worksheet 06.
2. Save the worksheet with Save As and name it Excel C4, Ex 05.
3. Split the window by completing the following steps:
   a. Click <u>W</u>indow and then <u>S</u>plit. (This causes the window to be split into four panes.)
   b. Drag both the horizontal and vertical gray lines by completing the following steps:
      1) Position the mouse pointer on the intersection between the horizontal and vertical lines until it turns into a four-headed black arrow.
      2) Hold down the left mouse button, drag up and to the left until the horizontal gray line is immediately below the first row and the vertical gray line is immediately to the right of the first column, and then release the mouse button.
   c. Freeze the window panes by clicking <u>W</u>indow and then <u>F</u>reeze Panes.
   d. Add two rows by completing the following steps:
      1) Select rows 18 and 19.
      2) Click <u>I</u>nsert and then <u>R</u>ows.
   e. Key the following text in the specified cells:

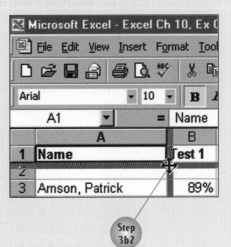

Step 3b2

A18	=	Nauer, Sheryl
B18	=	75
C18	=	83
D18	=	85
E18	=	78
F18	=	82
G18	=	80
H18	=	79
I18	=	82
J18	=	92
K18	=	90
L18	=	86
M18	=	84
A19	=	Nunez, James
B19	=	98
C19	=	96
D19	=	100
E19	=	90
F19	=	95
G19	=	93
H19	=	88
I19	=	91
J19	=	89
K19	=	100
L19	=	96
M19	=	98

f. Edit the text in the following cells:
    D3: Change *76%* to *92%*
    K6: Change *81%* to *74%*
    E8: Change *74%* to *90%*
    M12: Change *89%* to *95%*
    C14: Change *0%* to *70%* (Hint: Be sure to press Enter to change from
        the Edit mode to the Ready mode.)
g. Unfreeze the window panes by clicking Window and then Unfreeze Panes.
h. Remove the panes by clicking Window and then Remove Split.
4. Save the worksheet again with the same name (Excel C4, Ex 05).
5. Print the worksheet in landscape orientation and then close Excel C4, Ex 05.

Working with Windows

You can open multiple workbooks in Excel and arrange the open workbooks in the Excel window. With multiple workbooks open, you can cut and paste or copy and paste cell entries from one workbook to another using the same techniques discussed earlier in this chapter with the exception that you activate the destination workbook before executing the Paste command.

Opening Multiple Workbooks

With multiple workbooks open, you can move or copy information between workbooks or compare the contents of several workbooks. The maximum number of workbooks that you can have open at one time depends on the memory of your computer system and the amount of information in each workbook. When you open a new workbook, it is placed on top of the original workbook. Once multiple workbooks are opened, you can resize the workbooks to see all or a portion of them on the screen.

Multiple workbooks can be opened at one time at the Open dialog box. If workbooks are adjacent, display the Open dialog box, click the first workbook to be opened, hold down the Shift key, and then click the last workbook to be opened. If the workbooks are nonadjacent, click the first workbook to be opened, and then hold down the Ctrl key while clicking the remaining desired workbook names. Release the Shift key or the Ctrl key and then click the Open button.

To see what workbooks are currently open, click Window on the Menu bar. The names of the open workbooks display at the bottom of the drop-down menu. The workbook name with the check mark in front of it is the *active* workbook. The active workbook is the workbook containing the active cell. To make one of the other workbooks active, click the desired workbook.

Closing Multiple Workbooks

All open workbooks can be closed at the same time. To do this, hold down the Shift key, click File on the Menu bar, and then click Close All. Holding down the Shift key while clicking the File option causes the Close option to change to the Close All option.

exercise 6

Opening and Closing Multiple Workbooks

(Note: If you are using Microsoft Office on a network system that contains a virus checker, you may not be able to open multiple workbooks at one time.)

1. Open several workbooks at the same time by completing the following steps:
   a. Display the Open dialog box.
   b. Click the document named Excel Worksheet 02.
   c. Hold down the Ctrl key, click Excel Worksheet 04, and then click Excel Worksheet 06.
   d. Release the Ctrl key and then click the <u>O</u>pen button in the dialog box.
2. Make Excel Worksheet 02 the active document by clicking <u>W</u>indow and then <u>3</u>.
3. Make Excel Worksheet 04 the active document by clicking <u>W</u>indow and then <u>2</u>.
4. Close all open documents by completing the following steps:
   a. Hold down the Shift key.
   b. Click <u>F</u>ile on the Menu bar.
   c. Click <u>C</u>lose All.

Arranging Workbooks

If you have more than one workbook open, you can arrange the workbooks at the Arrange Windows dialog box shown in figure 4.3. To display this dialog box, open several workbooks, then click <u>W</u>indow and then <u>A</u>rrange.

Arrange Windows Dialog Box

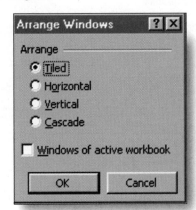

At the Arrange Windows dialog box, click <u>T</u>iled to display a portion of each open workbook. Figure 4.4 shows four open workbooks that have been tiled.

Tiled Workbooks

figure 4.4

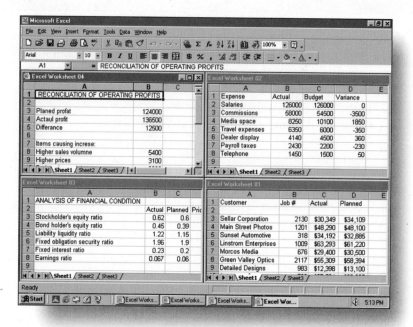

Choose the Horizontal option at the Arrange Windows dialog box and the open workbooks will be displayed across the screen. The Vertical option will display the open workbooks up and down the window. The last option, Cascade, will display the Title bar of each open workbook. Figure 4.5 shows four open workbooks that have been cascaded.

figure 4.5

Cascaded Workbooks

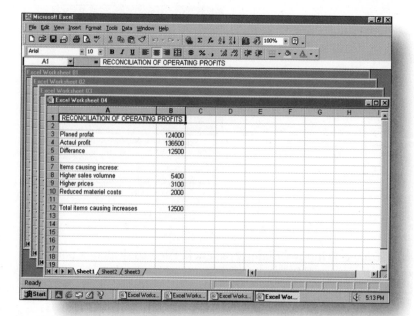

Arranging Workbooks

1. Open the following workbooks: Excel Worksheet 01, Excel Worksheet 02, Excel Worksheet 03, and Excel Worksheet 04.
2. Tile the workbooks by completing the following steps:
   a. Click Window and then Arrange.
   b. At the Arrange Windows dialog box, make sure Tiled is selected, and then click OK.
3. Tile the workbooks horizontally by completing the following steps:
   a. Click Window and then Arrange.
   b. At the Arrange Windows dialog box, click Horizontal.
   c. Click OK.
4. Cascade the workbooks by completing the following steps:
   a. Click Window and then Arrange.
   b. At the Arrange Windows dialog box, click Cascade.
   c. Click OK.
5. Close all the open workbooks by holding down the Shift key and then clicking File and then Close All.

Sizing and Moving Workbooks

Maximize

The Maximize and Minimize buttons in the upper right corner of the active workbook window can be used to change the size of the window. The Maximize button is the button in the upper right corner of the active document immediately to the left of the Close button. (The Close button is the button containing the X.) The Minimize button is located immediately to the left of the Maximize button.

Minimize

If you arrange all open workbooks and then click the Maximize button in the active workbook, the active workbook expands to fill the screen. In addition, the Maximize button changes to the Restore button. To return the active workbook back to its size before it was maximized, click the Restore button.

Close

Clicking the Minimize button causes the active workbook to be reduced and positioned as a button on the Taskbar. In addition, the Minimize button changes to the Restore button. To maximize a workbook that has been reduced, click the button on the Taskbar representing the workbook.

Restore

Minimizing, Maximizing, and Restoring Workbooks

1. Open Excel Worksheet 01.
2. Maximize Excel Worksheet 01 by clicking the Maximize button at the right side of the workbook Title bar. (The Maximize button is the button at the right side of the Title bar, immediately to the left of the Close button.)
3. Open Excel Worksheet 03 and Excel Worksheet 05.

4. Make the following changes to the open workbooks:
   a. Tile the workbooks.
   b. Make Excel Worksheet 01 the active workbook [Title bar displays with a blue background (the background color may vary depending on how Windows is customized)].
   c. Minimize Excel Worksheet 01 by clicking the Minimize button that displays at the right side of the Title bar.
   d. Make Excel Worksheet 03 the active workbook and then minimize it.
   e. . Minimize Excel Worksheet 05.
5. Close all workbooks by holding down the Shift key, then clicking File and then Close All.

Cut/copy and paste a worksheet between programs in the Microsoft Office suite in the same manner as you cut/copy and paste between worksheets in Excel.

Moving, Copying, and Pasting Data between Workbooks

With more than one workbook open, you can move, copy, and/or paste data from one workbook to another. To move, copy, and/or paste data between workbooks, use the cutting and pasting options you learned earlier in this chapter, together with the information about windows in this chapter.

exercise 9

Copying Selected Cells from One Open Worksheet to Another

1. At a blank worksheet, create the worksheet shown in figure 4.6 by completing the following steps (if a blank worksheet is not displayed, click the New button on the Standard toolbar):
   a. If you just completed exercise 8, click the Maximize button so the worksheet fills the entire worksheet window.
   b. Change the width of column A to 21.00.
   c. Select cells A1 through D1 click the Merge and Center button on the Formatting toolbar, and then click the Bold button.
   d. Select row 2, click the Bold button on the Formatting toolbar, and then click the Center button.
   e. Select cells B3 through B6 and then click the Center button on the Formatting toolbar.
   f. Key the text in the cells as shown in figure 4.6.
   g. Select cells C3 through D6, click the Currency Style button on the Formatting toolbar, and then click twice on the Decrease Decimal button.
2. Save the worksheet and name it Excel C4, Ex 09.
3. With Excel C4, Ex 09 still open, open Excel Worksheet 01.
4. With Excel Worksheet 01 the active worksheet, change the width of column A to 21.00.

5. Select and then copy text from Excel Worksheet 01 to Excel C4, Ex 09 by completing the following steps:
   a. With Excel Worksheet 01 the active workbook, select cells A5 through D10.
   b. Click the Copy button on the Standard toolbar.
   c. Click <u>W</u>indow and then click <u>2</u> Excel C4, Ex 09.
   d. Make cell A7 the active cell and then click the Paste button on the Standard toolbar.

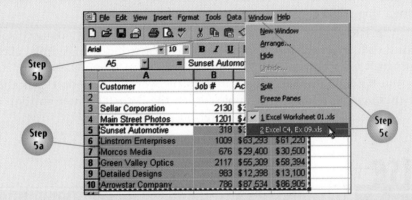

   e. Deselect the cells.
6. Select cells A1 through D12 in Excel C4, Ex 09 and then apply the Colorful 1 autoformat.
7. Save the workbook again with the same name (Excel C4, Ex 09).
8. Print and then close Excel C4, Ex 09.
9. Close Excel Worksheet 01 without saving the changes.

figure

4.6 **Exercise 9**

	A	B	C	D
1		FEBRUARY		
2	Customer	Job #	Actual	Planned
3	Real Photography	129	$ 42,350	$ 41,000
4	Jenkins Corporation	3310	$ 88,450	$ 90,000
5	Bridgway Electronics	1023	$ 19,340	$ 17,500
6	Moss Bay Productions	894	$ 68,340	$ 65,000
7				

Formatting with Format Painter

The Standard toolbar contains a button that can be used to copy formatting to different locations in the worksheet. This button is called the Format Painter and displays on the Standard toolbar as a paintbrush. To use the Format Painter button, make a cell active that contains the desired formatting, click the Format Painter button, and then click the cell or select cells to which you want the formatting applied.

Format
Painter

When you click the Format Painter button, the mouse pointer displays with a paintbrush attached. If you want to apply formatting a single time, click the Format Painter button once. If, however, you want to apply the character formatting in more than one location in the worksheet, double-click the Format Painter button. If you have double-clicked the Format Painter button, turn off the feature by clicking the Format Painter button once.

exercise 10

Formatting with Format Painter

1. Open Excel Worksheet 06.
2. Save the worksheet with Save As and name it Excel C4, Ex 10.
3. Use Format Painter to "paint" formatting to cells by completing these steps:
   a. Select cells B1 through B20 and then apply pale blue shading to the cells.
   b. Make a cell containing a percentage number in column B active.
   c. Double-click the Format painter button on the Standard toolbar.
   d. Select each of the following columns:
      Column D
      Column F
      Column H
      Column J
      Column L
   e. Select each of the following rows:
      Row 3
      Row 5
      Row 7
      Row 9
      Row 11
      Row 13
      Row 15
      Row 17
      Row 19
   f. Turn off Format Painter by clicking the Format Painter button on the Standard toolbar.
   g. Select row 1 and then click twice on the Bold button on the Formatting toolbar. (The Format Painter removed the bold formatting from the cells you formatted with pale blue shading. Selecting the row and then clicking the Bold button the first time removes bold from all headings. Clicking the Bold button the second time inserts bold formatting for the headings.)

4. Save the formatted worksheet with the same name (Excel C4, Ex 10).
5. Print Excel C4, Ex 10 in landscape orientation.
6. Close Excel C4, Ex 10.

Formatting with Styles

To automate the formatting of cells in a workbook, consider defining and applying a style. A style, which is a predefined set of formatting attributes such as font, font size, alignment, borders, shading, and so on, is particularly useful in large workbooks with data requiring a considerable amount of formatting.

There are several advantages to using a style to apply formatting. A style helps to ensure consistent formatting from one worksheet to another. All attributes for a particular style are defined only once and you do not have to redefine attributes over and over. If you need to change the formatting, you need only change the style, and all cells formatted with that style automatically reflect the change.

Defining a Style

Excel contains some common number styles that can be applied with buttons on the Formatting toolbar. For example, clicking the Currency Style button on the Formatting toolbar applies currency formatting to the cell or selected cells. The Percent Style and Comma Style buttons also apply styles to cells.

Two basic methods are available for defining your own style. You can define a style with formats already applied to a cell or you can display the Style dialog box, click the Modify button, and then choose formatting options at the Format Cells dialog box. Styles you create are only available in the workbook in which they are created.

To define a style with existing formatting, you would complete these steps:

1. Select the cell or cells containing the desired formatting.
2. Click Format and then Style.
3. At the Style dialog box, shown in figure 4.7, key a name for the new style in the Style name text box.
4. Click OK to close the dialog box.

4.7 **Style Dialog Box**

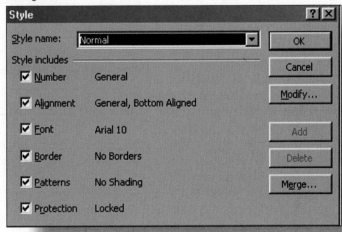

To define a new style without first applying the formatting, you would complete the following steps:

1. Click Format and then Style.
2. At the Style dialog box, key a name for the new style in the Style name text box.
3. Click the Modify button.
4. At the Format Cells dialog box, select the formats you want included in the style.
5. Click OK to close the Format Cells dialog box.
6. At the Style dialog box, remove the check mark from any formats that you do not want included in the style.
7. Click OK to define and apply the style to the selected cell. To define the style without applying it to the selected cell, click the Add button, and then click the Close button.

Applying a Style

To apply a style, select the cells you want to format, and then display the Style dialog box. At the Style dialog box, click the down-pointing triangle at the right side of the Style name text box, and then click the desired style name. Click OK to close the dialog box and apply the style.

Defining and Applying Styles

1. Open Excel Worksheet 02.
2. Save the worksheet with Save As and name it Excel C4, Ex 11.
3. Format a cell and then define a style with the formatting by completing the following steps:
   a. Make sure cell A1 is active.
   b. Change the font and apply a bottom border by completing the following steps:

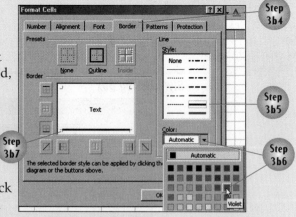

   1) Click Format and then Cells.
   2) At the Format Cells dialog box, click the Font tab.
   3) At the Font tab, change the font to Tahoma, the font style to Bold, the size to 12 points, and the color to Indigo. (Indigo is the second color from the right in the top row.)
   4) Click the Border tab.
   5) At the Format Cells dialog box with the Border tab selected, click the sixth Line Style option from the top in the second column.
   6) Click the down-pointing triangle at the right side of the Color option and then click the Violet color at the color palette (seventh color from the left in the third row from the top).
   7) Click the bottom border of the preview cell in the dialog box.
   8) Click OK to close the Format Cells dialog box.

c. With cell A1 still the active cell, define a style named *Title* with the formatting you just applied by completing the following steps:
   1) Click F̲ormat and then S̲tyle.
   2) At the Style dialog box, key **Title** in the S̲tyle name text box.
   3) Click the A̲dd button.
   4) Click the Close button.

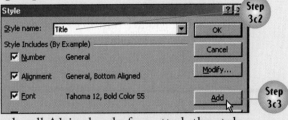

Step 3c2

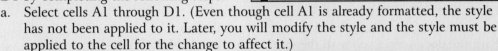

Step 3c3

4. Apply the Title style to cells A1 through D1 by completing the following steps:
   a. Select cells A1 through D1. (Even though cell A1 is already formatted, the style has not been applied to it. Later, you will modify the style and the style must be applied to the cell for the change to affect it.)
   b. Click F̲ormat and then S̲tyle.
   c. At the Style dialog box, click the down-pointing triangle at the right side of the S̲tyle name text box, and then click *Title* at the drop-down list.
   d. Click OK to close the Style dialog box.

Step 4d

Step 4c

5. Define a new style named *Font* without first applying the formatting by completing the following steps:
   a. Click in any empty cell.
   b. Click F̲ormat and then S̲tyle.
   c. At the Style dialog box, key **Font** in the S̲tyle name text box.
   d. Click the Modify button.
   e. At the Format Cells dialog box, click the Font tab.
   f. At the Format Cells dialog box with the Font tab selected, change the font to Tahoma, the size to 12, and the color to Indigo.
   g. Click the Patterns tab.
   h. At the Format Cells dialog box with the Patterns tab selected, click a light blue color of your choosing in the color palette.
   i. Click OK to close the Format Cells dialog box.
   j. At the Style dialog box, click the A̲dd button.
   k. Click the Close button.

Step 5c

Step 5k

Step 5d

Step 5j

6. Apply the Font style by completing the following steps:
   a. Select cells A2 through D8.
   b. Click F̲ormat and then S̲tyle.
   c. At the Style dialog box, click the down-pointing triangle at the right side of the S̲tyle name text box, and then click *Font* at the drop-down list.
   d. Click OK to close the Style dialog box.
7. Make the following changes to the worksheet:
   a. Select cells B2 through D8.
   b. Click the Currency Style button on the Formatting toolbar.
   c. Click twice on the Decrease Decimal button on the Formatting toolbar.
   d. Automatically adjust columns A through D.
8. Save the worksheet again with the same name (Excel C4, Ex 11).
9. Print Excel C4, Ex 11.
10. With Excel C4, Ex 11 still open, modify the Title style by completing the following steps:

a. Click in any empty cell.
b. Display the Style dialog box.
c. Click the down-pointing triangle at the right side of the Style name text box and then click *Title* at the drop-down list.
d. Click the Modify button.
e. At the Format Cells dialog box, click the Alignment tab.
f. At the Format Cells dialog box with the Alignment tab selected, click the down pointing triangle to the right of Horizontal option box, and then click *Center* at the drop-down list.
g. Click OK to close the Format Cells dialog box.
h. At the Style dialog box, click the Add button.
i. Click the Close button to close the Style dialog box.
11. Save the document again with the same name (Excel C4, Ex 11).
12. Print and then close Excel C4, Ex 11.

Copying Styles to Another Workbook

Styles you define are saved with the workbook in which they are created. You can, however, copy styles from one workbook to another. To do this, you would complete the following steps:

1. Open the workbook containing the styles you want to copy.
2. Open the workbook into which you want to copy the styles.
3. Display the Style dialog box.
4. At the Style dialog box, click the Merge button.
5. At the Merge Styles dialog box shown in figure 4.8, double-click the name of the workbook that contains the styles you want to copy.
6. Click OK to close the Style dialog box.

Merge Styles Dialog Box

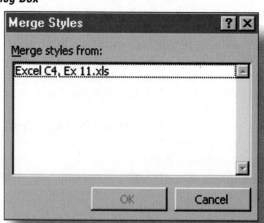

Removing a Style

If you apply a style to text and then decide you do not want the formatting applied, remove the style. To do this, select the cells formatted with the style you want to remove and then display the Style dialog box. At the Style dialog box, click the down-pointing triangle at the right side of the Style name text box, and then click *Normal* at the drop-down list.

Deleting a Style

Delete a style at the Style dialog box. To do this, display the Style dialog box, click the down-pointing triangle at the right side of the Style name text box. At the drop-down list that displays, click the style you want deleted, and then click the Delete button.

Copying and Removing Styles

1. Open Excel C4, Ex 11.
2. Open Excel Worksheet 13.
3. Save the document with Save As and name it Excel C4, Ex 12.
4. Delete column H.
5. Copy the styles in Excel C4, Ex 11 into Excel C4, Ex 12 by completing the following steps:
   a. Display the Style dialog box.
   b. At the Style dialog box, click the Merge button.
   c. At the Merge Styles dialog box, double-click *Excel C4, Ex 11.xls* in the Merge styles from list box.
   d. Click OK to close the Style dialog box.

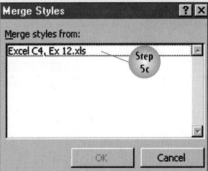

6. Modify the Font style by completing the following steps:
   a. Click in any empty cell.
   b. Display the Style dialog box.
   c. At the Style dialog box, click the down-pointing triangle at the right side of the Style name text box, and then click *Font*.
   d. Click the Modify button.
   e. At the Format Cells dialog box, click the Font tab.
   f. Change the font to *Arial* and the size to *10* point.
   g. Click OK to close the Format Cells dialog box.
   h. At the Style dialog box, click the Add button.
   i. Click the Close button to close the Style dialog box.
7. Apply the following styles:
   a. Select cells A1 through G2 and then apply the Title style.
   b. Select cells A3 through G8 and then apply the Font style.
8. Remove the Font style from cells B3 through B8 by completing the following steps:
   a. Select cells B3 through B8.
   b. Display the Style dialog box.
   c. At the Style dialog box, click the down-pointing triangle at the right side of the Style name text box, and then click *Normal*.
   d. Click OK to close the dialog box.
9. Complete steps similar to those in 8 to remove the style from cells D3 through D8 and cells F3 through F8.
10. Make the following changes to the document:

a. Change the width of columns B through G to 11.00.
b. Select cells B3 through G8, then click the Currency button on the Formatting toolbar, and then click twice on the Decrease Decimal button.
11. Save the worksheet again with the same name (Excel C4, Ex 12).
12. Print and then close Excel C4, Ex 12.
13. Close Excel C4, Ex 12.

Using Excel Templates

If it fits your needs, consider using an Excel template worksheet form.

Excel has included a number of *template* worksheet forms that are formatted for specific uses. For example, Excel has provided template forms for an expense statement, invoice, and purchase order. To view the templates available with Excel, click File and then New. This displays the New dialog box. At this dialog box, click the Spreadsheet Solutions tab and the template forms display as shown in figure 4.9.

figure
4.9

New Dialog Box with Spreadsheet Solutions Tab Selected

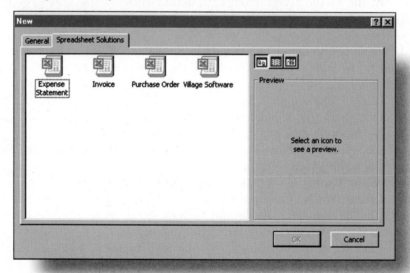

The templates in the New dialog box with the Spreadsheet Solutions tab selected are licensed to Microsoft by Village Software®. You can learn more about Village Software by double-clicking the Village Software template in the New dialog box.

Use the Expense template to itemize business expenses. The invoice is designed to help you prepare an invoice, which is an itemized list of goods shipped, specifying the price and terms of sale. Use the Purchase Order template to prepare a purchase order, which lists a description of products purchased, including quantity, number of units, and unit price.

Entering Data in a Template

Templates contain unique areas where information is entered at the keyboard. For example, in the Invoice template shown in figure 4.10, you enter information such as the customer name, address, and telephone number, and also the quantity, description, and unit price of products. To enter information in the appropriate location, position the mouse pointer (white plus sign) in the location where you want to key data, and then click the left mouse button. After keying the data, click the next location. You can also move the insertion point to another cell using the commands learned in chapter 1. For example, press the Tab key to make the next cell active, press Shift + Tab to make the previous cell active.

Invoice Template

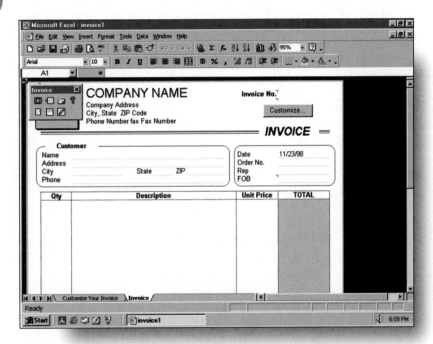

exercise 13

Preparing an Invoice Using a Template

(Note: The Invoice form created in this exercise will occupy a considerable amount of space on your disk. Consider creating the form in this exercise, printing it, and then closing it without saving it.)

1. Click File and then New.
2. At the New dialog box, click the Spreadsheet Solutions tab.
3. At the New dialog box with the Spreadsheet Solutions tab selected, double-click *Invoice*.
4. Depending on your system, Microsoft may display a message box telling you that the workbook you are opening contains macros. The message goes on to say, "Some macros may contain viruses that could be harmful to your computer. If you are sure this workbook is from a trusted source, click 'Enable Macros'." Check with your instructor to make sure your system is secure and, if it is, click Enable Macros.
5. If the Invoice form does not display at 100%, consider clicking the down-pointing

triangle at the right side of the Zoom button on the Standard toolbar and then clicking *100%* at the drop-down list.

6. Key data in the invoice by completing the following steps:
   a. Position the mouse pointer to the right of the Name option (on the light gray dotted line) in the Customer section of the invoice until it turns into a white plus sign.
   b. Click the left mouse button. (This should make the cell immediately to the right of Name active.)
   c. Key **IN-FLOW SYSTEMS** and then press Enter. (This makes the cell immediately to the right of the Address option active.)
   d. Key **320 Milander Way** and then press Enter. (This makes the cell immediately to the right of the City option active.)
   e. Key **Boston** and then press the Tab key twice. (This makes the cell immediately to the right of State active.)
   f. Key **MA** and then press the Tab key twice. (This makes the cell immediately to the right of ZIP active.)
   g. Key **02188**.
   h. Position the mouse pointer (white plus sign) to the right of the Phone option (on the light gray dotted line) and then click the left mouse button.
   i. Key **(617) 555-3900**.
   j. Position the mouse pointer (white plus sign) to the right of the Order No. option until it turns into a white plus sign and then click the left mouse button. (This should make the cell immediately to the right of Order No. active.)
   k. Key **2388-348** and then press Enter. (This makes the cell immediately to the right of Rep active.)
   l. Key **Jenkins** and then press Enter. (This makes the cell immediately to the right of FOB active.)
   m. Key **Boston**.
   n. Key the following data immediately below the specified heading (use the mouse, the Tab key, and/or the Enter key to make the desired cell active):

Qty.	=	**40**
Description	=	**Oscillator**
Unit Price	=	**340**
Qty.	=	**25**
Description	=	**Discriminator**
Unit Price	=	**570**
Qty.	=	**300**
Description	=	**Clamps**
Unit Price	=	**3.49**

Step 6

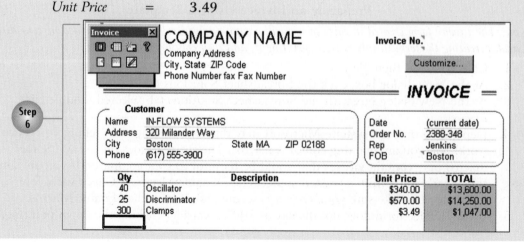

7. Save the completed invoice by completing the following steps (this step is optional; if you do not think you have enough room on your disk, print the form, and then close it without saving):
   a. Click File and then Save As.
   b. At the Save As dialog box, key **Excel C4, Ex 13** in the File name text box, and then press Enter or click Save.
8. Print and then close Excel C4, Ex 13.

When the Invoice template was displayed on the screen, did you notice small red triangles that displayed in various locations in the template? These small red triangles are comments that provide information about specific cells. To use a comment, position the mouse pointer on a small red triangle and a yellow box displays with information. For example, if you position the mouse pointer on the small red triangle above Invoice No., a yellow box displays as shown in figure 4.11.

figure
4.11

Invoice Comment

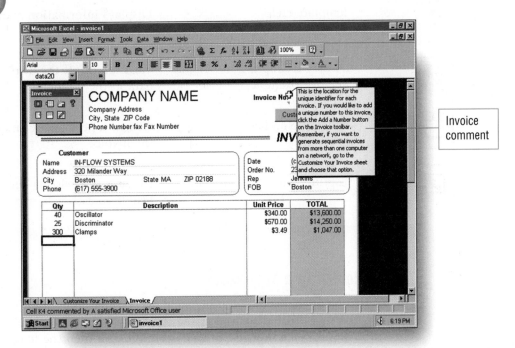

The Invoice toolbar that displays toward the upper left corner of the invoice contains buttons for performing functions in the template. There is a button that lets you hide the display of the red triangles. The buttons on the Invoice template are described in figure 4.12. The buttons that display in a template toolbar may vary slightly from those described in figure 4.12.

figure 4.12

Invoice Toolbar Buttons

Button	Name	Description
	Size to Screen/Return to Size	Reduces or expands the display of the invoice
	Hide Comments/ Display Comments	Hides or displays comments
	New Comment	Create your own note for a cell
	Template Help	Displays information about the template
	Display Example/ Remove Example	Turns on or off the display of example data in the template
	Assign a Number	Assigns a permanent unique number to the invoice
	Capture Data in a Database	Updates the existing Template Wizard Database with values from the template

Customizing a Template

Create customized templates for specific uses.

At the top of the invoice you prepared and printed in exercise 11, the text *COMPANY NAME* displayed at the top followed by *Company Address*, and so on. Information in a template can be customized and then the template can be saved with a new name. This allows you to create a customized template to use for subsequent invoices. You can also lock the customized template to prevent accidental changes to the customized information.

To customize a template, click the gray Customize button that generally displays in the upper right corner of a template. This causes a customize form to display. For example, if you click the Customize button at the Invoice template, the customize form displays as shown in figure 4.13.

figure
4.13

Invoice Customize Form

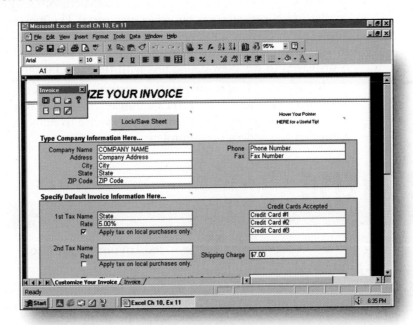

At the customize form shown in figure 4.13, key the information that you want to remain in the Invoice template for each use, and then click the gray Lock/Save Sheet button that displays toward the top of the invoice. When you click this button, the Lock/Save Sheet dialog box shown in figure 4.14 displays.

figure
4.14

Lock/Save Sheet Dialog Box

At the Lock/Save Sheet dialog box, specify whether you want to lock the invoice but not save it or lock it and save it as a template. If you want to use the template in the future, click Lock and save Template and then click OK. This displays the Save Template dialog box where you key a new name for the template. The default folder at the Save Template dialog box is the *Templates* folder. The new template you save will be saved in the *Templates* folder (rather than your disk in drive A). Key a new name for the template at the Save Template dialog box and then press Enter or click <u>S</u>ave. This displays a box containing information telling you that the new customized template has been saved to C:\WINDOWS\Application Data\Microsoft\Templates. *(Note: Depending on your system configuration, this folder may vary.)* The message also tells you that to begin using the new template, close the current invoice, and then open the new Invoice template from the New dialog box. A customized template that you create is displayed in the New dialog box with the General tab selected.

In exercise 14, you will create a customized Invoice template with the name XXX Invoice (where your initials are inserted instead of the XXX). Check with your instructor before completing this exercise to make sure your system will allow you to create a new template.

Creating a Customized Invoice Template

1. Click <u>F</u>ile and then <u>N</u>ew.
2. At the New dialog box, click the Spreadsheet Solutions tab.
3. At the New dialog box with the Spreadsheet Solutions tab selected, double-click *Invoice*.
4. If Microsoft displays the message box telling you that the workbook you are opening contains macros, click the <u>E</u>nable Macros button. *(Note: Be sure to check with your instructor before clicking this button.)*
5. At the Invoice template, click the gray Customize button that displays in the upper right corner of the Invoice template.
6. At the *CUSTOMIZE YOUR INVOICE* form that displays, key the following data in the specified cells. [To do this, position the mouse pointer (white plus sign) in the white area on top of the generic information (such as *COMPANY NAME*), click the left mouse button, and then key the text. Use the Enter key, the Tab key, Shift + Tab, and/or the mouse to move to the correct cell.]

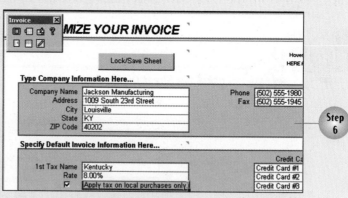

Step 6

Company Name	=	**Jackson Manufacturing**
Address	=	**1009 South 23rd Street**
City	=	**Louisville**
State	=	**KY**
ZIP Code	=	**40202**
Phone Number	=	**(502) 555-1980**
Fax Number	=	**(502) 555-1945**
1st Tax Name	=	**Kentucky**
Rate	=	8 *(Be sure to press Enter after keying 8.)*

7. Save the Invoice template with a new name by completing the following steps:
   a. Click the gray Lock/Save Sheet button that displays toward the top of the *CUSTOMIZE YOUR INVOICE* form.
   b. At the Lock/Save Sheet dialog box, click *Lock and save Template*, and then click OK.
   c. At the Save Template dialog box, key **XXX Invoice** (where your initials are inserted instead of the XXX), and then press Enter or click <u>S</u>ave.
   d. At the message telling you that the customized template has been saved to the directory, click OK.
8. Close the Invoice template.

When the *CUSTOMIZE YOUR INVOICE* form is displayed, tabs appear below the invoice at the left side of the horizontal scroll bar. The two tabs that display when customizing the Invoice template are Customize Your Invoice and Invoice. With these tabs you can move back and forth between the invoice and the customize form. You will notice similar types of tabs when customizing other templates.

exercise 15

Filling in a Customized Invoice Template

(Note: The Invoice form created in this exercise will occupy a considerable amount of space on your disk. Consider printing and then closing the Invoice form without saving it.)

1. Open the XXX Invoice template (where your initials display instead of the XXX) by completing the following steps:
   a. Click <u>F</u>ile and then <u>N</u>ew.
   b. At the New dialog box, click the General tab.
   c. At the New dialog box with the General tab selected, double-click the *XXX Invoice* icon (where your initials display instead of the *XXX*).
2. If Microsoft displays the message box telling you that the workbook you are opening contains macros, click the <u>E</u>nable Macros button. *(Note: Be sure to check with your instructor before clicking this button.)*
3. With the XXX Invoice template open, key the following data in the specified cells:

Name	=	**Seaside Marine Supplies**
Address	=	**1200 Camino Drive**
City	=	**San Diego**
State	=	**CA**
ZIP Code	=	**92031**
Phone	=	**(619) 555-9500**

Order No.	=	**231-202**
Rep	=	**Thornton**
FOB	=	**Kentucky**
Qty.	=	**3**
Description	=	**Propeller**
Unit Price	=	**725**
Qty.	=	**10**
Description	=	**Fuel Rover**
Unit Price	=	**210**
Qty.	=	**7**
Description	=	**Balancing Fan**
Unit Price	=	**95**

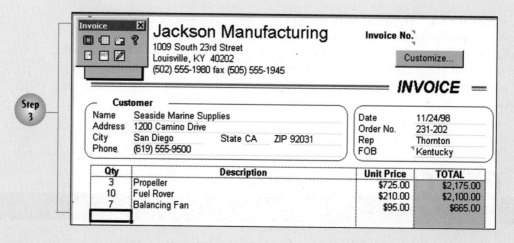

4. Delete information toward the bottom of the invoice by completing the following steps:
    a. Scroll down toward the bottom of the invoice until the text *Insert Fine Print Here* displays.
    b. Click anywhere in the text *Insert Fine Print Here* and then press the Delete key.
    c. Scroll down to the bottom of the invoice until the text *Insert Farewell Statement Here* displays.
    d. Click anywhere in the text *Insert Farewell Statement Here* and then press the Delete key.
5. Save the completed Invoice template in the normal manner to the *Chapter 04* folder on your disk in drive A with the name Excel C4, Ex 15. *(You will need to change the drive location at the Save As dialog box.)* (This step is optional. If you do not think you have room on your disk for this exercise, print the form and then close it without saving it.)
6. Print and then close Excel C4, Ex 15.

       The Invoice template automatically calculates the total price of each product ordered, and inserts a subtotal amount for all items, shipping and handling costs, sales tax, and a final total. This template includes formulas that calculate these amounts. In the next chapter, you will learn how to insert your own formula in a worksheet.

chapter summary

➤ Selected cells and cell contents can be moved in and between worksheets using the Cut, Copy, and Paste buttons on the Standard toolbar; dragging with the mouse; or with options from the Edit drop-down menu.

➤ Selected cells can be moved with the mouse by dragging the outline of the selected cells to the desired position.

➤ Selected cells can be copied with the mouse by holding down the Ctrl key and the left mouse button, dragging the outline of the selected cells to the desired location, and then releasing the left mouse button and then the Ctrl key.

➤ A variety of worksheets with related data can be created within a workbook.

➤ To print all worksheets in a workbook, click Entire workbook in the Print what section of the Print dialog box. You can also print specific worksheets by holding down the Ctrl key and then clicking the tabs of the worksheets you want printed.

➤ Perform maintenance activities, such as deleting and renaming, on worksheets within a workbook by clicking the *right* mouse button on a sheet tab, and then clicking the desired option at the pop-up menu.

➤ The worksheet window can be split into panes with the Split option from the Window drop-down menu or with the split bars on the horizontal and vertical scroll bars.

➤ Remove the split window by clicking Window and then Remove Split; or drag the split bars.

➤ Freeze window panes by clicking Window and then Freeze Panes. When panes are frozen, only the display of the pane with the active cell changes. Unfreeze window panes by clicking Window and then Unfreeze.

➤ Open multiple workbooks that are adjacent by displaying the Open dialog box, clicking the first workbook to be opened, holding down the Shift key, and then clicking the last workbook. If workbooks are nonadjacent, click the first workbook, hold down the Ctrl key, and then click the desired workbook names.

➤ If multiple workbooks are opened, click Window on the Menu bar to see a list of the open workbooks.

➤ Close all open workbooks at one time by holding down the Shift key and then clicking File and then Close All.

➤ Multiple workbooks can be arranged in a window with options from the Arrange Windows dialog box.

➤ Click the Maximize button located at the right side of the Title bar of the active workbook to make the workbook fill the entire window area. Click the Minimize button to shrink the active workbook to a button on the Taskbar. Click the Restore button to return the workbook back to its previous size.

➤ Data can be moved, copied, and/or pasted between workbooks.

➤ Objects can be copied from a document in one program (called the source program) and then pasted into a document in another program (called the destination program). When an object is pasted in the destination program, it becomes a part of that program and the object can be edited with only those tools available in the destination program.

➤ Automate formatting of cells with Format Painter.

➤ Automate the formatting of cells in a workbook by defining and then applying styles. A style is a predefined set of formatting attributes.

➤ A style helps to ensure consistent formatting from one worksheet to another. All formatting attributes for a particular style are defined only once. Modify a style and all cells to which the style is applied automatically reflect the change.

➤ Define a style with formats already applied to a cell or display the Style dialog box, click the Modify button, and then choose formatting options at the Format Cells dialog box.

➤ Define, apply, modify, remove, and delete styles at the Style dialog box.

➤ Styles are saved in the workbook in which they are created. Styles can be copied, however, to another workbook. Do this with the Merge button at the Style dialog box.

➤ Excel provides preformatted templates for creating forms such as an expense statement, invoice, or purchase order.

➤ Excel templates can be customized and the customized form can be locked and saved in the *Templates* folder.

➤ Templates contain unique areas where information is entered at the keyboard. These areas vary depending on the template.

➤ Each template contains comments that display as small red triangles and provide information about cells.

➤ A template contains a toolbar with buttons you can use to perform such actions as changing the size of the template, hiding or displaying comments, creating a note for a cell, displaying or removing an example, and assigning a number to the template. The buttons vary depending on the template displayed.

➤ To customize a template for personal use, click the gray Customize button that displays in the upper right corner of the template.

➤ A customized template that has been saved displays in the New dialog box with the General tab selected.

➤ When the customize form is displayed, tabs display below the template form. Use these tabs to switch between the customize form and the template.

commands review

	Mouse/Keyboard
Split window into panes	Click Window, Split; or drag split bar
Freeze window panes	Click Window, Freeze Panes
Unfreeze window panes	Click Window, Unfreeze Panes
Remove window panes	Click Window, Remove Split
Display Arrange Windows dialog box	Click Window, Arrange
Turn on Format Painter	Click Format Painter button on Standard toolbar
Display Style dialog box	Click Format, Style
Display Merge Styles dialog box	At Style dialog box, click Merge button
Display New dialog box	Click File, New

thinking offline

Completion: In the space provided at the right, indicate the correct term, number, or symbol.

1. To copy selected cells with the mouse, hold down this key while dragging the outline of the selected cells to the desired location. _____

2. To split a window using a split bar, position the mouse pointer on the split bar until the mouse pointer turns into this. _____

3. Clicking <u>W</u>indow and then <u>S</u>plit causes the active worksheet to be split into this number of windows. _____

4. To see what workbooks are currently open, click this on the Menu bar. _____

5. To close all open workbooks at the same time, hold down this key while clicking <u>F</u>ile and then <u>C</u>lose All. _____

6. Arrange all open workbooks with options from this dialog box. _____

7. Click this button to shrink the active workbook to a button on the Taskbar. _____

8. Click this button to return the workbook back to its original size. _____

9. Click this button to make the active workbook fill the entire window area. _____

10. When copying and pasting data between programs, the program containing the original data to be copied is called this. _____

11. Click this button at the Style dialog box to display the Format Cells dialog box. _____

12. Click this tab at the New dialog box to display a list of Excel templates. _____

13. List the steps you would complete to open all of the following documents at one time: Excel Worksheet 02, Excel Worksheet 03, and Excel Worksheet 05.

    _____

    _____

    _____

    _____

14. List the steps you would complete to copy a range of cells from one workbook to another.

    _____

    _____

    _____

    _____

15. List the steps you would complete to display the *CUSTOMIZE YOUR PURCHASE ORDER* form.

_____

_____

_____

_____

working hands-on

Assessment 1

1. Open Excel Worksheet 03.
2. Save the worksheet with Save As and name it Excel C4, SA 01.
3. Make the following changes to the worksheet:
   a. Insert a column between columns C and D. (The new column will be column D.)
   b. Move the cells in column B to the blank column D.
   c. Delete the blank column B.
   d. Select cells B3 through D8 and then click the Percent Style button.
   e. Select cells A1 through D8 and then apply an autoformat of your choosing.
4. Save the worksheet again with the same name (Excel C4, SA 01).
5. Print and then close Excel C4, SA 01.

Assessment 2

1. Open Excel Worksheet 05.
2. Save the worksheet with Save As and name it Excel C4, SA 02.
3. Make the following changes:
   a. Copy cells A1 through C8 to *Sheet2*.
   b. With *Sheet2* active, make the following changes:
      A1: Change *January* to *February*
      B3: Change *35* to *40*
      B6: Change *24* to *20*
      B7: Change *15* to *20*
      C4: Change *$19.00* to *20.15*
      C6: Change *$16.45* to *17.45*
   c. Automatically adjust the width of column A.
   d. Copy cells A1 through C8 to *Sheet3*.
   e. With *Sheet3* active, make the following changes:
      A1: Change *February* to *March*
      B4: Change *20* to *35*
      B8: Change *15* to *20*
   f. Automatically adjust the width of column A.
4. Save the worksheets again with the same name (Excel C4, SA 02).
5. Print all worksheets in the Excel C4, SA 02 workbook.
6. Close Excel C4, SA 02.

Assessment 3

1. Open Excel Worksheet 09.
2. Save the worksheet with Save As and name it Excel C4, SA 03.
3. Make the following changes to the worksheet:
   a. Split the window.
   b. Drag the intersection of the horizontal and vertical gray lines so that the horizontal gray line is immediately below row 9 and the vertical gray line is immediately to the right of column A.
   c. Freeze the window panes.
   d. Add a new row 8 and then key the following in the specified cells:

A8	=	**Loaned Out**
B8	=	10
C8	=	0
D8	=	5
E8	=	0
F8	=	11
G8	=	3
H8	=	16
I8	=	0
J8	=	0
K8	=	5
L8	=	0
M8	=	0

   e. Remove the split.
   f. Select rows 1 through 10 and then change the row height to 18.00.
4. Save the worksheet again with the same name (Excel C4, SA 03).
5. Print the worksheet in landscape orientation (it will take two pages) so the row titles print on each page.
6. Close Excel C4, SA 03.

Assessment 4

1. Create the worksheet shown in figure 4.15 (change the width of column A to 21.00).
2. Save the worksheet and name it Excel C4, SA 04.
3. With Excel C4, SA 04 still open, open Excel Worksheet 09.
4. Select and copy the following cells from Excel Worksheet 09 to Excel C4, SA 04:
   a. Copy cells A3 through G3 in Excel Worksheet 09 and paste them into Excel C4, SA 04 beginning with cell A12.
   b. Copy cells A9 through G9 in Excel Worksheet 09 and paste them into Excel C4, SA 04 beginning with cell A13.
5. With Excel C4, SA 04 the active worksheet, apply an autoformat of your choosing to cells A1 through G13.
6. Save the worksheet again with the same name (Excel C4, SA 04).
7. Print Excel C4, SA 04 in landscape orientation and centered horizontally and vertically on the page.
8. Close Excel C4, SA 04.
9. Close Excel Worksheet 09 without saving the changes.

figure
4.15

Assessment 4

	A	B	C	D	E	F	G	H
1		EQUIPMENT USAGE REPORT						
2		January	February	March	April	May	June	
3	Machine #12							
4	Total Hours Available	2,300	2,430	2,530	2,400	2,440	2,240	
5	In Use	2,040	2,105	2,320	2,180	2,050	1,995	
6								
7	Machine #25							
8	Total Hours Available	2,100	2,240	2,450	2,105	2,390	1,950	
9	In Use	1,800	1,935	2,110	1,750	2,215	1,645	
10								
11	Machine #30							
12								

Assessment 5

1. At a clear worksheet, define the following styles:
   a. Define a style named Heading that contains the following formatting:
      1) 14-point Times New Roman bold in Blue-Gray color
      2) Horizontal alignment of Center
      3) Double-line top and bottom border in Dark Red color
      4) Light purple shading
   b. Define a style named Column 01 that contains the following formatting:
      1) 12-point Times New Roman in Blue-Gray color
      2) Light purple shading
   c. Define a style named Column 02 that contains 12-point Times New Roman in Blue-Gray color.
2. Save the worksheet and name it Excel C4, Style 01.
3. With Excel C4, Style 01 open, open Excel Worksheet 09.
4. Save the worksheet with Save As and name it Excel C4, SA 05.
5. Copy the styles from Excel C4, Style 01 into Excel C4, SA 05. *(Hint: Do this through the Style dialog box.)*
6. Select cells A1 through M1 and then click the Merge and Center button on the Formatting toolbar.
7. Apply the following styles:
   a. Select cells A1 through M2 and then apply the Heading style.
   b. Select cells A3 through A9 and then apply the Column 01 style.
   c. Select cells B3 through G9 and then apply the Column 02 style.
   d. Select cells H3 through M9 and then apply the Column 01 style.
8. Automatically adjust the widths of columns A through M.
9. Save the worksheet again with the same name (Excel C4, SA 05).
10. Print Excel C4, SA 05 on one page in Landscape orientation. *(Hint: Change the orientation and scaling at the Page Setup dialog box with the Page tab selected.)*
11. With Excel C4, SA 05 still open, modify the following styles:
    a. Modify Heading so it changes the font color to Indigo (instead of Blue-Gray) and inserts a solid, thick top and bottom border in Violet (instead of a double-line top and bottom border in Dark Red).
    b. Modify Column 02 so it adds a font style of Bold Italic (leave all the other formatting attributes).
12. Save the worksheet again with the same name (Excel C4, SA 05).

13. Print Excel Ch 4, SA 05 on one page and in Landscape orientation.
14. Close Excel C4, SA 05.
15. Close Excel C4, Style 01.

Assessment 6

1. Create a customized template with the Purchase Order template. At the *CUSTOMIZE YOUR PURCHASE ORDER* form, key the following data in the specified cells:

COMPANY NAME	=	K & N Corporation
Company Address	=	897 North 112th Street
City	=	White Plains
State	=	NY
ZIP Code	=	10609
Phone Number	=	(201) 555-4321
Fax Number	=	(201) 555-4330
1st Tax Name	=	New York
Rate	=	8.2 *(Be sure to press Enter after keying 8.2.)*

2. Click the Lock/Save Sheet button and save the customized Purchase Order template with the name XXX Purchase Order (where your initials are inserted instead of the XXX).
3. Close the Purchase Order template.
4. Display the New dialog box with the General tab selected, and then double-click XXX Purchase Order (where your initials display instead of the XXX) and then key the following data in the specified cells:

In the Vendor section:

Name	=	Evergreen Services
Address	=	1209 Princeville Drive
City	=	Pickerington
State	=	OH
ZIP Code	=	43145
Phone	=	(614) 555-9766

In the Ship To section:

Name	=	K & N Corporation
Address	=	897 North 112th Street
City	=	White Plains
State	=	NY
ZIP Code	=	10609
Phone	=	(201) 555-4321
Qty.	=	120
Units	=	dozen
Description	=	Heater ring
Unit Price	=	24.95
Qty.	=	10
Units	=	boxes
Description	=	Wheel bands
Unit Price	=	79.50
Qty.	=	7
Units	=	dozen
Description	=	Repair kit, 21B
Unit Price	=	19.50

5. Save the completed Purchase Order in the normal manner to the chapter 04 folder on your disk in drive A with the name Excel C4, SA 06.
6. Print and then close Excel C4, SA 06.

Assessment 7

1. Delete the XXX Invoice template you created in this chapter by completing the following steps:
   a. Click File and then New.
   b. At the New dialog box with the General tab selected, position the arrow pointer on *XXX Invoice* (where your initials display instead of the *XXX*), and then click the *right* mouse button.
   c. At the pop-up menu that displays, click Delete.
   d. At the dialog box asking if you are sure you want to send the *XXX Invoice* to the Recycle Bin, click Yes.
2. Complete steps similar to those in steps 1a through 1d to delete *XXX Purchase Order*.

Assessment 8

1. In this chapter, you learned about features that automate the formatting of cells in a worksheet such as Format Painter and Styles. Another formatting feature is Conditional Formatting. Use Excel's Help feature to learn about Conditional Formatting.
2. Open Excel Worksheet 06.
3. Save the worksheet with Save As and name it Excel C4, SA 08.
4. Select cells B3 through M20 and then use Conditional Formatting to display all percentages between 95% and 100% in red and with a red border.
5. Save the worksheet again with the same name (Excel C4, SA 08).
6. Print and then close Excel C4, SA 08.

Chapter 05C

Inserting Formulas in a Worksheet

PERFORMANCE OBJECTIVES

Upon successful completion of chapter 5, you will be able to:

- Insert a formula in a cell using the AutoSum button.
- Key a formula in the Formula bar.
- Use the Paste Function feature to insert a formula in a cell.
- Write formulas with the AVERAGE, MAX, MIN, COUNT, SLN, DDB, FV, PMT, DATE, NOW, and IF functions.
- Name a range of cells and use a range in a formula.
- Create an absolute and mixed cell reference.
- Automatically outline a worksheet.
- Link cells between worksheets.
- Link worksheets using 3-D references.
- Plan and create a worksheet.

Excel is a powerful decision-making tool containing data that can be manipulated to answer "what if" situations. Insert a formula in a worksheet and then manipulate the data to make projections, answer specific questions, and use as a planning tool. For example, the manager of a department might use an Excel worksheet to prepare a department budget and then determine the impact on the budget of hiring a new employee or increasing the volume of production.

Insert a formula in a worksheet to perform calculations on values. A formula contains a mathematical operator, value, cell reference, cell range, and a function. Formulas can be written that add, subtract, multiply, and/or divide values. Formulas can also be written that calculate averages, percentages, minimum and maximum values, and much more. Excel includes an AutoSum button on the Standard toolbar that inserts a formula to calculate the total of a range of cells. Paste Function is an Excel feature that offers a variety of functions to create a formula.

Using the AutoSum Button

To perform a calculation in a worksheet, make active the cell in which you want to insert the formula (this cell should be empty). Key the formula in the cell and the formula displays in the cell as well as the Formula bar. When the formula is completed, and you exit the cell, the result of the formula displays in the active cell while the actual formula displays in the Formula bar.

You can also enter a formula in the Formula bar located below the Formatting toolbar. To do this, click in the Formula bar text box, key the desired formula and then press Enter or click the Enter button (contains a green check mark) on the Formula toolbar.

One of the advantages of using formulas in a worksheet is that cell entries can be changed and the formula will automatically recalculate the values and insert the result in the cell containing the formula. This is what makes an Excel worksheet a decision-making tool.

In addition to keying a formula in a cell, you can also use the AutoSum button on the Standard toolbar. The AutoSum button adds numbers automatically with the SUM function. When you click the AutoSum button, Excel looks for a range of cells containing numbers above the active cell if there are none there, then it looks to the left of the active cell. Excel suggests the range of cells to be added. If the suggested range is not correct, drag through the desired range with the mouse, and then press Enter. You can also just double-click the AutoSum button and this will insert the SUM function with the range Excel chooses.

(Before completing computer exercises, delete the Chapter 04C *folder on your disk. Next, copy the* Chapter 05C *folder from the CD that accompanies this textbook to your disk and make* Chapter 05C *the active folder.)*

Enter

AutoSum

Use the AutoSum button to automatically add numbers in a range of cells.

Hint

exercise 1

Adding Values with the AutoSum Button

1. Open Excel Worksheet 02.
2. Save the worksheet with Save As and name it Excel C5, Ex 01.
3. Calculate the sum of cells by completing the following steps:
   a. Make B9 the active cell.
   b. Click the AutoSum button on the Standard toolbar.
   c. Excel inserts the formula =SUM(B2:B8) in cell B9. This is the correct range of cells, so press Enter.

Step 3b

AutoSum

	A	B	C	D	E
1	Expense	Actual	Budget	Variance	
2	Salaries	126000	126000	0	
3	Commissions	58000	54500	-3500	
4	Media space	8250	10100	1850	
5	Travel expenses	6350	6000	-350	
6	Dealer display	4140	4500	360	
7	Payroll taxes	2430	2200	230	
8	Telephone	1450	1500	50	
9		=SUM(B2:B8)			

PMT =SUM(B2:B8)

Step 3c

  d. Make C9 the active cell.
  e. Click the AutoSum button on the Standard toolbar.
  f. Excel inserts the formula *=SUM(C2:C8)* in cell C9. This is the correct range of cells, so press Enter.
  g. Make D9 the active cell.
  h. Double-click the AutoSum button on the Standard toolbar. (This inserts the formula *=SUM(D2:D8)* in cell D9 and inserts the sum *-1820*.)
4. Select cells A1 through D9 and then apply the Accounting 1 autoformat.
5. Save the worksheet again with the same name (Excel C5, Ex 01).
6. Print Excel C5, Ex 01.
7. Make the following changes to cell entries:
   B4: Change *8,250.00* to *9550*
   D4: Change *1,850.00* to *550*
   B7: Change *2,430.00* to *2050*
   D7: Change *(230.00)* to *150*
8. Save the worksheet again with the same name (Excel C5, Ex 01).
9. Print and then close Excel C5, Ex 01.

Writing Formulas with Mathematical Operators

The AutoSum button on the Standard toolbar essentially creates the formula for you. You can also write your own formulas using mathematical operators. Commonly used mathematical formulas and their functions are described in figure 5.1.

  When writing your own formula, begin the formula with the equals (=) sign. For example, to divide cell B2 by cell C2 and insert the result in cell D2, you would make D2 the active cell, and then key **=B2/C2**.

After keying a formula in a cell, press the Enter key, the Tab key, Shift + Tab, or click the Enter button on the Formula bar.

figure

5.1   *Mathematical Operators*

To perform this function	Key this operator
Addition	+
Subtraction	-
Multiplication	*
Division	/
Percent	%
Exponentiation	^

If there are two or more operators in a formula, Excel uses the same order of operations used in algebra. From left to right in a formula, this order, called the *order of operations*, is: negations (negative number—a number preceded by -) first, then percents (%), then exponentiations (^), followed by multiplications (*), divisions (/), additions (+), and finally subtractions (-). If you want to change the order of operations, use parentheses around the part of the formula you want calculated first.

Copying a Formula with Relative Cell References

In many worksheets, the same basic formula is used repetitively. In a situation where a formula is copied to other locations in a worksheet, use a *relative cell reference*. Copy a formula containing relative cell references and the cell references change. For example, if you enter the formula *=SUM(A2:C2)* in cell D2 and then copy it relatively to cell D3, the formula in cell D3 displays as *=SUM(A3:C3)*. (Additional information on cell references is discussed later in this chapter in the "Using an Absolute Cell Reference in a Formula" section.)

To copy a formula relatively in a worksheet, use the Fill option from the Edit drop-down menu. To do this, select the cell containing the formula as well as the cells to which you want the formula copied, and then click Edit. At the Edit drop-down menu, point to Fill. This causes another drop-down menu to display. The choices active in this drop-down menu will vary depending on the selected cells. For example, if you select cells down a column, options such as Down and Up will be active. If cells in a row are selected, options such as Right and Left will be active. Click the desired direction and the formula is copied relatively to the selected cells.

You can display formulas in a worksheet rather than the calculated values by pressing Ctrl + ` (accent grave).

exercise 2

Finding Variances by Inserting and Copying a Formula

1. Open Excel Worksheet 01.
2. Save the worksheet with Save As and name it Excel C5, Ex 02.
3. Make the following changes to the worksheet:
   a. Change the width of column A to 19.00.
   b. Make cell E1 active and then key **Variance**.
4. Insert a formula and then copy it to other cells by completing the following steps:
   a. Make E3 the active cell.
   b. Key the formula **=D3-C3**.
   c. Press Enter.
   d. Copy the formula to cells E4 through E10 by completing the following steps:
      1) Select cells E3 through E10.
      2) Click Edit, point to Fill, and then click Down.

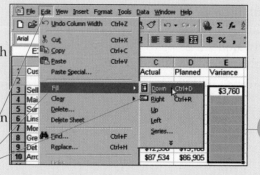

Step 4d2

Step 4d1

5. Select cells A1 through E10 and then apply the Colorful 1 autoformat.
6. Select cells B3 through B10 and then change the alignment to right.
7. Save the worksheet again with the same name (Excel C5, Ex 02).
8. Print Excel C5, Ex 02.
9. Make the following changes to cell contents:
   C4: Change $48,290 to 46425
   D6: Change $61,220 to 60000
   C8: Change $55,309 to 57415
   C9: Change $12,398 to 14115
10. Save the worksheet again with the same name (Excel C5, Ex 02).
11. Print and then close Excel C5, Ex 02.

Copying Formulas with the Fill Handle

Use the Autofill fill handle to copy a formula up, down, left, or right within a worksheet. To use the fill handle, insert the desired data in the cell (text, value, formula, etc.). With the cell active, position the mouse pointer (white plus sign) on the fill handle until the mouse pointer turns into a thin black cross. Hold down the left mouse button, drag and select the desired cells, and then release the mouse button. If you are dragging a cell containing a formula, a relative version of the formula is copied to the selected cells. You will use the fill handle in exercise 3 to copy a formula to adjacent cells.

Use the AutoFill fill handle to copy a relative version of a formula.

 exercise 3

Calculating Salary by Inserting and Copying a Formula with the Fill Handle

1. Open Excel Worksheet 05.
2. Save the worksheet with Save As and name it Excel C5, Ex 03.
3. Make cell D2 active, turn on bold, change the alignment to center, and then key **Salary**.
4. Insert a formula and then copy it to other cells using the fill handle by completing the following steps:
   a. Make D3 the active cell.
   b. Click the Formula bar text box and then key **=C3*B3**.
   c. Click the Enter button on the formula bar.
   d. Copy the formula to cells D4 through D8 by completing the following steps:
      1) Make cell D3 active.
      2) Position the mouse pointer (white plus sign) on the fill handle that displays at the lower right corner of cell D3 until the pointer turns into a thin black cross.
      3) Hold down the left mouse button, drag down to cell D8, and then release the mouse button.

	A	B	C	D
1	January			
2	Name	Hours	Rate	Salary
3	Carolyn Bentley	35	$23.15	$810.25
4	Lindon Cassini	20	$19.00	$380.00
5	Michelle DeFord	40	$18.75	$750.00
6	Javier Farias	24	$16.45	$394.80
7	Deborah Gould	15	$11.50	$172.50
8	William Jarman	15	$11.50	$172.50

Step
4d3

5. Save the worksheet again with the same name (Excel C5, Ex 03).
6. Print Excel C5, Ex 03.
7. Make the following changes to cell contents:
> B4: Change *20* to *28*
> C5: Change *$18.75* to *19.10*
> B7: Change *15* to *24*
8. Save the worksheet again with the same name (Excel C5, Ex 03).
9. Print and then close Excel C5, Ex 03.

Writing a Formula by Pointing

In exercises 2 and 3, you wrote formulas using cell references such as =C3-B3. Another method for writing a formula is to "point" to the specific cells that are to be part of the formula. Creating a formula by pointing is more accurate than keying the cell reference since a mistake can happen when entering the cell reference.

To write a formula by pointing, click the cell that will contain the formula, key the equals sign to begin the formula, and then click the cell you want to reference in the formula. This inserts a moving border around the cell and also changes the mode from *Enter* to *Point*. (The word *Point* displays at the left side of the Status bar.) Key the desired mathematical operator and then click the next cell reference. Continue in this manner until all cell references are specified and then press the Enter key. This ends the formula and inserts the result of the calculation of the formula in the active cell. When writing a formula by pointing, you can also select a range of cells you want included in a formula.

exercise 4

Writing a Formula by Pointing that Calculates Percentage of Down Time

1. Open Excel Worksheet 09.
2. Save the worksheet with Save As and name it Excel C5, Ex 04.
3. Make the following changes to the worksheet:
   a. Make cell A11 active and then key **Percentage of Down Time**.
   b. Enter a formula by pointing that computes the percentage of equipment down time by completing the following steps:
   1) Make cell B11 active.
   2) Key the equals sign followed by the left parenthesis (=().
   3) Click cell B3. (This inserts a moving border around the cell and the mode changes from *Enter* to *Point*.)
   4) Key the minus symbol (-).
   5) Click cell B9.
   6) Key the right parenthesis followed by the forward slash ()/).
   7) Click cell B3.
   8) Make sure the formula looks like this: *=(B3-B9)/B3* and then press Enter.

	A	B	
1			
2	**Hours**	January	**Step 3b7**
3	Total Hours Available	2,300	
4	Avoidable Delays	19	
5	Unavoidable Delays	9	
6	Repairs	5	
7	Servicing	6	
8	Unassigned	128	
9	In Use	2,040	
10			**Step 3b8**
11	Percentage of Down Time	=(B3-B9)/B3	
12			

c. Make cell B11 active and then click the Percent Style button on the Formatting toolbar.

d. With cell B11 still active, position the mouse pointer on the fill handle, drag across to cell M11, and then release the mouse button.

e. Enter a formula by dragging through a range of cells by completing the following steps:
 1) Click in cell A13 and then key **Hours Available Jan – June.**
 2) Click in cell B13 and then click the AutoSum button on the Standard toolbar.
 3) Select cells B3 through G3.
 4) Click the Enter key on the Formula bar.

f. Click in cell A14 and then key **Hours Available July – Dec.**

g. Click in cell B14 and then complete steps similar to those in steps 3e2 through 3e4 to create a formula that totals hours available from July through December.

4. Save the worksheet again with the same name (Excel C5, Ex 04).

5. Print the worksheet in landscape orientation horizontally and vertically centered on the page and with column A titles repeated at the left side of the worksheet on the second page.

6. Close Excel C5, Ex 04.

exercise 5

Writing a Formula by Pointing that Calculates Percentage of Actual Budget

1. Open Excel Worksheet 02.
2. Save the worksheet with Save As and name it Excel C5, Ex 05.
3. Make the following changes to the worksheet:
 a. Delete column D.
 b. Make cell D1 active and then key **% of Actual**.
 c. Enter a formula by pointing that calculates the percentage of actual budget by completing the following steps:
 1) Make cell D2 active.
 2) Key the equals sign (=).
 3) Click cell C2. (This inserts a moving border around the cell and the mode changes from *Enter* to *Point*.)
 4) Key the forward slash symbol (/).
 5) Click cell B2.
 6) Make sure the formula looks like this: *=C2/B2* and then press Enter.

	A	B	C	D
1	Expense	Actual	Budget	% of Actual
2	Salaries	126000	126000	=C2/B2
3	Commissions	58000	54500	
4	Media space	8250	10100	
5	Travel expenses	6350	6000	Step 3c
6	Dealer display	4140	4500	
7	Payroll taxes	2430	2200	
8	Telephone	1450	1500	

 d. Make cell D2 active and then click the Percent Style button on the Formatting toolbar.
 e. With cell D2 still active, position the mouse pointer on the fill handle, drag down to cell D8, and then release the mouse button.
 f. Select cells B2 through C8 and then click the Currency Style button on the Formatting toolbar.
 g. Automatically increase the width of column D to accommodate the column heading.
 h. Select cells A1 through D8 and then apply the Classic 2 autoformat.
4. Save the worksheet again with the same name (Excel C5, Ex 05).
5. Print the worksheet horizontally and vertically centered on the page.
6. Close Excel C5, Ex 05.

Inserting a Formula with the Paste Function Button

In exercise 1, the AutoSum button inserted a formula that began with =SUM. This part of the formula is called a *function*. A function is a built-in formula. Using a function takes fewer keystrokes when creating a formula. For example, the =SUM function saved you from having to key each cell to be included in the formula with the plus (+) symbol between cell entries.

Excel provides other functions that can be used to write formulas. A function operates on what is referred to as an *argument*. An argument may consist of a constant, a cell reference, or another function (referred to as a nested function). In exercise 1, when you made cell B10 active and then clicked the AutoSum button, the formula =SUM(B3:B9) was inserted in the cell. The cell range (B3:B9) is an example of a cell reference argument. An argument may also contain a *constant*. A constant is a value entered directly into the formula. For example, if you enter the formula =SUM(B3:B9,100), the cell range B3:B9 is a cell reference argument and 100 is a constant. In this formula, 100 is always added to the sum of the cells. If a function is included in an argument within a function, it is called a *nested function*. (You will learn about nested functions later in this chapter.)

Paste Function

When a value calculated by the formula is inserted in a cell, this process is referred to as *returning the result*. The term *returning* refers to the process of calculating the formula and the term *result* refers to the value inserted in the cell.

You can key a function in a cell in a worksheet or you can use the Paste Function button on the Standard toolbar to help you write the formula. When you click the Paste Function button, or click Insert and then Function, the Paste Function dialog box displays as shown in figure 5.2.

Depending on your system, the Office Assistant may ask if you would like help with the feature. If you know the formula you want to write and do not need help from the Office Assistant, either leave the yellow message box displayed or close it by clicking the blue circle that precedes the option "No, don't provide help now." If you would like assistance on how to write a formula and what function to use, click the blue circle preceding "Yes, please provide help," located in the yellow message box.

> **Hint**
> If you need to display a specific cell or cells behind the formula palette, move the palette by clicking and dragging it.

figure 5.2

First Paste Function Dialog Box

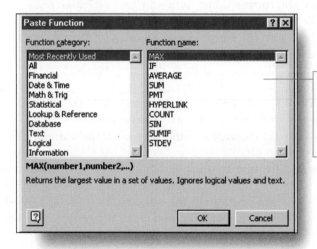

The functions in this list box vary. The most recently used function displays in this list box.

At the Paste Function dialog box, function categories display in a list box at the left and function names display in a list box at the right. The list of function names will change depending on what is selected in the function categories list box. For example, if you click *All* in the Function category list box, a much longer list of functions displays in the Function name list box.

Choose a function in the Function name list box and then click OK. This displays a formula palette, like the one shown in figure 5.3. At this palette, enter in the Number1 text box the range of cells you want included in the formula, enter any constants that are to be included as part of the formula, or enter another function. After entering a range of cells, a constant, or another function, click the OK button. More than one argument can be included in a function. If the function you are creating contains more than one argument, press the Tab key to move the insertion point to the Number2 text box, and then enter the second argument.

figure 5.3

Example Formula Palette

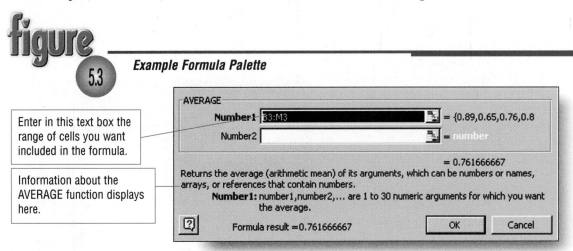

Enter in this text box the range of cells you want included in the formula.

Information about the AVERAGE function displays here.

Writing Formulas with Functions

Excel includes over 200 functions that are divided into nine different categories including Financial, Date & Time, Math & Trig, Statistical, Lookup & Reference, Database, Text, Logical, and Information. Clicking the AutoSum button on the Standard toolbar automatically adds numbers with the SUM function. The SUM function is included in the Math & Trig category. In some sections in this chapter, you will write formulas with functions in other categories including Statistical, Financial, Date & Time, and Logical.

Writing Formulas with Statistical Functions

In this section, you will learn to write formulas with the statistical functions AVERAGE, MAX, MIN, and COUNT. The AVERAGE function returns the average (arithmetic mean) of the arguments. The MAX function returns the largest value in a set of values and the MIN function returns the smallest number in a set of values. Use the COUNT function to count the number of cells that contain numbers within the list of arguments.

Finding Averages

A common function in a formula is the AVERAGE function. With this function, a range of cells is added together and then divided by the number of cell entries. In exercise 6 you will use the AVERAGE function, which will add all test scores for a student and then divide that number by the total number of tests. You will use the Paste Function feature to simplify the creation of the formula containing an AVERAGE function.

One of the advantages to using formulas in a worksheet is the ability to easily manipulate data to answer certain questions. In exercise 6 you will learn the impact of retaking certain tests on the final average score.

Averaging Test Scores in a Worksheet

1. Open Excel Worksheet 06.
2. Save the worksheet with Save As and name it Excel C5, Ex 06.
3. Make cell N1 the active cell, turn on bold, and then key **Average**.
4. Use the Paste Function feature to find the average of test scores and copy the formula down by completing the following steps:

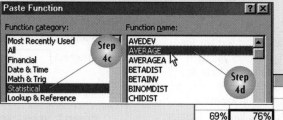

   a. Make N3 the active cell.
   b. Click the Paste Function button on the Standard toolbar.
   c. At the Paste Function dialog box, click *Statistical* in the Function category list box.
   d. Click *AVERAGE* in the Function name list box.
   e. Click OK.
   f. At the formula palette, make sure *B3:M3* displays in the Number 1 text box. (If not, key **B3:M3** in the Number 1 text box.)
   g. Click OK.

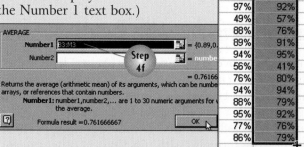

   h. Copy the formula by completing the following steps:
      1) Make cell N3 active.
      2) Position the mouse pointer on the fill handle until the pointer turns into a thin black cross.
      3) Hold down the left mouse button, drag down to cell N20, and then release the mouse button.
5. Save the worksheet again with the same name (Excel C5, Ex 06).
6. Specify that you want the names printed on each page of the worksheet and then print the worksheet by completing the following steps:

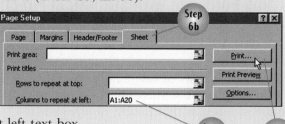

   a. Click File and then Page Setup.
   b. At the Page Setup dialog box, click the Sheet tab.
   c. Click inside the Columns to repeat at left text box.
   d. Key **A1:A20**.
   e. Click the Print button at the right side of the dialog box.

    f.   At the Print dialog box, click OK.
7. After viewing the averages of test scores, you notice that a couple of people have a low
    average. You decide to see what happens to the average score if students make up tests
    where they scored the lowest. You decide that a student can make up to 70% on a
    retake of the test. Make the following changes to test scores to see how the changes
    will affect the test average.
            L5: Change *45%* to *70%*
            M5: Change *49%* to *70%*
            C10: Change *45%* to *70%*
            M10: Change *49%* to *70%*
            C14: Change *0%* to *70%*
            I14: Change *0%* to *70%*
            J14: Change *0%* to *70%*
8. Save the worksheet again with the same name (Excel C5, Ex 06).
9. Print in landscape orientation and then close Excel C5, Ex 06. (Compare the test
    averages for Jack Calahan, Stephanie Flanery, and Kathleen Kwieciak to see what the
    effect of retaking the tests has on their final test averages.)

When a formula such as the AVERAGE formula you inserted in a cell in
exercise 6 calculates cell entries, it ignores certain cell entries. The AVERAGE
function will ignore text in cells and blank cells (not zeros). For example, in the
worksheet containing test scores, a couple of cells contained a 0% entry. This
entry was included in the averaging of the test scores. If you did not want that
particular test to be included in the average, enter text in the cell such as *N/A* (for
not applicable) or leave the cell blank.

Finding Maximum and Minimum Values

The MAX function is used in a formula to return the maximum value in a cell
range and the MIN function returns the minimum value in a cell range. As an
example, you could use the MAX and MIN functions in a worksheet containing
employee hours to determine which employee worked the most hours and which
worked the least. In a worksheet containing sales commissions, you could use the
MAX and MIN functions to determine the salesperson who earned the most
commission dollars and the one who earned the least.

Insert a MAX and MIN function into a formula in the same manner as an
AVERAGE function. In exercise 7, you will use the Paste Function feature to
insert MAX and MIN functions in cells to determine the highest test score
average and the lowest test score average.

exercise 7

Finding Maximum and Minimum Values in a Worksheet

1. Open Excel C5, Ex 06.
2. Save the worksheet with Save As and name it Excel C5, Ex 07.
3. Key the following in the specified cells:
   - A22: Turn on bold and then key **Highest Test Average**.
   - A23: Turn on bold and then key **Lowest Test Average**.
   - A24: Turn on bold and then key **Average of All Tests**.
4. Insert the following formulas in the worksheet:
   a. Insert a formula to identify the highest test score average by completing the following steps:
      1) Make cell B22 active.
      2) Click the Paste Function button on the Standard toolbar.
      3) At the Paste Function dialog box, click *Statistical* in the Function category list box.
      4) Click *MAX* in the Function name list box. (You will need to scroll down the list to display *MAX*.)
      5) Click OK.
      6) At the formula palette, key **N3:N20** in the Number 1 text box, and then click OK.

   b. Insert a formula to identify the lowest test score average by completing the following steps:
      1) Make cell B23 active.
      2) Click the Paste Function button on the Standard toolbar.
      3) At the Paste Function dialog box, make sure *Statistical* is selected in the Function category list box, and then click *MIN* in the Function name list box.
      4) Click OK.
      5) At the formula palette, key **N3:N20** in the Number 1 text box, and then click OK.
   c. Insert a formula to determine the average of all test scores by completing the following steps:
      1) Make cell B24 active.
      2) Click the Paste Function button on the Standard toolbar.
      3) At the Paste Function dialog box, make sure *Statistical* is selected in the Function category list box, and then click *AVERAGE* in the Function name list box.
      4) Click OK.
      5) At the formula palette, key **N3:N20** in the Number 1 text box, and then click OK.
5. Save the worksheet again with the same name (Excel C5, Ex 07).
6. Print Excel C5, Ex 07 in landscape orientation. (Check with your instructor first to determine if your printer is capable of landscape printing.)

7. Change the 70% values (which were previously 0%) in cells C14, I14, and J14 to *N/A*. (This will cause the average of test scores for Kathy Kwieciak to increase and also will change the minimum number and average of all test scores.)
8. Save the worksheet again with the same name (Excel C5, Ex 07).
9. Print Excel C5, Ex 07 in landscape orientation.
10. Close Excel C5, Ex 07.

Counting Numbers in a Range

Use the COUNT function to count the numeric values in a range. For example, in a range of cells containing cells with text and cells with numbers, you can count how many cells in the range contain numbers. In exercise 8, you will use the COUNT function to specify the number of students taking the midterm test and the number taking the final test. In this worksheet, a cell is left blank if a student did not take a test. If a value such as 0% was entered into the cell, the COUNT function would count this as a cell with a number.

Counting the Number of Students Taking Tests

1. Open Excel Worksheet 30.
2. Save the worksheet and name it Excel C5, Ex 08.
3. Count the number of students who have taken the midterm test by completing the following steps:
   a. Make cell A22 active.
   b. Key **Number of students** and then press Alt + Enter (this moves the insertion point down to the next line within the cell).
   c. Key **completing the midterm**.
   d. Make cell B22 active.
   e. Insert a formula counting the number of students who have taken the midterm test by completing the following steps:
      1) Click the Paste Function button on the Standard toolbar.
      2) At the Paste Function dialog box, click *Statistical* in the Function category list box.
      3) Scroll down the list of functions in the Function name list box until *COUNT* is visible and then double-click *COUNT*.
      4) At the formula palette, key **B3:B20** in the Value 1 text box, and then click OK.
4. Count the number of students who have taken the final test by completing the following steps:

   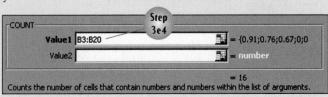

   a. Make cell A23 active.
   b. Key **Number of students** and then press Alt + Enter (this moves the insertion point down to the next line within the cell).
   c. Key **completing the final**.
   d. Make cell B23 active.

e. Insert a formula counting the number of students who have taken the final test by completing the following steps:
   1) Click the Paste Function button on the Standard toolbar.
   2) At the Paste Function dialog box, click *Statistical* in the Function category list box.
   3) Scroll down the list of functions in the Function name list box until *COUNT* is visible and then double-click *COUNT*.
   4) At the formula palette, key **C3:C20** in the Value 1 text box, and then click OK.
5. Save the worksheet again with the same name (Excel C5, Ex 08).
6. Print Excel C5, Ex 08.
7. Add test scores by completing the following steps:
   a. Make cell B14 active and then key **68%**.
   b. Make cell C14 active and then key **70%**.
   c. Make cell C19 active and then key **55%**.
   d. Press Enter.
8. Save the worksheet again with the same name (Excel C5, Ex 08).
9. Print and then close Excel C5, Ex 08.

Writing Formulas with Financial Functions

In this section, you will learn to write formulas with the financial functions SLN, DDB, FV, and PMT. The SLN function returns the straight-line depreciation of an asset for one period, while the DDB function returns the depreciation of an asset for a specified period of time using the double-declining balance method. Use the FV function to return the future value of an investment based on periodic, constant payments and a constant interest rate. The PMT function will calculate the payment for a loan based on constant payments and a constant interest rate.

Finding Depreciation Values

Assets within a company, such as equipment, can be depreciated over time. There are several methods for determining the amount of depreciation, such as the straight-line depreciation method, fixed-declining balance method, and the double-declining balance method. In determining depreciation, you need to create cell entries for some or all of the following categories: cost, salvage, life, period, and/or month. Figure 5.4 describes what each category should contain.

Depreciation Categories

cost	=	initial cost of the asset
salvage	=	value of asset at the end of the depreciation
life	=	number of periods over which the asset is being depreciated
period	=	period for which you want to calculate the depreciation (must use the same units as life category)
month	=	number of months in the first year (if omitted, 12 is used)

The straight-line method uses the categories cost, salvage, and life. The fixed-declining balance method uses all the categories shown in figure 5.4, and the double-declining balance method uses cost, salvage, life, and period. An optional category named factor can be included in the double-declining balance method. This category is the rate at which the balance declines. If no cell entry is included, the number 2 is assumed (which is why it is referred to as the double-declining balance method).

Determining Depreciation Using the Straight-Line Method

1. Open Excel Worksheet 07.
2. Save the worksheet with Save As and name it Excel C5, Ex 09.
3. Insert the function to determine straight-line depreciation by completing the following steps:
   a. Make cell E3 active.
   b. Click the Paste Function button on the Standard toolbar.
   c. At the Paste Function dialog box, click *Financial* in the Function category list box.
   d. Scroll down the Function name list until the function *SLN* is visible and then click *SLN*.
   e. Click OK.
   f. At the formula palette, key **B3** in the Cost category, and then press the Tab key.
   g. Key **C3** in the Salvage category and then press the Tab key.
   h. Key **D3** in the Life category.
   i. Click OK.
4. Copy the formula down to other cells by completing the following steps:
   a. Make cell E3 active.
   b. Using the fill handle, drag down to cell E10, and then release the mouse button.
5. Make the following formatting changes to the worksheet:
   a. Select cells A1 through E10 and then apply the Classic 3 autoformat.
   b. Select cells D3 through D10 and then click the Center button on the Formatting toolbar.
   c. Select cells E3 through E10 and then click the Currency Style button on the Formatting toolbar.

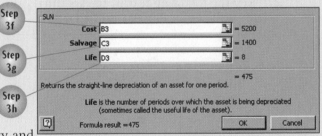

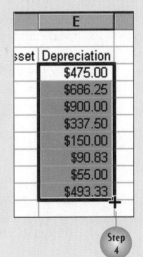

6. Save the worksheet again with the same name (Excel C5, Ex 09).
7. Print Excel C5, Ex 09 horizontally and vertically centered on the page.
8. Close Excel C5, Ex 09.

When you clicked the Financial option in the Function <u>c</u>ategory in step 3c of exercise 9, Excel displayed information below the list box that showed the order of categories in the formula. At the formula palette, as a cell designation was entered in each category, such as Cost, Salvage, Life, and so on, Excel displayed information about the category toward the bottom of the palette. This information can be very helpful in understanding the categories of a formula and what functions Excel uses when creating a formula with the Paste Function feature. Try experimenting with other function names to see what Excel uses to build the formula.

 exercise 10

Determining Depreciation Using the Fixed-Declining Method

1. Open Excel Worksheet 07.
2. Save the worksheet with Save As and name it Excel C5, Ex 10.
3. Add a column by completing the following steps:
    a. Make any cell in column E active.
    b. Click <u>I</u>nsert and then <u>C</u>olumns.
    c. Key the following text in the specified cells:

E2	=	**Period of Dep.**
E3	=	1 *(Hint: Use the fill handle to copy the 1s.)*
E4	=	1
E5	=	1
E6	=	1
E7	=	1
E8	=	1
E9	=	1
E10	=	1

4. Add another column by completing the following steps:
    a. Make any cell in column F active.
    b. Click <u>I</u>nsert and then <u>C</u>olumns.
    c. Key the following text in the specified cells:

F2	=	**Months in Period**
F3	=	12 *(Hint: Use the fill handle to copy the 12s.)*
F4	=	12
F5	=	12
F6	=	12
F7	=	12
F8	=	12
F9	=	12
F10	=	12

    d. Automatically adjust the width of columns E and F.

5. Insert the function to determine fixed-declining depreciation by completing the following steps:
   a. Make cell G3 active.
   b. Click the Paste Function button on the Standard toolbar.
   c. At the Paste Function dialog box, make sure *Financial* is selected in the Function category list box.
   d. Click *DB* in the Function name list box and then click OK.
   e. At the formula palette, key **B3** in the Cost category, and then press the Tab key.
   f. Key **C3** in the Salvage category and then press the Tab key.
   g. Key **D3** in the Life category and then press the Tab key.
   h. Key **E3** in the Period category and then press the Tab key.
   i. Key **F3** in the Month category.
   j. Click OK.
6. Copy the formula down to cells G4 through G10.
7. Make the following formatting changes to the worksheet:
   a. Select cells A1 through G10 and then apply the Classic 3 autoformat.
   b. Select cells D3 through F10 and then click the Center button on the Formatting toolbar.
   c. Select cells G3 through G10 and then click the Currency Style button on the Formatting toolbar.
8. Save the worksheet again with the same name (Excel C5, Ex 10).
9. Print Excel C5, Ex 10 in landscape orientation.
10. Close Excel C5, Ex 10.

E	F	G
HY		
Period of Dep.	Months in Period	Depreciation
1	12	$785.20
1	12	$1,210.39
1	12	$1,489.50
1	12	$516.15
1	12	$234.40
1	12	$134.36
1	12	$92.88
1	12	$770.43

Step 6

exercise 11

Determining Depreciation Using the Double-Declining Method

1. Open Excel Worksheet 07.
2. Save the worksheet with Save As and name it Excel C5, Ex 11.
3. Add a column between columns D and E and then key the following text in the specified cells:

E2	=	**Period of Dep.**
E3	=	1 *(Hint: Use the fill handle to copy the 1s.)*
E4	=	1
E5	=	1
E6	=	1
E7	=	1
E8	=	1
E9	=	1
E10	=	1

4. Insert the function to determine double-declining depreciation by completing the following steps:
   a. Make cell F3 active.
   b. Click the Paste Function button on the Standard toolbar.
   c. At the Paste Function dialog box, make sure *Financial* is selected in the Function category list box.
   d. Click *DDB* in the Function name list box and then click OK.
   e. At the formula palette, key **B3** in the Cost category, and then press the Tab key.
   f. Key **C3** in the Salvage category and then press the Tab key.
   g. Key **D3** in the Life category and then press the Tab key.
   h. Key **E3** in the Period category.
   i. Click OK.
5. Copy the formula down to cells F4 through F10.
6. Make the following formatting changes to the worksheet:
   a. Select cells A1 through F10 and then apply the Classic 3 autoformat.
   b. Select cells D3 through E10 and then click the Center button on the Formatting toolbar.
   c. Select cells F3 through F10 and then click the Currency Style button on the Formatting toolbar.
7. Save the worksheet again with the same name (Excel C5, Ex 11).
8. Print Excel C5, Ex 11 in landscape orientation.
9. Close Excel C5, Ex 11.

E	F
Period of Dep.	Depreciation
1	$1,300.00
1	$1,622.50
1	$2,250.00
1	$925.00
1	$400.00
1	$281.67
1	$143.33
1	$1,403.33

Step
5

Finding the Periodic Payments for a Loan

The PMT function finds the periodic payment for a loan based on constant payments and a constant interest rate. The PMT function contains the arguments nper, pv, fv, and type. The nper argument is the number of payments that will be made to an investment or loan, pv is the current value of amounts to be received or paid in the future, fv is the value of a loan or investment at the end of all periods, and type determines whether calculation will be based on payments made in arrears (at the end of each period) or in advance (at the beginning of each period).

exercise 12

Calculating Payments

1. Open Excel Worksheet 31.
2. Save the worksheet with Save As and name it Excel C5, Ex 12.
3. The owner of Real Photography is interested in purchasing a new developer and needs to determine monthly payments on three different models. Insert a formula that calculates monthly payments and then copy that formula by completing the following steps:
   a. Position the insertion point in cell E7.
   b. Click the Paste Function button on the Standard toolbar.
   c. At the Paste Function dialog box, click *Financial* in the Function category list box. ·

d. Click *PMT* in the Function name list box.
e. Click OK.
f. At the formula palette, key **C7/12** in the Rate text box. (This tells Excel to divide the interest rate by 12 months.)
g. Press the Tab key. (This moves the insertion point to the Nper text box).

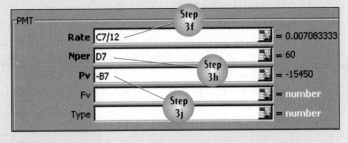

h. Key **D7**. (This is the total number of months in the payment period).
i. Press the Tab key. (This moves the insertion point to the Pv text box.)
j. Key **-B7**. (Excel displays the result of the PMT function as a negative number since the loan represents a negative cash flow to the borrower. Insert a minus sign before B7 to show the monthly payment as a positive number rather than a negative number.)
k. Click OK. (This closes the dialog box and also inserts the monthly payment of *$316.98* in cell E7.)
l. Copy the formula in cell E7 down to cells E8 and E9.

4. Insert a formula in cell F7 that calculates the total amount of the payments by completing the following steps:
a. Make cell F7 active.
b. Key **=E7*D7** and then press Enter.
c. Make cell F7 active and then copy the formula down to cells F8 and F9.

5. Insert a formula in cell G7 that calculates the total amount of interest paid by completing the following steps:
a. Make cell G7 active.
b. Key **=F7-B7** and then press Enter.
c. Make cell G7 active and then copy the formula down to cells G8 and G9.

6. Save the worksheet again with the same name (Excel C5, Ex 12).
7. Print and then close Excel C5, Ex 12.

Finding the Future Value of a Series of Payments

The FV function calculates the future value of a series of equal payments or an annuity. Use this function to determine information such as how much money can be earned in an investment account with a specific interest rate and over a specific period of time.

exercise 13

Finding the Future Value on an Investment

1. Open Excel Worksheet 32.
2. Save the worksheet with Save As and name it Excel C5, Ex 13.
3. The owner of Real Photography has decided to save money to purchase a new developer and wants to compute how much money can be earned by investing the

money in an investment account that returns a 9% annual interest. The owner determines that $1,200 per month can be invested in the account for three years. Complete the following steps to determine the future value of the investment account by completing the following steps:

a. Make cell C6 active.
b. Click the Paste Function button on the Standard toolbar.
c. At the Paste Function dialog box, click *Financial* in the Function category list box.
d. Click *FV* in the Function name list box.
e. Click OK.
f. At the formula palette, key **C3/12** in the Rate text box.
g. Press the Tab key.
h. Key **C4** in the Nper text box.
i. Press the Tab key.
j. Key **C5** in the Pmt text box.
k. Click OK. (This closes the dialog box and also inserts the future value of $49,383.26 in cell C6.)

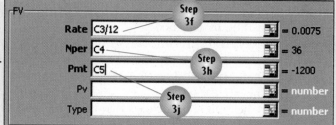

4. Save the worksheet again with the same name (Excel C5, Ex 13).
5. Print Excel C5, Ex 13.
6. The owner decides to determine the future return after two years. To do this, change the amount in cell C4 from *36* to *24* and then press Enter. (This recalculates the future investment amount in cell C6.)
7. Save the worksheet again with the same name (Excel C5, Ex 13).
8. Print and then close C5, Ex 13.

Writing Formulas with Date & Time Functions

In this section, you will learn to write formulas with the date and time functions NOW and DATE. The NOW function returns the serial number of the current date and time. The DATE function returns the serial number that represents a particular date. Excel can make calculations using dates because the dates are represented as serial numbers. To calculate a date's serial number, Excel counts the days since the beginning of the twentieth century. The date serial number for January 1, 1900 is 1. The date serial number for January 1, 2000, is 36,526.

Using the DATE and NOW Functions

1. Open Excel Worksheet 33.
2. Save the worksheet with Save As and name it Excel C5, Ex 14.
3. This worksheet establishes overdue dates for accounts. Enter a formula in cell D5 that returns the serial number for the date March 21, 2001 by completing the following steps:
    a. Make cell D5 active.
    b. Click the Paste Function button on the Standard toolbar.

c. At the Paste Function dialog box, click Date & Time in the Function category.
d. Click *DATE* in the Function name list box.
e. Click OK.
f. At the formula palette, key **2001** in the Year text box.
g. Press the Tab key and then key **03** in the Month text box.
h. Press the Tab key and then key **21** in the Day text box.
i. Click OK.

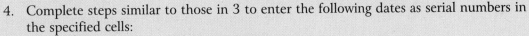

4. Complete steps similar to those in 3 to enter the following dates as serial numbers in the specified cells:

D6	=	March 27, 2001
D7	=	April 2, 2001
D8	=	April 10, 2001

5. Enter a formula in cell F5 that inserts the due date (the purchase date plus the number of days in the Terms column) by completing the following steps:
   a. Make cell F5 active.
   b. Key **=D5+E5** and then press Enter.
   c. Make cell F5 active and then copy the formula down to cells F6, F7, and F8.
6. Make cell A10 active and then key your name.
7. Insert the current date as a serial number by completing the following steps:
   a. Make cell A11 active.
   b. Click the Paste Function button on the Standard toolbar.
   c. At the Paste Function dialog box, make sure *Date & Time* is selected in the Function category list box, and then click *NOW* in the Function name list box.
   d. Click OK.
   e. At the formula palette telling you that the function takes no argument, click OK.
   f. With cell A11 still active, click the Align Left button on the Formatting toolbar.
8. Save the worksheet again with the same name (Excel C5, Ex 14).
9. Print and then close Excel C5, Ex 14.

Writing a Formula with the IF Logical Function

The IF function is considered a *conditional function*. With the IF function you can perform conditional tests on values and formulas. A question that can be answered with true or false is considered a *logical test*. The IF function makes a logical test and then performs a particular action if the answer is true and another action if the answer is false.

For example, an IF function can be used to write a formula that calculates a salesperson's bonus as 10 percent if the quota of $100,000 is met or exceeded and zero if the quota is less than $100,000. That formula would look like this: =IF(quota=>100000,quota*0.1,0). There are three parts to the formula—the condition or logical test IF(quota=>100000), action taken if the condition or logical test is true (quota*0.1), and the action taken if the condition or logical test is false (0). Commas separate the condition and the actions. In the bonus formula, if the quota is equal to or greater than $100,000, then the quota is multiplied by 10%. If the quota is less than $100,000, then the bonus is zero.

In exercise 15, you will write a formula with cell references rather than cell data. The formula in exercise 15 is =IF(C2>B2,C2*0.15,0). In this formula the condition or logical test is whether or not the number in cell C2 is greater than the number in cell B2. If the condition is true and the number is greater, then the number in cell C2 is multiplied by 0.15 (providing a 15% bonus). If the condition is false and the number in cell C2 is less than the number in cell B2, then nothing happens (no bonus). Notice how commas are used to separate the logical test from the actions.

Revising a Formula

Revise a formula by making active the cell containing the formula and then editing the formula in the cell or in the Formula bar text box. After revising the formula, press Enter or click the Enter button on the Formula bar and Excel will recalculate the result of the formula.

Writing a Formula with an IF Function

1. Open Excel Worksheet 10.
2. Save the worksheet with Save As and name it Excel C5, Ex 15.
3. Write a formula with the IF function by completing the following steps: (The formula will determine if the quota has been met and, if it has, will insert the bonus [15% of the actual sales]. If the quota has not been met, the formula will insert a zero.)
   a. Make cell D2 active.
   b. Key **=IF(C2>B2,C2*0.15,0)** and then press Enter.
   c. Make cell D2 active and then use the fill handle to copy the formula to cells D3 through D7.
   d. Select cells D2 through D7 and then click the Currency Style button on the Formatting toolbar.
4. Print the worksheet.
5. Revise the formula so it will insert a 25% bonus if the quota has been met by completing the following steps:
   a. Make cell D2 active.
   b. Click in the Formula bar and then edit the formula so it displays as *IF(C2>B2,C2*0.25,0)* and then click the Enter button on the Formula bar.
   c. Copy the formula down to cells D3 through D7.
6. Save the worksheet again with the same name (Excel C5, Ex 15).
7. Print and then close Excel C5, Ex 15.

C	D
Actual Sales	**Bonus**
$ 103,295.00	15494.25
$ 129,890.00	0
$ 133,255.00	19988.25
$ 94,350.00	14152.5
$ 167,410.00	25111.5
$ 109,980.00	0

Currency Style — Step 3c

D
Bonus
$ 15,494.25
$ -
$ 19,988.25
$ 14,152.50
$ 25,111.50
$ -

Step 3d

Writing a Nested IF Condition

In exercise 15, the IF function had only two possible actions—the actual sales times 15 percent or a zero. In a formula where more than two actions are required, use nested IF functions. For example, in exercise 16, you will write a formula with IF conditions that has four possible actions—a letter grade of A, B, C, or D. When writing nested IF conditions, insert symbols such as commas, quotation marks, and parentheses in the proper locations. If you want an IF condition to insert text, insert quotation marks before and after the text. The formula you will be writing in exercise 16 is shown below.

=IF(E2>89,"A",IF(E2>79,"B",IF(E2>69,"C",IF(E2>59,"D"))))

This formula begins with the condition =IF(E2>89,"A",. If the number in cell E2 is greater than 89 then the condition is met and the grade of A is returned. The formula continues with a nested condition, IF(E2>79,"B",. If the number in cell E2 does not meet the first condition (greater than 89) then Excel looks to the next condition—is the number in cell E2 greater than 79. If it is, then the grade of B is inserted in cell E2. The formula continues with another nested condition, IF(E2>69,"C",. If the number in cell E2 does not match the first condition, Excel looks to the second condition, and if that condition is not met, then Excel looks to the third condition. If the number in cell E2 is greater than 69, then the grade of C is inserted in cell E2. The final nested condition is IF(E2>59,"D". If the first three conditions are not met but this one is, then the grade of D is inserted in cell E2. The four parentheses at the end of the formula end each condition in the formula.

If you enter a complicated formula in a worksheet, consider protecting the worksheet. To do this, click Tools, point to Protection, and then click Protect Sheet. At the Protect Sheet dialog box, enter a password, and then click OK.

Hint

exercise 16

Writing a Formula with Nested IF Conditions

1. Open Excel Worksheet 11.
2. Save the worksheet with Save As and name it Excel C5, Ex 16.
3. Insert a formula to average the scores by completing the following steps:
   a. Make cell E2 active.
   b. Key **=AVERAGE(B2:D2)** and then press Enter.
   c. Make cell E2 active and then copy the formula down to cells E3 through E6.
   d. With cells E2 through E6 still selected, click the Decrease Decimal button on the Formatting toolbar five times.
4. Insert a formula with nested IF conditions by completing the following steps:
   a. Make cell F2 active.
   b. Key **=IF(E2>89,"A",IF(E2>79,"B",IF(E2>69,"C",IF(E2>59,"D"))))** and then press Enter.
   c. Make cell F2 active and then use the fill handle to copy the formula down to cells F3 through F6.
   d. With cells F2 through F6 still selected, click the Center button on the Formatting toolbar.
5. Save the worksheet again with the same name (Excel C5, Ex 16).
6. Print and then close Excel C5, Ex 16.

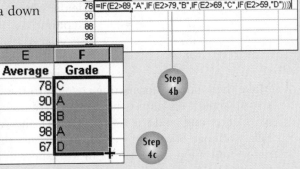

As you keyed the formula with nested IF conditions in step 4b of exercise 16, did you notice that the parentheses were different colors? Each color represents a condition. The four right parentheses at the end of the formula ended each of the conditions and each matched in color a left parenthesis. If an average in column E in Excel C5, Ex 16 is less than 59, the nested formula inserts "FALSE" in the cell. If you want the formula to insert a letter grade, such as "F," instead of FALSE, include another nested IF condition in the formula.

Working with Ranges

A selected group of cells is referred to as a *range*. As you learned in an earlier chapter, a range of cells can be formatted, moved, copied, or deleted. A range of cells can also be named. Name a range of cells to quickly move the insertion point to the range or use a named range as part of a formula.

To name a range, select the cells, and then click in the Name Box button on the Formula bar (first button from the left on the Formula Bar). Key a name for the range (do not use a space) and then press Enter. To move the insertion point to a specific range and select the range, click the down-pointing triangle at the right side of the Name Box button and then click the range name.

A range name can be used in a formula. For example, if a range is named Profit and you wanted to insert the average of all cells in the Profit range, you would make the desired cell active and then key **=AVERAGE(Profit)**. A named range can be used in the current worksheet or in another worksheet within the workbook.

exercise 17

Naming a Range and Using a Range in a Formula

1. Open Excel Worksheet 09.
2. Save the worksheet with Save As and name it Excel C5, Ex 17.
3. Click the *Sheet2* tab and then key the following text in the specified cell:

A1	=	**EQUIPMENT USAGE REPORT**
A2	=	**Yearly Hours**
A3	=	**Avoidable Delays**
A4	=	**Unavoidable Delays**
A5	=	**Total Delay Hours**
A6	=	(leave blank)
A7	=	**Repairs**
A8	=	**Servicing**
A9	=	**Total Repair/Servicing Hours**

4. Make the following formatting changes to the worksheet:
    a. Automatically adjust the width of column A.
    b. Center and bold the text in cells A1 and A2.
5. Select a range of cells in worksheet 1, name the range, and use it in a formula in worksheet 2 by completing the following steps:
    a. Make worksheet 1 active by clicking the *Sheet1* tab.
    b. Select cells B4 through M4.
    c. Click in the Name Box button on the Formula bar.
    d. Key **adhours** (for Avoidable Delays Hours) and then press Enter.
    e. Click the *Sheet2* tab to make worksheet 2 active.

f.   Make cell B3 active.
g.   Key the equation **=SUM(adhours)** and then press Enter.

Step 5g

6.   Make worksheet 1 active and then complete the following steps:
a.   Select cells B5 through M5 and then name the range udhours.
b.   Make worksheet 2 active, make cell B4 active, and then insert the equation *=SUM(udhours)*.
c.   Make worksheet 1 active.
d.   Select cells B6 through M6 and then name the range rhours.
e.   Make worksheet 2 active, make cell B7 active, and then insert the equation *=SUM(rhours)*.
f.   Make worksheet 1 active.
g.   Select cells B7 through M7 and then name the range shours.
h.   Make worksheet 2 active, make cell B8 active, and then insert the equation *=SUM(shours)*.

	A	B	
1	EQUIPMENT USAGE REPORT		
2	Yearly Hours		
3	Avoidable Delays	=SUM(adhours)	
4	Unavoidable Delays		
5	Total Delay Hours		
6			
7	Repairs		
8	Servicing		
9	Total Repair/Servicing Hours		

7.   With worksheet 2 still active, make the following changes:
a.   Make cell B5 active.
b.   Click the AutoSum button on the Standard toolbar and then press Enter.
c.   Make cell B9 active.
d.   Double-click the AutoSum button on the Standard toolbar.
8.   Save the workbook again with the same name (Excel C5, Ex 17).
9.   Print worksheet 2.
10. Make worksheet 1 active and then move to the range adhours by clicking the down-pointing triangle at the right side of the Name Box button and then clicking *adhours* at the drop-down list.
11. Close Excel C5, Ex 17.

Using Absolute and Mixed Cell References in Formulas

A reference identifies a cell or a range of cells in a worksheet and can be relative, absolute, or mixed. Relative cell references refer to cells relative to a position in a formula. Absolute references refer to cells in a specific location. A relative cell reference adjusts when a formula is copied while an absolute cell reference remains constant when a formula is copied. A mixed cell reference does both—either the column remains absolute and the row is relative or the column is relative and the row is absolute. Distinguish between relative, absolute, and mixed cell references using the dollar sign ($). Key a dollar sign before the column and/or row cell reference in a formula to specify that the column or row is an absolute cell reference.

Using an Absolute Cell Reference in a Formula

In this chapter you have learned to copy a relative formula. For example, if the formula =SUM(A2:C2) in cell D2 is copied relatively to cell D3, the formula changes to =SUM(A3:C3). In some situations, you may want a formula to contain an absolute cell reference, which always refers to a cell in a specific location. In exercise 18, you will add a column for projected job earnings and then perform "what if" situations using a formula with an absolute cell reference.

To identify an absolute cell reference, insert a $ symbol before the row and also the column. For example, the absolute cell reference C12 would be keyed as *$C$12* in a formula.

exercise 18

Inserting and Copying a Formula with an Absolute Cell Reference

1. Open Excel Worksheet 01.
2. Save the worksheet with Save As and name it Excel C5, Ex 18.
3. Make the following changes to the worksheet:
   a. Delete columns B and D by completing the following steps:
      1) Click the column B header (the letter B at the top of the column).
      2) Hold down the Ctrl key and then click the column D header. (This selects column B and column D.)
      3) Click Edit and then Delete.
   b. Key **Projected** in C1.
   c. Center and bold the text in cells A1 through C1.
4. Determine the effect on actual job earnings with a 20% increase by completing the following steps:
   a. Key **% Increase/Decrease** in cell A12.
   b. Key **1.2** in cell B12 and then press Enter. (This number will be used in a formula to determine a 20% increase.)
   c. Make cell B12 the active cell and make sure the number formatting is General. (If it is not, click Format and then Cells. At the Format Cells dialog box, click the Number tab, click *General* in the Category list box, and then click OK.)
   d. Make cell C3 active, key the formula **=B3*$B$12**, and then press Enter.
   e. Automatically adjust the width of column C.
   f. Make cell C3 active and then use the fill handle to copy the formula to cells C4 through C10.
   g. Select cells B3 through C10 and then click the Currency Style button on the Formatting toolbar.
   h. With cells B3 through C10 still selected, click twice on the Decrease Decimal button on the Formatting toolbar.
5. Save and then print the worksheet.

Step 3a1

Step 3a2

Step 3a3

	File	Edit	View	Insert	Format	Tools	Data	Window	Help
		Undo Column Width	Ctrl+Z						
	Cut		Ctrl+X						
	Copy		Ctrl+C						
	Paste		Ctrl+V						
	Paste Special...								
	Fill		▶						
	Clear		▶						
	Delete								
	Delete Sheet								

	B	C	D
1	#	Actual	Planned
2			
3	2130	$30,349	$34,109
4	1201	$48,290	$48,100
5	318	$34,192	$32,885
6	1009	$63,293	$61,220

Step 4d

	A	B	C
1	Customer	Actual	Projected
2			
3	Sellar Corporation	$30,349	=B3*$B$12
4	Main Street Photos	$48,290	
5	Sunset Automotive	$34,192	
6	Linstrom Enterprises	$63,293	
7	Morcos Media	$29,400	
8	Green Valley Optics	$55,309	
9	Detailed Designs	$12,398	
10	Arrowstar Company	$87,534	
11			
12	% Increase/Decrease	1.2	

Step 4a

Step 4b

B	C
Actual	Projected
$30,349	36418.8
$48,290	57948
$34,192	41030.4
$63,293	75951.6
$29,400	35280
$55,309	66370.8
$12,398	14877.6
$87,534	105040.8
	1.2

Step 4f

6. With the worksheet still open, determine the effect on actual job earnings with a 10%
    decrease by completing the following steps:
    a. Make B12 active.
    b. Key **0.9** and then press Enter.
7. Save and then print the worksheet.
8. Determine the effects on actual job
    earnings with a 10% increase. (To do
    this, key **1.1** in cell B12.)
9. Save, print, and then close Excel C5,
    Ex 18.

	A	B	C
1	Customer	Actual	Projected
2			
3	Sellar Corporation	$ 30,349	$ 27,314
4	Main Street Photos	$ 48,290	$ 43,461
5	Sunset Automotive	$ 34,192	$ 30,773
6	Linstrom Enterprises	$ 63,293	$ 56,964
7	Morcos Media	$ 29,400	$ 26,460
8	Green Valley Optics	$ 55,309	$ 49,778
9	Detailed Designs	$ 12,398	$ 11,158
10	Arrowstar Company	$ 87,534	$ 78,781
11			
12	% Increase/Decrease	0.9	
13			

Step
6b

Using a Mixed Cell Reference in a Formula

The formula you created in step 4d in exercise 18 contained a relative cell
reference (B3) and an absolute cell reference ($B$12). A formula can also contain
a mixed cell reference. In a mixed cell reference either the column remains
absolute and the row is relative or the column is relative and the row is absolute.
In exercise 19, you will create the formula =$A3*B$2. In the first cell reference in
the formula, $A3, the column is absolute and the row is relative. In the second
cell reference, B$2, the column is relative and the row is absolute. The formula
containing the mixed cell references allows you to fill in the column and row data
using only one formula.

exercise 19

Determining Simple Interest Using a Formula with Mixed Cell References

1. Open Excel Worksheet 12.
2. Save the worksheet with Save As and name it Excel C5, Ex 19.
3. Insert a formula containing mixed cell references by completing the following steps:
    a. Make cell B3 the active cell.
    b. Key the formula =$A3*B$2 and then press Enter.

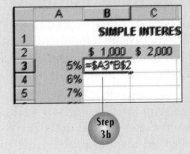

	A	B	C
1		SIMPLE INTERES	
2		$ 1,000	$ 2,000
3		5%	=$A3*B$2
4		6%	
5		7%	

Step
3b

4. Copy the formula down and to the right by completing the following steps:
   a. Make cell B3 active and then use the fill handle to copy the formula down to cell B13.
   b. Make cell B3 active and then use the fill handle to copy the formula across to cell F3.
   c. Make cell C3 active and then use the fill handle to copy the formula down to cell C13.
   d. Make cell D3 active and then use the fill handle to copy the formula down to cell D13.
   e. Make cell E3 active and then use the fill handle to copy the formula down to cell E13.
   f. Make cell F3 active and then use the fill handle to copy the formula down to cell F13.

	A	B
1		SIMPLE I
2		$ 1,000 $
3	5%	$ 50
4	6%	$ 60
5	7%	$ 70
6	8%	$ 80
7	9%	$ 90
8	10%	$ 100
9	11%	$ 110
10	12%	$ 120
11	13%	$ 130
12	14%	$ 140
13	15%	$ 150
14		

Step 4a

	A	B	C	D	E	F
1		SIMPLE INTEREST LOAN TABLE				
2		$ 1,000	$ 2,000	$ 3,000	$ 4,000	$ 5,000
3	5%	$ 50	$ 100	$ 150	$ 200	$ 250
4	6%	$ 60				

Step 4b

5. Save the worksheet again with the same name (Excel C5, Ex 19).
6. Print the worksheet centered horizontally and vertically on the page.
7. Close Excel C5, Ex 19.

	A	B	C
1		SIMPLE INTERES	
2		$ 1,000	$ 2,000
3	5%	$ 50	$ 100
4	6%	$ 60	$ 120
5	7%	$ 70	$ 140
6	8%	$ 80	$ 160
7	9%	$ 90	$ 180
8	10%	$ 100	$ 200
9	11%	$ 110	$ 220
10	12%	$ 120	$ 240
11	13%	$ 130	$ 260
12	14%	$ 140	$ 280
13	15%	$ 150	$ 300

Step 4c

You had to key only one formula in exercise 19 to create the data in the simple interest table. The mixed cell references allowed you to copy the formula down columns and across rows.

Linking Cells between Worksheets

In workbooks containing multiple worksheets or between related workbooks there may be data in cells that create a link between worksheets or workbooks. When data is linked, a change made in a linked cell is automatically made to the other cells in the link. Links can be made with individual cells or with a range of cells.

Linking cells between worksheets creates what is called a *dynamic link*. Dynamic links are useful in worksheets or workbooks that need to maintain consistency and control over critical data. The worksheet that contains the original data is called the *source* worksheet and the worksheet relying on the source worksheet for the data in the link is called the *dependent* worksheet.

To create a link, make active the cell containing the data to be linked (or select the cells), and then click the Copy button on the toolbar. Make active the worksheet where you want to paste the cell or cells and then click Edit and then Paste Special. This causes the Paste Special dialog box to display as shown in figure 5.5.

figure
5.5   Paste Special Dialog Box

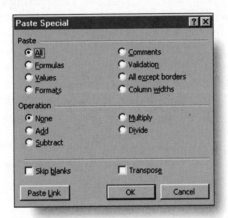

At the Paste Special dialog box, specify what in the cell you want to copy and what operators you want to include, and then click the Paste Link button at the bottom left side of the dialog box. When a change is made to the cell or cells in the source worksheet, the change is automatically made to the linked cell or cells in the dependent worksheet.

exercise 20

Linking Cells between Worksheets

1. Open Excel Worksheet 02.
2. Save the worksheet with Save As and name it Excel C5, Ex 20.
3. Make the following changes to the worksheet:
   a. Insert a new row at the beginning of the worksheet.
   b. Make A1 the active cell.
   c. Click the Bold button and then key **FIRST HALF, 2000**.
   d. Align the text in cell A1 between columns A, B, C, and D (use the Merge and Center button).
   e. Delete the data in cells D3 through D9. (You are deleting the amounts in these cells because you are going to insert a formula instead.)

f. Select cells B3 through D9, click the Currency Style button on the Standard toolbar, and then click twice the Decrease Decimal button on the Standard toolbar.

g. Make cell D3 active, key the formula **=C3-B3**, and then press Enter.

h. Copy the formula in cell D3 down to cells D4 through D9.

i. Automatically adjust the width of columns A, B, C, and D.

4. Save the worksheet again with the same name (Excel C5, Ex 20).

Step 3h

	A	B	C	D
1	FIRST HALF, 2000			
2	Expense	Actual	Budget	Variance
3	Salaries	$126,000	$126,000	$ -
4	Commissions	$ 58,000	$ 54,500	$ (3,500)
5	Media space	$ 8,250	$ 10,100	$ 1,850
6	Travel expenses	$ 6,350	$ 6,000	$ (350)
7	Dealer display	$ 4,140	$ 4,500	$ 360
8	Payroll taxes	$ 2,430	$ 2,200	$ (230)
9	Telephone	$ 1,450	$ 1,500	$ 50
10				

5. Copy the data in the worksheet to *Sheet2* by completing the following steps:

a. Select cells A1 through D9.

b. Click the Copy button on the Standard toolbar.

c. Click the *Sheet2* tab that displays to the left of the horizontal scroll bar.

d. With cell A1 the active cell, click the Paste button on the Standard toolbar.

e. Automatically adjust the width of columns A, B, C, and D.

f. Select cells C3 through C9 and then delete the cell data.

6. Link cells C3 through C9·from *Sheet1* to *Sheet2* by completing the following steps:

a. Click the *Sheet1* tab.

b. With *Sheet1* displayed, select cells C3 through C9.

c. Click the Copy button on the Standard toolbar.

d. Click the *Sheet2* tab.

e. Make cell C3 active.

Step 6f

f. Click Edit and then Paste Special.

g. At the Paste Special dialog box, make sure All is selected in the Paste section of the dialog box, and then click the Paste Link button.

Step 6e

7. With *Sheet2* still the active worksheet, make the following changes to the specified cells:

A1: Change *FIRST HALF, 2000* to *SECOND HALF, 2000*

B3: Change *$126,000* to *123,500*

B4: Change *$58,000* to *53,000*

B6: Change *$6,350* to *6,125*

8. Make *Sheet1* the active worksheet and then make the following changes to some of the linked cells:

C3: Change *$126,000* to *128,000*

C4: Change *$54,500* to *56,000*

C8: Change *$2,200* to *2,400*

9. Click the *Sheet2* tab and notice that the values in cells C3, C4, and C8 automatically changed. (This is because they are linked to *Sheet1*.)

10. Save the workbook again with the same name (Excel C5, Ex 20).

11. Print both worksheets in the workbook.

12. Close Excel C5, Ex 20.

Linking Worksheets Using 3-D References

In a multiple worksheet workbook, you can use a 3-D reference to analyze data in the same cell or range of cells. A 3-D reference includes the cell or range of cells, preceded by a range of worksheet names. For example, you can add all the values contained in cells in B2 through B5 in worksheets 1 and 2 in a workbook using a 3-D reference. To do this, you would complete these basic steps:

1. Make active the cell where you want to enter the function.
2. Key **=SUM(** and then click the *Sheet1* tab.
3. Hold down the Shift key and then click the *Sheet2* tab.
4. Select cells B2 through B5 in the worksheet.
5. Key **)** and then press Enter.

exercise 21

Linking Worksheets with a 3-D Reference

1. Open Excel Worksheet 34.
2. Save the workbook with Save As and name it Excel C5, Ex 21.
3. Link worksheets 1, 2, and 3 with a 3-D reference by completing the following steps:
    a. Make cell B10 active.
    b. Click the Center button and then the Bold button on the Formatting toolbar.
    c. Key **January Sales** and then press Alt + Enter.
    d. Key **1998-2001** and then press Enter.
    e. With cell B11 active, insert a formula with a 3-D reference by completing the following steps:
        1) Key **=SUM(**.
        2) Hold down the Shift key and then click the *Sheet3* tab.
        3) Select cells B3 through B8.
        4) Key **)** (this is the closing parenthesis that ends the formula) and then press Enter.
        5) Make cell B11 active.
        6) Click the Currency Style button on the Formatting toolbar and then click twice on the Decrease Decimal button.

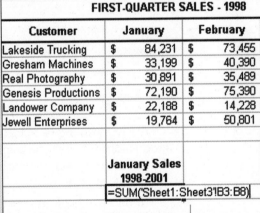

FIRST-QUARTER SALES - 1998		
Customer	**January**	**February**
Lakeside Trucking	$ 84,231	$ 73,455
Gresham Machines	$ 33,199	$ 40,390
Real Photography	$ 30,891	$ 35,489
Genesis Productions	$ 72,190	$ 75,390
Landower Company	$ 22,188	$ 14,228
Jewell Enterprises	$ 19,764	$ 50,801
January Sales 1998-2001		
=SUM('Sheet1:Sheet3'!B3:B8)		

Step 3e1-3e4

4. Complete steps similar to those in 3 to add February sales for 1998-2001. (Insert the heading *February Sales 1998-2001* [on two lines] in cell C10 and insert the formula with the 3-D reference in cell C11.)
5. Complete steps similar to those in 3 to add March sales for 1998-2001. (Insert the heading *March Sales 1998-2001* [on two lines] in cell D10 and insert the formula with the 3-D reference in cell D11.)
6. Save the workbook again with the same name (Excel C5, Ex 21).
7. Print worksheet 1 of the workbook.
8. Close Excel C5, Ex 21.

Automatically Outlining a Worksheet

Apply outlining to a worksheet to display specific rows and columns such as subtotals and totals. Apply an automatic outline to a worksheet by clicking Data, pointing to Group and Outline, and then clicking Auto Outline. Figure 5.6 shows a worksheet with outlining applied and identifies outlining buttons.

figure
5.6

Worksheet with Outlining Applied

Column Level Buttons

Hide Details Button

This line specifies a group of cells that are included in a subtotal.

Hours	January	February	March	April	May	June	1st Half	July
					EQUIPMENT USAGE REPORT			
Total Hours Available	2,300	2,430	2,530	2,400	2,440	2,240	14,340	2,5
Avoidable Delays	19	12	16	20	14	15	96	
Unavoidable Delays	9	8	6	12	9	10	54	
Repairs	5	7	12	9	10	6	49	
Servicing	6	13	7	6	4	5	41	
Unassigned	128	95	85	135	95	75	613	1
In Use	2,040	2,105	2,320	2,180	2,050	1,995	12,690	2,3

Apply outlining to a document containing rows or columns that summarize data. For example, if you apply outlining to a document with subtotals and totals, you can then display the entire worksheet, only subtotals and totals in the worksheet, or only totals.

In the workbook in figure 5.6, notice the lines that display above the column headers. These lines identify a group of cells that are part of a subtotal or total. The button with the hyphen on it is called the Hide Details button. Click this button and all cells in the group are hidden except the subtotal or total cell. The Hide Details button changes to the Show Details button (a button with a plus symbol on it). Click the Show Details button to show all cells in the group.

You can also specify what cells to display by clicking a Column Level button (see figure 5.6). For example, in the worksheet shown in figure 5.6, click the Column Level 1 button to display the total column, and click the Column Level 2 button to display subtotal and total columns. Clicking the Column Level 3 button displays all cells in the worksheet.

Hide Details

Show Details

exercise 22

Applying Automatic Outlining

1. Open Excel Worksheet 09.
2. Save the worksheet with Save As and name it Excel C5, Ex 22.
3. Make the following changes to the worksheet:
   a. Insert a new column by completing the following steps:
      1) Make any cell in column H active.
      2) Click Insert and then Columns.
      3) Key **1st Half** in cell H2 (in the new column).
      4) Make cell H3 active, key **=SUM(B3:G3)**, and then press Enter.
      5) Make cell H3 active again and then copy the formula down to cells H4 through H9.
   b. Create another subtotal column by completing the following steps:
      1) Key **2nd Half** centered and bolded in cell O2.
      2) Make cell O3 active, key **=SUM(I3:N3)**, and then press Enter.
      3) Make cell O3 active again and then copy the formula down to cells O4 through O9.
   c. Create a total column by completing the following steps:
      1) Key **Total** centered and bolded in cell P2.
      2) Make cell P3 active, key **=H3+O3**, and then press Enter.
      3) Make cell P3 active again and then copy the formula down to cells P4 through P9.
   d. Apply automatic outlining to the worksheet by completing the following steps:
      1) Make cell A1 active.
      2) Click Data, point to Group and Outline, and then click Auto Outline.
   e. Display only subtotals and totals by clicking the Column Level 2 button.
   f. Print the worksheet.
   g. Display only the total by clicking the Column Level 1 button.
   h. Print the worksheet.
4. Save and then close Excel C5, Ex 22.

	G	H
	|	T USAGE REPORT
	June	1st Half
	2,240	14,340
	15	96
	10	54
	6	49
	5	41
	75	613
	1,995	12,690

Step 3a3

	N	O
	December	2nd Half
	2,210	14,490
	5	53
	7	52
	8	55
	12	52
	120	716
	1,830	12,540

Step 3a5

Step 3b1

	O	P
	2nd Half	Total
	14,490	28,830
	53	149
	52	106
	55	104
	52	93
	716	1,329
	12,540	25,230

Step 3b3

Step 3c1

Step 3c3

Step 3e

	A	H	O	P
1	EQUIPMENT USAGE REPORT			
2	Hours	1st Half	2nd Half	Total
3	Total Hours Available	14,340	14,490	28,830
4	Avoidable Delays	96	53	149
5	Unavoidable Delays	54	52	106
6	Repairs	49	55	104
7	Servicing	41	52	93
8	Unassigned	613	716	1,329
9	In Use	12,690	12,540	25,230

Planning a Worksheet

The worksheets you have worked with so far have already been basically planned. If you need to plan a worksheet yourself, there are some steps you can follow. These are basic steps—you may think of additional steps or additional information to help you plan a worksheet.

Before entering data in a worksheet, plan the worksheet. **Hint**

- **Step 1: Identify the purpose of the worksheet.** The more definite you are about your purpose, the easier organizing your data into an effective worksheet will be. Consider things such as the purpose of the worksheet, the intended audience, the desired output or results, and the data required.
- **Step 2: Design the worksheet.** To do this, you need to determine how the data is to be organized, the titles of columns and rows, and how to emphasize important information. Designing the worksheet also includes determining any calculations that need to be performed.
- **Step 3: Create a sketch of the worksheet.** A diagram or sketch can help create a logical and well-ordered worksheet. With a sketch, you can experiment with alternative column and row configurations and titles and headings. When creating a sketch, start with the heading or title of the worksheet, which should provide a quick overview of what the data represents in the worksheet. Determine appropriate column and row titles that clearly identify the data.
- **Step 4: Enter the data in the worksheet.** Key the data in the worksheet, including the worksheet title, column titles, row titles, and data within cells. Enter any required formulas into the worksheet and then format the worksheet to make it appealing and easy to read.
- **Step 5: Test the worksheet data.** After preparing the worksheet and inserting any necessary formulas, check the data to be sure that the calculations are performed correctly. Consider verifying the formula results by completing the formula on a calculator.

exercise 23

Planning and Creating a Worksheet

1. Look at the data shown in figure 5.7. (The first paragraph is simply a description of the data—do not include this in the worksheet.) After reviewing the data, complete the following steps:
   a. Create a sketch of how you think the worksheet should be organized.
   b. Create a worksheet from the sketch. (Be sure to include the necessary formula to calculate the total costs.)
   c. Apply formatting to enhance the appearance of the worksheet.
2. Save the worksheet and name it Excel C5, Ex 23.
3. Print and then close Excel C5, Ex 23.

Exercise 23

The following data itemizes budgeted direct labor hours and dollars by department for planning purposes. This data is prepared quarterly and sent to the plant manager and production manager.

DIRECT LABOR BUDGET

	Labor Rate	Total Hours	Total Costs
April			
Assembly	12.75	723	
Electronics	16.32	580	
Machining	27.34	442	
May			
Assembly	12.75	702	
Electronics	16.32	615	
Machining	27.34	428	
June			
Assembly	12.75	694	
Electronics	16.32	643	
Machining	27.34	389	

chapter summary

➤ Key a formula in a cell and the formula displays in the cell as well as in the Formula bar. If cell entries are changed, a formula will automatically recalculate the values and insert the result in the cell.

➤ Use the AutoSum button on the Standard toolbar to automatically add numbers in rows or columns.

➤ Create your own formula with commonly used operators such as addition (+), subtraction (-), multiplication (*), division (/), percent (%), and exponentiation (^). When writing a formula, begin with the equals (=) sign.

➤ Copy a formula to other cells in a row or column with the F<u>i</u>ll option from the <u>E</u>dit drop-down menu or with the fill handle that displays in the bottom right corner of the active cell.

➤ Excel includes over 200 functions that are divided into nine categories. Use the Paste Function feature to create formulas using built-in functions.

➤ A function operates on an argument, which may consist of a cell reference, a constant, or another function. When a value calculated by a formula is inserted in a cell, this is referred to as returning the result.

➤ Use the IF function, considered a conditional function, to perform conditional tests on values and formulas.

➤ Use nested IF functions in a formula where more than two actions are required.

➤ A selected group of cells is referred to as a range. A range can be named and used in a formula. Name a range by keying the name in the Name Box button on the Formula bar.

➤ A reference identifies a cell or a range of cells in a worksheet and can be relative or absolute. Identify an absolute cell reference by inserting a $ symbol before the column and row.

➤ Cells can be linked between worksheets and workbooks. The worksheet containing the original cell is called the source worksheet and the worksheet relying on the source worksheet for the data in the link is called the dependent worksheet. To create a link, copy data in a cell, and then paste it with <u>E</u>dit and then Paste <u>S</u>pecial. At the Paste Special dialog box, click Paste <u>L</u>ink.

➤ In a multiple worksheet workbook, use a 3-D reference to analyze data in the same cell or range of cells.

➤ Apply outlining to a worksheet to display specific rows and columns such as subtotals and totals.

➤ Plan a worksheet by completing these basic steps: identify the purpose of the worksheet, design the worksheet, create a sketch of the worksheet, enter the data in the worksheet, and test the worksheet data.

commands review

	Mouse/Keyboard
Automatically insert sum	Click AutoSum button on Standard toolbar
Display Paste Function dialog box	Click Paste Function button on Standard toolbar; or click <u>I</u>nsert, <u>F</u>unction
Display Paste Special dialog box	Click <u>E</u>dit, Paste <u>S</u>pecial
Apply automatic outlining	Click <u>D</u>ata, point to <u>G</u>roup and Outline, click <u>A</u>uto Outline

thinking offline

Completion: In the space provided at the right, indicate the correct term, symbol, or value.

1. Begin a formula with this sign. _____

2. Click this button on the Standard toolbar to automatically add numbers in cells. _____

3. This is the operator for division that is used when writing a formula. _____

4. This is the operator for multiplication that is used when writing a formula. _____

5. This is the name of the small black box located at the bottom right corner of a cell that can be used to copy a formula to adjacent cells. _____

6. A function operates on this, which may consist of a constant, a cell reference, or another function. _____

7. This function is considered a conditional function. _____

8. To identify an absolute cell reference, key this symbol before the column and row. _____

9. In worksheets that are linked, the worksheet containing the cell with the original data is called this. _____

10. When linking data in a cell, click this button at the Paste Special dialog box. _____

11. In a multiple worksheet workbook, use this reference to analyze data in the same cell or range of cells. _____

12. Apply automatic outlining to a worksheet by clicking this option on the Menu bar, pointing to <u>G</u>roup and Outline, and then clicking <u>A</u>uto Outline. _____

13. Suppose that cell B2 contains the budgeted amount and cell C2 contains the actual amount. Write the formula below (including the IF conditions) that would insert the word "under" if the actual amount was less than the budgeted amount and insert the word "over" if the actual amount was greater than the budgeted amount.

_____

_____

14. List the steps you would complete to link the data in cell B2 in *Sheet1* with cell B2 in *Sheet2*.

_____

_____

_____

working hands-on

Assessment 1

1. Create a worksheet with the information shown in figure 5.8 with the following specifications:
   a. Key the data shown in figure 5.8 with the appropriate formatting.
   b. Insert the formula to calculate the difference (actual amount minus the budget amount) and then copy the formula down to the other cells.
   c. Use AutoSum to insert the total amounts.
   d. Format the numbers in cells as currency with zero decimal places.
2. Save the worksheet and name it Excel C5, SA 01.
3. Print Excel C5, SA 01 centered horizontally and vertically on the page.
4. Close Excel C5, SA 01.

figure

5.8   *Assessment 1*

SUMMARY OF PERFORMANCE

	Actual	Budget	Difference
Northeast division	2,505,250	2,250,000	
Southeast division	1,895,200	1,550,000	
Northwest division	2,330,540	2,200,000	
Southwest division	1,850,340	1,950,500	
Total			

Assessment 2

1. Open Excel Worksheet 13.
2. Save the worksheet with Save As and name it Excel C5, SA 02.
3. Make the following changes to the worksheet:
   a. Determine the average monthly sales using the AVERAGE function.
   b. Format the numbers in cell B3 through H8 as currency with zero decimal places.
   c. Automatically adjust columns B through H.
4. Save the worksheet again with the same name (Excel C5, SA 02).
5. Change the top margin to 2 inches and then print Excel C5, SA 02.
6. Close Excel C5, SA 02.

Assessment 3

1. Open Excel C5, SA 02.
2. Save the worksheet with Save As and name it Excel C5, SA 03.
3. Make the following changes to the worksheet:
    a. Total each monthly column. (Create an appropriate title for the row.)
    b. Use the MAX function to determine the highest monthly total (for cells B3 through G8). (You determine where you want this maximum monthly total to appear in the worksheet. Be sure to include a cell title.)
    c. Use the MIN function to determine the lowest monthly total (for cells B3 through G8). (You determine where you want this minimum monthly total to appear in the worksheet. Be sure to include a cell title.)
4. Save the worksheet again with the same name (Excel C5, SA 03).
5. Print the worksheet in Landscape orientation and then close Excel C5, SA 03.

Assessment 4

1. Open Excel Worksheet 08.
2. Save the worksheet with Save As and name it Excel C5, SA 04.
3. Insert a formula in cell E3 that calculates depreciation using the straight-line method.
4. Copy the formula down to cells E4 through E9.
5. Make the following formatting changes to the worksheet:
    a. Select cells E3 through E9 and then click the Currency Style button on the Formatting toolbar.
    b. Select cells A1 through E9 and then apply an autoformat of your choosing. (Make sure values and numbers are displayed properly.)
6. Save the worksheet again with the same name (Excel C5, SA 04).
7. Print Excel C5, SA 04 centered horizontally and vertically on the page.
8. Close Excel C5, SA 04.

Assessment 5

1. Open Excel Worksheet 35.
2. Save the worksheet with Save As and name it Excel C5, SA 05.
3. The manager of Clearline Manufacturing is interested in refinancing a loan for either $125,000 or $300,000 and wants to determine the monthly payments, total payments, and total interest paid. Insert a formula with the following specifications:
    a. Make cell E5 active.
    b. Use the Paste Function button on the Standard toolbar to insert a formula using the PMT function. At the formula palette, enter the following:

Rate	=	C5/12
Nper	=	D5
Pv	=	-B5

    c. Copy the formula in cell E5 down to cells E6 through E8.
4. Insert a formula in cell F5 that multiplies the amount in E5 by the amount in D5.
5. Insert a formula in cell G5 that subtracts the amount in F5 from the amount in B5.
6. Copy the formulas in F5 and G5 down through row 8.
7. Save the worksheet again with the same name (Excel C5, SA 05).
8. Print and then close Excel C5, SA 05.

Assessment 6

1. Open Excel Worksheet 32.
2. Save the worksheet with Save As and name it Excel C5, SA 06.
3. Make the following changes to the worksheet:
   a. Change the percentage in cell C3 from *9%* to *10%*.
   b. Change the number in cell C4 from *36* to *60*.
   c. Change the amount in cell C5 from *($1,200)* to *-500*.
   d. Use the FV function to insert a formula that calculates the future value of the investment. *(Hint: For help with the formula, refer to exercise 13.)*
4. Save the worksheet again with the same name (Excel C5, SA 06).
5. Print Excel C5, SA 06.

Assessment 7

1. Create the worksheet shown in figure 5.9 with the following specifications:
   a. Format the cells as shown in figure 5.9. (Before keying the percentages in cells B6 through B12, select the cells and then click the Percent Style button and then the Center button.)
   b. Key the data shown in the cells in figure 5.9.
   c. Make cell C6 active and then insert the formula =$B$3*B6. (In this formula, B3 is identified as an absolute cell reference because the budget amount remains in cell B3.)
   d. Copy the formula in cell C6 down to cell C12.
   e. Format the numbers in cells C6 through C12 as currency with zero decimal places. (If necessary, automatically adjust the column width.)
2. Save the workbook and name it Excel C5, SA 07.
3. With Excel C5, SA 07 open, copy the cells in the worksheet to *Sheet2* and *Sheet3* by completing the following steps:
   a. Select cells A1 through C12 and then copy the selected cells to *Sheet2*.
   b. Copy the selected cells to *Sheet3*.
4. With *Sheet3* displayed, make the following changes:
   a. Automatically adjust the widths of columns A, B, and C.
   b. Make the following changes to the specified cells:
       A5: Change *Production Department* to *Finance Department*
       B6: Change *15%* to *14*
       B7: Change *3%* to *2*
       B9: Change *9%* to *8*
       B10: Change *5%* to *4*
   c. Delete *$1,200,000* in cell B3.
5. Make *Sheet2* active and then make the following changes:
   a. Automatically adjust the widths of columns A, B, and C.
   b. Make the following changes to the specified cells:
       A5: Change *Production Department* to *Personnel Department*
       B6: Change *15%* to *13*
       B7: Change *3%* to *2*
       B9: Change *9%* to *6*
       B10: Change *5%* to *4*
   c. Delete *$1,200,000* in cell B3.
6. Make *Sheet1* active and then link the annual budget amount ($1,200,000) in cell B3 to cell B3 in *Sheet2* and B3 in *Sheet3*. *(Hint: Do this by copying and then pasting with Paste Link at the Paste Special dialog box.)*

7. Make *Sheet1* the active worksheet and then save the workbook again with the same name (Excel C5, SA 07).
8. Rename *Sheet1 Production,* rename *Sheet2 Personnel,* and rename *Sheet3 Finance.*
9. Print the entire workbook.
10. With Excel C5, SA 07 still open, determine the impact on the budget of a 10% increase in the annual budget. To do this, change the amount in cell B3 in *Sheet1* to *1,320,000.* (This will change the amounts in *Sheet2* and *Sheet3* because the cell was linked.)
11. Print the entire workbook.
12. With Excel C5, SA 07 still open, determine the impact on the budget of a 10% decrease in the annual budget. To do this, change the amount in cell B3 to *1,080,000.*
13. Save, print (the entire workbook), and then close Excel C5, SA 07.

Assessment 7

	A	B	C
1	SELLAR CORPORATION		
2			
3	Annual Budget	$1,200,000	
4			
5	Prodution Department	% of Budget	Total
6	Salaries	15%	
7	Benefits	3%	
8	Payroll taxes	2%	
9	Operating costs	9%	
10	Training	5%	
11	Supplies	2%	
12	Miscellaneous	1%	
13			

Assessment 8

1. Open Excel Worksheet 01.
2. Save the worksheet with Save As and name it Excel C5, SA 08.
3. Make the following changes to the worksheet:
   a. Key **Difference** in cell E1.
   b. Insert the formula =D3-C3 in cell E3 and then copy it down to E4 through E10.
   c. Select cells E3 through E10 and then name the range Difference.
   d. Key **Max Difference** in cell A13.
   e. Insert the formula =MAX(Difference) in cell B13.
   f. Key **Min Difference** in cell A14.
   g. Insert the formula =MIN(Difference) in cell B14.
   h. Key **Ave Difference** in cell A15.
   i. Insert the formula =AVERAGE(Difference) in cell B15.
   j. Select cells C3 through E10 and then click the Currency Style button on the Formatting toolbar.
   k. Select cells B13 through B15 and then click the Currency Style button on the Formatting toolbar.

      l.   Bold and center the text in cells A1 through E1.

      m. Center the text in cells B3 through B10.

4. Save the worksheet again with the same name (Excel C5, SA 08).

5. Print Excel C5, SA 08.

6. Make the following changes to the worksheet:

      a.   Change *63,293.00* in cell C6 to *55,500.00*.

      b.   Change *12,398.00* in cell C9 to *13,450.00*.

      c.   Create the header *Customer Jobs* that prints centered at the top of the page. (Create this header at the Page Setup dialog box with the Header/Footer tab selected.)

7. Save, print, and then close Excel C5, SA 08.

Assessment 9

1. Open Excel C5, SA 08.

2. Save the worksheet with Save As and name it Excel C5, SA 09.

3. Make the following changes to the worksheet:

      a.   Make cell F1 active and then key **Bonus**.

      b.   Make cell F3 active and then insert the following formula to provide a 10% bonus for those jobs that were under the planned amount: =IF(E3>0,C3*0.1,0).

      c.   Copy the formula in cell F3 down to cells F4 through F10.

      d.   Select cells F3 through F10 and then click the Currency Style button on the Formatting toolbar.

4. Save the worksheet again with the same name (Excel C5, SA 09).

5. Print and then close Excel C5, SA 09.

Assessment 10

1. Open Excel Worksheet 14.

2. Save the worksheet with Save As and name it Excel C5, SA 10.

3. Make the following changes to the worksheet:

      a.   Insert a formula using an absolute reference to determine the projected quotas at ten percent of the current quotas.

      b.   Save the worksheet and name it Excel C5, SA 10.

      c.   Print Excel C5, SA 10.

      d.   Determine the projected quotas at fifteen percent of the current quota by changing cell A14 to *15% Increase* and cell B14 to *1.15*.

      e.   Save and then print Excel C5, SA 10.

      f.   Determine the projected quotas at twenty percent of the current quota.

4. Save, print, and then close Excel C5, SA 10.

Assessment 11

1. Open Excel Worksheet 34.

2. Save the workbook with Save As and name it Excel C5, SA 11.

3. Make the following changes to the workbook:

      a.   Insert the heading *Average January Sales 1998-2001* (on multiple lines) in cell B10.

      b.   Insert a formula in cell B11 with a 3-D reference that averages the total in cells B3 through B8 in *Sheet1*, *Sheet2*, and *Sheet3*.

   c. Make cell B11 active and then change to the Currency Style with zero decimal places.

   d. Insert the heading *Average February Sales 1998-2001* (on multiple lines) in cell C10.

   e. Insert a formula in cell C11 with a 3-D reference that averages the total in cells C3 through C8 in *Sheet1*, *Sheet2*, and *Sheet3*.

   f. Make cell C11 active and then change to the Currency Style with zero decimal places.

   g. Insert the heading *Average March Sales 1998-2001* (on multiple lines) in cell D10.

   h. Insert a formula in cell D11 with a 3-D reference that averages the total in cells D3 through D8 in *Sheet1*, *Sheet2*, and *Sheet3*.

   i. Make cell D11 active and then change to the Currency Style with zero decimal places.

4. Save the workbook again with the same name (Excel C5, SA 11).

5. Print worksheet 1 of the workbook.

6. Close Excel C5, SA 11.

Assessment 12

1. Learn about specific options in the Options dialog box by completing the following steps:

   a. Display the Options dialog box by clicking Tools and then Options.

   b. At the Options dialog box, click the View tab.

   c. Read information about each of the options in the Window options section of the dialog box. (To do this, click the Help button [displays with a question mark] that displays in the upper right corner of the dialog box, and then click the desired option.)

2. After reading information about the options in the Window options section, complete the following steps:

   a. Open Excel C5, SA 04.

   b. Save the worksheet with Save As and name it Excel C5, SA 12.

   c. Display the formulas in column E (rather than the results) using information you learned from the Options dialog box.

3. Save the worksheet again with the same name (Excel C5, SA 12).

4. Print and then close Excel C5, SA 12.

Chapter 06C

Creating a Chart in Excel

P E R F O R M A N C E   O B J E C T I V E S

Upon successful completion of chapter 6, you will be able to:
- Create a chart with data in an Excel worksheet.
- Create a chart in a separate worksheet.
- Print a selected chart and print a worksheet containing a chart.
- Size, move, and delete a chart.
- Change the type of chart.
- Choose a custom chart type.
- Change data in a chart.
- Add, delete, and customize elements in a chart.

In the previous Excel chapters, you learned to create data in worksheets. While a worksheet does an adequate job of representing data, you can present some data more visually by charting the data. A chart is sometimes referred to as a *graph* and is a picture of numeric data. In this chapter, you will learn to create and customize charts in Excel.

Creating a Chart

In Excel, create a chart by selecting cells containing the data you want to chart, and then clicking the Chart Wizard button on the Standard toolbar. There are four steps involved in creating a chart with the Chart Wizard. Suppose you wanted to create a chart with the worksheet shown in figure 6.1. To create the chart with the Chart Wizard, you would complete the following steps:

 The Chart Wizard automates the process of creating charts.

Chart
Wizard

1. Select the cells containing data (in the worksheet in figure 6.1, this would be cells A1 through C4).
2. Click the Chart Wizard button on the Standard toolbar.
3. At the Chart Wizard - Step 1 of 4 - Chart Type dialog box shown in figure 6.2, choose the desired chart type and chart sub-type, and then click the Next > button.

Press F11 to create a chart using the Chart Wizard with all default settings.

4. At the Chart Wizard - Step 2 of 4 - Chart Source Data dialog box shown in figure 6.3, make sure the data range displays correctly (for the chart in figure 6.1, the range will display as =*Sheet1!$A$1:$C$4*), and then click the Next > button.

5. At the Chart Wizard - Step 3 of 4 - Chart Options dialog box shown in figure 6.4, make any changes to the chart, and then click the Next > button.

6. At the Chart Wizard - Step 4 of 4 - Chart Location dialog box shown in figure 6.5, specify where you want the chart inserted, and then click the Finish button.

If the chart was created with all the default settings at the Chart Wizard dialog boxes, the chart would display below the cells containing data as shown in figure 6.6.

figure

6.1

Excel Worksheet

	A	B	C	D
1	**Salesperson**	**June**	**July**	
2	Chaney	$34,239	$39,224	
3	Ferraro	$23,240	$28,985	
4	Jimenez	$56,892	$58,450	
5				
6				

figure

6.2

Chart Wizard - Step 1 of 4 - Chart Type Dialog Box

Choose a chart type from this list.

Choose a chart sub-type from these examples.

figure
6.3

Chart Wizard - Step 2 of 4 - Chart Source Data Dialog Box

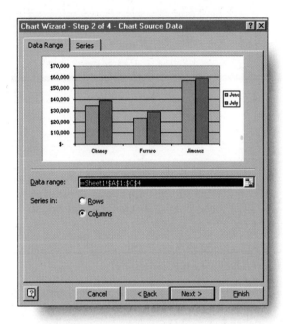

figure
6.4

Chart Wizard - Step 3 of 4 - Chart Options Dialog Box

Add and/or format chart elements with options from this dialog box with various tabs selected.

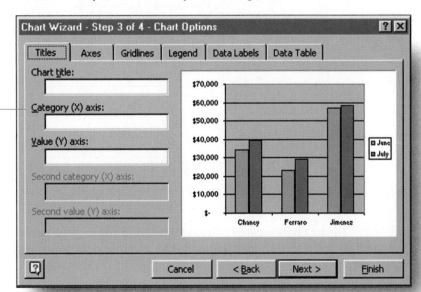

figure

6.5

Chart Wizard - Step 4 of 4 - Chart Location Dialog Box

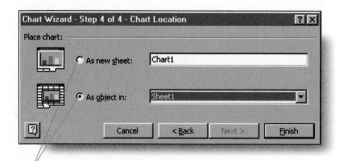

To insert the chart in the active worksheet, leave this at the default setting of As object in. Choose As new sheet option to create the chart in a separate sheet.

figure

6.6

Chart Based on Excel Worksheet

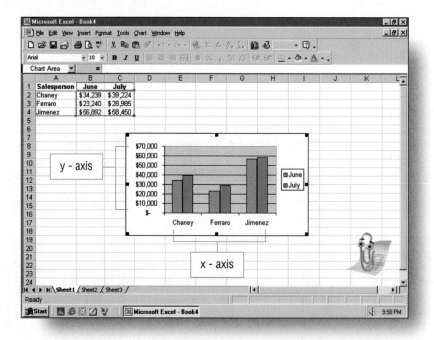

Preview the chart at step 1 of the Chart Wizard by positioning the arrow pointer on the Press and Hold to View Sample button and then holding down the left mouse button.

Hint

In the chart created in Excel, shown in figure 6.6, the left vertical side of the chart is referred to as the y-axis. The y-axis contains tick marks with amounts displaying the value at that particular point on the axis. The values in the chart in figure 6.6 are broken into tick marks by ten thousands beginning with zero and continuing to 70,000. The values for the y-axis will vary depending on the data in the table. The names in the first column are used for the x-axis, which runs along the bottom of the chart.

(Before completing computer exercises, delete the Chapter 05C *folder on your disk. Next, copy the* Chapter 06C *folder from the CD that accompanies this textbook to your disk and make* Chapter 06C *the active folder.)*

Creating a Chart in Excel with Data in a Worksheet

1. Open Excel Worksheet 15.
2. Save the worksheet with Save As and name it Excel C6, Ex 01.
3. Create a chart using the Chart Wizard by completing the following steps:
   a. Select cells A1 through E5.
   b. Click the Chart Wizard button on the Standard toolbar.

Step 3b

	A	B	C	D	E	F	G	H	I
1	Region	1st Qtr.	2nd Qtr.	3rd Qtr.	4th Qtr.				
2	Northwest	300,560	320,250	287,460	360,745				
3	Southwest	579,290	620,485	490,125	635,340				
4	Northeast	890,355	845,380	795,460	890,425				
5	Southeast	290,450	320,765	270,450	300,455				

Step 3a

   c. At the Chart Wizard - Step 1 of 4 - Chart Type dialog box, click the Next > button.
   d. At the Chart Wizard - Step 2 of 4 - Chart Source Data dialog box, make sure the data range displays as *=Sheet1!$A$1:$E$5* and then click the Next > button.
   e. At the Chart Wizard - Step 3 of 4 - Chart Options dialog box, click the Next > button.
   f. At the Chart Wizard - Step 4 of 4 - Chart Location dialog box, make sure the As object in option is selected and that *Sheet1* displays in the text box, and then click the Finish button.
   g. Click outside the chart to deselect the chart.
4. Save the worksheet again with the same name (Excel C6, Ex 01).
5. Print and then close Excel C6, Ex 01.

Printing Only the Chart

In a worksheet containing data in cells as well as a chart, you can print only the chart. To do this, click the chart to select it and then display the Print dialog box. At the Print dialog box, *Selected Chart* will automatically be selected in the Print what section. Click OK to print only the selected chart.

Previewing a Chart

Preview a chart by clicking the Print Preview button on the Standard toolbar or by clicking File and then Print Preview. This displays the worksheet containing the chart in Print Preview (refer to figure 8.13, page 348). After previewing the chart, click the Close button, or print the worksheet by clicking the Print button on the Print Preview toolbar and then clicking OK at the Print dialog box.

Previewing and Printing Only the Chart in Excel

1. Open Excel C6, Ex 01.
2. Preview the chart by completing the following steps:
   a. Click the Print Preview button on the Standard toolbar.
   b. In Print Preview, click the Zoom button to make the display of the worksheet bigger.
   c. Click the Zoom button again to return to the full-page view.
   d. Click the Close button to close Print Preview.
3. Print only the chart by completing the following steps:
   a. Click the chart to select it.
   b. Click File and then Print.
   c. At the Print dialog box, make sure *Selected Chart* is selected in the Print what section of the dialog box and then click OK.
4. Close Excel C6, Ex 01.

Creating a Chart in a Separate Worksheet

The chart you created in exercise 1 was inserted in the same worksheet as the cells containing data. You cannot delete the data (displaying only the chart) because the data in the chart will also be deleted. If you want to create a chart in a worksheet by itself, click the As new sheet option at the Chart Wizard - Step 4 of 4 - Chart Location dialog box. When the chart is completed, it displays in a separate sheet and fills most of the page. The sheet containing the chart is labeled *Chart1*. This sheet label displays on a tab located toward the bottom of the screen. The worksheet containing the data is located in Sheet 1. You can move between the chart and the worksheet by clicking the desired tab.

Creating a Chart in a Separate Excel Worksheet

1. Open Excel Worksheet 15.
2. Save the worksheet with Save As and name it Excel C6, Ex 03.
3. Create a chart as a separate sheet using the Chart Wizard by completing the following steps:
   a. Select cells A1 through E5.
   b. Click the Chart Wizard button on the Standard toolbar.
   c. At the Chart Wizard - Step 1 of 4 - Chart Type dialog box, click the Next > button.
   d. At the Chart Wizard - Step 2 of 4 - Chart Source Data dialog box, make sure the data range displays as =*Sheet1!$A$1:$E$5*, and then click the Next > button.
   e. At the Chart Wizard - Step 3 of 4 - Chart Options dialog box, click the Next > button.
   f. At the Chart Wizard - Step 4 of 4 - Chart Location dialog box, click As new sheet, and then click the Finish button.

4. Save the workbook (two sheets) again with the same name (Excel C6, Ex 03).
5. Print only the sheet containing the chart. (To do this, make sure the sheet containing the chart displays, and then click the Print button on the Standard toolbar.)
6. Close Excel C6, Ex 03.

Deleting a Chart

A chart can be deleted by clicking once in the chart to select it and then pressing the Delete key. If a chart created in a new worksheet is deleted, the chart is deleted but the worksheet is not. To delete the chart as well as the worksheet, position the mouse pointer on the *Chart1* tab, and then click the *right* mouse button. At the pop-up menu that displays, click the left mouse button on <u>D</u>elete. At the message box telling you that selected sheets will be permanently deleted, click OK.

Sizing and Moving a Chart

The size of a chart created in the same worksheet as the data containing cells can be changed. To do this, click the chart once to select it (this inserts black square sizing handles around the chart), and then drag the sizing handles in the desired direction.

A chart created with data in a worksheet can be moved by selecting the chart and then dragging it with the mouse. To move a chart, click once inside the chart to select it. Position the arrow pointer inside the chart, hold down the left mouse button, drag the outline of the chart to the desired location, and then release the button.

exercise 4

Sizing a Chart

1. Open Excel C6, Ex 01.
2. Save the worksheet with Save As and name it Excel C6, Ex 04.
3. Size the chart by completing the following steps:
   a. Select the chart by positioning the arrow pointer in the white portion of the chart just inside the chart border until a yellow box with the words *Chart Area* displays (takes approximately one second) next to the arrow pointer and then clicking the left mouse button. (Do not click on a chart element. This selects the element, not the entire chart.)

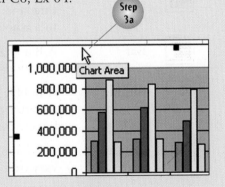

b. Position the arrow pointer on the black square sizing handle located in the middle of the bottom border until the arrow pointer turns into a double-headed arrow pointing up and down.

c. Hold down the left mouse button, drag the outline of the bottom border of the chart down approximately five rows, and then release the mouse button.

d. Position the arrow pointer on the black square sizing handle located in the middle of the right border until the arrow pointer turns into a double-headed arrow pointing left and right.

e. Hold down the left mouse button, drag the outline of the border to the right approximately two columns, and then release the mouse button.

f. Deselect the chart. (To do this, click in an empty cell somewhere in the worksheet.)

4. Save the worksheet again with the same name (Excel C6, Ex 04).
5. Change the page orientation to landscape and then print Excel C6, Ex 04.
6. Close Excel C6, Ex 04.

Changing the Chart Type

In exercises 1 and 3, you created a column chart, which is the default. The Chart Wizard offers 14 basic chart types along with built-in autoformats that can be applied to save time to get the desired look for the chart. Figure 6.7 shows an illustration and explanation of the 14 chart types.

figure

6.7   *Chart Types*

	Area	An Area chart emphasizes the magnitude of change, rather than time and the rate of change. It also shows the relationship of parts to a whole by displaying the sum of the plotted values.
	Bar	A Bar chart shows individual figures at a specific time or shows variations between components but not in relationship to the whole.
	Bubble	A Bubble chart compares sets of three values in a manner similar to a scatter chart with the third value displayed as the size of the bubble marker.
	Column	A Column chart compares separate (noncontinuous) items as they vary over time.

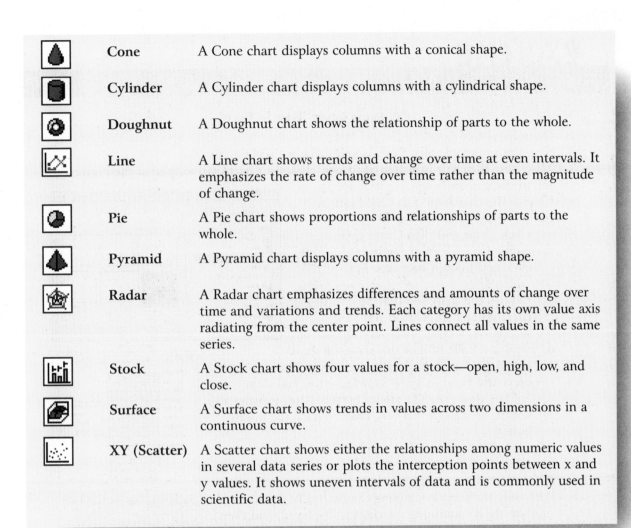

	Cone	A Cone chart displays columns with a conical shape.
	Cylinder	A Cylinder chart displays columns with a cylindrical shape.
	Doughnut	A Doughnut chart shows the relationship of parts to the whole.
	Line	A Line chart shows trends and change over time at even intervals. It emphasizes the rate of change over time rather than the magnitude of change.
	Pie	A Pie chart shows proportions and relationships of parts to the whole.
	Pyramid	A Pyramid chart displays columns with a pyramid shape.
	Radar	A Radar chart emphasizes differences and amounts of change over time and variations and trends. Each category has its own value axis radiating from the center point. Lines connect all values in the same series.
	Stock	A Stock chart shows four values for a stock—open, high, low, and close.
	Surface	A Surface chart shows trends in values across two dimensions in a continuous curve.
	XY (Scatter)	A Scatter chart shows either the relationships among numeric values in several data series or plots the interception points between x and y values. It shows uneven intervals of data and is commonly used in scientific data.

You can choose a chart type in step 1 of the Chart Wizard steps or change the chart type for an existing chart. When creating a chart with the Chart Wizard, choose the desired chart type and sub-type at the first Chart Wizard dialog box. To change the chart type for an existing chart, make sure the chart is active and then click Chart and then Chart Type. This displays the Chart Type dialog box. Choose the desired chart type and chart sub-type at this dialog box and then click the OK button.

You can also change the chart type in an existing chart with a shortcut menu. To do this, position the arrow pointer in a white portion of the chart (inside the chart but outside any chart element), and then click the *right* mouse button. At the shortcut menu that displays, click Chart Type. This displays the Chart Type dialog box that contains the same options at the Chart Wizard - Step 1 of 4 - Chart Type dialog box.

exercise 5

Changing Chart Type in Excel

1. Open Excel C6, Ex 03.
2. Save the workbook with Save As and name it Excel C6, Ex 05.
3. Make sure the chart is displayed. If not, click the *Chart1* tab located at the bottom of the worksheet window.
4. Change the chart type to a Line chart by completing the following steps:

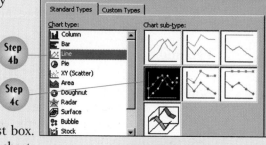

   a. Click Chart and then Chart Type.
   b. At the Chart Type dialog box, click *Line* in the Chart type list box.

   Step 4b

   c. Change the chart sub-type by clicking the first chart in the second row in the Chart sub-type list box.

   Step 4c

   d. View a sample of how this sub-type chart will display by positioning the arrow pointer on the Press and Hold to View Sample button and then holding down the left mouse button. After viewing a sample of the selected Line chart, release the mouse button.
   e. Click OK to close the dialog box.
5. Save the workbook again with the same name (Excel C6, Ex 05).
6. Print only the sheet containing the chart. (To do this, make sure the sheet containing the chart is displayed, and then click the Print button on the Standard toolbar.)
7. With Excel C6, Ex 05 still open, change the chart type to Bar by completing the following steps:
   a. Click Chart and then Chart Type.
   b. At the Chart Wizard dialog box, click *Bar* in the Chart type list box.
   c. Change the chart sub-type by clicking the first chart in the second row in the Chart sub-type list box.

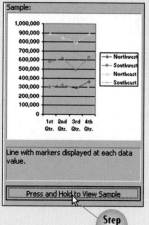

Step 4d

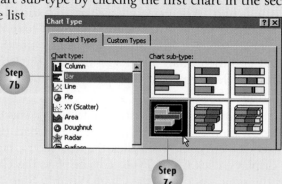

Step 7b

Step 7c

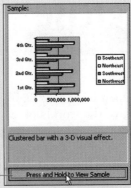

Sample:

Clustered bar with a 3-D visual effect.

Press and Hold to View Sample

d. View a sample of how this sub-type chart will display by positioning the arrow pointer on the Press and Hold to <u>V</u>iew Sample button and then holding down the left mouse button. After viewing a sample of the selected Bar chart, release the mouse button.
   e. Click OK to close the dialog box.
8. Save the workbook again with the same name (Excel C6, Ex 05).
9. Print only the sheet containing the chart and then close Excel C6, Ex 05.

Step 7d

Choosing a Custom Chart Type

The chart feature offers a variety of preformatted custom charts. A custom chart can be chosen in step 1 of the Chart Wizard steps or a custom chart type can be chosen for an existing chart. To choose a custom chart type while creating a chart, click the Custom Types tab at the Chart Wizard - Step 1 of 4 - Chart Type dialog box.

A variety of preformatted custom charts are available. Use one of these custom charts if the formatting is appropriate.

Hint

You can also choose a custom chart for an existing chart. To do this, click <u>C</u>hart and then Chart <u>T</u>ype. At the Chart Type dialog box, click the Custom Types tab. This displays the Chart Type dialog box as shown in figure 6.8. You can also display the Chart Type dialog box by positioning the arrow pointer in the chart, clicking the *right* mouse button, and then clicking Chart <u>T</u>ype at the shortcut menu. At the Chart Type dialog box with the Custom Types tab selected, click the desired custom chart type in the <u>C</u>hart type list box.

figure 6.8

Chart Type Dialog Box with Custom Types Tab Selected

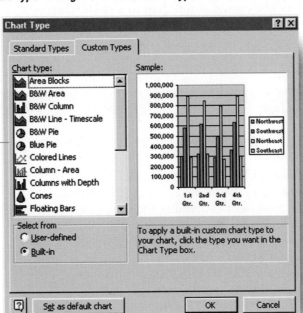

Choose a custom chart type from this list box and preview it at the right in the Sample box.

exercise 6

Choosing a Custom Chart Type

1. Open Excel C6, Ex 03.
2. Save the workbook with Save As and name it Excel C6, Ex 06.
3. Choose a custom chart type by completing the following steps:
   a. Click Chart and then Chart Type.
   b. At the Chart Type dialog box, click the Custom Types tab.
   c. At the Chart Type dialog box with the Custom Types tab selected, click *Columns with Depth* in the Chart type list box.
   d. Click OK to close the Chart Type dialog box.
4. Save the workbook again with the same name (Excel C6, Ex 06).
5. Print only the sheet containing the chart. (To do this, make sure the sheet containing the chart displays, and then click the Print button on the Standard toolbar.)
6. Close Excel C6, Ex 06.

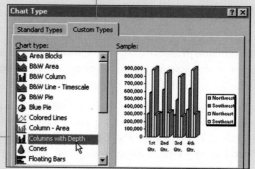

Step 3b

Step 3c

Changing Data in Cells

The Excel chart feature uses data in cells to create a chart. This data can be changed and the chart will reflect the changes. When a change is made to data in a worksheet, the change is also made to any chart created with the cells in the worksheet. The change is reflected in a chart whether it is located in the same worksheet as the changed cells or in a new sheet.

exercise 7

Changing Numbers in an Excel Worksheet

1. Open Excel C6, Ex 03.
2. Save the workbook with Save As and name it Excel C6, Ex 07.
3. Make the following changes to the data in cells in *Sheet1*:
   a. Make sure the worksheet containing the cells (not the chart) is active. If not, click the *Sheet1* tab located at the bottom of the worksheet window.
   b. Make the following changes to the specified cells:
      - C2: Change *320,250* to *295,785*
      - D3: Change *490,125* to *550,350*
      - C5: Change *320,765* to *298,460*
      - E5: Change *300,455* to *275,490*

4. Display the worksheet containing the chart (Chart1).
5. Save the workbook again with the same name (Excel C6, Ex 07).
6. Print only the sheet containing the chart.
7. Close Excel C6, Ex 07.

Changing the Data Series

When a chart is created, the Chart Wizard uses the data in the first column (except the first cell) to create the x-axis (the information along the bottom of the chart) and uses the data in the first row (except the first cell) to create the legend. For example, in the chart in figure 6.6, the names (Chaney, Ferraro, and Jimenez) were used for the x-axis (along the bottom of the chart) and the months (June and July) were used for the legend.

When a chart is created, the option <u>R</u>ows is selected by default at the Chart Wizard - Step 2 of 4 - Chart Source Data dialog box. This can be changed to Col<u>u</u>mns and the data in the first column (except the first cell) will be used to create the x-axis and the data in the first row will be used to create the legend.

Change the data series in an existing chart by making the chart active and then clicking <u>C</u>hart and then <u>S</u>ource Data. This displays the Source Data dialog box shown in figure 6.9. Another method for displaying the Source Data dialog box is to position the arrow pointer in a white portion of the chart (inside the chart but outside any chart element) and then click the *right* mouse button. At the shortcut menu that displays, click Source <u>D</u>ata. The Source Data dialog box contains the same options as the Chart Wizard - Step 2 of 4 - Chart Source Data dialog box.

A data series is information represented on the chart by bars, lines, columns, pie slices, etc.

figure
6.9

Source Data Dialog Box with Data Range Tab Selected

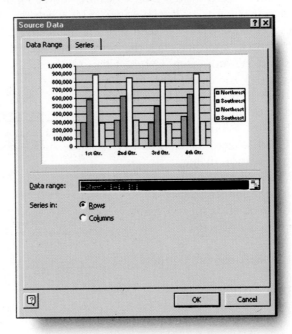

exercise

Changing Data Series in an Excel Chart

1. Open Excel C6, Ex 01.
2. Save the workbook with Save As and name it Excel C6, Ex 08.
3. Change the data series by completing the following steps:
   a. Position the arrow pointer in a white portion of the chart (inside the chart but outside any chart element) and then click the *right* mouse button.
   b. At the shortcut menu that displays, click Source Data.
   c. At the Source Data dialog box, click the Columns option.
   d. Click OK to close the Source Data dialog box.
   e. Click outside the chart to deselect it.
4. Save the workbook again with the same name (Excel C6, Ex 08).
5. Print and then close Excel C6, Ex 08.

exercise 9

Creating a Pie Chart in Excel Using Chart Wizard

1. Open Excel Worksheet 16.
2. Save the worksheet with Save As and name it Excel C6, Ex 09.
3. Create a pie chart by completing the following steps:
   a. Select cells A4 through B10.
   b. Click the Chart Wizard button on the Standard toolbar.
   c. At the Chart Wizard - Step 1 of 4 - Chart Type dialog box, click *Pie* in the Chart type list box, and then click the Next > button.
   d. At the Chart Wizard - Step 2 of 4 - Chart Source Data dialog box, make sure the data range displays as =*Sheet1!$A$4:$B$10*. Click the Rows option to see what happens to the pie when the data series is changed, click Columns to return the data series back, and then click the Next > button.
   e. At the Chart Wizard - Step 3 of 4 - Chart Options dialog box, click the Data Labels tab.
   f. At the dialog box with the Data Labels tab selected, click Show percent.
   g. Click the Next > button.
   h. At the Chart Wizard - Step 4 of 4 - Chart Location dialog box, click As new sheet and then click the Finish button.
4. Save the workbook (two sheets) again with the same name (Excel C6, Ex 09).
5. Print only the sheet containing the chart.
6. Close Excel C6, Ex 09.

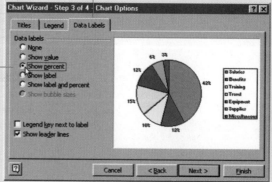

Adding Chart Elements

Certain chart elements are automatically inserted in a chart created by the Chart Wizard including a chart legend and labels for the x-axis and y-axis. Add other chart elements such as a chart title and data labels at the Chart Wizard - Step 3 of 4 - Chart Options dialog box. Add chart elements to an existing chart by making the chart active and then clicking <u>C</u>hart and then Chart <u>O</u>ptions. This displays the Chart Options dialog box shown in figure 6.10. Another method for displaying this dialog box is to position the arrow pointer in a white portion of the chart (inside the chart but outside any chart element), click the *right* mouse button, and then click Chart <u>O</u>ptions. The Chart Options dialog box contains the same options as the Chart Wizard - Step 3 of 4 - Chart Options dialog box.

The legend identifies which data series is represented by which data marker.

Hint

figure
6.10

Chart Options Dialog Box with Data Labels Tab Selected

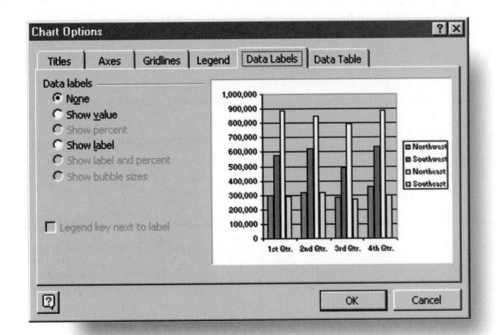

exercise 10

Adding a Title to a Chart and Changing the Legend Location

1. Open Excel C6, Ex 09.
2. Save the workbook with Save As and name it Excel C6, Ex 10.
3. Add a title and data labels to the chart and change the location of the chart legend by completing the following steps:

   a. Make sure the sheet (*Chart1*) containing the pie chart displays.
   b. Click Chart and then Chart Options.
   c. At the Chart Options dialog box, click the Titles tab. (Skip this step if the Titles tab is already selected.)
   d. Click inside the Chart title text box and then key **DEPARTMENT EXPENSES BY PERCENTAGE**.
   e. Click the Data Labels tab.
   f. Click the Legend key next to label check box.
   g. Click the Legend tab.
   h. At the Chart Options dialog box with the Legend tab selected, click Left.
   i. Click the OK button to close the dialog box.
4. Save the workbook again with the same name (Excel C6, Ex 10).
5. Print only the sheet containing the pie chart.
6. Close Excel C6, Ex 10.

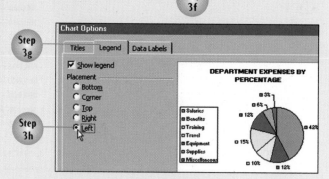

Moving/Sizing Chart Elements

When additional elements are added to a chart, the chart can become quite full and elements may overlap. If elements in a chart overlap, an element can be selected and then moved. To select an element, position the arrow pointer on a portion of the element, and then click the left mouse button. This causes sizing handles to display around the element. Position the mouse pointer toward the edge of the selected element until it turns into an arrow pointer, hold down the left mouse button, drag the element to the desired location, and then release the mouse button. To change the size of an element, drag the sizing handles in the desired direction.

Deleting/Removing Chart Elements

Chart elements can be selected by clicking the desired element. Once an element is selected, it can be moved and it can also be deleted. To delete a selected element, press the Delete key. If you delete a chart element in a chart and then decide you want it redisplayed in the chart, immediately click the Undo button on the Standard toolbar.

Moving/Sizing/Adding Chart Elements

1. Open Excel C6, Ex 10.
2. Save the workbook with Save As and name it Excel C6, Ex 11.
3. Move and size chart elements by completing the following steps:
    a. Move the legend to the right side of the chart by completing the following steps:
        1) Click the legend to select it.
        2) With the arrow pointer positioned in the legend, hold down the left mouse button, drag the outline of the legend to the right side of the chart, and then release the mouse button.
    b. Move the pie to the left by completing the following steps:
        1) Select the pie. To do this, position the arrow pointer in a white portion of the chart immediately outside the pie (a yellow box displays with *Plot Area* inside) and then click the left mouse button. (This should insert a square border around the pie. If not, try selecting the pie again.)
        2) With the pie selected (square border around the pie), position the arrow pointer inside the square border that displays around the pie (not inside the pie), hold down the left mouse button, drag the outline of the pie to the left until it looks balanced with the legend, and then release the mouse button.

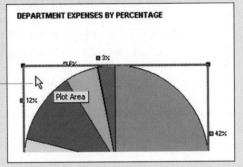

    c. Increase the size of the legend by completing the following steps:
        1) Click the legend to select it.
        2) Use the sizing handles that display around the legend to increase the size. (You determine the direction to drag the sizing handles and the final size of the legend. Make sure the pie and legend are balanced.)

4. Save the workbook again with the same name (Excel C6, Ex 11).
5. Print only the sheet containing the pie chart.
6. With Excel C6, Ex 11 still open, remove the legend, change the data labels, and move the pie by completing the following steps:
   a. Delete the legend by completing the following steps:
      1) Click the legend to select it.
      2) Press the Delete key.
   b. Change the data labels by completing the following steps:
      1) Position the arrow pointer in a white portion of the chart (outside any chart element) and then click the *right* mouse button.
      2) At the shortcut menu that displays, click Chart Options.
      3) At the Chart Options dialog box, click the Data Labels tab.
      4) At the Chart Options dialog box with the Data Labels tab selected, click the Show label and percent option.
      5) Click OK to close the Chart Options dialog box.
   c. Move the pie by completing the following steps:
      1) Make sure the pie is selected. (If the pie is not selected, select it by positioning the arrow pointer in a white portion of the chart immediately outside the pie [a yellow box displays with *Plot Area* inside] and then clicking the left mouse button).
      2) With the pie selected (square border around the pie), position the arrow pointer inside the square border that displays around the pie (not inside the pie), hold down the left mouse button, drag the outline of the pie until it looks centered between the left and right sides of the chart, and then release the mouse button.
7. Save the workbook again with the same name (Excel C6, Ex 11).
8. Print only the sheet containing the pie chart.
9. Close Excel C6, Ex 11.

Step 6b3

Chart Options

| Titles | Legend | Data Labels |

Data labels
- None
- Show value
- Show percent
- Show label
- Show label and percent
- Show bubble sizes

Step 6b4

Adding Gridlines

Gridlines can be added to a chart for the category, series, and value. Depending on the chart, some but not all of these options may be available. To add gridlines, display the Chart Options dialog box and then click the Gridlines tab. This displays the Chart Options dialog box with the Gridlines tab selected as shown in figure 6.11. At this dialog box, insert a check mark in those options for which you want gridlines.

figure 6.11

Chart Options Dialog Box with Gridlines Tab Selected

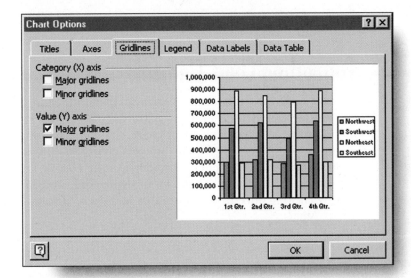

exercise 12

Adding Gridlines to a Chart

1. Open Excel C6, Ex 03.
2. Save the workbook with Save As and name it Excel C6, Ex 12.
3. Add gridlines to the chart by completing the following steps:
   a. Make sure the sheet containing the chart is displayed. (If not, click the *Chart1* tab located toward the bottom of the screen.)
   b. Click Chart and then Chart Options.
   c. At the Chart Options dialog box, click the Gridlines tab.
   d. At the Chart Options dialog box with the Gridlines tab selected, insert a check mark in the two options in the Category (X) axis section and also the two options in the Value (Y) axis section.
   e. Click OK to close the Chart Options dialog box.

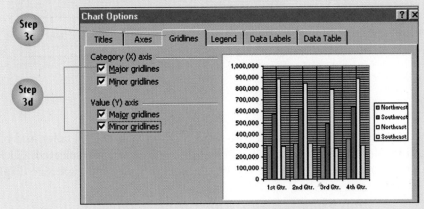

4. Save the workbook again with the same name (Excel C6, Ex 12).
5. Print only the sheet containing the chart.
6. Close Excel C6, Ex 12.

Formatting Chart Elements

A variety of formatting options are available for a chart or chart elements. Formatting can include adding a pattern, changing background and foreground colors of the selected element or chart, changing the font, and changing the alignment or placement. To customize a chart, double-click in the chart area (outside any chart element). This displays the Format Chart Area dialog box with the Patterns tab selected as shown in figure 6.12. You can also display this dialog box by clicking once in the chart area and then clicking Format and then Selected Chart Area.

Format Chart Area Dialog Box with Patterns Tab Selected

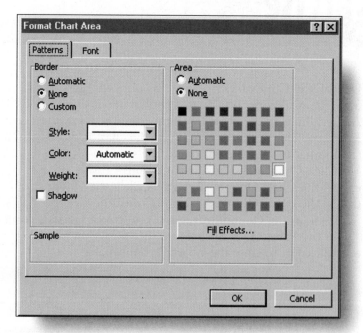

Customize the chart area by adding a pattern and/or fill color and background at the Format Chart Area dialog box with the Patterns tab selected. Click the Font tab and options for changing the typeface, type style, and type size display.

The font and pattern of chart elements can also be customized along with additional formatting for specific elements. For example, if you double-click a chart title, the Format Chart Title dialog box displays. (You can also display this dialog box by clicking once on the title and then clicking Format and then Selected Chart Title.) This dialog box contains three tabs—Patterns, Font, and Alignment. Clicking the Patterns or the Font tab displays the same options as those available at the Format Chart Area dialog box. Click the Alignment tab and options for changing the text alignment (horizontal or vertical) display along with options for the title orientation.

Double-click a chart legend and the Format Legend dialog box displays with three tabs—Patterns, Font, and Placement. (You can also display this dialog box by clicking once on the legend and then clicking Format and then Selected Legend.) Clicking the Patterns or the Font tab displays the same options as those available at the Format Chart Area dialog box. Click the Placement tab to display options for specifying the location of the legend in relation to the chart.

Each chart element contains a formatting dialog box. To display this dialog box, double-click the desired chart element. For example, double-click text in either the x-axis or the y-axis and the Format Axis dialog box displays.

exercise 13

Customizing Elements in an Excel Chart

1. Open Excel Worksheet 19.
2. Save the worksheet with Save As and name it Excel C6, Ex 13.
3. Create a Column chart with the data in the worksheet by completing the following steps:
   a. Select cells A4 through C7.
   b. Click the Chart Wizard button on the Standard toolbar.
   c. At the Chart Wizard - Step 1 of 4 - Chart Type dialog box, click the Next > button.
   d. At the Chart Wizard - Step 2 of 4 - Chart Source Data dialog box, make sure the data range displays as =*Sheet1!$A$4:$C$7* and then click the Next > button.
   e. At the Chart Wizard - Step 3 of 4 - Chart Options dialog box, make the following changes:
      1) Click the Titles tab.
      2) Click inside the Chart title text box and then key **NORTHWEST REGION**.
      3) Click the Next > button.
   f. At the Chart Wizard - Step 4 of 4 - Chart Location dialog box, click the As new sheet option, and then click the Finish button.
4. Change the font for the title and legend and add a border and shading by completing the following steps:
   a. Double-click the title *NORTHWEST REGION*.
   b. At the Format Chart Title dialog box, click the Font tab, and then change the font to 24-point Century Schoolbook bold (or a similar serif typeface).
   c. Click the Patterns tab.
   d. Click the white circle before Custom in the Border section of the dialog box.

e. Click the down-pointing triangle to the right of the <u>W</u>eight text box. From the drop-down menu that displays, click the third option.

f. Click the check box before the Sha<u>d</u>ow option.

g. Add light green color by clicking the fourth color from the left in the fifth row.

h. Click OK to close the Format Chart Title dialog box.

5. Format the legend with the same options as the title (complete steps similar to those in step 4, except change the font to 10-point Century Schoolbook bold [instead of 24-point].)

6. With the legend still selected, increase the width by dragging the left, middle sizing handle to the left so the legend slightly overlaps the chart. (Make sure *# of computers* is completely visible in the legend.)

7. Save the workbook again with the same name (Excel C6, Ex 13).

8. Print only the sheet containing the chart.

9. Close Excel C6, Ex 13.

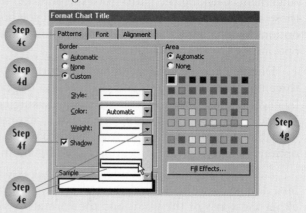

Changing Element Colors

Fill Color

A fill color can be added to a chart or a chart element with the Fill Color button on the Formatting toolbar. To add a fill color, select the chart or the chart element, and then click the down-pointing triangle at the right side of the Fill Color button on the Formatting toolbar. This displays a palette of color choices as shown in figure 6.13. Click the desired color on the palette.

6.13 *Fill Color Button Palette*

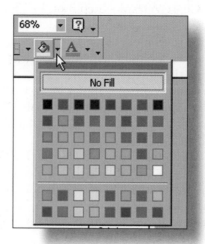

Changing Element Colors in a Chart

1. Open Excel C6, Ex 09.
2. Save the workbook with Save As and name it Excel C6, Ex 14.
3. Change the colors of the pieces of the pie by completing the following steps:
   a. Change the color of the piece of pie representing Salaries to red by completing the following steps:
      1) Position the arrow pointer on the Salaries piece of pie and then click the left mouse button. (Make sure the sizing handles surround only the Salaries piece of pie. You may need to experiment a few times to select the piece correctly.)
      2) Click the down-pointing triangle at the right of the Fill Color button on the Formatting toolbar.
      3) At the color palette, click the red color (first color in the third row).

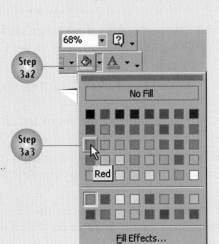

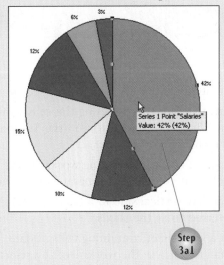

   b. Change the color of the Miscellaneous piece of pie to green by completing steps similar to those in step 3a. (You determine the shade of green.)
   c. Change the color of the Supplies piece of pie to yellow by completing steps similar to those in step 3a. (You determine the shade of yellow.)
   d. Change the color of the Equipment piece of pie to blue by completing steps similar to those in step 3a. (You determine the shade of blue.)
   e. Change the color of the Travel piece of pie to violet by completing steps similar to those in step 3a.
   f. Change the color of the Training piece of pie to light turquoise by completing steps similar to those in step 3a.
   g. Change the color of the Benefits piece of pie to a color you have not used on the other pieces of pie by completing steps similar to those in step 3a.

4. Add a background color to the chart by completing the following steps:
    a. Select the entire chart. (To do this, position the arrow pointer inside the chart window but outside the chart, and then click the left mouse button.)
    b. Click the down-pointing triangle at the right of the Fill Color button on the Formatting toolbar.
    c. From the color palette that displays, click a light blue color of your choosing.
5. Save the workbook again with the same name (Excel C6, Ex 14).
6. Print only the sheet containing the Pie chart.
7. Close Excel C6, Ex 14.

chapter summary

➤ Create a chart with data in an Excel worksheet. A chart is a visual presentation of data.

➤ Create a chart by selecting the cells containing the data to be charted and then clicking the Chart Wizard button on the Standard toolbar. Complete the four steps in the Chart Wizard.

➤ Insert a chart in the same worksheet as the cells containing data or in a separate sheet. If a chart is created in a separate sheet, the sheet is named *Chart1*.

➤ The left vertical side of a chart is referred to as the y-axis, and the bottom of the chart is referred to as the x-axis.

➤ In a worksheet containing cells of data as well as a chart, the chart can be printed (rather than all data in the worksheet) by selecting the chart first and then displaying the Print dialog box.

➤ To delete a chart in a worksheet, click the chart to select it, and then press the Delete key. To delete a chart created in a separate sheet, position the mouse pointer on the chart tab, click the right mouse button, and then click Delete.

➤ Change the size of a chart in an Excel worksheet by clicking the chart and then dragging the sizing handles in the desired direction. To move a chart, select the chart, position the arrow pointer inside the chart, hold down the left mouse button, drag the outline of the chart to the desired location, and then release the mouse button.

➤ Fourteen basic chart types are available and include Area, Bar, Bubble, Column, Cone, Cylinder, Doughnut, Line, Pie, Pyramid, Radar, Stock, Surface, and XY (scatter).

➤ The default chart type is a Column chart. This can be changed at the first Chart Wizard dialog box or at the Chart Type dialog box.

➤ A variety of custom charts are available at the Chart Type dialog box with the Custom Types tab selected.

➤ Change data in a cell used to create a chart and the data in the chart reflects the change.

➤ Chart elements can be added to a chart at the step 3 Chart Wizard dialog box or at the Chart Options dialog box.

➤ Move a chart element by selecting the element and then dragging the element to the desired location.

➤ Size a chart element by selecting the chart element and then dragging a sizing handle to the desired size.

➤ Delete a chart element by selecting the element and then pressing the Delete key.

➤ Customize the formatting of a chart element by double-clicking the element. This causes a formatting dialog box to display. The options at the dialog box will vary depending on the chart element.

➤ Add fill color to a chart or a chart element by selecting the chart or element and then clicking the Fill Color button on the Formatting toolbar. Click the desired color at the palette of color choices that displays.

commands review

	Mouse
Create a chart	Select the cells and then click the Chart Wizard button on the Standard toolbar; complete steps 1 through 4 of the Chart Wizard
Chart Type dialog box	Make chart active; click Chart, then Chart Type
Source Data dialog box	Make chart active; click Chart, then Source Data
Chart Options dialog box	Make chart active; click Chart, then Chart Options
Format Chart Area dialog box	Double-click in chart area outside any chart element
Format Chart Title dialog box	Double-click chart title
Format Legend dialog box	Double-click chart legend

thinking offline

Completion: In the space provided at the right, indicate the correct term or command.

1. Create a chart by selecting the cells containing data and then clicking this button on the Standard toolbar.

2. To create a chart as a separate worksheet, click this option at the Chart Wizard - Step 4 of 4 - Chart Location dialog box.

3. Change the size of a selected chart by dragging these.

4. This axis is located at the bottom of the chart.

5. Double-click a legend in a chart and this dialog box displays.

6. Choose a custom chart type at the Chart Type dialog box with this tab selected.

7. Double-click in a chart area and this dialog box displays.

8. Add fill color to a chart element by selecting the element and then clicking this button on the Formatting toolbar.

9. List the steps you would complete to create a default chart in Excel with cells A1 through D8 and insert the chart in a separate worksheet.

working hands-on

Assessment 1

1. Open Excel Worksheet 01.
2. Save the worksheet with Save As and name it Excel C6, SA 01.
3. Make the following changes to the worksheet:
   a. Delete column B.
   b. Delete row 2.
4. Select cells A1 through C9 and then create a chart in a separate sheet with the following specifications:
   a. At step 1 of the Chart Wizard do not make any changes.
   b. At step 2, make sure the proper cell range displays.
   c. At step 3, add the title *COMPANY SALES*.
   d. At step 4, specify that the chart is to be created as a new sheet.
   e. After the chart is created, change the font size of the title to 24 points.
5. Save the workbook again with the same name (Excel C6, SA 01).
6. Print only the sheet containing the chart.
7. Close Excel C6, SA 01.

Assessment 2

1. Open Excel Worksheet 22.
2. Save the worksheet with Save As and name it Excel C6, SA 02.
3. Select cells A1 through E3 and then create a chart in a new worksheet with the following specifications:
   a. At step 1 of the Chart Wizard, choose the Line chart type.
   b. At step 2, make sure the proper cell range displays.
   c. At step 3, add the title *COMPANY SALES*.
   d. At step 4, specify that the chart is to be created as a new sheet.

4. After the chart is created, make the following customizations:
   a. Add a light background color to the entire chart.
   b. Add a complementary light background color to the legend.
   c. Change the legend font to a serif typeface (you determine the typeface).
   d. Change the font for the title *COMPANY SALES* to the same serif typeface you chose for the legend and increase the font size.
   e. If some of the text in the legend is not visible, select the legend and then increase the size of the legend.
5. Save the workbook again with the same name (Excel C6, SA 02).
6. Print only the sheet containing the chart.
7. Close Excel C6, SA 02.

Assessment 3

1. Open Excel Worksheet 03.
2. Save the worksheet with Save As and name it Excel C6, SA 03.
3. Make the following changes to the worksheet:
   a. Delete column D.
   b. Select cells B3 through C8 and then click the Percent Style button on the Standard toolbar.
4. Select cells A2 through C8 and then create a chart in a new sheet with the default settings in Chart Wizard, except add the chart title *ANALYSIS OF FINANCIAL CONDITION*.
5. Make the following changes to the chart:
   a. Change the color of the bars in the chart (you determine the colors).
   b. Change the font of the title and add a border (you determine the font and border style).
   c. Change the background shading of the chart to light turquoise.
   d. Add the following gridlines: <u>M</u>ajor gridlines in *Category (X) Axis* and Minor gridlines in *Value (Y) Axis*.
6. Save the workbook again with the same name (Excel C6, SA 03).
7. Print only the sheet containing the chart.
8. Close Excel C6, SA 03.

Assessment 4

1. At a clear worksheet window, create a worksheet with the following data:

    Fund Allocations

Fund	Percentage
Annuities	23%
Stocks	42%
Bonds	15%
Money Market	20%

2. Create a pie chart as a separate worksheet with the data with the following specifications:
   a. Create a title for the pie chart.
   b. Add data labels to the chart.
   c. Add any other enhancements that will improve the visual presentation of the data.
3. Save the workbook and name it Excel C6, SA 04.
4. Print only the sheet containing the chart.
5. Close Excel C6, SA 04.

Assessment 5

1. Open Excel C6, SA 04.
2. Save the workbook with Save As and name it Excel C6, SA 05.
3. Choose a custom chart type at the Chart Type dialog box with the Custom Types tab selected. (Choose a custom pie chart.)
4. Save the workbook again with the same name (Excel C6, SA 05).
5. Print only the sheet containing the chart.
6. Close Excel C6, SA 05.

Assessment 6

1. Open Excel Worksheet 18.
2. Save the workbook with Save As and name it Excel C6, SA 06.
3. Look at the data in the worksheet and then create a chart to represent the data. Add a title to the chart and add any other enhancements to improve the visual display of the chart.
4. Save the workbook again with the same name (Excel C6, SA 06).
5. Print the chart and then close Excel C6, SA 06.

Assessment 7

1. Use Excel's Help feature to learn more about an XY (scatter) chart.
2. After reading the information presented by Help, create a worksheet with the data shown in figure 6.14. Create a scatter chart from the data in a separate sheet and create an appropriate title for the chart. (Excel will change the date *July 1* to *1-Jul* and change the other dates in the same manner. The XY scatter chart will display time in five-day intervals.)
3. Save the completed workbook and name it Excel C6, SA 07.
4. Print both sheets of the workbook (the sheet containing the data in cells and the sheet containing the chart).
5. Close Excel C6, SA 07.

figure

6.14   *Assessment 7*

HIGHLAND PARK ATTENDANCE		
Week	Projected	Actual
July 1	35,000	42,678
July 8	33,000	41,065
July 15	30,000	34,742
July 22	28,000	29,781
July 29	28,000	26,208

 Chapter 07C

Inserting Clip Art Images and Creating Maps

PERFORMANCE OBJECTIVES

Upon successful completion of chapter 7, you will be able to:

- Insert, size, and move a clip art image in an Excel worksheet.
- Use the Map feature to create a map from data in an Excel worksheet.
- Customize a map created in an Excel worksheet.
- Copy and paste a map from an Excel worksheet to a Word document.
- Draw arrows and objects using the Drawing toolbar to annotate a worksheet.

Microsoft Office contains several tools you can use in Excel to create special objects. In this chapter, you will learn to use two of these tools—Clip Gallery and Map. With Clip Gallery, you can insert images into a document to add visual appeal. With Map you can use data in an Excel worksheet to create a map. The Drawing toolbar contains tools you can use to draw attention to cells in a worksheet. For example, you could draw an arrow to highlight the highest sales.

Adding Clip Art to Worksheets

Microsoft Office includes a gallery of clip art images that can be inserted in an Office application such as Word, Excel, or PowerPoint. The steps to insert a clip art image into any of the Office applications are basically the same. To insert a clip art image, click Insert, point to Picture, and then click Clip Art. This displays the Insert ClipArt dialog box with the Pictures tab selected as shown in figure 7.1.

INTEGRATED TOPIC

7.1

Insert ClipArt Dialog Box with Pictures Tab Selected

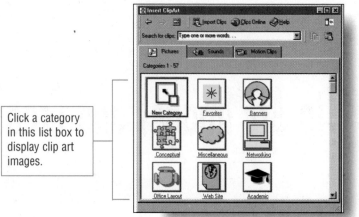

Click a category in this list box to display clip art images.

Insert
Clip Art

Alt + Home is the keyboard command to display all categories in the Insert ClipArt dialog box.

Increase the size of the Insert ClipArt dialog box by dragging a border.

Back

All Categories

Another method for displaying the Insert ClipArt dialog box is to click the Insert Clip Art button on the Drawing toolbar. To display the Drawing toolbar, position the mouse pointer on the Standard or Formatting toolbar, click the *right* mouse button, and then click Drawing at the drop-down list. You can also display clip art categories and images by clicking Insert and then Object. At the Object dialog box with the Create New tab selected, double-click *Microsoft Clip Gallery* in the list box. This displays the Microsoft Clip Gallery that contains the same options as the Insert ClipArt dialog box.

At the Insert ClipArt dialog box with the Pictures tab selected, click a category in the category list box. This displays a list of clip art available for the category. To insert a clip art image in the document, click the desired clip art, and then click the Insert clip button at the top of the callout side menu that displays. Remove the Insert ClipArt dialog box from the screen by clicking the Close button (contains an X) located in the upper right corner of the dialog box.

Maneuver through categories and clip art at the Insert ClipArt dialog box using buttons on the toolbar that displays at the top of the dialog box. For example, click the Back button to display clip art for the previously selected category. To redisplay all categories, click the All Categories button. (See figure 7.2.)

7.2

Insert ClipArt Dialog Box Buttons

Forward

Back   All Categories

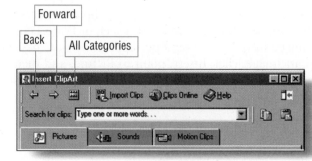

When you click a clip art image, a callout side menu displays containing several buttons as shown in figure 7.3. Click the Insert clip button to insert the image in the document. Click the Preview clip to view how the clip art image will display in the document. If you want to add a clip art image to the Favorites category or to any other category, click the Add clip to Favorites or other category button. This expands the side menu and displays an option for entering the desired category. The side menu will continue to display expanded until you click the button again. Clicking the Find similar clips button on the callout side menu causes the side menu to expand and display with keywords for searching. The side menu will remain expanded until you click the button again.

Insert clip

Preview clip

Add clip to
Favorites or
other category

Clip Art Callout Side Menu Buttons

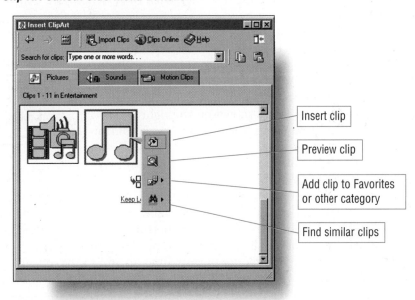

Sizing a Clip Art Image

Once a clip art image is inserted in a document, it can be sized using the white sizing handles that display around a selected clip art image. To change the size of a clip art image, click in the image to select it, and then position the mouse pointer on a sizing handle until the pointer turns into a double-headed arrow. Hold down the left mouse button, drag the sizing handle in or out to decrease or increase the size of the image, and then release the mouse button.

Use the middle sizing handle at the left or right side of the image to make the image wider or thinner. Use the middle sizing handle at the top or bottom of the image to make the image taller or shorter. Use the sizing handle at a corner of the image to change both the width and height at the same time.

Use sizing handles to
change the size
of an image.

Moving and Deleting a Clip Art Image

Move a clip art image by dragging the image. To do this, click once on the image to select it. Position the arrow pointer on the image, hold down the left mouse button, drag the outline of the image to the desired position, and then release the mouse button. To deselect an image, click anywhere in the worksheet outside the picture. Delete a clip art image from a document by clicking the image to select it and then pressing the Delete key.

exercise 1

Inserting and Sizing a Clip Art Image in an Excel Worksheet

1. Open Excel and then open Excel Worksheet 03.
2. Save the document with Save As and name it Excel C7, Ex 01.
3. Make the following changes to the worksheet:
   a. Select the first four rows of the worksheet and then click <u>I</u>nsert and then <u>R</u>ows. (This inserts four new rows at the beginning of the worksheet.)
   b. Double-click in cell A2, key **MYLAN COMPUTERS**, and then press Enter.
   c. Select cells A1 through D12 and then apply the Accounting 1 autoformat.
   d. Select cells B7 through D12 and then click the Percent Style button on the Formatting toolbar.
4. Insert an image in the worksheet by completing the following steps:
   a. Make cell B1 the active cell.
   b. Click <u>I</u>nsert, point to <u>P</u>icture, and then click <u>C</u>lip Art.
   c. At the Insert ClipArt dialog box, click the *Science & Technology* category in the category list box.
   d. Click once on the image shown on the right
   e. At the callout side menu, click the Insert clip button (top button).
   f. Click the Close button (contains an X) that displays in the upper right corner of the dialog box.
   g. Decrease the size of the clip art image by completing the following steps:
      1) Click the image to select it (white sizing handles display around the image).
      2) Position the mouse pointer on the bottom right sizing handle until the pointer turns into a diagonally pointing two-headed arrow.
      3) Hold down the left mouse button, drag up and to the left until the outline of the image fits within cells B1 through D5 and then release the mouse button.
   h. If necessary, move the image so it is centered within cells B1 through D4.
   i. Click outside the image to deselect it.
5. Save the worksheet again with the same name (Excel C7, Ex 01).
6. Print the worksheet horizontally and vertically centered on the page.
7. Close Excel C7, Ex 01 and then exit Excel.

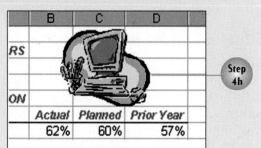

Searching for Clip Art Images

You can search for specific types of clip art images or for a specific image at the Insert ClipArt dialog box. To do this, display the Insert ClipArt dialog box, click in the Search for clips text box, and then key the type of clip art image desired or key the specific name. Press the Enter key and clip art images display that match what you entered.

Formatting Clip Art Images

Format clip art images using a variety of methods. The formatting available depends on the program in which the clip art is inserted. Moving and sizing clip art images is considered formatting. Other formatting available includes adding fill color and border lines, increasing or decreasing the brightness or contrast, choosing a wrapping style, and cropping the image. A variety of methods are available for changing the formatting of a clip art image. In this section, formatting will focus on using the buttons on the Picture toolbar.

Use buttons on the Picture toolbar to format a clip art image in Word, PowerPoint, or Excel.

Formatting Clip Art Images in Excel

Format an image in an Excel worksheet with buttons on the Picture toolbar shown in figure 7.4. To display this toolbar, click a clip art image. (If the toolbar does not display, position the mouse pointer on the image, click the *right* mouse button, and then click Show Picture Toolbar at the shortcut menu.) The buttons on the Picture toolbar are described in figure 7.5.

Excel Picture Toolbar

Excel Picture Toolbar Buttons

Click this button	Named	To do this
Insert Picture icon	Insert Picture	display the Insert Picture dialog box with a list of subfolders containing additional images
Image Control icon	Image Control	display a drop-down list with options for controlling how the image displays. Options include <u>A</u>utomatic, <u>G</u>rayscale, <u>B</u>lack & White, and <u>W</u>atermark
More Contrast icon	More Contrast	increase contrast of the image
Less Contrast icon	Less Contrast	decrease contrast of the image
More Brightness icon	More Brightness	increase brightness of the image

Click this button	Named	To do this
	Less Brightness	decrease brightness of the image
	Crop	crop image so only a specific portion of the image is visible
	Line Style	insert a border around the image and specify the border line style
	Format Picture	display Format Picture dialog box with options for formatting the image: tabs in the dialog box include Colors and Lines, Size, Layout, Picture, and Web
	Set Transparent Color	this button is available only for drawing objects
	Reset Picture	reset picture to its original size, position, and color

exercise 2

Formatting a Clip Art Image in Excel

1. Open Excel Worksheet 13.
2. Save the worksheet with Save As and name it Excel C7, Ex 02.
3. Make the following changes to the worksheet:
   a. Delete column H.
   b. Insert a row at the beginning of the worksheet.
   c. Change the height of the new row to 99.0.
   d. Select cells A1 through G1 and then click the Merge and Center button on the Formatting toolbar.
   e. With cell A1 the active cell, make the following changes:
      1) Display the Format Cells dialog box. (To do this, click Format and then Cells.)
      2) At the Format Cells dialog box, click the Alignment tab.
      3) At the Format Cells dialog box with the Alignment tab selected, change the Horizontal option to *Right* and the Vertical option to *Center* (in the Text alignment section).
      4) Click the Font tab.
      5) At the Format Cells dialog box with the Font tab selected, change the font to 34-point Arial bold.
      6) Click OK to close the dialog box.
   f. Key **Global Transport**.

4. Insert and format a clip art image by completing the following steps:
   a. Click outside cell A1 and then click cell A1 again.
   b. Display the Insert ClipArt dialog box.
   c. At the Insert ClipArt dialog box, click the *Maps* category.
   d. Click the image shown above and then click the Insert clip button. (The location of the image may vary.)

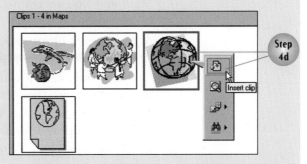

   e. Close the Insert ClipArt dialog box.
   f. Change the size of the image by completing the following steps:
      1) Click the image to select it.
      2) Click the Format Picture button on the Picture toolbar. (If the Picture toolbar is not visible, click View, point to Toolbars, and then click show Picture Toolbar.)
      3) At the Format Picture dialog box, click the Size tab.

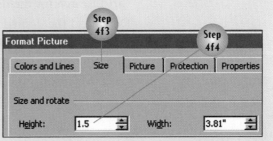

      4) Select the current measurement in the Height text box (in the Size and rotate section) and then key **1.5**.
      5) Click OK to close the dialog box.
   g. Click twice on the More Brightness button on the Picture toolbar.
5. Save the workbook again with the same name (Excel C7, Ex 02).
6. Print the worksheet centered horizontally and vertically on the page.
7. Close Excel C7, Ex 02.

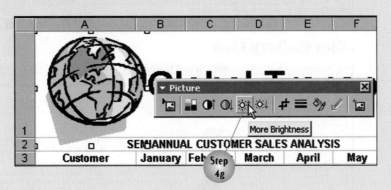

Downloading Clip Art

The Microsoft Web site offers a clip gallery with hundreds of clip art images you can download. To display the Microsoft Clip Gallery, you must have access to the Internet. To download a clip art image, you would complete these basic steps:

1. Make sure you are connected to the Internet and then display the Insert ClipArt dialog box.

2. At the Insert ClipArt dialog box, click the Clips Online button that displays towards the top of the dialog box.

3. At the message telling you to click OK to browse additional clips from a special Web page, click the OK button.

4. At the End-User License Agreement page, read the agreement, and then click the Accept button if you accept the terms of the agreement.

5. At the Microsoft Clip Gallery shown in figure 7.6 (your screen may vary), search for the desired image.

6. Download the desired image by clicking the download button that displays below the image.

7. Close the Insert ClipArt dialog box.

8. Close Microsoft Internet Explorer.

figure 7.6

Microsoft Clip Gallery Live Web Page

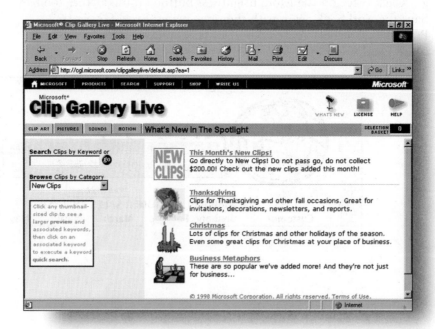

A downloaded clip is usually inserted in the Downloaded Clips category. To insert a downloaded clip art, display the Insert ClipArt dialog box, display the Downloaded Clips category, click the desired image, and then click the Insert clip button.

Deleting Downloaded Clip Art

Delete a clip art image from the Insert ClipArt dialog box by right-clicking the image and then clicking the <u>D</u>elete option from the shortcut menu. At the message telling you to click OK to delete the clip from all Clip Gallery categories, click the OK button.

Downloading a Clip Art Image from the Microsoft Clip Gallery

(*Note: Check with your instructor before completing this exercise to determine if you can download clip art with your system configuration.*)

1. Open Excel Worksheet 07.
2. Save the worksheet with Save As and name it Excel C7, Ex 03.
3. Make the following changes to the worksheet:
   a. Delete column E.
   b. Change the height of the first row to 100.
   c. With cell A1 the active cell, make the following changes
      1) Display the Format Cells dialog box with the Alignment tab selected.
      2) Change the <u>H</u>orizontal alignment to *Right* and the <u>V</u>ertical alignment to *Center*.
      3) Click the Font tab and then change the font style to Bold and the size to 14.
      4) Close the Format Cells dialog box.
4. Download a clip from the Microsoft Clip Gallery by completing the following steps:
   a. Make sure you are connected to the Internet.
   b. Display the Insert ClipArt dialog box.
   c. At the Insert ClipArt dialog box, click the <u>C</u>lips Online button.
   d. At the message telling you to click OK to browse additional clips from a special Web page, click the OK button.
   e. At the End-User License Agreement page, read the agreement, and then click the Accept button if you accept the terms of the agreement.
   f. At the Microsoft Clip Gallery (see figure 7.6), click in the Search text box and then key **Photography**.
   g. Click the go button that displays at the right side of the Search text box.
   h. When the photography clip images display, click the image of the camera. (This displays the image as a miniature in the box below the Browse text box.)
   i. Click the download button that displays immediately below the image (contains a small down-pointing red arrow).

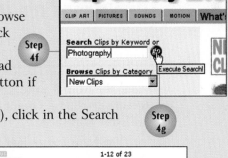

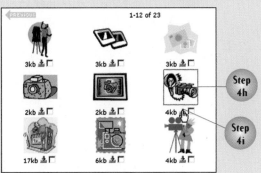

j. At the Insert ClipArt dialog box with the camera image displayed, click the Close button.

k. Click File and then Close to close the Microsoft Internet Explorer.

5. Insert and size the camera image by completing the following steps:
   a. With cell A1 the active cell, display the Insert ClipArt dialog box.
   b. At the Insert ClipArt dialog box, click the *Downloaded Clips* category.
   c. Click the camera image and then click the Insert clip button.
   d. Close the Insert ClipArt dialog box.
   e. Decrease the size of the image so it fits inside cell A1.

6. Save the worksheet again with the same name (Excel C7, Ex 03).

7. Print the worksheet centered horizontally and vertically on the page.

8. Delete the downloaded clip by completing the following steps:
   a. Display the Insert ClipArt dialog box.
   b. At the ClipArt dialog box, click the *Downloaded Clips* category.
   c. Right-click the camera image you downloaded and then click Delete at the shortcut menu.
   d. At the message telling you to click OK to delete the clip from all Clip Gallery categories, click the OK button.
   e. Close the Insert ClipArt dialog box.

9. Close Excel C7, Ex 03.

Step
5e

Displaying Data in a Map

Data in a worksheet can be difficult to analyze and may not have the intended impact. Inserting data in a chart, as you learned in chapter 6, presents data in a form that is more easily analyzed. Visual impact for some data can be achieved by using the Map feature to display data that is geographic in nature. The Map feature displays geographic areas and information for data that is established in an Excel worksheet.

The Map feature will create a map and display data for the following areas: Australia, Canada, Europe, Mexico, North America, UK Standard Regions, US with AK & HI Inset, United States in North America, and World Countries.

Creating a Map

A map can be created using worksheet data such as product sales for specific states or provinces, population data, or international sales figures. Data that you want to insert in a map must be created in columns in an Excel worksheet. Figure 7.7 shows columns of data in an Excel worksheet that have been used to create a map.

You must use geographic regions that the Map feature recognizes.

 **figure 7.7**

Map Created with Data in a Worksheet

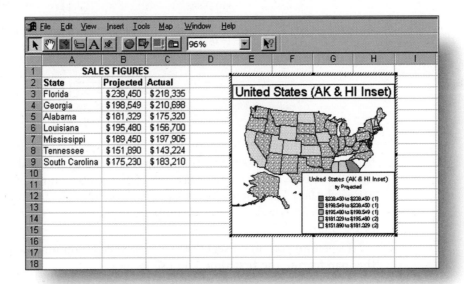

The map shown in figure 7.7 was created with all default settings. This map can be customized in a variety of ways. For example, you can display specific states, add color to the states, and change the column used to obtain data. In exercise 4, you will create the map shown in figure 7.7, and then learn how to customize the map.

Create a map by selecting specific cells in a worksheet and then clicking the Map button on the Standard toolbar. If the Map button does not display on the Standard toolbar, you can add it to the toolbar by completing the following steps:

Map

1. Click Tools and then Customize.

2. At the Customize dialog box, click the Commands tab.

3. At the Customize dialog box with the Commands tab selected, click *Insert* in the Categories list box (see figure 7.8).

4. Scroll down the Commands list box until *Map* displays (see figure 7.8).

5. Position the arrow pointer on *Map*, hold down the left mouse button, drag to the location on the Standard toolbar where you want the Map button inserted, and then release the mouse button.

6. Click the Close button to close the Customize dialog box.

figure
7.8
Customize Dialog Box with Commands Tab Selected

Click Insert in the Categories list box.

Scroll down the Commands list box until Map displays. Position arrow pointer on Map and then drag to desired position on toolbar.

If you do not add the Map button on the Standard toolbar, display the Map feature by clicking Insert and then Object. At the Object dialog box, scroll down the Object type list box until *Microsoft Map* is visible and then double-click *Microsoft Map*. These steps insert the map over the selected cells in the worksheet. If this is the method you use to complete exercises, you may need to modify some of the steps.

Depending on how Excel 2000 was installed, you may be prompted to install the map feature the first time you use it.

exercise
4

Creating a Map with an Excel Worksheet

(Note: If you are using a disk for saving exercise documents, you may want to delete the documents created earlier in this chapter. Check with your instructor before deleting any documents.)

1. Open Excel Worksheet 18.
2. Save the worksheet and name it Excel C7, Ex 04.
3. Create a map with the data in the worksheet by completing the following steps:
   a. Select cells A2 through C9.
   b. Click the Map button on the Standard toolbar. (This causes the arrow pointer to turn into crosshairs.)
   c. Position the crosshairs in the upper left corner of cell E2, hold down the left mouse button, drag the crosshairs to the bottom right corner of cell H15, and then release the mouse button.
   d. At the Multiple Maps Available dialog box, shown in figure 7.9, make sure *United States (AK & HI Inset)* is selected in the list box, and then click OK.

e. At the Microsoft Map Control dialog box, shown in figure 7.10, click the Close button that displays in the upper right corner of the dialog box. (You can also close the dialog box by clicking the Show/Hide Microsoft Map Control button on the Map toolbar.)

f. Deselect the map by clicking in the worksheet area, outside the map.

4. Save the worksheet again with the same name (Excel C7, Ex 04).

5. Print the worksheet (and map) centered horizontally and vertically on the page.

6. Close Excel C7, Ex 04.

Multiple Maps Available Dialog Box

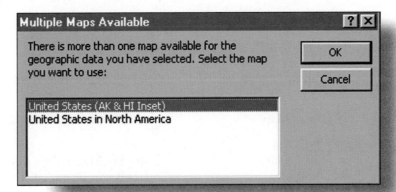

Microsoft Map Control Dialog Box

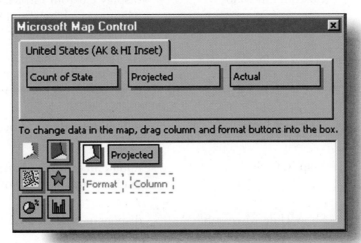

Customizing a Map

A data map can be customized in a variety of ways. Specific states or provinces can be displayed (rather than the entire North American continent), color can be added to specified states or provinces, dots can be used to indicate data, and different columns of data can be reflected in the map.

If changes are made to data in the worksheet used to create a map, click the Map Refresh button.

Changes can be made to the map with options and buttons at the Microsoft Map Control dialog box shown in figure 7.10 or with buttons on the Map toolbar. Figure 7.11 identifies each button on the Map toolbar and the function performed by the button.

Map Toolbar Buttons

Click this button	Named	To do this
	Select Objects	select objects in a data map and then move, size, or delete
	Grabber	move map within frame
	Center Map	specify the center of the map
	Map Labels	display Map Labels dialog box where labels can be added to features
	Add Text	add text to map
	Custom Pin Map	display Custom Pin Map dialog box where special "push-pins" can be added to mark specific locations
	Display Entire	zoom out and display map and all map features centered in the frame
	Redraw Map	redraw map that has been stretched
	Map Refresh	update map when changes have been made to data in the worksheet
	Show/Hide Microsoft Map Control	display or hide Microsoft Map Control dialog box
96%	Zoom Percentage of Map	zoom in on or zoom out of a specific area in a map

Zooming In on Specific States

Zoom in on a specific area in a map using the Zoom Percentage of Map button on the Map toolbar along with the Grabber button. To do this, click the down-pointing triangle at the right side of the Zoom Percentage of Map button. At the drop-down menu that displays, click a higher percentage number to zoom in on the map. Finding the right percentage may take some time. You can also change the percentage of zoom by selecting the current percentage in the Zoom Percentage of Map button and then keying the desired percentage. After changing the zoom percentage, click the Grabber button on the Map toolbar. Position the arrow pointer (displays as a hand) in the map, hold down the left mouse button, drag the map until the desired location displays, and then release the mouse button.

96%

Zoom
Percentage of
Map

Adding Labels

Labels can help the reader better understand the data displayed on the map. Click the Map Labels button on the Map toolbar and the Map Labels dialog box displays like the one shown in figure 7.12. At this dialog box, you can choose to label features based on the map displayed. For example, if the United States map displays, position the mouse pointer on a location on the map and a label displays. If you position the mouse pointer on a state, the state name displays. If you want the label to remain, click the left mouse button. You can also label values in the map by choosing the Values from option at the bottom of the dialog box. In exercise 5, you will add value labels to states showing the projected sales.

Grabber

Map Labels

Add labels to a map to help the reader better understand the data.

Map Labels Dialog Box

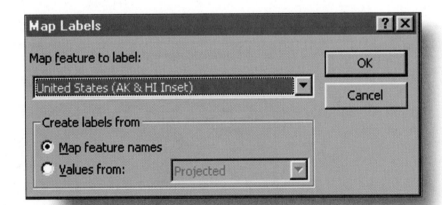

Zooming In on Specific States in a Map and Adding Value Labels

1. Open Excel C7, Ex 04.
2. Save the worksheet and name it Excel C7, Ex 05.
3. Zoom in on the specific states in the worksheet by completing the following steps:
   a. Double-click the map. (This displays the Map toolbar.)
   b. Click the Map Refresh button on the Map toolbar.
   c. Click the down-pointing triangle at the right side of the Zoom Percentage of Map button and then click *250%* at the drop-down menu. (This changes the size of the map to 250% of the original size.)
   d. Click the Grabber button on the Map toolbar.
   e. Position the mouse pointer (hand) on the map, hold down the left mouse button, drag the map to display the states in white and shades of gray as shown in figure 7.13, and then release the mouse button.
4. Add value labels to the states by completing the following steps:
   a. Click the Map Labels button on the Map toolbar.
   b. At the Map Labels dialog box, click in the white circle preceding <u>V</u>alues from (located toward the bottom of the dialog box).
   c. Click OK to close the dialog box.
   d. Click once on each state. (This will add the value.)
   e. Click the Select Objects button on the Map toolbar. (This returns the mouse pointer to an arrow pointer.)
   f. If you are not satisfied with the location of a value, click once on the value to select it, and then drag the value to the desired location.
5. Click outside the map to deselect it.
6. Save the worksheet again with the same name (Excel C7, Ex 05).
7. Print the worksheet (and map) centered horizontally and vertically on the page.
8. Close Excel C7, Ex 05.

figure
7.13

Exercise 5, Map of Specific States with Values Added

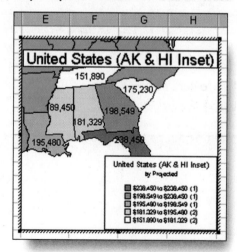

Remove a value label from a map by right-clicking the value and then clicking Clear at the pop-up menu that displays. If you want to format the value, right-click the value and then click Format Font. This displays the Font dialog box where you can change the font for the label.

Customizing a Legend and Title

By default, a legend is included in a data map. In figure 7.7, this default legend contains shaded boxes followed by the amounts of projected sales. A legend can be compacted displaying less information. To do this, right-click the legend, and then click Compact at the pop-up menu. This displays only two shaded boxes followed by *Projected*. You can also compact a legend at the Format Properties dialog box with the Legend Options tab selected as shown in figure 7.14. To display this dialog box, double-click the legend. To display the legend in compact form, insert a check mark in the Use Compact Format check box.

Format Properties Dialog Box with Legend Options Tab Selected

If a legend has been compacted and you would like to return it to its expanded form, display the Format Properties dialog box with the Legend Options tab selected and then remove the check mark from the Use Compact Format option. Removing the check mark makes the Title and Subtitle options available. Accept the title and subtitle provided or key your own. You can also right-click the legend and then click Compact. This removes the check mark preceding Compact and returns the legend to its expanded format.

If you do not want the legend to display in the map, right-click the legend, and then click Hide. You can also display the Format Properties dialog box with the Legend Options tab selected and then remove the check mark from the Show Legend option that displays at the bottom left corner of the dialog box.

The map shown in figure 7.7 displays with the title *United States (AK & HI Inset)*. This title may not accurately reflect the data in the table. You can change text in the title by double-clicking the title, deleting the existing text, and then keying the desired text. Format the text in the title by right-clicking the title and then clicking <u>F</u>ormat Font at the pop-up menu. This displays the Font dialog box where a different font can be chosen. If you do not want a title in the map, right-click the title, and then click <u>H</u>ide at the pop-up menu.

The legend and/or title can be moved within the map. To do this, click once in the title or legend and then use the mouse to drag the title or legend to the desired location.

exercise 6

Customizing the Legend and Changing the Title in a Map

1. Open Excel C7, Ex 05.
2. Save the worksheet and name it Excel C7, Ex 06.
3. Customize the legend so it appears as shown in figure 7.15 by completing the following steps:
   a. Double-click the map. (This displays the Map toolbar.)
   b. Click the Map Refresh button on the Map toolbar.
   c. Double-click the legend. (This displays the Format Properties dialog box with the Legend Options tab selected.)
   d. Make sure the text *United States (AK & HI Inset)* is selected in the Title text box and then press the Delete key. (This deletes the title.)
   e. Key **Projected Sales** in the Title text box.
   f. Select and then delete *by Projected* that displays in the Subtitle text box. (Do not key a subtitle.)
   g. Click OK.
4. Remove the title by right-clicking the title *United States (AK & HI Inset)* and then clicking <u>H</u>ide at the pop-up menu.
5. Move the legend down to the lower right corner as shown in figure 7.15. To do this, click once on the legend to select it, and then drag the legend to the desired location.
6. Click the Grabber tool and then move the map of the states up so more of Florida displays as shown in figure 7.15.
7. Click outside the map to deselect it.
8. Save the worksheet again with the same name (Excel C7, Ex 06).
9. Print the worksheet (and map) horizontally and vertically centered on the page.
10. Close Excel C7, Ex 06.

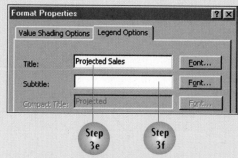

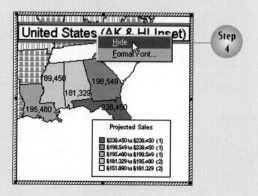

7.15

Exercise 6, Map with Title Removed and Legend Customized

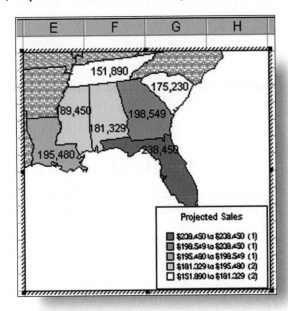

The legend in Excel C7, Ex 06 identifies the shading used for the states and the value range within the shade. The legend will display five different shades. There are, however, seven states specified in the map. The same color shading is used more than once for two states, Alabama and Mississippi, and also for two other states, South Carolina and Tennessee.

Customizing a Map at the Map Control Dialog Box

The map shown in figure 7.7 used the values in the *Projected* column to create the shading for the states and the legend. Other columns of data can be used for the map with options at the Microsoft Map Control dialog box, shown in figure 7.10. For an existing map, display this dialog box by clicking the Show/Hide Microsoft Map Control button on the Map toolbar.

Column buttons display at the top of the Microsoft Map Control dialog box. These column buttons vary depending on the worksheet. In the Microsoft Map Control dialog box shown in figure 7.10, the column buttons display with Count of State, Projected, and Actual. The Map feature used the column headings in the worksheet for the column buttons. Notice that the Projected column button also displays below in the white box in the dialog box. The Projected button displays because this column of data was used in the map. If you want the map to display data from a different column, drag that column button down into the white box on top of the original column. When you release the mouse button, the data automatically changes in the map and the legend title changes.

Show/Hide
Microsoft Map
Control

Formatting buttons display along the left side of the dialog box. The name and purpose of these buttons is described in figure 7.16.

figure 7.16

Microsoft Map Control Formatting Buttons

This button	Named	Produces this effect
	Value Shading	shades map features according to numeric values
	Category Shading	colors map features according to category
	Dot Density	displays numeric data as a quantity of dots
	Graduated Symbol	displays numeric data as various sizes of symbols
	Pie Chart	displays data for specific area in a pie chart
	Column Chart	displays data for specific area in a column chart

Category
Shading

Use the formatting buttons to customize the formatting of the map. By default, the states in the map shown in figure 7.7 display in shades from white to dark gray. Choose the Category Shading button to display the states in varying colors. To do this, you would drag the Category Shading button into the white box where the Projected button displays. When you position the arrow pointer on a formatting button, the pointer turns into a hand holding a handle. As you drag the button into the white box, the pointer turns into a hand holding a handle connected to a drawer.

exercise 7

Changing Column Data and Shading in a Map

1. Open Excel C7, Ex 06.
2. Save the worksheet and name it Excel C7, Ex 07.
3. Change the data in the map from the *Projected* column to the *Actual* column and change the shading to Category Shading as shown in figure 7.17 by completing the following steps:
   a. Double-click the map. (This displays the Map toolbar.)
   b. Click the Map Refresh button on the Map toolbar.
   c. Click the Show/Hide Microsoft Map Control button on the Map toolbar.

d. At the Microsoft Map Control dialog box, position the arrow pointer on the Actual button that displays at the top of the dialog box, hold down the left mouse button, drag the button so it is positioned on top of the Projected button in the white area of the dialog box, and then release the mouse button.

e. Position the arrow pointer on the Category Shading button that displays at the left side of the dialog box, hold down the left mouse button, drag the button so it is positioned on top of the Value Shading button in the white area of the dialog box, and then release the mouse button.

f. Click the Close button to close the Microsoft Map Control dialog box.

4. Edit the legend by completing the following steps:
   a. Double-click the legend. (This displays the Format Properties dialog box with the Legend Options tab selected.)
   b. At the Format Properties dialog box with the Legend Options tab selected, change the title to **Actual Sales**.
   c. Click OK to close the dialog box.

5. Remove the value labels from the states. To do this, position the arrow pointer on a value, click the right mouse button, and then click the left mouse button on the Clear option that displays in the pop-up menu. (Do this for each value.)

6. If necessary, move the legend so it appears as shown in figure 7.17. (To do this, click the legend once to select it and then drag the outline of the legend to the desired location.)

7. Click outside the map to deselect it.

8. Save the worksheet again with the same name (Excel C7, Ex 07).

9. Print the worksheet (and map) centered horizontally and vertically on the page.

10. Close Excel C7, Ex 07.

figure 7.17

Exercise 7, Map Displaying Data for Actual Column

A map can display data from more than one column. For example, in exercise 8 you will create a map that displays data for the number of households owning a computer and that also displays data for the number of households that are connected to an on-line service. To display data for more than one column, drag the column button from the top of the Microsoft Map Control dialog box to just below the first row in the white box. The data in the second row will display as a series of density dots. This display can be changed to symbols of varying sizes.

exercise 8

Creating a Map Displaying Data from Two Columns

1. Open Excel Worksheet 19.
2. Save the worksheet with Save As and name it Excel C7, Ex 08.
3. Create the map shown in figure 7.18 by completing the following steps:
   a. Select cells A4 through C7.
   b. Click the Map button on the Standard toolbar. (This causes the arrow pointer to turn into crosshairs.)
   c. Position the crosshairs in the upper left corner of cell E2, hold down the left mouse button, drag the crosshairs to the bottom right corner of cell H15, and then release the mouse button.
   d. At the Multiple Maps Available dialog box, make sure *United States (AK & HI Inset)* is selected in the list box, and then click OK.
   e. At the Microsoft Map Control dialog box, make the following changes:

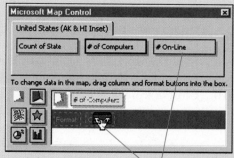

   1) Position the arrow pointer (turns into a hand holding a handle) on the # On-Line button located at the top of the dialog box, drag the button to the second row in the white box where the word *Column* displays surrounded by a dashed line border, and then release the mouse button.
   2) Position the arrow pointer (turns into a hand holding a handle) on the Category Shading button at the left side of the dialog box, hold down the left mouse button, drag the button to the Value Shading button located in the first row of the white box, and then release the mouse button.

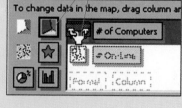

   3) Click the Close button located in the upper right corner of the Data Map Control dialog box. (If this button is not visible, drag the dialog box to the left until it is visible.)
   f. Edit the legend pertaining to dots by completing the following steps:
   1) Double-click the legend containing the title *United States (AK & HI Inset)* and the subtitle *by # On-Line* (along with information on 1 dot equalling 2,000).

2) At the Format Properties dialog box with the Legend Options tab selected, key **On-Line Users** in the Title text box. (The current title should already be selected when the dialog box is displayed.)

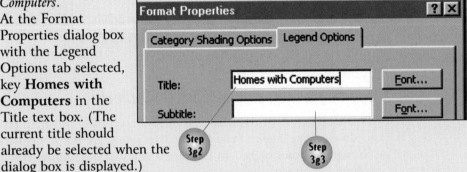

3) Select and then delete the text that displays in the Subtitle text box.
4) Click OK to close the Format Properties dialog box.

g. Edit and then move the legend that displays the number of computers by completing the following steps:
1) Double-click the legend containing the title *United States (AK & HI Inset)* and the subtitle *by # of Computers*.
2) At the Format Properties dialog box with the Legend Options tab selected, key **Homes with Computers** in the Title text box. (The current title should already be selected when the dialog box is displayed.)
3) Select and then delete the text that displays in the Subtitle text box.
4) Click OK to close the Format Properties dialog box.
5) With the legend selected (a thick gray border surrounds the legend), drag the legend to the bottom left corner of the map as shown in figure 7.18.

h. Click the legend containing the title *On-Line Users* and then drag the legend to the bottom right corner of the map as shown in figure 7.18.

i. Hide the title in the map. (To do this, right-click the title, and then click <u>H</u>ide at the pop-up menu.)

j. Zoom in on the three states displaying data in the map (Washington, Oregon, and Idaho). To do this, complete the following steps:
1) Click the down-pointing triangle at the right side of the Zoom Percentage of Map button on the Map toolbar and then click *400%* at the drop-down list.
2) Click the Grabber button on the Map toolbar.
3) Position the mouse pointer (hand) in the map and then drag the map until the three states display as shown in figure 7.18.

k. Click outside the map to deselect it.

4. Save the worksheet again with the same name (Excel C7, Ex 08).
5. Print the worksheet (and map) centered horizontally and vertically on the page.
6. Close Excel C7, Ex 08.

figure
7.18

Exercise 8, Map Displaying Data from Two Columns

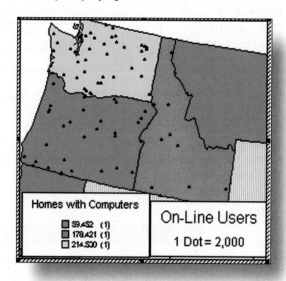

Copying a Map into a Word Document

A map created with the Map feature can be copied and then pasted in a Word document. The steps to copy and paste a map are the same as copying and pasting any other object. In exercise 9 you will be copying and pasting a map into a Word document.

exercise 9

Copying and Pasting a Map into a Word Document

1. Open Word.
2. With Word the active program, open Word Memo 01.
3. Save the memo with Save As and name it Word C7, Ex 09.
4. With Word C7, Ex 09 open, change to the Print Layout view and then change the Zoom to *Whole Page*.
5. Make Excel the active program and then open Excel C7, Ex 08.
6. Save the worksheet with Save As and name it Excel C7, Ex 09.
7. Copy and paste the map into the Word memo by completing the following steps:
   a. Click once on the map to select it.
   b. Click the Copy button on the Standard toolbar.
   c. Make Word the active program.
   d. Click the Paste button on the Standard toolbar.

8. Drag the map so it is positioned between the first and second paragraphs in the body of the memo.
9. Click outside the map to deselect it.
10. Change the Zoom back to *100%*.
11. Save the document again with the same name (Word C7, Ex 09).
12. Print and then close Word C7, Ex 09.
13. Exit Word.
14. Close Excel C7, Ex 09 saving the changes and then exit Excel.

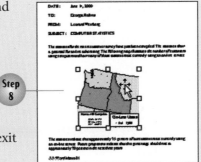

Drawing Lines and Objects

With buttons on the Drawing toolbar, you can draw a variety of shapes such as circles, squares, rectangles, and ovals, as well as straight lines, free form lines, lines with arrowheads, and much more. Draw lines or text boxes to add emphasis or insert explanatory notes to a value in a worksheet.

To display the Drawing toolbar, shown in figure 7.19, click the Drawing button on the Standard toolbar; or, position the mouse pointer on the Standard or Formatting toolbar, click the *right* mouse button, and then click *Drawing* at the drop-down list. A description of each button is provided in figure 7.20.

figure 7.19   *Drawing Toolbar*

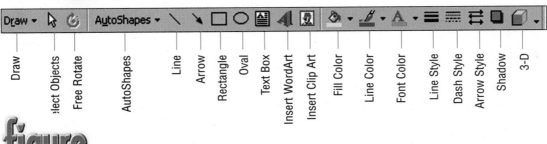

Draw | Select Objects | Free Rotate | AutoShapes | Line | Arrow | Rectangle | Oval | Text Box | Insert WordArt | Insert Clip Art | Fill Color | Line Color | Font Color | Line Style | Dash Style | Arrow Style | Shadow | 3-D

figure 7.20   *Drawing Toolbar*

Click this button	Named	To do this
Draw ▾	Draw	Display a pop-up menu with options for grouping and positioning drawings.
▸	Select Objects	Select text or objects.
⟳	Free Rotate	Rotate selected object to any degree by dragging a corner of the object in the desired direction.

AutoShapes	AutoShapes	Display a palette of shapes that can be drawn in a document. (To draw a shape circumscribed within a perfect square, hold down the Shift key while drawing the shape.)
	Line	Draw a line in a document.
	Arrow	Insert a line with an arrowhead. (To draw at 15-degree angles, hold down the Shift key.)
	Rectangle	Draw a rectangle in a document. (To draw a perfect square, hold down the Shift key while drawing the shape.)
	Oval	Draw an oval in a document. (To draw a perfect circle, hold down the Shift key while drawing the shape.)
	Text Box	Create text in a text box. (To add text that does not wrap, click the button, click in the document, then key the text. To add text that does wrap, click the button, drag to create a box, then key the text.)
	Insert WordArt	Insert a Microsoft Office drawing object.
	Insert Clip Art	Display the Insert ClipArt dialog box.
	Fill Color	Fill selected object with a color, pattern, texture, or shaded fill.
	Line Color	Change color of selected line.
	Font Color	Format selected text with a color.
	Line Style	Change thickness of selected line or change it to a compound line.
	Dash Style	Change style of selected line, arc, or border to dashed.
	Arrow Style	Add arrowheads to a selected line, arc, or open free-form.
	Shadow	Add or remove an object shadow.
	3-D	Add or remove a 3-D effect.

With some of the buttons on the Drawing toolbar, you can draw a shape. If you draw a shape with the Line button or the Arrow button, the shape you draw is considered a *line drawing*. If you draw a shape with the Rectangle or Oval button, the shape you draw is considered an *enclosed object*.

If you want to draw the same shape more than once, double-click the shape button on the Drawing toolbar. After drawing the shapes, click the button again to deactivate it.

Use the Rectangle button on the Drawing toolbar to draw a square or rectangle in a worksheet. If you want to draw a square, hold down the Shift key while drawing the shape. The Shift key keeps all sides of the drawn object equal. Use the Oval button to draw a circle or an oval object. To draw a circle, hold down the Shift key while drawing the object.

exercise 10

Drawing an Arrow and Text Box in a Worksheet

1. Open Excel Worksheet 18.
2. Save the worksheet with Save As and name it Excel C7, Ex 10.
3. Draw an arrow and text box to emphasize the Actual sales for Georgia by completing the following steps:

   Step 3b

   a. Click the Arrow button on the Drawing toolbar.
   b. Position the cross hairs pointer in the middle of cell D4 at the right column boundary line, hold down the Shift key, then drag the crosshairs to the left of the cell as shown and then release the left mouse button and Shift.

	A	B	C	D
1	SALES FIGURES			
2	State	Projected	Actual	
3	Florida	$238,450	$218,335	
4	Georgia	$198,549	$210,698	□◄———□
5	Alabama	$181,329	$175,320	
6	Louisiana	$195,480	$156,700	

   c. Click the Text Box tool on the Drawing toolbar.
   d. Position the pointer at the top left corner of cell E4, hold down the left mouse button, drag the pointer to the bottom right corner of cell F5, then release the left mouse button.
   e. Click the Center button on the Formatting toolbar.
   f. Key 6% over Projected!
   g. Click outside the text box to deselect it.
4. Decrease the height of the text box by completing the following steps:

   Step 4b

   a. Click the text box to display the white sizing handles.
   b. Position the pointer on the middle bottom sizing handle then drag the handle up to decrease the height as shown.

	A	B	C	D	E	F
1	SALES FIGURES					
2	State	Projected	Actual			
3	Florida	$238,450	$218,335			
4	Georgia	$198,549	$210,698	◄———	6% over Projected!	
5	Alabama	$181,329	$175,320			
6	Louisiana	$195,480	$156,700			

5. Save the revised worksheet with the same name (Excel C7, Ex 10).
6. Print and then close Excel C7, Ex 10.

Changing Objects

Shapes drawn using tools on the Drawing toolbar are referred to as objects. An object can be customized in a variety of ways. For example, an object can be selected and then moved, copied, or deleted; or the size of the object can be changed.

Selecting an Object

After an object has been created in a document, you may decide to make changes or delete the object. To do this, the object must be selected. To select an enclosed object, position the mouse pointer anywhere inside the object (the mouse pointer displays with a four-headed arrow attached) and then click the left mouse button. To select a line, position the mouse pointer on the line until the pointer turns into an arrow with a four-headed arrow attached, and then click the left mouse button. When an object is selected, it displays surrounded by white sizing handles. Once an object is selected, it can be edited, such as changing the fill and the line, it can be moved, or it can be deleted.

If a document screen contains more than one object, you can select several objects at once using the Select Objects button on the Drawing toolbar. To do this, click the Select Objects button, position the crosshairs in the upper left corner of the area containing the objects, hold down the left mouse button, drag the outline to the lower right corner of the area containing the objects, and then release the mouse button. You can also select more than one object by holding down the Shift key as you click each object.

Each object in the selected area displays surrounded by white sizing handles. Objects in the selected area are connected. For example, if you move one of the objects in the selected area, the other objects move relatively.

Deleting an Object

An object you have drawn can be deleted from the document screen. To do this, select the object, and then press the Delete key.

Moving an Object

An object can be moved to a different location in this document. To do this with an enclosed object, position the mouse pointer inside the object (mouse pointer displays with a four-headed arrow attached), hold down the left mouse button, drag the outline of the object to the new location, and then release the mouse button. If you selected more than one object, moving one of the objects will also move the other objects. To move a line, select the line, and then position the mouse pointer on the line until it turns into an arrow with a four-headed arrow attached. Hold down the left mouse button, drag the outline of the line to the desired location, and then release the mouse button.

You can move a selected object with the keyboard by pressing one of the arrow keys. For example, to move an object down the screen, select the object, and then press the down arrow key.

Copying an Object

Moving an object removes the object from its original position and inserts it into a new location. If you want the object to stay in its original location and an exact copy to be inserted in a new location, use the Ctrl key while dragging the object.

chapter summary

➤ Clip art images are available from the Insert ClipArt dialog box. The steps to insert a clip art image into any of the Office applications are basically the same.

➤ Display the Insert ClipArt dialog box by clicking Insert, pointing to Picture, and then clicking Clip Art or clicking the Insert ClipArt button on the Drawing toolbar. Display the Microsoft Clip Gallery (which contains the same images as the Insert ClipArt dialog box) by clicking Insert and then Object. At the Object dialog box with the Create New tab selected, double-click *Microsoft Clip Gallery* in the list box.

➤ To insert a clip art image in a worksheet, click the desired image in the Insert ClipArt dialog box, and then click the Insert clip button that displays at the callout side menu.

➤ A clip art image inserted in a document can be moved by selecting and then dragging the image.

➤ Size a clip art image using the sizing handles that display around the image when the image is selected.

➤ Use buttons on the Picture toolbar to customize a clip art image.

➤ The Microsoft Web site offers a clip gallery with hundreds of clip art images you can download. To display the Microsoft Clip Gallery, make sure you are connected to the Internet, and then click the Clips Online button that displays towards the top of the Insert ClipArt dialog box.

➤ Use the Map feature to display data that is geographic in nature.

➤ The Map feature will create maps for Australia, Canada, Europe, Mexico, North America, UK Standard Regions, US with AK & HI Inset, United States in North America, and World Countries.

➤ Use the Map feature on geographic data in an Excel worksheet. Data must be created in columns to create a map.

➤ To create a map, select the cells containing the data, click the Map button on the Excel Standard toolbar, and then draw a border in which the map will be inserted.

➤ Customize a map with buttons on the Map toolbar. With these buttons, you can move the map using the Grabber tool, add map labels, add text, display the entire map, redraw the map, refresh the map, display the Microsoft Map Control dialog box, or zoom in on or zoom out of a specific area of a map.

➤ Customize a title or legend in a map by right-clicking the object and then clicking the desired option.

➤ A map can also be customized with options at the Microsoft Map Control dialog box. With options at this dialog box, you can change the shading option, display numeric data as a quantity of dots or as various sizes of symbols, or display data in a pie chart or column chart.

➤ A map, like any other object, can be copied and then pasted into another Office application.

➤ Use buttons from the Drawing toolbar to draw objects on a worksheet.

commands review

	Mouse/Keyboard
Display Insert ClipArt dialog box	Click Insert, point to Picture, then click Clip Art
Display Microsoft Clip Gallery	Click Insert, Object, then double-click *Microsoft Clip Gallery*
Display the on-line Microsoft Clip Gallery	Click the Clips Online button in the Insert ClipArt dialog box
Create a map in Excel	Select cells, click Map button on Standard toolbar, draw frame
Display Map Labels dialog box	Click the Map Labels button on the Map toolbar
Display Format Properties dialog with Legend Options tab selected	Double-click legend; or right-click legend, then click Edit
Display Drawing toolbar	Right-click Standard or Formatting toolbar, then click Drawing

thinking offline

Completion: In the space provided at the right, indicate the correct term, symbol, or command.

1. Click Insert, point to this, and then click Clip Art to display the Insert ClipArt dialog box.

2. Click this button on the Picture toolbar to decrease the brightness of the image.

3. Click this button at the Insert ClipArt dialog box to display the on-line Microsoft Clip Gallery.

4. Click this button on the picture toolbar to display a dialog box with options to format the image.

5. A map can be created with data in this program.

6. Click this button on the Map toolbar to move the map within the frame.

7. Click this button on the Map toolbar to display a dialog box where you can add labels to map features.

8. Drag this button in the Map Control dialog box to the desired row in the white area to color the map features according to category.

       _____

9. Double-clicking a legend in a map will cause this dialog box to display.

       _____

10. Click this button on the Drawing toolbar to draw a rectangular shape in the worksheet that you can key text into.

       _____

11. Look at the data in the columns below. Suppose this data were established in an Excel worksheet. List below the basic steps you would complete to create a map with the data.

State	# Franchises
Alaska	14
Washington	21
Oregon	19
Idaho	10

_____

_____

_____

_____

working hands-on

Assessment 1

1. Open Excel Worksheet 05.
2. Save the document with Save As and name it Excel C7, SA 01.
3. Make the changes to the worksheet as shown in figure 7.21 by completing the following steps:
   a. Insert two rows at the beginning of the worksheet.
   b. Turn on bold and then key **LIGHTHOUSE FINANCING** in cell A1.
   c. Center the text *LIGHTHOUSE FINANCING* across columns A, B, and C.
   d. Make cell D1 the active cell.
   e. Insert the clip art image shown in figure 7.21. (At the Insert ClipArt dialog box, key **lighthouse** in the Search for clips text box.)
   f. Change the size of the image so the bottom of the image is aligned with the bottom of row 10 and the right side of the image is aligned with the right side of column E.
   g. Deselect the image.

4. Save the worksheet again with the same name (Excel C7, SA 01).
5. Print the worksheet centered horizontally and vertically on the page.
6. Close Excel C7, SA 01 and then exit Excel.

figure
7.21

Assessment 1

	A	B	C	D	E	F
1	LIGHTHOUSE FINANCING					
2						
3		January				
4	**Name**	**Hours**	**Rate**			
5	Carolyn Bentley	35	$23.15			
6	Lindon Cassini	20	$19.00			
7	Michelle DeFord	40	$18.75			
8	Javier Farias	24	$16.45			
9	Deborah Gould	15	$11.50			
10	William Jarman	15	$11.50			
11						

Assessment 2

1. Open Excel Worksheet 20.
2. Save the worksheet with Save As and name it Excel C7, SA 02.
3. Create a map like the one shown in figure 7.22 with the data in the worksheet, using these specifications:
   a. Create a map of the United States.
   b. Zoom in on the states specified in the worksheet (as shown in figure 7.22).
   c. Edit the legend so the title displays as *# of Customers* and the subtitle is deleted.
   d. Move the legend, if necessary, so it is positioned in the same location as shown in figure 7.22.
   e. Hide the title.
4. Save the worksheet again with the same name (Excel C7, SA 02).
5. Print the worksheet (and map) centered horizontally and vertically on the page.
6. Close Excel C7, SA 02.

figure
7.22

Assessment 2

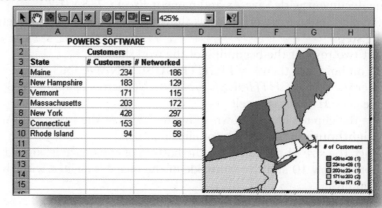

Assessment 3

1. Open Excel C7, SA 02.
2. Save the worksheet with Save As and name it Excel C7, SA 03.
3. Make the following changes to the map:
   a. Display the Map toolbar.
   b. Refresh the map.
   c. Display the Microsoft Map Control dialog box and then change the data column from *# Customers* to *# Networked*.
   d. At the Microsoft Map Control dialog box, change the shading button in the white area from *Value Shading* to *Category Shading*.
   e. Change the title of the legend to *# Networked*.
   f. If necessary, move the legend to the bottom right corner.
4. Save the worksheet again with the same name (Excel C7, SA 03).
5. Print the worksheet (and map) horizontally and vertically centered on the page.
6. Close Excel C7, SA 03.

Assessment 4

1. Open excel Worksheet 20.
2. Draw an arrow pointing to the value 172 in cell C7 that is approximately the width of one column.
3. Draw a text box that connects to the arrow and key the text **85% of customers are networked!**
4. If necessary, adjust the height and/or width of the text box to improve the display.
5. Save the revised worksheet with the same name (Excel C7, SA 04).
6. Print and then close Excel C7, SA 04.

Assessment 5

1. Objects drawn with the Drawing toolbar can be customized with buttons on the Drawing toolbar. Use Excel's Help feature to find information on how to change the color of drawn objects and how to change the font and color of text in drawn objects.
2. Using the information you found in Help, open Excel C7, SA 04.
3. Save the worksheet with Save As and name it Excel C7, SA 05.
4. Change the font and color of the text inside the text box.
5. Change the background color inside the text box.
6. Save the revised worksheet with the same name (Excel C7, SA 05).
7. Print and then close Excel C7, SA 05.

Performance Assessments

Excel CPA

EXCEL

ASSESSING CORE PROFICIENCIES

In this book, you have learned to create, save, print, edit, and format Excel worksheets. You have also learned how to perform file management tasks, save workbooks as Web pages with hyperlinks, and work with multiple windows; move, copy, and paste data between programs; insert a clip art image in a Word document or Excel worksheet; download a clip art image from the on-line Microsoft Clip Gallery; and create a map with data in an Excel worksheet.

(Note: Before completing computer exercises, delete the Chapter 07C *folder on your disk. Next, copy the* Excel CPA *folder from the CD that accompanies this textbook to your disk. Instructions for copying and deleting a folder are printed on the inside of the back cover of this textbook.)*

Assessment 1

1. Create the Excel worksheet shown in figure C1.1. Format the cells as you see them in the figure. (Include a formula in cell D3 that subtracts the Quota sales from the Actual sales. Copy the formula down to D9.)
2. Save the completed worksheet and name it Excel CPA 01.
3. Print the worksheet with gridlines and centered horizontally and vertically on the page.
4. Close Excel CPA 01.

	A	B	C	D	E
1	SALES QUOTA REPORT				
2	Salesperson	Quota	Actual	Over/(Under)	
3	Chavis	$ 55,000	$ 63,450		
4	Hampton	$ 85,000	$ 74,000		
5	Martindale	$ 48,000	$ 51,250		
6	Enriquez	$ 93,000	$ 86,300		
7	Gorham	$ 45,000	$ 42,350		
8	Kline	$ 75,000	$ 78,560		
9	McGuinness	$ 65,000	$ 71,450		

Figure C1.1 • Assessment 1

Assessment 2

1. Open Excel CPA 01.
2. Save the worksheet with Save As and name it Excel CPA 02.
3. Make the following changes to the worksheet:
   a. Add a row above row 7.
   b. Key the following data in the specified cells:

A7	=	**Dillinger**
B7	=	**95,000**
C7	=	**89,650**

   c. Make cell E2 the active cell and then key **% of Quota**.
   d. Insert a formula in cell E3 that divides the actual amount by the quota. Copy this formula down to the other cells. (The result will be a decimal point. Select the decimal numbers that are a result of the formula and then click the Percent Style button on the Formatting toolbar.)
   e. Select cells A1 through E10 and then apply an autoformat of your choosing.
4. Save the worksheet again with the same name (Excel CPA 02).
5. Print and then close Excel CPA 02.

Assessment 3

1. Open Excel CPA 02.
2. Save the worksheet with Save As and name it Excel CPA 03.
3. Sort the names of the salespersons alphabetically in ascending order.
4. Save the worksheet again with the same name (Excel CPA 03).
5. Print Excel CPA 03, centered horizontally and vertically on the page.
6. Sort the quota amounts in column B in descending order.
7. Save the worksheet again with the same name (Excel CPA 03).
8. Print Excel CPA 03, centered horizontally and vertically on the page.
9. Close Excel CPA 03.

Assessment 4

1. Open Excel Worksheet 06.
2. Save the worksheet with Save As and name it Excel CPA 04.
3. Make the following changes to the worksheet:
   a. Delete row 2.
   b. Insert a formula to average test scores for each student.
   c. Sort the data in the worksheet by the average test scores in *ascending* order.
   d. Select all cells in the worksheet and then change the font to 11-point Tahoma (or a similar sans serif typeface).
   e. Automatically adjust the widths of columns A through N.
   f. Add shading (you determine the color) to the first row.

g. Create the header *Student Test Scores* that prints at the top center on both pages.

h. Create a footer that prints *Page x* (where *x* represents the correct page number) at the bottom center on both pages.

4. Save the worksheet again with the same name (Excel CPA 04).

5. Print the worksheet so the column titles (names) print on both pages.

6. Close Excel CPA 04.

Assessment 5

1. Open Excel Worksheet 17.

2. Save the worksheet with Save As and name it Excel CPA 05.

3. Complete the following steps:

   a. Select cells A1 through C11 and then copy the cells to *Sheet2*.

   b. With *Sheet2* displayed, make the following changes:

      1) Automatically adjust the width of columns A, B, and C.
      2) Delete the contents of cell B2.
      3) Change the contents of the following cells:
         A6: Change *January* to *July*
         A7: Change *February* to *August*
         A8: Change *March* to *September*
         A9: Change *April* to *October*
         A10: Change *May* to *November*
         A11: Change *June* to *December*
         B6: Change *8.30%* to *8.10%*
         B8: Change *9.30%* to *8.70%*

   c. Make *Sheet1* active and then copy cell B2 and paste link it to cell B2 in *Sheet2*.

   d. Make *Sheet1* active and then determine the effect on projected monthly earnings if the projected yearly income is increased by 10%.

4. Save the workbook (two worksheets) again with the same name (Excel CPA 05).

5. Print both worksheets of the workbook so they are centered horizontally and vertically on each page.

6. Determine the effect on projected monthly earnings if the projected yearly income is increased by 20%.

7. Save the workbook again with the same name (Excel CPA 05).

8. Print both worksheets of the workbook so they are centered horizontally and vertically on each page.

9. Close Excel CPA 05.

Assessment 6

1. Open Excel Worksheet 36.

2. Save the worksheet with Save As and name it Excel CPA 06.

3. Using the DATE function, enter a formula in each of the specified cells that returns the serial number for the specified date:

C5	=	February 6, 2001
C6	=	February 8, 2001
C7	=	March 2, 2001
C8	=	March 2, 2001

4. Enter a formula in cell E5 that inserts the due date (date of service plus the number of days in the Terms column).
5. Make cell A10 active and then key your name.
6. Make cell A11 active and then use the NOW function to insert the current date as a serial number.
7. Save the worksheet again with the same name (Excel CPA 06).
8. Print and then close Excel CPA 06.

Assessment 7

1. Plan and prepare a worksheet with the information shown in figure C1.2. Apply formatting of your choosing to the worksheet either with an autoformat or with formatting at the Format Cells dialog box.
2. Insert a clip art image of your choosing to the right of the product list and order information. Resize and format the image as desired.
3. Save the completed worksheet and name it Excel CPA 07.
4. Print and then close Excel CPA 07.

Prepare a weekly summary of orders taken that itemizes the product coming into the company and the average order size.

The products and average order size include:

Black and gold wall clock—$2,450 worth of orders, average order size of $125
Traveling alarm clock—$1,358 worth of orders, average order size of $195
Waterproof watch—$890 worth of orders, average order size of $90
Dashboard clock—$2,135 worth of orders, average order size of $230
Pyramid clock—$3,050 worth of orders, average order size of $375
Gold chain watch—$755 worth of orders, average order size of $80

In the worksheet, total the amount ordered, and also calculate the average weekly order size. Sort the data in the worksheet by the order amount in descending order.

Figure C1.2 • Assessment 7

Assessment 8

1. Open Excel and then key the following information in a worksheet:

Country	Total Sales
Denmark	$85,345
Finland	$71,450
Norway	$135,230
Sweden	$118,895

2. Using the data just entered in the worksheet, create a column chart as a separate sheet.
3. Save the workbook (worksheet plus chart sheet) and name it Excel CPA 08.
4. Print only the sheet containing the chart.
5. Change the column chart to a line chart of your choosing.
6. Save the worksheet (and chart) again with the same name (Excel CPA 08).
7. Print only the sheet containing the chart.
8. Close Excel CPA 08.

Assessment 9

1. Open Excel Worksheet 40.
2. Save the worksheet with Save As and name it Excel CPA 09.
3. Create a map like the one shown in figure C1.3 with the data in the worksheet with these specifications:
   a. Create a Canadian map.
   b. Increase the zoom to approximately 100%.
   c. Hide the title.
   d. Move the legend as shown in figure C1.3.
4. Save the worksheet again with the same name (Excel CPA 09).
5. Print the worksheet (and map) centered horizontally and vertically on the page.
6. Close Excel CPA 09.

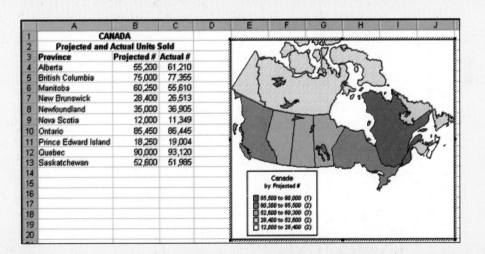

Figure C1.3 • Assessment 9

Assessment 10

1. Open Excel CPA 09.
2. Save the worksheet with Save As and name it Excel CPA 10.
3. Make the following changes to the map:
   a. Display the Microsoft Map Control dialog box and then change the data column from *Projected #* to *Actual #*.
   b. At the Microsoft Map Control dialog box, change the shading button in the white area from Value Shading to Category Shading.
   c. At the Format Properties dialog box with the Legend Options tab selected, change the title to *Actual Units Sold* and delete the subtitle.
4. Save the worksheet again with the same name (Excel CPA 10).
5. Print the worksheet (and map) centered horizontally and vertically on the page.
6. Close Excel CPA 10.

Assessment 11

1. Open Travel Advantage Worksheet 01.
2. Create a new folder on your disk named *Travel Web Page*.
3. Save Travel Advantage Worksheet 01 as a Web page in the Travel Web Page folder. Name the Web page *Travel Web Page*.
4. Preview the Web page in the default browser window.
5. Connect to the Internet and search for sites that might be of interest to tourists for each of the cities in Travel Web Page. Write down the URL for the best Web page you find for each city.
6. Create a hyperlink in Travel Web Page for each city to jump to the URL you wrote down from step 5.
7. Test the hyperlinks to make sure you entered the URLs correctly by clicking each hyperlink and then closing the browser application window to return to Travel Web Page.
8. Save the revised Web page using the same name (Travel Web Page).
9. Print and then close Travel Web Page.

WRITING ACTIVITIES

The following activities give you the opportunity to practice your writing skills along with demonstrating an understanding of some of the important Excel features you have mastered in this book. Use correct grammar, appropriate word choices, and clear sentence constructions.

Activity one

Suppose that you are the accounting assistant in the financial department of McCormack Funds and you have been asked to prepare a yearly proposed department budget. The total amount for the department is $1,450,000. You are given the percentages for the proposed budget items, which are: Salaries, 45%; Benefits, 12%; Training, 14%; Administrative Costs, 10%; Equipment, 11%; and Supplies, 8%. Create a worksheet with this information that shows the projected yearly budget, the budget items in the department, the percentage of the budget, and the amount for each item. After the worksheet is completed, save it and name it Excel CPA, Act 01. Print and then close Excel CPA, Act 01.

Activity two

Prepare a worksheet in Excel for Carefree Travels that includes the following information:

Scandinavian Tours

Country	Tours Booked
Norway	52
Sweden	62
Finland	29
Denmark	38

Use the information in the worksheet to create a bar chart as a separate worksheet. Save the workbook (worksheet and chart) and name it Excel CPA, Act 02. Print only the sheet containing the chart. Close Excel CPA, Act 02.

Activity three

Prepare a worksheet for Carefree Travels that advertises a snow skiing trip. Include the following information in the announcement:

Include the following text (you can edit the text as you see fit):

Ski the Slopes of Whistler
Picture the crystal clear blue sky, the glistening snow-covered mountains, and the cool alpine air. You can book your vacation today at special discount prices.

Include the following bulleted items:
- Round-trip air transportation: $95
- Seven nights' hotel accommodations: $1,250
- Four all-day ski passes: $375
- Compact rental car with unlimited mileage: $150

A bonus feature includes a two-for-one discount at many of the local ski resorts, including ski passes and ski school (included at no charge).

Calculate the total price of the ski package.

Include an appropriate clip art image (consider downloading an image from the on-line Microsoft Clip Gallery) in the worksheet. Save the completed announcement and name it Excel CPA, Act 03. Print and then close Excel CPA, Act 03. Save Excel CPA, Act 03 as a Web page and name it Excel CPA Whistler Web Page. Preview the Web page in the default browser window.

INTERNET ACTIVITY

Make sure you are connected to the Internet and then explore at least three of the sites listed below. Take notes on which part of the site was the most helpful and interesting to you. (*Note: Web sites change. If you get an error message telling you that you have reached a site that is no longer active or has changed its address, connect to the search directory site www.search-beat.com. Click Travel Directory in the Themes list box [you will need to scroll down the list to display this option] and then use resources from this site to jump to various country sites.*)

- www.africanet.com
- www.france.com
- www.okspain.org
- www.portugal.org
- www.tourindia.com

In Word, prepare a memo on the sites you visited that addresses the following:

- Compare how the sites are organized. Which site was the most helpful for actually planning a trip? Why? Though organized differently, do they offer essentially the same information or very different information?
- Which site had the most persuasive advertisements and photos? Were any so persuasive or enticing that they changed your mind about where you want to travel?
- What sites taught you the most about the geography, culture, and people of the country?

In Excel, create a travel planning worksheet for three countries you would like to visit. Include the following information in the worksheet:

- airline costs
- hotel costs (off-season and in-season rates if available)
- estimated meal costs
- entertainment costs
- car rental costs

If you cannot find specific information from all sites, leave the column(s) blank.

Index

objects, 250
page breaks, 68–69
rows, 60–61
styles, 132–134
workbooks, 92–95
worksheets, 118–119
Dependent worksheets, 178
Depreciation
double-declining balance,
164–165, 167–168
fixed-declining balance, 164–166
straight-line, 164–165
Designing worksheets, 184–185
Detect and Repair feature, 49
Disabling Office Assistant, 45,
47–48
Disks, workbooks, 10
Display Entire button (Map
toolbar), 236
Displaying
cell addresses, 6
comments, 138
data, 232
Delete dialog box, 60
invoice examples, 138
maps, 236
Page Setup dialog box, 62
Save As dialog box, 90
toolbars, 4
Division (/) mathematical
operator, 153–154
Documents
cutting and pasting in
workbooks, 98
default settings, 13–14
selecting in workbooks, 92
Dollar sign ($), 27
Dots, maps, 242
Dots per inch (DPI), 63
Double-declining balance
depreciation method,
164–165, 167–168
Doughnut chart, 203
Downloading clip art images,
230–232
Drawing
lines, 247–249
objects, 247–249
Insert Clip Art button, 224,
247–248
Drives, workbooks, 98
Drop-down menus, 12–13
Dynamic links of cells, 178

E-mail, 104–105
Editing
chart types, 202–205
column width, 21–24
data in cells, 10, 206–207
fonts, 20–21, 35–36
formulas, 172
margins, 18, 66–67
page orientation, 64–65
print quality, 74
row height, 25–27
series in cells, 207–208
Elements in charts
adding, 209–212
background, 214
color, 216
deleting, 211–212
fills, 214
fonts, 215
moving, 210–212
patterns, 214–215
sizing, 210
worksheets, 73
Enclosed objects, 249
Enter button (Formula toolbar),
10, 152
Entering cell data, 6–9
Error correction in cells, 7–8
Exiting Excel, 12
Expanding drop-down menus,
12–13
Expense template, 135
Exponentiation (^) mathematical
operator, 153–154

Files
copying in workbooks, 95–96
naming, 10
Fill Color button
Drawing toolbar, 247–248
Format Cells dialog box, 39
Formatting toolbar, 17, 216–218
Fill handle
AutoFill, 9
chart elements, 214
formulas, 155–156

Financial functions
DDB (double-declining
depreciation), 164–168
FV (future values), 164, 169–170
PMT (payment), 164, 168–169
SLN (straight-line
depreciation), 164
Find Similar Clips button (Insert
ClipArt dialog box), 225
Finding data, 76
First-rank menu options, 12
Fixed declining balance
depreciation, 164–166
Folders
creating, 90–91
deleting, 92, 99
naming, 91
workbooks, 90, 98
Font buttons
Drawing toolbar, 247–248
Formatting toolbar, 17, 35–36
Fonts
chart elements, 215
color, 35–36
editing, 20–21, 35–36
Footers, 63–66
Format Chart Area dialog box, 214
Format Properties dialog box, 239
Formatting, 38
alignment, 33
AutoFormat feature, 42–44
characters, 19–20
clip art images, 227–229
Fill Color button, 39
fonts, 35–36
numbers, 27–32
pages, 61
styles
applying, 130
copying, 132–134
defining, 129–132
deleting, 132–134
worksheets, 76, 128–129
Formatting toolbar buttons, 4–5
Align Left/Right, 17, 32
Bold, 17
Borders, 17, 36–37
Center, 32
Comma Style, 17, 28
Currency Style, 17, 28
Decrease Decimal, 17, 28
Decrease Indent, 17, 32
Fill Color, 17, 216–218

workbooks, 11, 89–90, 100, 122–123
Operators, mathematical, 151
 addition (+), 153–154
 division (/), 153–154
 exponentiation (^), 153–154
 multiplication (*), 153–154
 order of operators, 154
 percent (%), 153–154
 subtraction (-), 153–154
Options in menus, 12
Options button (AutoFormat dialog box), 43
Order of operations, 154
Orientation, pages, 62, 64–65
Outlining worksheets, 182–183
Oval button (Drawing toolbar), 247–248

Pages
 breaks, 68–70
 formatting, 61
 margins, 18, 62, 66–67
 numbering, 63–64
 orientation, 62, 64–65
 setup, 61–62
Panes, windows, freezing, 120–122
Paste Special dialog box, 179
Pasting, 114
 functions, 158–159
 workbooks, 126–127
Patterns
 cells, 39–42
 chart elements, 214–215
Payments
 future values, 169
 loans, 168
Percent (%) mathematical operator, 153–154
Percentages (%), 17, 27–28, 31
Picture toolbar buttons
 Crop, 228
 Format Picture, 228
 Image Control, 227
 Insert Picture, 227
 Less Brightness, 228
 Less Contrast, 227
 Line Style, 228
 More Brightness, 227
 More Contrast, 227
 Reset Picture, 228

Set Transparent Color, 228
Pie charts, 203, 208, 242
Pipe symbol (|), 10
Planning worksheets, 184–185
PMT financial function, 164, 168–169
Pointers
 cells, 7
 formulas, writing, 156–157
Portrait orientation, 62
Previewing
 charts, 198–200
 clip art, 225
 Web pages from workbooks, 106–108
 worksheets, 12, 17–18
 zoom settings, 18
Printing
 charts, 199–200
 columns
  headings, 72–73
  titles, 70–72
 gridlines, 72
 previewing, 17–18, 62, 199
 quality, 63, 74
 rows
  headings, 72–73
  titles, 70–72
 workbooks, 11–12, 100, 116–117
 worksheets, 11-12, 17–18, 73–74
Properties button (Print dialog box), 74
Protecting worksheets, 173
Purchase Order template, 135
Purpose of worksheets, 184, 185
Push-pins in maps, 236
Pyramid chart, 203

Quality of printing, 63, 74
Question mark (?), 10
Quotation mark ("), 10

Radar chart, 203
Ranges of cells
 naming, 174–175
 numbers, 163–164
 values, 161–163

Rectangle button (Drawing toolbar), 247–248
Recycle Bin, 93–95
Redo button (Standard toolbar), 75
Redrawing maps, 236
References
 3-D, 181
 cells, 175–178
Refreshing maps, 236
Relative cell references, 154–156
Renaming
 workbooks, 98–99
 worksheets, 103, 118
Replacing data, 77–78
Reset Picture button (Picture toolbar), 228
Restoring workbooks, 125–126
Returning the result in formulas, 158–159
Rotating cell data, 33–34
Rows
 boundaries, 25–26
 clearing, 61
 deleting, 60–61
 headings, 72–73
 height, 25–27
 inserting, 57–59
 numbering, 5
 selecting, 15–16
 titles, 70–72

Sample CD documents, 13–14
Save As dialog box, 10, 90, 106
Save button (Standard toolbar), 10–11
Save Template dialog box, 139
Saving
 sample documents, 13–14
 templates, 139–140
 Web pages, 105, 107–108
 workbooks, 10–11
Scatter (XY) chart, 203
Scientific numbers, 31
ScreenTips feature, 49–50
Scroll bars, 4–5, 7
Searches
 clip art images, 226
 Web pages, 90
Second-rank menu options, 12
Security, 173

Excel

EXPERT LEVEL

MICROSOFT® EXCEL 2000

EXPERT LEVEL MOUS SKILLS

Coding No.	SKILL	Pages
XL2000E.1	**Importing and exporting data**	
XL2000E.1.1	Import data from text files (insert, drag and drop)	270-273, 291-293
XL2000E.1.2	Import from other applications	283, 286
XL2000E.1.3	Import a table from an HTML file (insert, drag and drop – including HTML round tripping)	283-285
XL2000E.1.4	Export to other applications	275, 276-277
XL2000E.2	**Using templates**	
XL2000E.2.1	Apply templates	44
XL2000E.2.2	Edit templates	51-52
XL2000E.2.3	Create templates	49
XL2000E.3	**Using multiple workbooks**	
XL2000E.3.1	Using a workspace	59-60
XL2000E.3.2	Link workbooks	62-63
XL2000E.4	**Formatting numbers**	
XL2000E.4.1	Apply number formats (accounting, currency, number)	4-5
XL2000E.4.2	Create custom number formats	5-7
XL2000E.4.3	Use conditional formatting	21-22
XL2000E.5	**Printing workbooks**	
XL2000E.5.1	Print and preview multiple worksheets	258
XL2000E.5.2	Use the Report Manager	259-260
XL2000E.6	**Working with named ranges**	
XL2000E.6.1	Add and delete a named range	97-99
XL2000E.6.2	Use a named range in a formula	99
XL2000E.6.3	Use Lookup Functions (Hlookup or Vlookup)	99-100
XL2000E.7	**Working with toolbars**	
XL2000E.7.1	Hide and display toolbars	223
XL2000E.7.2	Customize a toolbar	223-225
XL2000E.7.3	Assign a macro to a command button	214-215
XL2000E.8	**Using macros**	
XL2000E.8.1	Record macros	210-211
XL2000E.8.2	Run macros	212-213
XL2000E.8.3	Edit macros	215-216
XL2000E.9	**Auditing a worksheet**	
XL2000E.9.1	Work with the Auditing Toolbar	228-229
XL2000E.9.2	Trace errors (find and fix errors)	229
XL2000E.9.3	Trace precedents (find cells referred to in a specific formula)	229
XL2000E.9.4	Trace dependents (find formulas that refer to a specific cell)	229
XL2000E.10	**Displaying and Formatting Data**	
XL2000E.10.1	Apply conditional formats	22
XL2000E.10.2	Perform single and multi-level sorts	127-128
XL2000E.10.3	Use grouping and outlines	135-136
XL2000E.10.4	Use data forms	119
XL2000E.10.5	Use subtotaling	139-140
XL2000E.10.6	Apply data filters	143-145
XL2000E.10.7	Extract data	147-148, 149-150
XL2000E.10.8	Query databases	288-289
XL2000E.10.9	Use data validation	121-124
XL2000E.11	**Using analysis tools**	
XL2000E.11.1	Use PivotTable autoformat	170
XL2000E.11.2	Use Goal Seek	193
XL2000E.11.3	Create pivot chart reports	181-183
XL2000E.11.4	Work with Scenarios	199-200
XL2000E.11.5	Use Solver	195-196
XL2000E.11.6	Use data analysis and PivotTables	161-165, 175-177
XL2000E.11.7	Create interactive PivotTables for the Web	189
XL2000E.11.8	Add fields to a PivotTable using the Web browser	189
XL2000E.12	**Collaborating with workgroups**	
XL2000E.12.1	Create, edit, and remove a comment	253-254
XL2000E.12.2	Apply and remove worksheet and workbook protection	240, 242-244
XL2000E.12.3	Change workbook properties	238-240
XL2000E.12.4	Apply and remove file passwords	241-242
XL2000E.12.5	Track changes (highlight, accept, and reject)	248-249
XL2000E.12.6	Create a shared workbook	67-68, 238
XL2000E.12.7	Merge workbooks	254

Chapter 01E

Formatting Excel Worksheets Using Advanced Formatting Techniques

PERFORMANCE OBJECTIVES

Upon successful completion of chapter 1, you will be able to:

- Apply accounting, fraction, and scientific formats.
- Create and apply custom formats.
- Format large labels.
- Automatically adjust column widths and row heights.
- Create, apply, and edit styles.
- Use the Format Painter.
- Format a worksheet by adding borders and shading.
- Apply formatting to a worksheet using one of Excel's predesigned AutoFormats.
- Create and use conditional formatting.
- Adjust the layout of a worksheet.
- Use the Paste Special Command.
- Hide and unhide rows, columns, and sheets.
- Rename sheets.
- Format large worksheets.

Excel includes many formatting features beyond basic options found on the Formatting toolbar. Although the most common use of worksheets may be to manipulate financial data, they are also used in many other fields including science and engineering. Some of these specialized fields make use of Excel's more advanced formatting features such as using fraction and scientific number formats. In some cases, the numbering format that is needed for a particular worksheet may not be included as one of Excel's preset number formats, in which case a custom format can be created. In other cases, a particular format may be needed in only certain circumstances, in which case a conditional format can be created. Especially large worksheets can also present a formatting challenge as you try to get the worksheet to fit on as few pages as possible while at the same time being as easy to read and understand as possible.

In this chapter you will learn many advanced formatting techniques that will help you manage not only the most complex or challenging worksheet but the most basic worksheet as well. These techniques will help save you time and will help to make your worksheets as readable as possible.

The three frequently used number formats, Currency, Comma, and Percent, are available as buttons on the Formatting toolbar.

Applying Number Formats

In Excel there are twelve categories by which numbers can be formatted. These categories are found in the Format Cells dialog box, which is accessed either by clicking Format and then Cells or by right-clicking the cell to be formatted and clicking Format Cells from the shortcut menu. Click the Number tab on the Format Cells dialog box, and all the available categories are displayed in the Category list box as shown in figure 1.1.

figure 1.1

Excel's Number Formats

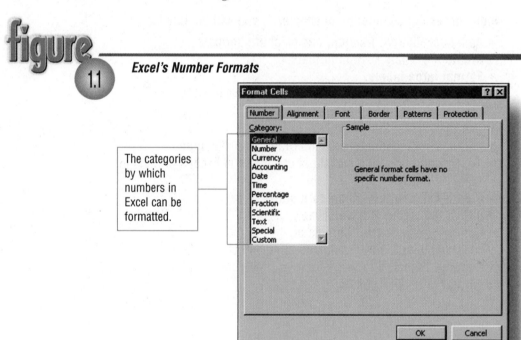

The categories by which numbers in Excel can be formatted.

The first three categories listed, General, Number, and Currency, are probably the three most frequently used categories. But some of the more specialized categories such as Accounting, Fraction, and Scientific are quite useful as well. The difference between the Currency and Accounting formats is that the Accounting format lines up the currency symbols and the Currency format does not. The Fraction format enables you to display how fractions are displayed in the cells. The Scientific format is used for very large or very small numbers. Engineers and scientists often use the Scientific format, which is also called scientific notation. For example, the Andromeda Galaxy (the closest one to our Milky Way galaxy) contains at least 200,000,000,000 stars. It is common for scientists to work with such large numbers so they must use an easier way to write them than having to enter all those zeros. If you entered the number 250,000,000,000, for example, and formatted it as Scientific, it would look like 2.5E+11 on the worksheet. The number after the E refers to how many places to the right you have to move the decimal point.

Creating Custom Formats

The last option in the <u>C</u>ategory list box on the Format Cells dialog box is *Custom*. This option allows you to create your own format. To create a custom format, first select the cells to which you want the format applied, right-click one of the selected cells, click <u>F</u>ormat Cells from the shortcut menu, and click the Number tab. Click *Custom*, the last option in the <u>C</u>ategory list box. The <u>T</u>ype box is displayed as shown in figure 1.2. The default data that is entered into the Type box depends on the current format of the selected cells.

A custom numeric format can have up to four parts: a positive number format, a negative number format, a format for zeros, and a format for text. Semicolons are used to separate the parts.

figure 1.2

The Custom Option from the Category List Box

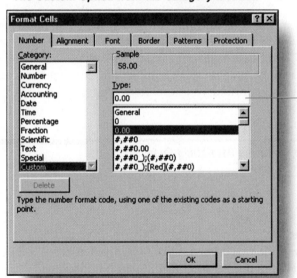

The Type box becomes available when the Custom option from the Category list box is selected.

To create a custom format, enter the desired format in the <u>T</u>ype box. If you are entering text that you want to appear, you must enclose the text with quotation marks. For example, you want to create a custom format that uses the text *meters*. You would place the insertion point to the right of the last entry in the <u>T</u>ype box, press the spacebar once and enter "meters" as shown in figure 1.3.

figure
1.3

Creating a Custom Format in the Type Box

When adding text
for a custom
format, the text
must be enclosed
in quotation
marks.

There are numeric, date, and time formatting codes that can be used when creating custom formats. These codes are listed in table 1.1. As is shown in figure 1.4, once you have created a custom format, it is added to the end of the Type list box so that you can use it again. If you want to delete a custom format that you have created, select the format you want to delete from the Type list box and click the Delete button.

table
1.1

Numeric, Date, and Time Formatting Codes

Code	Description
Numeric Formatting Codes	
#	Used to hold the place for a digit. Insignificant zeros are not displayed.
0	Used to hold the place for a digit. Zeros are displayed.
?	Used to hold the place for a digit. Insignificant zeros are represented by a space.
.	Decimal point.
,	Thousands separator.
%	Percent sign. Entry is multiplied by 100.
;	Used to separate positive number format from negative number format.
_	Used to skip the width of the next character. For example, entering _) skips the width of the right parenthesis character.
/	Used as a separator for fractions.
"text"	Quotation marks are used to insert specified text.
[color]	Braces are used to format entry as specified color.
@	Used to hold the place where user-input text is to appear.

(Table 1.1 continued)

Date Formatting Codes

m	Displays the month as a number (1, 2, 3, …10, 11, 12).
mm	Displays the month as a number with a leading zero (01, 02, 03…).
mmm	Displays month as a three-letter abbreviation (Jan, Feb, Mar…).
mmmm	Displays month as a complete name (January, February, March…).
d	Displays the day of the month as a number (2, 18, 29).
dd	Displays the day of the month as a number with a leading zero (01, 04, 08).
ddd	Displays the day of the week as a three-letter abbreviation (Mon, Tue, Wed).
dddd	Displays the day of the week as a complete name (Monday, Tuesday, Wednesday).
yy	Displays the year as a two digit number (92, 94, 98).
yyyy	Displays the year as a complete number (1994, 1998, 2000).

Time Formatting Codes

h	Displays the hour as a number (1, 8, 10).
hh	Displays the hour as a number with a leading zero (03, 05, 08).
m	Displays the minutes as a number (5, 38, 46).
mm	Displays the minutes as a number with a leading zero (03, 06, 09).
s	Displays the seconds as a number (7, 34, 56).
ss	Displays the seconds as a number with a leading zero (03, 05, 08).
AM/PM	Displays either AM or PM to indicate AM or PM time.
A/P	Displays either A or P to indicate AM or PM time.

figure
1.4

Applying and Deleting a Custom Format

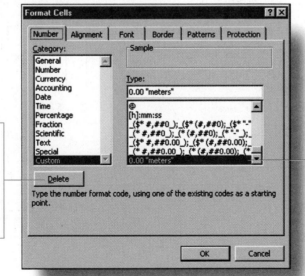

To delete a custom format, select the format to be deleted from the Type list box and press the Delete button.

When you create a custom format, it is added to the end of the Type list. To apply the format elsewhere in the worksheet, simply select the custom format from the Type list box.

Formatting Large Labels

Labels are used as headings to identify the contents of a row or column. If a label on a worksheet is quite large, it may make the worksheet's format look awkward. For example, if the longest entry in a column is only 5 digits, but the label for that column is 50 characters, there will be a lot of wasted space since the column has to be wide enough to accommodate the label.

Merge and Center Button

There are a couple of different ways in which large labels can be handled in Excel. First, if the label does not have to be confined to one column, the Merge and Center button is useful for centering a label across several columns. To use the Merge and Center button, first enter the label and then select all the cells across which the label is to be centered. Next, click the Merge and Center button. All the cells that were selected are merged into one cell and the label is centered within that one cell. Using the Merge and Center button is useful, for example, for centering a label over an entire worksheet that is made up of many columns.

There are several methods for handling large labels and they are found on the Alignment tab of the Format Cells dialog box which is shown in figure 1.5. To access these options, right-click the cell containing the label and click Format Cells on the shortcut menu. On the Format Cells dialog box, click the Alignment tab.

If at a later time you wish to undo the effects of using the Merge and Center button, right-click the merged cell, click Format cells, click the Alignment tab, click the Merge cells check box so that it is no longer selected, and click OK.

Hint

figure 1.5

The Format Cell Dialog Box with Alignment Tab Selected

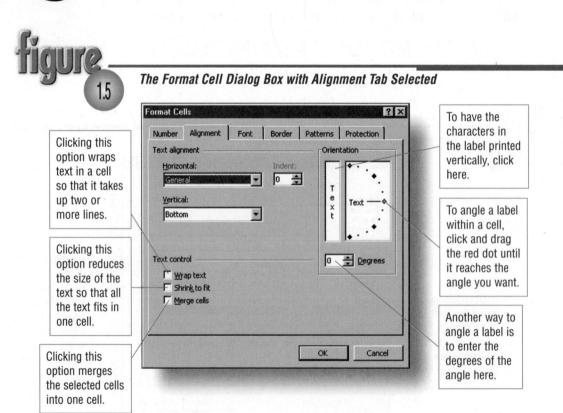

Clicking this option wraps text in a cell so that it takes up two or more lines.

Clicking this option reduces the size of the text so that all the text fits in one cell.

Clicking this option merges the selected cells into one cell.

To have the characters in the label printed vertically, click here.

To angle a label within a cell, click and drag the red dot until it reaches the angle you want.

Another way to angle a label is to enter the degrees of the angle here.

The options under Text Control help you manage large labels. Selecting the Wrap text option wraps the label within the cell so that it takes up two or more lines. Selecting the Shrink to fit option reduces the label as necessary in order to make it all fit within one cell. If two or more cells have been selected, selecting the Merge cells option merges the selected cells into one cell.

The Orientation feature offers another way to handle large labels. By clicking and dragging the red dot you can angle the label within the cell. As you drag the red dot, the degrees of the angle are displayed in the Degrees box. You can also just enter the degrees of the angle for the label in the Degrees box. If you want the text in the label to be printed vertically, with one character directly underneath another, click the third option under Orientation.

Automatically Adjusting Column Widths and Row Heights

The AutoFit option allows you to automatically adjust the width of one or more columns or the height of one or more rows to fit the longest or highest entry. To use this option to adjust the width of columns, first select all the columns to be adjusted. Click Format and then point to Column. Click AutoFit Selection on the Column submenu. The columns are automatically adjusted so that each column is wide enough to display the widest entry in that particular column. To use the AutoFit option to adjust the height of rows, first select all the rows to be adjusted. Click Format and then point to Row. Click Autofit on the Row submenu. The rows are automatically adjusted so that each row is high enough to display the highest entry in that row.

You can also automatically adjust the width of columns by double-clicking on the right column heading border. If you want to use this method to automatically adjust the width of several columns at one time, first select the columns and then double-click on the right heading border of any one of the selected columns. Each column is automatically adjusted to display the widest entry in that column. This method also works for automatically adjusting row heights. Simply double-click the bottom row heading border and the row will automatically adjust to display the highest entry in that row. To adjust the height of several rows at a time, select the rows to be adjusted and double-click the bottom row heading border of any one of the selected rows. Each row is automatically adjusted to display the highest entry in that row.

Adjust the column to the width you want it to be *before* issuing the command to Wrap Text.

If under Orientation you choose to have the labels displayed vertically, you should also make a selection from the Vertical drop-down list box, under Text alignment. A vertical label can be placed within a cell at the top, in the center, at the bottom or justified.

If you want to specify an exact column width or row height, click either Format, Column, and Width or Format, Row, and Height and key the desired dimension in the dialog box that is displayed.

(Before completing computer exercises, copy the Chapter 01E *folder from the CD that accompanies this textbook to your disk. Steps on how to copy a folder are presented on the inside back cover of this textbook.)*

Applying Scientific and Custom Formats, Adjusting Column Widths, and Formatting Large Labels

1. Open Excel.
2. Open Excel Worksheet E1-01.
3. Save the file using the Save As command and name it Excel E1, Ex 01.
4. Create a custom header by completing the following steps:
   a. Click File and then click Page Setup.
   b. Click the Header/Footer tab.
   c. Click the Custom Header button.
   d. Enter your name in the Left section box.
   e. Click the Right section box to select it. Click the Filename button. This will automatically insert the name of the file. Your screen should look like the accompanying illustration.
   f. Click the OK button twice.

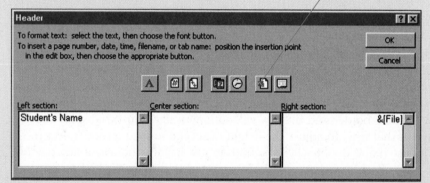

5. An astronomy class at Redwood Community College wants to calculate how far certain stars are from the sun in miles. In order to do this they have to convert the distance measured in light years into miles. The formula to accomplish this is the number of light years multiplied by the speed of light times seconds in a minute, times minutes in an hour, times hours in a day, times days in a year. Key the following formula in cell C4:

$$=B4*186000*60*60*24*365.25$$

6. The number is too large to be displayed. Widen the column by completing these steps:
   a. Position the mouse pointer on the column boundary between columns C and D until it turns into a double-headed arrow pointing left and right.
   b. Double-click.

7. The number that is displayed is very large and would be more appropriately displayed in scientific notation. Change the format of this number to scientific notation by completing the following steps:
    a. Right click cell C4.
    b. On the shortcut menu, click <u>F</u>ormat Cells.
    c. On the Format Cells dialog box, click the Number tab if necessary.
        1) Click *Scientific* in the <u>C</u>ategory list box.
        2) Click OK.

	A	B	C
1	Some Nearby Stars		
2			
3		Distance from the Sun in Light Years	Distance from the Sun in Miles
4	Proxima Centauri	4.2	2.5E+13
5	α Centauri	4.3	

Step 8b

8. Copy the formula in cell C4 to cells C5 through C16 by completing the following steps.
    a. Select cell C4.
    b. Place the mouse pointer over the AutoFill fill handle in the lower right corner of cell C4. The mouse pointer should look like a plus sign.
    c. Double-click on the AutoFill fill handle in the lower right corner of cell C4.
9. Create the custom format *ly*, which stands for light years, for the numbers in column B by completing the following steps:
    a. Select cells B4 through B16.
    b. Right-click on one of the selected cells.
    c. On the shortcut menu, click <u>F</u>ormat Cells.
    d. On the Format Cells dialog box, click the Number tab if necessary.
        1) In the <u>C</u>ategory list box, click *Custom*.
        2) In the <u>T</u>ype box, click to the right of the last zero.
        3) Press the space bar once and enter "**ly**". Be sure to include both sets of quotation marks.
        4) Click OK. The label *ly* now appears in cells B4 through B16.

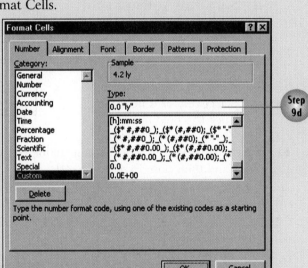

Step 9d

10. Create the custom format *miles* for the numbers in column C by completing the following steps:
    a. Select cells C4 through C16.
    b. Right-click on one of the selected cells.
    c. On the shortcut menu, click <u>F</u>ormat Cells.
    d. On the Format Cells dialog box, click the Number tab if necessary.
        1) In the <u>C</u>ategory list box, click *Custom*.

2) In the Type box, click to the right of the last zero.

3) Press the space bar once and enter "**miles**". Be sure to include both sets of quotation marks.

4) Click OK. The label *miles* now appears in cells C4 through C16.

11. Format the three column labels so that they are at an angle by completing the following steps:

a. Select cells A3 through C3.

b. Right-click one of the selected cells.

c. On the shortcut menu, click Format Cells.

d. Click the Alignment tab.

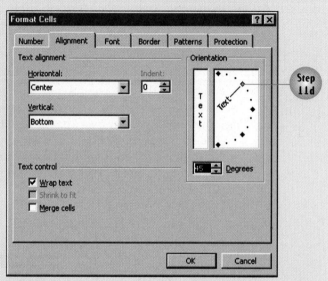

Step 11d

1) Click and drag the red dot in the Orientation box until 45 is displayed in the Degrees box.

2) Click OK.

12. Apply the Merge and Center command on cells A1 through D1 by completing the following steps:

a. Select cells A1 through D1.

b. Click the Merge and Center button.

13. Change the formatting of the title "Some Nearby Stars" by completing the following steps:

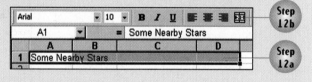

Step 12b

Step 12a

a. Select cell A1 if necessary.

b. Click the Bold button.

c. Change the Font Size to 12.

14. Save the worksheet with the same name (Excel E1, Ex 01).

15. Print and then close Excel E1, Ex 01.

Creating, Applying, and Editing Styles

When working with large worksheets or a workbook that has many worksheets, it is a good idea to apply formatting using styles. A style is a predefined set of formatting attributes such as font, font size, alignment, color, borders, and so on. In fact all the options available from the Format Cells dialog box can be defined as part of a particular style. Once a style has been defined, that style can be applied to any cell in a worksheet. Applying formatting using styles has several advantages. First, styles help to assure that the formatting from one worksheet to another is consistent. Second, all the attributes for a particular style have to be defined one time only. If you decide to use the same formatting over and over you do not have to keep redefining each attribute of the format. Third, if a change needs to be made to the style, you only have to make that change one time in the style's definition, and then that change is automatically reflected in all the cells where the style has been applied thus saving a lot of time.

To create a style, select the cells to which the style is to be applied. Click Format and then Style. The Style dialog box, as shown in figure 1.6, is displayed. Each one of the check boxes on the Style dialog box corresponds to one of the tabs on the Format Cells dialog box. To create a new style, enter the name of the style in the Style name box. If any of the options listed on the Style dialog box are not going to be part of the style you are going to create, click in the check boxes next to those options so that they are no longer selected. Click the Modify button and the Format Cells dialog box appears. Make the selections you want for the style from the Format Cells dialog box and click OK. The Style dialog box is displayed and the attributes you selected will be listed. Click OK again and the style will be applied to the selected cells. To apply the style to other cells, simply select those cells, click Format and then click Style. Click the down arrow to the right of the Style name box and select the name of the style you want to apply from the drop-down list. Click OK and the style is applied to the selected cells. To delete a style, click the down arrow to the right of the Style name box, select the name of the style to be deleted and click the Delete button.

The Normal style applies to all unformatted cells in the worksheet. If you modify the Normal style, all the unformatted cells in the worksheet will be changed to reflect whatever modification you make.

figure 1.6

The Style Dialog Box

The options on the Style dialog box correspond to the tabs in the Format Cells dialog box.

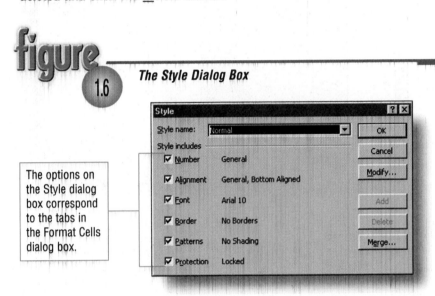

Using the Format Painter Button

The Format Painter button allows you to copy the format of one or more cells and apply it to other cells in the worksheet. To use the Format Painter button, select the cell or cells with the formatting you want to copy. Click the Format Painter button on the Standard toolbar. The mouse pointer changes to a paintbrush next to a cross as shown in figure 1.7. Select the cells to which you want the copied formatting applied. Clicking the Format Painter button one time allows you to apply the copied formatting one time. If you double-click the Format Painter button, you can apply the copied formatting as many times as you want. When you have finished applying the copied formatting, click the Format Painter button again to turn the feature off.

Format Painter Button

When using the Format Painter, the target cell or cells (the cell(s) to which the copied format is to be applied) can be in a different worksheet.

figure
1.7 — *Using the Format Painter Button*

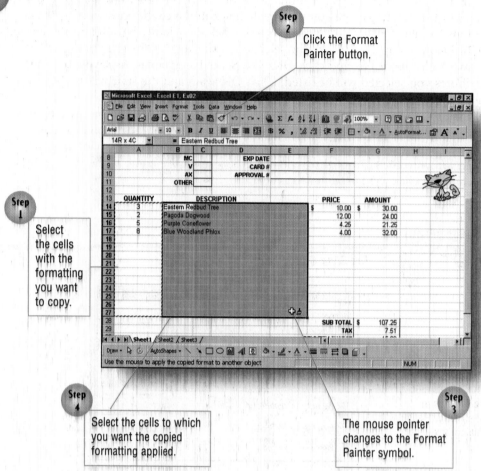

Step 2 — Click the Format Painter button.

Step 1 — Select the cells with the formatting you want to copy.

Step 4 — Select the cells to which you want the copied formatting applied.

Step 3 — The mouse pointer changes to the Format Painter symbol.

Applying Borders and Shading

There are two ways to apply borders and shading to cells in a worksheet. You can either use a dialog box or a button on the toolbar. To apply borders using a dialog box, select the cells to which you want to add borders, right-click one of the selected cells, click Format Cells on the shortcut menu, and click the Border tab. You can make border selections from the dialog box shown in figure 1.8. You can also apply shading to a cell from this dialog box.

You must select the line style and line color (found under Line in the dialog box) *before* selecting a border style (the buttons under Presets and Border on the dialog box). Any line style or color you select after selecting the border style will not go into effect.

Hint

figure 1.8

Applying Borders and Shading Using the Dialog Box

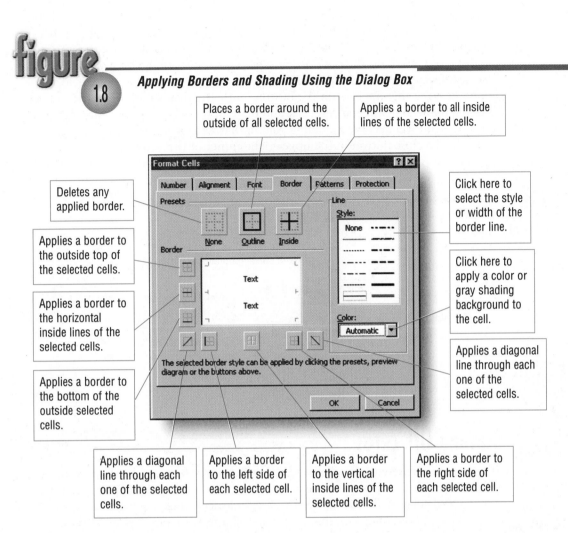

Places a border around the outside of all selected cells.

Applies a border to all inside lines of the selected cells.

Deletes any applied border.

Click here to select the style or width of the border line.

Applies a border to the outside top of the selected cells.

Click here to apply a color or gray shading background to the cell.

Applies a border to the horizontal inside lines of the selected cells.

Applies a diagonal line through each one of the selected cells.

Applies a border to the bottom of the outside selected cells.

Applies a diagonal line through each one of the selected cells.

Applies a border to the left side of each selected cell.

Applies a border to the vertical inside lines of the selected cells.

Applies a border to the right side of each selected cell.

To apply borders using the toolbar, click the down arrow to the right of the Borders button on the Formatting toolbar and the border options shown in figure 1.9 are displayed. Click on the button that represents the border style you want. The last selected border style becomes the default for the button on the toolbar. To apply the style that appears on the button on the toolbar, simply click the button. You can click and drag on the menu options blue title bar and they will become a floating palette that you can place anywhere on the worksheet. The palette will be displayed until you click the close box in the upper right corner of the palette.

figure 1.9

Applying Borders Using the Toolbar

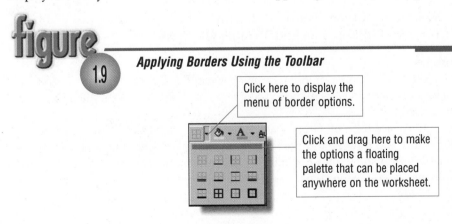

Click here to display the menu of border options.

Click and drag here to make the options a floating palette that can be placed anywhere on the worksheet.

To apply shading using the toolbar, click the down arrow to the right of the Fill Color button on the Formatting toolbar and the options shown in figure 1.10 are displayed. Click on the option that represents the shading you want to apply. The last selected color becomes the default for the button on the toolbar. To apply the color that appears on the button on the toolbar, simply click the button. Like the borders menu, you can click and drag on the menu options blue title bar and the menu will become a floating palette that remains on the worksheet until you click the close button in the upper right corner of the window.

Applying Shading Using the Toolbar

Click here to display the menu of shading options.

Click and drag here to make the options a floating palette that can be placed anywhere on the worksheet.

Another way to hide zeros is to select the range of cells where you do not want zeros to be displayed, right-click the selected cells, click Format Cells from the shortcut menu, click the Number tab, click Custom from the Category list box, and key # in the Type box. Click OK.

Turning Off Zeros

If a formula is entered into a cell and the cells being referenced by the formula are empty, a zero will be placed in the cell. In some situations, you may not want this zero to be displayed. To turn off zeros in a worksheet, click Tools and then Options. From the Options dialog box that appears, click the View tab. Under Window options, there is a check box for Zero values. If you do not want zeros to be displayed in a worksheet, this check box should be empty. Click the check box so that it is not selected and click OK.

exercise 2

Using Styles, the Format Painter Button, Custom Formats, Borders and Shading, and Turning Off Zeros

1. Open Excel Worksheet E1-02.
2. Save the file using the Save As command and name it Excel E1, Ex 02.
3. Create a custom header that has your name left-aligned and the name of the file, Excel E1, Ex 02, right-aligned.
4. This worksheet is an invoice used by Greenspace Architects. Greenspace Architects is a nursery that sells plants and flowers and provides landscaping services. The invoice needs to be formatted. Add some lines for filling in the information at the top of the invoice by completing the following steps:

a. Select cells B3 through E3 and right-click one of the selected cells.

b. Click <u>F</u>ormat Cells on the shortcut menu.

c. Click the Border tab on the Format Cells dialog box.

d. Click the second option in the first column in the <u>S</u>tyle list box.

e. Click the button to apply a border to the bottom of the cell.

f. Click OK.

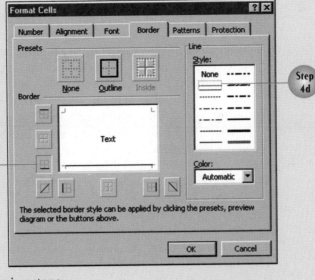

5. Use the Format Painter button to apply the border to the other cells where it is needed at the top of the invoice by completing the following steps:

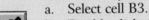

a. Select cell B3.

b. Double-click the Format Painter button.

c. Select cell G2.

d. Select cells B4 through E4.

e. Select cells B5 through C5.

f. Select cells B6 through C6.

g. Select cell E5.

h. Select cells G5 through G6.

i. Select cells E8 through F10.

j. Click the Format Painter button to turn it off.

6. The cells next to the labels MC (for Master Card), V (for Visa), and AX (for American Express) are supposed to be check boxes. Place a border around these cells by completing the following steps:

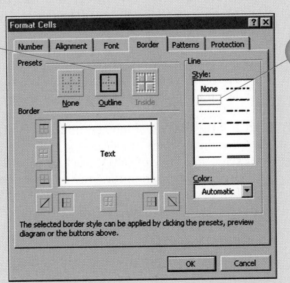

a. Right-click cell C8.

b. Click <u>F</u>ormat Cells on the shortcut menu.

c. If necessary, click the Border tab on the Format Cells dialog box.

d. Click the second option in the first column in the <u>S</u>tyle box.

e. Under Presets, click the <u>O</u>utline button.

f. Click OK.

g. Double-click the Format Painter button.

h. Select cells C8 through C11.

i. Click the Format Painter button to turn it off.

7. Place borders around the ordering information to make it easier to read by completing the following steps:

a. Select cells A14 through A27.
b. Click the down arrow to the right of the Borders button.
c. Click the Outside Borders button, the third button on the last row.
d. Each block of cells that is to be outlined by the border has to be selected separately. Select cells B14 through E27, hold down the Ctrl key, and select cells F14 through F27, cells G14 through G27, G28 through G30, and G31. The Outside Borders button is now the active Border button on the Formatting toolbar. Click the Borders button to apply the outside borders format.

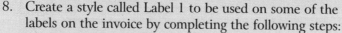

8. Create a style called Label 1 to be used on some of the labels on the invoice by completing the following steps:
a. Select cell A3.
b. Click F̲ormat and then S̲tyle.
c. Change the name in the S̲tyle name box to *Label 1*.
d. Click the N̲umber check box so that there is no longer a check mark in it.
e. Click the M̲odify button.
f. Click the Alignment tab and from the H̲orizontal drop-down menu, select *Right*.
g. Click the Font tab and in the F̲ont Style list box click *Bold*.
h. Click the down arrow to the right of the C̲olor box and click Green, the fourth button in the second row.
i. Click the OK button twice.

9. Apply the Label 1 style to the invoice by completing the following steps:
a. Select cells A4 through A6, hold down the Ctrl key, and select the following cells: D5, F5, F6, B8, B9, B10, B11, D8, D9, D10, F28, F29, F30.
b. Click F̲ormat and then S̲tyle.
c. Click the down arrow to the right of the S̲tyle Name box and select *Label 1*.
d. Click OK.

10. You want to create another style that is similar to the Label 1 style. The easiest way to do this is to start by selecting a cell that uses the Label 1 style. Many of the options you want for the new style will be automatically selected. Create a style called Label 2 by completing the following steps:
a. Select cell A3.
b. Click F̲ormat and then S̲tyle.
c. Change the name in the S̲tyle name box to *Label 2*.
d. Click the N̲umber check box so that there is no longer a check mark in it.
e. Click the M̲odify button.
f. Click the Alignment tab and from the H̲orizontal drop-down menu, select *Center*.
g. Click the OK button twice.
h. Change the Style of cell A3 back to Label 1 by clicking F̲ormat and then S̲tyle and selecting *Label 1* from the S̲tyle name list box.
i. Click OK.

11. Apply the Label 2 style to the invoice by completing the following steps:
a. Select cells A13 through G13.
b. Click F̲ormat and then S̲tyle.
c. Click the down arrow to the right of the S̲tyle name box and click *Label 2*.
d. Click OK.

12. Create a style called Label 3 to be used on some of the labels on the invoice by completing the following steps:
a. Select cell E2.
b. Click F̲ormat and then S̲tyle.

    c.   Change the name in the Style name box to *Label 3*.

    d.   Click the Number check box so that there is no longer a check mark in it.

    e.   Click the Modify button.

    f.   Click the Alignment tab and from the Horizontal drop-down menu, select *Right*.

    g.   Click the Font tab.

        1) From the Font style list box, select *Bold*.

        2) From the Size list box, select *12*.

        3) Click the down arrow to the right of the Color box and select white, the last option in the fifth row.

    h.   Click the Patterns tab and select the green that is the fourth option in the second row.

    i.   Click the OK button twice.

13. Apply the Label 3 style to cell F31 by selecting cell F31, clicking Format and then Style, and selecting *Label 3* from the Style name list box.

14. You decide that the font size for the style Label 1 is too large and you want to change it. Edit the Label 1 style by completing the following steps:

    a.   Select cell A3.

    b.   Click Format and then Style. Make sure that *Label 1* is in the Style name box.

    c.   Click the Modify button.

    d.   Click the Font tab.

    e.   From the Size list box, select *9*.

    f.   Click the OK button twice.

15. You are going to format the numbers on the Invoice so that they are displayed as prices by creating a custom format for the Number format. You want to include one space to the right of any entry formatted as Number. Complete the following steps:

    a.   Select cells F14 through F27.

    b.   Right-click one of the selected cells.

    c.   Select Format Cells on the shortcut menu.

    d.   Click the Number tab.

        1) You want your custom format based on the Number format so first select *Number* from the Category list box and then select *Custom*.

        2) 0.00 should appear in the Type box. You want to include a space equal to the size of the right parenthesis character to the right of the entry. The symbol for inserting this space is _). Place the insertion point to the right of the last zero in the Type box and press the underline key and then the right parenthesis key.

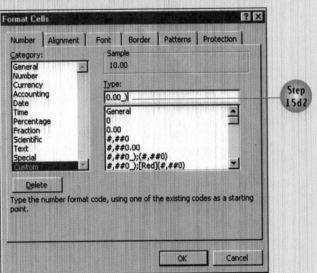

    e.   Click OK.

    f.   Cells F14 through F27 should still be selected. Click the Format Painter button.

    g.   Select cells G14 through G31.

16. You want the first value in a list to be displayed with a dollar sign in front of it. Apply the accounting format to these cells by completing the following steps:
    a. Select cell F14, hold down the Ctrl key, and select cells G14, G28, and G31.
    b. Right-click one of the selected cells.
    c. Select Format Cells on the shortcut menu.
    d. Click the Number tab and select *Accounting* from the Category list box. Make sure a 2 is displayed in the Decimal places box and a dollar sign is displayed in the Symbol box. If necessary, click the down arrow to the right of the Symbol box and select the dollar sign.
    e. Click OK.
17. The formulas in some of the cells in column G do not have any corresponding data for making the calculations so zeros are displayed. Turn off these zeros by completing the following steps:
    a. Click Tools and then Options.
    b. Click the View tab.
    c. Click the Zero values check box so that there is no longer a check mark in it.
    d. Click OK.
18. You want to make the prices in the Amount column stand out by adding some shading. Complete the following steps:
    a. Select cells G14 through G31.
    b. Click the down arrow next to the Fill color button on the Formatting toolbar.
    c. Click the palest green color, the fourth option in the last row.
19. Make sure none of the outside borders you set in step 7 have been lost. There should be an outside border around the following cells: A14:A27, B14:E27, F14:F27, G14:G27, G28:G30, and G31. Reset any missing borders.
20. Save the worksheet with the same name (Excel E1, Ex 02).
21. Print and then close Excel E1, Ex 02.

Using AutoFormat

Excel includes many predesigned formats that can be easily applied to a worksheet. To use a predesigned format, select the cells to which the format is to apply. Click Format and then AutoFormat. The AutoFormat dialog box is shown in figure 1.11. A preview of what each format looks like is displayed. To select a format, click its preview. There are seventeen different predesigned formats available. Use the scroll bar to see more of the formats.

figure

1.11

The AutoFormat Dialog Box

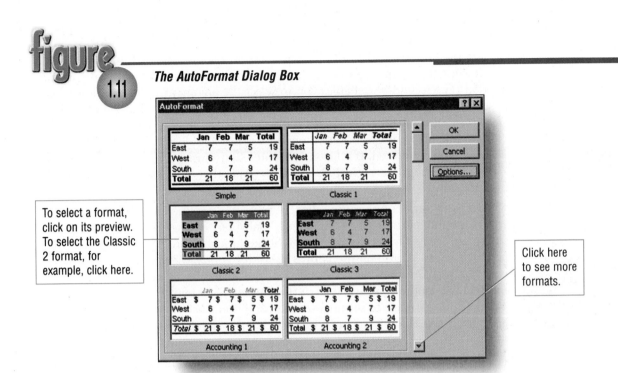

To select a format, click on its preview. To select the Classic 2 format, for example, click here.

Click here to see more formats.

Using Conditional Formatting

There may be times when you want to format cells in a particular way only if they meet a specific condition. For example, you may want to be alerted if sales figures dip below a specific number and therefore want only those entries to be displayed in red. Conditional formatting allows you to specify how cells that meet a specific condition should be formatted. To use conditional formatting, first select the cells to which the formatting should apply. Click Format and then Conditional Formatting. The Conditional Formatting dialog box, as shown in figure 1.12, is displayed.

figure

1.12

The Conditional Formatting Dialog Box

Click here to display the list of arguments.

Enter values here.

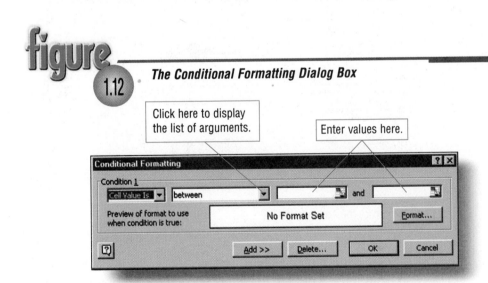

The default entry for the first box is *Cell Value Is*. This is the option you will want in most cases, particularly if the formula in the cell results in a value. If however, the formula in the cell produces a result such as True or False, you would want to click the down arrow at the right side of the first box and select the *Formula Is* option. The second box enables you to select the argument. Click the down arrow at the right side of the box to see the list of arguments which includes *not between, equal to, not equal to, greater than, less than, greater than or equal to*, and *less than or equal to*. In the remaining box or boxes you enter a constant value or formula if the *Cell Value Is* option is selected. If a formula is entered, it must begin with an equal sign. If the *Formula Is* option is selected, enter a formula that evaluates to a logical value of true or false.

To set the formatting for the cells that meet the condition you have defined, click the <u>F</u>ormat button. The Format Cells dialog box appears. Using this dialog box you can set <u>F</u>ont style, <u>U</u>nderline, <u>C</u>olor, Stri<u>k</u>ethrough, Border, and Patterns. Once you click the OK button on the Format Cells dialog box, the Conditional Formatting dialog box appears again. A preview of what the entries in the cells that meet the condition will look like is displayed in the Preview of format to use when condition is true box. If you want to set up a second condition, click the Add button. The dialog box expands to include a section for defining the second condition, as is shown in figure 1.13. You can define formatting for up to three conditions.

Conditional formatting can also be used for formatting nonnumeric data, such as text strings. Say, for example, the words "Pass" and "Fail" are text strings entered in a worksheet and you want all the "Pass" text strings to be green and all the "Fail" text strings to be red. In order to conditionally format these text strings, the *Cell Value Is* option should be selected in the first box on the Conditional Formatting dialog box, the *equal to* option should be selected in the second box, and either **Pass** or **Fail** should be entered in the third box.

When using conditional formatting, the Number, Alignment, and Protection tabs are not available on the Format Cells dialog box. The options from these tabs cannot be changed using conditional formatting.

figure
1.13

Adding a Second Condition for Conditional Formatting

A preview of what the formatting will look like in cells where the condition is true is displayed here.

When you click the Add button, a section for defining another condition is displayed.

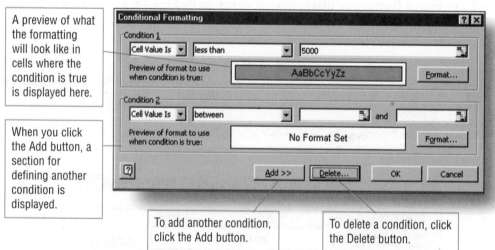

To add another condition, click the Add button.

To delete a condition, click the Delete button.

. To delete a condition, click the <u>D</u>elete button. The Delete Conditional Format dialog box shown in figure 1.14 is displayed. Simply select the condition you want to delete and click OK.

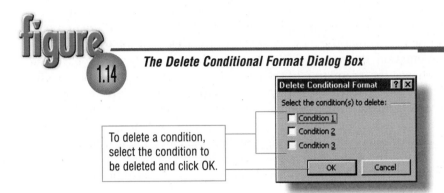

figure 1.14

The Delete Conditional Format Dialog Box

To delete a condition, select the condition to be deleted and click OK.

Adjusting the Layout of a Worksheet

In order to have a worksheet print on one page, adjustments to the layout of the worksheet are often necessary. There are several things you can do to adjust the layout of a worksheet in order to have it print on one page. First, you can make the margins smaller by clicking File and then Page Setup. On the Page Setup dialog box, click the Margins tab. As shown in figure 1.15, there is a box for the Top, Bottom, Left, and Right margins. To change the margins, you can either select the current entry and enter a new margin setting, or you can click the up or down arrow to the right of the box to make the margin larger or smaller. You can also adjust the distance of the header from the top of the page and the footer from the bottom of the page. In the Center on page section, you can select the Horizontally check box to have the worksheet centered horizontally on the page or the Vertically check box to have the worksheet centered vertically on the page.

> The distance entered in the Header and Footer boxes must be less than the distance entered in the Top and Bottom margin boxes or else the data in the worksheet will overlap the header or footer when the worksheet is printed.
>
> *Hint*

figure 1.15

The Page Setup Dialog Box with Margins Tab Selected

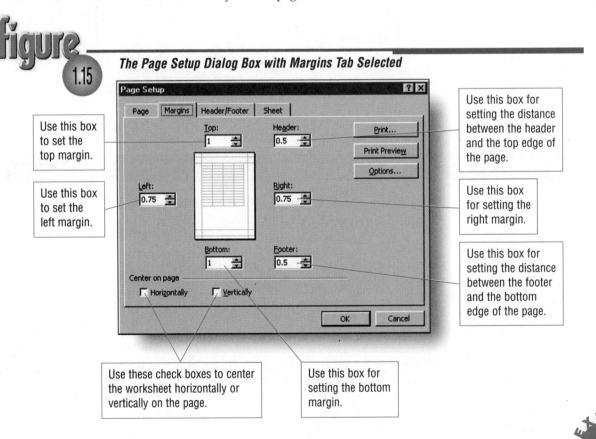

Use this box to set the top margin.

Use this box to set the left margin.

Use these check boxes to center the worksheet horizontally or vertically on the page.

Use this box for setting the bottom margin.

Use this box for setting the distance between the header and the top edge of the page.

Use this box for setting the right margin.

Use this box for setting the distance between the footer and the bottom edge of the page.

In many cases worksheets are wider than they are long and would be more appropriately printed in landscape rather than portrait. With portrait orientation the page is oriented so that the narrowest edge of the page is at the top. With landscape orientation, the page is oriented so that the widest edge of the page is at the top. To change the orientation of the page, click File and then Page Setup. On the Page Setup dialog box, click the Page tab. As shown in figure 1.16, the options for Portrait and Landscape orientation are on this tab. You can also scale the size of the worksheet. To reduce the worksheet size by a specific percentage of its full size, either select the current entry in the Adjust to box and enter a new scaling percentage or click the up or down arrow to the right of the Adjust to box to increase or reduce the scaling percentage. Use the Fit to option to fit the worksheet onto a specified number of pages.

Column widths, row heights, page margins, and page breaks determine the number of columns and rows that print on a page. Another way to adjust exactly what data fits on a printed page is to adjust the settings for these options.

Hint

figure
1.16

The Page Setup Dialog Box with Page Tab Selected

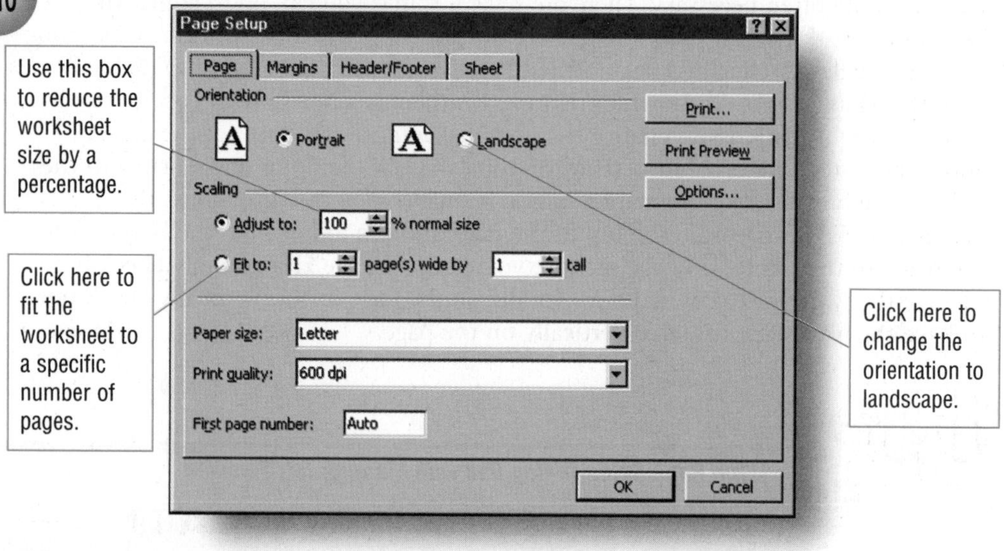

Use this box to reduce the worksheet size by a percentage.

Click here to fit the worksheet to a specific number of pages.

Click here to change the orientation to landscape.

Page Setup dialog box showing Page, Margins, Header/Footer, Sheet tabs. Orientation: Portrait (selected), Landscape. Scaling: Adjust to 100 % normal size; Fit to 1 page(s) wide by 1 tall. Paper size: Letter. Print quality: 600 dpi. First page number: Auto. Buttons: Print..., Print Preview, Options..., OK, Cancel.

exercise 3

Using AutoFormat, Creating a Conditional Format, and Adjusting the Layout of the Worksheet

1. Open Excel Worksheet E1-03.
2. Save the file with Save As and name it Excel E1, Ex 03.
3. Create a custom header that has your name left-aligned and the name of the file, Excel E1, Ex 03, right-aligned.
4. Copper Clad Incorporated is a manufacturing company that designs and manufactures printed circuit boards. The company has a sales force of twelve sales representatives who are responsible for selling their printed circuit boards across the United States. This worksheet records each sales representative's sales for each month in the year 2000. Format the worksheet using AutoFormat by completing the following steps:

a. Select cells A5 through N18 by completing the following steps:
   1) Click cell A5 to select it.
   2) Move the mouse pointer to the bottom edge of cell A5. The mouse pointer should turn into an arrow.
   3) Press the Shift key. While holding down the Shift key, double-click the bottom edge of cell A5. Cells A5 through A19 should be selected.
   4) Move the mouse pointer to the right edge of the selected cells. The mouse pointer should turn into an arrow.
   5) Press the Shift key. While holding down the Shift key, double-click the right edge of the selected cells. Cells A5 through N18 should now be selected.

b. Click Format and then AutoFormat.

c. Select the Accounting 2 Style.

d. Click OK.

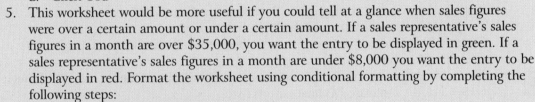

Step 4c

5. This worksheet would be more useful if you could tell at a glance when sales figures were over a certain amount or under a certain amount. If a sales representative's sales figures in a month are over $35,000, you want the entry to be displayed in green. If a sales representative's sales figures in a month are under $8,000 you want the entry to be displayed in red. Format the worksheet using conditional formatting by completing the following steps:

a. Select cells B6 through M17.

b. Click Format and then Conditional Formatting.

c. Click the down arrow to the right of the second box in the Conditional Formatting dialog box and select *greater than*.

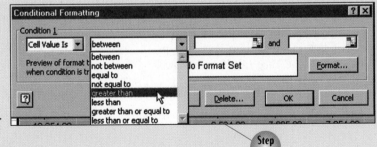

Step 5c

d. Enter **35000** in the third box.

e. Click the Format button.

f. If necessary, click the Font tab.
   1) Click *Bold* on the Font style list box.
   2) Click the down arrow at the right side of the Color box.
   3) Click the Sea Green button, the fourth button in the third row.
   4) Click OK. In the Preview of format to use when condition is true box, the letters should be green.

g. Click the Add button.

h. Under Condition 2, click the down arrow to the right of the second box in the Conditional Formatting dialog box and select *less than*.

Step 5g

i. Enter **8000** in the third box.

j. Click the Format button.

k. If necessary, click the Font tab.
   1) Click *Bold* on the Font style list box.
   2) Click the down arrow at the right side of the Color box.
   3) Click the Red button, the first button in the third row.
   4) Click OK. In the Preview of format to use when condition is true box, the letters should be red.

l. Click OK.

6. As it is currently formatted, the worksheet will not fit on one page. Complete the following steps to adjust the worksheet so that it will fit onto one page.

a. Click File and then Page Setup.

b. Click the Page tab if necessary.

c. Click the Landscape option.

d. Click the Margins tab.
   1) Select the current setting in the Top box and enter **0.75**.
   2) Select the current setting in the Left box and enter **0.5**.
   3) Select the current setting in the Bottom box and enter **0.5**.
   4) Select the current setting in the Right box and enter **0.5**.

e. Click the Print Preview button. The worksheet still will not fit on one page.

f. Click the Close button.

g. To save room, you do not want any decimal places displayed. Select cells B6 through N18. Click the Decrease Decimal button twice.

h. You want to automatically adjust the widths of the columns now that the numbers in the cells are not as wide. Cells B6 through N18 should still be selected. Click Format, point to Column and click AutoFit Selection.

i. Click the Print Preview button. The worksheet still does not fit on one page, but it is getting close. Click the Close button.

j. Click File and then Page Setup.

k. Click the Page tab if necessary.

l. Under Scaling, click the Fit to option. The page(s) wide by box and tall box should both display *1*.

m. Click OK.

7. Save the worksheet with the same name (Excel E1, Ex 03).

8. Print and then close Excel E1, Ex 03.

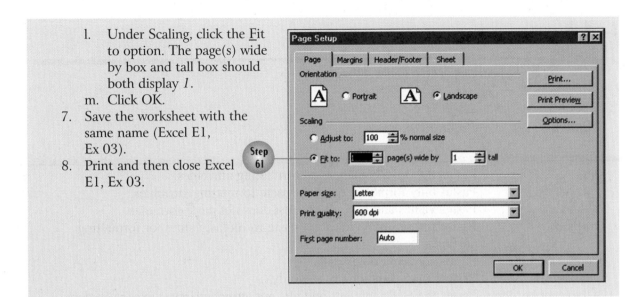

Step 61

Using the Paste Special Command

When you use the Paste command, the entire contents of the cell or cells, including formulas and formats, are pasted. There may be times when you want to copy the contents of a cell, but you do not want to paste its format or you want to paste just the values and not the formulas. The Paste Special command allows you to do this. To access the Paste Special command, you first have to copy some cells and then click Edit and Paste Special. The Paste Special dialog box, as shown in figure 1.17 is displayed.

figure 1.17

The Paste Special Dialog Box

The Paste Special dialog box provides options for many unique pasting situations. Table 1.2 describes all the options on the Paste Special dialog box. All the options under Paste relate to what is going to be pasted. All the options under Operation relate to how the copied cells are to be combined with the cells to which they are being copied. The copied cells could, for example, be added to the cells into which they are pasted.

table

1.2 *The Paste Special Dialog Box*

Option	Description
Paste	
All	Pastes the cell's contents and formatting attributes.
Formulas	Pastes only formulas; does not paste formatting attributes.
Values	Pastes values and formula results; does not paste formulas.
Formats	Pastes formats only; does not paste formulas, values, or formatting attributes.
Comments	Pastes comment notes only.
Validation	Pastes data validation criteria only.
All except borders	Pastes the cell's contents and all formatting attributes except borders.
Column widths	Pastes the column widths only; does not paste formulas, values, or formatting attributes.
Operation	
None	The contents of the copied cells replace the contents of the cells into which they are being pasted.
Add	The contents of the copied cells are added to the contents of the cells into which they are being pasted.
Subtract	The contents of the copied cells are subtracted from the contents of the cells into which they are being pasted.
Multiply	The contents of the copied cells are multiplied by the contents of the cells into which they are being pasted.
Divide	The cells into which the copied cells are being pasted are divided by the copied cells.
Skip blanks	Any blank cells that are copied will not replace the contents of the cells into which they are pasted.
Transpose	Places the contents of rows into columns and the contents of columns into rows.

Another way to hide a row is by dragging the bottom border of the row heading to the top border of the row heading. A column can be hidden by dragging the right border of the column heading to the left border of the column heading.

Hint

Hiding and Unhiding Rows, Columns, and Sheets

There may be times when you do not want certain columns displayed. Say for example you had a worksheet open that contained confidential payroll information. You could hide specific columns so that the confidential information would not be visible to anyone passing by your computer. To hide a column or columns, first select the columns to be hidden. Click Format, point to Column, and click Hide. The columns are then hidden. You can tell if a column is hidden because its column header will not be displayed. If you hid column F, the column headers displayed at the top of the worksheet would be D, E, G, H, and so on. To unhide a hidden column, select the column to the left and the column to the right of the hidden column. Click Format, select Column, and click Unhide.

EXPERT *E-28*

Chapter One

The process for hiding and unhiding rows is the same as for columns. First select the row or rows to be hidden. Click Format, select Row and click Hide. The rows are then hidden. You can tell if a row is hidden because its row header will not be displayed. To unhide a hidden row, select the row above and the row below the hidden row. Click Format, select Row, and click Unhide.

If a row or column is hidden, it will not print.

To hide a sheet, click the tab for that sheet so that it is displayed. Click Format, select Sheet, and click Hide. The sheet is hidden and its tab is no longer displayed. To unhide a hidden sheet, click Format, select Sheet, and click Unhide. The Unhide dialog box shown in figure 1.18 is displayed. Select the sheet to be unhidden and click OK.

figure
1.18

The Unhide Dialog Box

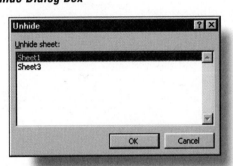

exercise 4

Using the Paste Special Dialog Box and Hiding and Unhiding Columns

1. Open Excel Worksheet E1-04.
2. Save the file using the Save As command and name it Excel E1, Ex 04.
3. Create a custom header that has your name left-aligned and the name of the file, Excel E1, Ex 04, right-aligned.
4. This worksheet is for a company called Performance Threads: Theatrical Fabrics, Draperies and Supplies. Performance Threads is a company that supplies the entertainment industry (theatre, film, and television) with a full line of theatrical fabrics, stage draperies, scenic, and production supplies. This worksheet lists some prices of ornate tassels the company sells. Format the numbers in this worksheet by completing the following steps:
   a. Select cells B4 through G4.
   b. Right-click one of the selected cells.
   c. Click on Format Cells from the shortcut menu.
   d. Click the Number tab if necessary.
   e. Click *Fraction* in the Category list box.
   f. Click *Up to one digit (1/4)* in the Type list box if necessary.
   g. Click OK.
   h. Select cells B5 through G5. Hold down the Ctrl key and select cells B7 through G7.
    i. Click the Currency Style button on the Formatting toolbar.

j.   Select cells B6 through G6.

    k.   Click the Percent Style button on the Formatting toolbar.

5.   Adjust the widths of columns E, F, and G by completing the following steps:

    a.   Select columns E, F, and G.

    b.   Double-click the column header border between column E and F.

6.   The data is not very easy to read as it is currently arranged on the worksheet. Transposing the columns and rows would make the data easier to understand. Transpose the columns and rows by completing the following steps:

    a.   Select cells A3 through G7.

    b.   Click the Copy button on the Standard toolbar.

    c.   Click cell A9.

    d.   Click the Edit menu and click Paste Special.

    e.   Click the Transpose check box in the Paste Special dialog box.

    f.   Click OK.

    g.   Now you need to delete the old data. Select rows 3 through 7, click Edit and then click Delete.

7.   Adjust the widths of the columns by completing the following steps:

    a.   Select columns A through E.

    b.   Double-click on any one of the selected column header borders.

8.   You want to delete column D. Select cell E5 and notice that the formula in cell E5 references cell D5. If you delete column D, error messages will appear in column E. In order to delete column D, you must first change the formulas to values. Complete the following steps to change the formulas to values:

    a.   Select cells E5 through E10.

    b.   Click the Copy button on the Standard toolbar.

    c.   Select cell E5.

    d.   Click the Edit menu and click Paste Special.

    e.   Under Paste, click the Values option.

    f.   Click OK. Notice that now there are values, not formulas, in cells E5 through E10.

    g.   Press Esc to turn off the copy border.

9.   Delete column D by completing the following steps:

    a.   Select column D.

    b.   Click Edit and then click Delete.

10.   You want to do some quick calculations. Sales representatives earn 8% commission on sales they make. Complete the following steps to quickly calculate what 8% of the price Per Dozen is.

    a.   Enter **8% Commission** in cell E4.

    b.   Enter .08 in cell E5.

    c.   Double-click on the AutoFill fill handle in the lower right corner of cell E5.

    d.   Select cells D5 through D10.

    e.   Click the Copy button on the Standard toolbar.

    f.   Select cell E5.

    g.   Click Edit and click Paste Special.

h.   In the Operation section, click the <u>M</u>ultiply option.
i.   Click OK.
j.   Press Esc to turn off the copy border.
11.   Someone has asked to see the prices for the tassels. You want to hide column E, the sales representatives' commission, before you show them to this person. Hide column E by completing the following steps:
a.   Select column E.
b.   Click F<u>o</u>rmat, point to <u>C</u>olumn and click <u>H</u>ide.
12.   Print the worksheet with the column hidden.
13.   Unhide the column by completing the following steps:
a.   Select columns D and F.
b.   Click F<u>o</u>rmat, point to <u>C</u>olumn and click <u>U</u>nhide.
14.   Save the worksheet with the same name (Excel E1, Ex 04). Close Excel E1, Ex 04.

Using the Page Break Preview Command

The Page Break Preview command enables you to see where page breaks are going to occur. In addition, you can edit where the page breaks are going to appear in this preview mode. If you adjust a page break so that more data is going to appear on a page, Excel automatically scales the data so that it will fit on the page. There are two ways to access the Page Break Preview command. One way is to click <u>V</u>iew and then click <u>P</u>age Break Preview. The second way is to click the Print Preview button on the Standard toolbar and then to click the Page Break Pre<u>v</u>iew button. A display similar to the one shown in figure 1.19 appears. The blue lines indicate the current page breaks. By clicking and dragging on these lines you can adjust where the page breaks will occur. To return to the Normal view, click the Print Preview button and then click the Normal <u>V</u>iew button.

Any rows and/or columns you may have defined as print titles to repeat on every page are not displayed in Page Break Preview. They are only displayed in Print Preview.

figure 1.19

Page Break Preview Mode

Click and drag the blue lines to adjust the page breaks.

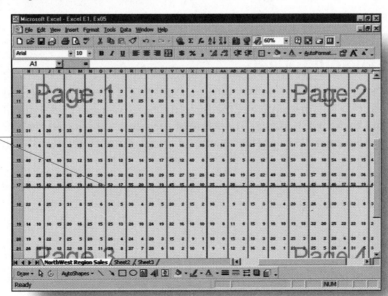

Changing Page Order

As you can see in figure 1.19, a worksheet can be both too wide to fit on one page as well as be too long to fit on one page. When this occurs, Excel can either print all the pages going across first and then print the pages going down, or it can print all the pages going down first and then print the pages going across. In figure 1.19, the pages going across will be printed first (as indicated by the Page 1 and Page 2 labels), and then the pages going down (as indicated by the Page 3 and Page 4 labels). The default setting is to print all the pages going down first and then print all the pages going across. To change this, Click File, Page Setup, and then click the Sheet tab. As shown in figure 1.20, the options for changing the order in which the pages are printed are found under Page order.

Selecting the Order Worksheet Pages Are Printed

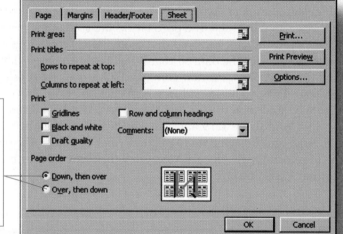

If worksheet pages are both too wide and too long to fit on one page, they either can be printed going down first and then across, or printed going across first and then going down.

Renaming Sheets

The default names on the Sheet tabs are *Sheet1*, *Sheet2*, *Sheet3*, and so on. If you want a more descriptive name for your sheets you can click Format, point to Sheet, and then click Rename. The name of the currently selected sheet is highlighted. Simply enter the new sheet name and press Enter to rename the sheet.

exercise 5

Transposing Data, Creating a Custom Format, Using Page Break Preview, Changing Page Order, Renaming Sheets, Hiding and Unhiding Columns

1. Open Excel Worksheet E1-05.
2. Save the file using the Save <u>A</u>s command and name it Excel E1, Ex 05.
3. Create a custom header that has your name left-aligned and the name of the file, Excel E1, Ex 05, right-aligned.
4. The Whitewater Canoe and Kayak Corporation is a company that makes and sells custom made canoes and kayaks and related sporting supplies to dealers around the country. This worksheet shows the number of canoes and kayaks Whitewater Canoe and Kayak's resellers ordered each month for the years 2000 and 2001. The data is not very easy to understand the way it is currently formatted. It would be easier to understand if the columns displayed the dates and the rows displayed the resellers. Complete the following steps to transpose the rows and columns.
   a. Click cell A3 to select it. Move the mouse pointer to the bottom edge of cell A3. When the mouse pointer turns into an arrow, hold down the Shift key and double-click. Cells A3 through A51 should be selected. Move the mouse pointer to the right edge of the selected cells. When the mouse pointer turns into an arrow, hold down the Shift key and double-click. Cells A3 through U51 should be selected.

   b. Click the Copy button.
   c. Select cell A53.
   d. Click <u>E</u>dit and then Paste <u>S</u>pecial.
   e. Click the Transpo<u>s</u>e check box in the Paste Special Dialog box.
   f. Click OK.
   g. Now you need to delete the old data. Select rows 3 through 51, click <u>E</u>dit and then click <u>D</u>elete.
   h. Select columns A through AW.
   i. Click F<u>o</u>rmat, point to <u>C</u>olumn, and click <u>A</u>utoFit Selection.
   j. Click in any cell so that the columns are no longer selected.
   k. Drag the right column heading border to column A until column A is 9.86 points wide.
   l. Select rows 6 through 24.
   m. Click F<u>o</u>rmat, point to <u>R</u>ow, click <u>A</u>utoFit.
5. You could save a considerable amount of space if all the "Canoes" and "Kayaks" labels were angled. Angle the labels by completing the following steps:
   a. Select row 4.
   b. Right click on any one of the selected cells and click <u>F</u>ormat Cells on the shortcut menu.
   c. Click the Alignment tab.
   d. Click the red dot in the Orientation box and drag it until *60* is displayed in the <u>D</u>egrees box.
   e. Click OK.
6. Use the Merge and Center button to merge cells B5 and C5, D5 and E5, F5 and G5, H5 and I5, and so on until the two cells for each date are merged.
7. Adding borders around the two columns that represent one month would make the worksheet easier to understand. Complete the following steps to add the borders:

a.   Select cells B4 through C24.

b.   Right click on any one of the selected cells and click Format Cells from the shortcut menu.

c.   Click the Border tab.

d.   Under Presets, click the Outline button.

e.   Click OK.

f.   Cells B4 through C24 should still be selected. Double-click the Format Painter button.

g.   Click cell D4. The format is applied. Click cell F4. The format is applied. Continue clicking every other cell until the cells representing each month have a border around them.

h.   Click the Format Painter button to turn it off.

8.   You want to create a custom format so that the numbers are indented from the right side of the cell. Complete the following steps to create the custom format.

a.   Select cells B6 through AW24.

b.   Right-click on any one of the selected cells and click ·Format Cells from the shortcut menu.

c.   Click the Number tab.

d.   Click *Custom* in the Category list box.

e.   In the Type box, enter **0_0**.

f.   Click OK.

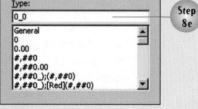

9.   Complete the following steps to use the AutoFit command to reduce the widths of the columns:

a.   Select columns B through AW.

b.   Click Format, point to Column and click AutoFit Selection.

10. Adding shading to the numbers would also make them easier to read. Complete the following steps to add shading:

a.   Select cells B6 through AW24.

b.   Click the down arrow to the right of the Fill Color button.

c.   Click the Light Green button, the fourth button in the last row.

11. Adjust the layout of the worksheet by changing the orientation to landscape and setting the left and right margins to 0.5 inches.

12. You need your labels to appear on each page. Complete the following steps to select rows 4 and 5 to repeat at the top of each page and column A to repeat at the left of each page:

a.   Click File and then click Page Setup.

b.   Click the Sheet tab.

c.   Click the button to the right of the Rows to repeat at top box.

d.   Select rows 4 and 5.

e.   Click the button at the right side of the Page Setup - Rows to repeat at top dialog box that appears.

f. Click the button at the right side of the <u>C</u>olumns to repeat at left box.

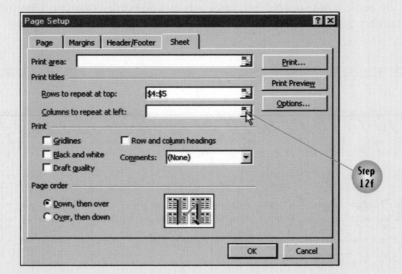

Step
12f

g. Select column A.
h. Click the button at the right side of the Page Setup - Columns to repeat at left dialog box that appears.

Step
12h

i. Change the Page Order by selecting the O<u>v</u>er, then down option under Page order.

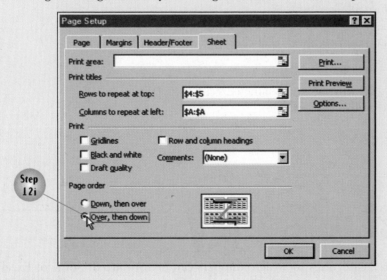

Step
12i

j. Click OK.
13. Complete the following steps to use Page Break Preview to change the page breaks.
a. Click the Print Preview button.
b. Click the Page Break Pre<u>v</u>iew button. If the Welcome to Page Break Preview dialog box is displayed, click the OK button.

c. Currently, page 1 breaks in the middle of the figures for December 2000. Click and drag the vertical blue dotted line until it is on the border between December 2000 and January 2001.

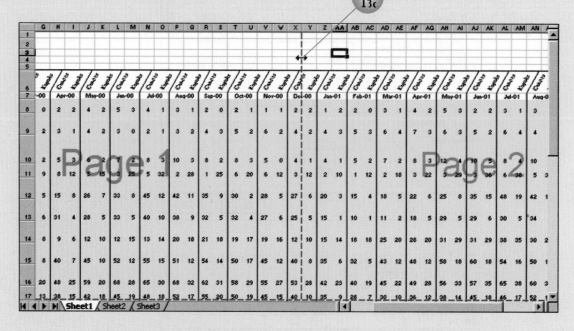

d. Drag the horizontal blue dotted line until it is between rows 17 and 18.
e. Click the Print Preview button.
f. Click the Normal View button.
14. Rename the sheet by completing the following steps:
    a. Click Format, point to Sheet, and click Rename.
    b. Key **Sales**.
    c. Press Enter.
15. Save the worksheet with the same name (Excel E1, Ex 05).
16. Print and then close Excel E1, Ex 05.

chapter summary

➤ Excel includes 12 categories by which numbers can be formatted. Some of Excel's more specialized number formats include Accounting, Fraction, and Scientific.

➤ The main difference between the Currency and Accounting formats is that the Accounting format aligns the currency symbols at the left side of the cell and the Currency format does not.

➤ The Scientific format is used for very large or very small numbers.

➤ When you create a custom format, the format you create is added to the bottom of the Type list box, where it can be selected and used as often as needed.

➤ Use the Alignment tab of the Format Cells dialog box to manage large labels by wrapping the text within a cell, shrinking the cell's entry to fit within one cell, or rotating the label a specified number of degrees.

➤ When you automatically adjust the width of a column or the height of a row, the column is displayed at its optimum width or the row is displayed at its optimum height.

➤ A style is a predefined set of formatting attributes. Each one of the check boxes on the Style dialog box corresponds to one of the tabs on the Format Cells dialog box. There are several advantages to using styles. Using styles helps to assure that the formatting from one worksheet to another is consistent, enables you to define the attributes for a particular style one time only, and simplifies editing.

➤ Excel includes 17 different predesigned formats.

➤ The layout of large worksheets often needs to be adjusted in order to have the worksheet print on as few pages as possible. Reduce the margins at the Page Setup dialog box with the Margins tab selected. Change the orientation to landscape and reduce the worksheet size by a percentage of its full size at the Page Setup dialog box with the Page tab selected.

commands review

	Mouse/Keyboard
Apply number format	Click Format, Cells
Create a custom format	Click Format, Cells, and select *Custom*
Format large labels	Click Format, Cells, Alignment tab
Automatically adjust column widths	Click Format, Column, AutoFit Selection
Automatically adjust row height	Click Format, Row, AutoFit
Create a style	Click Format, Style
Apply borders	Click Format, Cells, Border tab
Apply shading	Click Format, Cells, Border tab
Turn off zeros	Click Tools, Options, View tab
Apply a predesigned format	Click Format, AutoFormat
Create a conditional format	Click Format, Conditional Formatting
Transpose columns/rows	Click Edit, Paste Special, Transpose check box
Hide columns	Click Format, Column, Hide
Hide rows	Click Format, Row, Hide
Unhide columns	Click Format, Column, Unhide
Unhide rows	Click Format, Row, Unhide
Adjust page breaks	Click View, Page Break Preview
Change order pages are printed	Click File, Page Setup, Sheet tab
Rename sheets	Click Format, Sheet, Rename

thinking offline

Completion: In the space provided at the right, indicate the correct term, command, or symbol.

1. This numbering format is used to display very large or very small numbers.

2. To create a custom format that uses text, the text must be enclosed by these characters.

3. To center a label across all the columns in a worksheet, click this button on the Formatting toolbar.

4. A label can be formatted so that it prints at an angle at the Format Cells dialog box with this tab selected.

5. Double-click on this location to automatically adjust a column so that the widest entry in the column fits in one cell.

6. These are what each one of the check boxes on the Style dialog box corresponds to.

7. To apply the formatting from one cell to another cell, click this button on the Standard toolbar.

8. Turn off zeros with an option at the Options dialog box with this tab selected.

9. Scale the size of the worksheet by a specific percentage of its full size at the Page Setup dialog box with this tab selected.

10. Use this dialog box to add the values in copied cells to the values in the cells into which they are being pasted.

11. If you are currently viewing a worksheet in the Page Break Preview mode and you want to return to the Normal view, you must click this button on the Standard toolbar.

12. Change the order in which worksheet pages are printed at the Page Setup dialog box with this tab selected.

13. List the advantages of applying formatting using styles.

14. List the steps you would complete to create a conditional format that printed all values greater than 150 as blue and italicized.

15. Column J is currently hidden. List the steps you would take to unhide it.

working hands-on

Assessment 1

1. Open Excel Worksheet E1-06.
2. Save the worksheet using the Save <u>A</u>s command and name it Excel E1, SA 01.
3. Create a custom header that has your name left-aligned and the file name right-aligned.
4. Center the label in cell A5 across columns A, B, and C.
5. Format the numbers in cells A8 through A12 as fractions, up to one digit.
6. Create a custom format for the numbers in cells A8 through A12. The format should read *inches*.
7. Center and bold each of the labels in row 7.
8. Format the numbers in cells C8 through C12 as Accounting.
9. Add a light yellow shading to the cells C8 through C12.
10. Save the worksheet again with the same name (Excel E1, SA 01).
11. Print and then close Excel E1, SA 01.

Assessment 2

1. Open Excel Worksheet E1-07.
2. Save the worksheet using the Save <u>A</u>s command and name it Excel E1, SA 02.
3. Create a custom header that has your name left-aligned and the file name right-aligned.
4. Align the labels in cells B6 through G6 so that they are at a 75 degree angle.
5. Automatically adjust the widths of columns B through G.
6. Center the label in cell A5 across columns A through G.
7. Print the worksheet.
8. Copy cells A7 through A10 to cells A13 through A16.
9. Enter the label **Projections** in cell A12.
10. You want to know how many sections would be offered if the number of sections was increased by 2 for each semester. Enter 2 in cells B13 through G16.
11. Copy cells B7 through G10. Use the Paste Special command to add the values in these cells to the values in cells B13 through G16.
12. Print the worksheet again.
13. Save the worksheet again with the same name (Excel E1, SA 02).
14. Close Excel E1, SA 02.

Assessment 3

1. Open Excel Worksheet E1-08.
2. Save the worksheet using the Save <u>A</u>s command and name it Excel E1, SA 03.
3. Create a custom header that has your name left-aligned and the file name right-aligned.
4. Center the label in A7 across columns A through F.
5. Create a custom format for cells A9 through A14 that does not display the leading zero and adds two single quotation marks to the right of the number to indicate the symbol for inches. *(Hint: You may need to refer to table 1.1. The single quotation marks should be treated like text when creating the format.)*

6. Create a custom format for cells B9 through F14 that displays only one decimal place and adds the capital letter A, which is the symbol for amps, to the right of the numbers.
7. Place a border around each cell from cell A7 through cell F14. *(Hint: Use the Borders button on the Formatting toolbar and select the All Borders option, the second button on the last row.)*
8. Add a light green shading to cell A7.
9. Automatically adjust the widths of columns B through F so that they are just wide enough to display the widest entry in each column.
10. Save the worksheet again with the same name (Excel E1, SA 03) and print it.
11. Close Excel E1, SA 03.

Assessment 4

1. Open Excel Worksheet E1-09.
2. Save the worksheet using the Save <u>A</u>s command and name it Excel E1, SA 04.
3. Create a custom header that has your name left-aligned and the file name right-aligned.
4. Format the numbers in column B as fractions, up to one digit.
5. Create a custom format for cells B7 through B10 that adds "lbs" to the right of the numbers. Apply this custom format to cells B14 through B17 and cells B21 through B24.
6. Format the numbers in column C as Accounting with two decimal places and the dollar sign displayed.
7. Select cell A5. Create a style called Header 1. The font for the Header 1 style should be the Century Gothic font (or another sans serif font), the font style should be italic, the size should be 12, and the color should be green.
8. Apply the Header 1 style to cells A12 and A19.
9. Select cell A6. Create a style called Header 2. The horizontal alignment for the Header 2 style should be centered, the font should be Century Gothic (or another sans serif font), the font style should be bold, the size should be 11, and there should be an outside border around the cell.
10. Apply the Header 2 style to cells B6, C6, A13, B13, C13, A20, B20, C20.
11. Print the worksheet.
12. Edit the Header 1 style so that the font style is bold italic instead of just italic.
13. Edit the Header 2 style so that it includes a light green background.
14. Print the worksheet again.
15. Save the worksheet again with the same name (Excel E1, SA 04).
16. Close Excel E1, SA 04.

Assessment 5

1. Open Excel Worksheet E1-10.
2. Save the worksheet using the Save <u>A</u>s command and name it Excel E1, SA 05.
3. Create a custom header that has your name left-aligned and the file name right-aligned.
4. Apply the AutoFormat style List 1 to cells A7 through B29 as well as to cells D7 through E29.
5. Center the label in cell A6 across columns A and B. Center the label in cell D6 across cells D6 and E6. Center the label in cell A5 across cells A5 through E5.

6. Create a conditional format to apply to the numbers in cells B8 through B29 and cells E8 through E29. If a number is less than 75, it should be displayed in the bold italic font style and the color orange. If a number is greater than 250, it should be displayed in the bold italic font style and the color blue.
7. Save the worksheet again with the same name (Excel E1, SA 05) and print it.
8. Close Excel E1, SA 05.

Assessment 6

1. Open Excel Worksheet E1-11.
2. Save the worksheet using the Save <u>A</u>s command and name it Excel E1, SA 06.
3. Create a custom header that has your name left-aligned and the file name right-aligned.
4. Using the Paste Special command, transpose the entries in cells A5 through K13. *(Hint: You will have to paste the cells to a clear part of the worksheet and then delete the original entries.)*
5. Apply the AutoFormat style Classic 2 to the appropriate cells in the worksheet.
6. Print the worksheet.
7. Hide columns containing the Hourly Rate figures and the Gross Pay figures.
8. Print the worksheet again.
9. Unhide columns that were hidden in step 7.
10. Save the worksheet again with the same name (Excel E1, SA 06).
11. Close Excel E1, SA 06.

Assessment 7

1. Open Excel Worksheet E1-12.
2. Save the worksheet using the Save <u>A</u>s command and name it Excel E1, SA 07.
3. Create a custom header that has your name left-aligned and the file name right-aligned.
4. Angle the labels in row 4 so that they are at a 60 degree angle.
5. Adjust the width of columns B through Y using the <u>A</u>utoFit Selection command.
6. Change the page orientation to landscape. Scale the page so that it fits to 1 page wide by 2 pages tall.
7. Set up the sheet so that rows 2 through 4 print at the top of every page. Set the left and right margins to 0.5 inch.
8. Use the Page Break Preview command to adjust the page breaks so that the temperatures for the state of Montana are printed at the top of page two.
9. Create a conditional format to apply to all the temperatures. If a temperature is between 70 and 82 degrees, it should display as bold and the cell should be shaded with pale blue.
10. Save the worksheet again with the same name (Excel E1, SA 07) and print it.
11. Close Excel E1, SA 07.

Assessment 8

1. Open Excel Worksheet E1-13.
2. Save the worksheet using the Save <u>A</u>s command and name it Excel E1, SA 08.
3. Create a custom header that has your name left-aligned and the file name right-aligned.
4. Select cell A4. Create a style named Header 1. The style should use the font Tahoma (or another sans serif font), the font style bold italic, the font size 14, and the color plum.

Assessment 8

1. Open Excel Worksheet E1-13.
2. Save the worksheet using the Save <u>A</u>s command and name it Excel E1, SA 08.
3. Create a custom header that has your name left-aligned and the file name right-aligned.
4. Select cell A4. Create a style named Header 1. The style should use the font Tahoma (or another sans serif font), the font style bold italic, the font size 14, and the color plum.
5. Apply the Header 1 style to cells A14 and A23.
6. Select cells A5 through G5. Create a style named Header 2. The style should use the font Tahoma (or another sans serif font), the font style bold, the font size 10. In addition, it should have a very light gray background and the horizontal alignment should be centered.
7. Apply the Header 2 style to cells A15 through G15 and cells A24 through G24.
8. Select cells G6 through G11, G16 through G20, and G25 through G30. Create a conditional format that displays any value greater than 12 as bold and red.
9. Automatically adjust the width of the columns so that all of the labels can be read.
10. Save the worksheet again with the same name (Excel E1, SA 08) and print it.
11. Close Excel E1, SA 08.

Assessment 9

1. Use Excel's Office Assistant to learn how you can remove conditional formats. *(Hint: Click <u>H</u>elp and Microsoft Excel <u>H</u>elp. Either at the Office Assistant or on the <u>A</u>nswer Wizard tab, key the question "**How do I remove a conditional format?**" and click <u>S</u>earch. At the list of topics that displays, click* Remove conditional formats. *Read and then print the information displayed in the Help dialog box.)*
2. Open Excel E1, SA 08. Save the worksheet using the Save <u>A</u>s command and name it Excel E1, SA 09.
3. Create a custom header that has your name left-aligned and the file name right-aligned.
4. Select cells G6 through G11, G16 through G20, and G25 through G30. Using the help information you printed in step 1, remove the conditional formatting from these cells.
5. Print Excel E1, SA 09.
6. Save the worksheet using the same file name (Excel E1, SA 09) and close it.

Chapter 02E

Working with Templates and Workbooks

2

PERFORMANCE OBJECTIVES

Upon successful completion of chapter 2, you will be able to:

- Use an existing Excel template.
- Create a new template.
- Edit a template.
- Automatically collect data with an existing template.
- Create and use a workspace file.
- Open multiple workbooks.
- Copy several worksheets into a new workbook.
- Consolidate data into a list.
- Link workbooks.
- Share workbooks.

Many people in an organization often need to share data and use the same workbooks. Excel includes several features that facilitate the sharing of data and workbooks. A template can be created that anyone in an organization could use as often as desired. A template serves as a pattern for a worksheet. The template includes data that would remain the same every time the worksheet was used. Certain labels and formulas, for example, might never change in a particular worksheet so they could become a part of the template that anyone in the organization could then use. Being able to work with multiple workbooks at the same time is another feature that makes it easy for people to share workbooks. Several worksheets can be merged into a new workbook. Specific cells in one workbook can be linked to another workbook, making it easy to share data. Two people can even edit the same workbook at the same time. In this chapter you will learn ways to share data using Excel.

Using Excel Templates

Oftentimes worksheets are used over and over again for the same purpose. Calculating a monthly profit and loss statement is a routine task performed in most businesses. Much of the data contained in a monthly profit and loss worksheet would be the same from month to month, such as the labels and the formulas. The only thing that would change from one month to the next would be the actual numbers. Whenever you have a situation where the basic format of a worksheet is going to be used repeatedly, using a template is a good idea. A template is like a form that gets filled out over and over again. You retrieve a template that has been created, fill in the relevant data, and save it. When the Save command is given, the Save As box automatically appears so that you can give the file a new name. That way, you always have the original template file to use over again.

The templates for all the Office 2000 applications are stored in the same folder. The default template folder for all the Office 2000 applications is:

<root drive>\<windows folder>\Application Data\Microsoft\Templates

The only exception to this is if Profiles are in use. Profiles allow multiple users to personalize settings on the computer. In that case, the default template folder is:

<root drive>\<windows folder>\Profiles\<username>\Application Data\Microsoft\Templates

Excel comes with a template for an Expense Statement, an Invoice, and a Purchase Order. These templates are accessed by clicking File and New to display the New dialog box and then clicking the Spreadsheet Solutions tab. The templates you see in figure 2.1 are licensed to Microsoft by Village Software®. Clicking the Village Software icon provides you with information about the company.

Four additional templates, Loan Manager, Car Lease, Production Tracking, and Personal Budgeter, can be downloaded for free from Microsoft's Web site, http://www.microsoft.com.

Hint

Templates must be saved in the Template folder. If you try saving a template in any other folder, Excel will not recognize it as a template.

Hint

You cannot access the templates by clicking the New button on the Standard toolbar or by using the Ctrl+N shortcut key. The only way to access the templates is by clicking File and then clicking New.

Hint

figure 2.1

Excel's Predesigned Templates

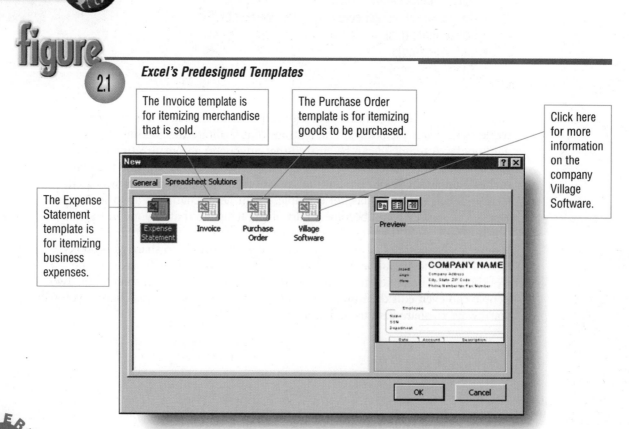

The Invoice template is for itemizing merchandise that is sold.

The Purchase Order template is for itemizing goods to be purchased.

Click here for more information on the company Village Software.

The Expense Statement template is for itemizing business expenses.

(Before completing computer exercises, delete the Chapter 01E *folder on your disk. Next, copy the* Chapter 02E *folder from the CD that accompanies this textbook to your disk and then make* Chapter 02E *the active folder. Follow this procedure when starting the computer exercises for each chapter.)*

Using an Existing Template

(Note: To complete this exercise, Excel's templates must be installed on your computer system.)

1. Open Excel.
2. Click File and New.
3. Click the Spreadsheet Solutions tab on the New dialog box.
4. Double-click the icon for the Expense Statement template. A dialog box may appear warning you that the file contains macros and that macros may contain viruses. Macros are used to automate some of the functions that this template performs. This is a reliable template, and it should not contain any viruses. Click the Enable Macros button.
5. Throughout the template are small red triangles. Move the mouse pointer so that it is over the small red triangle to the right of the word *Date*. A note appears instructing the user as to what type of data should be keyed at this location. Move the mouse pointer over the other red triangles in the worksheet to read those notes.

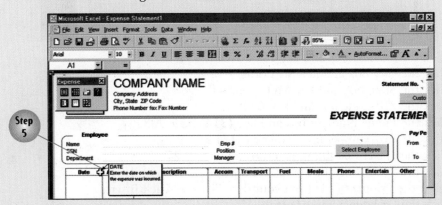

6. The Expense toolbar at the top of the template has seven buttons. Click the Display Example/Remove Example button to see what the expense statement would look like with data filled in. Click the Display Example/Remove Example button again to remove the data.

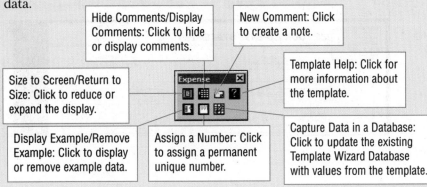

7. Before you key data in the template, you want to customize it for an actual company. Customize the template by completing the following steps:

a. Click the Customize button in the upper right corner of the template. You may have to scroll right to see this button.

b. Click the Company Name box and key **Copper Clad Incorporated.**

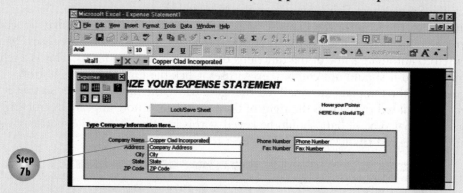

c. Click the Address box and key **1986 Avenue H**.
d. Click the City box and key **St. Louis**.
e. Click the State box and key **MO**.
f. Click the ZIP Code box and key **63155**.
g. Click the Phone Number box and key **(314) 555-9031**.
h. Click the Fax Number box and key **(314) 555-9035**.
i. Click the Travel Reimbursement box and key **0.27**.
j. Click the Select Logo button at the bottom of the template.
k. Select the Copper.tif file from your data disk and click Insert.
l. Click the Lock/Save Sheet button.

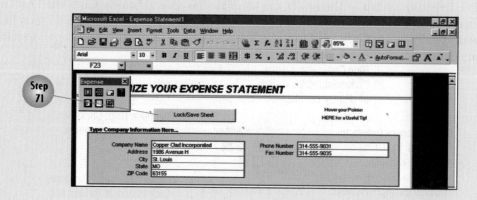

m. Check to make sure the *Lock and save Template* option is selected. If it is not, select it.

n. Click OK.

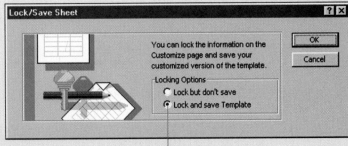

o. The Save Template dialog box is displayed. The default templates folder is in the Save in box. Save the template in the default templates folder rather than on your disk in drive A. Key the following in the File name box:

Copper Clad Expense Statement

p. Click Save.

q. Read the Expense information box that appears and click OK. Before you can start to use the template, you must first close it. Click File and then Close.

r. Click File and then New.

s. If necessary, click the General tab on the New Dialog box.

t. Double-click the icon for the Copper Clad Expense Statement.xlt file.

u. Click the Enable Macros button.

8. You are ready to use the customized template. You can move around the Expense Statement using the Tab key. Under the Employee section, key the following data:

Name:	**Lucinda Getz**
Emp #:	**293**
SSN:	**555-63-1234**
Position:	**Sales Representative**
Department:	**Sales**
Manager:	**Mark Wilcox**
Pay Period From:	**12/6**
Pay Period To:	**12/19**

Key the following data into the expense statement:

Date	Account	Description	Accom	Fuel	Meals	Phone
12/9	1473-96	Service Call		33.75	15.60	
12/14	2783-92	Update Orders	85.74	126.90	32.40	2.45

Your screen should look like the following illustration:

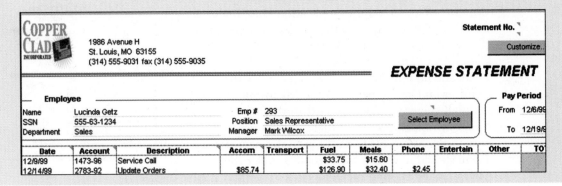

9. Create a custom header by completing the following steps:
   a. Click File and then click Page Setup.
   b. Click the Header/Footer tab.
   c. Click the Custom Header button.
   d. Key your name in the Left section box.
   e. Click in the Right section box and click the Insert File Name button.
   f. Click the OK button twice.
10. Save the worksheet by completing the following steps:
    a. Click File and click Save.
    b. The Template File - Save to Database dialog box appears. If you had the proper database set up, you could save the data as a record in a database. Click the Continue without updating option.
    c. Click OK.
    d. The Save As dialog box appears. Notice that the name of the file has been changed to Copper Clad Expense Statement1. Save the Copper Clad Expense Statement1 file on your data disk in drive A.

Template File - Save to Database

The contents of this workbook have not been saved as a record in the database.

OK   Step 10c

Cancel

What would you like to do?

○ Create a new record

● Continue without updating   Step 10b

11. Print and then close the Copper Clad Expense Statement1 file.
12. You need to delete the template you created from the Templates folder. This exercise assumes the default user template folder is found:

   <root drive>\<Windows folder>\Application Data\Microsoft\Templates

   If this is not the location of the default user template folder on the computer system you are using, you will need to ask your instructor for help.
   a. Click the Start button.
   b. Click Programs.
   c. Click Windows Explorer.
   d. In the Folders pane, there should be a plus sign next to the root directory, which in may cases will be (C:). If there is, click it. If there is a minus sign next to the root directory, skip to the next step.
   e. There should now be a list of folders under the root directory. Find the Windows folder. If there is a plus sign next to the Windows folder, click it. If there is a minus sign next to the Windows folder, skip to the next step.
   f. There should now be a list of folders under the Windows folder. Find the Application Data folder. If there is a plus sign next to the Application Data folder, click it. If there is a minus sign next to the Application Data folder, skip to the next step.
   g. There should now be a list of folders under the Application Data folder. Find the Microsoft folder. If there is a plus sign next to the Microsoft folder, click it. If there is a minus sign next to the Microsoft folder, skip to the next step.
   h. There should now be a list of folders under the Microsoft folder. Find the Templates folder and double-click it.

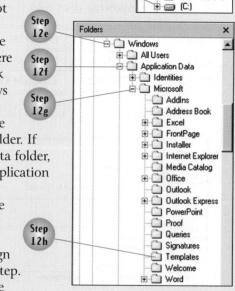

Step 12d

Folders
☑ Desktop
⊟ 💻 My Computer
   ⊞ 💾 3½ Floppy (A:)
   ⊞ 💿 (C:)

Step 12e

Step 12f

Step 12g

Step 12h

Folders
⊟ 📁 Windows
   ⊞ 📁 All Users
   ⊟ 📁 Application Data
      ⊞ 📁 Identities
      ⊟ 📁 Microsoft
         📁 AddIns
         📁 Address Book
         ⊞ 📁 Excel
         ⊞ 📁 FrontPage
         ⊞ 📁 Installer
         ⊞ 📁 Internet Explorer
         📁 Media Catalog
         ⊞ 📁 Office
         📁 Outlook
         ⊞ 📁 Outlook Express
         📁 PowerPoint
         📁 Proof
         📁 Queries
         📁 Signatures
         📁 Templates
         📁 Welcome
         ⊞ 📁 Word

i. Click the icon for the Copper Clad Expense Statement template.
j. Click the Delete button. Click the Yes button.

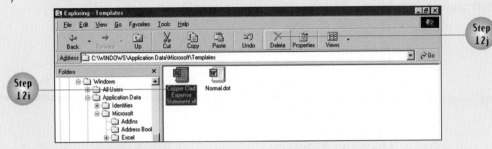

Step 12j

Step 12i

k. Close Windows Explorer.
13. Close Excel.

Creating a New Template

Creating a template is simply a matter of creating a workbook and then saving the workbook as a template. The workbook should contain the standard data that would be used over and over again each time the workbook is used. The two biggest advantages of using templates are they save you time since much of the data is already entered and they insure consistency in the appearance of workbooks.

Since Excel saves workbooks using the extension .xls and it saves templates using the extension .xlt, being able to see the filename extension is quite useful. If you cannot view the extensions, you cannot tell which files are templates and which files are workbooks. If the extensions are not displayed, the option to hide them must be selected. To show filename extensions use either My Computer or Windows Explorer to find the folder containing the files whose extensions you want to see. Click the folder to select it and then click View and Folder Options. Click the View tab on the Folder Options dialog box. Under Advanced settings, the check box for the *Hide file extensions for known file types* option will be selected. Click the box so that it is no longer selected and then click OK. The exercises in this book assume that the file extensions are not hidden.

Creating a Template

1. Open a new Excel workbook.
2. Create a custom header by completing the following steps:
   a. Click File and then click Page Setup.
   b. Click the Header/Footer tab.
   c. Click the Custom Header button.
   d. Key your name in the Left section box.
   e. Click the Right section box and then click the Insert File Name button.

f.   Click the OK button twice.
3. You are going to create a monthly income statement as a template so that it can be used over again each month. Key the following data in the cells indicated:

Cell	Data
A4	Whitewater Canoe and Kayak Corporation
A5	Income Statement
A7	For the Month Ending:
A9	Sales
A10	Less: cost of goods sold
A11	Gross margin
A13	Operating expenses:
A14	Wages expense
A15	Depreciation expense
A16	Insurance expense
A17	Operating income
A19	Other Expenses:
A20	Interest expense
A21	Net income

4. Save the file on your data disk in drive A. For now, just save it as a regular workbook file. Name the file Excel E2, Ex 02.
5. Format the worksheet by completing the following steps:
    a. Automatically adjust the width of column A so that the name of the company fits in one cell.
    b. Center the data in A4 across columns A, B, C, and D. Center the data in A5 across columns A, B, C, and D.
    c. Format cells A7, A11, A17, and A21 so that data entered into them will be right-aligned in the cell.
    d. Format the data in cells A4, A5, and A7 so that the font style is bold and the font size is 12.
    e. Format cells C9 through D21 so that numbers entered into those cells are displayed in the Accounting format with zero decimal places and the dollar sign symbol displayed.
    f. Format cell B7 so that data entered in that cell displays as the month (Mar, for example) and year only.
    g. Place a single line border on the bottom of cells D10, C16, D16, and D20. Place a double line border on the bottom of cell D21.
6. Enter the following formulas in the cells indicated:

Cell	Formula
D11	=D9-D10
D16	=SUM(C14:C16)
D17	=D11-D16
D21	=D17-D20

7. Your screen should now look like the illustration at the right. You are now ready to save the file as a template. Complete the following steps to save the file as a template.

a. Click File and Save As.

b. When the Save As dialog box appears, click the down arrow to the right of the Save as type box.

c. Click Template (*.xlt).

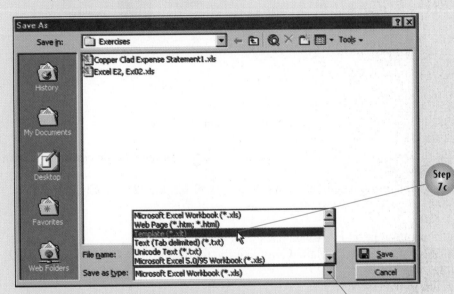

	A	B	C	D
3				
4	**Whitewater Canoe and Kayak Corporation**			
5	**Income Statement**			
6				
7	**For the Month Ending:**			
8				
9	Sales			
10	Less: cost of goods sold			
11	Gross margin			$ -
12				
13	Operating expenses:			
14	Wages expense			
15	Depreciation expense			
16	Insurance expense		$	-
17	Operating income		$	-
18				
19	Other Expenses:			
20	Interest expense			
21	Net income			$ -

Step 7c

If the extensions are not displayed in the Save as type list box, select the drive where your data disk is located and then click View and Folder Options. Click the View tab. Under Advanced settings, click the check box for the *Hide File Extensions for known file types* option so that it is not selected. Click OK.

Step 7b

d. Notice that the file name automatically changed to Excel E2, Ex 02.xlt and that the Templates folder is in the Save in box. Click Save.

8. Close the Excel E2, Ex 02.xlt template. You must close the template file before you can make a new worksheet based on it.

Editing a Template

Once the template is edited, you must close it before you start to use it. If you don't, the additions you make to it will be saved as part of the template.

Once a template has been created, you can easily edit it to make changes that might be needed at a later time. To edit a template, click File and New and then double-click the icon for the template to be edited from the General tab on the New dialog box. Make the necessary changes to the template and click the Save button. When the Save As dialog box appears, click the down arrow to the right of the Save as type box and click the Template (*.xlt) option. In the File name box enter the original name of the template and click the Save button. When the warning dialog box appears asking if you want to replace the original template file, click Yes. The edited template will then be saved.

exercise 3

Applying and Editing Templates

1. Complete the following steps to open the Excel E2, Ex 02.xlt template.
   a. Click File and then New.
   b. If necessary, click the General tab on the New dialog box.
   c. Double-click the Excel E2, Ex 02.xlt icon.
2. Enter the following data in the cells indicated:

Cell	Data
B7	April
D9	90000
D10	50000
C14	5000
C15	1000
C16	1500
D20	800

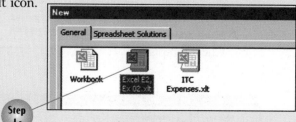

Step 1c

3. Complete the following steps to save the worksheet.

   a. Click the Save button.
   b. Check the Save in box to make sure that the file is going to be saved on your data disk in drive A.
   c. Currently the name in the File name box is Excel E2, Ex 021.xls. Change the filename to **Excel E2, Ex 02-a.xls**.
   d. Click Save.
4. Print and then close Excel E2, Ex 02-a.xls.
5. You now need to edit the template. Complete the following steps to edit the Excel E2, Ex 02.xlt template.
   a. Click File and then New.
   b. If necessary, click the General tab on the New dialog box.
   c. Double-click the Excel E2, Ex 02.xlt icon.
   d. Insert a new row 15.
   e. Key **Rent expense** in cell A15.
   f. Click the Save button.
   g. When the Save As dialog box appears, click the down arrow to the right of the Save as type box and click Template (*.xlt).
   h. Change the name in the File name box to **Excel E2, Ex 02.xlt**.
   i. Click Save.
   j. When the warning box appears asking if you want to replace the existing file, click Yes.
6. Close the Excel E2, Ex 02.xlt template. You must close the template file before you can make a new worksheet based on it.
7. Complete the following steps to open the Excel E2, Ex 02.xlt template.
   a. Click File and then New.
   b. If necessary, click the General tab on the New dialog box.

   c.   Double-click the Excel E2, Ex 02.xlt icon. Notice that the new Rent Expense category is now in the template.

8. Enter the following data in the cells indicated:

Cell	Data
B7	May
D9	93000
D10	49500
C14	5000
C15	2200
C16	1000
C17	1500
D21	800

9. Complete the following steps to save the worksheet.
   a.   Click the Save button.
   b.   Check the Save in box to make sure that the file is going to be saved on your data disk in drive A.
   c.   Currently the name in the File name box is Excel E2, Ex 02.xls. Change the filename to **Excel E2, Ex 02-b.xls**.
   d.   Click Save.

10. Print and then close Excel E2, Ex 02-b.xls.

11. You need to delete the template you created from the Templates folder. This exercise assumes the default user template folder is found:

<root drive>\<Windows folder>\Application Data\Microsoft\Templates

If this is not the location of the default user template folder on the computer system you are using, you will need to ask your instructor for help.

   a.   Click the Start button.
   b.   Point to Programs.
   c.   Click Windows Explorer.
   d.   In the Folders pane, there should be a plus sign next to the root directory, which in many cases will be (C:). If there is, click it. If there is a minus sign next to the root directory, skip to the next step.
   e.   There should now be a list of folders under the root directory. Find the Windows folder. If there is a plus sign next to the Windows folder, click it. If there is a minus sign next to the Windows folder, skip to the next step.
   f.   There should now be a list of folders under the Windows folder. Find the Application Data folder. If there is a plus sign next to the Application Data folder, click it. If there is a minus sign next to the Application Data folder, skip to the next step.
   g.   There should now be a list of folders under the Application Data folder. Find the Microsoft folder. If there is a plus sign next to the Microsoft folder, click it. If there is a minus sign next to the Microsoft folder, skip to the next step.
   h.   There should now be a list of folders under the Microsoft folder. Find the Templates folder and double-click it.

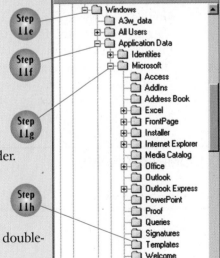

    i. Click the icon for the Excel E2, Ex 02.xlt template.
    j. Click the Delete button. Click the Yes button.
    k. Close Windows Explorer.
12. Close Excel.

Automating Data Collection with a Built-In Template

One of the templates that comes with Excel automatically collects any data entered into it and places the data in a single list. The Expense Statement template already includes all the automation work necessary to collect the data into a single list. Whenever workbooks based on the Expense Statement template are saved, the data entered into each workbook is automatically copied to a list that is linked or attached to the workbook. That way, all the data from any expense statement can be consolidated into one list.

In Excel a list is also referred to as a database. A database in Excel is simply a worksheet that has been organized into columns, which are called fields, and rows which are called records. At the top of each column is a label, or field name. There can be no blank columns or rows within the database. Using lists or databases in Excel will be covered in more detail in chapter 6.

Collecting Data Automatically with a Built-in Template

(Note: In order to have room on your disk to save the file you will be creating in this exercise, you will need to delete the Copper Clad Expense Statement1.xls file you created in exercise 1. Check with your instructor to make sure it is all right to delete this file.)

1. Open Excel.
2. Click File and New.
3. Click the Spreadsheet Solutions tab on the New dialog box.
4. Double-click the icon for the Expense Statement template. When a dialog box appears warning you that the file contains macros and macros may contain viruses, click the Enable Macros button.
5. Create a custom header that displays your name at the left margin and the name of the file at the right margin.
6. Customize the template by completing the following steps:
   a. Click the Customize button in the upper right corner of the template. You may have to scroll right to see it.

COMPANY NAME

Company Address
City, State ZIP Code
Phone Number fax Fax Number

Statement No.

Customize...

Step 6a

EXPENSE STATEMENT

b. Move to the Company Name box and key **Whitewater Canoe and Kayak**.

c. Move to the Address box and key **34982 Olympia Blvd**.

d. Move to the City box and key **Seattle**.

e. Move to the State box and key **WA**.

f. Move to the ZIP Code box and key **98101**.

g. Move to the Phone Number box and key **(206) 555-8937**.

h. Move to the Fax Number box and key **(206) 555-8940**.

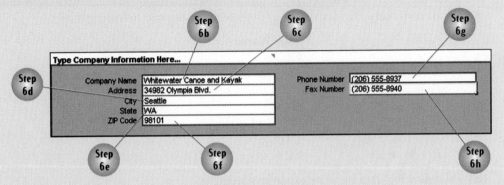

7. Look at the information in the section titled Specify Default Expense Statement Information Here. You will have to scroll down to see the whole section. The Common Database box and the Template Wizard Database box provide you with information you will need later. The location displayed in the Common Database box is where the consolidated list of expenses will be found. The Template Wizard Database box tells you what this file will be named, which is expdb.xls. Write down the path name in the Template Wizard Database box so that you will be able to find the file later on in this exercise. If you wanted to use a list other than the default expdb.xls, you would have to create it using the Template Wizard.

8. Scroll to the bottom of the expense statement. Click the Select Logo button. Select the

Whitewtr.tif file from your data disk and click Insert.

9. Save the template by completing the following steps:

a. Click the Lock/Save Sheet button near the top of the expense statement.

b. Check to make sure the *Lock and save Template* option is selected. If it is not, select it.

c. Click OK.

d. The Save Template dialog box is displayed. The default templates folder is in the Save in box. Save the template in the default templates folder rather than on your disk in drive A. Key the following in the File name box:

Whitewater Expense Statement

e. Click Save.

f. Read the Expense information box that appears regarding saving customized template and click OK.

g. Click File and then Close.

h. Click File and then New.

i. If necessary, click the General tab on the New dialog box.

j. Double-click the icon for the Whitewater Expense Statement.xlt file.

k. Click the Enable Macros button.

10. You are ready to use the customized template. For the employee name you are going to enter your own name. Under the Employee section, key the following data:

Name:	**Your Name**
Emp #:	**18**
SSN:	**555-90-3321**
Position:	**Sales Representative**
Department:	**Sales**
Manager:	**Brenda Lopez**
Pay Period From:	**4/10**
Pay Period To:	**4/23**

Key the following data into the expense statement:

Date	Description	Accom	Transportation	Meals	Phone
4/12	**Trade Show**	**118.00**	**43.00**	**45.59**	**5.25**
4/13	**Trade Show**	**118.00**	**56.00**	**38.92**	**1.75**

Your screen should look like the following illustration.

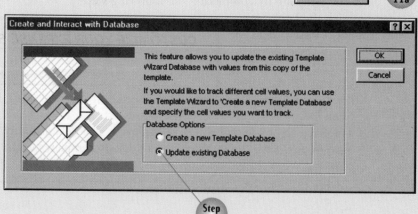

11. Complete the following steps to write the data to a database:

a. Click the Capture Data in a Database button on the Expense toolbar.

Step 11a

b. The Create and Interact with Database dialog box appears. Make sure the *Update existing database* option is selected. Click OK.

Create and Interact with Database

This feature allows you to update the existing Template Wizard Database with values from this copy of the template.

If you would like to track different cell values, you can use the Template Wizard to 'Create a new Template Database' and specify the cell values you want to track.

Database Options

○ Create a new Template Database

◉ Update existing Database

OK

Cancel

Step 11b

c. The Template File - Save to Database dialog box appears. Make sure that the *Create a New Record* option is selected. Click OK.

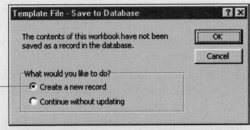

12. Save the worksheet by completing the following steps:

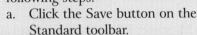

a. Click the Save button on the Standard toolbar.

b. The Template File - Save to Database dialog box appears. Click the *Continue without updating* option and then click OK.

c. The Save As dialog box appears. Notice that the name of the file has been changed to Whitewater Expense Statement1. Save the Whitewater Expense Statement1 file on your data disk in drive A.

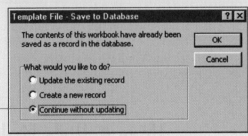

13. Print and then close the Whitewater Expense Statement1 file.

14. Now you want to look at the expenses database to make sure the data from the Expense Statement was entered. Complete the following steps to view the expenses database:

a. Click File and then Open.

b. You need to find the expdb.xls file. The path name you wrote down in step 7 will direct you to this file. In most cases, you will need to locate and open the Program Files folder, the Microsoft Office folder, the Office folder, and then double-click the Library folder. The expdb.xls file should be in the Library folder. Double-click the icon for the expdb.xls file to open it.

15. The expdb.xls file should minimally display one row that contains your name in column B along with the other data you entered. Notice that all the expenses listed in the expense statement were consolidated into one total that is listed in column J. There may be other entries in this database. Every time a worksheet based on the Expense Statement template is created and saved, a new row containing the data from that worksheet will be entered in the expdb.xls file.

16. Delete the row containing your name in column B from the worksheet. Save and close the worksheet.

17. You need to delete the template you created from the Templates folder. If the default user template folder is not found in the following location,

        \<root drive\>\\\<Windows folder\>\Application Data\Microsoft\Templates

you will need to ask your instructor for help.

a. Click the Start button.

b. Click Programs.

c. Click Windows Explorer.

d. In the Folders pane, there should be a plus sign next to the root directory, which in many cases will be (C:). If there is, click it. If there is a minus sign next to the root directory, skip to the next step.

e. There should now be a list of folders under the root directory. Find the Windows folder. If there is a plus sign next to the Windows folder, click it. If there is a minus sign next to the Windows folder, skip to the next step.

f. There should now be a list of folders under the Windows folder. Find the Application Data folder. If there is a plus sign next to the Application Data folder, click it. If there is a minus sign next to the Application Data folder, skip to the next step.

g. There should now be a list of folders under the Application Data folder. Find the Microsoft folder. If there is a plus sign next to the Microsoft folder, click it. If there is a minus sign next to the Microsoft folder, skip to the next step.

h. There should now be a list of folders under the Microsoft folder. Find the Templates folder and double-click it.

i. Click the icon for the Whitewater Expense Statement template.

j. Click the Delete button. Click the Yes button.

k. Close Windows Explorer.

18. Close Excel.

Using Multiple Workbooks

You can easily work with data from different workbooks at the same time using Excel. By creating a workspace you can open several workbooks at the same time with just one step. Once several workbooks are open, you can copy all the data from the open workbooks into a new workbook, and consolidate the data from several workbooks into one worksheet.

Arranging Multiple Workbooks in the Desktop

In order to work with more than one workbook at a time, the workbooks must be arranged so that you can easily read the data contained in each one. To arrange multiple workbooks, click Window and then Arrange. As shown in figure 2.2, there are four options for arranging windows in the desktop: Tiled, Horizontal, Vertical, and Cascade. Select one of these options and click OK and the open workbooks will be arranged so that the data from each workbook can be viewed at the same time.

The Arrange Windows Dialog Box

Using a Workspace

If you frequently work with the same group of workbooks you may want to create a customized workspace. A customized workspace allows you to open a group of workbooks in one step. Information about the open files, such as their locations, window sizes, and screen positions, are stored in a workspace file. Then, instead of opening each individual workbook, all you have to do is open the workspace file and all the individual workbooks that are a part of the file are opened.

To create a workspace, first open the workbooks you want to be included in the workspace and size and position them as you want them to appear each time the workspace file is opened. Click File. You may need to expand the File menu in order to click Save Workspace. Enter a name for the workspace file in the File name box. The extension for a workspace file is .xlw. Whenever you want to open the group of workbooks together, open the workspace file.

Merging Multiple Workbooks into a Single Workbook

Once you have multiple workbooks open at the same time, you can easily copy worksheets from each workbook into a single workbook. To copy a worksheet from one workbook to another, press the Ctrl key and drag the sheet tab of the worksheet you want to copy to the sheet tabs in the workbook where you want to place the copied worksheet.

> Once multiple worksheets have been copied into a single workbook, if they are not in the order you would like, you can easily change their positions. To change the position of a worksheet in a workbook, simply click on the worksheet tab and drag it to the new location.
>
> Hint

exercise 5

Using a Workspace and Merging Worksheets into a Workbook

1. Open Excel.
2. The sales figures for individual sales representatives of Copper Clad Incorporated for the last quarter of 1999 are stored in three separate workbooks. Since these three workbooks are frequently used at the same time, you want to create a workspace for them. Open OctSales.xls, NovSales.xls, and DecSales.xls.
3. All three workbooks are open, but you cannot see them because they are on top of one another. Complete the following steps to adjust how the workbooks are displayed on your desktop:
   a. Click Window and Arrange.
   b. Click the Vertical option on the Arrange Windows dialog box and click OK. The workbooks are now arranged next to each other.
4. Create a workspace by completing the following steps:
   a. Click File. If necessary, expand the menu by clicking the down arrow at the bottom of the menu. Click Save Workspace.
   b. The Save Workspace dialog box appears. Key the following in the File name box:
      Last Quarter.xlw
   c. Click Save.

5. Close the OctSales.xls, NovSales.xls, and DecSales.xls workbooks.
6. Open the workspace you just created by completing the following steps:
   a. Click File and Open.
   b. The Open dialog box is displayed. Click *Last Quarter.xlw* to select it.
   c. Click Open. The workspace you created is now open.
7. Open a new workbook and copy the October 99 worksheet, the November 99 worksheet, and the December 99 worksheet into the new workbook by completing the following steps:

   a. Click the New button on the Standard toolbar to open a new workbook.
   b. Click Window and Arrange.
   c. Click the Tiled option on the Arrange Windows dialog box and click OK. Four workbooks should now be displayed, the new blank workbook and Dec Sales.xls, Nov Sales.xls, and Oct Sales.xls.
   d. Click on the Oct Sales.xls sheet to make it active.
   e. Press the Ctrl key and drag the October 99 sheet tab to the new workbook placing it to the left of the Sheet1 tab.
   f. Click on the Nov Sales.xls sheet to make it active.
   g. Press the Ctrl key and drag the November 99 sheet tab to the new workbook, placing it between the October 99 tab and the Sheet1 tab.
   h. Click on the Dec Sales.xls sheet to make it active.
   i. Press the Ctrl key and drag the December 99 sheet tab to the new workbook placing it between the November 99 tab and the Sheet1 tab.
8. The worksheets are now all copied into the new workbook. Close the Dec Sales.xls, Nov Sales.xls, and Oct Sales.xls files. You have to make each workbook active and then close it. Click the Maximize button on the new workbook. Save the new workbook on the data disk using the file name Excel E2, Ex 05.
9. Close Excel E2, Ex 05.

Consolidating Data from Several Worksheets into a List

If the data you want to consolidate is in many different workbooks, you might want to first copy the data to be consolidated into a single workbook. The consolidation process will be easier if the data is all in one workbook.

If you have several worksheets in one workbook or several worksheets from different workbooks, data from each worksheet can be consolidated on a separate worksheet. To consolidate the data, click Data and then Consolidate. The Consolidate dialog box shown in figure 2.3 appears. You first have to decide what function you want performed on the consolidated data. Figure 2.4 shows you the options from the Function drop-down menu. Next you have to select all the references you want consolidated. If you want the consolidated data to include labels, you can select the appropriate check boxes in the Use labels in section. When all the selections have been made, click OK. The data is then all consolidated onto one worksheet.

figure

2.3

The Consolidate Dialog Box

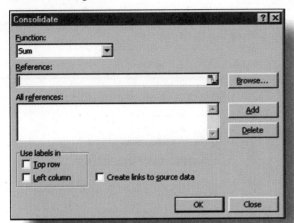

figure

2.4

Functions That Can Be Performed on Consolidated Data

exercise

6

Consolidating Data into a List

1. Open Excel E2, Ex 05.
2. Save the workbook with the Save <u>A</u>s command and name it Excel E2, Ex 06.
3. You want to consolidate the figures on the three separate worksheets into one worksheet. Complete the following steps to consolidate the data:
    a. Click the *Sheet1* tab.
    b. Click F<u>o</u>rmat, point to S<u>h</u>eet, and click <u>R</u>ename. Key the following: **Last Qtr 99.**
    c. Click cell A1 on the Last Qtr 99 worksheet.
    d. Click <u>D</u>ata and Con<u>s</u>olidate.
    e. Check to make sure that Sum is displayed in the <u>F</u>unction box.
    f. If necessary, click in the <u>R</u>eference box. The insertion point must be in the <u>R</u>eference box.

g. Click the October 99 sheet tab. You may have to scroll to the left to see it.

h. If the Consolidate dialog box is in the way, click on the title bar and drag it to the right. Select cells A1 through B17.

i. Click the Add button.

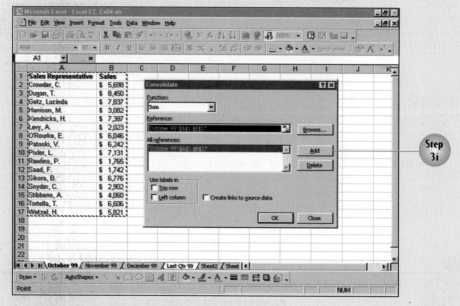

Step 3i

j. Click the November 99 sheet tab.

k. Select cells A1 through B17.

l. Click the Add button.

m. Click the December 99 sheet tab.

n. Select cells A1 through B17.

o. Click the Add button.

p. In the Use labels in section, click the Top row check box and the Left column check box.

q. Click OK.

4. The data is consolidated in the Last Qtr 99 worksheet. If necessary, click the Last Qtr 99 sheet tab. Widen column A to display all the names. Add a custom header that displays your name at the left margin and the file name at the right margin. Print the Last Qtr 99 worksheet.

5. Save the workbook with the same name (Excel E2, Ex 06).

6. Close Excel E2, Ex 06.

Linking Workbooks

When you link worksheets, you are entering a formula that refers to another worksheet, which is why you always begin the link by keying the equal sign.

In many cases, worksheets utilize data that is already located in another worksheet. For example, someone preparing a quarterly report would need the figures from the monthly reports for each month in the quarter. Instead of re-entering all that data into the quarterly report, with Excel you can link the quarterly report worksheet to the monthly reports worksheets. Once a link has been established, if the data in the worksheet to which you have linked is changed, the link will automatically update itself to reflect any changes when the worksheet is opened. A link can be established between worksheets in the same workbook, between worksheets in different workbooks, and even to data found on company intranets or the Internet.

To link worksheets, click the cell where the linked data will be placed and key =
to begin the link. Locate the worksheet where the data you want to link to is stored,
click the cell to be linked, and press Enter. The worksheet containing the linked data
will appear with the appropriate data displayed in the linked cell. Links can even be
used in formulas and functions.

It is a good idea to
give the data you want
to link to a range
name. You can then
easily link to
that data
using the
range name.

Hint

exercise 7

Using a Workspace and Linking Workbooks

1. Before starting this exercise, you need to remove the read-only attribute from the Region
    Sales Oct, Region Sales Nov, and Region Sales Dec files. To remove the read-only
    attribute from the Region Sales Oct file, complete the following steps:
    a. Using either Windows Explorer or My Computer, navigate to the Region Sales Oct
        file on your data disk.
    b. Right click the Region Sales Oct file.
    c. From the short-cut menu that is displayed, click Properties.
    d. Click the General tab on the File Properties dialog box that is displayed.
    e. In the Attributes section toward the bottom of the dialog box, click the Read-only
        check box so that it is no longer selected.
    f. Click OK.
2. Repeat step 1 to remove the read-only attribute from the Region Sales Nov and Region
    Sales Dec files. When you have finished, close either Windows Explorer or My
    Computer.
3. Open Excel.
4. The quarterly sales figures by regions for the sales representatives of Copper Clad
    Incorporated for the last quarter of 1999 are stored in three separate workbooks. Create
    a workspace for these three workbooks by completing the following steps:
    a. Open Region Sales Oct, Region Sales Nov, and Region Sales Dec.
    b. Click Window and Arrange.
    c. Click the Vertical option on the Arrange Windows dialog box and click OK. You can
        now see all three workbooks.
    d. Click File. If necessary, expand the menu by clicking the down arrow at the bottom
        of the menu. Click Save Workspace.
    e. The Save Workspace dialog box appears. Key the following in the File name box:
        4th Quarter Sales.xlw
    f. Click Save.
5. Close the Region Sales Oct, Region Sales Nov, and Region Sales Dec workbooks.
6. Open the workspace you just created by completing the following steps:
    a. Click File and Open.
    b. The Open dialog box is displayed. Click *4th Quarter Sales.xlw* to select it.
    c. Click Open. The workspace you created is now open.
    d. Open Fourth Qtr Summary.
    e. Click Window and Arrange.

f. Click the Tiled option on the Arrange Windows dialog box and click OK. There are now four worksheets displayed.

7. The Fourth Qtr Summary workbook is going to summarize the data found in the other three workbooks. Click cell B5 in the Fourth Qtr Summary workbook. In this cell, you want the total for the North Region's sales in October, November, and December. Complete the following steps to link the three subtotals for the North Region's sales to the Fourth Qtr Summary workbook (you may need to scroll down in each window in order to select the necessary cell):

a. In cell B5 on the Fourth Qtr Summary workbook, key =.

b. Click the Region Sales Oct workbook and then click cell C7 in that workbook. Notice that a reference to that cell immediately appears in the Fourth Qtr Summary workbook.

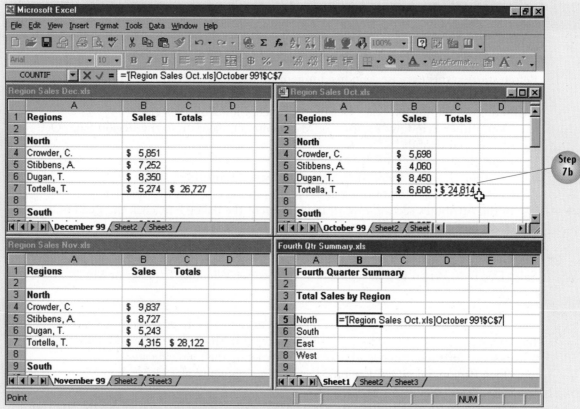

Step 7b

c. The insertion point should be back in cell B5 on the Fourth Qtr Summary workbook to the right of the reference to the linked cell. Key +.

d. Click the Region Sales Nov workbook to make it active and then click cell C7 in that workbook.

e. Key +.

f. Click the Region Sales Dec workbook to make it active and then click cell C7 in that workbook.

g. Press Enter. The total for the North Region's sales for the months of October, November, and December appear in cell B5 in the Fourth Quarter Summary workbook.

8. Complete the following steps to link the three subtotals for the South Region's sales to the Fourth Qtr Summary workbook (you may need to scroll down in each window in order to select the necessary cell):

    a. In cell B6 on the Fourth Qtr Summary workbook, key =.

    b. Click the Region Sales Oct workbook to make it active and then click cell C13 in that workbook.

    c. Key +.

    d. Click the Region Sales Nov workbook to make it active and then click cell C13 in that workbook.

    e. Key +.

    f. Click the Region Sales Dec workbook to make it active and then click cell C13 in that workbook.

    g. Press Enter. The total for the South Region's sales for the months of October, November, and December appear in cell B6 in the Fourth Quarter Summary workbook.

9. Complete the following steps to link the three subtotals for the East Region's sales to the Fourth Qtr Summary workbook (you may need to scroll down in each window in order to select the necessary cell):

    a. In cell B7 on the Fourth Qtr Summary workbook, key =.

    b. Click the Region Sales Oct workbook to make it active and then click cell C19 in that workbook.

    c. Key +.

    d. Click the Region Sales Nov workbook to make it active and then click cell C19 in that workbook.

    e. Key +.

    f. Click the Region Sales Dec workbook to make it active and then click cell C19 in that workbook.

    g. Press Enter. The total for the East Region's sales for the months of October, November, and December appear in cell B7 in the Fourth Quarter Summary workbook.

10. Complete the following steps to link the three subtotals for the West Region's sales to the Fourth Qtr Summary workbook (you may need to scroll down in each window in order to select the necessary cell):

    a. In cell B8 on the Fourth Qtr Summary workbook, key =.

    b. Click the Region Sales Oct workbook to make it active and then click cell C25 in that workbook.

    c. Key +.

    d. Click the Region Sales Nov workbook to make it active and then click cell C25 in that workbook.

    e. Key +.

    f. Click the Region Sales Dec workbook to make it active and then click cell C25 in that workbook.

    g. Press Enter. The total for the South Region's sales for the months of October, November, and December appear in cell B8 in the Fourth Quarter Summary workbook. Enter a function in cell B10 in the Fourth Qtr Summary workbook to add together the sales for the North, South, East and West regions.

11. Next you want to use a link in an Excel function. In the Fourth Qtr Summary workbook, scroll down until you can see cells A14 through B19. In this area of the worksheet you want to calculate the average sales for each region for the third quarter. Complete the following steps to create the necessary links:

    a. On the Fourth Qtr Summary workbook, click cell B16.

    b. On the Standard toolbar, click the Paste Function button. The Paste Function dialog box appears.

c. In the Function category list box, click *Statistical*.
d. In the Function name list box, click *AVERAGE*.
e. Click OK. The Formula Palette opens.
f. On the Region Sales Oct workbook, click cell C7. The reference to cell C7 appears in the Formula Palette. If the Formula Palette gets in the way, you can move it by clicking on it and dragging it to a new location.

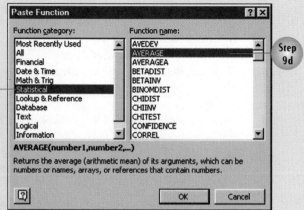

Step 9c

Step 9d

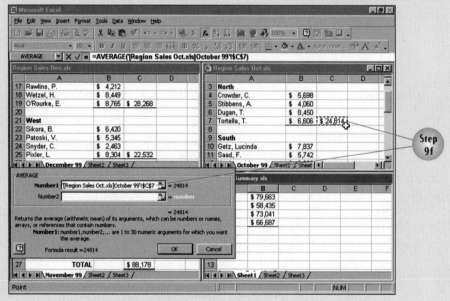

Step 9f

g. Key , (a comma).
h. Click the Region Sales Nov workbook to activate it and then click cell C7.
i. Key , (a comma).
j. Click the Region Sales Dec workbook to activate it and then click cell C7.
k. Press Enter.

12. Complete steps similar to step 9 to find the average sales for the South Region. Use cell B17 in the Fourth Qtr Summary workbook and cell C13 in the monthly workbooks.

13. Complete steps similar to step 9 to find the average sales for the East Region. Use cell B18 in the Fourth Qtr Summary workbook and cell C19 in the monthly workbooks.

14. Complete steps similar to step 9 to find the average sales for the West Region. Use cell B19 in the Fourth Qtr Summary workbook and cell C25 in the monthly workbooks.

15. Close the Region Sales Oct, Region Sales Nov, and Region Sales Dec workbooks. Save the Fourth Qtr Summary workbook using the file name Excel E2, Ex 07.

16. Create a header for the workbook that displays your name at the left margin and the name of the file at the right margin.

17. Print the Excel E2, Ex 07 workbook and then close it.

18. Someone just discovered there are some mistakes on the Region Sales Dec workbook. Open this workbook and make the following changes:

Cell	Sales
B7	5798
B10	3001
B24	2609

Save and close the revised workbook.

19. Open the Excel E2, Ex 07 workbook. A dialog box appears asking if you want to update the workbook with changes made to the linked workbook. Click Yes.

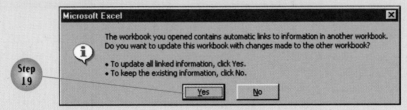

Step 19

Microsoft Excel

The workbook you opened contains automatic links to information in another workbook. Do you want to update this workbook with changes made to the other workbook?

- To update all linked information, click Yes.
- To keep the existing information, click No.

[Yes]   [No]

20. Print the Excel E2, Ex 07 workbook again. Notice how the figures have changed.
21. Save the worksheet with the same name (Excel E2, Ex 07) and close it.

Sharing Workbooks

Excel has many workgroup features, that is, features that make it easy for people to collaborate while using Excel. For example, people can share the same workbook and can even be using it at the same time. More than one person can make changes to the shared file at the same time. To share a workbook, click Tools and Share Workbook. The Share Workbook dialog box, shown in figure 2.5, appears. On the Editing tab, click the Allow changes by more than one user at the same time option. You can tell that a workbook is shared because the word [Shared] is displayed in the title bar next to the workbook name. Once the option for sharing a workbook has been selected, additional sharing options can be selected from the Advanced Tab on the Share Workbook dialog box as shown in figure 2.6. Table 2.1 describes the options.

Some features are not available when you use a shared workbook. Merging cells, inserting or deleting blocks of cells, deleting worksheets, and defining or applying conditional formats are a few examples of things you cannot do in a shared workbook. To use these features the workbook must be removed from shared use.

Hint

figure
2.5

The Share Workbook Dialog Box with Edit Tab Selected

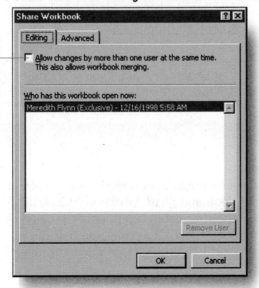

Click here to allow multiple users to edit a workbook at the same time.

Share Workbook

| Editing | Advanced |

☐ Allow changes by more than one user at the same time.
This also allows workbook merging.

Who has this workbook open now:

Meredith Flynn (Exclusive) - 12/16/1998 5:58 AM

[Remove User]

[OK]   [Cancel]

EXPERT

figure
2.6

The Share Workbook Dialog Box with Advanced Tab Selected

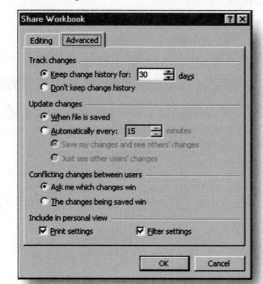

table
2.1

Advanced Options for Sharing Workbooks

Option	Description
Track changes	Sets the time period for how long Excel keeps the change history. The change history keeps track of how conflicting changes to the workbook were resolved.
Update changes	Sets when everyone's changes will be saved. They can be saved when the file is saved or at a regular time interval.
Conflicting changes between users	Sets how to resolve different changes made to the same data. Either your changes are saved over the other users' or Excel can prompt you to choose which change should be saved.

When you no longer want to share a workbook, you can turn the sharing option off by clicking Tools and Share Workbook. Click the Allow changes by more than one user at the same time check box to remove the check mark and then click OK. A warning box will be displayed alerting you that the workbook will no longer be available for shared use. Clicking Yes removes the workbook from shared use.

exercise 8

Sharing Workbooks

1. Open Excel Worksheet E2-01 from your data disk.
2. Save the document using the Save As command and name it Excel E2, Ex 08.
3. Create a custom header with your name displayed at the left margin and the file name displayed at the right margin.
4. Assume you are the head of personnel at Whitewater Canoe and Kayak Corporation. Changes need to be made to the employee records. You need to confer with Shirley Aultman, the office manager, regarding these changes. The easiest way to do this is for the two of you to share the worksheet. In order to tell which person is accessing which worksheet, you have to assign user names to the worksheets. Complete the following steps to change the user name:
   a. Click Tools and Options.
   b. Click the General tab on the Options dialog box.
   c. Look in the User name box. Write down on a piece of paper the name that is currently entered. When you complete this exercise, you will change the name back.
   d. Enter your name in the User name box.
   e. Click OK.

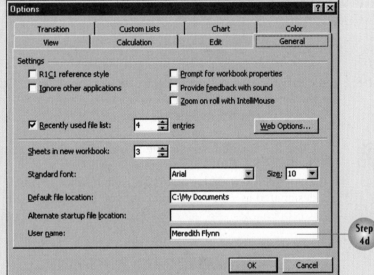

Step 4d

5. Click the Save button on the Standard toolbar.
6. To simulate sharing workbooks, you are going to open another copy of Excel. For the simulation to work, you must open Excel from the Start button. Click the Start button, point to Programs, and open another copy of Excel.

7. You now have a second copy of Excel running with an unnamed worksheet on the screen. You need to change the user name for this copy of Excel. This will be the copy being run by the office manager. Complete the following steps to change the user name:
   a. Click Tools and Options.
   b. Click the General tab on the Options dialog box.
   c. In the User name box, key **Shirley Aultman**.
   d. Click OK.
   e. Right-click the Windows taskbar and click Tile Windows Horizontally.

f. Make sure the copy of Excel that currently has the workbook Excel E2, Ex 08 open is on top. If necessary, rearrange the two windows by clicking and dragging on the title bars.

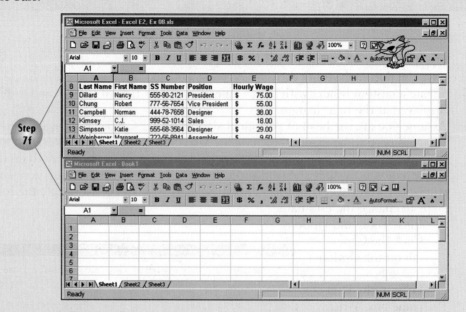

8. You currently have the Excel E2, Ex 08 workbook open. Complete the following steps to see what happens if Shirley tries to open the same workbook.
    a. If necessary, click in Shirley's copy of the program (the one on the bottom) to make sure it is the active program.

    b. Click the Open button on the Standard toolbar of Shirley's program and try to open the Excel E2, Ex 08 file on your data disk.
    c. The File in Use dialog box is displayed. Since Excel E2, Ex 08 has not been designated as a shared workbook, you cannot make any changes to it once it is open.

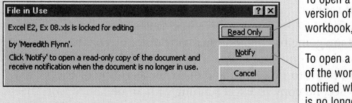

    d. Click Cancel.
9. Complete the following steps to designate Excel E2, Ex 08 as a shared workbook.
    a. Click in the window for Excel E2, Ex 08 (the top window) to make it active.
    b. On the menu bar of the top window, click <u>T</u>ools and S<u>h</u>are Workbook.

c. Click the <u>A</u>llow changes by more than one user at the same time check box to select it.

d. Click OK.

e. A dialog box is displayed notifying you that the workbook will be saved. Click OK.

10. Complete the following steps to open a copy of the shared workbook.

a. Click in Shirley's copy of the program (the one on the bottom) to select it.

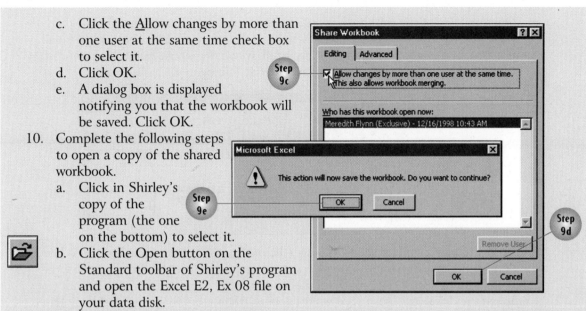

b. Click the Open button on the Standard toolbar of Shirley's program and open the Excel E2, Ex 08 file on your data disk.

11. The workbook is now open in both program windows. Notice that the word [Shared] appears in the title bar of both windows. Complete the following steps to make changes to the worksheet.

a. Access Shirley's copy of the workbook (the one on the bottom). Scroll to the bottom of the list and enter the following data for an employee that was just hired:

Cell	Data
A27	**Goldman**
B27	**Rona**
C27	**555-30-8311**
D27	**Assistant**
E27	**7.50**

b. Click the Save button on the Standard toolbar of Shirley's copy of the workbook.

c. Access your copy of the workbook (the one on top). One of the employees was promoted and you need to make the necessary changes. Make the following changes to the contents of the cells listed.

Cell	Data
D17	**Assistant Manager**
E17	**8.75**

d. Adjust the width of column D so that the complete position title is displayed.

e. Click the Save button on the Standard toolbar of your copy of the workbook.

f. An information box appears notifying you that your workbook was updated with changes made by someone else. Excel updates the workbook whenever it is saved. Click OK.

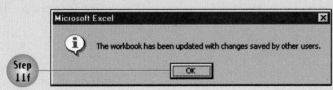

g. On your copy of the workbook, scroll down so that row 27 is displayed. The data on the new employee, entered by Shirley, appears in your worksheet. Notice the small triangles in the upper left corner of each cell. Move the mouse pointer over one of those triangles. Information on the change that Shirley made is displayed.

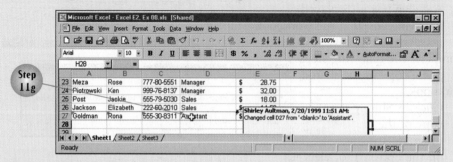

h. Access Shirley's copy of the workbook (the one on the bottom) and save it. When you are notified that the workbook has been updated, click OK. Look at cells D17 and E17 in Shirley's copy of the workbook to see the changes you made in your copy.

12. Complete the following steps to see what happens when users sharing a workbook enter conflicting data into the same cell:

a. In Shirley's copy of the workbook (the one on the bottom) change the data in cell E14 to 10.75. Save the workbook.

b. In your copy of the workbook (the one on the top) change the data in cell E14 to 10.25. Save the workbook.

c. The Resolve Conflicts dialog box appears, notifying you that there have been conflicting changes made to the worksheet. The first person who saves the workbook after conflicting changes have been entered is the one who gets to resolve the conflict. Click the Accept Mine button.

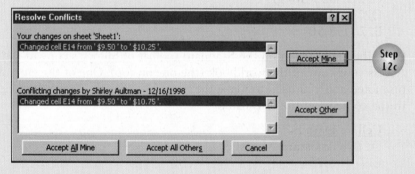

d. Access Shirley's copy of the workbook and save it. When the dialog box appears informing you the workbook has been updated, click OK. Notice that 10.25 is now entered in cell E14 in Shirley's workbook.

e. Shirley still has an opportunity to reject your changes. On the menu bar in Shirley's copy (the one on the bottom), click Tools and, if necessary, wait a moment for the Track Changes option to display. Point to the Track Changes option and click Accept or Reject Changes.

f. The Select Changes to Accept or Reject dialog box is displayed. You can limit the changes that you review using this dialog box. Click OK to accept the default options.

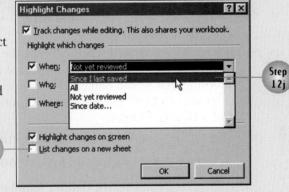

Step 12f

g. The Accept or Reject Changes dialog box is displayed. Click the Accept button until your dialog box displays the conflicting numbers entered in cell E14.

> The conflicting values for cell E14 should be displayed.

h. Shirley is going to reject your change to cell E14. Click the second option in the list, the option originally entered by Shirley, and click Accept. Save the workbook.

Step 12g

i. Access your copy of the workbook (the one on top) and click the Save button. Click OK when the dialog box appears notifying you that changes were made by other users. Now you want to look at a history of the changes that were made. Click Tools on the menu bar of your copy of the workbook, point to Track Changes, and click Highlight Changes.

j. The Highlight Changes dialog box is displayed. Click the down arrow at the right side of the When box. Select the *Since I last saved* option.

Step 12j

k. Click the check box to List changes on a new sheet. A check mark should be in the box.

l. Click OK. A new sheet tab is added to the worksheet called History. On this worksheet you can see that Shirley rejected your change in cell E14.

Step 12k

m. Save your worksheet (the one on top). Notice that the History sheet tab is no longer displayed. You cannot make any changes to the History worksheet and it is hidden when not needed.

13. Print a copy of your worksheet.

14. Access Shirley's copy of the workbook (the one on the bottom). Change the user name back to the original entry and exit the workbook by completing the following steps:

a. Click Tools and Options.

b. Click the General tab.

c. In the User name box, key the name that was originally displayed when you started the exercise. Click the Save button to save the file.

d. Click OK.

e. Click File on the menu bar in Shirley's workbook and click Exit. (You may have to scroll down the menu options in order to display the Exit option.)

15. Access your copy of the workbook. Maximize the window. Complete the following steps to designate that the workbook is no longer to be shared.
    a. Click Tools and Share Workbook.
    b. Click the Allow changes by more than one user at the same time check box so that it is no longer selected.
    c. Click OK.
    d. When the dialog box is displayed asking if you want to remove the workbook from shared use, click Yes.
16. Complete the following steps to change the user name back to the original entry.
    a. Click Tools and Options.
    b. Click the General tab.
    c. In the User name box, key the name that was originally displayed when you started the exercise.
    d. Click OK.
17. Save the worksheet with the same name (Excel E2, Ex 08) and close it.

chapter summary

➤ If a workbook is used repeatedly for the same purpose, a template should be created for it. A template saves the basic format of a workbook so that labels, formats, formulas—anything that would remain the same each time the workbook is used—do not have to be entered each time. Excel comes with a template for an Expense Statement, an Invoice, and a Purchase Order.

➤ The default template folder for the Office 2000 applications is:

   <root drive>\<windows folder>\Application Data\Microsoft\Templates

If Profiles are in use, the default template folder is:

   <root drive>\<windows folder>\Profiles\<username>\Application Data\Microsoft\Templates

➤ Create a new template by entering the data that will be used repeatedly into the worksheet, clicking File and then Save As. The Save As dialog box is displayed. Save the file as a template by clicking the down arrow to the right of the Save as type box, selecting Template (*.xlt) from the drop-down menu and clicking Save.

➤ Edit a new template by clicking File and New. Open to template to be edited by clicking the General tab and double-clicking the appropriate icon. Make the changes to the template and click the Save button on the Standard toolbar. When the Save As dialog box is displayed, click the down arrow to the right of the Save as type box, select Template (*.xlt) from the drop-down menu and click Save. Save the file by clicking Yes when the warning dialog box appears asking if you want to replace the original file.

Chapter Two

- Excel's built-in Expense Statement template allows you to automatically collect data and place it in a single list.
- A list in Excel is also called a database. A database in Excel is a worksheet that has been organized into columns, which are called fields, and rows, which are called records. A label, or field name, is at the top of each column.
- Creating a workspace allows you to open several workbooks at the same time with just one step. A workspace file uses the extension .xlw.
- Data from one worksheet can be consolidated into another worksheet. For example, data from one worksheet could be consolidated by adding it to the data in another worksheet.
- If a link has been established from cell A5 in *Sheet1* to cell D10 in *Sheet2*, for example, whatever data is entered in cell D10 will automatically appear in cell A5. If the data in cell D10 is changed, then the data in cell A5 will be automatically updated to reflect that change.
- If a workbook is shared, then more than one person can use it and make changes to it at the same time.

commands review

	Mouse/Keyboard
Access Excel's built-in templates	Click File, New, Spreadsheet Solutions tab
Display file extensions using Windows Explorer or My Computer	Click View, Folder Options, View tab
Save a template	Click File, Save As, the down arrow to the right of the Save as type box, Template (*.xlt)
Create a workspace	Click File, Save Workspace
Arrange multiple worksheets	Click Window, Arrange
Copy multiple worksheets into a single workbook	Press Ctrl key, drag sheet tab of copied worksheet to sheet tabs in workbook where copied worksheet is to be placed
Consolidate data	Click Data, Consolidate
Link workbooks	Key =, click the cell to be linked, press Enter
Share workbook	Click Tools, Share Workbook

thinking offline

Completion: In the space provided at the right, indicate the correct term, command, or symbol.

1. This dialog box automatically appears whenever you try to save a template.

2. Click this tab on the New dialog box to access Excel's built-in templates.

3. Excel automatically adds this extension on to the file name of a template.

4. Click this tab on the New dialog box to access the templates that you create.

5. This is another term for a list in Excel.

6. This is the extension given to workspace files.

7. Click this option on the menu bar in order to arrange multiple windows on the desktop.

8. Press this key while dragging the sheet tab of a worksheet you want to copy to a different workbook.

9. Click this option on the menu bar in order to consolidate data.

10. This is the first thing you key into a cell that is to contain linked data.

11. This is displayed in the title bar next to the workbook name of a workbook that is currently being shared.

12. In order to allow two or more people to make changes to a workbook at the same time, you have to access this dialog box.

13. List the advantages of using templates.

14. List the steps you would take to link cell E5 in a workbook named Quarterly Profits to cell F15 in a workbook named January Sales.

15. List the steps you would take to display the file extensions to the file names of the files in a folder called Quarterly Statements.

working hands-on

(Note: In order to have room on your disk to save the files you will be creating, you will need to delete the Whitewater Expense Statement1.xls file you created in exercise 4. Check with your instructor to make sure it is all right to delete this file.)

Assessment 1

1. Open Excel.
2. Open Excel's built-in template named Invoice. Enable the macros.
3. Click the Customize button. Enter the following data in the Type Company Information Here box:

Company Name	**Whitewater Canoe & Kayak**
Address	**34982 Olympia Blvd**
City	**Seattle**
State	**WA**
ZIP Code	**98101**
Phone	**(206) 555-8937**
Fax	**(206) 555-8940**

4. In the Specify Default Invoice Information here box, delete $7.00 from the Shipping Charge box. Leave this box empty.
5. Scroll down to the Formatted Information box. Click the Select Logo button. Insert the Whitewtr.tif file which is located on your student data disk. Click the Change Plate Font button. Change the font size to 8.
6. Click the Lock/Save Sheet button. Click OK. Save the template in the default template folder using the file name **Whitewater Invoice**.
7. When the Invoice dialog box appears, click OK. Close the Whitewater Invoice template.
8. Open the Whitewater Invoice template.
9. Enable the macros. Enter the following customer information:

Name:	**Rocky Mountain Outfitters**
Address:	**39853 Highway 50**
City:	**Howard**
State:	**CO**
ZIP:	**81233**
Phone:	**(719) 555-8032**
Order No.	**RT-594**
Rep.	**Jackson**

10. Enter the following information:

Qty	Description	Unit Price
3	15' Pathfinder, vinyl trim, forest green	1149
2	14' 6" Trekker, vinyl trim, spruce	1199
4	12' Excursion, red	679

11. Toward the bottom of the invoice in the Payment Details section, click the Check option.
12. At the bottom of the invoice, click where it says "Insert Fine Print Here". Key the following: **Shipping charges included in unit price**
13. At the bottom of the invoice, click where it says "Insert Farewell Statement Here". Key the following: **River Adventure Specialists**
14. Create a custom header that prints your name at the left margin and the file name at the right margin.
15. Save the worksheet on your student data disk. When the Template File - Save to Database dialog box appears, click the Continue without updating option. Save the worksheet using the file name Excel E2, SA 01.
16. Print the Excel E2, SA 01 file and close it.
17. Delete the Whitewater Invoice.xlt file from the default user template folder.

Assessment 2

(Note: In order to have room on your disk to save the files you will be creating, you will need to delete the Excel E2, SA 01.xls file you created in assessment 1. Check with your instructor to make sure it is all right to delete this file.)

1. Open Excel Worksheet E2-02.
2. You are going to create a template. Enter the following data:

Cell	Data
B12	1st Quarter
C12	2nd Quarter
D12	3rd Quarter
E12	4th Quarter
F12	TOTAL
A13	Operating Costs
A14	Selling Expenses
A15	General Administrative
A16	Total Costs and Expenses
B16	=SUM(B13:B15)
F13	=SUM(B13:E13)

3. Bold and center the labels in row 12.
4. Bold the label in cell A16.
5. Adjust the column widths so that the labels all fit in the columns.
6. Copy the function in cell B16 to cells C16 through F16.
7. Copy the function in cell F13 to cells F14 and F15.
8. Place a single line border at the bottom of cells B15 through F15. Place a double line border at the bottom of cells B16 through F16.
9. Save the file as a template in the default user template folder. Name the template Excel Worksheet E2-02.xlt.
10. Close the Excel Worksheet E2-02.xlt template.
11. Open the template Excel Worksheet E2-02.xlt.

12. Enter the following data:

Cell	Data
B13	21589
B14	15733
B15	7036
C13	23579
C14	21627
C15	9458
D13	26722
D14	24691
D15	10499
E13	31834
E14	25637
E15	14675

13. Create a custom header that prints your name at the left margin and the file name at the right margin.
14. Save the worksheet on your student data disk using the file name Excel E2, SA 02-A.
15. Print and then close the Excel E2, SA 02-A file.
16. Open the template Excel Worksheet E2-02.xlt.
17. Edit the template by entering the following data:

Cell	Data
G12	AVERAGE
G13	=AVERAGE(B13:E13)

18. Copy the function in cell G13 to cells G14 and G15. *(Hint: Ignore the Divide by zero error message. This message will go away as soon as data is entered into the worksheet.)*
19. Save the file as a template in the default user template folder. Name the template Excel Worksheet E2-02.xlt. Replace the existing file.
20. Close the Excel Worksheet E2-02.xlt template.
21. Open the template Excel Worksheet E2-02.xlt.
22. Enter the following data:

Cell	Data
B13	20201
B14	14354
B15	6991
C13	24002
C14	20823
C15	9324
D13	25624
D14	23951
D15	11056
E13	30089
E14	24394
E15	13987

23. Create a custom header that prints your name at the left margin and the file name at the right margin.

24. Save the worksheet on your student data disk using the file name Excel E2, SA 02-B.
25. Print and then close the Excel E2, SA 02-B file.
26. Delete the Excel Worksheet E2-02.xlt file from the default user template folder.

Assessment 3

1. Open Excel.
2. Open Net Income 1st Qtr, Net Income 2nd Qtr, Net Income 3rd Qtr, and Net Income 4th Qtr. Arrange the workbooks using the Window Arrange command. Select the Tiled option. Save a workspace for the four files. Name the workspace Income.
3. Close the four files. Open Income.xlw.
4. Open a new workbook. Arrange the five workbooks using the Window Arrange command. Use the Tiled option.
5. Copy the 1st Qtr worksheet, 2nd Qtr worksheet, 3rd Qtr worksheet, and 4th Qtr worksheet into the workbook you opened in step 3.
6. Close the Net Income 1st Qtr, Net Income 2nd Qtr, Net Income 3rd Qtr, and Net Income 4th Qtr workbooks.
7. Maximize the new workbook and save it on the student data disk using the file name Excel E2, SA 03.
8. Rename the *Sheet1* tab to TOTALS.
9. Copy the labels in cells A11 through A22 in the 1st Qtr worksheet to cells A11 through A22 in the TOTALS worksheet. Automatically adjust the width of column A so that the labels all fit in the column.
10. Click cell B10 in the TOTALS worksheet. Consolidate the data in cells E10 through E22 on the 1st Qtr, 2nd Qtr, 3rd Qtr, and 4th Qtr worksheets so that the totals on each worksheet are added together. Use the labels in the top row. Adjust the width of column B so that the consolidated data is displayed.
11. If necessary, click the TOTALS sheet tab. Add a custom header that displays your name at the left margin and the file name at the right margin. Print the TOTALS worksheet.
12. Save the workbook with the same name (Excel E2, SA 03).
13. Close Excel E2, SA 03.

Assessment 4

1. Open Excel.
2. Open Fall Enrollment, Spring Enrollment, and Summer Enrollment. Arrange the workbooks using the Window Arrange command. Select the Vertical option. Save a workspace for the three files. Name the workspace Enrollment.
3. Close the three files. Open Enrollment.xlw.
4. Open a new workbook. Arrange the four workbooks using the Window Arrange command. Use the Tiled option.
5. Copy the Fall, Spring, and Summer worksheets into the workbook you opened in step 3.
6. Close the Fall Enrollment, Spring Enrollment, and Summer Enrollment workbooks.
7. Maximize the new workbook and save it on the student data disk using the file name Excel E2, SA 04.
8. Rename the *Sheet1* tab to AVERAGE ENROLLMENT.
9. Copy the labels in cells A13 through A18 in the Fall worksheet to cells A13 through A18 in the AVERAGE ENROLLMENT worksheet. Automatically adjust the width of column A so that the labels all fit in the column.

10. Click cell B14 in the AVERAGE ENROLLMENT worksheet. Consolidate the data in cells D14 through D18 on the Fall, Spring, and Summer worksheets so that the average of the data is calculated. Do not use any labels.
11. If necessary, click the AVERAGE ENROLLMENT sheet tab. Key the label **Average Enrollment** in cell B13. Bold the label in B13.
12. Adjust the width of column B so that the label fits in the column.
13. Format cells B14 through B18 to the Number format with no decimal places displayed.
14. Add a custom header that displays your name at the left margin and the name of the workbook, Excel E2, SA 04, at the right margin.
15. Print the AVERAGE ENROLLMENT worksheet.
16. Save the workbook with the same name (Excel E2, SA 04) and close it.

Assessment 5

1. Before starting this exercise, you need to remove the read-only attribute from the Net Income 1st Qtr, Net Income 2nd Qtr, Net Income 3rd Qtr, and Net Income 4th Qtr files. To remove the read-only attribute from the Net Income 1st Qtr file, complete the following steps:
   a. Using either Windows Explorer or My Computer, navigate to the Net Income 1st Qtr file on your data disk.
   b. Right click the Net Income 1st Qtr file.
   c. From the short-cut menu that is displayed, click Properties.
   d. Click the General tab on the File Properties dialog box that is displayed.
   e. In the Attributes section toward the bottom of the dialog box, click the Read-only check box so that it is no longer selected.
   f. Click OK.
2. Repeat step 1 to remove the read-only attribute from the Net Income 2nd Qtr, Net Income 3rd Qtr, and Net Income 4th Qtr files. When you have finished, close either Windows Explorer or My Computer.
3. Open Excel Worksheet E2-03. Save it as Excel E2, SA 05.
4. Open the Income.xlw file you created in assessment 3. Use the Windows Arrange command to arrange the windows vertically.
5. Link cell B13 in the Excel E2, SA 05 worksheet to cell E11 in the Net Income 1st Qtr worksheet.
6. Link cell B14 in the Excel E2, SA 05 worksheet to cell E11 in the Net Income 2nd Qtr worksheet.
7. Link cell B15 in the Excel E2, SA 05 worksheet to cell E11 in the Net Income 3rd Qtr worksheet.
8. Link cell B16 in the Excel E2, SA 05 worksheet to cell E11 in the Net Income 4th Qtr worksheet.
9. Close the Net Income 1st Qtr, Net Income 2nd Qtr, Net Income 3rd Qtr, and Net Income 4th Qtr workbooks. Maximize the window for the Excel E2, SA 05 file.
10. Add a custom header to the Excel E2, SA 05 worksheet that displays your name at the left margin and the file name at the right margin.
11. Print the Excel E2, SA 05 worksheet.
12. Open the Net Income 2nd Qtr workbook. Key the following into cell C11: **69302**
13. Save and close the Net Income 2nd Qtr workbook.
14. Notice the updated value in cell B14. Print the Excel E2, SA 05 worksheet again.
15. Save the workbook with the same name (Excel E2, SA 05) and close it.

Assessment 6

(Note: In order to have room on your disk to save the files you will be creating, you will need to delete the Excel E2, SA 02-A.xls and Excel E2, SA 02-B.xls files you created in assessment 2. Check with your instructor to make sure it is all right to delete these files.)

1. Open 4th Qtr Sales.xlw. You created this file in exercise 7.
2. Open Excel Worksheet E2-04. Save it as Excel E2, SA 06. Use the Windows Arrange command to arrange the windows vertically.
3. Link cell B14 in the Excel E2, SA 06 worksheet to cell C27 in the Region Sales Oct worksheet.
4. Link cell C14 in the Excel E2, SA 06 worksheet to cell C27 in the Region Sales Nov worksheet.
5. Link cell D14 in the Excel E2, SA 06 worksheet to cell C27 in the Region Sales Dec worksheet.
6. Close the Region Sales Oct, Region Sales Nov, and Region Sales Dec workbooks. Maximize the window for the Exel E2, SA 06 file.
7. Add a custom header to the Excel E2, SA 06 worksheet that displays your name at the left margin and the file name at the right margin.
8. Print the Excel E2, SA 06 worksheet.
9. Open the Region Sales Oct workbook. Key the following into cell B11: **6742**
10. Save and close the Region Sales Oct workbook.
11. Notice the updated value in cell B14. Print the Excel E2, SA 06 worksheet again.
12. Save the workbook with the same name (Excel E2, SA 06) and close it.

Assessment 7

1. Open Excel Worksheet E2-05. Save it as Excel E2, SA 07.
2. Create a custom header with your name displayed at the left margin and the file name at the right margin.
3. The Production Manager, Ed Snyder, and the Vice President of Finance, Beverly Peterson, both need to make changes to Copper Clad's budget figures for January and February. They are going to do this by sharing the workbook. Click Tools and Options. Click the General tab on the Options dialog box. Look in the User name box. Write down on a piece of paper the name that is currently entered. When you complete this assessment exercise you will change the name back to what is currently entered. Assign the user name Ed Snyder to the workbook that is currently open.
4. Click Tools and Share Workbook. Click the Allow changes by more than one user at the same time check box to select it. Click OK. Click OK to save the workbook.
5. Start another copy of the Excel program by clicking the Start button, selecting Programs and opening another copy of Excel. Change the user name for this copy of Excel to Beverly Peterson.
6. Right-click the taskbar and click Tile Windows Horizontally.
7. Click in Beverly's copy of Excel to select it and open the E2, SA 07 file. Beverly's copy of Excel should be on the top. If it's not, rearrange the windows so it is.

8. The workbook is now open in both program windows. Notice that the word [Shared] appears in the title bar of both windows. Access Beverly's copy of the workbook (on the top) and make the following changes:

Cell	Data
B14	16309
C14	19986
B17	8.50
C17	8.50

9. Save the worksheet.
10. Access Ed Snyder's copy of the workbook (on the bottom) and make the following changes:

Cell	Data
B15	.75
C15	.75

11. Save the workbook. When the information box appears telling you the workbook has been updated with changes saved by other users, click OK. Move the mouse pointer over the blue triangles to read about the changes that were made.
12. Access Beverly's copy of the workbook and save it. When the information box appears telling you the workbook has been updated with changes saved by other users, click OK. Move the mouse pointer over the maroon triangles to read about the changes that were made.
13. In Beverly's copy of the workbook, enter 0.5 in cells B15 and C15. Save the workbook. In Ed's copy of the workbook (on the bottom) enter 1 in cells B15 and C15. Save the workbook. The Resolve Conflict dialog box is displayed. Click the Accept All Mine button.
14. Access Beverly's copy of the workbook and save it. When the dialog box appears informing you the workbook has been updated, click OK. Click Tools on the menu bar in Beverly's workbook and point to the Track Changes option. Click Accept or Reject Changes. Click OK to accept the default options. Click the Accept button until the dialog box displays the conflicting values entered in cell B15. Click the second option in the list, Ed Snyder's change to 0.75 and click the Accept button. When the dialog box displays the conflicting values entered for C15, click the second option in the list, Ed Snyder's change to 0.75 and click the Accept button. Save the workbook.
15. Access Ed Snyder's copy of the workbook (on the bottom) and click the Save button. Click OK when the dialog box appears notifying you that changes were made by other users. Look at a history of the changes that were made by clicking Tools on the menu bar of Ed's copy of the workbook, pointing to Track Changes and clicking Highlight Changes. Click the down arrow at the right side of the When box. Select the *Since I last saved* option. Click the check box next to List changes on a new sheet. A check mark should be in the box. Click OK. A new sheet tab is added to the worksheet called History. On this worksheet you can see that Beverly rejected your changes in cells B15 and C15.
16. Save Ed's copy of the workbook (on the bottom). Print a copy of the workbook.
17. Access Beverly's copy of the workbook. Change the user name back to the original entry by clicking Tools and Options. Click the General tab. In the User name box, key the name that was originally displayed when you started the exercise. Click OK. Save the workbook. Click File on the menu bar in Beverly's workbook and click Exit.

18. Access Ed's copy of the workbook. Maximize the window. Designate that the workbook should no longer be shared by clicking <u>T</u>ools and S<u>h</u>are Workbook. Click the <u>A</u>llow changes by more than one user at the same time check box so that it is no longer selected. Click OK. When the dialog box is displayed asking if you want to remove the workbook from shared use, click <u>Y</u>es.
19. If necessary change the user name back to the original entry.
20. Save the worksheet with the same name (Excel E2, SA 07) and close it.

Assessment 8

(Note: In order to have room on your disk to save the file you will be creating, you will need to delete the Excel E2, SA 07.xls file you created in assessment 7. Check with your instructor to make sure it is all right to delete this file.)

1. When cells that supply data to a link are changed, Excel will not automatically update the link if the workbook containing the link is closed. Use Excel's Office Assistant to learn how you can manually update links. *(Hint: Click <u>H</u>elp and Microsoft Excel <u>H</u>elp. At the Office Assistant or the <u>A</u>nswer Wizard tab, key the question "**How do I update a link manually?**" and click <u>S</u>earch. At the list of topics that displays, click* Update a linked object manually. *Read and then print the information displayed in the Help dialog box.)*
2. Open the Region Sales Nov workbook. Key the following into cell B17: **6090**. Save the workbook using the same name. Close the workbook.
3. Open Excel E2, SA 06. When the dialog box appears asking if you want to update this workbook with changes made to another workbook, click <u>N</u>o. Save the worksheet using the Save <u>A</u>s command and name it Excel E2, SA 08.
4. Using the help information you printed in step 1, update the linked objects in this workbook manually.
5. Print Excel E2, SA 08.
6. Save the worksheet using the same file name (Excel E2, SA 08) and close it.

Chapter 03E

Using Advanced Functions

PERFORMANCE OBJECTIVES

Upon successful completion of chapter 3, you will be able to:

- Use the PMT function.
- Use the PV function.
- Use the ROUND function.
- Use the RAND function.
- Use the SUMIF function.
- Use the COUNTIF function.
- Name a Range.
- Use a Named Range in a Formula.
- Use the VLOOKUP function.
- Use the IF function.
- Use array formulas.

Excel includes many functions that make the task of creating a worksheet much easier. A function is a built-in formula. Functions perform complex mathematical, financial, data-manipulation, and logical operations. Excel includes over 200 functions that are divided into the following nine categories:

Financial
Date and Time
Math and Trig
Statistical
Lookup and Reference
Database
Text
Logical
Information

Functions include two parts. The first part is the name of the function, which always immediately follows the equal sign. The second part of the function is the argument. The argument contains the data needed by the function to perform the necessary calculations or data manipulations. The argument may contain numbers, formulas, cell references, range names, or other functions, which are called nested functions. In this chapter you will learn how to use some advanced functions as well as how to work with named ranges and use them in formulas and functions.

Entering a Function

Paste Function
Button

Functions can be keyed directly into a cell or entered using the Edit Formula button or the Paste Function button. To enter a function using the Paste Function button, click the Paste Function button on the Standard toolbar. The Paste function dialog box as shown in figure 3.1 is displayed. First you must select a category from the Function category list box. All the functions for that particular category are then listed in the Function name box. Next, select the particular function you want from the Function name list and click OK.

figure 3.1

The Paste Function Dialog Box

If you select the Function category *Most Recently Used* on the Paste Function dialog box, a list of the ten most recently used functions appears in the Function name list box. This is a quick way to select a function that was used recently.

First, select a category from the Function category list box.

A description of the function name currently selected in the Function name box is displayed.

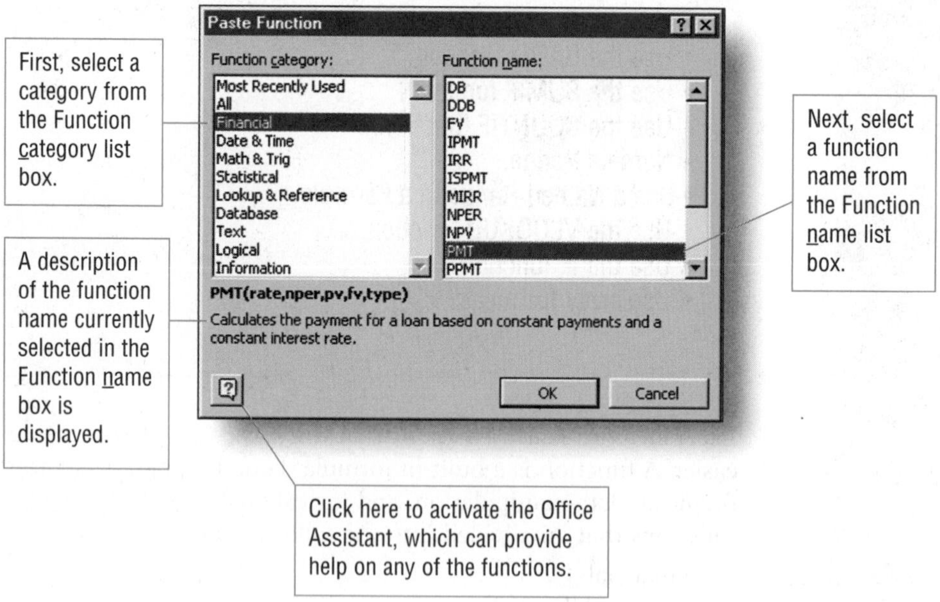

Paste Function

Function category:
- Most Recently Used
- All
- Financial
- Date & Time
- Math & Trig
- Statistical
- Lookup & Reference
- Database
- Text
- Logical
- Information

Function name:
- DB
- DDB
- FV
- IPMT
- IRR
- ISPMT
- MIRR
- NPER
- NPV
- PMT
- PPMT

PMT(rate,nper,pv,fv,type)
Calculates the payment for a loan based on constant payments and a constant interest rate.

OK   Cancel

Next, select a function name from the Function name list box.

Click here to activate the Office Assistant, which can provide help on any of the functions.

If the Formula Palette covers up cells on the worksheet which you want to select, you can easily move it by clicking on it and dragging it to a new location.

Figure 3.2 shows the Formula Palette for the PMT function. You enter the data to be used in the formula using the Formula Palette. Next to each argument name is a box. If the argument name is bold, then that particular argument is required by the function and must have data assigned to it. Cell references, ranges, range names, and formulas may be entered into an argument box. You can either key the data into the argument box or select the appropriate cells from the worksheet to enter them into the argument box. Once the necessary data is entered into the argument boxes, click OK.

figure 3.2

The Formula Palette

Argument Names

If an argument name is bold, data must be entered in its box.

If an argument name is not bold, entering data in its box is optional.

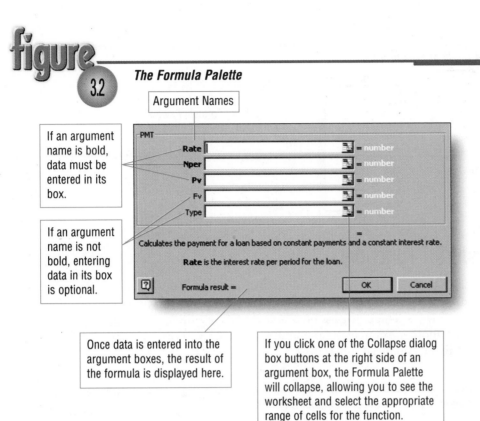

Once data is entered into the argument boxes, the result of the formula is displayed here.

If you click one of the Collapse dialog box buttons at the right side of an argument box, the Formula Palette will collapse, allowing you to see the worksheet and select the appropriate range of cells for the function.

Two other ways to insert a function are to click Insert and Function or to press Shift and F3.

Another way to enter functions is by clicking the Edit Formula button on the Formula bar. When you click this button, an abbreviated version of the Formula Palette appears, as shown in figure 3.3.

Edit Formula Button

figure 3.3

An Abbreviated Version of the Formula Palette

Click here to see a list of common functions.

The Edit Formula Button

The function is entered here.

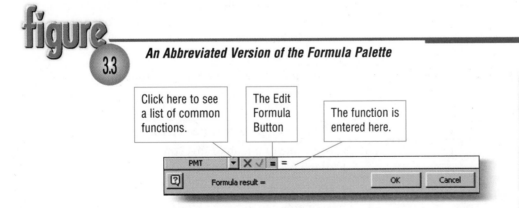

To see a list of commonly used functions, click the down arrow to the right of the Name box. The drop-down menu shown in figure 3.4 appears. If you select one of the functions from the list, an expanded Formula Palette for that particular function is displayed. If you select the last option, *More Functions,* the Paste Function dialog box is displayed. From this dialog box you can select any function you want.

When you edit a function that has more than one set of parentheses, each set of parentheses is displayed as the same color so you can tell which opening parenthesis goes with which closing parenthesis. Also when editing a function, if you place the insertion point anywhere within a reference to a range of cells (B5:B25, for example) the reference is displayed in a color and a border with a matching color is placed around that range on the worksheet.

figure 3.4

A Menu of Function Options

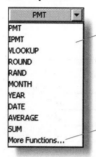

Selecting any of these options displays the expanded Formula Palette for that particular function.

Click this option to display the Paste Function dialog box.

Use range names whenever possible in functions.

Financial Functions

Excel includes many financial functions that are used for calculating loan details, annuities, and investment analyses, for example. An annuity is a periodic series of equal payments. The mortgage on a house is one example of an annuity. A car loan would be another example of an annuity. Table 3.1 describes the common arguments used in Excel's financial functions.

table 3.1

Arguments Used in Excel's Financial Functions

Argument	Argument Name	Description
Present value	Pv	The current value of amounts to be received or paid in the future discounted at some interest rate; the amount that must be invested today at some interest rate to accumulate to some specified future value.
Number of periods	Nper	The number of payments that will be made to an investment or loan. For example, a five-year loan with monthly payments would have 60 periods.
Payment	Pmt	The amount paid or collected for each period.
Future value	Fv	The value of a loan or investment at the end of all the periods.
Rate		The interest rate being charged or paid.
Type		Payments can either be made in arrears (at the end of each period) or in advance (at the beginning of each period). The Type argument determines whether the calculation will be based on payments made in arrears or in advance. Type is the number 0 (payments in arrears) or 1 (payments in advance). If Type is omitted, it is assumed to be 0.

The PMT Function

The PMT function calculates the periodic payment of a loan based on constant payments and a constant interest rate. The format for the PMT function is

=PMT(rate, nper, pv)

Rate is the interest rate per period. Nper is the total number of payments to be made. Pv is the present value of the amount borrowed. Look at the following PMT function:

=PMT(8%/12,60,–13000)

This formula will calculate how much each payment would be if you borrowed $13,000 at 8% interest and were going to repay the loan in 60 installments. Because the payments are made monthly, the interest rate must also be monthly; therefore the annual rate of interest, or 8%, must be divided by 12. If the loan is for five years, that means there are 60 payments ($5 \times 12 = 60$). The present value of the amount borrowed is –13,000, or minus 13,000, because no payments have yet been made. For all arguments, cash you pay out is represented by a negative number and cash you receive is represented by a positive number.

exercise

Using the PMT Function

1. Open Excel Worksheet E3-01.
2. Save the worksheet using the Save <u>A</u>s command and name it Excel E3, Ex 01.
3. Create a custom header that displays your name at the left margin and the file name at the right margin.
4. Primrose Decorators is a decorating business owned and operated by Georgia and Paul Sorenson. They have outgrown their current facility and need to relocate. Their plans for relocation must include an approximation of what they can afford to pay for a mortgage. This worksheet is designed to make such an estimate. Look over the worksheet. The interest rate per period is in cell D5. The term of the loan is in row 8 and the amount of money being borrowed is in column B. Complete the following steps to compute the loan payments:

   a. Select cell C9.
   b. Click the Paste Function button on the Standard toolbar.
   c. When the Paste Function dialog box appears, click Financial in the Function <u>c</u>ategory list box.
   d. Click *PMT* in the Function <u>n</u>ame list box.
   e. Click OK.

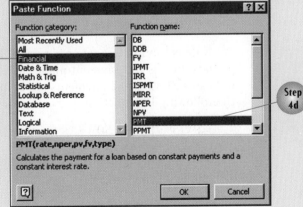

f. The Formula Palette box appears. This is where you enter the data needed for the function. Data must be entered for the arguments that are bold. Entering data for the arguments that are not bold is optional. Click on a gray portion of the Formula Palette box and drag it to the lower right corner of the screen. Make sure the insertion point is in the Rate box. Click cell D5. Press F4 to make the reference to D5 absolute. Key the following: /12.

g. Place the insertion point in the Nper box. Click cell C8. Press F4 to make the reference to C8 absolute. Key the following: *12.

h. Place the insertion point in the Pv box. Press the minus sign key (or hyphen) and click cell B9.

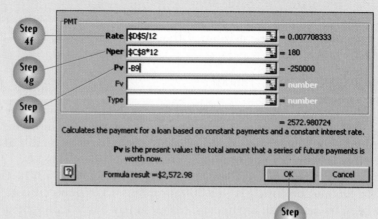

i. Click OK.

j. Copy the function in cell C9 to cells C10 through C17.

5. Repeat step 4 to enter the appropriate functions into cells D9, E9, F9, and G9. Copy the functions as needed. Adjust column widths as needed.

6. The Sorensons do not want to spend more than $3,000 a month on a mortgage. Format cells C9 through G17 so that any value less than or equal to 3,000 is displayed as bold and in the color green.

7. Shade cells B8 through G8 and cells B9 through B17 with a light green color.

8. Print the worksheet.

9. The Sorensons think they may be able to get a better interest rate. Enter .08 in cell D5. Print the worksheet again.

10. Save the worksheet with the same name (Excel E3, Ex 01) and close the worksheet.

The PV Function

The PV function calculates the present value that the total amount of a series of future payments is worth right now. The format for the PV function is:

=PV(**rate, nper, pmt,** fv,type)

Rate is the interest rate per period. Nper is the total number of payment periods. Pmt is the payment made each period. Fv is the future value and type indicates whether the payments are being made in arrears or in advance. Look at the following PV function:

=PV(5%/12,60,150)

This formula will calculate the present value of 60 payments of $150 with a 5% annual percentage rate.

exercise 2

Using the PV Function

1. Open Excel Worksheet E3-02.
2. Save the worksheet using the Save <u>A</u>s command and name it Excel E3, Ex 02.
3. Create a custom header that displays your name at the left margin and the file name at the right margin.
4. There is a machine that Copper Clad Incorporated is considering purchasing, since having this machine would generate significant cash savings. The machine costs $35,000. The accountant has to decide whether or not investing $35,000 in the purchase of this machine is a wise investment. Copper Clad has to make an 18% rate of return on this capital investment in order to make the investment worth it. The company expects to generate a cash savings of $6,500 for the life of the machine, which is estimated to be 15 years. Complete the following steps to use the PV function to make the necessary calculations:

   a. Key **18%** in cell B4.
   b. Key **15** in cell B5.
   c. Key **6500** in cell B6. Format the value in cell B6 as currency with no decimals displayed.

   d. Select cell B8. Click the Paste Function button.
      1) Click *Financial* in the Function <u>c</u>ategory list box.
      2) Click *PV* in the Function <u>n</u>ame list box.
      3) Click OK.
   e. The Formula Palette is displayed. Drag the Formula Palette to the lower right corner of the screen so you can see cells A4 through B8. The insertion point should be in the Rate box. Click cell B4.
   f. Place the insertion point in the Nper box. Click cell B5.
   g. Place the insertion point in the Pmt box. Click cell B6.
   h. Click OK.

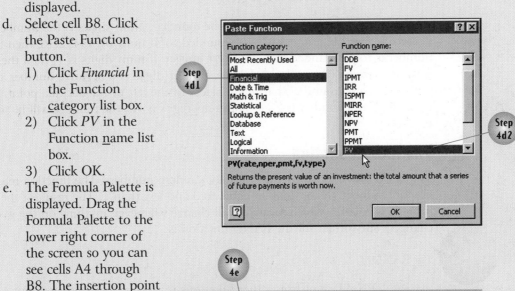

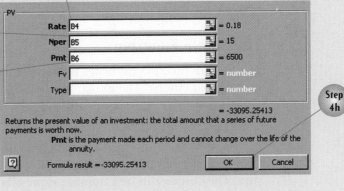

5. The present value of the money is displayed as a negative number because this represents money that would be paid out. The present value of the money is $33,095.25, which is less than the $35,000 cost of the machine. Therefore, this is not a wise investment for the Copper Clad company. The accountant advises the president of Copper Clad that unless the price of the machine can be negotiated down to $33,095, the company should not invest in the machine.

6. Save the worksheet with the same name (Excel E3, Ex 02).

7. Print and close the worksheet.

Math and Trig Functions

Excel includes many math and trigonometric functions. These functions perform a wide variety of calculations such as sines, cosines, factorials, exponents, and logs. The following section introduces you to three of Excel's Math and Trig functions.

The ROUND Function

The ROUND function rounds a number to a specified number of digits. The format for the ROUND function is:

ROUND(**number, num_digits**)

Number is the number that is to be rounded. Num_digits is the number of decimal places the number is to be rounded to. If num_digits is zero, then the number is to be rounded to the nearest integer. If num_digits is 1, then the number is to be rounded to one decimal place. If num_digits is a negative number, then the number is to be rounded that many places to the left of the decimal point. For example, if the number is 2345 and num_digits is –2, the number will be rounded to 2300.

The RAND Function

Pressing F9 recalculates the RAND function.

The RAND function is used to calculate random numbers. The function returns a random number greater than or equal to 0 and less than 1. The result of the formula is volatile, which means it will change whenever anything on the worksheet changes. The format for the RAND function is:

RAND()

RAND is different from other functions in that it does not have any arguments.

The SUMIF Function

The SUMIF function calculates the total of only those cells that meet a given condition or criteria. The format for the SUMIF function is:

SUMIF(**range,criteria**, sum_range)

Range is the range of the cells that are to be evaluated by the function. Criteria is the condition or criteria the cell is to match if it is to be included in the sum. The criteria can be a number, expression, or text. Sum_range are the actual cells to sum. For example, look at the following worksheet fragment:

Using the data from this worksheet fragment, the following SUMIF function would add together only those commissions that were made on sales greater than or equal to $25,000:

SUMIF(B2:B6,">=25000",C2:C6)

The value that would be returned for this function is 7320.

	A	B	C
1	Sales Rep	Sales	Commission
2	Hyde, Paul	$25,000	$3,000
3	Snyder, Holly	$36,000	$4,320
4	Jackson, Donna	$13,000	$1,560
5	Carter, Bob	$19,000	$2,280
6	Adamski, Steve	$23,000	$2,760

exercise 3

Using the ROUND, RAND, and SUMIF Functions

1. Open Excel Worksheet E3-03.
2. Save the worksheet using the Save As command and name it Excel E3, Ex 03.
3. Create a custom header that displays your name at the left margin and the file name at the right margin.
4. This is the start of a worksheet that calculates the commissions earned on sales. The sales figures are not yet available, so you need to use the RAND function to generate some figures. Complete the following steps to generate sales figures using the RAND function:

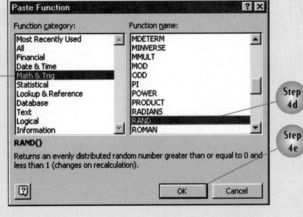

   a. Click cell B5.
   b. Click the Paste Function button.
   c. Click *Math & Trig* from the Function category list box.
   d. Click *RAND* from the Function name list box.
   e. Click OK.
   f. The RAND function generates numbers between 0 and 1. You want to generate numbers between 0 and 100,000, so you have to multiply the function by 100,000. Key ***100000**.
   g. Click OK.
5. The sales figures need to be rounded to the nearest 100. To do this, you will need to create a nested function. Complete the following steps to nest the current RAND function inside a ROUND function:
   a. If necessary, click cell B5 to select it.
   b. In the Formula Bar, place the insertion point between the equal sign and the letter "R". Key the following: **ROUND(**.

c. In the Formula Bar, place the insertion point after the last zero in 100000. Key the following: **, -2)**. When you have finished, the nested function in the Formula Bar should be:

$$=ROUND(RAND()*100000,-2)$$

d. Click the Enter button on the Formula Bar.

e. Double-click the AutoFill handle in the lower right corner of cell B5 to copy the cell to cells B6 through B16.

6. Copper Clad Incorporated pays its sales representatives a 10% commission. Complete the following steps to calculate the commissions on the sales.

a. Click cell C5 to select it.

b. Key the following in cell C5: **=B5*.1**.

c. Click the Enter button on the Formula Bar.

d. Double-click the AutoFill handle in the lower right corner of cell C5 to copy the formula.

7. You may notice that every time you change something on the worksheet, the random numbers change. That is because they are volatile. Next you want to calculate the commissions paid on sales over $40,000. Complete the following steps to use the SUMIF function to make the calculation:

a. Click cell F3 to select it.

b. Click the Paste Function button on the Standard toolbar.

c. Click *Math & Trig* from the Function category list box.

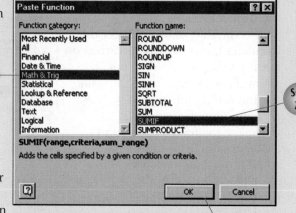

d. Click *SUMIF* from the Function name list box.

e. Click OK.

f. The Formula Palette is displayed. Click and drag the palette to the lower right corner of the screen.

g. The insertion point should be in the Range box. On the worksheet select cells B5 through B16.

h. Place the insertion point in the Criteria box.

i. Key the following: **>40000**.

j. Place the insertion point in the Sum_range box.

k. On the worksheet select cells C5 through C16. When you have finished, your screen should look similar to the one below. Your values will be different because the RAND function is being used.

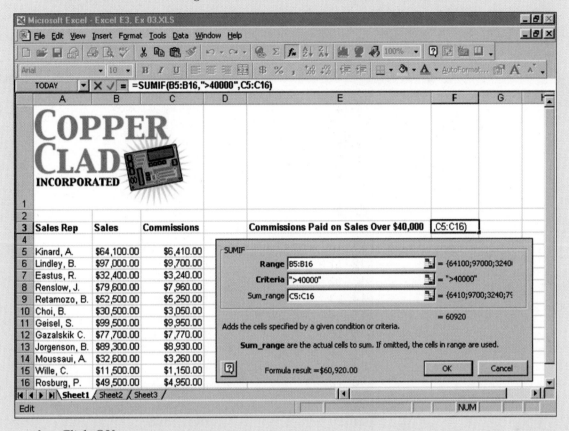

l. Click OK.
8. Repeat step 7 to enter a SUMIF function in cell F6 that calculates the commissions paid on sales over $80,000.
9. Save the worksheet with the same name (Excel E3, Ex 03).
10. Print and close the worksheet.

Statistical Functions

Excel's statistical functions are used on lists of data. Some of the simpler statistical functions are AVERAGE, MAX, and MIN. Excel also includes very complex statistical functions that can calculate deviations, distributions, correlations, and slopes, for example.

The COUNTIF Function

The COUNTIF function counts the number of cells in a given range that meet a specific condition. The format for the COUNTIF function is:

COUNTIF(**range**, **criteria**)

The range is the range of cells to be counted. The criteria is the condition that must be met in order for that cell to be counted. The condition can be a number, expression, or text. Suppose, for example, you had a worksheet that kept track of the weather for the past month. Look at the following segment from this worksheet:

	A	B
1	Day of the Month	Cloud Report
2	1	Overcast
3	2	Partly Cloudy
4	3	Overcast
5	4	Overcast
6	5	Partly Cloudy
7	6	Partly Cloudy
8	7	Partly Cloudy
9	8	Clear
10	9	Clear
11	10	Partly Cloudy
12	11	Clear
13	12	Overcast
14	13	Overcast
15	14	Overcast
16	15	Partly Cloudy
17	16	Clear
18	17	Clear
19	18	Overcast
20	19	Overcast
21	20	Overcast
22	21	Partly Cloudy
23	22	Clear
24	23	Overcast
25	24	Overcast
26	25	Overcast
27	26	Partly Cloudy
28	27	Partly Cloudy
29	28	Clear
30	29	Overcast
31	30	Overcast
32	31	Overcast

Using this worksheet segment, the COUNTIF function =COUNTIF(B2:B32,"Clear") would return 7.

Using the COUNTIF Function

1. Open Excel Worksheet E3-04.
2. Save the worksheet using the Save <u>A</u>s command and name it Excel E3, Ex 04.
3. Create a custom header that displays your name at the left margin and the file name at the right margin.
4. This worksheet keeps track of grades for a CS100 class at Redwood Community College. The instructor wants to know how many students received A's, how many received B's, how many received C's, and so on. Complete the following steps to use the COUNTIF function to find out how many students received A's:

   a. Select cell O6.

   b. Click the Paste function button on the Standard toolbar.

   c. Click *Statistical* in the Function <u>c</u>ategory list box.

   d. Click *COUNTIF* in the Function <u>n</u>ame list box.

   e. Click OK.

   f. The Formula Palette is displayed and the insertion point is in the Range box. Key the following in the Range box: **$M$6:$M$58**.

   g. Place the insertion point in the Criteria box. Key "**A**" in the Criteria box.

   h. Click OK.

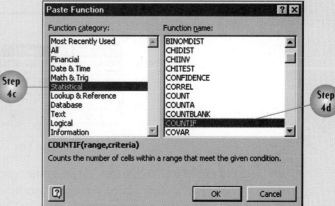

5. Click cell O6 if necessary. Double-click the AutoFill handle to copy the formula. Click cell O7 and edit the function to count the number of B's. Click cell O8 and edit the function to count the number of C's. Click cell O9 and edit the function to count the number of D's. Click cell O10 and edit the function to count the number of F's.
6. Change the orientation of the page to landscape.
7. Select rows 3 through 5 as a print title to repeat at the top of each page.
8. Save the worksheet with the same name (Excel E3, Ex 04).
9. Print and close the worksheet.

Naming a Range

You can define a name that can be used to represent specific cells in a worksheet. The name you create should describe the range of cells. The name *January_Sales*, for example, could be defined for the range of cells containing the January sales figures. When naming a cell or range of cells, the first character of the name must be a letter or an underscore character. The other characters in the name can be letters, numbers, periods, and underscore characters. Spaces are not allowed in names so use either the underscore character or a period to separate the words used in a name, such as *May_Sales* or *Third.Quarter*. Even though uppercase and lowercase letters can be used in a name, they are not case sensitive. That is, if you created the name *Sales_Tax* and then created a second name *sales_tax*, the second name would simply replace the first.

Any worksheet in a workbook can utilize the names you create. For example, if the name *Freight_Cost* is the name for the range of cells C5 through H25 on *Sheet1*, you can use that name on any other sheet in the workbook to refer to the cells C5 through H25 on *Sheet1*.

To create a name for a cell or a range of cells, select the cell or range of cells to be named. Click the Name box at the left side of the formula bar as shown in figure 3.5. Key the name for the cell or cells and press Enter.

figure
3.5

Name Box in Formula Bar

Name Box

If you want to change a range name, click Insert, point to Name, and then click Define. The Define Name dialog box shown in figure 3.6 is displayed. In the Names in workbook list, click the name you want to change. In the Names in workbook box, select the name to be changed and key the new name. Click Add. To delete the original name, in the Names in workbook list click the name to be deleted and then click Delete. Notice in the Refers to box at the bottom of the dialog box the cells to which the name refers are displayed. If you want to change the cells to which the name is to refer, change the cell references in the Refers to box.

figure
3.6

Define Name Dialog Box

Names in workbook box

Names in workbook list

The Refers to box displays the cells to which the selected name refers.

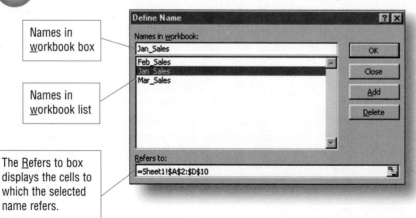

You can select a named range by clicking the down arrow to the right of the Name box and clicking the range to be selected from the drop-down list that appears. If you want to select two or more named ranges, click the first range from the drop-down list, hold down the Ctrl key and click the other ranges.

Using a Named Range in a Formula

Range names can be used in formulas in place of the references to the cells. For example, say the sales figures for January are in cells B5 through B30. To find the total of these figures you could use the function =SUM(B5:B30). If you named the range of cells B5 through B30 *Jan_Sales*, you could also use the formula =SUM(Jan_Sales). One of the advantages of using range names in formulas is that the purpose of the formula is easier to understand. Looking at the formula =SUM(B5:B30) does not provide you with any information about what is being added. But by looking at the formula =SUM(Jan_Sales) you know the sales figures for the month of January are being added.

Range names use absolute cell references by default.

Lookup and Reference Functions

When worksheets contain long lists of data, you need a way to be able to find specific information within the list. Excel's Lookup and Reference functions provide a way to extract certain information from a list. These functions can return cell references when the information is found or they can return the actual contents of the found cell.

The VLOOKUP Function

The VLOOKUP function searches for a value in the leftmost column of a table on the worksheet and then enters a value from a specific column, in the same row as the value it found, into a different location in the worksheet. The format for the VLOOKUP function is:

=VLOOKUP(**lookup_value,table_array,col_index_num**)

The lookup_value is the value to be found in the first column of the table that is being searched. The lookup_value can be a value, text, or reference. The table_array is the table, or range, of information in which data is looked up. The col_index_num is the column number in the table from which the matching value should be returned. The first column in the table or range is column 1, the second column is column 2, and so on. For example, look at the table in figure 3.7. This table shows how much various salaries increase year by year if the increase rate is 5%. To look up how much you would be earning in four years if your starting salary was $25,000, you would use the following VLOOKUP function:

The #N/A error often occurs when using the VLOOKUP function. It means that a required match was not available.

=VLOOKUP(25000,B5:G16,5)

The lookup_value is 25,000, or your starting salary. The table_array, or the range of the table, is B5 through G16. The col_index_num is 5 because the fifth column lists the salaries people earn after having worked for four years. This VLOOKUP function would return the value $30,388.

figure

3.7

A Lookup Table

The col_index_num is the column number in the table where the returned value should be found, in this case the fifth column.

The VLOOKUP function looks up the look_up value in the first column of the table.

The table_array is the range of cells that make up the entire table. In this case the table_array is B5:G16.

	A	B	C	D	E	F	G
1	Salary Increases at 5%						
2							
3				NUMBER OF YEARS WORKED			
4		Starting	1	2	3	4	5
5	SALARY	$ 10,000	$ 10,500	$ 11,025	$ 11,576	$ 12,155	$ 12,763
6		$ 15,000	$ 15,750	$ 16,538	$ 17,364	$ 18,233	$ 19,144
7		$ 20,000	$ 21,000	$ 22,050	$ 23,153	$ 24,310	$ 25,526
8		$ 25,000	$ 26,250	$ 27,563	$ 28,941	$ 30,388	$ 31,907
9		$ 30,000	$ 31,500	$ 33,075	$ 34,729	$ 36,465	$ 38,288
10		$ 35,000	$ 36,750	$ 38,588	$ 40,517	$ 42,543	$ 44,670
11		$ 40,000	$ 42,000	$ 44,100	$ 46,305	$ 48,620	$ 51,051
12		$ 45,000	$ 47,250	$ 49,613	$ 52,093	$ 54,698	$ 57,433
13		$ 50,000	$ 52,500	$ 55,125	$ 57,881	$ 60,775	$ 63,814
14		$ 55,000	$ 57,750	$ 60,638	$ 63,669	$ 66,853	$ 70,195
15		$ 60,000	$ 63,000	$ 66,150	$ 69,458	$ 72,930	$ 76,577
16		$ 65,000	$ 68,250	$ 71,663	$ 75,246	$ 79,008	$ 82,958
17							

The returned value is in the same row as the look_up value and the same column as the col_index_num.

There are cases when the lookup value does not exactly match a value in the first column of the VLOOKUP table. If this happens, the function looks in the first column of the table for the largest value that is less than or equal to the lookup value. Say, for example, your starting salary was $28,000 and you wanted to use the VLOOKUP table in figure 3.7. The VLOOKUP function would look in the first column of the table for the largest value that is less than or equal to $28,000. The value it would find would be $25,000. So, using the VLOOKUP function to look up how much you would be earning in four years if your starting salary was $28,000 would return the same value, $30,388.

exercise 5

Using Named Ranges and the VLOOKUP Function

1. Open Excel Worksheet E3-05.
2. Save the worksheet using the Save As command and name it Excel E3, Ex 05.
3. Create a custom header that displays your name at the left margin and the file name at the right margin.

4. This worksheet keeps track of grades for a CS100 class at Redwood Community College. The instructor wants to use the VLOOKUP function to automatically calculate if a student's grade is an A, B, C, D, or F. VLOOKUP tables must always be sorted in ascending order. Key the following into the cells indicated to enter the VLOOKUP table:

Cell	Data
O6	50%
O7	60%
O8	70%
O9	80%
O10	90%
P6	F
P7	D
P8	C
P9	B
P10	A

5. Name the table you just entered Lookup_Grade by completing the following steps:
   a. Select cells O6 through P10.
   b. Click the Name box and key **Lookup_Grade**.
   c. Press Enter.
6. Complete the following steps to enter a VLOOKUP function that will look up the appropriate grade for the first student:
   a. Click cell M6 to select it.
   b. Click the Paste Function button on the Standard toolbar.
   c. Click *Lookup & Reference* in the Function category list box.
   d. Click *VLOOKUP* in the Function name list box.
   e. Click OK.
   f. The Formula Palette is displayed and the insertion point is in the Lookup_value box. Key **$L6** in the Lookup_value box. You are going to be copying the formula so the reference to column L has to be absolute.
   g. Place the insertion point in the Table_array box. You are going to use the range name to refer to the table. Key **Lookup_Grade**.
   h. Place the insertion point in the Col_index_num box and key **2**.
   i. Click OK.

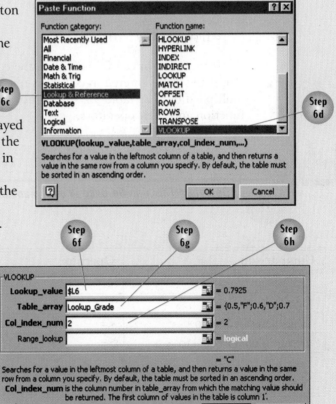

7. Double-click the AutoFill handle in the lower-right corner of cell M6 to copy the function to cells M7 through M58.
8. Change the orientation of the page to landscape.
9. Select rows 3 through 5 as a print title to repeat at the top of each page.
10. Save the worksheet with the same name (Excel E3, Ex 05).
11. Print and close the worksheet.

Logical Functions

Excel's logical functions are used to perform logical tests, which test whether or not a statement is true or false. Depending on the outcome of the logical test, a specific result is returned.

Using the IF Function

An IF function is a logical function that sets up a conditional statement to test data. If the condition is true, one value will be returned. If the condition is false, another value will be returned. The format for an IF statement is:

=IF(logical_test,value_if_true,value_if_false)

The logical_test is a condition that can be evaluated as being true or false. The value_if_true is the value that should be returned if the logical_test is true. The value_if_false is the value that should be returned if the logical_test is false. Look at the following IF function:

=IF(B7=1, C7*.10, C7*.12)

If the value in cell B7 is 1, then the contents of cell C7 will be multiplied by .10. If the value entered in cell B7 is not 1, then the contents of cell C7 will be multiplied by .12. Table 3.2 shows the conditions that can be used in an IF function and their operators.

3.2   *Operators That Can Be Used in an IF Function*

Comparison	Operator
Less than	<
Greater than	>
Less than or equal to	<=
Greater than or equal to	>=
Equal to	=
Not equal to	<>

exercise 6

Using the IF Function

(Note: You will need to delete some files from your disk in order to make room on your disk for the file you will be creating in this exercise. The following files could be deleted from your disk: Excel Worksheet E3-01, Excel Worksheet E3-02, Excel Worksheet E3-03, Excel Worksheet E3-04, and Excel Worksheet E3-05. Check with your instructor to make sure it is all right to delete these files.)

1. Open Excel Worksheet E3-06. This worksheet is located on your student data disk.
2. Save the worksheet using the Save <u>A</u>s command and name it Excel E3, Ex 06.
3. Create a custom header that displays your name at the left margin and the file name at the right margin.
4. Sales representatives for Whitewater Canoe and Kayak Corporation earn a commission on their sales. Sales representatives who are managers earn a 12 percent commission. If a sales representative earns 10 percent the commission code is 1. If a sales representative earns 12 percent the commission code is 2. Complete the following steps to use an IF function to calculate the commission amount for C.J. Kimsey:

    a. Click cell D8 to select it.
    b. Click the Paste Function button on the Standard toolbar.
    c. Click *Logical* in the Function category list box.
    d. Click *IF* in the Function name list box.
    e. Click OK.
    f. The Formula Palette is displayed and the insertion point is in the Logical_test box. Key **B8=1** in the Logical_test box.
    g. Place the insertion point in the Value_if_true box.
    h. Key **C8*.10** in the Value_if_true box.
    i. Place the insertion point in the Value_if_false box.
    j. Key **C8*.12** in the Value_if_false box.
    k. Click OK.
5. Double-click the AutoFill handle in the lower-right corner of cell D8 to copy the function to cells D9 through D13.
6. Whitewater Canoe and Kayak Corporation has decided to give a bonus to sales representatives who sell more than $85,000 in merchandise. If a sales representative sells more than $85,000 in merchandise, he or she earns a 2 percent bonus. If not, no bonus is earned. Complete the following steps to use the IF function to calculate the sales representatives' bonuses.

Paste Function dialog box showing:

Paste Function

Function category:
Most Recently Used
All
Financial
Date & Time
Math & Trig
Statistical
Lookup & Reference
Database
Text
Logical
Information

Function name:
AND
FALSE
IF
NOT
OR
TRUE

IF(logical_test,value_if_true,value_if_false)
Returns one value if a condition you specify evaluates to TRUE and another value if it evaluates to FALSE.

OK   Cancel

Step 4c

Step 4d

a. Click cell E6 and key **Bonus**.
b. Add a border to the bottom of cell E6 to match the border on the bottom of cell D6.
c. Click cell E8 to select it.

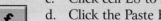

d. Click the Paste Function button on the Standard toolbar.
e. Click *Logical* in the Function category list box.
f. Click *IF* in the Function name list box.
g. Click OK.
h. The Formula Palette is displayed and the insertion point is in the Logical_test box. Key **C8>85000** in the Logical_test box.
i. Place the insertion point in the Value_if_true box.
j. Key **C8*.02** in the Value_if_true box.
k. Place the insertion point in the Value_if_false box.
l. Key **0** in the Value_if_false box.
m. Click OK.

7. Double-click the AutoFill handle in the lower-right corner of cell E8 to copy the function to cells E9 through E13.
8. Format the cells from E8 through E18 as currency with zero decimal places.
9. Save the worksheet with the same name (Excel E3, Ex 06).
10. Print and close the worksheet.

Using Array Formulas

An array formula is a formula in which the arguments used in the functions that make up the formula are arrays rather than individual numbers. An array is a group of elements that form a complete unit. Array formulas perform multiple calculations that can produce multiple results. The array formula does this by operating on a range of cells rather than just one cell. With an array formula, the same formula is repeated for a range of cells.

For example, look at the worksheet fragment in figure 3.8.

An Example of an Array Formula

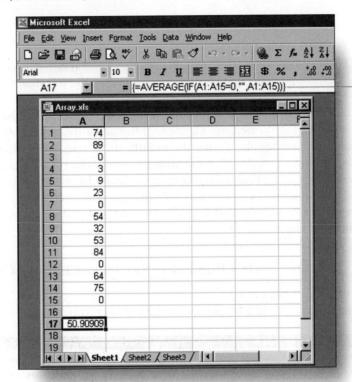

An array formula is always displayed surrounded by braces { }.

Excel's AVERAGE function includes zeros as part of the average. Suppose you wanted to be able to find the average of all non-zero values. An array formula such as the one used in figure 3.8 enables you to do this. By entering the array formula shown in figure 3.8, you are instructing the =AVERAGE function to go through the range A1 to A15 to compare the value in each cell to zero. If the value is zero, it is to be ignored—nothing is assigned to it. If a value is not zero, it is to become a part of the range of cells used in the AVERAGE function. In this case the array formula operates on the range of cells A1 through A15 basically "removing" all the zeros from the range allowing the AVERAGE function to apply to what is left.

An array formula is created the same way as you would create a regular formula. The only difference is that instead of pressing Enter to enter the formula, you press Ctrl+Shift+Enter. Once you press Ctrl+Shift+Enter, Excel automatically surrounds the formula with braces {}. You must press Ctrl+Shift+Enter each time you enter an array formula and each time you edit an array formula. If you try entering an array formula by just pressing Enter, a #VALUE! error is displayed.

If more than one range is used in an array formula, all the ranges must contain the same number of cells. If they do not, an error is returned.

Using an Array Formula

1. Open Excel Worksheet E3-07.
2. Save the worksheet using the Save <u>A</u>s command and name it Excel E3, Ex 07.
3. Create a custom header that displays your name at the left margin and the file name at the right margin.
4. This worksheet keeps track of how many units of each type of canoe or kayak the sales representatives for Whitewater Canoe and Kayak Corporation sold. As sales representatives made sales during the month, those sales were entered into the worksheet. Now the Sales Manager wants to know the total units each sales representative sold of each type of canoe or kayak. In order to make this calculation, you need to use an array formula. Complete the following steps to enter an array formula that calculates how many Pathfinders were sold by Claxton:
   a. Click cell G6 to select it.
   b. Key the following in cell G6:

   =SUM((A6:A38="Pathfinder")*(B6:B38="Claxton")*C6:C38)

   c. Press Ctrl+Shift+Enter
   d. Your screen should look similar to the one shown here.

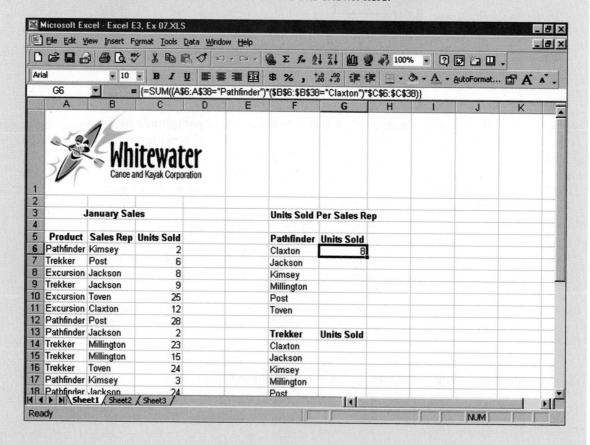

Look at the array formula you entered. The formula looks at the data in the three ranges A6 through A38, B6 through B38, and C6 through C38. If the first cell looked at (A6) is Pathfinder, a 1, which represents the value True, is returned. If A6 is not Pathfinder, a 0, which represents the value False, is returned. If B6 is Claxton, a 1 is returned; if it is not, a 0 is returned. Then C6 is returned and the three values (in this case 1, 0, and 2) are multiplied together. As the array formula loops through all the rows, the results are added together.

5. Complete the following steps to enter an array formula that calculates how many Pathfinders were sold by Jackson:
   a. Click cell G7 to select it.
   b. Key the following in cell G7:

   =SUM((A6:A38="Pathfinder")*(B6:B38="Jackson")*C6:C38)

   c. Press Ctrl+Shift+Enter.

6. Complete the following steps to enter an array formula that calculates how many Pathfinders were sold by Kimsey:
   a. Click cell G8 to select it.
   b. Key the following in cell G8:

   =SUM((A6:A38="Pathfinder")*(B6:B38="Kimsey")*C6:C38)

   c. Press Ctrl+Shift+Enter.

7. Complete the following steps to enter an array formula that calculates how many Pathfinders were sold by Millington:
   a. Click cell G9 to select it.
   b. Key the following in cell G9:

   =SUM((A6:A38="Pathfinder")*(B6:B38="Millington")*C6:C38)

   c. Press Ctrl+Shift+Enter.

8. Complete the following steps to enter an array formula that calculates how many Pathfinders were sold by Post:
   a. Click cell G10 to select it.
   b. Key the following in cell G10:

   =SUM((A6:A38="Pathfinder")*(B6:B38="Post")*C6:C38)

   c. Press Ctrl+Shift+Enter.

9. Complete the following steps to enter an array formula that calculates how many Pathfinders were sold by Toven:
   a. Click cell G11 to select it.
   b. Key the following in cell G11:

   =SUM((A6:A38="Pathfinder")*(B6:B38="Toven")*C6:C38)

   c. Press Ctrl+Shift+Enter.

10. To calculate the units sold for Trekkers, complete the following steps:
    a. Click cell G6.
    b. Place the insertion point between the A and the 6 in the Formula bar and press F4. The reference to A6 is now absolute ($A$6).
    c. Place the insertion point between the A and the 38 in the Formula bar and press F4. The reference to A38 is now absolute ($A$38).
    d. Place the insertion point between the B and the 6 in the Formula bar and press F4. The reference to B6 is now absolute ($B$6).

e. Place the insertion point between the B and the 38 in the Formula bar and press F4. The reference to B38 is now absolute ($B$38).

f. Place the insertion point between the C and the 6 in the Formula bar and press F4. The reference to C6 is now absolute ($C$6).

g. Place the insertion point between the C and the 38 in the Formula bar and press F4. The reference to C38 is now absolute ($C$38).

h. Press Ctrl+Shift+Enter.

i. Press the Copy button on the Standard toolbar.

j. Click cell G14.

k. Press the Paste button on the Standard toolbar.

l. In the Formula bar delete "Pathfinder" and replace it with "Trekker." Be sure to press Ctrl+Shift+Enter to enter the function. The function should look like this.

$${=SUM((\$A\$6:\$A\$38="Trekker")*(\$B\$6:\$B\$38="Claxton")*\$C\$6:\$C\$38)}$$

m. Copy the function in cell G14 to cells G15 through G19.

n. Click cell G15. Delete "Claxton" and replace it with "Jackson." Be sure to press Ctrl+Shift+Enter to enter the function. The function should look like this:

$${=SUM((\$A\$6:\$A\$38="Trekker")*(\$B\$6:\$B\$38="Jackson")*\$C\$6:\$C\$38)}$$

o. Click cell G16. Delete "Claxton" and replace it with "Kimsey." Be sure to press Ctrl+Shift+Enter to enter the function. The function should look like this:

$${=SUM((\$A\$6:\$A\$38="Trekker")*(\$B\$6:\$B\$38="Kimsey")*\$C\$6:\$C\$38)}$$

p. Click cell G17. Delete "Claxton" and replace it with "Millington." Be sure to press Ctrl+Shift+Enter to enter the function. The function should look like this:

$${=SUM((\$A\$6:\$A\$38="Trekker")*(\$B\$6:\$B\$38="Millington")*\$C\$6:\$C\$38)}$$

q. Click cell G18. Delete "Claxton" and replace it with "Post." Be sure to press Ctrl+Shift+Enter to enter the function. The function should look like this:

$${=SUM((\$A\$6:\$A\$38="Trekker")*(\$B\$6:\$B\$38="Post")*\$C\$6:\$C\$38)}$$

r. Click cell G19. Delete "Claxton" and replace it with "Toven." Be sure to press Ctrl+Shift+Enter to enter the function. The function should look like this:

$${=SUM((\$A\$6:\$A\$38="Trekker")*(\$B\$6:\$B\$38="Toven")*\$C\$6:\$C\$38)}$$

11. Repeat step 10 to calculate how many Excursions were sold by each sales representative.
12. Save the worksheet with the same name (Excel E3, Ex 07).
13. Print and close the worksheet.

chapter summary

➤ A function is a built-in formula. Functions include two parts: the function name and the argument. The argument, which may contain numbers, formulas, cell references, range names, or other functions, provides the data needed by the function to perform the calculation or data manipulation.

➤ A function can be entered using the Paste Function button on the Standard toolbar or the Edit Formula button on the Formula bar.

➤ Financial functions are used for calculating financial data such as loan details, annuities, and investment analyses.

➤ An annuity is a periodic series of equal payments.

➤ The PMT function calculates the periodic payment of a loan based on constant payments and a constant interest rate. The format for the PMT function is: =PMT(rate,nper,pv)

➤ The PV function calculates the present value that the total amount of a series of future payments is worth right now. The format for the PV function is: =PV(rate,nper,pmt, fv,type)

➤ The ROUND function rounds a number to a specified number of digits. The format for the ROUND function is: =ROUND(number,num_digits)

➤ The RAND function calculates random numbers. The format of the RAND function is: =RAND()

➤ The SUMIF function calculates the total of specific cells that meet a given condition or criteria. The format for the SUMIF function is: =SUMIF(range,criteria,sum_range)

➤ The COUNTIF function counts the number of cells in a given range that meet a specific condition. The format for the COUNTIF function is: =COUNTIF(range,criteria)

➤ Names can be assigned to a specific cell or range of cells. The first character in a range name must be an underscore or a letter. The rest of the characters can be letters, numbers, the underscore character, or periods. You cannot use spaces in a range name.

➤ Range names can be used in formulas in place of the references to the cells. The formula =AVERAGE(Exam1_Grades) would average the values entered in the range of cells named *Exam1_Grades*. Using range names in formulas makes it easier to understand the purpose of the formula.

➤ Excel's Lookup and Reference functions provide a way to find specific information within a list of data.

➤ The VLOOKUP function searches for a value in the first column of a table. Upon finding that value, it enters into a different location in the worksheet a value from the table that is in a specific column in the same row as the value that was found in the first column. The format for the VLOOKUP function is: =VLOOKUP(lookup_value,table_array, col_index_num)

➤ Logical functions perform logical tests to see whether or not a statement is true or false. Specific results are returned depending on the outcome of the logical test.

➤ The IF function sets up a conditional statement to test data. If the condition is true, one value is returned. If the condition is false, a different value is returned. The format for the IF statements is: =IF(logical_test, value_if_true,value_if_false)

➤ Array formulas perform multiple calculations that can produce multiple results. To enter an array formula, press Ctrl+Shift+Enter. Array formulas are always surrounded by braces.

commands review

	Mouse/Keyboard
Entering an array formula	Ctrl + Shift + Enter
Naming a range	Click the Name box, key the name, press Enter
Change a range name	Click Insert, point to Name, click Define

thinking offline

Completion: In the space provided at the right, indicate the correct term, command, or symbol.

1. This term refers to the second part of a function.

2. This term refers to a periodic series of equal payments, such as the mortgage on a house.

3. A three-year loan with monthly payments would have this many periods.

4. This formula calculates what the monthly payments would be on a 5-year, $15,000 loan at a 6% annual interest rate.

5. This formula rounds the number 589.345 to the nearest integer.

6. This formula will generate random numbers between 0 and 100.

7. The result of a RAND function is said to be this term because the result automatically changes whenever anything on the worksheet changes.

8. This function does not have any arguments.

9. This function would add together the values in cells B5:B25 only if the values are greater than zero.

10. This function would count the number of cells in a given range where the values are greater than 250.

EXPERT

E-110

11. Click here in order to create a name for a selected range of cells. _____

12. This function would look up the value in cell B5 in a table located in cells D20:G35 in the third column of the table. _____

13. If the value in cell C6 is less than 60, this function will add 5 to it. If the value in cell C6 is greater than 60, the value will not change. _____

14. Press these keys to enter an array formula. _____

15. Explain an advantage to using range names in formulas.

    _____

    _____

    _____

16. Explain what is wrong with the following array formula. Edit the formula so that it is correct.

    {=SUM(IF(A5:I5=B5:B10,1,0))}

    _____

    _____

    _____

17. Suppose you correctly edited the array formula from the previous question, but the #VALUE! error is displayed. Explain what you did wrong and what you must do to fix it.

    _____

    _____

    _____

working hands-on

Assessment 1

(Note: In order to have room on your disk to save all the files you will be creating in the following assessments you will need to delete some files from your disk. You may delete the following files: Excel E3, Ex 01; Excel E3, Ex 02; Excel E3, Ex 03; Excel E3, Ex 04; Excel E3, Ex 05; Excel E3, Ex 06; and Excel E3, Ex 07. Check with your instructor to make sure it is all right to delete these files.)

1. Open Excel Worksheet E3-08.
2. Save the worksheet using the Save <u>A</u>s command and name it Excel E3, SA 01.
3. Create a custom header with your name displayed at the left margin and the file name displayed at the right margin.

4. Georgia and Paul Sorenson, the owners of Primrose Decorators, have made a decision on the building they want to buy in order to expand their business. Now they want to create a loan amortization table that calculates their payments. Name cell B5 *Rate*. Name cell B6 *Term*. Name cell B7 *Principal*. Name cell B9 *Monthly_Payment*. In cell B9, enter a PMT function that will calculate their monthly payments. Be sure to use the range names in the formula.

5. Enter a formula in cell B11 that will calculate the total amount paid on the loan. This would be the monthly payment times the total number of payments being made. Be sure to use range names in the formula. Use the ROUND function so that the result is rounded to two decimal places. Format the result as currency.

6. Enter a formula in cell B12 that calculates the total interest paid for the loan. This would be the total amount paid minus the principal. Use a range name in the formula.

7. The first entry on the payment schedule, the principal owed at the beginning of the loan is already entered in cell B15. In cell C15, enter a formula that calculates one month's interest on the loan. One month's interest would be the principal times the interest rate. But remember you have to divide the annual interest rate by 12 to get the interest for one month. Use the cell reference B15 to refer to the principal. Use the range name *Rate* to refer to the interest rate. Use the ROUND function so that the result is rounded to two decimal places. Format the result as currency.

8. In cell D15 enter a formula that will calculate how much of the payment goes toward the principal, which would be the monthly payment minus how much was paid to interest. Be sure to use the *Monthly_Payment* range name in the formula.

9. Enter a formula in cell E15 that calculates the principal owed after the payment is made, which would be the principal minus the amount paid to the principal. Use the cell reference B15 to refer to the principal.

10. Key =**E15** in cell B16 to enter the new principal.

11. Click cell B16 to select it. Double-click the AutoFill handle to copy cell B16 to cells B17 through B180.

12. Click cell C15 to select it. Double-click the AutoFill handle.

13. Click cell D15 to select it. Double-click the AutoFill handle.

14. Click cell E15 to select it. Double-click the AutoFill handle.

15. Select row 14 as a print title to be repeated at the top of each page when the worksheet is printed.

16. Save the workbook with the same name (E3, SA 01).

17. Print and close E3, SA 01.

Assessment 2

1. Open Excel Worksheet E3-09.

2. Save the worksheet using the Save <u>A</u>s command and name it Excel E3, SA 02.

3. Create a custom header with your name displayed at the left margin and the file name displayed at the right margin.

4. You recently entered a contest and won the grand prize. You can take this prize in one of two payments. With Option A you will be paid $10,000 now and $3,500 each year for the next five years. With Option B you will not be paid any cash now, but you will be paid $6,000 a year for the next five years. You need to determine which option is the better deal. In cell B3 use the PV function to calculate the present value of $3,500 paid annually for the next five years. Assume the appropriate interest rate is 12%. Remember that the result will be displayed as a negative number because the present value is assumed to be cash that will be paid out.

5. In cell B4, use the PV function to calculate the present value of the one time payment of $10,000. The appropriate interest rate would be 0% because you would be getting the money immediately.
6. In cell B6 enter a formula that adds together the present value of the installment payments and the present value of the cash you would receive now.
7. In cell B11 use the PV function to calculate the present value of $6,000 paid annually for the next five years. Assume the appropriate interest rate is 12%.
8. In terms of the present value, which option is the better deal?
9. Save the workbook with the same name (E3, SA 02).
10. Print and close E3, SA 02.

Assessment 3

1. Open Excel Worksheet E3-10.
2. Save the worksheet using the Save As command and name it Excel E3, SA 03.
3. Create a custom header with your name displayed at the left margin and the file name displayed at the right margin.
4. The EastWest Crossroads Company is a company that sells imported and unique gifts through the mail. This worksheet helps the manager in charge of the warehouse keep track of daily shipping expenses. Shipping expenses depend upon two things: the weight of the package and the zone to which it is being shipped. There are six different shipping zones. Look at cells J6 through P42. This is the table that must be used to look up how much it costs to ship a package. Now look at cells A6 through F54. This is the form the manager used to calculate the shipping expense together with the total charge for each item shipped.
5. Name the range of cells J8 through P42 *Shipping*.
6. Click cell E7 to select it. Use the VLOOKUP function to enter a formula that finds the shipping expenses for the packages shipped to zone 1. The formula should look up the weight of the package (D7) in the range of cells named *Shipping*. (Be sure to use the range name in the formula.) The costs of shipping packages to zone 1 are found in column 2 of the table.
7. Cell E7 should still be selected. Double-click the AutoFill handle to copy the formula.
8. Enter a formula in F7 that adds together the charge and the shipping expense. Double-click the AutoFill handle to copy the formula.
9. Click cell E15 to select it. Use the VLOOKUP function to enter a formula that finds the shipping expenses for packages shipped to zone 2.
10. Cell E15 should still be selected. Double-click the AutoFill handle to copy the formula.
11. Enter a formula in cell F15 that adds together the charge and the shipping expense. Double-click the AutoFill handle to copy the formula.
12. Enter the appropriate VLOOKUP function in cell E23 to find the shipping expense for zone 3. Copy the formula. Enter the appropriate formula in cell F23 to add together the charge and the shipping expense. Copy the formula.
13. Enter the appropriate VLOOKUP function in cell E31 to find the shipping expense for zone 4. Copy the formula. Enter the appropriate formula in cell F31 to add together the charge and the shipping expense. Copy the formula.
14. Enter the appropriate VLOOKUP function in cell E39 to find the shipping expense for zone 5. Copy the formula. Enter the appropriate formula in cell F39 to add together the charge and the shipping expense. Copy the formula.
15. Enter the appropriate VLOOKUP function in cell E47 to find the shipping expense for zone 6. Copy the formula. Enter the appropriate formula in cell F47 to add together the charge and the shipping expense. Copy the formula.

16. Adjust the width of column F to automatically display the widest entry.
17. Enter today's date in cell B4.
18. Insert a page break so that zones 1, 2, and 3 print on one page and zones 4, 5, and 6 print on a second page.
19. Print the first two pages of the worksheet.
20. Save the workbook with the same name (E3, SA 03).
21. Close E3, SA 03.

Assessment 4

1. Open Excel Worksheet E3-11.
2. Save the worksheet using the Save As command and name it Excel E3, SA 04.
3. Create a custom header with your name displayed at the left margin and the file name displayed at the right margin.
4. This worksheet is used to keep track of Whitewater Canoe and Kayak's weekly payroll. Scroll horizontally and vertically to view the entire worksheet.
5. In cell I9 enter a formula that calculates the total hours worked by Norman Campbell. Copy the formula to cells I10 through I13.
6. In cell K9 use the IF function to enter a formula that calculates the regular pay. If an employee works 40 hours or less during the week, the regular pay would be the hours worked times the wage. If an employee works more than 40 hours a week, the regular pay would be the wage times 40. Enter the appropriate IF function in cell K9. Copy the formula to cells K10 through K13. Format cells K9 through K13 as currency.
7. In cell L9 use the IF function to enter a formula that calculates overtime. If an employee works more than 40 hours during the week, he or she gets paid time-and-a-half on all the hours over 40 that were worked. If the employee does not work more than 40 hours, no overtime pay is earned. *(Hint: Time-and-a-half would be 1.5 times the regular wage. Remember, time-and-a-half is paid only on the hours that are worked over the normal 40 hours.)* Copy the formula to cells L10 through L13. Format cells L9 through L13 as currency.
8. Enter a formula in M9 that calculates the gross pay (regular pay plus overtime). Copy the formula to cells M10 through M13.
9. Use the IF function to enter a formula in cell N9 that calculates the deduction for FICA. Look at the tax table in cells D17 through F21. If the gross pay is less than $600, one set of tax percentages is to be used. If the gross pay is greater than or equal to $600, a different set of tax percentages is to be used. Click cell N9 to select it and enter the following formula:

$$=IF(M9<600, M9*\$E\$18, M9*\$F\$18)$$

   If the value in M9, which is gross pay, is less than 600, the gross pay will be multiplied by cell E18, which is the FICA tax for gross pay less than $600. If the value in M9 is not less than 600, then the gross pay will be multiplied by cell F18, which is the FICA tax for gross pay that is greater than or equal to $600. Copy the formula to cells N10 through N13. Format cells N9 through N13 as currency.
10. Use the appropriate IF function to enter a formula in cell O9 to calculate the deduction for federal tax. Be sure to reference the cells for federal tax from the tax table. Copy the formula to cells O10 through O13. Format cells O9 through O13 as currency.
11. Use the appropriate IF function to enter a formula in cell P9 to calculate the deduction for state tax. Be sure to reference the cells for state tax from the tax table. Copy the formula to cells P10 through P13. Format cells P9 through P13 as currency.

12. Use the appropriate IF function to enter a formula in cell Q9 to calculate the deduction for local tax. Be sure to reference the cells for local tax from the tax table. Copy the formula to cells Q10 through Q13. Format cells Q9 through Q13 as currency.
13. Enter a formula in cell R9 to calculate the net pay (gross pay minus FICA, federal tax, state tax, and local tax). Copy the formula to cells R10 through R13.
14. Adjust the page set up so that the orientation of the page is landscape, row 7 is printed at the top of every page, and columns A and B repeat at the left of every page. Center the worksheet on the page horizontally.
15. Save the worksheet with the same name (E3, SA 04).
16. Print and close the worksheet.

Assessment 5

1. Open Excel Worksheet E3-12.
2. Save the worksheet using the Save As command and name it Excel E3, SA 05.
3. Create a custom header with your name displayed at the left margin and the file name displayed at the right margin.
4. This worksheet is a running tabulation of how many Pathfinders, Trekkers, and Excursions were sold during January by Whitewater Canoe and Kayak's sales representatives. You need to calculate the total units that were sold for each product. Name the range of cells C6 through C38 *Units_Sold*. Name the range of cells A6 through A38 *Product*.
5. Click in cell F5 to select it. Using the SUMIF function, enter a formula that calculates the total number of Pathfinders that were sold in January. Use the range names *Product* and *Units_Sold* in the function.
6. Click in cell F6 to select it. Using the SUMIF function, enter a formula that calculates the total number of Trekkers that were sold in January. Use the range names *Product* and *Units_Sold* in the function.
7. Click in cell F7 to select it. Using the SUMIF function, enter a formula that calculates the total number of Excursions that were sold in January. Use the range names *Product* and *Units_Sold* in the function.
8. Save the worksheet with the same name (E3, SA 05).
9. Print and close the worksheet.

Assessment 6

1. Open Excel Worksheet E3-13.
2. Save the worksheet using the Save As command and name it Excel E3, SA 06.
3. Create a custom header with your name displayed at the left margin and the file name displayed at the right margin.
4. This worksheet is used by Performance Threads, a company that supplies the entertainment industry with theatrical fabrics, stage draperies, scenic, and production supplies, to keep track of its inventory of velour fabrics at both its New York and Los Angeles warehouses. You want to add a couple of functions to this worksheet, but the current inventory figures have not yet arrived so you need to enter some dummy values to make sure your functions are going to work. You want to use the RAND function to generate numbers between 1 and 300. These numbers have to be whole numbers so you have to use the ROUND function as well. Click cell B8 and key the following formula:

   =ROUND((RAND()*300),0)

Multiplying the RAND function by 300 produces random numbers between 1 and 300. Copy the formula to cells B9 through B29.

5. Click cell E8. Use the RAND and ROUND functions to generate a whole number between 1 and 300. Copy the formula to cells E9 through E29.

6. Key the following label in both cell A31 and D31:

 # Fabrics with Bolts > 200

Automatically adjust the widths of columns A and D.

7. Name the range of cells B8 through B29 *NY_Bolts*. Name the range of cells E8 through E29 *LA_Bolts*.

8. Click cell B31. Use the COUNTIF function to count how many cells in the range B8:B29 contain values greater than 200. Use the range name *NY_Bolts* in the formula.

9. Click cell E31. Use the COUNTIF function to count how many cells in the range E8:E29 contain values greater than 200. Use the range name *LA_Bolts* in the formula.

10. Save the workbook with the same name (Excel E3, SA 06).

11. Print and close the worksheet.

Chapter 04E

Working with Lists

Upon successful completion of chapter 4, you will be able to:

- Enter data using the Data Form.
- Use data validation.
- Sort a list.
- Perform a multi-level sort on a list.
- Create a custom list.
- Find and display records using the Data Form.
- Edit records using the Data Form.
- Delete records using the Data Form.
- Outline a worksheet.
- Subtotal a list.
- Filter a list using AutoFilter.
- Create a custom AutoFilter.
- Filter a list using advanced filtering.

In Excel, a list is a series of worksheet rows containing similar sets of data that are identified by labels in the top row. Employee names, addresses, and telephone numbers would be an example of a list. Each column in a list contains similar information based on the label for that column. Column A, for example, might be labeled "Last Name" and contain last names, column B might be labeled "First Name" and contain first names, column C might be labeled "Address" and contain street addresses, and so on. In a list, the labels have to be in the top row; they cannot be in the first column. There are no blank rows in a list.

Excel automatically recognizes a list as a database. A database is used for performing record-keeping tasks such as keeping track of all of a company's incoming orders or keeping track of inventory. As shown in figure 4.1, each row in the list is a record, while each column in the list is a field. The labels in the first row of the list are the field names. A value found in a single cell is called a field value.

The list range is the range of cells that contains all the records, fields, and field names of the list. Once you have your Excel data organized as a list, certain database operations can be performed, such as sorting data, finding specific data, and subtotaling data. The purpose of this chapter is to teach you how to create and use lists in Excel.

figure 4.1

An Excel List

Each column is a field.

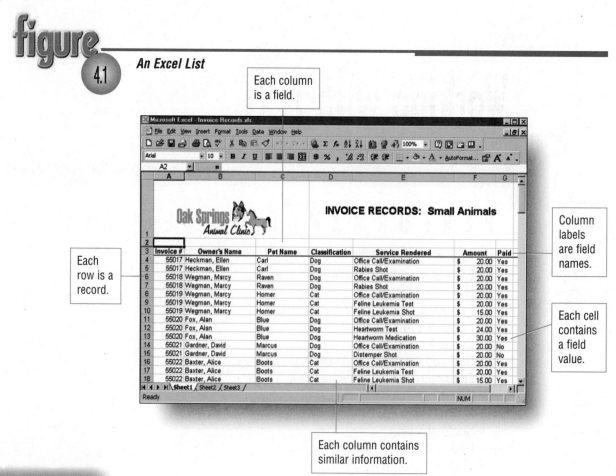

INVOICE RECORDS: Small Animals

Column labels are field names.

Each row is a record.

Each cell contains a field value.

Each column contains similar information.

Creating a List

Certain rules must be followed when creating a list. The first row of the list must contain the labels or field names. The labels should be formatted differently from the rest of the data in the list. Use bold, italics, or cell borders (or a combination of the three) to differentiate them from the list data. There cannot be any blank rows in the list, which means there cannot be a blank row between the labels and the data.

Only one list should be stored on a worksheet. If you have several related lists, store each one on a separate worksheet. You cannot have any extraneous data stored in columns or rows adjacent to the list, or they might be considered to be a part of the list. It is best not to store any data on the worksheet other than the list itself.

Entering Data Using the Data Form

Data can be entered either by entering it into the individual cells on the worksheet or by using the Data Form. To enter data using the Data Form, select any cell in the list. Click Data. If necessary, expand the menu by clicking the down arrow at the bottom of the list. Click the Form option once it appears. The Data Form dialog box as shown in figure 4.2 is displayed. Each field name with a corresponding box is displayed. Click the New button. A new blank record is displayed. The appropriate data can be entered into each box. If more records are to be added, press Enter and another new blank record will be displayed. Once you have completed entering the data, click the Close button to return to the worksheet.

When using Data Form to enter records, the record is placed on the worksheet when you move to another record or close the Data Form.

Hint

If a field in the list is a formula, the result of the formula is displayed in the Data Form as a label and cannot be edited.

Hint

figure 4.2

The Data Form Dialog Box

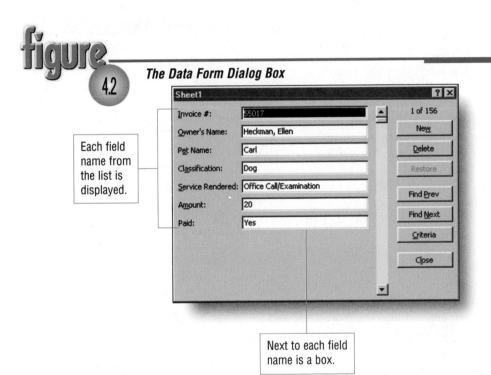

Each field name from the list is displayed.

Next to each field name is a box.

exercise 1

Entering List Data

1. Open Excel Worksheet E4-01.
2. Save the worksheet using the Save As command and name it Excel E4, Ex 01.
3. Create a custom header that displays your name at the left margin and the file name at the right margin.
4. This worksheet stores a list of invoice records for Oak Springs Animal Clinic. Three veterinarians work at the Oak Springs Animal Clinic and they specialize in both large and small animals. This worksheet keeps track of the invoices for their small animal business. You want to add three more records to the list. Complete the following steps to add three more records using the Data Form dialog box:
   a. Click cell A4.

b. Click Data. If necessary, click the down arrow at the bottom of the menu so that the Form option is displayed. Click Form.

c. The Data Form dialog box is displayed. The record that is displayed in the dialog box is the record from the row that is currently selected. Click the New button.

d. The insertion point is in the Invoice # box. Key the following: **55070**.

e. Press Tab. The insertion point moves to the Owner's Name box. Key **Henry, Irene**.

f. Press Tab. The insertion point moves to the Pet Name box. Key **Ralph**.

g. Press Tab. The insertion point moves to the Classification box. Key **Dog**.

h. Press Tab. The insertion point moves to the Service Rendered box. Key **Office Call/Examination**.

i. Press Tab. The insertion point moves to the Vet box. Key **Frobose**.

j. Press Tab. The insertion point moves to the Amount box. Key **20**.

k. Press Tab. The insertion point moves to the Paid box. Key **No**.

l. The data for the next record has now all been entered into the Data Form. Press Enter.

Step 4c

Enter the data in the boxes next to the field names.

5. The data has been entered into the worksheet and the boxes are all empty ready for another record to be entered. By now you should be familiar with entering data using the Data Form. Enter the following two records using the Data Form:

Invoice #:	**55070**
Owner's Name:	**Henry, Irene**
Pet Name:	**Ralph**
Classification:	**Dog**
Service Rendered:	**Distemper Shot**
Vet:	**Frobose**
Amount:	**20**
Paid:	**No**

Invoice #:	**55070**
Owner's Name:	**Henry, Irene**
Pet Name:	**Ralph**
Classification:	**Dog**
Service Rendered:	**Rabies Shot**
Vet:	**Frobose**
Amount:	**20**
Paid:	**No**

When you have finished entering the data click the Close button. If you accidentally press the Enter key instead of the Tab key before you have entered all the data in a record, you can click the Close button, scroll to the bottom of the worksheet and enter the data in the appropriate cells on the worksheet.

6. Adjust the page set up so that row 3 repeats as a print title at the top of each page.
7. Save the worksheet with the same name (Excel E4, Ex 01). You are going to use this worksheet in exercise 2.
8. Print and close the worksheet.

Using Data Validation

Excel's data validation feature allows you to specify the exact data that can be entered into a cell. This feature helps to prevent errors from being made when data is entered. Using the data validation feature, entries can be limited to the options on a list. Allowing a user to enter data by selecting it from a list also eliminates having to key in the exact same entry over and over again.

To use the data validation feature, select the cells that have data you want to validate. You can either select an entire column or only specific cells within a column. Click Data and Validation. The Data Validation dialog box as shown in figure 4.3 is displayed. The entries on the Settings tab allow you to establish the validation criteria. As shown in figure 4.3, clicking the down arrow to the right of the Allow box displays a drop-down menu that lists the options for what can be allowed into the selected cells. The options available on the Settings tab change when something other than Any value is entered in the Allow box.

Selecting a specific type of data from the Allow list box does not affect the cell formatting. Use the Format Cells dialog box to format the cells as numbers, dates, or time.

figure
4.3

The Data Validation Dialog Box with the Settings Tab Selected

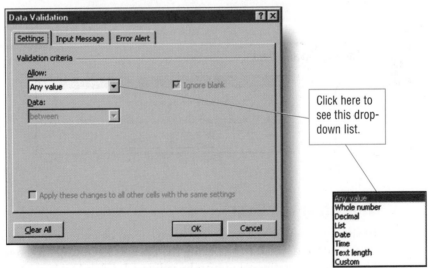

Click here to see this drop-down list.

If you select *Whole number, Decimal, Date, Time,* or *Text Length* from the drop-down menu for the Allow box, the Data box is activated as shown in figure 4.4. Clicking the down arrow to the right of the Data box displays a drop-down list that lists the Data operator options shown in figure 4.4. Select one of the data operators and enter the Minimum and Maximum values.

figure
4.4

Validating Numeric Data

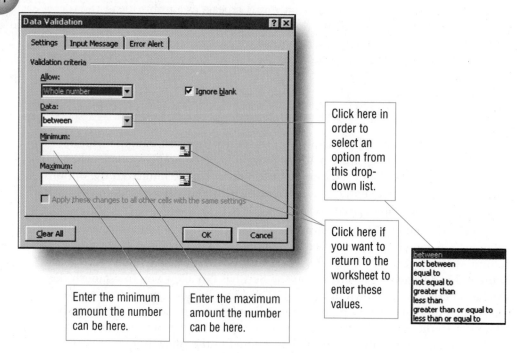

Click here in order to select an option from this drop-down list.

Click here if you want to return to the worksheet to enter these values.

Enter the minimum amount the number can be here.

Enter the maximum amount the number can be here.

For example, you can set the data validation for a cell so that a whole number greater than or equal to 100 must be entered. If someone tries entering 98 into the cell, the error message shown in figure 4.5 is displayed.

figure
4.5

Entering Invalid Data

Validating List Data

In situations where the same few items are to be entered into a column, you can create a drop-down list containing the options from which the user must choose. First select the entire column to be validated. Click Data and Validation. Click the down arrow to the right of the Allow box and select *List*. Enter the options to be included in the list in the Source box. To select the options from the worksheet, click the Cell Reference button to the right of the Source box as shown in figure 4.6.

figure 4.6

Validating List Data

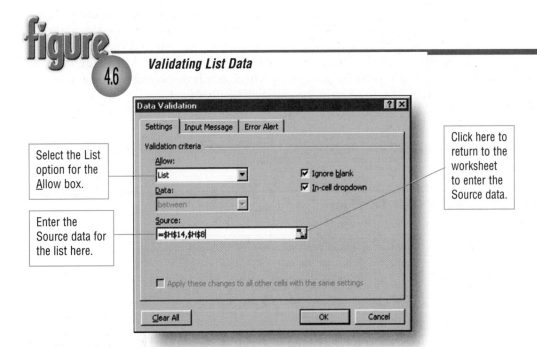

Select the List option for the Allow box.

Enter the Source data for the list here.

Click here to return to the worksheet to enter the Source data.

Including Input and Error Messages

You can include messages that will display if a user tries to enter invalid data. To include an input message, click the Input Message tab on the Data Validation dialog box. As shown in figure 4.7, you need to enter the title for the Title bar and the input message. Make sure the Show input message when cell is selected check box is selected. When a user selects the cell, the Input message will be displayed.

figure 4.7

Including an Input Message

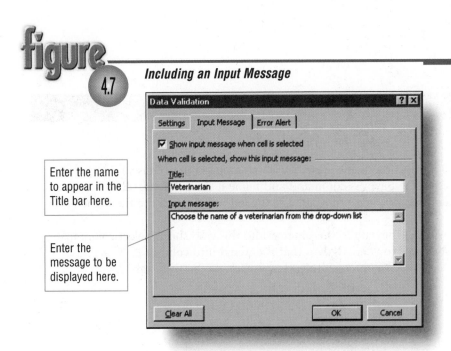

Enter the name to appear in the Title bar here.

Enter the message to be displayed here.

To include an error message, click the Error Alert tab. As shown in figure 4.8, you need to select the style for the error alert, which can either be Stop, Warning, or Information. You also need to enter the title for the Title bar and the error message to be displayed when someone tries to enter invalid data. Make sure the Show error alert after invalid data is entered check box is displayed. When a user tries to enter invalid data, the error message will be displayed.

Including an Error Message

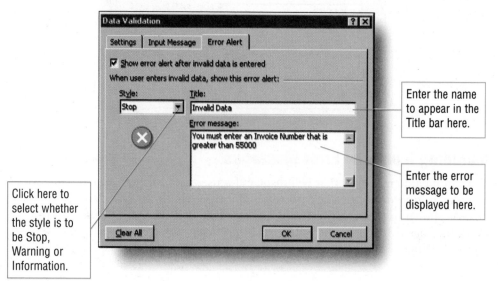

Enter the name to appear in the Title bar here.

Enter the error message to be displayed here.

Click here to select whether the style is to be Stop, Warning or Information.

Using Data Validation

1. Open Excel E4, Ex 01. This is the worksheet that was completed in exercise 1.
2. Save the worksheet using the Save As command and name it Excel E4, Ex 02.
3. Create a custom header that displays your name at the left margin and the file name at the right margin.
4. You want to validate some of the data that is entered into this worksheet. Select column A. Complete the following steps to validate data that is entered into column A:
   a. Click Data and then click Validation. If necessary, click the Settings tab.

b. Click the down arrow to the right of the <u>A</u>llow box. Select *Whole number*.

c. Click the down arrow to the right of the <u>D</u>ata box. Select *greater than or equal to*.

d. Place the insertion point in the <u>M</u>inimum box. Key the following: **55000**.

e. Click the Input Message tab.

f. Key the following in the <u>T</u>itle box: **Invoice Number**.

g. Key the following in the Input message box: **Enter an invoice number. Invoice numbers start at 55000.**

h. Click the Error Alert tab.

i. Key the following in the <u>T</u>itle box: **Error**.

j. Key the following in the <u>E</u>rror message box: **Invoice numbers must be greater than 55000.**

k. Make sure the *Stop* option is selected in the St<u>y</u>le box.

l. Click OK.

5. The only entry made in column F is the name of one of the veterinarians. Select column F. Complete the following steps to create a drop-down list of options for column F:

a. Click <u>D</u>ata and then click Validation. Click the Settings tab.

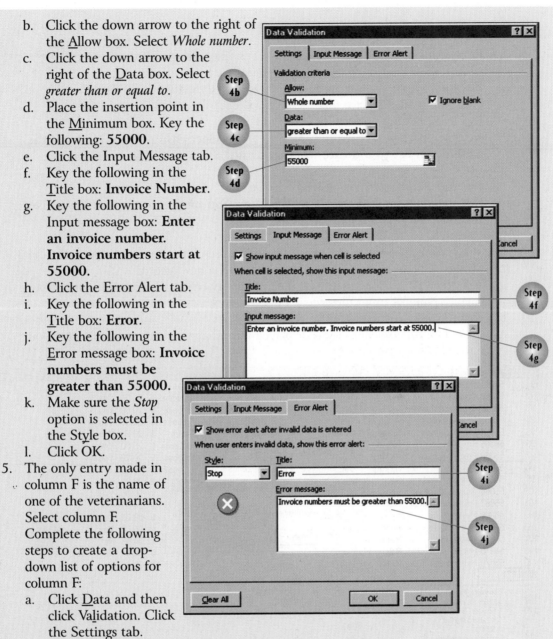

b. Click the down arrow to the right of the <u>A</u>llow box. Select *List*.

c. Place the insertion point in the <u>S</u>ource box. Key **Frobose, Ketner, Martin**.

d. Click the Input Message tab.

e. Key the following in the <u>T</u>itle box: **Veterinarian**.

f. Key the following in the Input message box: **Select one of the veterinarian's names from the drop-down list.**

g. Click the Error Alert tab.

h. Key the following in the <u>T</u>itle box: **Error**.

i. Key the following in the <u>E</u>rror message box: **You must select a name from the drop-down list.**

j. Click OK.

EXPERT

6. The only entries made in column H are Yes or No. Select column H. Complete the following steps to create a drop-down list of options for column H:
   a. Click Data and then click Validation. Click the Settings tab.
   b. Click the down arrow to the right of the Allow box. Select *List*.
   c. Place the insertion point in the Source box. Key the following: **Yes, No**.
   d. Click the Input Message tab.
   e. Key the following in the Title box: **Paid**.
   f. Key the following in the Input message box: **Select either Yes or No from the drop-down list to indicate whether or not the invoice has been paid.**
   g. Click the Error Alert tab.
   h. Key the following in the Title box: **Error**.
   i. Key the following in the Error message box: **You must select either Yes or No from the drop-down list.**
   j. Click OK.
7. Use the vertical split bar at the top of the vertical scroll bar to freeze rows 1, 2, and 3 in the window. Complete the following steps to enter a new record:
   a. Select cell A107. This should be the first empty cell at the end of the list. Notice the Invoice Number input message is displayed.
   b. Key the following in cell A107: **5571**.
   c. Press Tab. An error message is displayed informing you the invoice number you entered is not large enough.

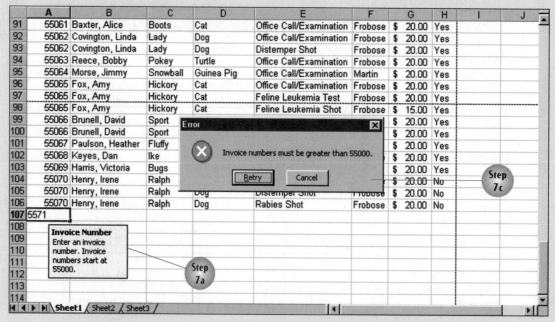

   d. Click the Retry button.
   e. Key the following: **55071**.
   f. Press Tab. Key the following: **Mason, Anita**.
   g. Press Tab. Key the following: **Snickers**.
   h. Press Tab. Key the following: **Dog**.
   i. Press Tab. Start to key **Office Call/Examination**. As soon as the first couple of characters are entered, Excel automatically fills in the rest.

j. Press Tab. The Veterinarian input message is displayed. A down arrow automatically is displayed to the right of the cell.

Step 7j

107	55071	Mason, Anita	Snickers	Dog	Office Call/Examination		▼
108							
109						**Veterinarian**	
110						Select one of the	
111						veterinarian's names from the	
112						drop-down list.	
113							

k. Click the down arrow to the right of the cell and select *Martin* from the drop-down list.

l. Press Tab. Key the following: **20**.

m. Press Tab. The Paid input message is displayed. A down arrow automatically is displayed to the right of the cell.

n. Click the down arrow to the right of the cell and select *Yes* from the drop-down list.

8. By now you should be familiar with entering data using data validation. Enter the following records in rows 108 and 109:

Invoice #:	55071
Owner's Name:	**Mason, Anita**
Pet Name:	**Snickers**
Classification:	**Dog**
Service Rendered:	**Heartworm Test**
Vet:	**Martin**
Amount:	24
Paid:	**Yes**
Invoice #:	55071
Owner's Name:	**Mason, Anita**
Pet Name:	**Snickers**
Classification:	**Dog**
Service Rendered:	**Heartworm Medication**
Vet:	**Martin**
Amount:	35
Paid:	**Yes**

9. Make any necessary adjustments so that all the columns fit on one page.

10. Save the worksheet with the same name (Excel E4, Ex 02). You are going to use this worksheet in exercise 3.

11. Print and close the worksheet.

Sorting a List

Excel's sort feature helps you organize the data in a list. Column fields can be quickly sorted in ascending or descending order. To sort the data in a column, select any cell in the column by which you want to sort. To sort in ascending order, click the Sort Ascending button on the Standard toolbar. To sort in descending order, click the Sort Descending button on the Standard toolbar.

Sort Ascending Button

Sort Descending Button

Performing a Multi-Level Sort

If you want to sort a list by more than one field, you can use the Sort dialog box. Suppose, for example, you wanted to sort first by a last name field and then by a first name field. To perform such a multi-level sort, select any cell in the list to be sorted. Click Data and then click Sort. The Sort dialog box shown in figure 4.9 is displayed.

figure 4.9

The Sort Dialog Box

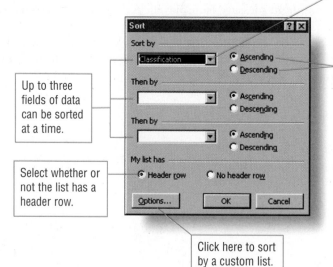

To select the field to be sorted, click here to display a drop-down list of all the field names in the list.

Select whether the field is to be sorted in ascending or descending order.

Up to three fields of data can be sorted at a time.

Select whether or not the list has a header row.

Click here to sort by a custom list.

If after performing a sort you did not get correct results, check to make sure there are no extra spaces at the beginning or end of a cell. Extra spaces affect how the data is sorted.

To select the first field to be sorted, click the down arrow to the right of the Sort by box. A list of all the field names is displayed. Select the field name of the column to be sorted first and select whether the sort should be in ascending or descending order. If you want to sort by a second field, click the down arrow to the right of the first Then by box and select the field name of the column to be sorted next, and so on. At the bottom of the dialog box select whether or not the list has a header row and click OK.

Creating a Custom List

A custom list can contain either text only or a mixed list of both text and numbers. If the list is to contain only numbers, before you key the list into the worksheet, format the cells as text. Key the list of numbers into the formatted cells.

There may be times when you want to sort by an unusual order, that is, not simply ascending or descending. You can do this by creating a custom list. To create a custom list, key the list into a worksheet and select all the cells containing the list. Click Tools and then click Options. Click the Custom Lists tab on the Options dialog box. As shown in figure 4.10, the selected cell range appears in the Import list from cells box. Click the Import button. The list is then displayed in the Custom lists box and the List entries box. Click the OK button.

figure 4.10

The Options Dialog Box with the Custom Lists Tab Selected

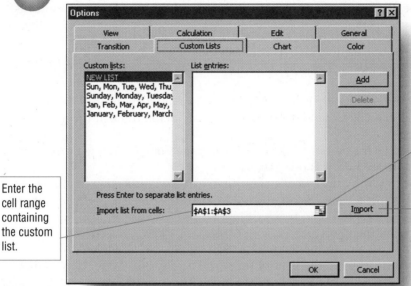

Click here to return to the worksheet in order to select the range of cells containing the custom list.

Enter the cell range containing the custom list.

Click here to import the selected list.

You can only use a custom list to sort the first or top level of the sort. Click the down arrow to the right of the Sort by list box and select the column for which the custom list was created. To sort that column using the custom list, click the Options button at the bottom of the Sort dialog box. The Sort Options dialog box shown in figure 4.11 is displayed. Click the down arrow to the right of the First key sort order box. The custom list will be included in the drop-down menu that appears. Select the custom list and click OK.

Another way to create a custom list is to click Tools, Options, and the Custom Lists tab. Click *NEW LIST* in the Custom lists box. Key the list into the List entries box starting with the first item on the list and pressing Enter after each item. Click the Add button after keying the list's last item. **Hint**

figure 4.11

The Sort Options Dialog Box

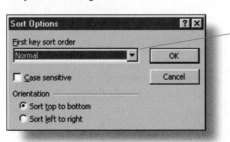

Click here to select a custom list.

Once a custom list is created, Excel saves it on the computer system so that it is always available. To delete a custom list, Click Tools and then Options. Click the Custom Lists tab on the Options dialog box. Select the custom list to be deleted from the Custom lists box and click the Delete button. Click OK. A box warning you that the list will be permanently deleted is displayed. Click OK.

EXPERT

Sorting a List, Performing a Multi-Level Sort, and Sorting by a Custom List

1. Open Excel E4, Ex 02. This is the worksheet that was completed in exercise 2.
2. Save the worksheet using the Save <u>A</u>s command and name it Excel E4, Ex 03.
3. Create a custom header that displays your name at the left margin and the file name at the right margin.
4. Right now the list is sorted by invoice number. You would like to sort it by owner's name. Click cell B4. Click the Sort Ascending button. Scroll through the list to see how it is now sorted.
5. Next try sorting the list by vet. Click cell F4. Click the Sort Ascending button. Scroll through the list to see how it is now sorted.
6. Now you want to sort by the owner's name first, by the classification of animal second, and finally by the pet's name. Select any cell in the list. Complete the following steps to perform the multi-level sort.
   a. Click <u>D</u>ata and then <u>S</u>ort.
   b. Click the down arrow to the right of the Sort by box. Select *Owner's Name*.
   c. Click the down arrow to the right of the first Then by box. Select *Classification*.
   d. Click the down arrow to the right of the second Then by box. Select *Pet Name*.
   e. Be sure that <u>H</u>eader row is selected at the bottom of the dialog box.
   f. Click OK.
   g. Scroll through the list to see how it is now sorted.

7. Make any necessary adjustments so that the columns all fit on one page. Print the sorted list.
8. The veterinarians want to be able to sort the list in order by who has worked at the clinic the longest. Dr. Ketner has worked there the longest, followed by Dr. Frobose, followed by Dr. Martin. Complete the following steps to create a custom list.
   a. Key **Ketner** in cell I4.
   b. Key **Frobose** in cell I5.
   c. Key **Martin** in cell I6.
   d. Select cells I4 through I6.
   e. Click <u>T</u>ools and then <u>O</u>ptions.
   f. Click the Custom Lists tab. Check to make sure that the cell range I4:I6 is in the Import list from cells box.
   g. Click the <u>I</u>mport button.

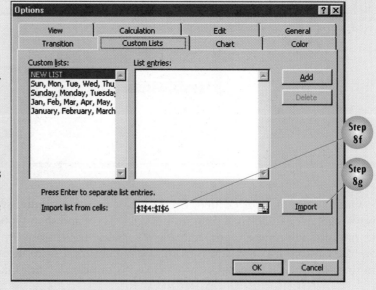

h. Click OK.

i. Delete cells I4:I6.

9. You are ready to sort using the custom list you just created. Complete the following steps to sort by the custom list:

a. Click any cell in the list.

b. Click Data and then Sort.

c. Click the down arrow to the right of the Sort by box. Select *Vet*.

d. Click the Options button at the bottom of the dialog box.

e. Click the down arrow key next to the First key sort order box. Select *Ketner, Frobose, Martin*.

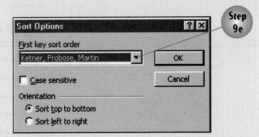

f. Click OK.

g. Click the down arrow to the right of the first Then by box. Select *Owner's name*.

h. Click the down arrow to the right of the second Then by box. Select *Classification*.

i. Click OK.

j. Scroll through the list to see how it is now sorted.

10. Make any necessary adjustments so that the columns all fit on one page. Print the sorted list.

11. Complete the following steps to delete the custom list you created:

a. Click Tools and then Options.

b. Select *Ketner, Frobose, Martin* in the Custom lists box.

c. Click the Delete button.

d. A warning box is displayed letting you know that the list will be permanently deleted. Click OK.

e. Click OK.

12. Save the worksheet with the same name (Excel E4, Ex 03). You are going to use this worksheet in exercise 4.

13. Close the worksheet.

Modifying Records

Updates usually have to be made to data lists. Records need to be deleted or edited in some way. In addition to allowing you to enter new records, you can also use the data form to search for, display, edit, and delete specific records.

Finding Records

To find specific records, select any cell in the data list and click Data and then Form. Clicking the Find Prev button displays the previous record. Clicking the Find Next button displays the next record. Clicking the Criteria button allows you to enter specific criteria Excel will use when searching for the record. A blank record is displayed. You can enter the search criteria in the field name boxes. If you enter criteria in more than one field, in order to be found the record must contain the criteria in both fields. Using the criteria entered in figure 4.12, Excel will find all the records containing "Heckman, Ellen" in the Owner's Name field and "Cat" in the Classification field.

figure 4.12

Finding Specific Records

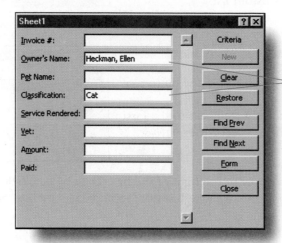

Enter the criteria for the records to be found in the field name boxes. In this case the records to be found must have "Heckman, Ellen" entered in the Owner's Name field and "Cat" entered in the Classification field.

The comparison operators listed in table 4.1 can be used as part of the search criteria. For example, if you wanted to find all the records where the Amount field was greater than 20, you would enter **>20** in the Amount box.

table 4.1

Comparison Operators

Operators	Description
=	Equals
>	Greater than
<	Less than
>=	Greater than or equal to
<=	Less than or equal to
<>	Not equal to

Once the search criteria have been entered in the boxes, click the Find Next button. The first record Excel finds is displayed. Click the find Next button until you hear a beep. The beep indicated that Excel could not find any more matches. To return to the worksheet, click the Close button.

Editing Records

Once a specific record has been located using the data form, you can make any changes to it right on the data form. Key the changes in the appropriate field name boxes. Remember to press Tab to move from field to field and press Enter to move from record to record. Once you click the Close button or move to a different record in the data form, whatever changes were made are entered into the worksheet. You can also edit records directly on the worksheet.

Deleting Records

Records can be deleted using the data form. Once the record to be deleted has been located using the data form, click the Delete button. A warning box is displayed letting you know that the record will be permanently deleted. Click OK to delete the record. You can also delete records by deleting the row containing the record from the worksheet.

If the record you are editing contains a formula, the formula is not recalculated until you move to another record or close the dialog box.

Clicking the Restore button undoes any changes you have made to the record currently displayed in the Data Form.

exercise 4

Finding, Editing, and Deleting Records

1. Open Excel E4, Ex 03. This is the worksheet that was completed in exercise 3.
2. Save the worksheet using the Save As command and name it Excel E4, Ex 04.
3. Create a custom header that displays your name at the left margin and the file name at the right margin.
4. First you want to find all the records where Heartworm Medication was the service rendered. Complete the following steps to use the data form to conduct the search:
   a. Click any cell in the data list.
   b. Click Data and then Form.
   c. Click the Criteria button.
   d. Key the following in the Service Rendered box: **Heartworm Medication**
   e. Click the Find Next button. The first record found is displayed. Click the Find Next button until no more records are found. How many records were found?
5. Complete the following steps to find all the records where the Heartworm Medication sold cost more than $50.00.

Sheet1		?X
Invoice #:		Criteria
Owner's Name:		New
Pet Name:		Clear
Classification:		Restore
Service Rendered:	Heartworm Medication	
Vet:		Find Prev
Amount:		Find Next
Paid:		Form
		Close

Step 4d
Step 4e

a. You want to start the search beginning with record 1. In order to do this, record 1 must be displayed. To display record 1, click the button on the scroll bar and drag it to the top. It should say 1 of 106 in the upper right corner of the dialog box. This means the record that is displayed is the first record out of a total of 106 records.

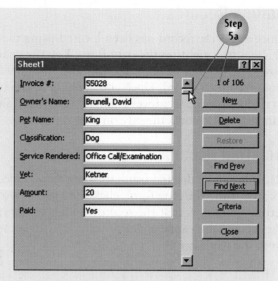

Step 5a

b. Click the Criteria button.

c. "Heartworm Medication" should still be entered in the Service Rendered box. Key **>50** in the Amount box.

d. Click the Find Next button. The first record found is displayed. Click the Find Next button until no more records are found. How many records were found this time?

6. Linda Covington has gotten married and wants her last name changed on all her records. Complete the following steps to make this change:

a. Use the scroll bar to move to record 1. The first record in the list should be displayed in the data form.

b. Click the Criteria button.

c. Delete the entries in the Service Rendered box and the Amount box.

d. Key the following in the Owner's name box: **Covington, Linda**.

e. Click the Find Next button.

f. Key the following in the Owner's name box: **Kale, Linda**.
   You must be sure to press the Enter key after keying the changes. The editing changes will not be made until the Enter key is pressed.

g. Click the Find Next button. Edit the next record that is found so that **Linda Kale** is in the Owner's name box.

h. Edit all Linda Covington's records to reflect her name change.

i. Click the Find Prev button to make sure there are no more records for Linda Covington. When you have finished, Excel should not be able to find any records for Linda Covington when you press either the Find Next or Find Prev buttons.

7. A mistake was made on invoice 55070. Irene Henry was charged for a rabies shot and her dog was not given a rabies shot. Complete the following steps to delete this record.

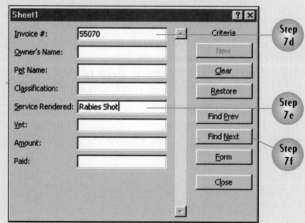

Step 7d

Step 7e

Step 7f

a. Use the scroll bar to move to record 1.

b. Click the Criteria button.

c. Delete the entry in the Owner's Name box.

d. Key **55070** in the Invoice # box.

e. Key **Rabies Shot** in the Service Rendered box.

f. Click the Find Next button.

g. Click the Delete button.

h. A warning box is displayed informing you that the record will be permanently deleted. Click OK.

i. Click the Close button.

8. Sort the list by Owner's Name first, Classification second, and Pet Name third.

9. Save the worksheet with the same name (Excel E4, Ex 04). You are going to use this worksheet in exercise 7.

10. Print and close the worksheet.

Outlining a Worksheet

When working with long lists of data, quickly finding the specific information you need could be difficult. One way to make locating information in a list easier is by outlining the worksheet. Once you outline a worksheet, a single mouse click will hide or reveal levels of detail within the worksheet. With an outline you can quickly display only the rows or columns that provide summaries. In figure 4.13, for example, the details for the East Central Region's sales are displayed. The details are hidden for the North Central and Northeast Regions' sales. In figure 4.13 there are three levels of detail. An outline can have up to eight levels of detail. Each inner level provides details for the preceding outer level. In figure 4.13, level 1 is the row displaying the Grand Total, level 2 are the rows displaying the totals for each of the regions, and level 3 are the detail rows for all the regions. To see a particular level of the outline, click the outline symbol that represents the number of the level you want to see. These symbols are located in the upper right corner of figure 4.13.

figure
4.13

A Worksheet Outline

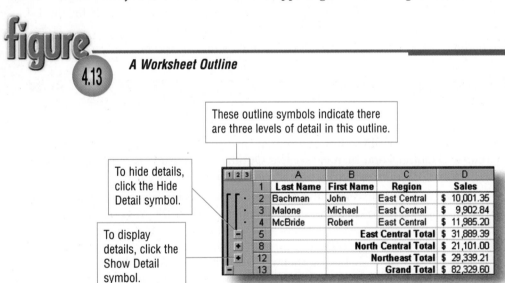

These outline symbols indicate there are three levels of detail in this outline.

To hide details, click the Hide Detail symbol.

To display details, click the Show Detail symbol.

	A	B	C	D
1	Last Name	First Name	Region	Sales
2	Bachman	John	East Central	$ 10,001.35
3	Malone	Michael	East Central	$ 9,902.84
4	McBride	Robert	East Central	$ 11,985.20
5			East Central Total	$ 31,889.39
8			North Central Total	$ 21,101.00
12			Northeast Total	$ 29,339.21
13			Grand Total	$ 82,329.60

In order to outline a worksheet automatically, it must contain formulas that summarize the data, such as formulas that find subtotals and a grand total. If the summary formulas are in columns, all the columns containing the summary formulas must be either to the right or left of the detail data. If the summary formulas are in rows, all the rows containing the summary formulas must be either below or above the detail data. That is, the summary formulas cannot be mixed in with the detail data.

Once you are sure the worksheet is set up correctly, select the range of cells to be outlined. If you want to outline the entire worksheet, click any cell in the worksheet. If you are outlining only a portion of the worksheet, select the range of cells to be outlined. Click Data, point to Group and Outline, and then click Auto Outline. The appropriate outline symbols are displayed. You can then hide and show levels of detail as explained in table 4.2.

table 4.2

Showing and Hiding Levels of Detail in an Outline

To Show Details	Click
The detail data for a group	The Show Detail symbol ⊞.
A specific level in an outline	The Row or Column Level symbol 1 2 3.
All detail in an outline	The Row or Column Level symbol for the lowest row or column. If there are three levels, the lowest level would be three.
To Hide Details	**Click**
The detail data for a group	The Hide Detail symbol ⊟.
A specific level in an outline	The preceding Row or Column Level symbol 1 2 3. For example, if an outline has three levels, hide the third level by clicking the symbol for level 2.
All detail in an outline	The first level symbol, which would be one.

To remove an outline, click any cell on the worksheet. Click Data, point to Group and Outline, and then click Clear Outline. The outline is removed. None of the data on the worksheet changes when an outline is removed.

Instead of having Excel automatically create an outline for you, you can create an outline manually. To create an outline manually, select the rows or columns that will be hidden when the details are not displayed. One outline area cannot be immediately adjacent to another. If you try, for example, to create one outline level that hides rows 5 through 10 and then try to create a second outline level that hides rows 11 through 15, you will end up with one outline level that hides rows 5 through 15. A row or column has to separate the two areas that you want to outline. In many cases that row or column will contain the summarization function, such as SUM or AVERAGE.

A shortcut for creating an outline manually is to select the rows or columns to be outlined and press Alt + Shift + right arrow.

To create an outline level, select the rows or columns to be outlined. Click Data, point to Group and Outline, and then click Group. The outline is created. To remove an outline, select the rows or columns that comprise the outline to be removed. If you want to clear an entire outline, click a single cell in the worksheet. Click Data, point to Group and Outline, and then click Ungroup. The outline is removed.

exercise 5

Outlining a Worksheet Manually

1. Open Excel Worksheet E4-02.
2. Save the worksheet using the Save As command and name it Excel E4, Ex 05.
3. Create a custom header that displays your name at the left margin and the file name at the right margin.
4. Scroll through the worksheet to look at the information stored in it. The records are sorted by veterinarian and there is a subtotal for the invoices for each veterinarian in rows 40, 73, and 111. You would like to be able to easily see just the subtotals. Creating an outline would allow you to do this. Create an outline for the worksheet manually by completing the following steps:
    a. Select row 4. Move the mouse pointer to the bottom of row 4. When the mouse pointer turns into an arrow, hold down the Shift key and double-click. Rows 4 through 39 should be selected.
    b. Click Data. If necessary, expand the drop-down menu. Point to Group and Outline, and then click Group.
    c. Select row 41. Move the mouse pointer to the bottom of row 41. When the mouse pointer turns into an arrow hold down the Shift key and double-click. Rows 41 through 72 should be selected.
    d. Click Data, point to Group and Outline, and then click Group.
    e. Select row 74. Move the mouse pointer to the bottom of row 74. When the mouse pointer turns into an arrow, hold down the Shift key and double-click. Rows 74 through 110 should be selected.
    f. Click Data, point to Group and Outline, and then click Group. The outline for the worksheet now has two levels.
5. Experiment with displaying different levels of the outline by completing the following steps:
    a. Click the level 1 Column Level symbol. Only the subtotals are displayed.

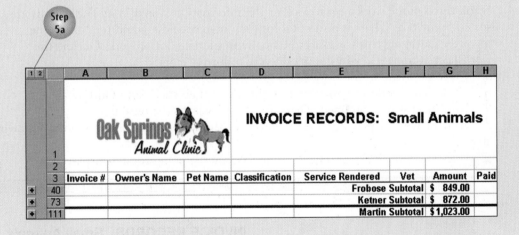

Step 5a

b. Print the worksheet.

c. Click the Show Detail symbol to the left of row 111. The details for Martin's invoices are now displayed. The Show Detail symbol changed to a Hide Detail symbol.

d. Print the worksheet.

e. Click the Hide Detail symbol to the left of row 111.

Step 5e									
	108	55071	Mason, Annie	Snickers	Dog	Office Call/Examination	Martin	$ 20.00	Yes
	109	55071	Mason, Annie	Snickers	Dog	Heartworm Test	Martin	$ 24.00	Yes
	110	55071	Mason, Annie	Snickers	Dog	Heartworm Medication	Martin	$ 35.00	Yes
	111						Martin Subtotal	$1,023.00	

6. Ungroup the records for Frobose by completing the following steps:

a. Click the Show Detail symbol to the left of row 40. The details for Frobose's invoices are now displayed.

b. Select row 4. Move the mouse pointer to the bottom of row 4. When the mouse pointer turns into an arrow, hold down the Shift key and double-click. Rows 4 through 39 should be selected.

c. Click Data, point to Group and Outline, and then click Ungroup. Frobose's records are no longer grouped.

7. To clear the outline for the rest of the worksheet, click Data, point to Group and Outline, and then click Clear Outline.

8. Save and close Excel E4, Ex 05.

exercise 6

Outlining a Worksheet Automatically

1. Open Excel Worksheet E4-03.

2. Save the worksheet using the Save As command and name it Excel E4, Ex 06.

3. Create a custom header that displays your name at the left margin and the file name at the right margin.

4. Scroll through the worksheet to look at the information stored in it. The records are sorted by invoice. There is a subtotal for each invoice and a grand total of all the invoices. Outlining this worksheet manually would be a lot of work. Outline the worksheet automatically by completing the following steps:

a. Click anywhere in the worksheet.

b. Click Data, point to Group and Outline, and then click Auto Outline. The worksheet is now outlined. There are three levels to the outline.

5. Experiment with displaying different levels of the outline by completing the following steps:

a. Click the level 1 Column Level symbol. Only the grand total is displayed.

Step 5a

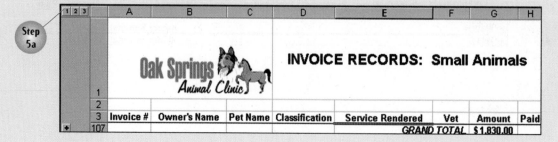

	A	B	C	D	E	F	G	H
				INVOICE RECORDS: Small Animals				
1								
2								
3	Invoice #	Owner's Name	Pet Name	Classification	Service Rendered	Vet	Amount	Paid
107					GRAND TOTAL		$1,830.00	

b. Print the worksheet.
c. Click the Show Detail symbol to the left of row 107.
d. Click the level 2 Column Level symbol. All the Invoice totals are displayed.
e. Click the Show Detail symbol to the left of row 17. The details for Invoice # 55020 are now displayed.
f. Print the worksheet.
g. Click the level 3 Column Level symbol. All the details are displayed.
6. To clear the outline for the worksheet, click Data, point to Group and Outline, and then click Clear Outline.
7. Save and close Excel E4, Ex 06.

Subtotaling a List

Data in a list can be summarized using subtotals. To subtotal a list you must first sort the list by the field on which you want the list subtotaled. For example, suppose you want a subtotal of each veterinarian's invoices. The list would first have to be sorted by veterinarian. Once the list is sorted by the field on which the subtotals are to be based, select any cell in the list. Click Data and then click Subtotals. The Subtotal dialog box as shown in figure 4.14 is displayed.

figure
4.14   *The Subtotal Dialog Box*

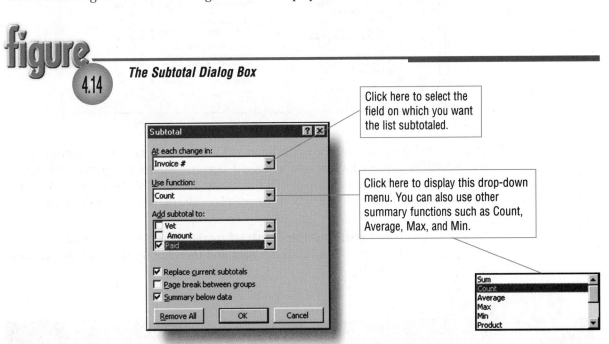

Click here to select the field on which you want the list subtotaled.

Click here to display this drop-down menu. You can also use other summary functions such as Count, Average, Max, and Min.

To select the field by which the list is to be subtotaled, click the down arrow to the right of the At each change in box. A list of all the field names is displayed. Click the appropriate field. Click the down arrow to the right of the Use function box. To find subtotals, click *Sum*. Other summary functions, such as Count, Average, Max, and Min, are also available. In the Add subtotal to box, click the check box next to the field containing the values that are to be subtotaled. Click OK. You are returned to the worksheet and the subtotals along with a grand total are displayed.

Subtotals are displayed in outline view. The Hide Detail Level buttons as shown in figure 4.15 allow you to display as much or as little of the data as you want. Suppose you only want to display the data subtotal and not all the individual records. Click the Hide Detail Level button for that subtotal and only that subtotal will be displayed. The Hide Detail Level button changes to a Show Detail Level button. To display the records, click the Show Detail Level button.

figure

4.15

Creating Subtotals

Level Symbols

Hide Detail Level Buttons

	A	B	C	D	E	F	G	H	I
3	Invoice #	Owner's Name	Pet Name	Classification	Service Rendered	Vet	Amount	Paid	
4	55022	Baxter, Alice	Boots	Cat	Office Call/Examination	Frobose	$ 20.00	Yes	
5	55022	Baxter, Alice	Boots	Cat	Feline Leukemia Test	Frobose	$ 20.00	Yes	
6	55022	Baxter, Alice	Boots	Cat	Feline Leukemia Shot	Frobose	$ 15.00	Yes	
7	55061	Baxter, Alice	Boots	Cat	Rabies Shot	Frobose	$ 20.00	Yes	
8	55061	Baxter, Alice	Boots	Cat	Office Call/Examination	Frobose	$ 20.00	Yes	
9		**Baxter, Alice Total**					$ 95.00		
10	55028	Brunell, David	King	Dog	Office Call/Examination	Ketner	$ 20.00	Yes	
11	55028	Brunell, David	King	Dog	Distemper Shot	Ketner	$ 20.00	Yes	
12	55066	Brunell, David	Sport	Dog	Office Call/Examination	Ketner	$ 20.00	Yes	
13	55066	Brunell, David	Sport	Dog	Distemper Shot	Ketner	$ 20.00	Yes	
14		**Brunell, David Total**					$ 80.00		
15	55029	Bruton, Joe	Patches	Dog	Office Call/Examination	Martin	$ 20.00	Yes	
16	55029	Bruton, Joe	Patches	Dog	Distemper Shot	Martin	$ 20.00	Yes	
17		**Bruton, Joe Total**					$ 40.00		
18	55030	Cavataio, Anthony	Rex	Dog	Office Call/Examination	Ketner	$ 20.00	Yes	
19	55030	Cavataio, Anthony	Rex	Dog	Distemper Shot	Ketner	$ 20.00	Yes	
20		**Cavataio, Anthony Total**					$ 40.00		
21	55020	Fox, Alan	Blue	Dog	Office Call/Examination	Ketner	$ 20.00	Yes	
22	55020	Fox, Alan	Blue	Dog	Heartworm Test	Ketner	$ 24.00	Yes	
23	55020	Fox, Alan	Blue	Dog	Heartworm Medication	Ketner	$ 30.00	Yes	
24	55057	Fox, Alan	Blue	Dog	Office Call/Examination	Ketner	$ 20.00	No	
25	55057	Fox, Alan	Blue	Dog	Distemper Shot	Ketner	$ 20.00	No	
26		**Fox, Alan Total**					$ 114.00		

The level symbols, also shown in figure 4.15, allow you to quickly control how much detail is displayed. Clicking the Level 1 button displays the grand total only. Clicking the Level 2 button displays all the subtotals. None of the individual records are displayed. Clicking the Level 3 button displays all the records, subtotals, and the grand total.

When you have finished working with subtotals, they can be removed by selecting any cell in the list and clicking Data and then Subtotals. Click the Remove All button and click OK.

exercise 7

Subtotaling a List

1. Open Excel E4, Ex 04. This is the worksheet that was completed in exercise 4.
2. Save the worksheet using the Save As command and name it Excel E4, Ex 07.
3. Create a custom header that displays your name at the left margin and the file name at the right margin.
4. Complete the following steps to subtotal the list by veterinarian:
   a. Sort the list in ascending order on the Vet field.
   b. Click Data and then Subtotals.

c. Click the down arrow to the right of the At each change in box. Select *Vet*.

d. Click the down arrow to the right of the Use function box. Select *Sum*.

e. Select the Amount check box. Deselect any other check boxes.

f. Click OK.

g. The subtotals have been created. Click the Level 2 button.

h. Adjust the width of columns F and G.

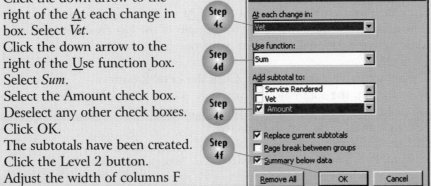

Step 4c
Step 4d
Step 4e
Step 4f

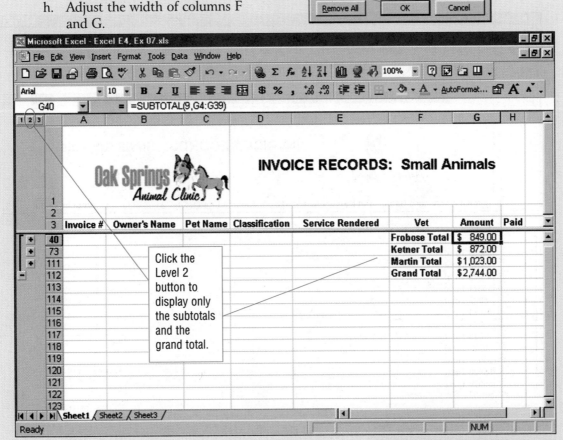

Click the Level 2 button to display only the subtotals and the grand total.

i. To see only the records for Dr. Frobose, click the Show Details button to the left of row 40.

j. To see all the individual records, click the Level 3 button. All of the records, subtotals, and the grand total are now displayed.

5. Complete the following steps to remove the subtotals:

a. If necessary, select a cell in the list.

b. Click Data and then Subtotals.

c. Click the Remove All button.

6. Complete the following steps to subtotal the list by invoice number:

a. Sort the list in ascending order on the invoice number field.

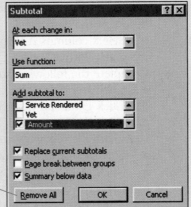

Step 5c

b. Click <u>D</u>ata and then Su<u>b</u>totals.
c. Click the down arrow to the right of the <u>A</u>t each change in box. Select *Invoice #*.
d. If necessary, click the down arrow to the right of the <u>U</u>se function box and select *Sum*.
e. Make sure the Amount check box is the only box selected.
f. Click OK.
g. The subtotals have been created. Click the Level 2 button.
7. You want to print the subtotals, but you only want to print the data in columns A and G. Complete the following steps to print the worksheet:
a. Select columns B through F. Press the Ctrl key and select column H. Columns B, C, D, E, F, and H should be selected.

Select columns B through F and column H.

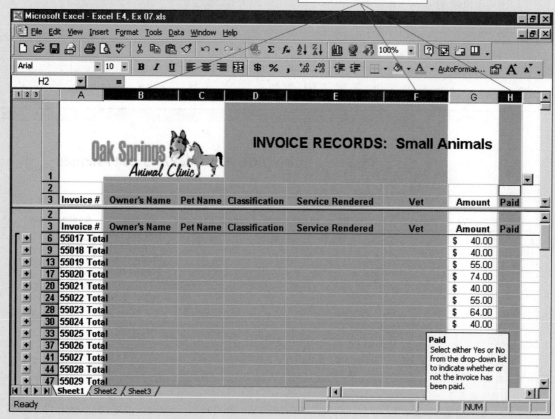

b. Click F<u>o</u>rmat, select <u>C</u>olumn, and then click <u>H</u>ide.
c. If necessary, adjust the column widths so that all the data is displayed.
d. Print the worksheet.
e. Select columns A through I.
f. Click F<u>o</u>rmat, select <u>C</u>olumn, and then click <u>U</u>nhide.
8. Complete the following steps to remove the subtotals:
a. Click any cell in the list.
b. Click <u>D</u>ata and then Su<u>b</u>totals.
c. Click the <u>R</u>emove All button.
9. Complete the following steps to subtotal the list by classification:
a. Sort the list in ascending order on the classification field.
b. Click <u>D</u>ata and then Su<u>b</u>totals.
c. Click the down arrow to the right of the <u>A</u>t each change in box. Select *Classification*.
d. If necessary, click the down arrow to the right of the <u>U</u>se function box and select *Sum*.

e. Make sure the Amount check box is the only check box selected.
f. Click OK.
g. The subtotals have been created. Click the Hide Detail Level button to the left of the Cat Total.
h. Click the Hide Detail Level button to the left of the Dog Total.
i. Hide columns E, F, and H.
j. Adjust the width of column D.
k. Print the worksheet.
l. Select rows C through I.
m. Click Format, select Column, and then click Unhide.

10. Complete the following steps to remove the subtotals:
a. Click any cell in the list.
b. Click Data and then Subtotals.
c. Click the Remove All button.

11. Save the worksheet with the same name (Excel E4, Ex 07). You are going to use this worksheet in exercise 8.

12. Close the worksheet.

Filtering a List

Another way of displaying only certain records in a list is by applying filters to display in the worksheet only those records that meet certain criteria. The records that do not meet the criteria are temporarily hidden from view.

Filtering a List Using AutoFilter

The quickest and easiest way to filter a list is by using the AutoFilter feature. To use AutoFilter, select any cell in the list to be filtered. Click Data, point to Filter, and then click AutoFilter. As shown in figure 4.16, drop-down lists appear next to each column heading. Click the down arrow to the right of the field name you want to filter. The drop-down list that appears allows you to display all the records in the list, display the top 10 records, create a custom filter, or select an entry that appears in one or more records on the list. As you can see in figure 4.16, if you select one of the cell entries, then only those records containing that entry are displayed. To go back to displaying all the records, click the down arrow to the right of the field name and select *All*.

The down arrow to the right of the column heading that was used to perform an AutoFilter turns blue after the filter has been applied. The row numbers of the displayed records are also blue. This alerts you to the fact that not all the records are currently displayed and also indicates which column has to be selected in order to display all the records.

figure
4.16

Using AutoFilter

When using AutoFilter, drop-down lists appear next to each column heading.

By selecting one of the cell entries that appears on the list, only the records containing that entry are displayed.

The number of records meeting the criteria is displayed in the Status bar.

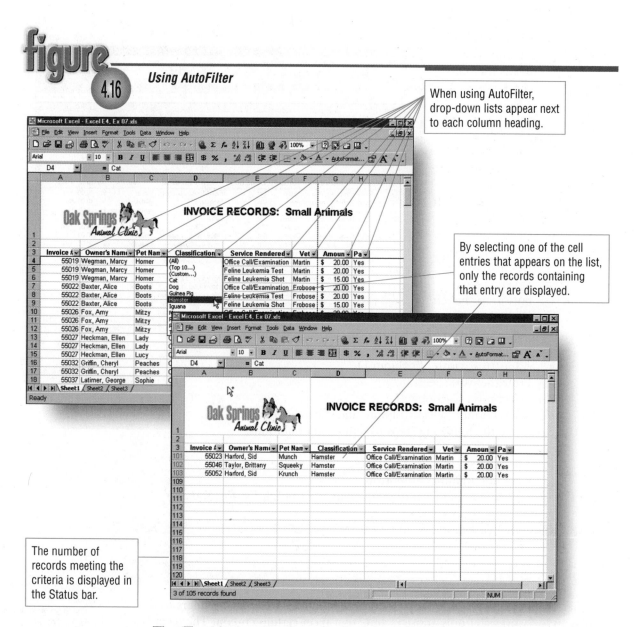

The (Top 10...) option from the drop-down list only works if there are values (rather than text) stored in that column. When you select it, the dialog box shown in figure 4.17 is displayed. You can choose whether you want to display the Top or Bottom Items or Percents. You can also indicate how many items (or percents) should be displayed. Click OK and the filtered records are displayed.

figure
4.17

The Top 10 AutoFilter Dialog Box

Creating a Custom AutoFilter

To create a custom AutoFilter, select any cell in the list, click Data, point to Filter, and then click AutoFilter. Click the down arrow to the right of the field name you want to filter. Select *(Custom...)*. The Custom AutoFilter dialog box is displayed. As shown in figure 4.18, to select a comparison operator, click the down arrow to the right of the first box under Show rows where. Select one of the comparison operators. Either click the down arrow to the right of the next box to select the data to be compared or key the data to be compared in the box. A second set of criteria can be entered in the bottom two boxes. If the And option is selected, both sets of criteria must be met by the record. If the Or option is selected, either one or the other set, but not necessarily both, of the criteria must be met by the record. Click OK to display the records that match the criteria. When you have finished with the filter, display all the records by clicking the down arrow to the right of the field name and selecting *All*.

You may apply more than one filter at a time.

To turn the AutoFilter feature off, click Data, point to Filter, and then click AutoFilter. The AutoFilter feature will then be turned off.

The Custom AutoFilter Dialog Box

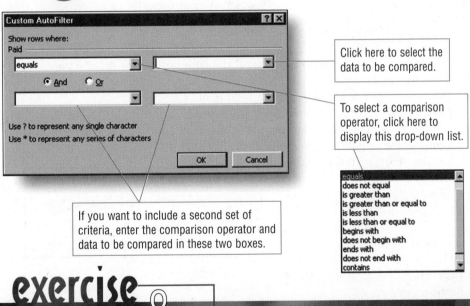

exercise 8

Using AutoFilter

1. Open Excel E4, Ex 07. This is the worksheet that was completed in exercise 7.
2. Save the worksheet using the Save As command and name it Excel E4, Ex 08.
3. Create a custom header that displays your name at the left margin and the file name at the right margin.
4. Sort the list in ascending order on the invoice # column.
5. First you want to see all the records where the invoices have not been paid. Complete the following steps to filter the records:

a. Click any cell in the list.
b. Click <u>D</u>ata, point to <u>F</u>ilter, and then click Auto<u>F</u>ilter. Drop-down lists appear next to all the field names.
c. Click the down arrow to the right of the field name Paid.
d. Click *No*.

	A	B	C	D	E	F	G	H	I
1			**INVOICE RECORDS: Small Animals**						
2									
3	Invoice #	Owner's Name	Pet Name	Classification	Service Rendered	Vet	Amount	Paid	
4	55017	Heckman, Ellen	Carl	Dog	Office Call/Examination	Frobose	$	(All)	
5	55017	Heckman, Ellen	Carl	Dog	Rabies Shot	Frobose	$	(Top 10...)	
6	55018	Wegman, Marcy	Raven	Dog	Office Call/Examination	Martin	$	(Custom...)	
7	55018	Wegman, Marcy	Raven	Dog	Rabies Shot	Martin	$	No	
8	55019	Wegman, Marcy	Homer	Cat	Office Call/Examination	Martin	$ 20.00	Yes	
9	55019	Wegman, Marcy	Homer	Cat	Feline Leukemia Test	Martin	$ 20.00	Yes	
10	55019	Wegman, Marcy	Homer	Cat	Feline Leukemia Shot	Martin	$ 15.00	Yes	
11	55020	Fox, Alan	Blue	Dog	Office Call/Examination	Ketner	$ 20.00	Yes	
12	55020	Fox, Alan	Blue	Dog	Heartworm Test	Ketner	$ 24.00	Yes	
13	55020	Fox, Alan	Blue	Dog	Heartworm Medication	Ketner	$ 30.00	Yes	
14	55021	Gardner, David	Marcus	Dog	Office Call/Examination	Frobose	$ 20.00	No	
15	55021	Gardner, David	Marcus	Dog	Distemper Shot	Frobose	$ 20.00	No	
16	55022	Baxter, Alice	Boots	Cat	Office Call/Examination	Frobose	$ 20.00	Yes	
17	55022	Baxter, Alice	Boots	Cat	Feline Leukemia Test	Frobose	$ 20.00	Yes	
18	55022	Baxter, Alice	Boots	Cat	Feline Leukemia Shot	Frobose	$ 15.00	Yes	

Sheet1 / Sheet2 / Sheet3 /

Step 5c

Step 5d

e. Adjust the widths of the columns so that all the columns will fit on one page.
f. Print the worksheet.
g. Click the down arrow to the right of the field name Paid.
h. Click *(All)*. All the records are once again displayed.
6. The veterinarians want to know which invoices contributed to the top 5 percent of their income. Complete the following steps to filter the records:
a. Click the down arrow to the right of the field name Amount.
b. Click *(Top 10…)*.
c. In the middle box key **5**.
d. Click the down arrow to the right of the last box. Click *Percent*.
e. Click OK.
f. Print the worksheet. The worksheet should fit on one page.
g. Click the down arrow to the right of the field name Amount.
h. Click *(All)*. All the records are once again displayed.

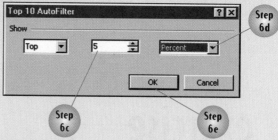

Top 10 AutoFilter
Show
Top | 5 | Percent
OK | Cancel

Step 6d

Step 6c

Step 6e

7. The veterinarians want to see the records of all the animals treated that were not dogs or cats. Sort the list in ascending order on the Classification field. Complete the following steps to create a custom filter.
a. Click the down arrow to the right of the field name Classification.
b. Click *Custom*. The Custom AutoFilter dialog box is displayed.
c. Click the down arrow to the right of the first box under Classification. Click *does not equal*.
d. Click the down arrow to the right of the second box in the first row. Click *Dog*.

e. Make sure the <u>A</u>nd option is selected.
f. Click the down arrow to the right of the first box in the second row. Click *does not equal*.
g. Click the down arrow to the right of the second box in the second row. Click *Cat.*
h. Click OK.
i. Adjust the column widths so that all the data can be seen, but the data all fits on one page.
j. Print the worksheet.
k. Click the down arrow to the right of the field name Classification.
l. Click *(All).* All the records are once again displayed.

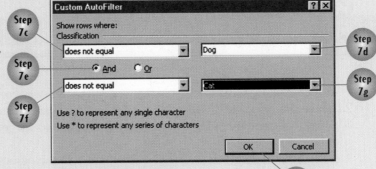

8. Complete the following steps to turn the AutoFilter feature off:
   a. Click any cell in the list.
   b. Click <u>D</u>ata, point to <u>F</u>ilter, and then click Auto<u>F</u>ilter. Drop-down lists should no longer be displayed next to the field names.
9. Save the worksheet with the same name (Excel E4, Ex 08). You are going to use this worksheet in exercise 9.
10. Close the worksheet.

Filtering a List Using Advanced Filters

Using advanced filters allows you to be very precise in searching for specific records. With an advanced filter you can denote the exact criteria to be found.

Extracting Unique Records

One task for which an advanced filter can be used is to create a list of unique values. To create a list of unique values, select the portion of the list to be extracted from. Click <u>D</u>ata, point to <u>F</u>ilter, and then click <u>A</u>dvanced Filter. The Advanced Filter dialog box shown in figure 4.19 is displayed.

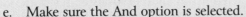

4.19 **The Advanced Filter Dialog Box**

Select this option to copy the extracted list to another location.

Select this option to extract unique records only.

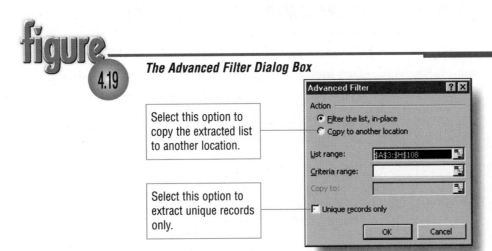

If you want to copy the extracted list to another location, select the Copy to another location option. Once that option is selected, the Copy to option becomes available and you can indicate the cell or cell range to where the extracted list should be copied. Finally, to extract unique records, select the Unique records only option.

Extracting Unique Records

1. Open Excel E4, Ex 08. This is the worksheet that was completed in exercise 8.
2. Save the worksheet using the Save As command and name it Excel E4, Ex 09.
3. Create a custom header that displays your name at the left margin and the file name at the right margin.
4. The veterinarians want a list of each client and the names of his or her pets. Sort the list first by owner's name, then by classification, and then by pet name.
5. You need to select the portion of the list you want to extract from, which would be columns B, C, and D. Complete the following steps to select the portion of the list.
   a. Click cell B3.
   b. While holding down the Shift key, double-click the bottom of the cell. Be sure you do not double-click the AutoFill handle. All of the field values in column B should be selected.
   c. While holding down the Shift key, press the right arrow key twice. All of the field values in columns B, C, and D should be selected.
   d. Click Data, point to Filter, and click Advanced Filter. The Advanced Filter dialog box is displayed.
   e. Click the Copy to another location option to select it.
   f. Make sure that **$B$3:$D$108** is entered in the List range box.
   g. Click the Collapse Dialog button at the right of the Copy to box. Click cell J3. Click the Expand Dialog button.
   h. Click the Unique records only option to select it.
   i. Click OK.

6. The unique records are copied to columns J, K, and L. Adjust the widths of these columns so that all the data can be seen.
7. Complete the following steps to print the unique records.
   a. Click cell J3. While holding down the Shift key, double-click the bottom of the cell. While still holding down the Shift key, press the right arrow key twice. Cells J3 through L51 should be selected.
   b. Click File, point to Print Area, and then click Set Print Area.
   c. Print the records.
8. Click File, point to Print Area, and then click Clear Print Area to clear the print area.
9. Save the worksheet with the same name (Excel E4, Ex 09).
10. Close the worksheet.

Using a Criteria Range

As shown in figure 4.20, the middle box on the Advanced Filter dialog box provides a place to enter a criteria range. Filtering a list using a criteria range is similar to filtering a list using AutoFilter, only instead of selecting the criteria from drop-down lists, the criteria is keyed into the worksheet in the criteria range. The criteria range is a range of cells that is set aside specifically as the place where the search conditions are entered. The criteria range is made up of one header row and one or more rows where the search condition is defined.

The Criteria Range in the Advanced Filter Dialog Box

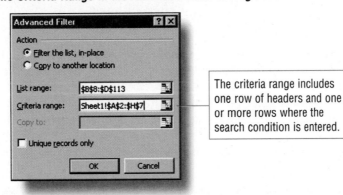

The criteria range includes one row of headers and one or more rows where the search condition is entered.

Typically the criteria range is placed in the rows above the list, so the first step is to insert four or more blank rows above the list that can be used for the criteria range. There must be at least one blank row between the criteria range and the list. Next, the header row or field names from the list have to be copied to the first blank row in the criteria range. The criteria is entered into the rows below the header row.

Several different types of conditions can be used with advanced filters. An advanced filter criteria can include one or more conditions applied to a single column. For example, the following criteria range would display rows containing either Frobose or Ketner in the Vet column.

Vet
Frobose
Ketner

You can also have a condition in one column or another. For example, the following criteria range would display rows containing either values greater than 50 in the Amount column or "No" in the Paid column.

Amount	Paid
>50	
	No

When conditions are entered in different rows, either one or the other condition may be met, but not necessarily both. If both conditions must be met, then the criteria must be placed in the same row. For example, the following criteria range would display only those rows containing both values greater than 50 in the Amount column and "No" in the Paid column.

Amount	Paid
>50	No

Once the criteria you want to match have been entered in the criteria range, click any cell in the list. Click Data, point to Filter, and then click Advanced Filter. The Advanced Filter dialog box shown in figure 4.20 is displayed. The range of cells for the criteria range, including the header row, must be entered in the Criteria range box. There must be at least one blank row between the criteria range and the list. Click OK and the records that are found are displayed.

exercise 10

Using a Criteria Range

1. Open Excel Worksheet E4-04.
2. Save the worksheet using the Save As command and name it Excel E4, Ex 10.
3. Create a custom header that displays your name at the left margin and the file name at the right margin.
4. Complete the following steps to set up a criteria range.
   a. Insert four blank rows above row 2. The header row for the list should now be in row 6.
   b. Copy cells A6 through H6 to cells A1 through H1. The header row should now be in both row 6 and in row 1.

ExcelE4, Ex 10.xls

Step 4b

	A	B	C	D	E	F	G	H	I
1	Invoice #	Owner's Name	Pet Name	Classification	Service Rendered	Vet	Amount	Paid	
2									
3									
4									
5									
6	Invoice #	Owner's Name	Pet Name	Classification	Service Rendered	Vet	Amount	Paid	
7	55017	Heckman, Ellen	Carl	Dog	Office Call/Examination	Frobose	$ 20.00	Yes	
8	55017	Heckman, Ellen	Carl	Dog	Rabies Shot	Frobose	$ 20.00	Yes	
9	55018	Wegman, Marcy	Raven	Dog	Office Call/Examination	Martin	$ 20.00	Yes	
10	55018	Wegman, Marcy	Raven	Dog	Rabies Shot	Martin	$ 20.00	Yes	
11	55019	Wegman, Marcy	Homer	Cat	Office Call/Examination	Martin	$ 20.00	Yes	

Sheet1 / Sheet2 / Sheet3 /

5. You want to find all the records of invoices that were either for Feline Leukemia Shots or Feline Leukemia Tests. Complete the following steps to enter the search criteria in the criteria range.
   a. Click cell E2. Key **Feline Leukemia Shot**.
   b. Click cell E3. Key **Feline Leukemia Test**.

ExcelE4, Ex 10.xls

Step 5a

Step 5b

	A	B	C	D	E	F	G	H	I
1	Invoice #	Owner's Name	Pet Name	Classification	Service Rendered	Vet	Amount	Paid	
2					Feline Leukemia Shot				
3					Feline Leukemia Test				
4									
5									
6	Invoice #	Owner's Name	Pet Name	Classification	Service Rendered	Vet	Amount	Paid	
7	55017	Heckman, Ellen	Carl	Dog	Office Call/Examination	Frobose	$ 20.00	Yes	
8	55017	Heckman, Ellen	Carl	Dog	Rabies Shot	Frobose	$ 20.00	Yes	
9	55018	Wegman, Marcy	Raven	Dog	Office Call/Examination	Martin	$ 20.00	Yes	
10	55018	Wegman, Marcy	Raven	Dog	Rabies Shot	Martin	$ 20.00	Yes	
11	55019	Wegman, Marcy	Homer	Cat	Office Call/Examination	Martin	$ 20.00	Yes	

Sheet1 / Sheet2 / Sheet3 /

6. If you name the criteria range Criteria, Excel will automatically recognize it as the criteria range. Complete the following steps to name the criteria range Criteria.
   a. Select cells A1 through H3.
   b. Click Insert, point to Name, and click Define.
   c. Key **Criteria**.
   d. Click OK.
7. Complete the following steps to apply the advanced criteria:
   a. Click any cell in the data list (not in the criteria range).
   b. Click Data, point to Filter, and then click Advanced Filter. The Advanced Filter dialog box appears. Excel automatically recognizes both the list range and the criteria range.
   c. Click OK. Only the records that meet the criteria are displayed.
   d. Print the worksheet.
   e. Click Data, point to Filter, and then click Show All.

Step 6c

Step 6d

Excel automatically recognizes the list range.

Because you named the criteria range "Criteria", Excel automatically recognized it.

8. Next you want to find either invoices that are over $50.00 or that have not been paid. Complete the following steps to apply the advanced criteria:
   a. Clear cells E2 and E3.
   b. Click cell G2. Key **>50**.
   c. Click cell H3. Key **No**.

	A	B	C	D	E	F	G	H	I
1	Invoice #	Owner's Name	Pet Name	Classification	Service Rendered	Vet	Amount	Paid	
2							>50		
3								No	
4									
5									
6	Invoice #	Owner's Name	Pet Name	Classification	Service Rendered	Vet	Amount	Paid	
7	55017	Heckman, Ellen	Carl	Dog	Office Call/Examination	Frobose	$ 20.00	Yes	
8	55017	Heckman, Ellen	Carl	Dog	Rabies Shot	Frobose	$ 20.00	Yes	
9	55018	Wegman, Marcy	Raven	Dog	Office Call/Examination	Martin	$ 20.00	Yes	

Excel E4, Ex 10.xls

Sheet1 / Sheet2 / Sheet3

Step 8b

Step 8c

   d. Click any cell in the data list (not in the criteria range).
   e. Click Data, point to Filter, and then click Advanced Filter. The Advanced Filter dialog box appears. Excel automatically recognizes both the list range and the criteria range.
   f. Click OK. Only the records that meet the criteria are displayed.
   g. Print the worksheet.
   h. Click Data, point to Filter, and then click Show All.
9. Now find the invoices that are both over $50.00 and have not been paid. Complete the following steps to apply the advanced criteria:
   a. Clear cell H3.

b. Click cell H2. Key **No**. The entries in the criteria range are now both in row 2.
c. Click any cell in the data list (not in the criteria range).
d. Click <u>D</u>ata, point to <u>F</u>ilter, and then click <u>A</u>dvanced Filter. The Advanced Filter dialog box appears.
e. Check to make sure the entry in the <u>L</u>ist range box is **$A$6:$H$106**.
f. The criteria range has to be changed because now it is A1 through H2, since the criteria are in row 2. Edit the entry in the <u>C</u>riteria Range box so that it says **$A$1:$H$2**.
g. Click OK. Only the records that meet the criteria are displayed.
h. Print the worksheet.
i. Click <u>D</u>ata, point to <u>F</u>ilter, and then click <u>S</u>how All.

10. Now find the invoices for when either Frobose spayed a cat, Martin spayed a cat, or Ketner spayed a cat. Complete the following steps to apply the advanced criteria:
a. Clear cells G2 and H2.
b. Key the following data in the cells indicated:

Cell	Data
D2	**Cat**
E2	**Spay**
F2	**Frobose**
D3	**Cat**
E3	**Spay**
F3	**Martin**
D4	**Cat**
E4	**Spay**
F4	**Ketner**

c. Click any cell in the data list (not in the criteria range).
d. Click <u>D</u>ata, point to <u>F</u>ilter, and then click <u>A</u>dvanced Filter. The Advanced Filter dialog box appears.
e. Check to make sure the entry in the <u>L</u>ist range box is **$A$6:$H$106**.
f. The criteria range has to be changed because now it is A1 through H4, since the criteria are in rows 2, 3, and 4. Edit the entry in the <u>C</u>riteria Range box so that it says **$A$1:$H$4**.
g. Click OK. Only the records that meet the criteria are displayed.
h. Print the worksheet.
i. Click <u>D</u>ata, point to <u>F</u>ilter, and then click <u>S</u>how All.

11. Save the worksheet with the same name (Excel E4, Ex 10).
12. Close the worksheet.

chapter summary

➤ A list is a labeled series of worksheet rows that contain similar sets of data such as student names and addresses. Each row in a list is a record. Each column in a list is a field. The labels in the first row of the list are field names. A value in a cell is a field value. The range of cells containing all the records, fields and field names is the list range.

➤ The first row of a list must contain labels or field names. There cannot be any blank rows in the list. There should not be any data in the rows or columns immediately adjacent to the list. Only one list can be stored on a worksheet.

➤ Records in an Excel list can be entered, edited, and deleted using a Data Form. Data Forms can be used to search for and find only those records that meet specific criteria.

➤ You can specify the exact data that can be entered into a cell using data validation. You can specify that the data being entered must meet specific criteria or that the data must be selected from a list.

➤ Sorting helps to organize the data in a list. Sort the data in a column by selecting any cell in the column to be sorted and clicking the Sort Ascending button to sort in ascending order or clicking the Sort Descending button to sort in descending order.

➤ To sort in an order other than ascending or descending, a custom list must be created. A custom list can be used to sort the first or top level of a sort only. Once a custom list has been created, it is always available.

➤ Outlining a worksheet provides a way to quickly find specific information in a long list of data. Levels of detail can be easily displayed or hidden by clicking the Show Detail symbol and the Hide Detail symbol. Rows or columns that provide a summary of the data using functions such as AVERAGE or SUM can be displayed quickly.

➤ When the data in a list is subtotaled using the subtotal command it is displayed in outline view. The list must be sorted by the field on which it is to be subtotaled before using the subtotal command. Levels of detail can be hidden or displayed in a list that has been subtotaled using the Show Detail symbol and the Hide Detail symbol.

➤ Filtering a list using AutoFilter temporarily displays only those records that meet certain criteria. Creating a custom AutoFilter enables the use of comparisons such as equals or is less than. An example of a custom AutoFilter search criterion might be Salary is greater than 50,000.

➤ An advanced filter extracts the unique records that meet specific criteria. The extracted data can be copied to a new location. With an advanced filter, a list is filtered using a criteria range. The criteria range usually is placed in the rows above the list. The header row (or field names) from the list has to be copied to the first row in the criteria range. The criteria used to filter the list are keyed into the criteria range. If the criteria are keyed into different rows, either one or the other condition may be met, but not necessarily both. If the criteria are keyed into the same row, then both conditions must be met.

commands review

	Mouse/Keyboard
Display the data form	Click Data, Form
Use data validation	Click Data, Validation
Perform a multi-level sort	Click Data, Sort
Create/Delete a custom list	Click Tools, Options, Custom Lists tab
Outline a worksheet manually	Click Data, Group and Outline, Group
Outline a worksheet automatically	Click Data, Group and Outline, Auto Outline
Subtotal a list	Click Data, Subtotals
Filter a list using AutoFilter	Click Data, Filter, AutoFilter
Filter a list using Advanced Filter	Click Data, Filter, Advanced Filter

thinking offline

Completion: In the space provided at the right, indicate the correct term, command, or symbol.

1. This term refers to the individual rows in a list.
2. This term refers to each column in a list.
3. Click this to display the data form.
4. Select this option from the drop-down list for the Allow box on the Data Validation dialog box if you want users to be able to enter data by selecting it from a list.
5. Click this tab on the Options dialog box to create a custom list.
6. This is the comparison operator that stands for not equal to.
7. Click this to subtotal a list.
8. Subtotals are displayed in this view.
9. This is what will be displayed if you click the Level 1 button after subtotaling a list.
10. Click this to turn the AutoFilter feature off.
11. Click this option on the Advanced Filters dialog box if you want to extract unique records from a list.
12. This term refers to the range of cells that is set aside as the area where the search conditions are entered when using Advanced Filters.

13. List the rule that must be followed when creating a list.

_____

_____

_____

14. Explain the difference between using the AutoFilter command and the Criteria button on a data form.

_____

_____

_____

15. Explain what records are going to be displayed using the following criteria range:

Sales Representative	Sales
Zimmerman	<1000
Robinson	<=1500

_____

_____

_____

working hands-on

(Note: In order to have room on your disk to save all the files you will be creating in the following assessments you will need to delete some files from your disk. You may delete the following files: Excel E4, Ex 01; Excel E4, Ex 02; Excel E4, Ex 03; Excel E4, Ex 04; Excel E4, Ex 05; Excel E4, Ex 06; Excel E4, Ex 07, Excel E4, Ex 08, Excel E4, Ex 09, and Excel E4, Ex 10. Check with your instructor to make sure it is all right to delete these files.)

Assessment 1

1. Open Excel Worksheet E4-05.
2. Save the worksheet using the Save <u>A</u>s command and name it Excel E4, SA 01.
3. Create a custom header with your name displayed at the left margin and the file name displayed at the right margin.

4. This worksheet keeps track of the profit the EastWest Crossroads Company makes on some of the items in its mail order catalog. Use the data form to add the following three records to the list:

Item Number	**GL-10-1**
Item	**Chinese Nesting Baskets**
Selling Price	**35**
Unit Cost	**18**

Item Number	**GM-39-1**
Item	**Asian Desk Set**
Selling Price	**125**
Unit Cost	**70**

Item Number	**GT-29-1**
Item	**Bird Box**
Selling Price	**85**
Unit Cost	**35**

5. The EastWest Crossroads Company no longer sells the Antler Bookends, Item Number GH-88-2. Use the data form to delete this record.
6. The cost of the Stained Glass Lamp, Item Number GH-82-2, has come down. Use the data form to edit this record so that the Selling Price is $225.00 and the Unit Cost is $150.00.
7. Adjust the page setup so that row 3 repeats at the top of each page as a print title.
8. Save the workbook with the same name (Excel E4, SA 01).
9. Print and close Excel E4, SA 01.

Assessment 2

1. Open Excel Worksheet E4-06.
2. Save the worksheet using the Save As command and name it Excel E4, SA 02.
3. Create a custom header with your name displayed at the left margin and the file name displayed at the right margin.
4. The Little Music Shop, a music store, sells opera CDs, videos, and laserdiscs. This worksheet is the beginning of a list to keep track of all the opera CDs, videos, and laserdiscs that the store sells. You want to use data validation to make it easier to enter more data into the list. The order numbers are all exactly six characters long. You want to set it up so that an order number that is anything other than six characters cannot be entered. Select column A and display the Data Validation dialog box. From the Allow drop-down list on the Settings tab, select *Text Length*. From the Data list box select *equal to*. Key **6** in the Length box.
5. Include an input message that has Order # for a title. The message should read, "Enter the 6-character order number."
6. Include an error message that has Error for a title. The message should read, "The order number must be exactly six characters long."
7. The only three entries that are ever made in the Medium column are Video, CD, or Laserdisc. Create a drop-down list from which the user can select Video, CD, or Laserdisc in order to enter data into column C.
8. Include an input message that has Medium for a title. The message should read, "Select an option from the drop-down list."

9. Include an error message that has Error for a title. The message should read, "The medium must be selected from the drop-down list."
10. The cost for any item in the list will never be over $100.00. Set up data validation so that any decimal entered into column D is less than or equal to $100.00.
11. Include an input message that has Cost for a title. The message should read, "Enter the cost of the video, CD, or laserdisc."
12. Include an error message that has Error for a title. The message should read, "The cost cannot be over $100.00."
13. Starting in row 18, enter the following records into the list:

Order #	Opera	Medium	Cost
COS09V	Cosi Fan Tutte	Video	44.95
COS61C	Cosi Fan Tutte	CD	37.95
DON40V	Don Carlo	Video	44.95
DON40L	Don Carlo	Laserdisc	79.95
DON79C	Don Carlo	CD	47.95

14. Save the workbook with the same name (Excel E4, SA 02).
15. Print and close Excel E4, SA 02.

Assessment 3

1. Open Excel Worksheet E4-07.
2. Save the worksheet using the Save As command and name it Excel E4, SA 03.
3. Create a custom header with your name displayed at the left margin and the file name displayed at the right margin.
4. Use the Sort Ascending button to sort the list by Order #. Print the worksheet.
5. Use the Sort Descending button to sort the list by Cost. Print the worksheet.
6. Perform a multi-level sort sorting first by Cost in descending order and then by Opera in ascending order. Print the list.
7. The Little Music Shop wants to be able to sort the list in the order of the popularity of the medium. Create the following custom list:

    CD
    Video
    Laserdisc

8. Sort the list first by the custom list created in step 7 in ascending order and then by Opera in ascending order. Print the worksheet.
9. Delete the custom list created in step 7.
10. Save the workbook with the same name (Excel E4, SA 03).
11. Close Excel E4, SA 03.

Assessment 4

1. Open Excel Worksheet E4-08.
2. Save the worksheet using the Save As command and name it Excel E4, SA 04.
3. Create a custom header with your name displayed at the left margin and the file name displayed at the right margin.
4. Outline the worksheet manually. Place all the records for CDs in one group, all the records for Videos in another group, and all the records for Laserdiscs in a third group.

5. Display only the average prices for the CDs, Videos, and Laserdiscs. Print the worksheet.
6. Display the details for the Videos. Print the worksheet.
7. Ungroup all the records for Videos.
8. Display the details for CDs and Laserdiscs.
9. Clear the outline for the entire worksheet.
10. Save the workbook with the same name (Excel E4, SA 04).
11. Close Excel E4, SA 04.

Assessment 5

1. Open Excel Worksheet E4-09.
2. Save the worksheet using the Save <u>A</u>s command and name it Excel E4, SA 05.
3. Create a custom header with your name displayed at the left margin and the file name displayed at the right margin.
4. This worksheet keeps track of The EastWest Crossroads Company invoices. There is an error in the address of Dennis Davis, which is invoice number 10-6119. Use the data form to find the record and change the address for Dennis Davis to P.O. Box 2860.
5. The invoice amount is currently incorrect on invoice 10-6118. Change the invoice amount to 82.58.
6. Sort the list in ascending order first by state, then by last name, and finally by first name.
7. Subtotal the Invoice Totals by State. Adjust the width of column H. Print the worksheet.
8. Collapse the list so that only the subtotals and grand total are displayed. Print the worksheet.
9. Expand the list so that all the details are displayed.
10. Remove the subtotals from the list.
11. Save the workbook with the same name (Excel E4, SA 05).
12. Close Excel E4, SA 05.

Assessment 6

1. Open Excel Worksheet E4-10.
2. Save the worksheet using the Save <u>A</u>s command and name it Excel E4, SA 06.
3. Create a custom header with your name displayed at the left margin and the file name displayed at the right margin.
4. Sort the list first by state in ascending order and then by Invoice Total in descending order.
5. Create a custom AutoFilter to find all of the invoices over $1,000. Print the worksheet.
6. Display all the records.
7. Create custom AutoFilters, one for the Invoice Totals and one for State, that will find all the invoices from either California or New York that are under $500. Print the worksheet.
8. Display all the records.
9. Turn the AutoFilter feature off.
10. Save the workbook with the same name (Excel E4, SA 06).
11. Close Excel E4, SA 06.

Assessment 7

1. Open Excel Worksheet E4-11.
2. Save the worksheet using the Save As command and name it Excel E4, SA 07.
3. Create a custom header with your name displayed at the left margin and the file name displayed at the right margin.
4. This worksheet keeps track of the salary and commissions for the sales representatives of Case 'n Crate, a company that manufactures and sells wooden products. Claire Hoag received a raise. Use the data form to find her record and change her salary to 1200.
5. The sales figures for Ria Munoz are incorrect. Use the data form to find her record and change the sales amount to 12299.76
6. Sort the list in ascending order first by region, next by percent commission, and finally by last name.
7. Subtotal the Total column by Region. Adjust the width of column H. Print the worksheet.
8. Use the Hide Detail button to hide the detail for The East Central region, the South Central region, the Southeast Region, and the Southwest region. Print the worksheet.
9. Expand the list so that all the details are displayed.
10. Remove the subtotals from the list.
11. Create a custom AutoFilter command to find all of the sales over $9,000. Print the worksheet.
12. Display all the records.
13. Create custom AutoFilters, one for Region and one for Sales to find all of the records from either the South Central region or the East Central region that have sales over $10,000. Print the worksheet.
14. Display all the records.
15. Use AutoFilter to find the records of the sales representatives whose sales are in the top 10 percent. Print the worksheet.
16. Turn the AutoFilter feature off.
17. Save the workbook with the same name (Excel E4, SA 07).
18. Close Excel E4, SA 07.

Assessment 8

1. Open Excel Worksheet E4-12.
2. Save the worksheet using the Save As command and name it Excel E4, SA 08.
3. Create a custom header with your name displayed at the left margin and the file name displayed at the right margin.
4. Sort the list in ascending order by Opera.
5. You want to create a unique list of the opera names. Select cells B3 through B39. Use Advanced Filter to copy the unique records only to cell F3.
6. Adjust the width of column F.
7. Print the worksheet.
8. Save the workbook with the same name (Excel E4, SA 08).
9. Close Excel E4, SA 08.

Assessment 9

1. Open Excel Worksheet E4-13.
2. Save the worksheet using the Save <u>A</u>s command and name it Excel E4, SA 09.
3. Create a custom header with your name displayed at the left margin and the file name displayed at the right margin.
4. Sort the list in ascending order by last name.
5. Set up a criteria range for this worksheet. Insert four blank rows above row 2.
6. Copy the labels from row 6 to row 1.
7. Name the range of cells A1 through H3 Criteria.
8. Use Advanced Filter to find the records from either the East Central or the North Central region. Filter the list in place. Print the worksheet.
9. Show all the records.
10. Sort the list in ascending order first by Region then by Sales.
11. Use Advanced Filter to find the records that are either from the Northeast region or the sales are over $12,000. Filter the list in place. Print the worksheet.
12. Show all the records.
13. Use Advanced Filter to find either the records that are from the East Central region that are over $10,000 or the records from the Southeast region that are over $10,000. Filter the list in place. Print the worksheet.
14. Show all the records.
15. Save the workbook with the same name (Excel E4, SA 09).
16. Close Excel Ch 11, SA 09.

Assessment 10

1. You want to know if wildcard characters can be used when filtering data. Use Microsoft Excel Help to search for the Help topic *Wildcard characters you can use to find text or numbers*. Read and print the Help topic.
2. Open Excel E4, SA 09. You created this file in Assessment 9. Save the worksheet using the Save <u>A</u>s command and name it Excel E4, SA 10.
3. Using the information from the Help topic, created an advanced filter using a wildcard character to find any region that ends with *west*. Make sure you use the correct criteria range for the filter. Filter the list in place. Print the worksheet.
4. Show all the records.
5. Save the workbook with the same name (Excel E4, SA 10) and close it.

Chapter 05E

Using Excel's Analysis Tools

PERFORMANCE OBJECTIVES

Upon successful completion of chapter 5, you will be able to:
- Create a PivotTable report using the PivotTable Wizard.
- Format a PivotTable report using AutoFormat.
- Sort and filter a PivotTable report.
- Hide and show detail in a PivotTable report.
- Analyze data using a PivotTable report.
- Create a PivotChart report.
- Create an interactive PivotTable for the Web.
- Analyze data using Goal Seek.
- Analyze data using Solver.
- Create Scenarios.

When worksheets become large and complex, being able to summarize and analyze the data stored in them becomes increasingly important. Excel includes a number of features to help you analyze data, such as PivotTable reports, PivotChart Reports, Goal Seek, Scenarios, and Solver. The purpose of this chapter is to show you how to analyze data using Excel's analysis tools.

Introduction to PivotTables

There are several layers of complexity involved when analyzing data in an Excel worksheet. Chapter 4 introduced you to some of the simpler ways to analyze data. The data form allows you to look up and retrieve specific records one record at a time. AutoFilter allows you to extract particular records from the list based on specific criteria. Advanced Filter allows you to create more complex search criteria for extracting records. PivotTables add another level of complexity for analyzing data. With PivotTables you can compare several facts about one element in a data list.

E-161

A PivotTable is an interactive table that quickly summarizes and analyzes large amounts of data. A PivotTable is interactive because you can easily rotate or "pivot" its rows and columns in order to summarize the data in a different way. The interactive PivotTable allows you to easily change the view of the data so that you can see more or less detail. PivotTable reports are useful when you have a long list of figures that you want to summarize in a variety of ways. The PivotTable report summarizes the data in one field by breaking it down according to the data in another field. Figure 5.1 illustrates an example of a PivotTable. The data list in columns A through D lists the first and second quarter sales by sales representative for all the sales regions. This data list is the source data for the PivotTable report in cells F1 through I10. The PivotTable report summarizes the data in the Sales field by breaking it down according to the data in the Region field and the Qtr field. This PivotTable report allows you to easily compare the first and second quarter sales for each sales region. As shown in figure 5.2, you can easily "pivot" the table and have the column field become the row field and vice versa.

figure 5.1

A PivotTable

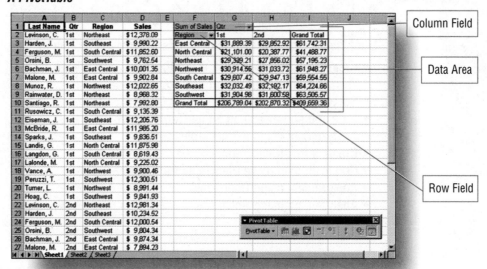

Column Field

Data Area

Row Field

figure 5.2

Pivoting a PivotTable

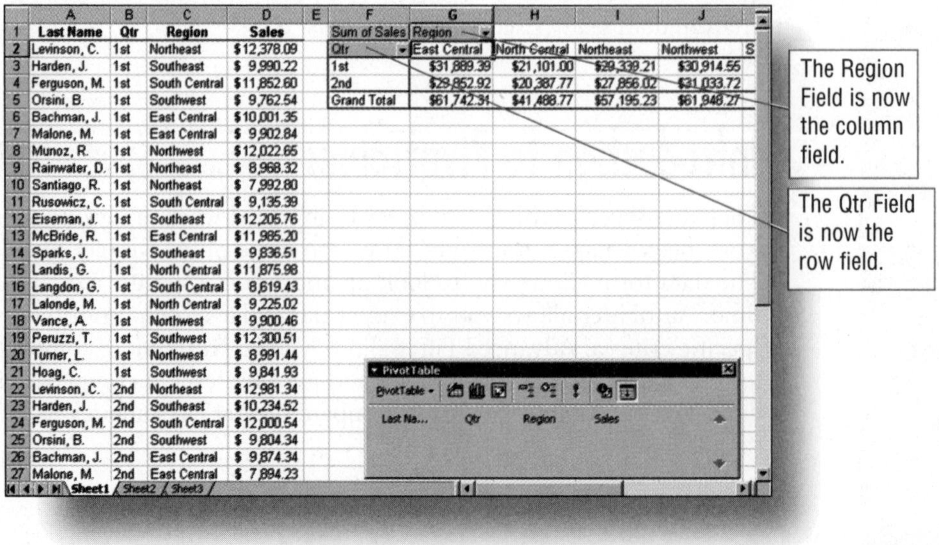

The Region Field is now the column field.

The Qtr Field is now the row field.

Creating a PivotTable

A PivotTable report is based on its source data. The source data for a PivotTable can be created from a list, a database, multiple Excel worksheets or another PivotTable. Chapter 4 covered how to set up a list in Excel. The rules for setting up a list in Excel that were covered in chapter 4 must be followed when using a list as the source data for a PivotTable report.

Instead of working with columns and rows, a PivotTable report works with fields and items. Each field in a PivotTable report corresponds to a column in the source data. The name of the field in the PivotTable report is the column header for that column in the list. Look at figure 5.3, for example. "Region" is a field in the PivotTable report and it corresponds to the Region column in the source data. An item in a PivotTable report is a unique value in a field. In figure 5.3, *1st* and *2nd* are items. The Qtr field contains the items 1st and 2nd. "Sum of Sales" is a data field. A data field is a field from the source list that contains data that is summarized in a PivotTable report. Data field values can be summarized in the PivotTable report using summary functions such as Sum, Count, or Average.

If you do not see the PivotTable and PivotChart Report button on the Standard toolbar, click the down arrow at the right edge of the toolbar and point to Add or Remove buttons. Click PivotTable and PivotChart Report.

figure
5.3

How Data Is Organized in a PivotTable Report

"Sum of Sales" is a data field. The data that is summarized comes from the data field.

"Qtr" is a field in this PivotTable report. It corresponds to the Qtr column in the source data.

"1st" and "2nd" are items. The Qtr field contains the items 1st and 2nd.

"Region" is a field in this PivotTable report. It corresponds to the Region column in the source data.

Sum of Sales	Qtr		
Region	1st	2nd	Grand Total
East Central	$31,889.39	$29,852.92	$61,742.31
North Central	$21,101.00	$20,387.77	$41,488.77
Northeast	$29,339.21	$27,856.02	$57,195.23
Northwest	$30,914.55	$31,033.72	$61,948.27
South Central	$29,607.42	$29,947.13	$59,554.55
Southeast	$32,032.49	$32,192.17	$64,224.66
Southwest	$31,904.98	$31,600.59	$63,505.57
Grand Total	$206,789.04	$202,870.32	$409,659.36

The PivotTable and PivotChart Report Button

When you are creating a PivotTable from an Excel list, the first step is to name the range of cells that make up the list *Database*. Excel will then automatically recognize the list as the data source. Excel's PivotTable Wizard takes you step-by-step through the process of creating a PivotTable. Figure 5.4 illustrates the three dialog boxes that make up the PivotTable Wizard. Once you have named your list *Database*, click Data and then click PivotTable and PivotChart Report. Step 1 of the PivotTable and PivotChart Wizard is displayed. You can also access the PivotTable Wizard by clicking the PivotTable and PivotChart Report button on the Standard toolbar. As shown in figure 5.4, you have to identify where the data source to be used is located and whether you want to create a PivotTable or a PivotChart. In step 2 you have to identify the range of cells that make up the data source. If you named the list *Database*, then Excel will automatically enter the correct range. In step 3 you have to identify whether you want the PivotTable placed on a new worksheet or on the same worksheet as the list. When you have made all the necessary selections, click the Finish button.

If you do not name the list to be used as a data source Database, another way to have Excel automatically recognize the list as the data source is to position the cell pointer in the list before activating the PivotTable Wizard.

The PivotTable and PivotChart Wizard

If the PivotTable Toolbar is not displayed, click View, point to Toolbars and click PivotTable.

In order for the field buttons to be displayed on the PivotTable toolbar, the toolbar must be undocked and the Display Fields button on the toolbar must be pressed in.

The order in which you should drag fields to the PivotTable Diagram is fields in the row, column, and page areas first. Drag fields to the data area last. Using this order helps to prevent delays when dropping fields from the PivotTable toolbar to the PivotTable diagram.

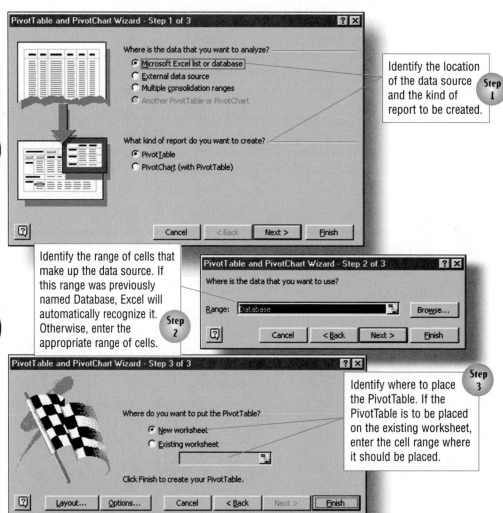

Once you click the Finish button, the PivotTable diagram and PivotTable toolbar is displayed as shown in figure 5.5. On the PivotTable toolbar is a group of field buttons. Drag the fields with data to be displayed in rows to the *Drop Row Fields Here* area of the diagram. Drag the fields with data to be displayed in columns to the *Drop Column Fields Here* area of the diagram. More than one field can be dragged to each area. Drag fields to be used as page fields to the *Drop Page Fields Here* area. To remove a field from the PivotTable, simply drag it off the diagram. To rearrange the fields in the PivotTable, simply drag them from one area to another.

figure

5.5

The PivotTable Diagram and PivotTable Toolbar

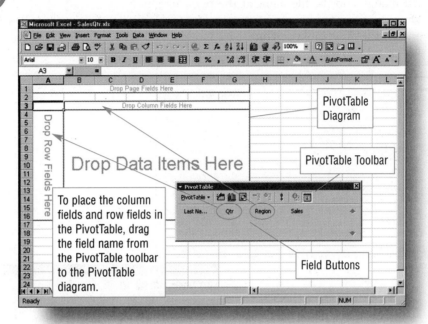

exercise

Creating a PivotTable and Filtering a PivotTable Report

1. Open Excel Worksheet E5-01.
2. Save the worksheet using the Save As command and name it Excel E5, Ex 01.
3. This worksheet contains a list of orders made to the Whitewater Canoe and Kayak Corporation by various stores. You are going to use this list to create a PivotTable. Complete the following steps to name the range of cells that comprises the list:
   a. Select cells A3 through F68.
   b. Click in the Name Box at the left side of the Formula Bar and key **Database**.
   c. Press Enter.
4. Complete the following steps to create the PivotTable.
   a. Click Data and then click PivotTable and PivotChart Report.
   b. The PivotTable and PivotChart Wizard - Step 1 of 3 dialog box is displayed. You want the default selections to analyze the data in a Microsoft Excel list or database and to create a PivotTable. Click Next.
   c. The PivotTable and PivotChart Wizard - Step 2 of 3 is displayed. Database should already be entered in the Range box. Click Next.
   d. The PivotTable and PivotChart Wizard - Step 3 of 3 dialog box is displayed. The default option is to put the PivotTable on a new worksheet, which is fine. Click Finish.

e. The PivotTable diagram and PivotTable toolbar is displayed. Double-click the worksheet tab and key **PivotTable**. Press Enter.

f. Create a custom header for the PivotTable worksheet that displays your name at the left margin and the file name at the right margin.

g. Drag the Store field button from the PivotTable toolbar to the *Drop Row Fields Here* area of the PivotTable diagram.

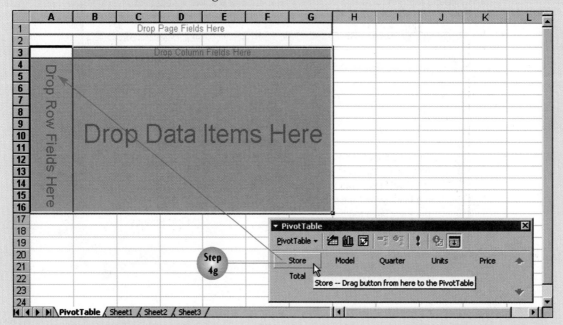

h. Drag the Model field button from the PivotTable toolbar to the *Drop Column Fields Here* area of the PivotTable diagram.

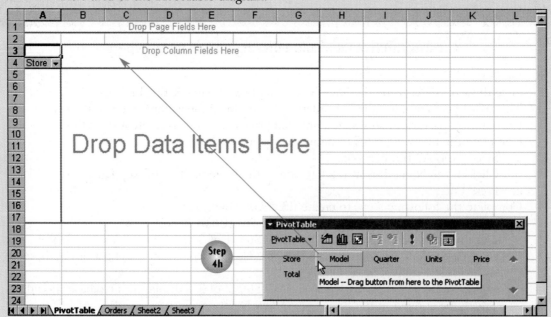

i. Drag the Units field button from the PivotTable toolbar to *the Drop Data Items Here* area of the PivotTable diagram.

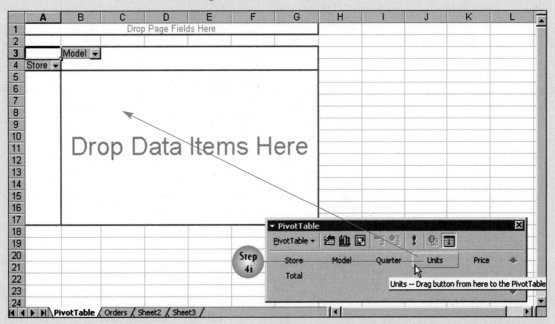

5. The PivotTable is displayed on the worksheet. The PivotTable summarizes how many units of each model were ordered by each store. Grand Totals for the total number of units that were ordered by each store and the total number units that were sold of each model are also displayed. Print the worksheet.

6. You want to rearrange the PivotTable so that you see the data as a summarized list. Complete the following steps to rearrange the PivotTable:

   a. Move the mouse pointer over the Model field button in the PivotTable diagram. Notice that the mouse pointer changes to a four-headed arrow shape.

   b. Click and drag the Model field button until it is under the Store field button. The Models are summarized in the first column, the Stores in the second, and the Totals are in the third column. Print the worksheet.

A	B	C	D	E	F
1	Drop Page Fields Here				
2					
3 Sum of Units	Model ▾				
4 Store ▾	Excursion	Pathfinder	Trekker	Grand Total	
5 Adventures Unlimited	32	52	20	104	
6 Backwoods Country	27	64	23	114	
7 Camping and More	67	15	114	196	
8 NorthWest Camping	47	40	12	99	
9 Outdoor Adventures	62	38	12	112	
10 Outdoor Sporting Goods	30	9	7	46	
11 The Canoe Shop		28	24	52	
12 Water Sports	66	103	17	186	
13 Grand Total	331	349	229	909	
14					
15					

Step 6a

Step 6b

   c. Click the Store field button on the PivotTable diagram and drag it over the Model field button on the PivotTable diagram. Now the Stores are summarized in the first column and the models in the second. Print the worksheet.

d. Now you want to display only the units sold of the Excursion. Click the down arrow to the right of the Model field button.

e. Click the Pathfinder and Trekker check boxes so that they are no longer selected.

f. Click OK. The only figure displayed now represents the units sold of the Excursions.

g. Click the down arrow to the right of the Model field button.

h. Click the Pathfinder check box and the Trekker check box so that they are selected. Click OK.

7. Data in the PivotTable can be filtered by dragging a field button to the Drop Page Fields Here area of the PivotTable diagram. Using a Page field allows you to display the data for a single item at a time. Complete the following steps to use a Page field:

a. Drag the Model button from the PivotTable diagram to the *Drop Page Fields Here* area of the PivotTable diagram.

b. Now the PivotTable is displaying the total for all the Models. Click the down arrow to the right of the cell that has (All) entered in it. Click *Pathfinder*.

c. Click OK. Now the PivotTable is displaying the total number of Pathfinders ordered by each store.

d. Click the down arrow to the right of the cell that now has Pathfinder entered in it and select *Excursion*. Click OK. Now the PivotTable is displaying the total number of Excursions ordered by each store.

e. Click the down arrow to the right of the cell that now has Excursion entered in it and select *All*. Click OK.

8. The PivotTable you have worked with so far has summarized the number of units sold. More than one field can be summarized at a time. Complete the following steps to add a second field to be summarized:

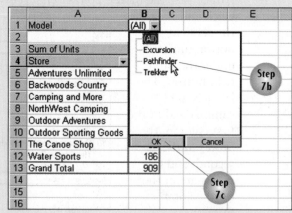

a. The Data Items area of the PivotTable now lists the total number of units ordered by each store. Click and drag the Total field button from the PivotTable toolbar to the cell under the Total column heading.

	A	B	C	D	E	F	G	H
1	Model	(All) ▾						
2								
3	Sum of Units							
4	Store	▾	Total					
5	Adventures Unlimited	104						
6	Backwoods Country	114						
7	Camping and More	196						
8	NorthWest Camping	99						
9	Outdoor Adventures	112						
10	Outdoor Sporting Goods	46						
11	The Canoe Shop	52						
12	Water Sports	186						
13	Grand Total	909						

PivotTable toolbar: PivotTable ▾ Store Model Quarter Units Price

Total

Total -- Drag button from here to the PivotTable

Step 8a

b. A summary for both the total number of units each store ordered together with the total cost for all the units is now displayed. Print the worksheet.

c. Drag the Data field button on the PivotTable so that it is under the Store field button on the PivotTable.

d. Print the worksheet.

9. Save the worksheet with the same name (Excel E5, Ex 01). You are going to use this worksheet in exercise 2.

10. Close the worksheet.

	A	B	C	D
1	Model	(All) ▾		
2				
3	Store	▾	Data ▾	Total
4	Adventures Unlimited	Sum of Units	104	
5		Sum of Total	105456	
6	Backwoods Country	Sum of Units	114	
7		Sum of Total	119446	
8	Camping and More	Sum of Units	196	
9		Sum of Total	199414	
10	NorthWest Camping	Sum of Units	99	
11		Sum of Total	92261	
12	Outdoor Adventures	Sum of Units	112	
13		Sum of Total	100148	
14	Outdoor Sporting Goods	Sum of Units	46	
15		Sum of Total	39104	
16	The Canoe Shop	Sum of Units	52	
17		Sum of Total	60948	
18	Water Sports	Sum of Units	186	
19		Sum of Total	183544	
20	Total Sum of Units		909	
21	Total Sum of Total		900321	
22				
23				
24				

Step 8c

◄ ◄ ► ►◄ \ PivotTable / Orders / Sheet2 / Sheet3 /

Formatting and Sorting a PivotTable

A PivotTable report can be formatted much the same way as the cells on a worksheet can be formatted. You can select all the cells belonging to a field by moving the mouse pointer to the top of the data field label if the data is in columns. The pointer turns into a down arrow. If the data is in rows, move the mouse pointer to the left of the data field label and the mouse pointer turns into an arrow pointing to the right. Once the mouse pointer turns into an arrow, click. All the items related to the particular data field are selected. When the items are selected, they can be formatted as you would format any other cell on the worksheet. You can also select and format a single data item.

You cannot use conditional formatting or data validation in a PivotTable Report.

The entire report can be formatted using the Format Report button on the PivotTable toolbar. When you click the Format Report button, the AutoFormat dialog box shown in figure 5.6 is displayed. Click one of the report styles and click OK.

The Format Report Button

If you need to sort or to change the order of items, you can manually move them. To move an item, drag the border of the item. As you drag, an I-shaped marker shows you the location of the item you are dragging. When you reach the location you want, release the mouse button and the item will appear in its new location.

figure 5.6

The AutoFormat Dialog Box

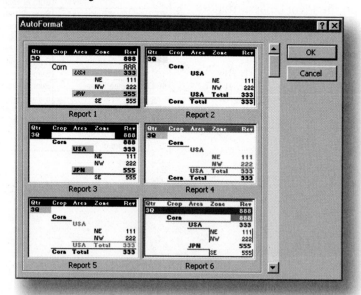

You can also control how the items in a field are sorted using the PivotTable Field Advanced Options dialog box, shown in figure 5.7. To display this dialog box, double-click a field button on the PivotTable and click the Advanced button. When Manual is selected under the AutoSort options you can manually move the items to the desired order. The Ascending option sorts the items in ascending order and the Descending option sorts the items in descending order. The AutoShow options allow you to manually select the items to be shown or to show only a specific number of the top or bottom items based on a specific field.

figure
5.7

The PivotTable Field Advanced Options Dialog Box

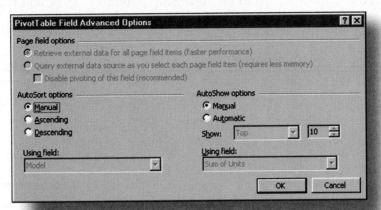

exercise 2

Formatting a PivotTable Report

1. Open Excel E5, Ex 01. You created this worksheet in exercise 1.
2. Save the worksheet using the Save <u>A</u>s command and name it Excel E5, Ex 02.
3. If necessary, click the PivotTable worksheet tab.
4. Edit the custom header so that the file name is displayed at the right margin.
5. Numbers from the Total field need to be formatted as currency. Before you can do that, however, you need to arrange the PivotTable report so that those numbers are displayed in columns by themselves. Complete the following steps to arrange the layout of the PivotTable report so the numbers that need to be formatted as currency are displayed in individual columns.
    a. Drag the Data field button in cell A3 to cell C3.

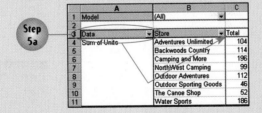

    b. Drag the Model page field button in cell A1 to the Data field button in cell B3.

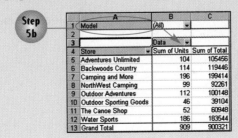

6. Complete the following steps to format the numbers from the Total field as currency.
    a. Place the mouse pointer over the top border of cell C5. It should turn into an arrow pointing down. Once the mouse pointer turns into an arrow pointing down, click. All the columns related to the Total field (columns C, E, G, and I) are selected.

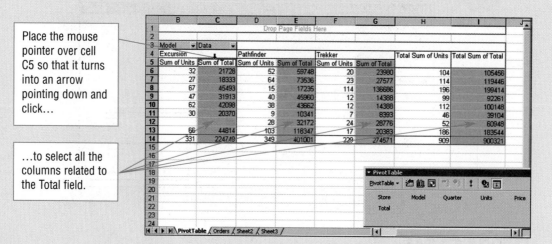

Place the mouse pointer over cell C5 so that it turns into an arrow pointing down and click...

...to select all the columns related to the Total field.

    b. Click the Currency Style button on the Formatting toolbar.
    c. Click the Decrease Decimal button on the Formatting toolbar twice.

7. Since the Camping and More store has placed the most orders, you would like to keep track of this one particular store in your PivotTable. Complete the following steps to format the entries for Camping and More:
    a. Place the mouse pointer to the left of row 8 (at the left side of cell A8). It should turn into an arrow pointing to the right. Once the pointer turns into an arrow pointing to the right, click. Row 8 in the PivotTable report should be selected.

Place the mouse pointer to the left of row 8 so that it turns into an arrow pointing to the right and click...

...to select row 8 in the PivotTable report.

    b. Click the down arrow to the right of the Fill Color button. Click the Pale Blue option, the sixth option in the fifth row.

c. Drag the Data field button in cell C3 to the Store field button in cell A5. The gray I-shaped pointer showing where the field will be inserted should be to the left of column A. Notice that each instance of Camping and More is highlighted in blue and that all the dollar amounts are still formatted as currency.

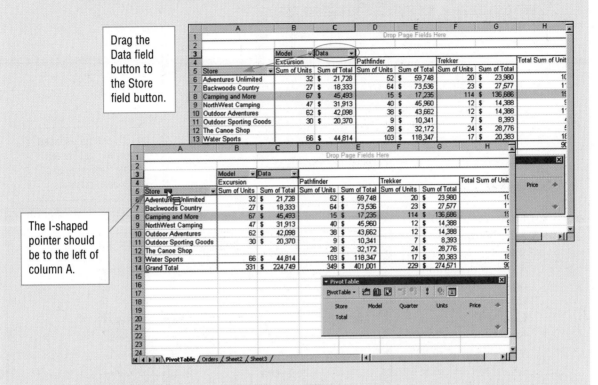

Drag the Data field button to the Store field button.

The I-shaped pointer should be to the left of column A.

d. Print the PivotTable worksheet.
8. Save the worksheet with the same name (Excel E5, Ex 02). You are going to use this worksheet in exercise 3.
9. Close the worksheet.

exercise 3

Sorting a PivotTable Report and Filtering a PivotTable Report

1. Open Excel E5, Ex 02. You created this worksheet in exercise 2.
2. Save the worksheet using the Save As command and name it Excel E5, Ex 03.
3. If necessary, click the PivotTable worksheet tab.
4. You want the models displayed in order from the model that sold the most number of units to the model that sold the least number of units. That order would be Pathfinder, Excursion, Trekker. Complete the following steps to change the order in which the models are displayed:
   a. Click cell C4.

b. Drag the right border of cell C4 until the I-shaped pointer is between the Pathfinder and Trekker columns.

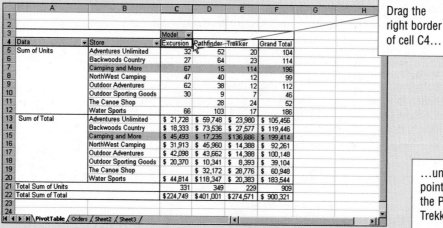

Drag the right border of cell C4...

...until the I-shaped pointer is between the Pathfinder and Trekker columns.

5. Now you want to sort the report so that the stores are listed in descending order according to their grand totals. Complete the following steps to sort the entire table:

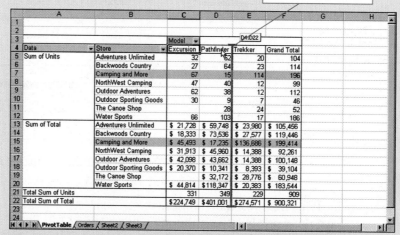

a. Double-click cell B4, the Store field button.

b. On the PivotTable Field dialog box, click Advanced.

c. The PivotTable Field Advanced Options dialog box appears. Under AutoSort options, click Descending.

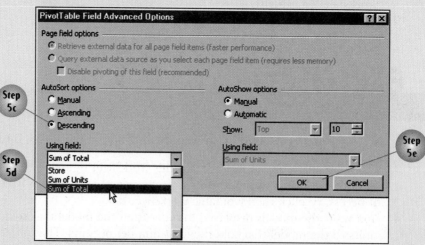

Step 5c

Step 5d

Step 5e

d. Click the down arrow to the right of the Using field box. Click *Sum of Total*.

e. Click OK.

f. Click OK again.

6. Now you want to display the top four stores according to the units ordered. Complete the following steps to filter the report:

a. Double-click cell B4, the Store field button.
b. On the PivotTable Field dialog box, click Advanced.
c. Under AutoShow options, click Automatic.
d. Make sure Top is selected in the first Show box. In the second Show box, enter 4.
e. Make sure Sum of Units is selected in the Using field box.
f. Click OK.
g. Click OK again. Only the top four stores are displayed. Notice that the Total Sum of Units, Total Sum of Total and Grand Total reflect only the orders from these top four stores.

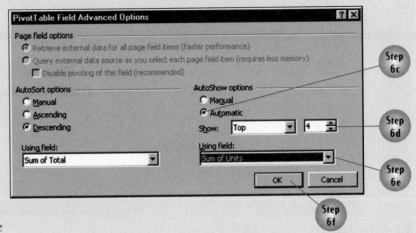

Step 6c

Step 6d

Step 6e

Step 6f

7. Print the PivotTable worksheet.
8. Turn the filter off by double-clicking cell B4, the Store field button, clicking Advanced, and under AutoShow options, clicking Manual. Click OK twice.
9. Save the worksheet with the same name (Excel E5, Ex 03). You are going to use this worksheet in exercise 4.
10. Close the worksheet.

Managing a PivotTable Report

If PivotTable Reports contain long lists of items, reading the information in them may become difficult. On the PivotTable toolbar there is a Hide Detail button and a Show Detail button. Hiding details for items in a PivotTable report can make the report easier to read. To hide details click the appropriate field button on the PivotTable report and then click the Hide Detail button on the PivotTable toolbar. To show the detail, click the field button again and click the Show Detail button on the PivotTable toolbar.

Hiding details for items is not the same as filtering items. There are two ways to filter items: by clicking the down arrow to the right of the field button on the PivotTable report and selecting the fields to be displayed, and by using a page field. When a list is filtered, the report assumes the items that are not displayed are not a part of the report at all. Therefore they are not included in any of the totals. When you hide details, the report assumes the items that are hidden are still a part of the report so even though the individual items are not displayed in the report, their numbers are still included in the totals.

At times it may be useful to see exactly which cells from the original list went into making a particular value in the report. To see the cells from the list that go into making a value in the report, double-click the cell containing the value you want to check. The appropriate rows from the original list are displayed.

You can remove subtotals and grand totals from a PivotTable report. To remove a subtotal, double-click the appropriate field button. The PivotTable Field dialog box shown in figure 5.8 is displayed. Select None if the subtotals are not to be displayed. To remove grand totals from a report, right-click on any cell in the

The Hide Detail Button

The Show Detail Button

A cell on the PivotTable Report must be selected in order for the PivotTable toolbar to be active.

PivotTable report and click Table Options on the shortcut menu. The PivotTable Options dialog box shown in figure 5.9 is displayed. On this dialog box there is a selection for Grand totals for columns and one for Grand totals for rows. If the grand totals are displayed in columns make sure the check box for the Grand totals for columns option is not selected. If the grand totals are displayed in rows make sure the check box for the Grand totals for rows option is not selected. Click OK.

figure 5.8

The PivotTable Field Dialog Box

If the subtotals are not to be displayed in a PivotTable report, select None.

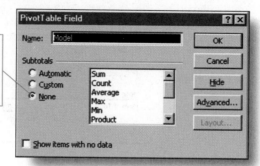

figure 5.9

The PivotTable Options Dialog Box

If the grand totals are not to be displayed in a PivotTable report, the Grand totals check boxes should not be selected.

If formatting is lost when you change the layout of a PivotTable report, click the down arrow to the right of the PivotTable button on the PivotTable toolbar, click Table Options, and make sure the Preserve formatting check box is selected. Changes to cell borders are not retained when you change the layout of a PivotTable report.

The PivotTable Wizard Button

You can manage the layout of the PivotTable report using the PivotTable Wizard. To do so, click the PivotTable Wizard button on the PivotTable toolbar. The PivotTable and PivotChart Wizard - Step 3 of 3 dialog box is displayed as in figure 5.4. Click the Layout button. The PivotTable and PivotChart Wizard - Layout dialog box as shown in figure 5.10 is displayed. You can rearrange the layout of the PivotTable report by dragging the field buttons on the right side of the dialog box to the PivotTable diagram in the middle of the dialog box. To remove a field from the PivotTable, drag the field button off the PivotTable diagram. When you have finished rearranging the report, click OK. The PivotTable and PivotChart Wizard - Step 3 of 3 dialog box is displayed again. Click Finish.

figure 5.10

The PivotTable and PivotChart Wizard - Layout Dialog Box

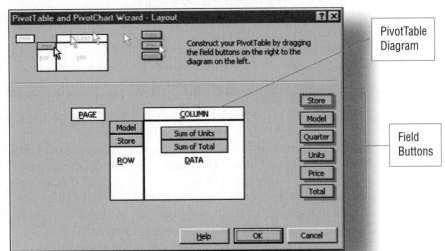

PivotTable Diagram

Field Buttons

exercise 4

Hiding Detail in a PivotTable Report,
Changing the Layout of a Report Using the PivotTable Wizard,
Removing Subtotals and Grand Totals from a PivotTable Report

1. Open Excel E5, Ex 03. You created this worksheet in exercise 3.
2. Save the worksheet using the Save <u>A</u>s command and name it Excel E5, Ex 04.
3. If necessary, click the PivotTable worksheet tab.
4. Edit the custom header so that the file name is displayed at the right margin.
5. Rearrange the layout of the PivotTable report by dragging the Model field button in cell C3 to the Data field button in cell A4. The I-shaped pointer should be to the left of column A.

Drag the Model field button to the Data field button.

The I-shaped pointer should be to the left of column A.

	A	B	C	D	E	F	G	H
1		Drop Page Fields Here						
2								
3			Model					
4	Data	Store	Pathfinder	Excursion	Trekker	Grand Total		
5	Sum of Units	Camping and More	15	67	114	196		
6		Water Sports	103	66	17	186		
7		Backwoods Country	64	27	23	114		
8		Adventures Unlimited	52	32	20	104		
9		Outdoor Adventures	38	62	12	112		
10		NorthWest Camping	40	47	12	99		
11		The Canoe Shop	28		24	52		
12		Outdoor Sporting Goods	9	30	7	46		
13	Sum of Total	Camping and More	$ 17,235	$ 45,493	$136,686	$ 199,414		
14		Water Sports	$118,347	$ 44,814	$ 20,383	$ 183,544		
15		Backwoods Country	$ 73,536	$ 18,333	$ 27,577	$ 119,446		
16		Adventures Unlimited	$ 59,748	$ 21,728	$ 23,980	$ 105,456		
17		Outdoor Adventures	$ 43,662	$ 42,098	$ 14,388	$ 100,148		
18		NorthWest Camping						
19		The Canoe Shop						
20		Outdoor Sporting Goods						
21	Total Sum of Units							
22	Total Sum of Total							
23								
24								

PivotTable ▾   Store   Model   Quarter   Units   Price   Total

Sheet1 **PivotTable** Orders Sheet2 Sheet3

6. You want to compare the orders for each model, but it is difficult to do that with all the stores listed. Complete the following steps to hide the detail.

   a. Click the Model field button in cell A3.

   b. Click the Hide Detail button on the PivotTable toolbar. Only the figures for the three models are displayed.

   c. Print the PivotTable worksheet.

   d. Next you want to show the details for the Excursion model only. Click cell A6.

   e. Click the Show Detail button on the PivotTable toolbar. The details for the Excursion model only are displayed.

   f. Display all the detail by clicking the Model field button in cell A3 and clicking the Show Detail button on the PivotTable toolbar.

7. Find the cell that displays the total number of units of the Trekker model ordered by the store Camping and More. The number is considerably higher than all the other orders and you want to see the cells in the source data that make up this value. Complete the following steps to see the values from the source data that this number summarizes.

   a. Double-click the cell showing the units ordered of Trekkers by Camping and More. The values from the data source are displayed.

   b. Click the PivotTable worksheet tab to return to the PivotTable report.

8. You want to rearrange the layout of the report using the PivotTable Wizard. Complete the following steps to use the PivotTable Wizard to change the layout of the report.

   a. Click the PivotTable Wizard button on the PivotTable toolbar.

   b. The PivotTable and PivotChart Wizard - Step 3 of 3 dialog box is displayed. Click Layout.

   c. The PivotTable and PivotChart Wizard - Layout dialog box is displayed. Drag the Quarter button to the COLUMN area on the PivotTable diagram.

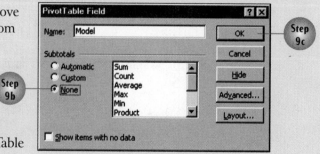

   d. Drag the Sum of Units field button off the PivotTable. The only button that should be in the DATA area on the PivotTable diagram is Sum of Total.

   e. Click OK.

   f. Click Finish.

9. Complete the following steps to remove the subtotals and the grand totals from the report:

   a. Double-click the Model field button in cell A4.

   b. Under Subtotals, click the None option.

   c. Click OK.

   d. Right-click any cell in the PivotTable

report.

e. Click Table Options on the shortcut menu.

f. Click the check box next to Grand totals for columns and the check box next to Grand totals for rows so that they are not selected.

g. Click OK.

10. Print the PivotTable worksheet.

11. Complete the following steps to display the subtotals and grand totals.

a. Double-click the Model field button in cell A4.

b. Under Subtotals, click the Automatic option.

c. Click OK.

d. Right-click any cell in the PivotTable report.

e. Click Table Options on the shortcut menu.

f. Click the check box next to Grand totals for columns and the check box next to Grand totals for rows so that they are selected.

g. Click OK.

12. Save the worksheet with the same name (Excel E5, Ex 04). You are going to use this worksheet in exercise 5.

13. Close the worksheet.

Step 9f → (points to PivotTable Options dialog)

Step 9g → (points to PivotTable Options dialog)

PivotTable Options dialog box:

Name: PivotTable9

Format options
- ☐ Grand totals for columns
- ☐ Grand totals for rows
- ☑ AutoFormat table
- ☐ Subtotal hidden page items
- ☐ Merge labels
- ☑ Preserve formatting
- ☑ Repeat item labels on each printed page
- ☐ Mark Totals with *

Page layout: Down, Then Over

Fields per column: 0

- ☐ For error values, show:
- ☑ For empty cells, show:
- ☐ Set print titles

Data options

Data source options:
- ☑ Save data with table layout
- ☑ Enable drilldown
- ☐ Refresh on open
- ☐ Refresh every 0 minutes

External data options:
- ☐ Save password
- ☐ Background query
- ☐ Optimize memory

[OK] [Cancel]

exercise 5

Formatting a PivotTable Report Using AutoFormat

1. Open Excel E5, Ex 04. You created this worksheet in exercise 4.
2. Save the worksheet using the Save As command and name it Excel E5, Ex 05.
3. If necessary, click the PivotTable worksheet tab.
4. To format the entire PivotTable report using AutoFormat, complete the following steps:
   a. Click the Format Report button on the PivotTable toolbar.

b.   The AutoFormat dialog box is displayed. Click the option for Report 4.
c.   Click OK.
d.   Use the Page Break Preview command to adjust the layout so that the first and second quarter figures print on the first page and the 3rd quarter figures, 4th quarter figures, and grand totals print on the second page.

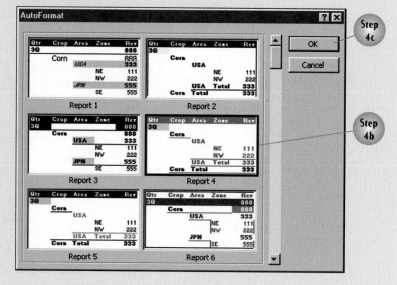

e.   Return to Normal view.
f.   When you used AutoFormat, all the currency formatting was lost. Place the mouse pointer over cell D3, the Total column. When the mouse pointer turns into an arrow pointing down, click to select all the numbers in the Total field. Format the numbers as currency with no decimal places. Adjust the column width if necessary.
5.   Print the PivotTable worksheet.
6.   Complete the following steps to change the layout of the PivotTable report and to select a different formatting style:
a.   Click the PivotTable Wizard button on the PivotTable toolbar.
b.   Click Layout.
c.   Drag the Model field button from the ROW area of the PivotTable diagram to the COLUMN area of the PivotTable diagram.
d.   Click OK.
e.   Click Finish.
f.   Click the Format Report button on the PivotTable toolbar.
g.   Scroll down to find the Table 6 option. Click the Table 6 option.
h.   Click OK.

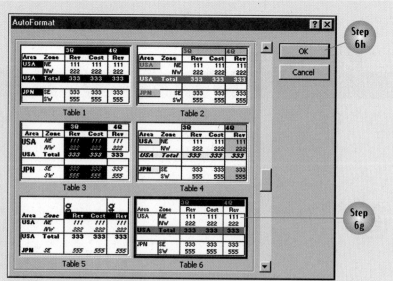

i.   The currency formatting is gone. Place the mouse pointer over cell F4, the Grand Total column. When the mouse pointer turns into an arrow pointing down, click to select all the numbers in the Grand Total field.

	A	B	C	D	E	F	G	H
3	Total		Model ▾					
4	Quarter ▾	Store ▾	Pathfinder	Excursion	Trekker	Grand Total		
5	1st	Adventures Unlimited		6111	5995	12106		
6		Backwoods Country		10185	5995	16180		
7		Camping and More		6111	38368	44479		
8		NorthWest Camping	18384			18384		
9		Outdoor Adventures	34470	1358		35828		
10		Outdoor Sporting Goods		4074		4074		
11		The Canoe Shop			9592	9592		
12		Water Sports	6894	10185	11990	29069		
13	1st Total		59748	38024	71940	169712		
14	2nd	Adventures Unlimited	45960	4074	14388	64422		
15		Backwoods Country	24129			24129		
16		Camping and More		27160	22781	49941		
17		NorthWest Camping		10185		10185		
18		Outdoor Adventures		16975		16975		
19		Outdoor Sporting Goods		3395	3597	6992		
20		Water Sports	22980	2716		25696		
21	2nd Total		93069	64505	40766	198340		
22	3rd	Adventures Unlimited		6111		6111		
23		Backwoods Country	9192	5432	21582	36206		
24		Camping and More	17235		38368	55603		
25		NorthWest Camping		19012	14388	33400		
26		Outdoor Adventures		23765	14388	38153		

PivotTable / Orders / Sheet2 / Sheet3 /

Step 6i

j.   Format the numbers as currency with no decimal places.
7. Print the PivotTable worksheet.
8. Save the worksheet with the same name (Excel E5, Ex 05).
9. Close the worksheet.

Creating PivotChart Reports

A PivotChart report is created from a PivotTable report. You can create the PivotChart report from scratch using the PivotTable and PivotChart Report Wizard. A PivotTable report will be created when you create the PivotChart report. Or you can create a PivotChart report based on an existing PivotTable report by clicking the Chart Wizard button on the Standard toolbar. Row fields in the PivotTable report become category fields in the PivotChart report. Column Fields in the PivotTable report become series fields in the PivotChart report. Since a PivotChart report is associated with a PivotTable report, changes made to the PivotTable report are reflected in the PivotChart report and vice versa.

The Chart
Wizard Button

To create a PivotChart report from scratch, name the Excel list that is going to be used as the data source *Database*. Click Data and then click PivotTable and PivotChart Report. The PivotTable and PivotChart Wizard - Step 1 of 3 dialog box is displayed. As shown in figure 5.11, you need to select PivotChart (with PivotTable) to create a PivotChart report. Click Next. The PivotTable and PivotChart Wizard - Step 2 of 3 dialog box will be displayed. Excel will automatically enter the Database range as the data source. Click Next. The PivotTable and PivotChart Wizard - Step 3 of 3 dialog box is displayed. Since PivotCharts must be linked to a PivotTable, Excel is going to automatically create a PivotTable. Specify whether you want the PivotTable on a new worksheet or the existing worksheet. The PivotChart will be created on a new worksheet. Click Finish.

figure 5.11

Creating a PivotChart Report Using the PivotTable and PivotChart Wizard

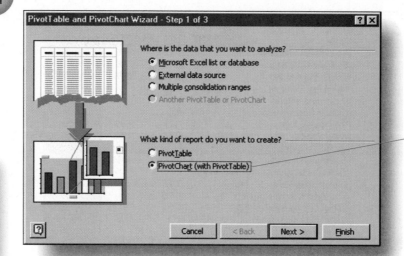

Select PivotChart (with PivotTable) to create a PivotChart report.

The order in which you should drag fields to the PivotChart diagram is fields in the series, category and page areas first. Drag fields to the data area last. Using this order helps to prevent delays when dropping fields from the PivotTable toolbar to the PivotChart diagram.

The PivotChart diagram shown in figure 5.12 is displayed. From the PivotTable toolbar, drag the field buttons for the fields you want to display in categories to the Drop More Category Fields Here area of the diagram. From the PivotTable toolbar, drag the fields to be displayed in series to the Drop More Series Fields here area of the PivotChart diagram. From the PivotTable toolbar, drag the fields containing the data to be compared or measured to the Drop Data Items Here area of the PivotTable diagram. You can rearrange the fields by dragging them from one area to another. Remove a field by dragging it off the PivotTable diagram.

figure 5.12

A PivotChart Diagram

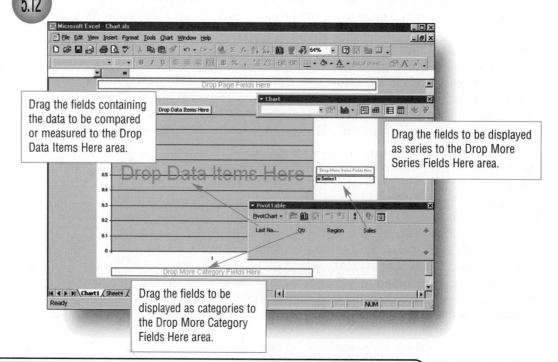

Drag the fields containing the data to be compared or measured to the Drop Data Items Here area.

Drag the fields to be displayed as series to the Drop More Series Fields Here area.

Drag the fields to be displayed as categories to the Drop More Category Fields Here area.

To create a PivotChart report from an existing PivotTable report, click any cell in the PivotTable report. Click the Chart Wizard button on the Standard toolbar. Excel automatically creates a stacked column chart on a new worksheet named Chart. Row fields in the PivotTable report are the category fields in the PivotChart report. Column fields in the PivotTable report are the series fields in the PivotChart report. To change the chart type, click the Chart Type button on the Chart toolbar. To make other changes, including changing the chart type, adding or editing titles, or changing the location of the chart, click the Chart Wizard button on the PivotTable toolbar.

The Chart
Type Button

exercise 6

Creating a PivotChart Report for an Existing PivotTable Report

1. Open Excel Worksheet E5-02.
2. Save the worksheet using the Save <u>A</u>s command and name it Excel E5, Ex 06.
3. Click the PivotTable worksheet tab, if necessary.
4. Complete the following steps to create a chart from this PivotTable report:
   a. Click any cell in the PivotTable report.
   b. Click the Chart Wizard button on the PivotTable toolbar. Excel automatically creates a stacked column chart on a chart sheet.
   c. Double-click the Chart1 worksheet tab.
   d. Key **PivotChart**.
   e. Press Enter.
5. Create a custom header for the PivotChart worksheet that displays your name at the left margin and the file name at the right margin.
6. You want to make some changes to the PivotChart report. Complete the following steps to edit the chart:
   a. Click the Chart Wizard button on the PivotTable toolbar. The Chart Wizard - Step 1 of 4 - Chart Type dialog box is displayed.
   b. Under <u>C</u>hart type, click Line.
   c. Under Chart sub-<u>t</u>ype, click the second option in the second row.
   d. Click Next.
   e. Click in the Chart <u>t</u>itle box. Key **Sales by Quarter**.
   f. Click in the <u>C</u>ategory (X) axis box. Key **Quarter**.
   g. Click in the <u>V</u>alue (Y) axis. Key **Sales**.
   h. Click Next.

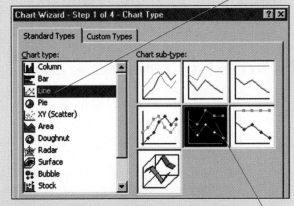

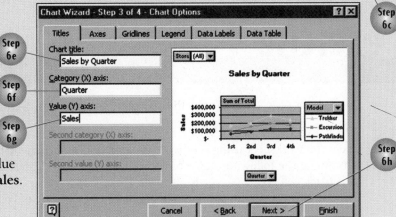

    i.   Accept the default entries for the Chart Wizard - Step 4 of 4 - Chart Location dialog box. Click Finish.

7.   Print the PivotChart worksheet.

8.   The PivotChart worksheet should still be displayed. Now you want to create a PivotChart report that shows the figures for the Camping and More store only. Complete the following steps to change the PivotChart report.

    a.   Click the down arrow to the right of the Store field button.

    b.   Click the *Camping and More* option.

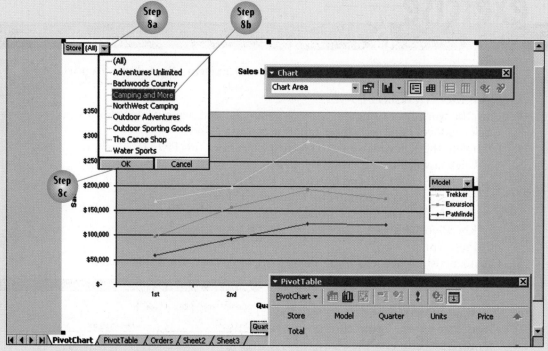

    c.   Click OK.

9.   Now only the figures for the store Camping and More are displayed. Print the PivotChart worksheet.

10. Display all the stores by clicking the down arrow to the right of the Store field button, clicking the *All* option and clicking OK.

11. Save the worksheet with the same name (Excel E5, Ex 06).

12. Close the worksheet.

Creating a PivotChart Report from Scratch

1.   Open Excel worksheet E5-03.

2.   Save the worksheet using the Save As command and name it Excel E5, Ex 07.

3.   Complete the following steps to name the data source *Database*:

    a.   Click cell A1.

    b.   Hold the Shift key and double-click the right border of cell A1.

c. Hold the Shift key and double-click the bottom border of cell A1. The entire list (A1:D81) should be selected.
d. Click the Name box.
e. Key **Database**.
f. Press Enter.
4. Complete the following steps to create a PivotChart report from scratch:
a. Click Data and then click PivotTable and PivotChart Report.
b. The PivotTable and PivotChart Wizard - Step 1 of 3 is displayed. Under What kind of report do you want to create? click the PivotChart (with PivotTable) option.

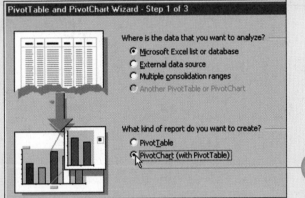

c. Click Next.
d. Excel should automatically recognize the Database range. Click Next.
e. Click Finish.
f. Double-click the Chart 1 sheet tab and key **PivotChart**.
g. Press Enter.
h. Drag the Last Name button from the PivotTable toolbar to the Drop Page Fields Here area of the PivotChart diagram.
i. Drag the Qtr button from the PivotTable toolbar to the Drop More Series Fields Here area of the PivotChart diagram.
j. Drag the Region button on the PivotTable toolbar to the Drop More Category Fields Here area of the PivotChart diagram.
k. Drag the Sales button on the PivotTable toolbar to the Drop Data Items Here area of the PivotChart diagram.

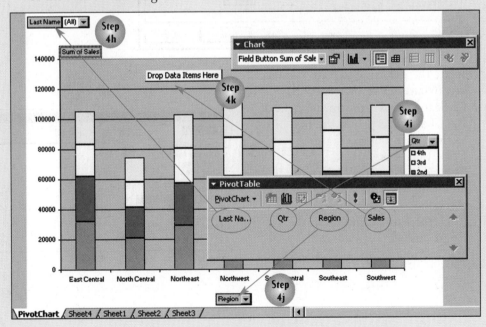

l. Create a custom header for the PivotChart worksheet that displays your name at the left margin and the file name at the right margin.

5. Complete the following steps to edit the PivotChart report.

a. Click the Chart Wizard button on the PivotTable toolbar.

b. Select the first option under the Chart sub-type.

c. Click Next.

d. Click in the Chart title box. Key **Sales by Region**.

e. Click in the Category (X) axis box. Key **Region**.

f. Click in the Value (Y) axis. Key **Sales**.

g. Click Next.

h. Accept the default entries on the Chart Wizard - Step 4 of 4 Chart Location dialog box by clicking Finish.

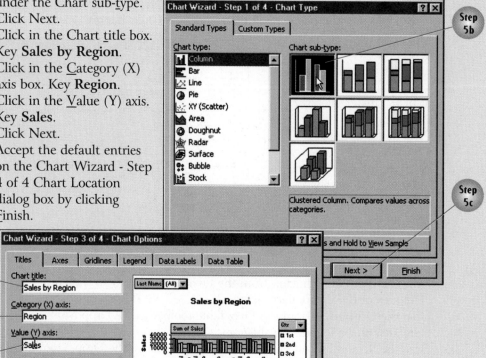

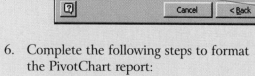

6. Complete the following steps to format the PivotChart report:

a. Click the down arrow to the right of the Chart Objects box, the first box in the Chart toolbar.

b. Click *Value Axis*.

c. The value axis is now selected. You want to format the numbers on the value axis as currency.

d. Click the Format button on the Chart toolbar.

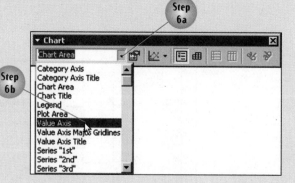

e. The Format Axis dialog box is displayed. Click the Number tab.
f. In the Category list box, click *Currency*.
g. Enter **0** in the Decimal places box.
h. Click OK.
i. Click the down arrow to the right of the first box in the Chart toolbar.
j. Click *Category Axis*.
k. Click the Angle Text Upward button on the Chart toolbar.

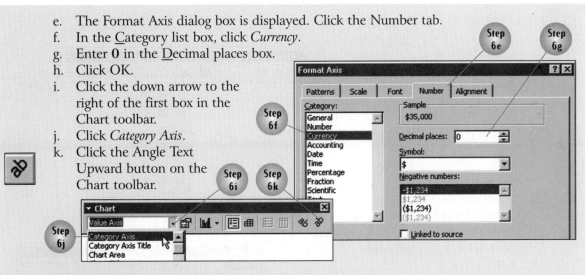

7. Print the PivotChart worksheet.
8. Now you want to see just the sales figures for Levinson. Complete the following steps to display the sales figures for one sales representative.
   a. Click the down arrow to the right of the Last Name field button.
   b. Click *Levinson, C.*
   c. Click OK.
   d. Print the PivotChart worksheet.
   e. Display all the sales representatives by clicking the down arrow to the right of the Last Name field button, clicking *(All)*, and clicking OK.

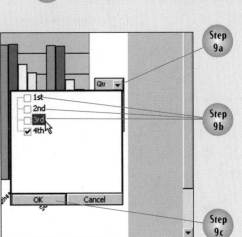

9. Complete the following steps to create a pie chart that illustrates the sales for the fourth quarter:
   a. Click the down arrow to the right of the Qtr field button.
   b. Click the 1st, 2nd, and 3rd check boxes so that they are no longer selected.
   c. Click OK.

d. Click the down arrow to the right of the Chart Type button on the Chart toolbar.

e. Click the 3-D Pie Chart option, the second option in the fifth row.

f. Click the down arrow to the right of the Chart Objects box, the first box in the Chart toolbar.

g. Click *Series "4th."*

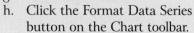

h. Click the Format Data Series button on the Chart toolbar.

i. Click the Data Labels tab on the Format Data Series dialog box.

j. In the Data labels section, click the *Show label and percent* option.

k. Click OK.

l. Click the chart title *Sales by Region* to select it. Once the chart title is selected, place the insertion point after the *n* in *Region*. Press the space bar once and key **4th Quarter**.

m. If the data label *Southwest 14%* is covered by the *Sum of Sales* field button, click the label to select it. When handles appear around that one data label only, click one of the borders around the label and drag it so that it is not being covered by the *Sum of Sales* field.

10. Print the PivotChart worksheet and save it with the same name (Excel E5, Ex 07.

11. Close the worksheet.

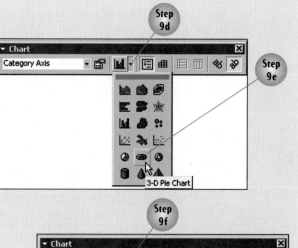

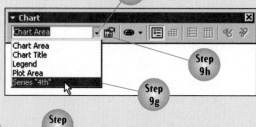

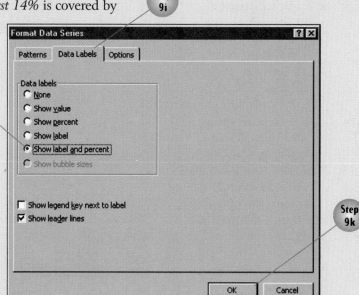

Creating Interactive PivotTables for the Web

A PivotTable report can be saved as a Web page and then published to a public location such as a Web server. Other users who have Microsoft Office Web Components installed can view the PivotTable report using version 4.01 or later of the Microsoft Internet Explorer Web browser. The Microsoft Office Web components are automatically installed when Microsoft Office 2000 is installed. An interactive PivotTable report that has been published in a public location is called a PivotTable list. Users can interact with a PivotTable list in many of the same ways as PivotTable reports can be manipulated in Excel. A PivotTable list on a Web page includes features and commands similar to an Excel PivotTable report.

One of the ways you can interact with a PivotTable list on a Web page is by adding fields to it or removing fields from it. Once the PivotTable has been saved as a Web page and is displayed in a Web browser, a toolbar appears above it. As shown in figure 5.13, a list of all the available fields that can be added to the PivotTable is displayed when the Field List button is clicked. To add a field to the PivotTable, click the field name in the list and then click OK. To remove a field from the PivotTable, simply click the field button representing that field and drag it off the PivotTable.

> When you place a PivotTable report on the Web it is called a PivotTable list.
>
> *Hint*

figure
5.13
Adding Fields to a PivotTable Using a Web Browser

> To add a field to a PivotTable using a Web browser, click the Field List button, click the field to be added from the PivotTable Field List that is displayed and click Add to.

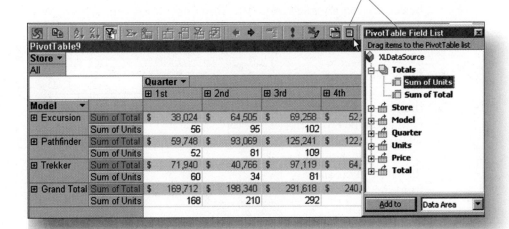

exercise 8

Creating an Interactive PivotTable for the Web

1. Open Excel worksheet E5-04.
2. Save the worksheet using the Save As command and name it Excel E5, Ex 08.
3. If necessary, click the PivotTable worksheet tab.
4. Complete the following steps to save the PivotTable report as a Web page:
   a. Click File and then click Save As Web Page.
   b. The Save As dialog box is displayed. Make sure Entire Workbook is selected.
   c. Click Publish.

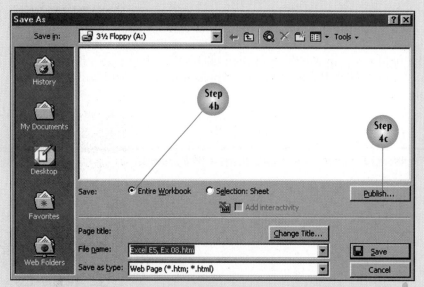

   d. Select *Items on PivotTable* from the drop-down list for the Choose box.
   e. Select *PivotTable* from the list under the Choose box.
   f. In the Viewing options section, click the Add interactivity with check box to select it.
   g. If necessary, choose *PivotTable functionality* from the drop-down list for the Add interactivity with box.
   h. Click the Open published web page in browser check box to select it.
   i. Click Publish.

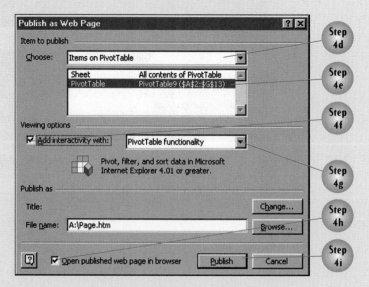

5. The PivotTable is displayed in Microsoft Internet Explorer. Complete the following steps to interact with the PivotTable as a Web page.

   a. You do not want to see the figures for the Sum of Units. Click one of the Sum of Units field buttons and drag it off the PivotTable.

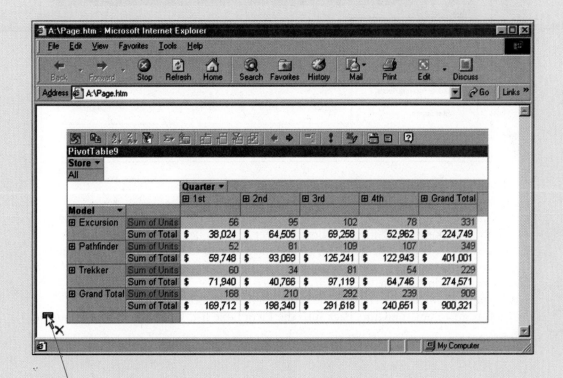

Click one of the Sum of Units field buttons and drag it off the PivotTable list to remove it.

b. You want to see the figures for the NorthWest Camping store only. Click the down arrow to the right of the Store field button.

c. Click the NorthWest Camping check box to select it.

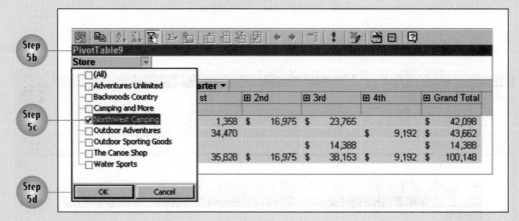

d. Click OK.
e. Click the Print button.
f. Display all the stores by clicking the down arrow to the right of the Store field button, clicking the (All) check box to select it, and clicking OK.
g. You want to display the detail for the Trekker model. Click the plus sign in the box next to Trekker.
h. Click the Print button.
i. Collapse the detail by clicking the minus sign in the box next to Trekker.
j. You want to put the Units back into the PivotTable list. Click the Field List button.

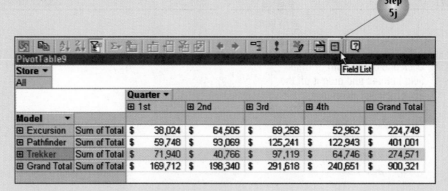

k. The PivotTable Field List dialog box is displayed. Click Sum of Units and drag the item to below the first Sum of Total field button.
l. Close the PivotTable Field List dialog box.

6. Close Microsoft Internet Explorer.
7. Save the worksheet with the same name (Excel E5, Ex 08) and close it.

Analyzing Data Using Goal Seek

Excel's Goal Seek is used to calculate a specified result by changing the value of another cell. Goal Seek adjusts the value in a specified cell until a formula dependent on that cell reaches the desired result. For example, suppose a company wanted to buy a machine costing $70,000. The company knows the interest that must be paid on the loan and they know their payments cannot exceed $4,000. What they need to know is the period of the loan or how many payments it will take to pay the loan off. They know the goal they are seeking—paying off a $70,000 loan at a specific interest rate with monthly payments of $4,000. Goal Seek can tell them what they need to do to reach that goal, that is, how many payments they will need to make.

To use the Goal Seek command, enter the formula and corresponding values in the worksheet. Click Tools and then either wait a few seconds or click the down arrow at the bottom of the menu for the Goal Seek option to be displayed. Click Goal Seek. The Goal Seek dialog box shown in figure 5.14, is displayed. Enter the cell reference to the cell containing the formula in the Set cell box. Enter the goal you are seeking in the To value box. Enter the cell reference to the cell containing the value that can change in the By changing cell box. The Goal Seek Status dialog box is displayed. The value on the worksheet has changed to display the goal being sought after. To enter the goal into the worksheet, click OK. To cancel Goal Seek and return the original value to the worksheet, click Cancel.

figure 5.14   *The Goal Seek Dialog Box*

Using Goal Seek

1. Open Excel worksheet E5-05.
2. Save the worksheet using the Save As command and name it Excel E5, Ex 09.
3. Create a custom header that displays your name at the left margin and the file name at the right margin.
4. This worksheet keeps track of the profit the EastWest Crossroads Company makes on each item it sells through its mail order catalog. View the item in row 16. Right now, item number GG-47-1 is only making a $5.00 profit. Complete the following steps to use Goal Seek to find out how much the selling price of the Mosaic Glass Bracelet would have to be to make an $8.00 profit.

a. Click <u>T</u>ools, click the down arrow at the bottom of the menu if necessary and click <u>G</u>oal Seek.

b. The Goal Seek dialog box appears. The current entry in the Se<u>t</u> cell box is already selected. Key **F16**.

c. Click the To <u>v</u>alue box and key **8.00**.

d. Click the By <u>c</u>hanging cell box and key **C16**.

e. Click OK.

f. The Goal Seek Status dialog box is displayed. Click OK.

5. Scroll down to view the item in row 43. Right now item GH-82-2, the Stained Glass Lamp, has a 30% markup. Complete the following steps to use Goal Seek to find out how much the selling price would have to be if the markup is 40%:

a. Click <u>T</u>ools and then click <u>G</u>oal Seek.

b. The Goal Seek dialog box appears. The current entry in the Se<u>t</u> cell box is already selected. Key **E43**.

c. Click the To <u>v</u>alue box and key **40%**.

d. Click the By <u>c</u>hanging cell box and key **C43**.

e. Click OK.

f. The Goal Seek Status dialog box is displayed. Click OK.

6. View the item in row 11. The Unit Cost of the Jakarta Drum is $65.00. Complete the following steps to use Goal Seek to find out how much that unit cost would have to decrease in order for the EastWest Crossroads Company to realize a 40% profit on the drum:

a. Click <u>T</u>ools and then click <u>G</u>oal Seek.

b. The Goal Seek dialog box appears. The current entry in the Se<u>t</u> cell box is already selected. Key **E11**.

c. Click the To <u>v</u>alue box and key **40%**.

d. Click the By <u>c</u>hanging cell box and key **D11**.

e. Click OK.

f. The Goal Seek Status dialog box is displayed. Click OK.

7. Save the worksheet with the same name (Excel E5, Ex 09) and print it.

8. Close the worksheet.

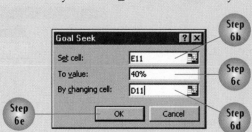

Analyzing Data Using Solver

Businesses can always meet their objectives in a number of different ways. What businesses must determine is which way is the most efficient way, or the way that will generate the maximum profit, or the way that will optimize the use of plant facilities. The variables involved in meeting the specific objective are subject to restrictions or constraints. For example, a constraint involved in determining the optimal use of plant facilities is that the plant cannot operate more than 24 hours a day. Using Excel's Solver, problems that have multiple variables that are interdependent can be solved. Excel's Goal Seek can arrive at a specific result in problems with only one changing variable. With Solver, you can arrive at a specific result in problems that have many changing variables.

Suppose a factory makes two different products using the same machine. The goal is to maximize the total net profit from these two products. The profit for each product is different. The time it takes the machine to produce each product is different. The machine can only run a certain number of hours a week. The products are shipped out at the end of each week so the products produced in one week cannot exceed the space available for storing them in the warehouse. There is a limit on the weekly demand for one of the products. As you can see, there are several variables involved: the net profit for each product, the machine time, the warehouse space, and the demand for one of the products. Each one of these variables has a constraint. The machine can run only a certain number of hours a week. The warehouse is a specific size. There is a limit to the number of one of the products that can be sold in a week. By taking into consideration all the variables and their constraints, Solver finds the optimal solution: the number of each product that should be produced in a week in order to maximize the total net profit.

To use Solver click Tools and then click Solver. If the Solver command is not on the Tools menu, the Solver add-in needs to be installed. The Solver Parameters dialog box shown in figure 5.15 is displayed. In the Set Target Cell box enter the cell reference or name for the target cell. The target cell must contain a formula. If the target cell is to be as large as possible, click Max. If it is to be as small as possible, click Min. If it is to be a specific value, click Value of and enter the Value in the Value of box. Enter a name or reference for each cell that can be adjusted to meet the target in the By Changing Cells box. Separate nonadjacent references using commas. If you want Solver to automatically propose the cells to be adjusted based on the target cell, click Guess. The cells to be adjusted must not contain formulas and the target cell must be dependent on them. An adjustment to the value in a cell listed in the By Changing Cells box must affect the value in the target cell. Any constraints to be applied are entered in the Subject to the Constraints box. Once you have defined the problem in the Solver Parameters dialog box, click Solve.

Once you click Solve, the Solver Results dialog box shown in figure 5.16 is displayed. Click Keep Solver Solution to keep the solution values on the worksheet. Click Restore Original Values to restore the original data. The Reports list box allows you to select the type of report you would like to see and places each report on a separate sheet in the workbook. The Answer Report displays the target cell, the changing cells, and the constraints. The Sensitivity Report presents the detailed sensitivity information about the target cell. The Limits Report displays how much the values of the changing cells can be increased or decreased without violating the constraints of the problem.

To install Solver, click Tools and Add-Ins. The Add-Ins dialog box is displayed. Click the Solver Add-in check box and click OK.

The Target Cell must be a single cell. Only one cell is optimized when using Solver.

figure
5.15

The Solver Parameters Dialog Box

Solver will optimize the result of the target cell.

Solver arrives at the optimal result for the target cell by modifying the cells entered in the By Changing Cells box.

Solver optimizes the result of the target cell by finding a maximum value, minimum value, or a specific value.

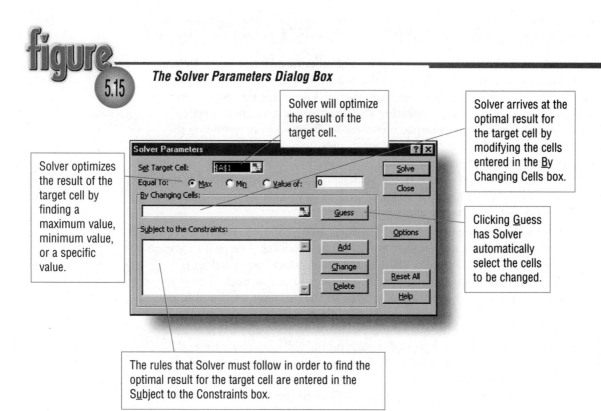

Clicking Guess has Solver automatically select the cells to be changed.

The rules that Solver must follow in order to find the optimal result for the target cell are entered in the Subject to the Constraints box.

figure
5.16

The Solver Results Dialog Box

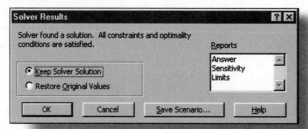

exercise 10

Defining and Solving a Problem Using Solver

1. Open Excel worksheet E5-06.
2. Save the worksheet using the Save As command and name it Excel E5, Ex 10.
3. Create a custom header that displays your name at the left margin and the file name at the right margin.

4. Copper Clad Incorporated makes modem circuit boards for three different modem manufacturers off a single production line. The production line runs 60 hours a week. A weekly production schedule is run where the week is spent producing the three different modem circuit boards and the output is stored in a warehouse during the week. At the end of each week, the modem boards are shipped to each modem manufacturer. It takes 3 hours to produce 100 boxes of Board A, 4 hours to produce 100 boxes of Board B, and 5 hours to produce 100 boxes of Board C. It takes 1.5 cubic feet to store a box of Board A, 2.5 cubic feet to store 1 box of Board B, and 3 cubic feet to store one box of Board C. The warehouse holds at most 2,000 cubic feet. The net profit per box of Board A is $75.00. The net profit per box of Board B is $100, and the net profit per box of Board C is $150. You can sell as many boxes as you can produce in a week to the companies that buy Board A and Board B. But the company that buys Board C will never purchase more than 250 boxes a week. You want to use Solver to determine a production plan that abides by all the constraints and maximizes the total net profit.

Look at the worksheet. The target cell, or the total net profit, is surrounded by a blue border. The changing cells, or the number of boxes produced for each modem board, are surrounded by a green border. The constraints on the variables are surrounded by a violet border. First, you are going to name some of the cells in order to make using Solver a little easier to understand. Complete the following steps to name the cells:

   a. Name cell F7 **Total_Profit**.
   b. Name cell G7 **Total_Space**.
   c. Name cell H7 **Total_Hours**.
   d. Name cell C11 **Available_Space**.
   e. Name cell C12 **Max_Boxes_Board_C**.
   f. Name cell C13 **Available_Hours**.

5. Complete the following steps to define the problem using Solver:
   a. Click <u>T</u>ools and then click Sol<u>v</u>er.
   b. Key **Total_Profit** in the Set Target Cell box.
   c. Make sure <u>M</u>ax is selected in the Equal to section.
   d. Key **$E$3:$E$5** in the By Changing Cells box.
   e. Next you must add the constraints. Click <u>A</u>dd.
   f. The Add Constraint dialog box is displayed. The first constraint you are going to add is the total space cannot exceed the space available.
      1) Key **Total_Space** in the Cell <u>R</u>eference box.
      2) Make sure the comparison operator <= is displayed in the middle box.
      3) Key **Available_Space** in the <u>C</u>onstraint box.
      4) Click <u>A</u>dd.

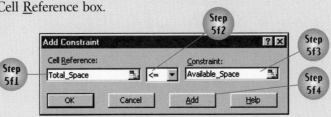

g. The Add Constraint dialog box is ready for you to enter the second constraint. The second constraint you are going to add is the maximum boxes produced of Board C can never exceed 250.
  1) Key **$E$5** in the Cell Reference box.
  2) Make sure the comparison operator <= is displayed in the middle box.
  3) Key **Max_Boxes_Board_C** in the Constraint box.
  4) Click Add.

h. The Add Constraint dialog box is ready for you to enter the third constraint, which is that the total hours can never exceed the available hours.
  1) Key **Total_Hours** in the Cell Reference box.
  2) Make sure the comparison operator <= is displayed in the middle box.
  3) Key **Available_Hours** in the Constraint box.
  4) Click Add.

i. The Add Constraint dialog box is ready for you to enter the fourth constraint, which is that the number of boxes that are produced of each modem board cannot be a negative number.
  1) Key **$E$3:$E$5** in the Cell Reference box.
  2) Click the down arrow to the right of the middle box. Click >=.
  3) Key **0** in the Constraint box.
  4) Click Add.

j. The Add Constraint dialog box is ready for you to enter the last constraint, which is that the number of boxes that are produced of each modem board has to be a whole number (an integer).
  1) Key **$E$3:$E$5** in the Cell Reference box.
  2) Click the down arrow to the right of the middle box. Click int.
  3) Click OK.

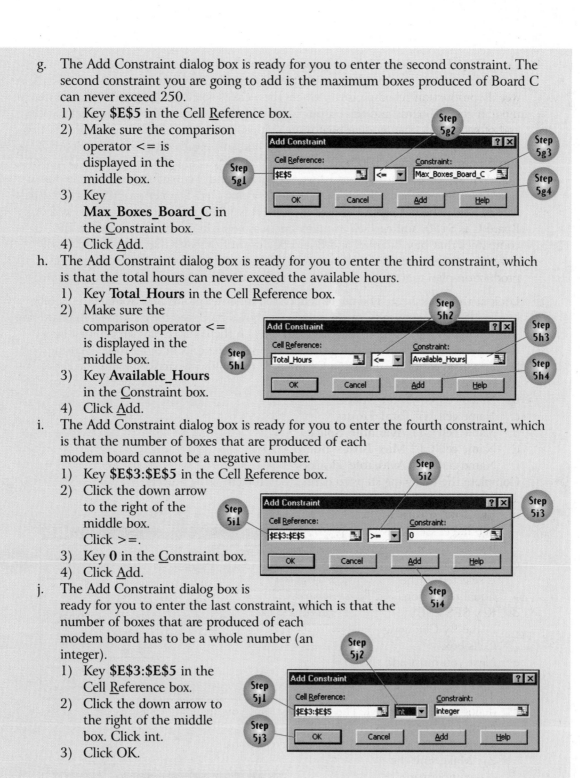

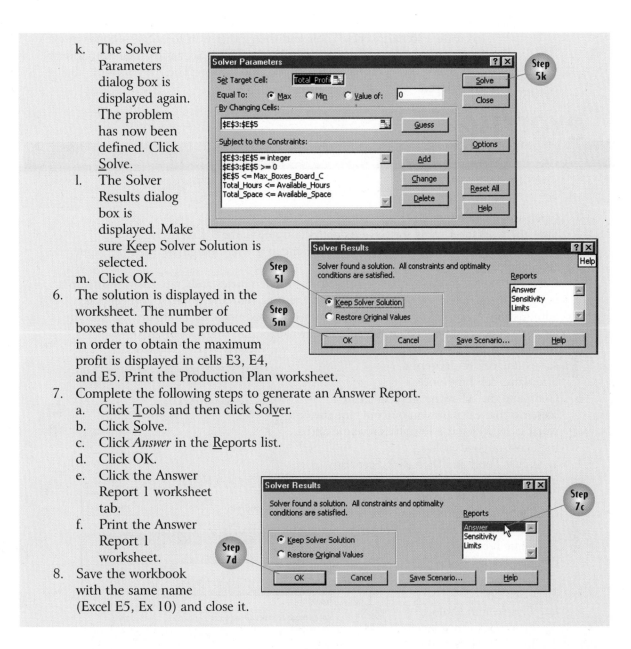

k. The Solver Parameters dialog box is displayed again. The problem has now been defined. Click Solve.

l. The Solver Results dialog box is displayed. Make sure <u>K</u>eep Solver Solution is selected.

m. Click OK.

6. The solution is displayed in the worksheet. The number of boxes that should be produced in order to obtain the maximum profit is displayed in cells E3, E4, and E5. Print the Production Plan worksheet.

7. Complete the following steps to generate an Answer Report.

   a. Click <u>T</u>ools and then click Sol<u>v</u>er.

   b. Click <u>S</u>olve.

   c. Click *Answer* in the <u>R</u>eports list.

   d. Click OK.

   e. Click the Answer Report 1 worksheet tab.

   f. Print the Answer Report 1 worksheet.

8. Save the workbook with the same name (Excel E5, Ex 10) and close it.

Creating Scenarios

Goal Seek and Solver provide one specific answer to a specific question. There are times, however, when examining several different answers to a question would be useful. Scenario Manager allows you to set up several different scenarios. Then you can examine how each scenario affects the final outcome. A company trying to establish a budget for the upcoming year does not know, for example, what the sales for the year will be. The sales figures obviously affect the rest of the budget. With the Scenario Manager you can create a "best case" and a "worst case" scenario. The best case scenario would show what the budget figures would look like if sales for the year were especially good. The worst cast scenario would show what the budget figures would look like if sales were especially poor.

Since creating scenarios changes the original values in cells, you might want to first create a scenario that uses those original values before creating scenarios that will change them. That way you will always be able to go back to the original values.

To create a scenario, click Tools and then either wait for a few seconds or click the down arrow at the bottom of the menu and click Scenarios. The Scenario Manager dialog box is displayed. Click the Add button. The Add Scenario dialog box is displayed.

Creating Scenarios

1. Open Excel worksheet E5-07.
2. Save the worksheet using the Save As command and name it Excel E5, Ex 11.
3. Create a custom header that displays your name at the left margin and the file name at the right margin.
4. Case 'N Crate, a company that manufactures wooden boxes and crates, is working on a budget for the upcoming year. Expenses for the year, rent and utilities, and general administrative, are known. What is not known is how much the company will earn in gross revenues and how much the company will spend on the cost of goods sold. Complete the following steps to name the cells with which you will be working:
   a. Name cell B5 **Revenue**.
   b. Name cell B6 **Goods**.
5. Complete the following steps to create a scenario that calculates an outcome for the worst case, which is a low gross revenue and a high cost of goods sold.
   a. Click Tools and then click Scenarios.
   b. The Scenario Manager dialog box is displayed. Click Add.
   c. The Add Scenario dialog box is displayed. Key **Worst Case** in the Scenario name box.
   d. Key **B5:B6** in the Changing cells box.
   e. Click OK.
   f. The Scenario Values dialog box is displayed. Key **2399128** in the Revenue box.
   g. Key **1963610** in the Goods box.
   h. Click Add.

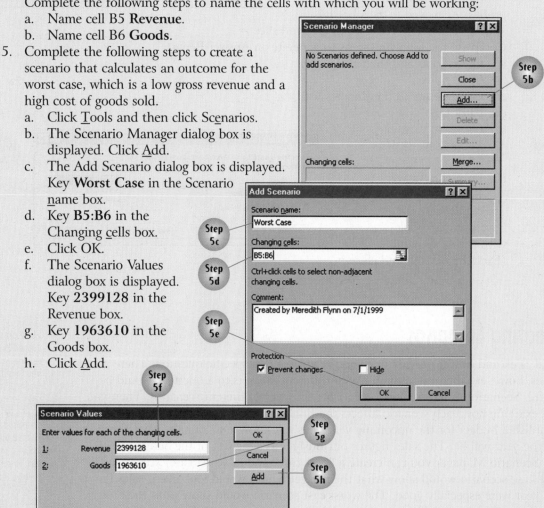

6. The Add Scenario dialog box is displayed again. Complete the following steps to create a second scenario that calculates a probable case:
   a. Key **Probable Case** in the Scenario name box.
   b. Make sure B5:B6 is still entered in the Changing cells box.
   c. Click OK.
   d. The Scenario Values dialog box is displayed. Key **3427325** in the Revenue box.
   e. Key **1785100** in the Goods box.
   f. Click Add.

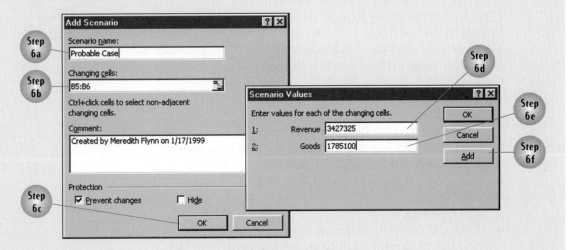

7. The Add Scenario dialog box is displayed again. Complete the following steps to create a third scenario that calculates the best case:
   a. Key **Best Case** in the Scenario name box.
   b. Make sure B5:B6 is still entered in the Changing cells box.
   c. Click OK.
   d. The Scenario Values dialog box is displayed. Key **4284156** in the Revenue box.
   e. Key **1428080** in the Goods box.
   f. Click OK.

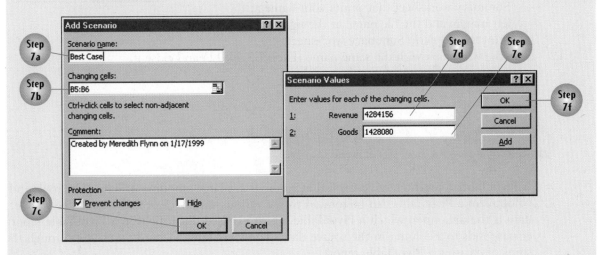

8. The Scenario Manager dialog box is displayed again. Complete the following steps to show the Worst Case scenario:

   Step 8a

   a. In the Scenarios list box, click *Worst Case*.
   b. Click Show.
   c. Click Close.
   d. Print the Projected Budget worksheet.

9. Complete the following steps to show the Probable Case scenario:
   a. Click Tools and then click Scenarios.
   b. In the Scenarios list box, click *Probable Case*.
   c. Click Show.
   d. Click Close.
   e. Print the Projected Budget worksheet.

10. Complete the following steps to show the Best Case scenario:
    a. Click Tools and then click Scenarios.
    b. In the Scenarios list box, click *Best Case*.
    c. Click Show.
    d. Click Close.
    e. Print the Projected Budget worksheet.

11. Complete the following steps to create a scenario summary:
    a. Click Tools and then click Scenarios.
    b. Click Summary.
    c. The Scenario Summary dialog box appears. Make sure the Scenario summary option is selected.
    d. Make sure B15 is entered in the Result cells box.
    e. Click OK.
    f. The Scenario Summary is created on a new worksheet. Create a custom header for the Scenario Summary worksheet that prints your name at the left margin and the file name at the right margin.
    g. Print the Scenario Summary worksheet.

12. Save the workbook with the same name (Excel E5, Ex 11) and close it.

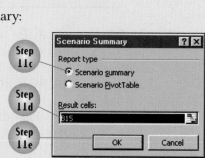

Step 8b

Step 8c

Step 11c

Step 11d

Step 11e

chapter summary

➤ A PivotTable is an interactive table that summarizes large amounts of data. The rows and columns of a PivotTable can be rotated to see various summaries of the data. The source data is the data upon which a PivotTable report is based. Each field in a PivotTable report corresponds to a column in the source data. The PivotTable Wizard takes you through the steps of creating a PivotTable report.

➤ A PivotTable report contains fields and items. Fields correspond to columns in the source data. Items are unique values in a field. The fields from the source list containing the data that is summarized in the PivotTable report are the data fields. Data fields can be summarized in a PivotTable report using summary functions such as Sum, Count, or Average.

➤ Format an entire PivotTable report by clicking the Format Report button on the PivotTable toolbar.

➤ Items on a PivotTable report can be hidden or filtered. Items are hidden and displayed by clicking the Hide Detail button and Show Detail button on the PivotTable toolbar. Items are filtered by clicking the down arrow to the right of the field button on the PivotTable report and selecting the fields to be displayed. Hidden items are still a part of the report and are included in the totals. Filtered items are not a part of the report and are not included in the totals.

➤ The layout of a PivotTable report can be changed by clicking the PivotTable Wizard button on the PivotTable toolbar and then clicking the Layout button on the PivotTable and PivotChart Wizard – Step 3 of 3 dialog box. The PivotTable and PivotChart Wizard – Layout dialog box containing the PivotTable diagram is displayed. Field buttons can be dragged on to and off the dialog box in order to rearrange the report.

➤ A PivotChart report is created from a PivotTable report. Row fields in a PivotTable report become category fields in a Pivot Chart report, and column fields in a PivotTable report become series fields in a PivotChart report. Changes made to the PivotTable report are reflected in the PivotChart report and vice versa.

➤ An interactive PivotTable that has been saved as a Web page and published to a public location such as a Web server is called a PivotTable list. Users can access a PivotTable list and interact with it in many of the same ways as PivotTable reports can be manipulated in Excel.

➤ The Goal Seek command calculates a specified result by changing the value of another cell until a formula dependent on that cell reaches the result specified.

➤ The Solver command calculates a specified result that is based on many changing variables. Solver is used to determine the "best" solution to a problem, that is, the solution that generates the most profit or utilizes resources in the most efficient way, for example. The variables that go into determining the solution can be subject to restrictions or constraints, such as an employee cannot work more than 40 hours a week. By analyzing the variables and their constraints, Solver finds the optimal solution.

➤ Several different answers, or scenarios, to a specific question can be set up using Excel's Scenario Manager. Each scenario can be examined to see how it affects the final outcome. For example, you can set up one scenario where sales are high and costs are low and a second scenario where sales are low and costs are high and then examine how the two scenarios affect profits.

commands review

	Mouse/Keyboard
Create a PivotTable	Click Data, PivotTable, and PivotChart Report
Sort the items in a field in a PivotTable report	Double-click a field button on the PivotTable and click Advanced
Remove subtotals from a PivotTable report	Double-click a field button on the PivotTable, click None
Remove grand totals from a PivotTable report	Right-click a cell in the PivotTable report, click Table Options
Create a PivotChart report	Click Data, PivotTable, and PivotChart Report

Use Goal Seek	Click <u>T</u>ools, <u>G</u>oal Seek
Use Solver	Click <u>T</u>ools, Sol<u>v</u>er
Create a Scenario	Click <u>T</u>ools, Sc<u>e</u>narios

thinking offline

Completion: In the space provided at the right, indicate the correct term, command, button, or symbol.

1. This term refers to a report that is used to quickly summarize and analyze large amounts of data.

2. This term refers to the list upon which a PivotTable report is based.

3. If you name the list this term, Excel will automatically recognize it as the data upon which to base a PivotTable report.

4. To select all the cells belonging to a field in a PivotTable report, the mouse pointer must turn into this symbol when you move it to the top of the data field label in a column.

5. To sort the fields in a PivotTable report, double-click a field button on the PivotTable and click this button.

6. To remove grand totals from a PivotTable report, right-click a cell in the report and click this option from the shortcut menu.

7. To manage the layout of a PivotTable report using the PivotTable Wizard, click the PivotTable and PivotChart Wizard button on the PivotTable toolbar and click this button.

8. This term refers to what you must have in order to create a PivotChart report.

9. This term refers to Excel's analysis tool that calculates a specified result by changing the value of one cell.

10. This term refers to Excel's analysis tool that calculates a specified result by changing several variables.

11. This term refers to Excel's analysis tool that allows you to examine how several different projected plans will affect the final outcome.

12. List the two ways you can filter items on a PivotTable report.

13. List the steps for creating a PivotChart report from scratch and for creating a PivotChart report based on an existing PivotTable.

_____

_____

_____

_____

14. List the steps for saving a PivotTable report as a Web page.

_____

_____

_____

_____

working hands-on

Assessment 1

1. Open Excel Worksheet E5-09.
2. Save the worksheet using the Save As command and name it Excel E5, SA 01.
3. Case 'N Crate is a company that manufactures wooden boxes, crates, and trays. They sell their products to businesses that use them for packaging fresh fruit and other specialty items. This worksheet keeps track of orders made the first quarter of the year. Name the list Database.
4. Create a PivotTable from the list. Place the PivotTable on a new worksheet. Rename the new worksheet PivotTable. *(Hint: Remember to press Enter after keying in the new worksheet name.)*
5. Create a custom header for the PivotTable worksheet with your name displayed at the left margin and the file name displayed at the right margin.
6. Drag the Region button to the Drop Page Fields Here area of the PivotTable diagram. Drag the Month and Sales Representative buttons to the Drop Row Fields Here area. Drag the Product button to the Drop Column Field here area. Drag the Total Order button to the Drop Data Items Here area.
7. Format the entire PivotTable report using the Table 8 format from the AutoFormat dialog box.
8. Format all the values for Boxes, Crates, Trays, all the subtotals, and the grand totals as currency with no decimal places.
9. Automatically adjust the width of columns A through F so that each column is at its optimal width.
10. Filter the PivotTable report so that only the orders for the South region are displayed. Print the PivotTable worksheet.
11. Display all the orders. Filter the PivotTable report so that only the orders for March are displayed. Print the PivotTable worksheet.

12. Display all the months. Change the layout of the PivotTable report so that Product is displayed as a row field and Month is displayed as a column field. Make any necessary adjustments so that the PivotTable report prints on one page. Print the PivotTable worksheet.

13. Adjust the layout of the PivotTable so that both the Month and Product are displayed as column fields. Hide the detail for the *Month* field. Make sure all the values are formatted as currency with no decimal places. Adjust column width if necessary. Print the PivotTable worksheet.

14. Save the workbook with the same name (E5, SA 01) and close it.

Assessment 2

1. Open Excel Worksheet E5-10.
2. Save the worksheet using the Save <u>A</u>s command and name it Excel E5, SA 02.
3. Nichols Dairy Ice Cream is a company that makes and sells its own ice cream. This list keeps track of ice cream orders. Name the list Database.
4. Create a PivotTable from the list. Place the PivotTable on a new worksheet. Rename the new worksheet PivotTable.
5. Create a custom header for the PivotTable worksheet with your name displayed at the left margin and the file name displayed at the right margin.
6. Drag the Month button to the Drop Page Fields Here area of the PivotTable diagram. Drag the Flavor and Customer buttons to the Drop Row Fields Here area. Drag the Type button to the Drop Column Fields Here area. Drag the Amount button to the Drop Data Items Here area.
7. Format the entire PivotTable report using the Table 4 format from the AutoFormat dialog box.
8. Format the values in the PivotTable report as currency with two decimal places.
9. Display the top 2 customers according to the total amount of their orders.
10. Adjust the page setup so that rows 1 through 4 repeat at the top as a print title.
11. Print the PivotTable worksheet.
12. Display all the customers.
13. Filter the report by selecting only Low Fat from the Type drop-down list.
14. Remove the grand totals from the report.
15. Print the PivotTable report.
16. Remove the filter from the Type field and display the grand totals in the PivotTable report. Print the PivotTable worksheet.
17. Save the workbook with the same name (Excel E5, SA 02) and close it.

Assessment 3

1. Open Excel Worksheet E5-11.
2. Save the worksheet using the Save <u>A</u>s command and name it Excel E5, SA 03.
3. Name the list Database.
4. Create a PivotChart using the PivotTable and PivotChart Wizard. Put the PivotTable that will be created on a new worksheet.
5. Drag the Paid button to the Drop Page Fields Here area of the PivotChart diagram. Drag the Vet button to the Drop More Series Fields Here area. Drag the Service Rendered button to the Drop More Category Fields Here area. Drag the Amount button to the Drop Data Items here area.
6. Click the Chart Wizard button on the PivotTable toolbar. Select the first option in the first row under Chart sub-type.

7. The chart title should be **Income from Services Rendered**. The title for the Category (X) axis should be **Veterinarian**. The title for the Value (Y) axis should be **Dollars**.
8. Place the chart on a new sheet. Rename the Chart1 worksheet tab PivotChart.
9. Create a custom header for the PivotTable worksheet with your name displayed at the left margin and the name of the file displayed at the right margin.
10. Format the numbers on the value axis as currency with no decimal places.
11. Angle the text on the category axis upward.
12. Print the PivotChart.
13. Filter the PivotChart so that in the Paid field only the No records are displayed and in the Veterinarian field only Martin's records are displayed.
14. Click the Chart Wizard button on the PivotTable toolbar. Select the Pie option under Chart type. Select the second option in the second row under Chart sub-type.
15. The chart title should be **Dr. Martin's Unpaid Invoices**.
16. The Data labels should show the percent.
17. Place the chart on a new sheet named PivotChart.
18. Print the PivotChart.
19. Save the workbook with the same name (Excel E5, SA 03) and close it.

Assessment 4

1. Open Excel Worksheet E5-12.
2. Save the worksheet using the Save As command and name it Excel E5, SA 04.
3. If necessary, click the PivotTable worksheet tab.
4. Save the PivotTable as a Web page. Use the same file name (Excel E5, SA 04). Click the Publish button. Click *PivotTable* from the list under the Choose box. The items you want to publish are the Items on PivotTable. Click the Add interactivity with check box and choose PivotTable functionality from the drop-down list. Make sure the Open published web page in browser check box is selected and click Publish.
5. In the File name box change the file name to A:\Nichols.htm.
6. You do not want to see the Sum of Amount figures. Drag one of the Sum of Amount field buttons off the PivotTable.
7. Display the figures for the Second Street Market only. Print the PivotTable.
8. Display all the stores.
9. Display the detail for Triple Mocha Madness ice cream by clicking the plus sign next to it. Print the PivotTable.
10. Collapse the detail for Triple Mocha Madness by clicking the minus sign.
11. Put the Sum of Amount button back on the PivotTable as a column field. Print the PivotTable.
12. Close Microsoft Internet Explorer.
13. Save the workbook with the same name (Excel E5, SA 04) and close it.

Assessment 5

1. Open Excel Worksheet E5-13.
2. Save the worksheet using the Save As command and name it Excel E5, SA 05.
3. Create a custom header for the Salary and Commissions worksheet with your name displayed at the left margin and the file name displayed at the right margin.
4. Using Goal Seek find the total amount Michael Malone sales would have to be in order for him to earn a total of $2,500. Enter that value into the worksheet.

5. Using Goal Seek find what percent commission Robert McBride would have to earn in order for his total income to be $3,500. Enter that value into the worksheet.
6. Using Goal Seek, find what Charles Levinson's salary would have to be in order for his total income to be $3,200.
7. Print the Salary & Commissions worksheet.
8. Save the workbook with the same name (Excel E5, SA 05) and close it.

Assessment 6

1. Open Excel Worksheet E5-14.
2. Save the worksheet using the Save <u>A</u>s command and name it Excel E5, SA 06.
3. Create a custom header for the worksheet with your name displayed at the left margin and the file name displayed at the right margin.
4. The production manager at Case 'N Crate has to figure out how many gross each of boxes and crates to produce in order to generate the most profit. Look over the worksheet carefully. The worksheet shows how many hours it takes to build and varnish a gross of boxes and a gross of crates. There is a limit on how many hours a week can be devoted to building and varnishing the boxes and crates because of the number of employees available.
5. Define the problem using Solver. The target cell is cell E8 and you are trying to find the maximum profit. The cells that can be changed are the number of gross of each to produce (B9 and C9). Add the two constraints. The resources used for carpentry cannot exceed 240 hours. The resources used for varnishing cannot exceed 100 hours.
6. Keep the Solver solution. Print the worksheet.
7. Save the workbook with the same name (Excel E5, SA 06) and close it.

Assessment 7

1. Open Excel Worksheet E5-15.
2. Save the worksheet using the Save <u>A</u>s command and name it Excel E5, SA 07.
3. Create a custom header for the Bad Debts worksheet with your name displayed at the left margin and the file name displayed at the right margin.
4. This worksheet is going to be used to project three scenarios. The veterinarians want to know how much money they are going to lose on uncollected accounts and how much this will affect the overall revenue of the company. The total bad debt is a percentage of the total uncollected accounts. Click cell B8. Key **=(B7*B6)+B5**.
5. The anticipated revenue is the gross revenue minus the total bad debt. Click cell B11. Key **=B10-B8**.
6. Name cell B6 *Uncollected*. Name cell B7 *BD_Allowance*.
7. Create a scenario named Worst Case. The changing cells should be B6 and B7. Enter **15500** as the uncollected amount. Enter **.3** as the bad debt allowance.
8. Create a scenario named Probable Case. The changing cells should be B6 and B7. Enter **8500** as the uncollected amount. Enter **.2** as the bad debt allowance.
9. Create a scenario named Best Case. The changing cells should be B6 and B7. Enter **3200** as the uncollected amount. Enter **.1** as the bad debt allowance.
10. Show the Worst Case Scenario. Print the Bad Debts worksheet.
11. Show the Probable Case Scenario. Print the Bad Debts worksheet.
12. Show the Best Case Scenario. Print the Bad Debts worksheet.
13. Save the workbook with the same name (Excel E5, SA 07) and close it.

Chapter 06E

Managing and Auditing Worksheets

6

PERFORMANCE OBJECTIVES

Upon successful completion of chapter 6, you will be able to:

- Record a macro.
- Run a macro.
- Edit a macro using the Microsoft Visual Basic editor.
- Assign a macro to a command button.
- Hide and display toolbars.
- Create a custom toolbar.
- Use the Auditing toolbar.
- Trace precedents.
- Trace dependents.
- Trace errors.

Excel includes a number of features that help you manage worksheets. Macros are useful for automating many tasks typically performed on a worksheet. They can save you time by automatically performing tasks that you do repeatedly, or tasks that involve the exact same sequence of steps. When you assign a macro to a command button, the macro is placed right on the worksheet to give you quick and easy access to it. You can also manage your worksheets by creating custom toolbars containing buttons for the commands you routinely use or the macros you have created. Making sure your worksheet is functioning properly is also a part of worksheet management. The auditing features that come with Excel 2000 help you trace the cells to which a formula refers, and to trace formulas that refer to a specific cell. If there is an error in the worksheet, Excel 2000's auditing feature will track down the source of the error. The purpose of this chapter is to introduce you to these features in Excel so that you can successfully manage and audit your worksheets.

Introduction to Macros

Macros are used to increase productivity by automating tasks that perform the same sequence of steps or automating tasks that are performed repeatedly. Instead of performing these same sequence of steps over and over every time you need to perform the task, you can record the steps in a macro and then by pressing a key or two the macro automatically performs the task for you. Once a macro has been created, it can be executed in a number of ways. A macro can be executed by selecting a menu item or pressing a particular key combination. You can also assign the macro to a toolbar button, or a graphic object on a worksheet.

Excel's macro recorder makes it easy to record a macro. The macro recorder works much like a tape recorder in that once it is turned on, it records every keystroke and mouse click you make until it is turned off. Macros can be used for very simple tasks such as formatting a worksheet and printing reports. Or they can be used for very complex tasks such as automating entire worksheets so that all the user has to do is retrieve the worksheet file and follow on-screen instructions. Planning each step the macro is to perform before actually recording the macro is very important as the macro recorder will record every step you perform, including the steps you take to correct any mistakes you make. In order for the macro to run as efficiently as possible any unnecessary keystrokes, such as those taken to fix a mistake, should not be a part of the macro.

The macro recorder does not record any uncompleted tasks. For example, if you open a dialog box, make some changes, and then click Cancel, then the macro recorder will record none of those actions.

Recording a Macro

Macros recorded in Excel are created automatically in the Visual Basic for Applications programming language, also known as VBA. Excel's Visual Basic toolbar can be quite useful when you are recording a macro. To display the Visual Basic toolbar shown in figure 6.1, right-click a toolbar that is currently displayed and click Visual Basic.

figure 6.1

The Visual Basic Toolbar

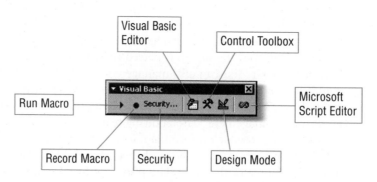

You can display the Record Macro dialog box shown in figure 6.2 by clicking the Record Macro button on the Visual Basic toolbar. You can also display this dialog box using the menus by clicking Tools and then either waiting a couple of seconds or clicking the down arrow at the bottom of the menu to display the Macro option. Select Macro and then click Record new Macro. A macro name that describes the purpose of the macro is entered in the Macro name box. The first letter of the macro name must be a letter. The other characters in the name can be numbers, letters, or the underscore character. A macro name cannot contain any spaces. A letter that will be pressed together with Ctrl to run the macro is entered in the Shortcut key box next to Ctrl. You can use lowercase or uppercase letters. You must use the same case when executing the macro. That is, if you enter a capital *T* in the Shortcut key box, pressing Ctrl and a lowercase *t* will not execute the macro. You can also select where the macro is to be stored. Figure 6.2 shows the drop-down menu that is displayed when the down arrow to the right of the Store macro in box is clicked. If Personal Macro Workbook is selected, the macro will be available whenever you use Excel. If either the New Workbook or This Workbook options are selected, the macro will be available to that workbook only. A description of the macro can be entered in the Description box. When you have finished filling out the dialog box, click OK.

If you open a workbook that contains macros, even if it is a workbook you have created yourself, Excel displays a warning message alerting you to the fact the workbook might contain a macro virus. If a workbook does contain a macro virus, Excel cannot disable or destroy the virus. If you are certain a workbook comes from a reliable source, click Enable Macros when the warning box appears. If you are uncertain about the reliability of the workbook's source, click Disable Macros. A macro virus can cause damage only if it is run.

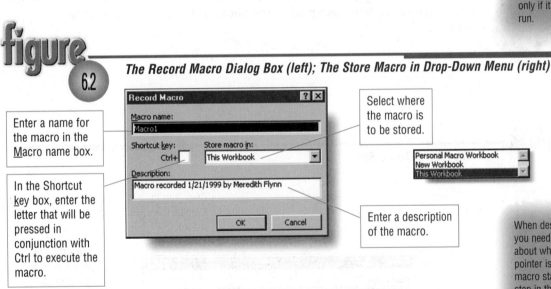

figure 6.2

The Record Macro Dialog Box (left); The Store Macro in Drop-Down Menu (right)

Enter a name for the macro in the Macro name box.

In the Shortcut key box, enter the letter that will be pressed in conjunction with Ctrl to execute the macro.

Select where the macro is to be stored.

Enter a description of the macro.

Once you click OK, the Stop Recording toolbar shown in figure 6.3 is displayed. There are two buttons on the toolbar. If part of your macro includes selecting cells, Excel will always select the exact same cells as were selected when the macro was created because the macro records absolute cell references. If the macro is to select cells no matter where the active cell is located when the macro is run, click the Relative Reference button. Relative references will be recorded until you either click the Stop button or click the Relative Reference button to turn the feature off. When you have finished entering the macro, click the Stop Recording button, which will stop the recording of the macro.

When designing a macro, you need to be careful about where the cell pointer is located when the macro starts. If the first step in the macro is to select a specific cell, then the macro starts executing in that cell. If the first step in the macro is *not* selecting a specific cell, then the macro is going to start executing in whatever cell happens to be selected when the macro was invoked. If that cell contains data, the data is going to be overwritten by any input that is part of the macro.

The Stop Recording Toolbar

Relative Reference

Stop Recording

Running a Macro

There are several ways to run a macro. One way is to click Tools, select Macro once it is displayed, and click Macros. The Macro Dialog box shown in figure 6.4 is displayed. You can also display this dialog box by clicking the Run Macro button on the Visual Basic toolbar. Select the name of the macro you want to run from the list box and click Run. The macro you selected is run. If you need to delete a macro, select the name of the macro you want to delete from the list box and click Delete. Clicking Options displays the Macro Options dialog box, shown in figure 6.5, where you can change the letter assigned to the Shortcut key command and the description.

6.4

The Macro Dialog Box

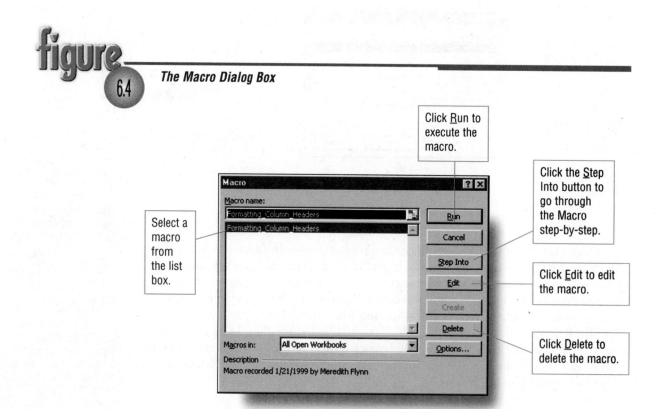

Click Run to execute the macro.

Click the Step Into button to go through the Macro step-by-step.

Select a macro from the list box.

Click Edit to edit the macro.

Click Delete to delete the macro.

figure 6.5

The Macro Options Dialog Box

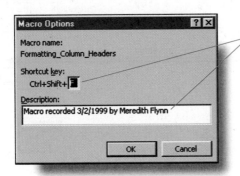

The Macro Options dialog box allows you to edit the Shortcut key used to run the macro and the description of the macro.

If a keyboard shortcut key has been assigned to the macro either in the Record Macro dialog box when the macro was first recorded or in the Macro Options dialog box after the macro was recorded, the macro can be run by simply pressing the keyboard shortcut key. For example, pressing Ctrl-F might run a macro that formats column headers.

exercise

Creating and Running a Macro

1. Open Excel.
2. Open Excel Worksheet E6-01.
3. Save the worksheet using the Save As command and name it Excel E6, Ex 01.
4. Create a custom header that displays your name at the left margin and the file name at the right margin.
5. Chris Robinson is a freelance PC technician. His company is called Bits Unlimited and he specializes in offering his PC consulting services to doctors' offices. This worksheet has been created to project his earnings for next year. You are going to create a macro that takes a figure from a cell in the current year and increases it by 5%. Complete the following steps to create the macro:
   a. Click cell H5.
   b. Click View, point to Toolbars, and click Visual Basic. The Visual Basic toolbar is displayed.
   c. Click the Record Macro button. The Record Macro dialog box is displayed.

Step 5c

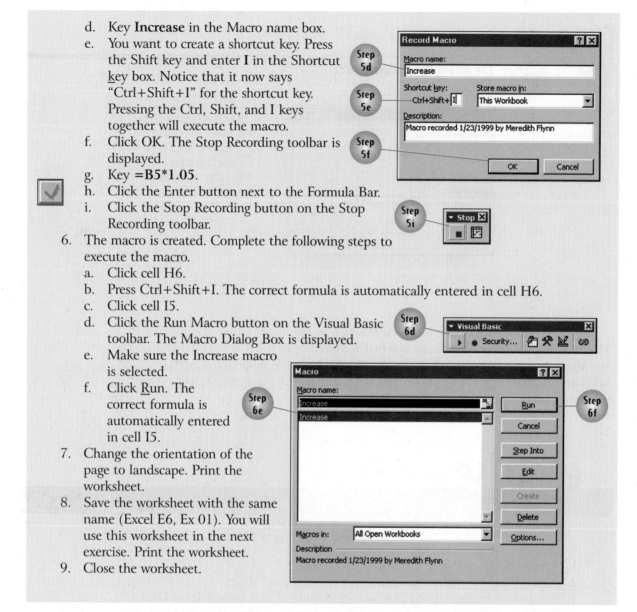

d. Key **Increase** in the Macro name box.

e. You want to create a shortcut key. Press the Shift key and enter **I** in the Shortcut key box. Notice that it now says "Ctrl+Shift+I" for the shortcut key. Pressing the Ctrl, Shift, and I keys together will execute the macro.

f. Click OK. The Stop Recording toolbar is displayed.

g. Key **=B5*1.05**.

h. Click the Enter button next to the Formula Bar.

i. Click the Stop Recording button on the Stop Recording toolbar.

6. The macro is created. Complete the following steps to execute the macro.

a. Click cell H6.

b. Press Ctrl+Shift+I. The correct formula is automatically entered in cell H6.

c. Click cell I5.

d. Click the Run Macro button on the Visual Basic toolbar. The Macro Dialog Box is displayed.

e. Make sure the Increase macro is selected.

f. Click Run. The correct formula is automatically entered in cell I5.

7. Change the orientation of the page to landscape. Print the worksheet.

8. Save the worksheet with the same name (Excel E6, Ex 01). You will use this worksheet in the next exercise. Print the worksheet.

9. Close the worksheet.

Assigning a Macro to a Command Button

You can run an existing macro from a command button placed on the worksheet. To assign a macro to a command button, display the Forms Toolbar shown in figure 6.6 and click the Button button. The mouse pointer turns into a crosshair and you can drag the control to the size you want. The default name of the button is Button 1, Button 2, and so on. To change the name of the button, select the default name and key in a new one. To change the format of the button, such as the size of the button or the font and font color used on the button, right-click the button and click Format Control on the shortcut menu. To assign a macro to the button, right-click the button and click Assign Macro. The Assign Macro dialog box shown in figure 6.7 is displayed. To assign the button to a macro that has already been created, select the macro name from the list and click OK. To record a macro to be assigned to the button, click Record.

 **figure**
6.6

The Forms Toolbar

Button button

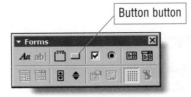

 **figure**
6.7

The Assign Macro Dialog Box

To assign a macro that has already been recorded to a command button, select the macro to be assigned and click OK.

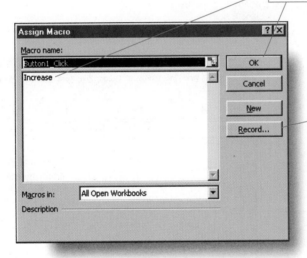

To record a macro to be assigned to a command button, click Record.

Editing a Macro

To edit a macro you first click the Run Macro button on the Visual Basic toolbar. When the Macro dialog box appears, select the macro to be edited and click Edit as shown in figure 6.8. The Visual Basic Editor appears as a new application. Macros are edited using the Visual Basic Editor.

In order to do much in the way of editing macros, you need to be familiar with the Visual Basic Editor.

figure
6.8 — *Editing a Macro*

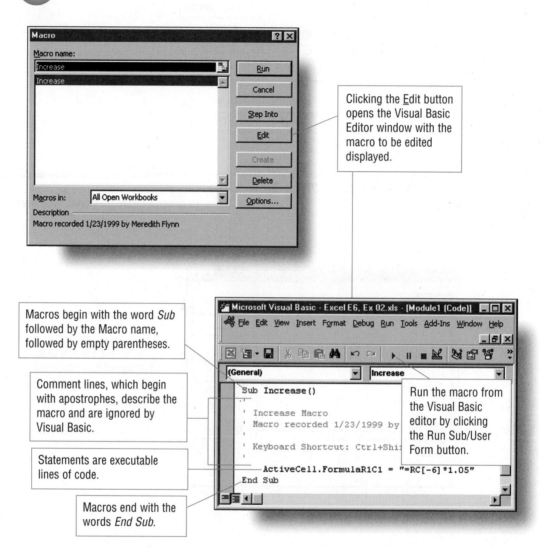

Clicking the Edit button opens the Visual Basic Editor window with the macro to be edited displayed.

Macros begin with the word *Sub* followed by the Macro name, followed by empty parentheses.

Comment lines, which begin with apostrophes, describe the macro and are ignored by Visual Basic.

Statements are executable lines of code.

Macros end with the words *End Sub*.

Run the macro from the Visual Basic editor by clicking the Run Sub/User Form button.

As you can see in figure 6.8, macros begin with the word Sub followed by the macro name followed by empty parentheses. The next few lines, which begin with apostrophes, are the comment lines. Comment lines describe the macro and are ignored by Visual Basic. After the comment lines is the macro. The executable lines of code in the macro are called statements. In the example in figure 6.8, the statement is made up of two parts that are separated by a period. Everything to the left of the period is the object. The object identifies the part of Excel that is to be affected. In figure 6.8, *ActiveCell* is the object. That is, the currently active cell is the cell that is going to be affected. Everything to the right of the period indicates how the object is to be affected. Edit the statements however necessary. You can run the edited macro right from the Visual Basic editor by clicking the Run Sub/User Form button.

Editing a Macro and Assigning a Macro to a Command Button

1. Open worksheet Excel E6, Ex 01. You created this worksheet in exercise 1.
2. Save the worksheet using the Save <u>A</u>s command and name it Excel E6, Ex 02.
3. Create a custom header that displays your name at the left margin and the file name at the right margin.
4. Click cell H6. Instead of having a macro that increases the income by 5%, you want it to increase the income by 6%. Complete the following steps to edit and execute the macro:
    a. If necessary, display the Visual Basic toolbar.
    b. Click the Run Macro button on the Visual Basic toolbar.

    c. Make sure the Increase macro is selected.
    d. Click <u>E</u>dit.
    e. The Visual Basic Editor appears as a new application. There should be three windows. The code window contains the code for the macro. Close the other two windows.

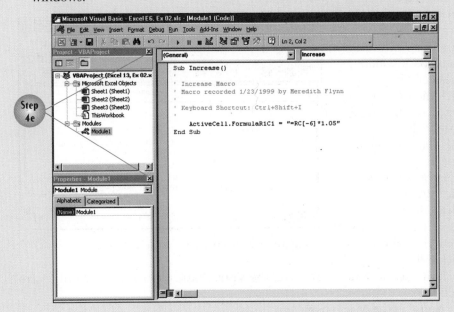

f. Resize the Microsoft Visual Basic to make it smaller so that you can see the worksheet behind it.

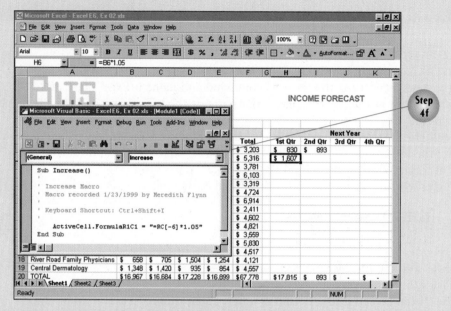

g. There is one statement line, *ActiveCell.FormulaR1C1 = "=RC[-6]*1.05"*. Edit this line so that the formula is *1.06 instead of *1.05.

h. Click the Run Sub/User Form button.

i. Close the Microsoft Visual Basic window.

j. Click cell I5.

k. Click the Run Macro button on the Visual Basic toolbar.

l. The Macro dialog box appears with the macro name Increase selected. Click Run.

m. Click cell H5.

n. Press Ctrl+Shift+I.

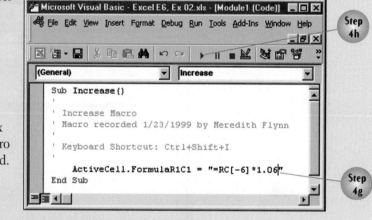

5. Complete the following steps to create and execute two more macros:

a. Click cell J5.

b. Click the Record Macro button on the Visual Basic toolbar. The Record Macro dialog box is displayed.

c. Key **Same** in the Macro name box.

d. You want to create a shortcut key. Click the Shortcut key box to select it. Press the Shift key and enter **S**. Notice that it now says *Ctrl+Shift+S* for the shortcut key. Pressing the Ctrl, Shift, and S keys together will execute the macro.

e. Click OK. The Stop Recording toolbar is displayed.

f. Key **=D5**.

g. Click the Enter button next to the Formula bar.

h. Click the Stop Recording button on the Stop Recording toolbar.

i. Click cell J6.

j. Press Ctrl+Shift+S.

k. Click cell I6.

l. Click the Record Macro button. The Record Macro dialog box is displayed.

m. Key **Decrease** in the Macro name box.

n. You want to create a shortcut key. Click the Shortcut key box. Press the Shift key and enter **D**.

o. Click OK. The Stop Recording toolbar is displayed.

p. Key **=C6-(C6*.04)**.

q. Click the Enter button next to the Formula Bar.

r. Click the Stop Recording button on the Stop Recording toolbar.

s. Click cell K5.

t. Press Ctrl+Shift+D.

6. Next you want to assign the Increase macro to a command button. Complete the following steps to assign the macro to a command button.

a. Click <u>V</u>iew, point to <u>T</u>oolbars, and click Forms. The Forms toolbar is displayed.

b. Click the Button button.

c. The mouse pointer changes to crosshairs. Underneath and a little to the left of the INCOME FORECAST header, click and drag a rectangle that is approximately 0.25 inches high and 0.75 inches wide. You will set the exact size in a later step.

d. The button appears along with the Assign Macro dialog box. Select the Macro name *Increase*.

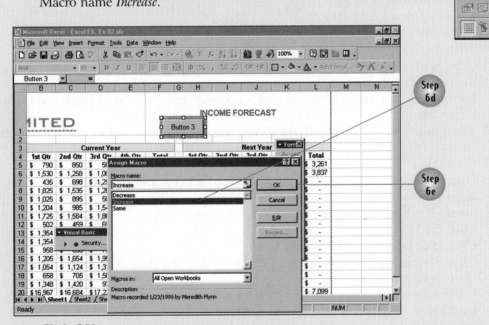

e. Click OK.

f. Drag across the text currently on the button to select it and key **Increase**.

g. Right-click one of the button's edges and click Format Control on the shortcut menu. The Format Control dialog box is displayed.

h. If necessary click the Font tab.

i. Click *Bold* from the Font style list box.

j. Click the down arrow to the right of the Color box and then click the Red button, the first button in the third row.

k. Click the Size tab. Enter **0.25"** in the Height box.

l. Enter **0.75"** in the Width box.

m. Click OK.

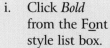

7. Complete the following steps to assign the Same macro to a command button.

   a. The Forms toolbar should still be displayed. Click the Button button.

   b. The mouse pointer changes to crosshairs. To the right of the Increase button, click and drag a rectangle that is approximately 0.25 inches high and 0.75 inches wide.

   c. The button appears along with the Assign Macro dialog box. Select the Macro name *Same*.

   d. Click OK.

   e. Drag across the text currently on the button to select it and key **Same**.

   f. Right-click one of the button's edges and click Format Control on the shortcut menu. The Format Control dialog box is displayed.

   g. Click the Font tab.

   h. Click Bold from the Font style list box.

   i. Click the down arrow to the right of the Color box and then click the Red button, the first button in the third row.

   j. Click the Size tab. Enter **0.25"** in the Height box; enter **0.75"** in the Width box.

   k. Click OK.

8. Complete the following steps to assign the Decrease macro to a command button.

   a. Click the Button button.

   b. The mouse pointer changes to crosshairs. To the right of the Same button, click and drag a rectangle that is approximately 0.25 inches high and 0.75 inches wide.

   c. The button appears along with the Assign Macro dialog box. Select the Macro name *Decrease*.

   d. Click OK.

   e. Drag across the text currently on the button to select it and key **Decrease**.

 f. Right-click one of the button's edges and click Format Control on the shortcut menu. The Format Control dialog box is displayed.

 g. Click the Font tab.

 h. Click Bold from the Font style list box.

 i. Click the down arrow to the right of the Color box and then click the Red button, the first button in the third row.

 j. Click the Size button. Enter **0.25″** in the Height box; enter **0.75″** in the Width box.

 k. Click OK.

 l. Close the Forms toolbar.

9. Complete the following steps to enter Macros from the command buttons.

 a. Click cell K6.

 b. Click the Decrease button.

 c. Click cell H7.

 d. Click the Same button.

10. To finish filling in the forecast, click the listed command button for each cell in the following list:

Cell	Command Button	Cell	Command Button
H8	Increase	J7	Same
H9	Increase	J8	Same
H10	Same	J9	Increase
H11	Increase	J10	Same
H12	Increase	J11	Increase
H13	Same	J12	Increase
H14	Increase	J13	Decrease
H15	Decrease	J14	Increase
H16	Decrease	J15	Same
H17	Decrease	J16	Increase
H18	Decrease	J17	Increase
H19	Decrease	J18	Increase
I7	Increase	J19	Same
I8	Decrease	K7	Increase
I9	Increase	K8	Decrease
I10	Decrease	K9	Increase
I11	Increase	K10	Same
I12	Increase	K11	Increase
I13	Increase	K12	Increase
I14	Same	K13	Same
I15	Decrease	K14	Increase
I16	Increase	K15	Increase
I17	Same	K16	Same
I18	Same	K17	Increase
I19	Decrease	K18	Increase
		K19	Same

11. Create another macro that uses conditional formatting to display the cells in the Total column that have values under $4,000 as red and those that have values over $6,000 as blue. Complete the following steps to create and execute the macro:

 a. Click cell F5.

 b. Click the Record Macro button on the Visual Basic toolbar.

 c. Key **Format** in the Macro name box.

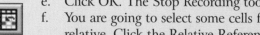

d.   Click the Shortcut key box. Press the Shift key and enter **F**.
e.   Click OK. The Stop Recording toolbar is displayed.
f.   You are going to select some cells for the macro, but you want their reference to be relative. Click the Relative Reference button on the Stop Recording toolbar. The button should appear to be pressed in.
g.   Select cells F5 through F19.
h.   Click F̲ormat and then click Con̲ditional Formatting. The Conditional Formatting dialog box appears.
i.   Add a condition that displays any value less than 4000 as bold and in the color red.
j.   Add a second condition that displays any value greater than 6000 as bold and in blue.

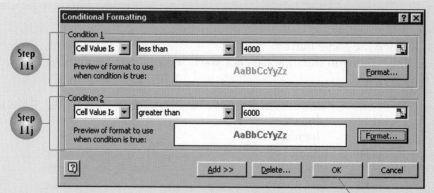

k.   Click OK.
l.   Click the Stop Recording button on the Stop Recording toolbar.
m.   Click cell L5.
n.   Press Ctrl+Shift+F.
12. Close the Visual Basic toolbar.
13. Print the worksheet.
14. Save the worksheet using the same name (Excel E6, Ex 02). Close the worksheet.

Working with Toolbars

The toolbars used in Office 2000 are quite flexible and adaptable. Toolbars can be docked or floating. They can be hidden or displayed. They can be reshaped. You can even make your own customized toolbar.

Floating and Docked Toolbars

Figure 6.9 shows examples of both docked and floating toolbars. A docked toolbar is attached to one of the program window's borders. A docked toolbar can be attached below the program title bar or to the left, right, or bottom border of the program window. A floating toolbar is not attached to the edge of the programming window. Toolbars can be moved to any location on the screen. To move a toolbar that is docked, drag the move handle located at the left side of the docked toolbar. To move a floating toolbar, drag the toolbar's title bar. When a toolbar is dragged to the border of the programming window or close to the edge of another docked toolbar, it becomes a docked toolbar. To undock a toolbar, drag the move handle at that toolbar's left side.

Docked and Floating Toolbars

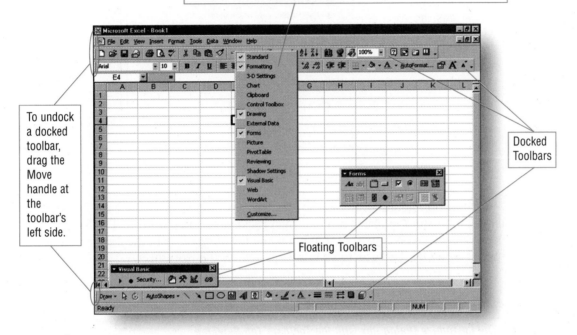

To display or hide a toolbar, right-click any displayed toolbar to see a complete menu of toolbars. Selecting a toolbar that has a check by it will close that toolbar. Selecting a toolbar that does not have a check by it will open that toolbar.

To undock a docked toolbar, drag the Move handle at the toolbar's left side.

Docked Toolbars

Floating Toolbars

Hiding and Displaying Toolbars

As shown in figure 6.9, you can hide and display toolbars by right-clicking on any displayed toolbar. A menu pops up listing all the toolbars. Toolbars with a check mark next to them are currently open. Those without check marks are currently hidden. Clicking on a hidden toolbar displays it and clicking on a displayed toolbar hides it. You can also hide and display toolbars by clicking View and Toolbars. The same menu appears that is displayed when you right-click a toolbar.

Customizing a Toolbar

There are a number of ways that toolbars can be customized. The default setting for Excel 2000 is to have the Standard and Formatting toolbars share one row. To change this default setting so that they appear on two rows, click Tools and then click Customize. The Customize dialog box appears. Click the Options tab. The dialog box will look like figure 6.10. Click the Standard and Formatting toolbars share one row check box so that it is no longer selected.

figure
6.10

The Customize Dialog Box with the Options Tab Selected

If you want the
Standard and
Formatting
toolbars displayed
on two rows, this
option should not
be selected.

As shown in figure 6.11, you can create a new toolbar by clicking the Toolbars tab on the Customize dialog box and then clicking the New button. The New Toolbar dialog box is displayed. Enter a name for the toolbar in the Toolbar name box and click OK. The new toolbar is displayed on the worksheet.

figure
6.11

The Customize Dialog Box with the Toolbars Tab Selected

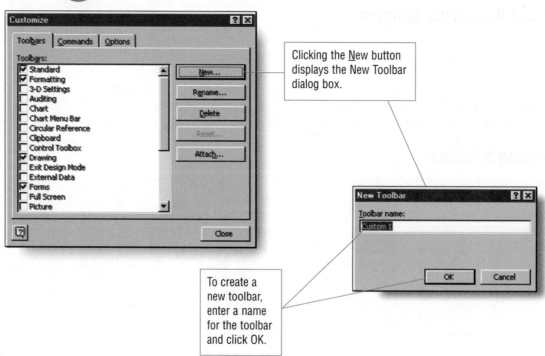

Clicking the New button
displays the New Toolbar
dialog box.

To create a
new toolbar,
enter a name
for the toolbar
and click OK.

Buttons can be added to a new toolbar a number of different ways. To place one of Excel's existing commands on the new toolbar, click the Commands tab on the Customize dialog box. Click the appropriate category of the command in the Categories list box. Drag the command from the Commands list box to the new toolbar. The appropriate button will appear on the toolbar.

figure

6.12

The Customize Dialog Box with the Commands Tab Selected

To place a button on a new toolbar, select the button's category from the Categories list

...and then drag the command from the Commands list box to the new toolbar.

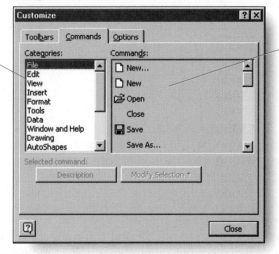

You can place a button that runs a macro on a toolbar by clicking the Commands tab on the Customize dialog box (shown in figure 6.12) and selecting Macros in the Categories list box. A custom button appears in the Commands list box. Drag this custom button to the toolbar. To change the name of the button, the image that appears on the button, and to assign the macro to the button, you right click the button on the toolbar.

You can delete a custom toolbar that you have created by clicking the Toolbars tab on the Customize dialog box (shown in figure 6.11). Select the toolbar you want to delete from the Toolbars list box and click Delete.

exercise 3

Creating Macros and Customizing a Toolbar

1. Open Excel worksheet E6-02.
2. Save the worksheet using the Save As command and name it Excel E6, Ex 03.
3. Click the 7 Percent worksheet tab. Press Shift and click the 8 Percent worksheet tab. All three worksheets should be selected. Create a custom header that displays your name at the left margin and the file name at the right margin.
4. When students come into the Financial Advisor's office at Redwood Community College, they often want to know what kind of payments they can expect on student loans. This worksheet helps students determine what the monthly payments on a student loan would be, depending on how much money they borrow, the interest rate, and the length of the loan. Complete the following steps for creating a macro that will enter the loan amounts:
   a. Click cell A7.

b. Display the Visual Basic toolbar by right-clicking on a toolbar and clicking Visual Basic.

c. Click the Record Macro button on the Visual Basic toolbar. The Record Macro dialog box is displayed.

d. Key **Amounts** in the Macro name box.

e. Click the Shortcut key box. Press the Shift key and enter **A**.

f. Click OK. The Stop Recording toolbar is displayed.

g. You do not want the cell references to be relative. Make sure the Relative References button on the Stop Recording toolbar is *not* pressed in. Key the following in the cells indicated:

Cell	Value
A7	10000
A8	15000
A9	20000
A10	25000
A11	30000
A12	35000
A13	40000
A14	45000
A15	50000
A16	55000
A17	60000

h. You are going to select some cells and you want the cell references to be relative. Click the Relative Reference button on the Stop Recording toolbar so that it is pressed in.

i. Select cells A7 through A17.

j. Format cells A7 through A17 as currency with no decimal places.

k. Click the Stop Recording button on the Stop Recording toolbar.

5. Complete the following steps to create a macro for entering the PMT function:

a. Click cell B7.

b. Click the Record Macro button on the Visual Basic toolbar.

c. Key **Payment** in the Macro name box.

d. Press the Shift key and enter **P** in the Shortcut key box. Notice that it now says *Ctrl+Shift+P* for the shortcut key.

e. Click OK. The Stop Recording toolbar is displayed.

f. Make sure the Relative Reference button on the Stop Recording toolbar is selected. It should appear to be pressed in.

g. Key **=PMT($B$4/12, B$5, -$A7)** in cell B7.

h. Click the Enter button next to the Formula Bar.

i. Copy the formula in cell B7 down to cell B17 and then across to column F.

j. Click the Stop Recording button on the Stop Recording toolbar.

6. Complete the following steps to create a custom toolbar that will include a button for the Amounts macro and a button for the Payment macro.

a. Click Tools and then click Customize.

b. If necessary, click the Toolbars tab.

c. Click New.

Step 6c

d. Key **Macros** in the Toolbar name box.
e. Click OK.
f. Click the Commands tab.
g. Select *Macros* from the Categories list box.
h. Drag the custom Button from the Commands list box to the Macros toolbar twice.
i. Since students often ask for the worksheet to be printed, having the Print button on the Macros toolbar would be convenient. Select *File* from the Categories list box.
j. Drag the Print command from the Commands list box to the Macros toolbar.

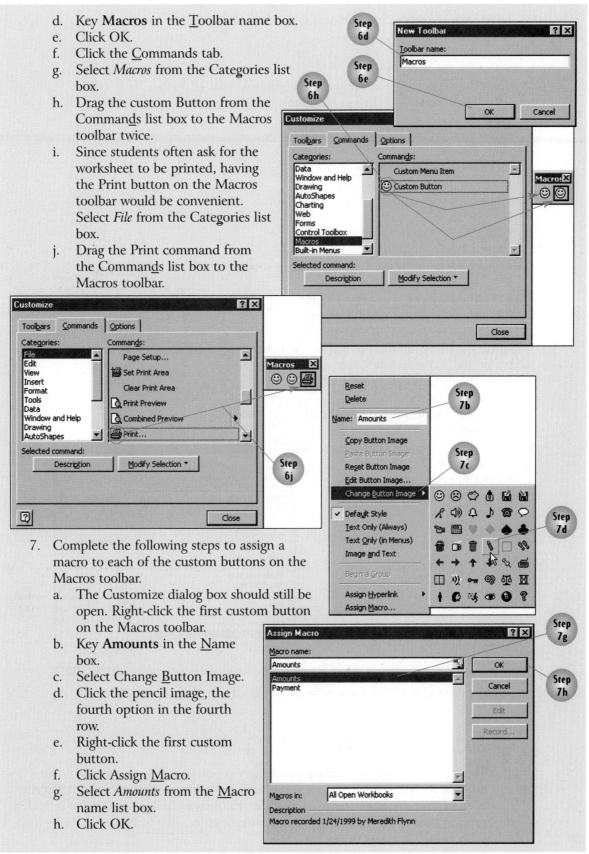

7. Complete the following steps to assign a macro to each of the custom buttons on the Macros toolbar.
   a. The Customize dialog box should still be open. Right-click the first custom button on the Macros toolbar.
   b. Key **Amounts** in the Name box.
   c. Select Change Button Image.
   d. Click the pencil image, the fourth option in the fourth row.
   e. Right-click the first custom button.
   f. Click Assign Macro.
   g. Select *Amounts* from the Macro name list box.
   h. Click OK.

i.   Right-click the second custom button on the Macros toolbar.
j.   Key **Payment** in the Name box.
k.   Select Change Button Image.
l.   Click the piggy bank button, the third option in row 1.
m.   Right-click the second custom button on the Macros toolbar.
n.   Click Assign Macro.
o.   Select *Payment* from the Macro name list box.
p.   Click OK.
q.   Close the Customize dialog box.
r.   Close the Visual Basic toolbar.

8.   Complete the following steps to use the Amounts and Payment macros on the 7.5 Percent worksheet.
a.   Click the 7.5 Percent worksheet tab.
b.   Click cell A7.
c.   Click the Amounts button on the Macros toolbar.
d.   Click cell B7.
e.   Click the Payment button on the Macros toolbar.
f.   Click the Print button on the Macros toolbar.
g.   Click OK.

9.   Complete the following steps to use the Amounts and Payment macros on the 8 Percent worksheet.
a.   Click the 8 Percent worksheet tab.
b.   Click cell A7.
c.   Click the Amounts button on the Macros toolbar.
d.   Click cell B7.
e.   Click the Payment button on the Macros toolbar.
f.   Click the Print button on the Macros toolbar.
g.   Click OK.

10.   Complete the following steps to delete the Macros toolbar.
a.   Right-click the Macros toolbar.
b.   Click Customize.
c.   Click the Toolbars tab.
d.   Select *Macros* from the Toolbars list box.
e.   Click Delete.
f.   Click OK.
g.   Close the Customize dialog box.

11.   Save the workbook using the same name (Excel E6, Ex 03) and close it.

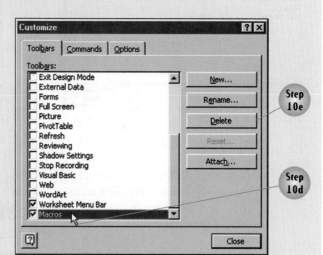

Auditing Workbooks

Making sure a large and complex worksheet is functioning accurately could be a difficult chore. Excel's built-in auditing features help to simplify that task. Excel's auditing features allow you to display tracer arrows to find precedents, or cells that provide data to a formula, dependents, or cells containing formulas that refer to other cells, and errors in any cell.

Displaying the Auditing Toolbar

To display the Auditing Toolbar, right-click a toolbar, and click Customize. Click the Toolbars tab and select Auditing from the Toolbars list box. The Auditing toolbar shown in figure 6.13 is displayed. You can also display the Auditing toolbar by clicking Tools, selecting Auditing, and clicking Show Auditing Toolbar. Table 6.1 describes the buttons found on the Auditing toolbar.

Displaying the Auditing Toolbar

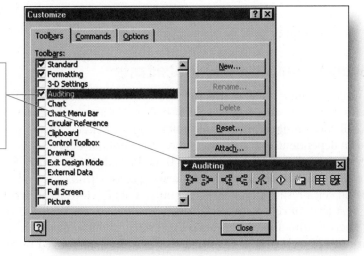

Select Auditing from the Toolbars list box and the Auditing toolbar will appear.

The Auditing Toolbar

 The Trace Precedents button displays a tracer arrow that indicates the source of the data for a formula.

 The Remove Precedent button removes tracer arrows generated by the Trace Precedents button.

 The Trace Dependents button displays a tracer arrow to indicate cells containing formulas with cell references for a specific cell.

 The Remove Dependent Arrows button removes the tracer arrows generated by the Trace Dependents button.

 The Remove All Arrows button removes all precedent tracer arrows and dependent tracer arrows.

 The Trace Error button finds cells contributing to an error in a cell.

The New Comment button allows you to write a comment that is attached to a cell.

 The Circle Invalid Data button circles cells containing data outside the valid range defined with the Validation feature.

 The Clear Validation Circles removes circles generated by the Circle Invalid Data button.

Black arrows pointing from a worksheet icon to the selected cell are an indication that the selected cell contains a reference to another worksheet or workbook.

Tracing Dependents and Precedents

A precedent cell is a cell that is referred to by a formula in another cell. For example, if cell G5 contains the formula =F5*1.05, F5 is a precedent to G5. A dependent cell is a cell containing a formula that refers to another cell. In the preceding example, G5 is a dependent of F5. To trace the precedents or dependents of a cell, select the appropriate cell and click either the Trace Precedents or Trace Dependents button. Blue tracer arrows are displayed indicating cells with a direct relationship to the selected cell's result. If you click the button again, additional arrows that indicate the next level of cells with a relationship to the selected cell's result are drawn. You can keep clicking the button until Excel beeps, which means there are no more relationships to be found. The tracer arrows can be removed by clicking the Remove Precedent Arrows button, Remove Dependent Arrows button, or the Remove All Arrows button.

Double-clicking a tracer arrow selects the cell at the other end of the arrow.

Tracing Errors

If an error result such as #DIV/0! is being displayed in a cell, clicking the cell containing the error and then clicking the Trace Error button draws red tracer arrows to the cells that are causing the error. To remove the tracer arrows, click the Remove All Arrows button.

Auditing a Worksheet

1. Open Excel Worksheet E6-03.
2. Save the worksheet using the Save As command and name it Excel E6, Ex 04.
3. Create a custom header that displays your name at the left margin and the file name at the right margin.
4. There are cells divided by zero error messages in this worksheet. Complete the following steps to find the cells causing this error.
   a. Right-click the Formatting toolbar and click Customize.
   b. Click the Toolbars tab.

c. Click the *Auditing* check box in the Toolbars list box to select it. The Auditing toolbar is displayed.

d. Click the Close button.

e. Click cell C5.

f. Click the Trace Error button on the Auditing toolbar. A red tracer arrow is drawn to cell D27.

g. Look at the formula in D27, which is =D25/D26. Now look at cell D26. It contains a zero. Click cell D26 and key **5**. Press Enter.

h. The red tracer line changes to a blue tracer line because the error was fixed.

i. Click cell D11.

j. Click the Trace Precedents button on the Auditing toolbar.

k. Click the Trace Precedents button a second time. You can now see that cells D4, D5, D7, D9, and D10 are all precedents to the contents of cell D11. The first level precedents are cells D9 and D10. The next level of precedents are D4, D5, and D7.

l. You can follow a trace by double-clicking one of the dots on the tracer line. The active cell immediately becomes the cell at the other end of the arrow. Double-click the blue dot in cell D4. Cell D9 is now the active cell.

m. Double-click the blue dot in cell D4 again to move the active cell back to cell D4.

n. Click Cell G11.

o. Click the Trace Dependents button. The tracer arrow that is drawn shows you that cell G16 contains a formula that refers to cell G11.

5. Print the worksheet.

6. Click the Remove All Arrows button on the Auditing toolbar.

7. Complete the following steps to enter a new comment for cell A5:

a. Click cell A5.

b. Click the New Comment button on the Auditing toolbar.

c. Key the following:

> **Figures for calculating the depreciation on new machine are found in cells C21 through D27.**

8. Close the Auditing toolbar.

9. Save the workbook using the same name (Excel E6, Ex 04) and close it.

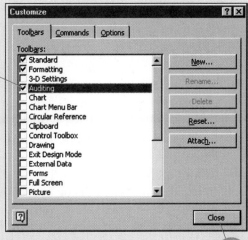

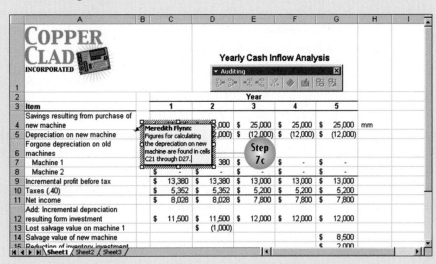

chapter summary

- Macros automate tasks that perform the same sequence of steps or tasks that are performed repeatedly. Excel's macro recorder records every keystroke and mouse click so that it can be played back at a later time.

- Excel macros are automatically created in the Visual Basic for Applications programming language.

- Record a macro by clicking Tools, selecting Macro, and then clicking Record new Macro. In the Record Macro dialog box, enter a macro name and, if desired a shortcut key and description. A macro name must begin with a letter but can contain numbers, letters, and the underscore character. A shortcut key is a letter that is pressed together with Ctrl or Ctrl+Shift in order to execute the macro.

- Planning the exact steps of a macro before recording it is important because everything that is entered, including mistakes and the keystrokes taken to fix the mistakes, is recorded and executed every time the macro is run.

- When selecting cells is a step to be included in a macro, you must know whether the selected cells should have an absolute cell reference or a relative cell reference. The default is for cells to have an absolute cell reference, which means the exact same cells will be selected each time the macro is executed. If the cells should have a relative cell reference, click the Relative Reference button on the Stop Recording toolbar. If the Relative Reference button appears to be pressed in when the cells are selected, the selected cells will have a relative reference. If the button is not pressed in, then the cells will have an absolute reference.

- Run a macro by pressing the shortcut key, pressing the Run Macro button on the Visual Basic toolbar, or by clicking Tools, selecting Macro, and clicking Macros.

- Macros can be run from a command button placed on the worksheet. Assign a macro to a command button by clicking the Button button on the Forms toolbar. The mouse pointer turns into a crosshair and you can click and drag to make the command button the size you want. Once the button has been placed on the worksheet you can change its name and format and assign a macro to it.

- Edit a macro by accessing the Macro dialog box, selecting the macro to be edited, and clicking Edit. The macro is displayed in the Microsoft Visual Basic Editor.

- Docked toolbars are attached to one of the program window's borders or to another toolbar. Floating toolbars are not attached to anything. Move a docked toolbar by dragging the move handle located at the left side of the docked toolbar. Move a floating toolbar by dragging the toolbar's title bar.

- Change the default setting so that Excel's Standard and Formatting toolbars are on two rows instead of one by clicking Tools and then Customize. Click the Options tab on the Customize dialog box. The Standard Formatting toolbars share one row check box should not be selected.

- Precedents are cells that provide data to a formula. Dependents are cells containing formulas that refer to other cells.

commands review

	Mouse/Keyboard
Display or hide toolbars	Click View, Toolbars
Record a macro	Click Tools, Macro, Record new Macro
Run a macro	Click Tools, Macro, Run
Delete a macro	Click Tools, Macro, Delete
Editing a macro's shortcut key command and/or description	Click Tools, Macro, Options
Change the format of a command button	Right-click the button, Format Control
Assign a macro to a command button	Right-click the button, Assign Macro
Change the default setting for toolbars	Click Tools, Customize, Options tab
Create a new toolbar	Click Tools, Customize, Toolbars tab, New
Place a button that runs an Excel command or a macro on a new toolbar	Click Tools, Customize, Commands
Delete a custom toolbar	Click Tools, Customize, Toolbars tab, Delete
Display the Auditing toolbar	Click Tools, Customize, Toolbars tab

thinking offline

Completion: In the space provided at the right, indicate the correct term, command, or button.

1. This term refers to the programming language in which Excel macros are created.

2. This is the toolbar that needs to be displayed in order to place a command button on a worksheet.

3. This term refers to the Editor used to edit Excel macros.

4. Display this box to edit a macro.

5. This is the term used to refer to the executable lines in a macro.

6. This is the button you click on the Forms toolbar if you want to place a command button on a worksheet.

7. When editing a macro, the comment lines describing the macro begin with this character.

8. This term describes a toolbar that is attached to the border of a program window.

9. If you right-click a toolbar, this is what appears.

10. This term refers to a cell that is referred to by a formula in another cell.

11. This is the term that refers to a cell containing a formula that refers to another cell. _____

12. If red tracer arrows appear on a worksheet you know that this button was pressed. _____

13. Explain why it is so important to carefully plan the steps of a macro before recording it.

_____

_____

_____

14. Explain the rules that must be followed for naming a macro.

_____

_____

_____

15. List the steps you would take to place a button that runs a macro on a toolbar.

_____

_____

_____

working hands-on

Assessment 1

1. Open Excel worksheet E6-04.
2. Save the worksheet using the Save <u>A</u>s command and name it Excel E6, SA 01.
3. This workbook is used by Chris Robinson to keep track of the software installed at all the offices where he works as a freelance PC technician. There are ten worksheets in the workbook. Each worksheet contains the records for a different office. Scroll through the worksheet tabs at the bottom of the window to see the ten tabs that are there.
4. Click on the Archer worksheet tab. Scroll to the end of the worksheet tabs. Press the Shift key. Click the River Road worksheet tab. All the worksheet tabs should be selected. Create a custom header that displays your name at the left margin and the file name at the right margin. Be sure to use the file name button for entering the file name in the header. The header will now appear on all the selected worksheets.

5. The applications installed on the various PCs and the NT Server at each office can be either served or local. If an application is local, it resides on the hard drive of that computer. If an application is served it resides on a different computer on the network. A served application can be either an image or a copy. A served image is a unique installation. A served copy is a copy of a served image. Chris needs to keep track of the number of each kind of installation there is at each office. Click the Archer worksheet tab. Record a macro called Count. You should be able to execute the macro with the shortcut key combination Ctrl+Shift+C. The macro should use absolute cell referencing and should include these steps:

   - In cell H4, enter a COUNTIF function that counts the number of times the letter I occurs in cells B4 through G4. *(Hint: Since the macro uses absolute cell referencing, make sure that selecting cell H4 is part of the macro.)*
   - Copy the function in cell H4 down through cell H8.
   - In cell I4, enter a COUNTIF function that counts the number of times the letter S occurs in cells B4 through G4.
   - Copy the function in cell I4 down through cell I8.
   - In cell J4, enter a COUNTIF function that counts the number of times the letter L appears in cells B4 through G4.
   - Copy the function in cell J4 down through cell J8.
   - Enter a SUM function in cell H9 that totals cells H4 through H8.
   - Copy the function in cell H9 to cells I9 and J9.
   - Enter a formula in cell H11 that adds together the values in cells H9 and J9.

6. Once the Count macro has been recorded, click on the Bateson worksheet tab.
7. Run the macro using the shortcut key combination Ctrl+Shift+C.
8. Print the Archer and Bateson worksheets.
9. Save the workbook using the same name (Excel E6, SA 01). This worksheet is used in the Assessment 2 exercise. Close the workbook.

Assessment 2

1. Open workbook Excel E6, SA 01. You created this workbook in the Assessment 1 exercise.
2. Save the worksheet using the Save As command and name it Excel E6, SA 02.
3. Click the Central worksheet tab.
4. Create a custom toolbar. Name the toolbar My Commands.
5. Place a button on the My Commands toolbar for the Count macro. The name of the button for the Count macro should be Count. Choose a different graphic image for the button other than the default. Assign the Count macro to the button.
6. Place a button for the print command on the My Commands toolbar.
7. Run the Count macro using the Count button on the My Commands toolbar.
8. Print the Central worksheet using the Print button on the My Commands toolbar.
9. Click the Doss worksheet tab.
10. Run the Count macro using the Count button on the My Commands toolbar.
11. Print the Doss worksheet using the Print button on the My Commands toolbar.
12. Click the Findlay worksheet tab.
13. Run the Count macro using the Count button on the My Commands toolbar.
14. Print the Findlay worksheet using the Print button on the My Commands toolbar.
15. Close the My Commands toolbar.
16. Save the workbook using the same name (Excel E6, SA 02). Close the workbook.

Assessment 3

1. Open Excel worksheet E6-05.
2. Save the worksheet using the Save <u>A</u>s command and name it Excel E6, SA 03.
3. Create a custom header for the worksheet that displays your name at the left margin and the file name at the right margin.
4. Create a macro that uses AutoFilter to display only the shade plants. Name the macro Shade.
5. Create a macro that uses AutoFilter to display all the plants. Name the macro All.
6. Create a macro that uses AutoFilter to display all the sun plants. Name the macro Sun.
7. Create a custom button on the worksheet. The button should be toward the top and to the right of the list. Assign the Shade macro to the button. Rename the button Shade. The letters on the button should be bold and the color sea green. The size of the button should be .25″ high and .75″ wide. On the Properties tab in the Format Control dialog box, the option <u>D</u>on't move or size with cells should be selected.
8. Create another custom button that is underneath the Shade custom button. Assign the Sun macro to the button. Rename the button Sun. The letters on the button should be bold and the color sea green. The size of the button should be .25″ high and .75″ wide. On the Properties tab in the Format Control dialog box, the option <u>D</u>on't move or size with cells should be selected.
9. Create another custom button that is underneath the Sun custom button. Assign the All macro to the button. Rename the button All. The letters on the button should be bold and the color sea green. The size of the button should be .25″ high and .75″ wide. On the Properties tab in the Format Control dialog box, the option <u>D</u>on't move or size with cells should be selected.
10. Click the Shade button. Print the worksheet.
11. Click the All button. *(Hint: You must click the All button before clicking either the Shade button or the Sun button.)* Print the worksheet.
12. Click the Sun button. Print the worksheet.
13. Click the All button.
14. Save the worksheet using the same name (Excel E6, SA 03) and close it.

Assessment 4

1. Open Excel worksheet E6-06.
2. Save the worksheet using the Save <u>A</u>s command and name it Excel E6, SA 04.
3. Create a custom header for the worksheet that displays your name at the left margin and the file name at the right margin.
4. Display the Auditing toolbar.
5. There is an error somewhere in this worksheet. Click cell F12. Click the Trace Error button. The tracer arrows indicate that the formula in cell E12 references cells J13 through K16, which are empty. Remove the tracer arrows. In the VLOOKUP function the references to the cells that make up the look up table should be absolute. Click cell E3. Edit the formula so that the references to the Look Up Table are absolute. Copy the formula to cells E4 through E22.
6. Click cell E3. Click the Trace Precedents button.
7. Click cell E6. Click the Trace Dependents button. Click the Trace Dependents button again.
8. Print the worksheet.
9. Remove all the tracer arrows.
10. Close the Auditing toolbar.
11. Save the worksheet using the same name (Excel E6, SA 04) and close it.

Chapter 07E

Collaborating with Workgroups

PERFORMANCE OBJECTIVES

Upon successful completion of chapter 7, you will be able to:

- Change workbook properties.
- Apply and remove passwords.
- Apply and remove workbook protection
- Apply and remove worksheet protection.
- Track changes in a shared workbook.
- Accept and reject tracked changes.
- Create, edit, and remove a comment.
- Merge workbooks.
- View multiple worksheets.
- Print multiple worksheets.
- Create and print a report using the Report Manager.

(Note: The Excel add-on program called Report Manager *must be loaded to complete exercise 5.)*

In chapter 2 you were introduced to sharing workbooks. In this chapter, you will learn more about sharing workbooks and the concept of workgroup computing. One of the goals of computer networks is to make it easy and efficient for people to work together in groups. The term *workgroup computing* refers to a group of people working on a common project using computer resources to share ideas, software, and data. Typically a workgroup is comprised of a small number of people who work at the same location.

Excel includes two groups of features that help promote workgroup computing: workgroup sharing features and security features. As you already know, several users, or members of a workgroup, can share a workbook. Each workgroup member can edit the workbook simultaneously. These workgroup sharing features help stimulate workgroup collaboration. Excel's security features allow you to prevent certain types of access to a shared workbook. All the features that help facilitate workgroup collaboration will be discussed in this chapter.

Benefits and Limitations of Sharing Workbooks

Typically in any kind of a business project there are several people involved. Those people directly involved in the project make up a workgroup. Often each individual in the workgroup is responsible for a certain aspect of the project. The manager of the project has to gather information from the workgroup members and consolidate that information in one place. One way for the manager to do this would be to collect hard copies of the data from individual workgroup members and then key all of the collected data into one workbook. But this method would be extremely inefficient. Instead, the workgroup members could all share the workbook and each member could key in his or her own data. Sharing workbooks increases productivity, saves time, and increases the likelihood that the data will be accurate.

There are some limitations involved when you work with shared workbooks. Security is an issue because anyone who has access to the network location where the shared workbook is stored has access to that shared workbook. You have to use workbook and/or worksheet protection to insure the information in the workbook is available only to those who should have access to it. In addition, some features are not available in shared workbooks. These features include deleting worksheets, merging cells, conditional formatting, using drawing tools, inserting or deleting blocks of cells, inserting or editing charts, pictures, objects, or hyperlinks, using the drawing tools, creating or editing PivotTables, creating or editing macros, and assigning passwords to individual worksheets or to the whole workbook.

Changing Workbook Properties

Workbook properties can be used to help administer shared workbooks. Each workbook has a set of properties. These properties keep track of general information about the workbook such as the size of the file and when it was last modified, who created it, the worksheets contained in it, and the title and subject of the workbook. As part of the workbook's properties, Excel also keeps track of who last modified the workbook and the total amount of time it took to edit it, which is useful information to know if you have to bill someone for a project according to the amount of time that you spent working on it.

To assign workbook properties, click File and then click Properties. The Properties dialog box similar to the one in figure 7.1 is displayed. When the Summary tab is selected, you can enter specific information such as the title and subject of the workbook and the author's name. Figure 7.2 shows the general properties that Excel tracks.

If you would like Excel to open the Properties dialog box automatically the first time a new workbook is saved, click Tools and Options. Click the General tab on the Options dialog box. Click the check box next to the Prompt for workbook properties option to select it.

figure
7.1

Properties Dialog Box with the Summary Tab Selected

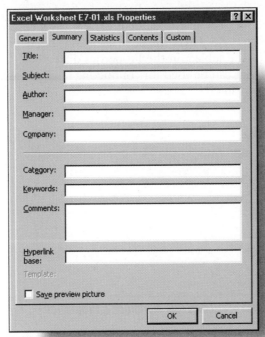

figure
7.2

Properties Dialog Box with the General Tab Selected

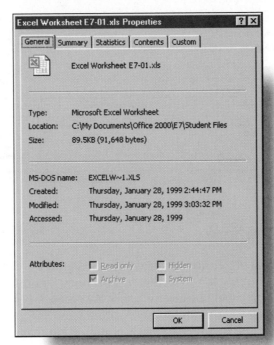

If you are going to use the same search criteria at another time, you can save it. After conducting the search, click the Save Search button at the bottom of the Find dialog box. Enter a name for the search criteria and click OK. To use a saved search, access the Find dialog box and click the Open Search button at the bottom of the dialog box. Select the name of the search and click Open. The search criteria are automatically entered in the Find dialog box.

An advantage of assigning properties to a workbook is that you can use those properties to search for a workbook. This is useful if you have forgotten the file name or forgotten where the file is saved. To search for a workbook by properties, click File and then click Open. Click the Tools button on the Open dialog box and then click Find. The Find dialog box is displayed where you can define the criteria for searching for the file. These criteria are based on the workbook properties. In the example shown in figure 7.3, Excel will search for workbooks that have Income Statement entered as the subject in the Properties dialog box. There are many different properties that can be used for conducting a search such as File Name, Keywords, Author, and so on.

figure 7.3

Searching for a Workbook Using the Workbook's Properties

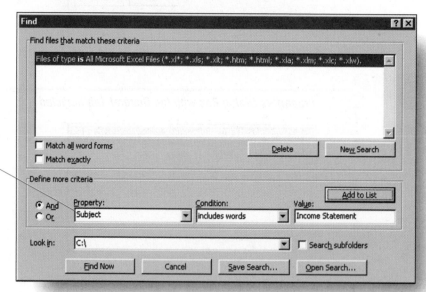

Excel will search for workbooks that have Income Statement entered as the subject in the Properties dialog box.

Protecting Workbooks

Workbooks often contain sensitive information. Sometimes a workbook should only be accessible to certain people within the organization. At other times, people within an organization should be able to access a workbook but not make any changes to it. You may want to prohibit users from removing a workbook from shared use. There are several different levels of protection that can be placed on a worksheet or workbook.

Applying and Removing Passwords

Password protection for an entire workbook is the highest level of protection a workbook can have. If a password has been assigned to a workbook, the workbook cannot be opened by anyone who does not know the password. When a password has been assigned to a workbook, that workbook cannot be shared.

To apply a password to a workbook, click File and then click Save As. Click the Tools button on the Save As dialog box and click General Options. The Save Options dialog box is displayed. Enter the password in the Password to open box. If a workbook is to be generally accessible but only certain people should be able to make changes to it, enter a password in the Password to modify box. Anyone will be able to open the workbook, but only those who know the password will be able to add changes.

As can be seen in figure 7.4, when the password is entered, asterisks are displayed in the box. Passwords can be up to 15 characters long. They are case sensitive which means that uppercase and lowercase does matter. If a password contains a capital letter, that letter must be capitalized when entering the password or the workbook will not open. The same is true with lowercase letters.

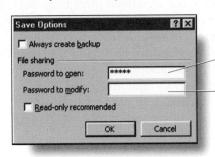

figure 7.4

Save Options Dialog Box

When the password is entered, asterisks are displayed.

If a user can have access to a workbook but not make any changes to it, enter a password here. Anyone can open the workbook, but only those who know the password can modify it.

Once the password has been entered, click OK. The Confirm Password dialog box shown in figure 7.5 is displayed. Enter the password again in the Reenter password to proceed box. Again the password is displayed in asterisks. A message appears in this dialog box warning you that if the password is lost or forgotten, there is no way to recover it and the workbook cannot be opened. If the warning box appears, asking if you want to replace the existing workbook with the open workbook, click Yes.

When you try to open a password-protected workbook, the dialog box shown in figure 7.5 is displayed. As you enter the password, asterisks are once again displayed. After entering the password, click OK. If the password was entered correctly, the workbook is opened.

7.5

Confirm Password Dialog box

To remove a password from a workbook, click File and then click Save As. Click the Tools button on the Save As dialog box and click General Options. Delete the asterisks from the Password to open box and click OK. When you click Save and a warning box appears, asking if you want to replace the existing file, click Yes.

Applying and Removing Worksheet and Workbook Protection

Shared workbooks also can be protected. To protect a shared workbook, click Tools, point to Protection, and click Protect and Share Workbook. The Protect Shared Workbook dialog box is displayed. Click the Sharing with track changes check box to select it. Enter a password if desired, and click OK.

You can protect a worksheet by hiding it from view or by locking its cells so that changes cannot be made to them. To hide an entire worksheet from view, click the worksheet to be hidden and then click Format, select Sheet, and click Hide. The worksheet that was selected is no longer displayed.

Once a worksheet is hidden, the workbook must be protected in order to prevent other users from redisplaying it. When a workbook is protected, other users cannot insert, delete, hide, move, or rename worksheets unless they know the password. To protect the workbook, click Tools, point to Protection, and click Protect Workbook. The Protect Workbook dialog box shown in figure 7.6 is displayed. The Structure check box should be selected in order for the underlying structure of the worksheet to be protected. Enter a password in the Password box and click OK. The password is case sensitive. Once you click OK the Confirm Password dialog box shown in figure 7.5 is displayed. Enter the password again and click OK.

7.6

Protect Workbook Dialog Box

If you want to display a worksheet that has been hidden, you must first remove the workbook protection. To remove workbook protection, click Tools, point to Protection, and click Unprotect Workbook. The Unprotect Workbook dialog box is displayed. Enter the Password in the Password box and click OK. You can then unhide the worksheet by clicking Format, pointing to Sheet, and clicking Unhide. The Unhide dialog box is displayed. Click the worksheet to be unhidden and click OK. The worksheet is once again displayed.

You also can protect individual cells from being changed. This feature is useful for protecting formulas that you want to make sure do not get overwritten with other data. When you use this feature to protect cells, all the cells on the worksheet are protected. You then have to indicate those cells that can be changed. Select the cells in the worksheet that can be changed and then click Format and Cells. Click the Protection tab on the Format Cells dialog box. As shown in figure 7.7, there are two options in the dialog box, Locked and Hidden.

Format Cells Dialog Box with the Protection Tab Selected

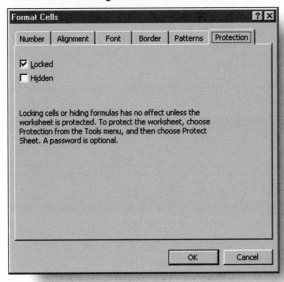

Click the Locked check box so that it is no longer selected. This will unlock the selected cells so that changes can be made to them. Click OK to close the Format Cells dialog box. Click Tools, select Protection, and click Protect Sheet. The Protect Sheet dialog box shown in figure 7.8 is displayed. The default is for Excel to protect everything in the worksheet except for the cells that you unlocked. An optional password can be entered in the Password box. The password is case sensitive. If you enter a password, you will have to reenter it in the Confirm Password dialog box.

Protect Sheet Dialog Box

Once the cells have been protected the warning box shown in figure 7.9 is displayed. To remove cell protection, click Tools, point to Protection, and click Unprotect Sheet. If the worksheet is password protected, you will have to enter the password in the Password box on the Unprotect Sheet dialog box and click OK.

Protect Sheet Warning Box

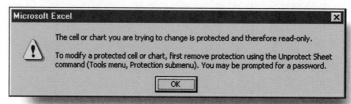

exercise

Changing Workbook Properties, Assigning a Workbook Password, and Protecting Worksheets and Workbooks

1. Open Excel.
2. Open Excel Worksheet E7-01.
3. Save the workbook using the Save As command and name it Excel E7, Ex 01.
4. Create a custom header for the Income Statement worksheet that displays your name at the left margin and the file name at the right margin.
5. This is an Income Statement worksheet for Copper Clad Incorporated that must be completed. But first, you want to enter some workbook properties. Complete the following steps to enter workbook properties for Excel E7, Ex 01.
    a. Click File and then click Properties. *(Hint: You may need to expand the menu.)*

b. Key **Year End Income Statement** in the Title box.

c. Key **Income Statement** in the Subject box.

d. Key your name in the Author box.

e. Key **Bates** in the Manager box.

f. Key **Copper Clad Incorporated** in the Company box.

g. Key **Year End Statement** in the Category box.

h. Key **Income Statement Year End** in the Keywords box.

i. Key the following in the Comments box: **This year-end income statement was put together in collaboration with Larry Ford, Vice President of Finance.**

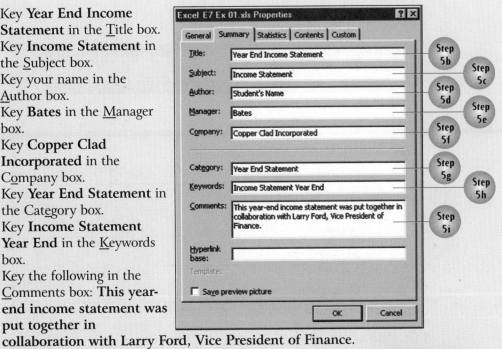

j. Click the General, Statistics, and Contents tabs and read the information provided on each tab.

k. Click the Summary tab.

l. Click OK.

6. Complete the following steps to assign a password to the workbook:

a. Click File and then click Save As.

b. Click the Tools button on the Save As dialog box and click General Options.

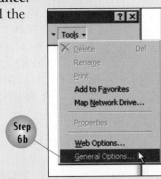

c. Key **C1401C** in the Password to open box on the Save Options dialog box. Only asterisks are displayed.

d. Click OK.

e. Key **C1401C** in the Reenter password to proceed box on the Confirm Password dialog box. Only asterisks are displayed.

f. Click OK.

g. Click Save.

h. The warning is displayed asking if you want to replace the existing file. Click Yes.

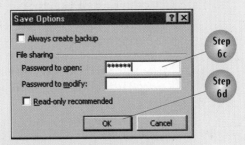

7. Close the Excel E7, Ex 01 workbook.

8. Complete the following steps to find the workbook based on its properties and open it:

a. Click File and then click Open.

b. Click the Tools button on the toolbar in the Open dialog box.

c. Click Find.

d. Click the down arrow to the right of the Property box.

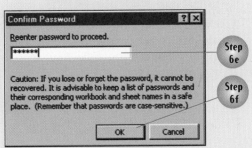

e. Click the *Category* option from the list box.

f. Key **Year End Statement** in the Value box.

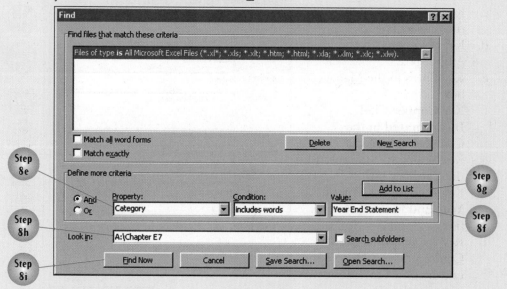

g. Click Add to List.

h. Make sure the drive where your files are located is displayed in the Look in box.

i. Click Find Now.

j. The Excel E7, Ex 01 file is selected. Click Open.

k. Key **C1401C** in the Password box on the Password dialog box.

l. Click OK.

9. Make sure the Income Statement worksheet is selected. Click cell C8. This cell is linked to a cell on the Cost of Goods Sold worksheet. The figures on this worksheet are confidential, so you want to hide this worksheet. Complete the following steps to hide the Cost of Goods Sold worksheet:

a. Click the Cost of Goods Sold worksheet tab.

b. Click Format, point to Sheet, and then click Hide.

c. Click Tools, point to Protection, and click Protect Workbook. The Protect Workbook dialog box is displayed.

d. Make sure the Structure option is selected.

e. Key **cg0128** in the Password box.

f. Click OK.

g. Key **cg0128** in the Reenter password to proceed box on the Confirm Password dialog box.

h. Click OK.

10. Click the Income Statement worksheet tab. Cells C7, C8, C9, C12, C16, C18, and C20 on the worksheet contain formulas. You want to make sure these formulas cannot be changed. Complete the following steps to protect the cells containing formulas:

a. Click cell B4. Press Ctrl and click the following cells in order to select them all:
B5, B6, B7, B11, B12, C13, C14, C15, C17, and C19

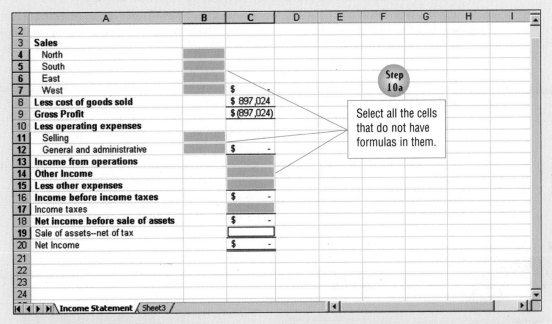

b. Click Format and then click Cells.
c. Click the Protection tab on the Format Cells dialog box.

The Locked check box should not be selected.

d. Click the Locked check box so that it is no longer selected.
e. Click OK.
f. Click Tools, point to Protection, and click Protect Sheet.
g. Key **IFY05ws** in the Password box on the Protect Sheet dialog box.
h. Click OK.
i. Key **IFY05ws** in the Reenter password to proceed box on the confirm Password dialog box.
j. Click OK.
k. Click cell C12 and try to delete it. A warning box appears saying that the cell is protected. Click OK. If a warning box does not appear, click Edit and Undo. Repeat steps a through j to protect the cells on the worksheet.

11. Save the workbook using the same name (Excel E7, Ex 01). You will be using this workbook in exercise 2. Close the workbook.

Tracking Changes

Excel can make it easy to track changes made to the contents of a cell by highlighting those changes. If a workbook is not already set up to be shared, when you use the Highlight Changes command, the workbook sharing feature is automatically turned on. Each user's changes are highlighted in a different color.

To track the changes, click Tools and then either wait for a few moments or click the down arrow at the bottom of the menu to display more options. Point to Track changes and then click Highlight Changes. Click the Track changes while editing check box as shown in figure 7.10. If you want to make specific limitations on the tracking feature, you can do so in the Highlight which changes area in the dialog box. You can select what to track according to when the changes were made, by whom they were made, or specifically where on the worksheet they were made. If none of these options are selected, Excel tracks changes made anywhere in the worksheet, by any user, at any time. Excel can track the changes either by highlighting them on the screen or by listing them on a new worksheet.

figure
7.10

Highlight Changes Dialog Box

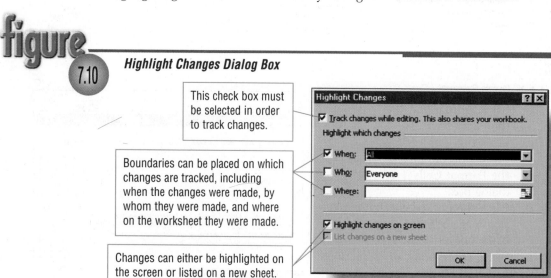

This check box must be selected in order to track changes.

Boundaries can be placed on which changes are tracked, including when the changes were made, by whom they were made, and where on the worksheet they were made.

Changes can either be highlighted on the screen or listed on a new sheet.

When any changes are made to the contents of a cell, a border appears around the cell and a revision triangle appears in the upper left corner of the cell. When the mouse pointer is moved over the revision triangle, a box is displayed that lists who made the change, when the change was made, and what the change was.

Accepting and Rejecting Tracked Changes

Tracked changes can either be accepted or rejected. They can either be accepted or rejected all at one time, or you can go through each change individually and decide whether to accept or reject it. To accept or reject tracked changes, click Tools, point to Track Changes and click Accept or Reject Changes. The Select Changes to Accept or Reject dialog box as shown in figure 7.11 is displayed. The changes to be viewed can be limited by when they were made, by whom they were made, or where on the worksheet they were made. Click OK and the Accept or Reject Changes dialog box shown in figure 7.12 is displayed. To accept just the one change that is displayed, click Accept. To reject just the one change that is displayed, click Reject. To accept all of the changes that were made, click Accept All. To reject all the changes that were made, click Reject all.

figure 7.11

Select Changes to Accept or Reject Dialog Box

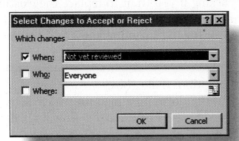

figure 7.12

Accept or Reject Changes Dialog Box

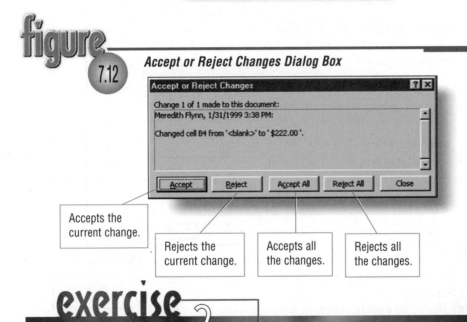

Accepts the current change.

Rejects the current change.

Accepts all the changes.

Rejects all the changes.

exercise 2

Tracking Changes to a Workbook and Accepting or Rejecting Changes to a Workbook

1. Open Excel E7, Ex 01. You created this worksheet in exercise 1. The password to open the workbook is C1401C.
2. Save the workbook using the Save <u>A</u>s command and name it Excel E7, Ex 02.
3. If necessary, edit the custom header for the Income Statement worksheet so that the current file name is displayed at the right margin.
4. You are going to be sharing this workbook and you cannot share a workbook that is password protected. Complete the following steps to remove the password protection from the workbook:
   a. Click <u>T</u>ools, point to <u>P</u>rotection, and click Unprotect <u>W</u>orkbook. The Unprotect Workbook dialog box is displayed.
   b. Key **cg0128** in the <u>P</u>assword box.
   c. Click OK.
   d. Click <u>F</u>ile and then click Save <u>A</u>s.
   e. Click the Tool<u>s</u> button on the Save As dialog box and then click <u>G</u>eneral Options.

f.   Delete all the asterisks from the Password to open box.

g.   Click OK.

h.   Click Save.

i.   When the warning appears asking if you want to replace the existing file, click Yes.

5.   Since you are going to be sharing the workbook, you need to change the user name so that you can keep track of who is using the shared workbook. Complete the following steps to change the user name:

a.   Click Tools and Options.

b.   Click the General tab on the Options dialog box.

c.   Look in the User name box. Write down on a piece of paper the name that is currently entered. When you complete this exercise you will change the name back to what is currently entered.

d.   Enter your name in the User name box.

e.   Click OK.

f.   Click the Save button on the Standard toolbar.

6.   Complete the following steps to turn on the tracking feature:

a.   Click Tools and point to Track Changes. You may need to expand the menu in order to see the Track Changes option.

Step 6c

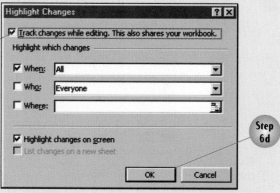

b.   Click Highlight Changes. The Highlight Changes dialog box is displayed.

c.   Click the Track changes while editing check box to select it.

Step 6d

d.   Click OK.

e.   Click OK to save the workbook.

7.   Look in the title bar. [Shared] should now be in the title bar after the workbook name. Complete the following steps to set up a second copy of the workbook:

a.   Click the Start button.

b.   Select Programs and open another copy of Excel.

c.   Right-click the task bar and click Tile Windows Vertically. Larry's copy should be on the right and your copy on the left. If necessary, rearrange the windows so your copy of the file is on the left.

d.   Click Tools and Options in the second copy of Excel.

e.   Click the General tab on the Options dialog box.

f.   In the User name box, key **Larry Ford**.

g.   Click OK.

h.   Open the Excel E7, Ex 02 workbook in the second copy of Excel.

8.   Larry Ford is the Vice President of Finance and he has some estimates you need to complete this income statement. Key the following values in the cells indicated in Larry's copy of Excel (the copy on the right):

Cell	Value
B4	333,300
B5	250,996
B6	345,023
B7	242,024
B11	94,039
B12	124,178

Save the workbook.

9. Click your copy of Excel (the one on the left). Save the workbook so that you can see the changes made by Larry Ford. Click OK when the information box appears notifying you that the workbook has been updated. Enter the remaining values into the worksheet.

Cell	Value
C13	86,101
C14	22,828
C15	21,765
C17	23,369
C19	24,349

Save the workbook.

10. Select Larry's copy of Excel (the one on the right) and save the workbook so that the changes you just made are displayed. Click OK when the information box is displayed notifying you that the workbook has been updated.

11. Notice that the changes you made are highlighted in one color on Larry Ford's copy of the worksheet and Larry's changes are highlighted in a different color on your copy. Click cell B4 on your copy of Excel (the one on the left). Position the mouse pointer on top of the revision triangle in the upper left corner of cell B4. The box explaining the change that was made should be displayed.

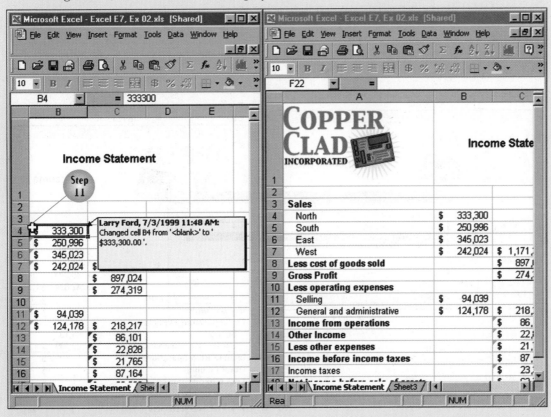

12. As you and Larry look over the figures each other made, you agree that some of the figures the other person entered are incorrect. Complete the following steps to make some changes to each worksheet:
   a. Click Larry's copy of Excel (the one on the right) to select it.

b. Click cell C17 and key **24,287**.
c. Click cell C19 and key **26,024**.
d. Save the workbook.
e. Click your copy of Excel (the one on the left) to select it.
f. Click cell B11 and key **96,102**.
g. Click cell B12 and key **122,189**.
h. Save the workbook.
i. Click OK when the box displays telling you the workbook has been updated.
j. Click Larry's copy of Excel (the one on the right) to select it.
k. Save the workbook.
l. Click OK when the box displays telling you the workbook has been updated.

13. Complete the following steps to accept or reject the tracked changes.
a. Click your copy of Excel (the one on the left) to select it.
b. Click Tools, point to Track Changes, and then click Accept or Reject Changes. The Select Changes to Accept or Reject dialog box is displayed.
c. Click OK. The Accept or Reject Changes dialog box is displayed.
d. The first change made is for cell B4. Notice that cell B4 has a moving border to indicate which cell is currently under consideration. Click Accept.
e. Accept all the changes until you get to the change for cell B11. After further investigation, you have decided Larry Ford's figure is correct. Click the option for *$94,039*, the figure Larry entered, to select it.

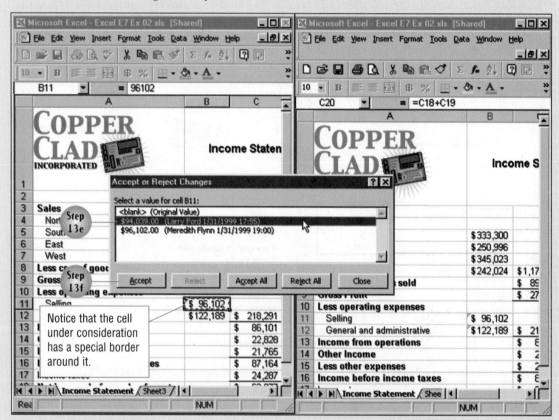

f. Click Accept.
g. You need to select which value to accept for cell B12. This time you think your figure is the correct one. Click the option for *$122,189* to select it.

    h.   Click Accept.

    i.   You want to accept all the rest of the changes, so click Accept All.

    j.   Print a copy of the worksheet.

14. Click Larry's copy of Excel (the one on the right). Complete the following steps to change the user name back to the original entry and exit Larry's copy of Excel.

    a.   Click Tools and then click Options.

    b.   Click the General tab.

    c.   In the User name box, key the name that was originally displayed when you started the exercise.

    d.   Click OK.

    e.   Save the file. Click File and then click Exit.

15. Maximize the window of your copy of Excel. Complete the following steps to turn off the track changes option:

    a.   Click Tools, point to Track Changes, and click Highlight Changes. The Highlight Changes dialog box is displayed.

    b.   Click the Track changes while editing check box so that it is no longer selected.

    c.   Click OK.

    d.   An information box is displayed asking if you want to remove the workbook from shared use. Click Yes.

16. Complete the following steps to change the user name back to the original entry.

    a.   Click Tools and then click Options.

    b.   Click the General tab.

    c.   In the User name box, key the name that was originally displayed when you started the exercise.

    d.   Click OK.

17. Complete the following steps to unhide the hidden worksheet:

    a.   Click Format, point to Sheet, and click Unhide.

    b.   Select *Cost of Goods Sold*.

    c.   Click OK.

18. Save the workbook with the same name (Excel E7, Ex 02) and close it.

Creating, Editing, and Removing a Comment

Comments can be added to any cell on a worksheet. Comments can be used to explain or clarify the contents of a cell. Comments are not printed when the worksheet is printed. If a cell has a comment attached to it, a small red triangle appears in the upper right corner of the cell. Passing the mouse pointer over this triangle displays the comment. To add a comment, right-click the cell to which the comment is to be added. Click Insert Comment from the shortcut menu. As shown in figure 7.13, the comment box appears with the name of the user who is entered on the General tab of the Options menu. Enter the comment and then click anywhere outside the comment box. To edit a comment, right-click the cell containing the comment to be edited and click Edit Comment from the shortcut menu. Make the necessary changes and click anywhere outside the comment. To delete a comment, right-click the cell containing the comment to be deleted and click Delete Comment.

You can review the comments in a workbook by clicking View and Comments. The reviewing toolbar is displayed. Click the Next Comment button or the Previous Comments button.

figure 7.13
Creating Comments

	A	B	C	D	E	F	G	H	I	J
1	Greenspace Architects			Weekly Time Records						
2		Nicole	Nolan	Ryan						
3	**Woodland Mall Project**	Meredith Flynn:								
4	Design Work									
5	Research									
6	Meetings									
7	On Site		1							
8	Vendor Relations			2						
9	Office Management		2	1						
10	Other									
11										
12	**Redwood Community College**									
13	Design Work			10	4					
14	Research		3	2	2					
15	Meetings		5		3					
16	On Site		10	5	5					
17	Vendor Relations		4		1					

Sheet1 / Sheet2 / Sheet3

When a comment is created, the name of the user automatically appears in the comment box.

Merging Workbooks

Another way of sharing workbooks is to send a copy of the shared workbook to different users. Each user can then make his or her own changes to the workbook. All those changes can then be merged into one workbook. The first step in merging workbooks is to open the shared workbook that will be used as the copy into which all the other copies will be merged. Next, click Tools and Merge Workbooks. If you are prompted to save the workbook, click OK. The Select Files to Merge Into Current Workbook dialog box is displayed. Choose the workbooks to be merged and click OK. As many workbooks as needed can be merged.

exercise 3

Creating, Editing, and Removing Comments, and Merging Workbooks

1. Open Excel Worksheet E7-02.
2. Save the workbook using the Save As command and name it Excel E7, Ex 03.
3. Create a custom header for the Time Sheet worksheet that displays your name at the left margin and the file name at the right margin.

4. This worksheet is used to keep track of the weekly project time spent by three of the employees at Greenspace Architects, a company that provides landscaping services.

5. Complete the following steps to add a comment to cell A3:
   a. Right-click cell A-3.
   b. Click Insert Comment on the shortcut menu.
   c. Key the following in the comment box:

   This project is nearing completion and therefore very few hours need to be devoted to it.

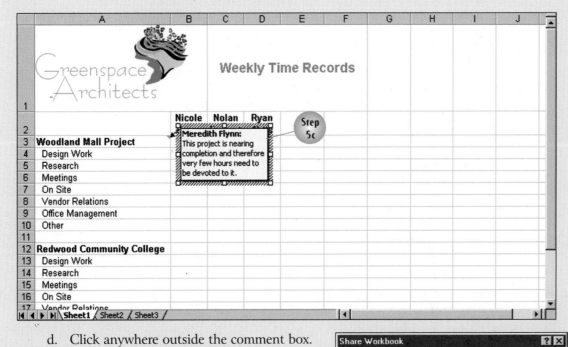

   d. Click anywhere outside the comment box.

6. Nicole, Nolan, and Ryan each need to enter their hours in this worksheet. Before they can do that, you need to set up the workbook as a shared workbook. Complete the following steps to designate Excel E7, Ex 03 as a shared workbook.
   a. Click Tools and then click Share Workbook.
   b. If necessary, click the Editing tab.
   c. Click the Allow changes by more than one user at the same time check box to select it.
   d. Click OK.
   e. Click OK to save the workbook.
   f. Close the Excel E7, Ex 03 workbook.

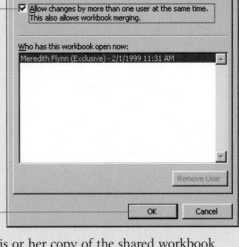

7. In order to simulate this shared workbook being sent to three different employees, you will have to open the file three times. Each employee would open up his or her copy of the shared workbook to enter the requested figures. Nicole is now ready to enter her hours in the weekly time sheet. Open Excel E7, Ex 03. It should say [Shared] in the title bar. Save the workbook using the Save As command and name it Nicole 9-18.

8. Key the following values in the cells indicated:

Cell	Value
B7	1
B9	2
B14	3
B15	5
B16	10
B17	4
B18	8
B19	4.5
B23	2
B25	4

9. Save the workbook using the same name (Nicole 9-18) and close it.
10. Nolan is now ready to enter his hours in the weekly time sheet. Open Excel E7, Ex 03. It should say [Shared] in the title bar. Save the workbook using the Save <u>A</u>s command and name it Nolan 9-18.
11. Key the following values in the cells indicated:

Cell	Value
C6	1
C8	2
C9	1
C13	10
C14	2
C16	5
C18	1
C22	15
C23	3
C24	2
C25	6

12. Save the workbook using the same name (Nolan 9-18) and close it.
13. Ryan is now ready to enter his hours in the weekly time sheet. Open Excel E7, Ex 03. It should say [Shared] in the title bar. Save the workbook using the Save <u>A</u>s command and name it Ryan 9-18.
14. Key the following values in the cells indicated:

Cell	Value
D13	4
D14	2
D15	3
D16	5
D17	1
D18	2
D19	2
D22	3
D23	2
D24	4
D25	6
D26	3
D27	2
D28	3

15. Save the workbook using the same name (Ryan 9-18) and close it.
16. You are now ready to merge the three workbooks into one workbook. Open Excel E7, Ex 03. Complete the following steps to merge the workbooks:
    a. Click Tools and then click Merge Workbooks. You may have to expand the menu to see the Merge Workbooks option.
    b. Click OK to save the workbook. The Select Files to Merge Into Current Workbook dialog box is displayed.
    c. Select the Nicole 9-18, Nolan 9-18, and Ryan 9-18 files.

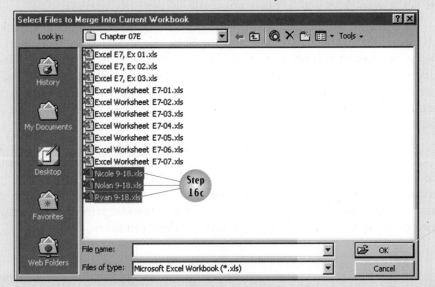

    d. Click OK. The values from the three workbooks are merged into the one workbook.
17. You no longer want this to be a shared workbook. Click Tools and Share Workbook. Click the Allow changes by more than one user at the same time check box so that it is no longer selected. Click OK and then click Yes.
18. Complete the following steps to edit the comment box.
    a. Right-click cell A3.
    b. Click Edit Comment from the shortcut menu.
    c. In the comment box delete the phrase *is nearing completion* and key the following to take its place:

       will be completed on 9/25

19. Save the workbook using the same name (Excel E7, Ex 03) and print it.
20. Close the workbook.

Working with Multiple Worksheets

When there is more than one worksheet in a workbook, you often want to perform the same command on two or more, or perhaps even on all of the worksheets in the workbook. For example, you might want to place the same header on all the worksheets. Or you might want to print two of the four worksheets. In order to perform a command on more than one worksheet at a time, you first need to select the worksheets. If more than one worksheet is selected, the command executed on the active worksheet will be made on all the selected worksheets.

To select two or more adjacent worksheets in a workbook, click the worksheet tab for the first worksheet, hold down the Shift key and click the worksheet tab for the last worksheet you want selected. To select two or more worksheets that are not adjacent, click the worksheet tab for the first worksheet, hold down the Ctrl key and then click the worksheet tab for each worksheet you want selected. To select all the worksheets in a workbook, right-click a worksheet tab and then click Select All Sheets on the shortcut menu.

If you wanted to view more than one worksheet at a time, for example, you would select all the worksheets to be viewed and click the Print Preview button on the Standard toolbar. The first worksheet would be displayed. Clicking the Next button would display the next worksheet and so on. If you wanted to print more than one worksheet at a time, select the worksheets to be printed before issuing the Print command. All of the selected worksheets will print.

Working with Multiple Worksheets

1. Open Excel Worksheet E7-03.
2. Save the workbook using the Save As command and name it Excel E7, Ex 04.
3. You want the custom header you create to appear on all the worksheets in this workbook. Complete the following steps to create a header that appears on all the worksheets:
   a. Right-click the North worksheet tab.
   b. Click Select All Sheets from the shortcut menu. Notice that the word *[Group]* now appears in the title bar to the right of the file name.
   c. Create a custom header for the North worksheet that displays your name at the left margin and the file name at the right margin.
4. You want to preview all the worksheets to make sure the header appears on all of them. All the worksheets should still be selected. Click the Print Preview button on the Standard toolbar. The first worksheet is displayed. Click the Next button. The next worksheet is displayed and the header appears at the top of it. Keep clicking Next until you have viewed all the worksheets. Click Close.
5. Click the North worksheet tab. Only the North worksheet is selected.
6. You want to print the South and West worksheet. Click the South worksheet tab. Press the Ctrl key and click the West worksheet tab. The two worksheets are now selected. Click the Print button on the Standard toolbar. The two worksheets should print.
7. Click the North worksheet tab. Only the North worksheet is selected.
8. Save the workbook using the same name (Excel E7, Ex 04) and close it.

Using the Report Manager

In the previous section you learned how to manage printing multiple worksheets by selecting them just prior to printing. Another way to manage printing multiple worksheets is by using the Report Manager. Worksheets and scenarios can be combined into reports. Reports are saved with the workbook and can be printed at any time using the Report Manager.

To define a report, click View and then click Report Manager. The Report Manager dialog box shown in figure 7.14 is displayed. To define a report, click Add. The Add Report dialog box shown in figure 7.15 is then displayed. Enter a name for the report in the Report Name box. You can then select a specific sheet, view, and/or scenario to add to the report. Once the selections have been made, click the Add button. Once you click the Add button, your selections are moved to the Sections in this Report list box. A section is any combination of a sheet, view, and scenario. Each section prints on its own page or pages. You can add as many sections to the report as is necessary. The Move Up and Move Down buttons allow you to change the order of the sections in the report. The Delete button allows you to remove a section from the report. If you want to number each page in the report, click the Use Continuous Page Numbers check box in order to select it.

To print a report, click View and then click Report Manager. Select the report you want to print from the Reports list box and click Print. The Print dialog box appears asking how many copies you want to print. Enter the number of copies and click OK.

When the report is printed, the sections are printed in the order in which they appear in the Sections in this Report list box.

figure 7.14

Report Manager Dialog Box

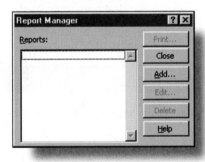

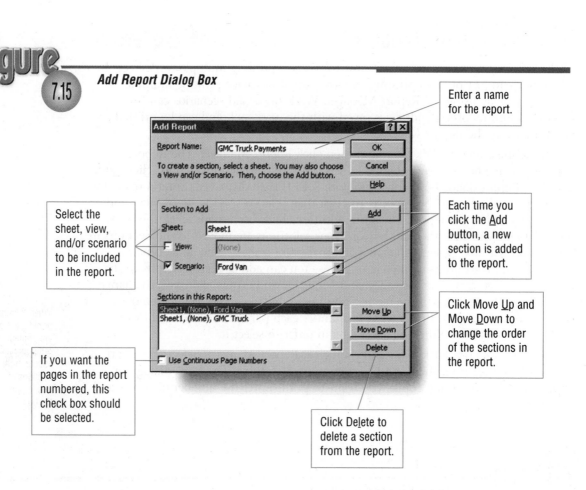

figure 7.15 — Add Report Dialog Box

Enter a name for the report.

Select the sheet, view, and/or scenario to be included in the report.

Each time you click the Add button, a new section is added to the report.

Click Move Up and Move Down to change the order of the sections in the report.

If you want the pages in the report numbered, this check box should be selected.

Click Delete to delete a section from the report.

exercise 5

Using the Report Manager

1. Open Excel Worksheet E7-04.
2. Save the workbook using the Save As command and name it Excel E7, Ex 05.
3. Chris Robinson, who owns his own company called Bits Unlimited, needs to buy either a truck or van for the company. Complete the following steps to create three scenarios on what the loan payments would be depending on the vehicle he buys.
   a. Select the range of cells A5 through B11.
   b. Click Insert, select Name, and click Create.
   c. Select the Left column check box. This is the only check box on the Create Names dialog box that should be selected.
   d. Click OK.
   e. Click Tools and then click Scenarios.
   f. Click Add.

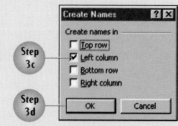

Step 3c

Step 3d

g. Key **98 Ford Truck** in the Scenario name box.
h. Key **B5:B9** in the Changing cells box.
i. Click OK.
j. Click OK to accept the default values in the Scenario Values dialog box.
k. Click Add.
l. Key **95 Ford Van** in the Scenario name box.
m. Click OK.
n. Change the entry in the Model box to **95 Ford Van**.
o. Change the amount in the Price box to **11995**.
p. Change the amount in the Down box to **0.4**.
q. Click Add.
r. Key **93 Dodge Truck** in the Scenario name box.
s. Click OK.
t. Change the entry in the Model box to **93 Dodge Truck**.
u. Change the amount in the Price box to **10993**.
v. Click OK.
w. Click Close.

4. You are now ready to create a report that will print each of the scenarios on a separate page. Complete the following steps to create the report:
   a. Click View and then click Report Manager.
   b. Click Add.
   c. Key **Loan Payments** in the Report Name box.
   d. Click the View check box so that it is no longer selected.
   e. Click the down arrow to the right of the Scenario box and click *98 Ford Truck*.
   f. Click Add.
   g. Click the down arrow to the right of the Scenario box and click *95 Ford Van*.
   h. Click Add.
   i. Click the down arrow to the right of the Scenario box and click *93 Dodge Truck*.
   j. Click Add.

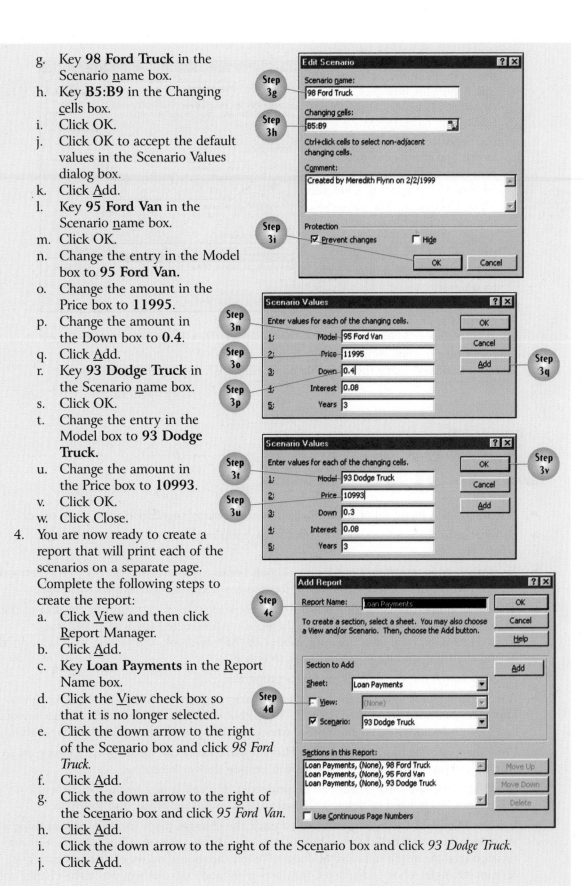

k. You want to change the order of the sections. In the Sections in this Report list box, click *Loan Payments, (None), 93 Dodge Truck* to select it. Click the Move Up button twice.

l. In the Sections in this Report list box, click *Loan Payments, (None), 95 Ford Van* to select it. Click the Move Up button. The scenarios are now in order from the oldest vehicle to the newest vehicle.

m. Click the Use Continuous Page Numbers check box to select it.

n. Click OK.

5. You are now ready to print the report. The Report Manager dialog box is displayed. Click Print. Click OK to accept the default of printing one copy.

6. Save the workbook using the same file name (Excel E7, Ex 05) and close it.

Add Report dialog box:

Report Name: Loan Payments

To create a section, select a sheet. You may also choose a View and/or Scenario. Then, choose the Add button.

OK — Step 4n

Cancel

Help

Section to Add — Add

Sheet: Loan Payments

☐ View: (None)

☑ Scenario: 93 Dodge Truck

Sections in this Report:
Loan Payments, (None), 93 Dodge Truck
Loan Payments, (None), 95 Ford Van
Loan Payments, (None), 98 Ford Truck

Move Up
Move Down
Delete

☑ Use Continuous Page Numbers — Step 4m

chapter summary

➤ A workgroup is made up of individuals who are working together on the same project.

➤ Being able to share a workbook enables workgroup members to work together more efficiently.

➤ Security is an issue when sharing a workbook because whoever has access to the network location where the shared workbook is located has access to that shared workbook.

➤ The set of properties belonging to each workbook includes such things as the size of the workbook, when it was last modified, the person who created the workbook, the worksheets it contains, the title and subject of the workbook, the person who last edited it, and the total amount of time it took to edit it.

➤ You can search for a workbook using its properties.

➤ A workbook can be completely protected by assigning a password to it. Only those who know the password are able to open it. A workbook can also be protected so that anyone can view the workbook but only those who know the password can make changes to it.

➤ Worksheets can be hidden from view. Hidden worksheets can be assigned a password so that only those knowing the password can unhide the worksheet.

➤ Individual cells on a worksheet can be protected. If a cell is protected, the contents of the cell cannot be changed or deleted. This feature is useful for protecting formulas.

➤ Use the Highlight Changes command to track the changes made by each person using a shared workbook. A cell that has been changed is displayed with a border around it and a revision triangle in the upper right corner. When the mouse pointer is passed over the revision triangle, a box is displayed that lists who made the change, when the change was made, and what the change was.

➤ Tracked changes can be accepted all at one time, rejected all at one time, or each change can be accepted or rejected individually.

➤ A comment is useful for explaining or clarifying the contents of a cell. Cells with comments attached to them have red comment triangles in the upper right corner of the cell. When the mouse pointer is passed over the comment triangle, a comment box is displayed.

➤ Each member in a workgroup can make changes to his or her own copy of a shared workbook. All those copies of the shared workbook then can be merged into one workbook.

➤ To select multiple worksheets that are adjacent to one another, click the first worksheet tab, press the Shift key and click the last worksheet tab. To select multiple copies of nonadjacent worksheets, press the Ctrl key and click the worksheet tab for each worksheet to be selected. Once multiple worksheets are selected, commands carried out on the active worksheet affect all the selected worksheets. For example, if several worksheets are selected and the print command is issued, all the selected worksheets will be printed.

➤ You can manage printing several worksheets, views, or scenarios using Excel's Report Manager. As many sections as needed can be added to a report. The report is saved with the workbook and can be printed at any time.

commands review

	Mouse/Keyboard
Assign workbook properties	Click File, Properties, Summary tab
To search for a workbook using workbook properties	Click File, Open, Tools button, Find
Apply/Remove a password to a workbook	Click File, Save As, Tools button, General Options
Hide a worksheet	Click Format, Sheet, Hide
Protect a workbook	Click Tools, Protection, Protect Workbook
Remove workbook protection	Click Tools, Protection, Unprotect Workbook
Unhide a worksheet	Click Format, Sheet, Unhide
Protect individual cells	Click Format, Cells, Protection tab
Protect a worksheet	Click Tools, Protection, Protect Sheet
Remove worksheet protection	Click Tools, Protection, Unprotect Sheet
Track changes in a shared workbook	Click Tools, Track Changes, Highlight Changes
Accept or reject tracked changes	Click Tools, Track Changes, Accept or Reject Changes
Add a comment	Right-click the cell, click Insert Comment
Edit a comment	Right-click the cell, click Edit Comment
Delete a comment	Right-click the cell, click Delete Comment
Merging shared workbooks	Click Tools, Merge Workbooks
Define/Print a report	Click View, Report Manager

thinking offline

Completion: In the space provided at the right, indicate the correct term, command, or button.

1. This term refers to all the people working together on the same project.

2. Click this tab to enter workbook properties such as a title and keywords.

3. This is what appears in the box when you enter a password.

4. When creating a password to be used for password protection, the password always is entered this many times.

5. If a worksheet is hidden, this is what must be protected in order to prevent other users from unhiding it.

6. When individual cells have been protected on a worksheet so that changes cannot be made to them, you also have to protect this.

7. The Highlight Changes command automatically turns this feature on.

8. The option for tracking changes is found on this menu.

9. This term refers to boxes attached to individual cells which contain information regarding the specific cell to which they are attached.

10. Press this key to select multiple worksheets that are adjacent to one another.

11. Press this key to select multiple worksheets that are not adjacent to one another.

12. This Microsoft Excel add-in program allows you to print multiple sheets or scenarios at the same time.

13. List the benefits of sharing workbooks.

_____

_____

_____

14. Explain what security issues you must consider when sharing a workbook.

_____

_____

_____

15. List the Excel features that are not available in a shared workbook.

_____

_____

_____

working hands-on

Assessment 1

1. Open Excel Worksheet E7-05.
2. Save the worksheet using the Save <u>A</u>s command and name it Excel E7, SA 01.
3. This workbook is the cash flow schedule for a ski shop that sells downhill and cross country ski supplies. Enter the following workbook properties:

Title:	**Cash Flow Schedule**
Author:	**Your name**
Company:	**Slope and Trail Ski Shop**
Category:	**Financial Statement**
Keywords:	**cash flow, financial**

4. Click <u>F</u>ile and then click Save <u>A</u>s. Click the Tools button on the Save As dialog box and click <u>G</u>eneral Options. Assign the following password to the workbook: **CM5!78sts**.
5. Close Excel E7, SA 01. You will be using this file in Assessment 2.

Assessment 2

1. Use the <u>F</u>ind command to find the file that includes the words *cash flow* as keywords. Open the file (it should be Excel E7, SA 01). The password to open the file is CM5!78sts.
2. Save the worksheet using the Save <u>A</u>s command and name it Excel E7, SA 02.
3. Select both worksheets. Create a custom header with your name displayed at the left margin and the file name displayed at the right margin.
4. The values in cells B9, C9, and D9 are linked to the Commissions worksheet, which is confidential. Hide the Commissions worksheet.
5. Protect the workbook by using the following password: 131!63C.
6. All the cells that currently have something entered in them contain formulas, which you want to protect, so these cells should remain locked. Select the cells that are empty which would be cells B3 through D5, B10 through D13, and B19. Format these cells so that they are no longer locked.
7. Protect the worksheet using the following password: W89**25s.
8. Save the workbook using the same name (Excel E7, SA 02) and close it. You will be using this file in Assessment 3.

Assessment 3

1. Open Excel E7, SA 02. The password to open the file is CM5!78sts.
2. Save the worksheet using the Save As command and name it Excel E7, SA 03.
3. If necessary, edit the custom header so that the current name of the file (Excel E7, SA 03) is displayed at the right margin.
4. Click Tools, point to Protection, and click Unprotect workbook to remove the workbook protection. The password for the workbook protection is 131!63C.
5. Click File and then click Save As. Click the Tools button and click General Options. Delete all the asterisks from the Password to Open box. Save the file, replacing the existing Excel E7, SA 03 file.
6. Change the user name to your name. Make sure you jot down the current user name so that you can change it back at the end of the exercise.
7. Use the Highlight Changes command to turn the tracking feature on. You want to track all the changes made by everyone. The word *[Shared]* should appear in the title bar.
8. Resize the Excel window so that it appears in the left half of the desktop.
9. Open a second copy of the Excel program. Resize the second copy so that it is displayed in the right half of the desktop. Change the user name for this copy of Excel to **Megan Bassett**.
10. Open Excel E7, SA 03 in the second copy of Excel. Megan has some of the figures that go into this worksheet and you have some of the figures. Key the following figures in the cells indicated on Megan's copy of Excel (the one on the right):

Cell	Value
B3	36,540
B4	6,000
B5	2,658.50
C3	43,960
C5	5,110
D3	33,271
D5	16,506

    Save the workbook.
11. Click your copy of Excel (the one on the left). Save it so that you can see the changes made by Megan.
12. Key the following figures in the cells indicated on your copy of Excel (the one on the left):

Cell	Value
B10	24,500
B11	10,720
B12	6,280
C10	24,500
C11	13,584
C12	6,589
D10	24,500
D11	13,072
D12	6,432
D13	2,000

    Save the workbook.

13. Click Megan's copy of Excel (the one on the right). Save it so that you can see the changes that were made. Megan knows the loan/interest repayment in March is supposed to be $2,200. Change the value in cell D13 to **2,200**. She also knows that the beginning cash balance in January was $750. Enter **750** in cell B19. Save the worksheet.
14. Change the user name back to the original entry. Save and exit Megan's copy of Excel.
15. Click your copy of Excel (the one on the left). Maximize the window. Save the worksheet to see the changes. Accept all the changes that were made to the worksheet.
16. Turn off the track changes options.
17. Unhide the Commissions worksheet.
18. Preview and print both the Cash Flow and the Commissions worksheets.
19. Change the user name back to what it was originally.
20. Save the workbook using the same file name (Excel E7, SA 03) and close it.

Assessment 4

1. Open Excel Worksheet E7-06.
2. Save the worksheet using the Save <u>A</u>s command and name it Excel E7, SA 04.
3. Create a custom header with your name displayed at the left margin and the name of the file displayed at the right margin.
4. Attach a comment to cell A5. The comment should read as follows: **This inventory reflects stock on hand as of December 15.**
5. Designate this workbook as a shared workbook.
6. Close the workbook.
7. Open the workbook and rename it New York Inventory.
8. Key the following values in the cells indicated:

Cell	Value		Cell	Value
B8	5		B19	8
B9	6		B20	5
B10	10		B21	14
B11	2		B22	2
B12	1		B23	19
B13	4		B24	30
B14	7		B25	18
B15	20		B26	0
B16	15		B27	28
B17	35		B28	25
B18	12		B29	6

9. Save the workbook using the same name (New York Inventory) and close it.
10. Open Excel E7, SA 04. Open the workbook and rename it Los Angeles Inventory.

11. Key the following values in the cells indicated:

Cell	Value		Cell	Value
E8	5		E19	4
E9	10		E20	6
E10	3		E21	0
E11	18		E22	13
E12	12		E23	18
E13	10		E24	22
E14	8		E25	8
E15	36		E26	5
E16	25		E27	31
E17	28		E28	24
E18	35		E29	22

12. Save the workbook using the same name (Los Angeles Inventory) and close it.
13. Open Excel E7, SA 04. Merge the New York Inventory workbook and the Los Angeles Inventory workbook into the Excel E7, SA 04 workbook.
14. Remove the workbook from shared use.
15. Edit the comment attached to cell A5 so the date is December 31 rather than December 15. Save the workbook using the same name (Excel E7, SA 04).
16. Print and then close the workbook.

Assessment 5

1. Open Excel Worksheet E7-07.
2. Save the worksheet using the Save As command and name it Excel E7, SA 05.
3. Create a custom header with your name displayed at the left margin and the name of the file displayed at the right margin.
4. You are going to use this worksheet to project three possible budgets. Expenses for the year are known. Create a scenario called *Worst Case* using the figures below. The Changing cells are B4 and B5.

Cell	Value
B4	1,199,564
B5	681,805

5. Add a new scenario called *Probable Case* that changes the figures in cells B4 and B5 to the following:

Cell	Value
B4	1,713,660
B5	892,550

6. Add a new scenario called *Best Case* that changes the figures in cells B4 and B5 to the following:

Cell	Value
B4	2,142,078
B5	714,040

7. Use the Report Manager to create a report called Projected Budget that will print each of the scenarios on a separate page. The order of the pages should be Probable Case, Best Case, Worst Case. The pages should have page numbers.
8. Print one copy of the Projected Budget report.
9. Save the workbook using the same name (Excel E7, SA 05) and close it.

Chapter 08E

Importing and Exporting Data

PERFORMANCE OBJECTIVES

Upon successful completion of chapter 8 you will be able to:

- Import data from text files.
- Export data to text files.
- Place a noninteractive worksheet on the Web.
- Place an interactive worksheet on the Web.
- Take an Excel workbook on a "round trip."
- Place an interactive chart on the Web.
- Import data from a Web page into Excel.
- Retrieve data from a Web page using Web Query.
- Query a database using Microsoft Query.
- Link an object in an Excel worksheet.
- Embed an object in an Excel worksheet.

In chapter 7 you were introduced to the concept of workgroup computing. People working together in a workgroup on a particular project often share not only data found in Excel workbooks, but data from other applications as well. Data in an Excel workbook may need to be accessed by another application or you may need to have the data from another application in an Excel workbook. When data from Excel is sent to another application, such as Word, the data is said to be exported from Excel. When data from another application, such as a Web browser, is sent to Excel, the data is said to be imported into Excel. Knowing how to import and export data to and from Excel enables you to share your Excel data across applications. One of the ways to accomplish this, which is covered in this chapter, is by linking or embedding objects.

Microsoft Excel 2000 includes many Web features. You can easily place worksheets and workbooks on the Web as well as import the data from a Web page into Excel. With the increasing popularity of intranets, which are described in this chapter, Excel data is frequently imported from and exported to Web pages as an easy way for people to share data.

INTEGRATED TOPIC

Importing from and Exporting to Text Files

A text file is a file that contains only printable letters, numbers and symbols, usually from the ASCII character set. There are no formatting codes in a text file. The strength of text files is that they are easily shared. The text file format is supported by nearly every application on every machine. The weakness of text files is that they cannot contain any formatting codes. If you need to share data with others, however, using text files can be a good solution.

Importing Data from Text Files

There are a number of reasons why you might have to import a text file. The source of the data might be a mainframe computer report, which has been saved as a text file so that it can be used on a personal computer. The data might come from an older application program, and the only way you might be able to open it in Excel 2000 is by saving the data from the older program as a text file. Data sent to you in e-mail messages might be in a text file format.

Excel provides automatic help when importing text files. There are two common formats for data that is arranged in rows and columns in a text file, a delimited text file and a fixed width text file. A delimited text file uses a special character or delimiter, which is often a comma or a tab, to separate one column from the next. In figure 8.1a, the delimiter is a comma. As shown in figure 8.1b, the number of characters and/or spaces in each column in a fixed width text file is set.

figure 8.1

Two Common Text File Formats

a. Delimited Text

```
Last Name, First Name, SS Number, Position, Hourly Wage
Dillard, Nancy, 555-90-2121, President, $75.00
Chung, Robert, 777-56-7654, Vice President, $55.00
Campbell, Norman, 444-78-7658, Designer, $38.00
Kimsey, C.J., 999-52-1014, Sales, $18.00
Simpson, Katie, 555-68-3564, $29.00
```

b. Fixed-Width Text

```
Last Name    First Name    SS Number      Position        Hourly Wage
Dillard      Nancy         555-90-2121    President        $75.00
Chung        Robert        777-56-7654    Vice President   $55.00
Campbell     Norman        444-78-7658    Designer         $38.00
Kimsey       C.J.          999-52-1014    Sales            $18.00
Simpson      Katie         555-68-3564    Designer         $29.00
```

To import a text file, click File and then click Open. The Open dialog box appears. Click the down arrow to the right of the Files of type box and select *Text Files*. All the files with the extension .txt will be displayed. Usually text files end with the extension .txt. If the text file you are trying to open has a different extension, select *All Files* from the Files of type list box. Locate the file to open and click Open. The Text Import Wizard - Step 1 of 3 dialog box, shown in figure 8.2, is displayed. You can select whether the file is Delimited or Fixed width, although Excel probably will make the proper selection for you automatically. You can also enter a value in the Start import at row box if you want the first row of the data to be a row other than 1.

Text files can be imported into Excel so that they are refreshable, which means they can be updated to the most recent version of the original data. To import text so that it is refreshable, click Data, point to Get External Data, and click Import Text File. Locate and double-click the text file to be imported. Follow the directions in the Text Import Wizard. To refresh the data when the original text changes, click the Refresh Data button on the External Data toolbar.

8.2 The Text Import Wizard - Step 1 of 3 Dialog Box

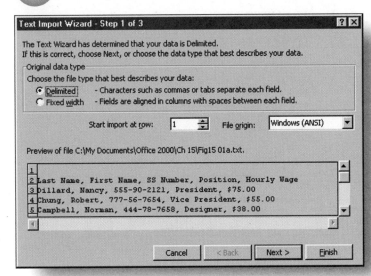

Click Next. The Text Import Wizard - Step 2 of 3 dialog box is displayed. As shown in figure 8.3, the dialog box that is displayed depends on whether the file is delimited or fixed width. If the file is delimited, the Step 2 dialog box allows you to set what character should be used as the delimiter. You also can select the Text qualifier, which typically is the quotation mark. Any text entered between text qualifiers would be placed in one column. For example "Vice President" indicates that the words *Vice President* make up the contents of a column. If the file is fixed width, the Step 2 dialog box allows you to set the column breaks.

figure
8.3

The Text Import Wizard - Step 2 of 3 Dialog Box

Step 2 Dialog Box for a Delimited File

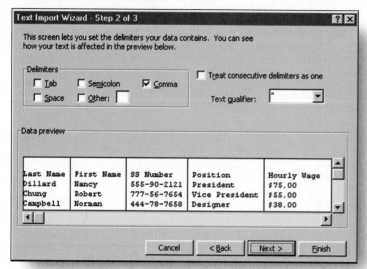

Step 2 Dialog Box for a Fixed Width File

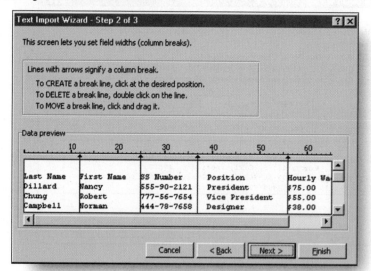

Click Next. The Text Import Wizard - Step 3 of 3 dialog box allows you to set the Data Format for each column. You can also select the Do not import column (skip) option if you do not want to import the data from a particular column or columns. Click Finish. The data is imported into an Excel worksheet.

Importing Data from Word Using Drag and Drop

Text from a Word document can be imported into an Excel workbook using drag and drop. To drag and drop between Word and Excel, arrange the windows so that you can see both applications. Select the text to be imported from the Word document. If you click on the selected text using the left mouse button and then drag it to a cell in an Excel worksheet, the text will be moved from the Word document to the Excel workbook. If you click on the selected text using the *right* mouse button and then drag it to a cell in an Excel worksheet, a shortcut menu appears giving you the option of moving the text, copying the text, linking the document, creating a hyperlink, or creating a shortcut.

exercise

Importing Data from Text Files

1. Open Excel.
2. Taylor Made, a company owned and operated by Linda Taylor, designs and makes custom clothing. Sales representatives for Taylor Made call on owners or managers of clothing stores and boutiques who might be interested in carrying Taylor Made clothes. These sales representatives e-mail information on new contacts back to the main office. The e-mail messages are saved as text files, which are then imported into an Excel worksheet. You are going to import one of these text files into an Excel worksheet. Complete the following steps to open the file.
   a. Click File and then click Open.
   b. Click the down arrow to the right of the Files of type box and select *Text Files*.
   c. Open the Contacts.txt file from your data disk.
3. The Text Import Wizard - Step 1 of 3 dialog box is displayed. This is a Delimited file and the data can be imported starting at row 1, so click Next to accept the default setting on this dialog box.
4. The Text Import Wizard - Step 2 of 3 dialog box is displayed. Complete the following steps:
   a. Click the Tab check box so that it is no longer selected.
   b. Click the Comma check box to select it.
   c. Click Next.
5. The Text Import Wizard - Step 3 of 3 dialog box is displayed. Complete the following steps.
   a. The first column in the Data preview area is selected. Under Column data format, click the Text option.

Step 4b

Step 4a

Text Import Wizard - Step 2 of 3 ? X

This screen lets you set the delimiters your data contains. You can see how your text is affected in the preview below.

Delimiters
☐ Tab ☐ Semicolon ☑ Comma ☐ Space ☐ Other: [ ]

☐ Treat consecutive delimiters as one

Text qualifier: [" ▼]

Data preview

Contact Name	Date of Contact	Phone	# of Stores
Teresa Repasz	2/8	316-555-2893	5
Rosemary Thorpe	2/10	716-555-2354	3
Joseph Cheney	2/10	716-555-9032	4
Rosalinda Cantu	2/12	717-555-2544	1

Cancel < Back Next > Finish

Step 5a **Step 4c**

Text Import Wizard - Step 3 of 3 ? X

This screen lets you select each column and set the Data Format.

'General' converts numeric values to numbers, date values to dates, and all remaining values to text.

Column data format
○ General
○ Text
○ Date: [MDY ▼]
○ Do not import column (skip)

Advanced...

Data preview

b. Click the second column, *Date of Contact*, to select it.
c. Click the <u>D</u>ate option.

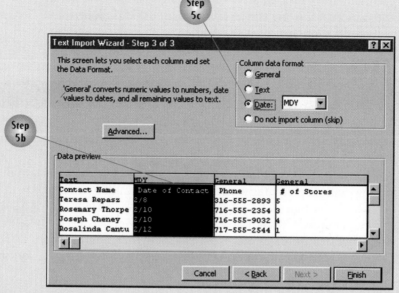

d. Click the third column, *Phone*, to select it.
e. Click the Text option.

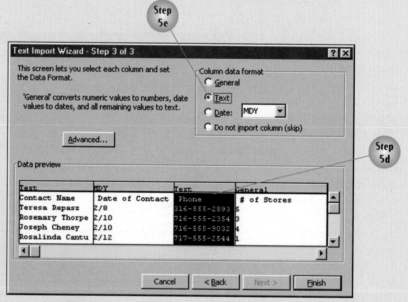

f. The last column, *# of Stores*, is already set as a General data format, which is what it
    should be. Click <u>F</u>inish.
6. Adjust the width of the columns so that all the data can be seen.
7. Click <u>F</u>ile and then click Save <u>A</u>s. Click the down arrow to the right of the Save as <u>t</u>ype
    box and select *Microsoft Excel Workbook*. Change the file name to Excel E8, Ex 01. Click
    <u>S</u>ave.
8. Create a custom header for the worksheet that displays your name at the left margin and
    the file name at the right margin.

9. Start Word and open the Memo.doc file on your data disk. Arrange the window for Word and the window for Excel so that you can see both applications. To drag and drop data from the Memo.doc file in Word to the Excel E8, Ex 01.xls file in Excel, complete the following steps:
   a. Select the name *Jane Mercereau* in the Memo.doc file.
   b. Right-click on the name *Jane Mercereau* and drag it to cell A13 in the Excel E8, Ex 01 file.
   c. From the shortcut menu that appears, select Copy Here.

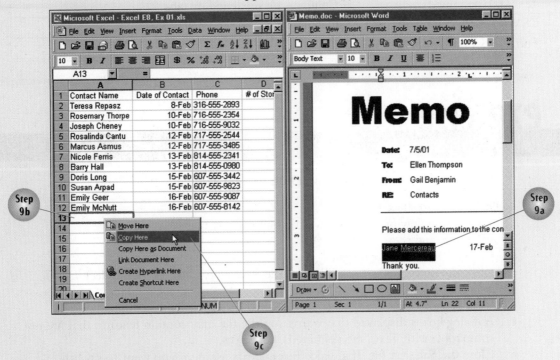

10. Repeat steps 9a through 9c to drag and drop the date *17-Feb* to cell B13, the phone number *607-555-0303* to cell C13, and the number *5* to cell D13.
11. Save the workbook again using the same file name (Excel E8, Ex 01) and print it.
12. Close the workbook.

Exporting Data to Text Files

There may be times when you want to share data with someone who does not have the Excel program. To do so, you can export the data in an Excel worksheet to a text file. To export a worksheet, open the worksheet, click File and then click Save As. Enter a name for the file in the file name box. Click the down arrow to the right of the Save as type box. The option you select from this list depends on the application that is going to use the file. Table 8.1 explains some of the text file options found in this list. Once you have made your selection, click Save.

table

Option	Description
Text (Tab delimited)	Columns are separated by tabs
CSV (Comma delimited)	Columns are separated by commas
Formatted Text (Space delimited)	Columns are a fixed width

exercise 2

Exporting Data to Text Files

1. Open Excel Worksheet E8-01.
2. Complete the following steps to save the file as a text file.
   a. Click <u>F</u>ile and then click Save <u>A</u>s.
   b. Change the file name to Sales.
   c. Click the down arrow to the right of the Save as <u>t</u>ype dialog box. Select *Text (Tab delimited)*.
   d. Click <u>S</u>ave.
   e. A dialog box is displayed that warns you the file may contain features that are not compatible with Text (Tab delimited). Click <u>Y</u>es.
   f. Close the Sales.txt file. If a dialog box appears asking if you want to save the changes you made, click <u>Y</u>es, click <u>S</u>ave, and click <u>Y</u>es again.
3. Start Microsoft Word and open the Sales.txt file. You may have to select *All Files (*.*)* from the Files of <u>t</u>ype selection box in order to display the Sales.txt file in the Open dialog box.
4. Select all the text in the document.
5. Set left tab stops at 1.5″ and 2.75″.
6. Save the file as a Word document using the file name Excel E8, Ex 02. You will have to select *Word Document (*.doc)* from the Files of <u>t</u>ype selection box on the Open dialog box.
7. Enter a header that prints your name at the left margin and the file name, Excel E8, Ex 02, at the right margin.
8. Save the Word file again using the same file name (Excel E8, Ex 02) and print it.
9. Exit Microsoft Word.

Accessing and Placing Data on the Web

Shortly after the World Wide Web appeared on the scene in the late 1980s, businesses began to take advantage of the capability to develop company intranets. An intranet is a local area or wide area network that provides an organization or business with services similar to those provided by the Internet without necessarily being connected to the Internet. Since about 1995 intranets have become increasingly popular in corporate computing because of the availability of inexpensive or, in some cases, free commercial browser and Web server software. An intranet is an excellent way to distribute information within a company. Employees find the graphical user interface of the Web easy to use. Intranets allow employees to easily access and share information. The HTML markup language used to create Web pages can be used on every desktop system. Therefore, even if some employees are using a Windows environment, some Macintosh, and others UNIX, all can access the company's intranet.

Excel 2000 incorporates many Web capabilities. You can export a workbook, worksheet, chart, or graph to HTML and then make it available on an HTTP site, on an FTP site, in a Web server, or on a network server. Users can then access the file using a Web browser. One of the advantages of putting Excel data on the Web is that people do not have to have Excel installed in order to interact with the data. All they need is a Web browser.

Placing Excel Data on the Web

The data that you export to the Web can either be interactive or noninteractive. If the Excel data on the Web is interactive, users can enter, format, calculate, analyze, sort, and filter the data. If it is noninteractive, users will be able to view the data but they will not be able to make any changes to it.

To place Excel data on the Web, select the worksheet to be put on a Web page. Click File. You may have to expand the menu to see the Save as Web Page option. When the Save as Web Page option is displayed, select it. The Save As dialog box is displayed. Click Publish. The Publish As Web Page dialog box is displayed. In the Choose list box you can select to publish a range of cells, all the items on an entire sheet, or previously published items. If the data is to be interactive, click the Add interactivity with check box. You can choose to have either spreadsheet functionality or PivotTable functionality. Clicking Change displays the Set Title dialog box. Anything you enter here will be centered over the published data. In the File name box you must select the drive, folder, Web folder, Web server, or FTP location where the Web page should be published or saved. Click the Browse button to help you find the proper location. To view the published Web page as it will appear on the Web, make sure the Open published Web page in browser check box is selected. When all the selections have been made, click Publish.

Placing a Noninteractive Worksheet on the Web

1. Open Excel Worksheet E8-03.
2. Save the workbook using the Save As command and name it Excel E8, Ex 03.
3. Complete the following steps to save noninteractive data on the Web:
   a. Select cells A1 through D7.
   b. Click File. If necessary, either wait a few moments or click the down arrow at the bottom of the menu. Click Save as Web Page.

Worksheets you place on the Web should be no more than six columns wide. If the worksheet contains more than six columns, it may be too wide to fit in the browser window or the columns will be so narrow they will be hard to read. If possible, the worksheet should be no more than about twelve rows long. The larger the worksheet, the longer it will take to download.

If you get a message saying the file name cannot be accessed when you try to publish Excel data as a Web page, the amount of data you are trying to save might be too large, especially if the data is to be interactive. Break the worksheet up into two or more worksheets so that you can save a smaller amount of data.

c. The Save As dialog box appears. Click Publish.

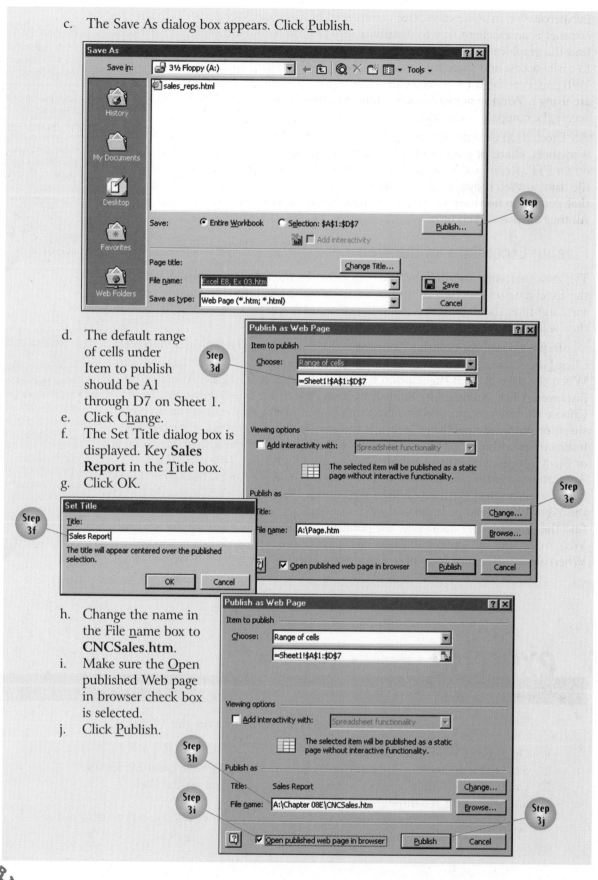

d. The default range of cells under Item to publish should be A1 through D7 on Sheet 1.
e. Click Change.
f. The Set Title dialog box is displayed. Key **Sales Report** in the Title box.
g. Click OK.

h. Change the name in the File name box to **CNCSales.htm**.
i. Make sure the Open published Web page in browser check box is selected.
j. Click Publish.

4. The Web page is displayed in Internet Explorer. Click the Print button to print the Web page.
5. Close Internet Explorer.
6. Save the workbook using the same file name (Excel E8, Ex 03) and close it.

Step 4

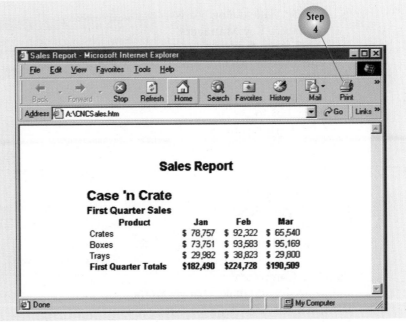

exercise 4

Placing an Interactive Worksheet on the Web

(Note: To complete this exercise, you must have Microsoft Office Web Components installed with Office 2000.)

1. Open Excel Worksheet E8-04.
2. Save the workbook using the Save As command and name it Excel E8, Ex 04.
3. Managers at Case 'N Crate need to compute sales representatives' earnings on a weekly basis. The sales representatives earn a commission based on their sales for the week. Those sales representatives who are a category 1 also receive a flat weekly salary of $200. This worksheet automatically calculates the earnings. The managers want it published on the company's intranet so they can use it to make the weekly calculations. Complete the following steps to save this worksheet as interactive data on the Web:
   a. Click File and then click Save as Web Page.
   b. The Save As dialog box appears. Click Publish.
   c. Make sure *Items on Sheet1* is selected in the Choose box.
   d. Click the Add interactivity with check box.
   e. Make sure *Spreadsheet functionality* is selected in the Add interactivity with list box.
   f. Click Change.

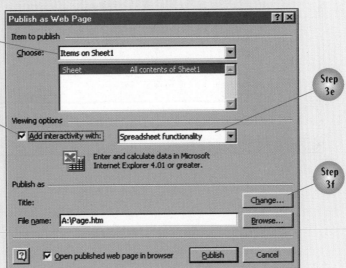

g. The Set Title dialog box is displayed. Key **Managers' Worksheet for Calculating Earnings** in the Title box.

h. Click OK.

i. Change the name in the File name box to **CNCEarnings.htm**.

j. Make sure the Open published Web page in browser check box is selected.

k. Click Publish.

4. The Web page is displayed in Internet Explorer as an interactive data file. Complete the following steps to make changes to the worksheet.

a. Click cell A5.

b. To sort the worksheet by sales representatives, click the Sort Ascending button and then click *Sales Rep* from the drop-down list.

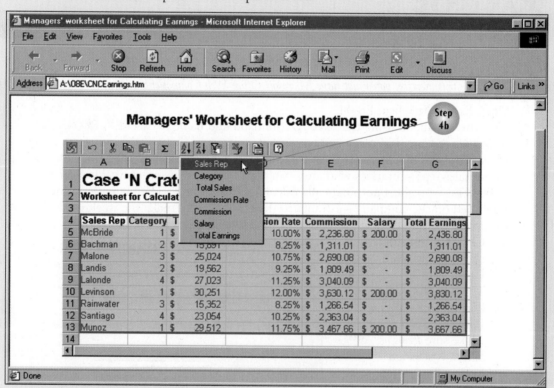

c. Key the following values in the cells indicated:

Cell	Value
C5	18,252
C6	31,350
C7	17,652
C8	33,467
C9	22,406
C10	28,309
C11	24,892
C12	13,902
C13	27,346

d. Change the value in cell B6 to 1.
e. Click the AutoFilter button.
f. Click the down arrow to the right of the Salary column.
g. Click the check box next to the $ - option so that it is no longer selected.
h. Click OK. Only the sales representatives who earn the $200 salary are displayed.
i. Click the Print button to print the worksheet.

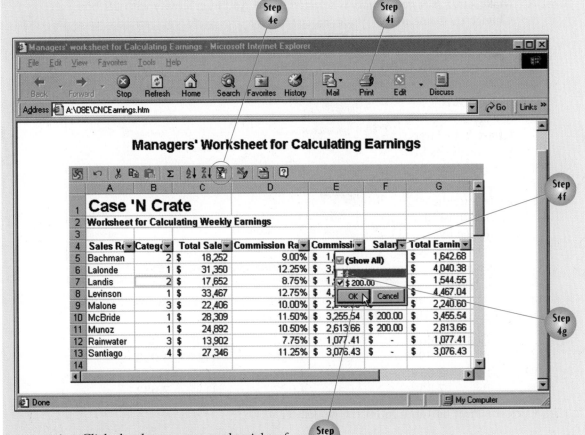

j. Click the down arrow to the right of the Salary label.
k. Click the check box next to (Show All) to select it.
l. Click OK.
5. Close Internet Explorer.
6. Save the workbook using the same file name (Excel E8, Ex 04) and close it.

exercise 5

Placing an Interactive Chart on the Web

(Note: To complete this exercise, you must have Microsoft Office Web Components installed with Office 2000.)

1. Open Excel Worksheet E8-05.
2. Save the workbook using the Save As command and name it Excel E8, Ex 05.
3. This chart can be used by the sales representatives at Case 'N Crate to track their first-quarter sales. Management at Case 'N Crate would like this chart put on the company intranet so the sales representatives can chart their own sales. Complete these steps to save the chart on a Web page.
   a. Click File and then click Save as Web Page.
   b. The Save As dialog box appears. Click Publish.
   c. Select *Chart* from the Choose list box.
   d. Click the Add interactivity with check box.
   e. Make sure *Chart functionality* is selected in the Add interactivity with list box.
   f. Change the name in the File name box to **CNCChart.htm**
   g. Click Change.
   h. The Set Title dialog box is displayed. Key **Chart Your First Quarter Sales** in the Title box.
   i. Click OK.
   j. Make sure the Open published Web page in browser check box is selected.
   k. Click Publish.

   [Dialog box: Publish as Web Page]

   Item to publish
   Choose: Items on Sheet1
   | Sheet | All contents of Sheet1 |
   | Chart | Chart 1 (Line) |

   Viewing options
   ☑ Add interactivity with: Chart functionality

   Chart and supporting data can be updated in Microsoft Internet Explorer 4.01 or greater.

   Publish as
   Title:
   File name: A:\08E\CNCChart.htm
   Change...   Browse...

   ☑ Open published web page in browser   Publish   Cancel

   (Callouts: Step 3c, Step 3d, Step 3f, Step 3j, Step 3e, Step 3g, Step 3k)

4. The Web page is displayed in Internet Explorer. The chart is interactive. Key the following values in the cells indicated to make changes to the chart:

Cell	Value	Cell	Value	Cell	Value
B2	1,895	C2	3,926	D2	4,053
B3	2,058	C3	8,502	D3	5,021
B4	7,358	C4	4,987	D4	7,932

5. Click the Print button to print the worksheet.

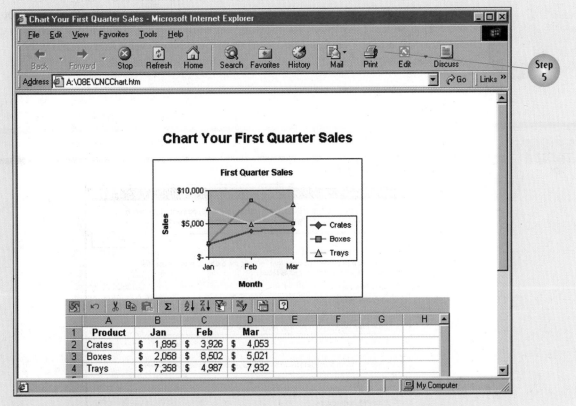

Step 5

6. Close Internet Explorer.
7. Save the workbook using the same file name (Excel E8, Ex 05) and close it.

Importing Data from a Web Page into Excel

There are many ways to import data from a Web page into Excel. Depending on which method you choose, some of the data might display differently in Excel than it does on the Web page.

Simply copying and pasting is one way to import data from a Web page into Excel. Select the data you want to import and right-click on any of the cells. From the shortcut menu that appears, click Copy. Click an appropriate cell on the worksheet into which you want to import the copied data and click the Paste button on the Standard toolbar. The data from the Web page is copied into the worksheet.

Data from a Web page can be imported into Excel using drag and drop. First select the data to be imported from the Web page and then click the selected data and drag it to the desired cell in Excel.

The Object command from the Insert menu enables you to insert a Web page in an Excel worksheet. When the object is inserted, an icon for the Web page is displayed. Double-clicking the icon opens the Web page in Internet explorer.

You can import data from a Web page into Excel from the Web browser by clicking the Export to Excel toolbar button. When you click the Export to Excel button, a read-only copy of the data immediately appears in Excel. Using the Save As command and giving the file a new name allows you to save the data permanently as an Excel worksheet.

Export to Excel

Another way to import data from a Web page into Excel is by using a Web Query. A Web Query allows you to specify exactly which parts of the Web page you want to import and how much formatting you want to keep. To create a Web query, click Data, select Get External Data, and then click New Web Query. Follow the directions in the New Web Query dialog box shown in figure 8.4.

figure

8.4

New Web Query Dialog Box

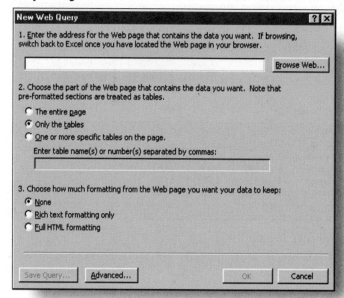

Finally, you can open any .html file in Excel by using the Open command on the File menu. This method imports the entire Web page, although some content, such as .gif image files, might be lost.

Round-Tripping an Excel Workbook

With the Web technology that is integrated into Excel 2000, you can take an Excel workbook on what is called a *round trip* from the Excel 2000 application to a Web browser and then back to the Excel 2000 application. To start this trip, click File and then Save as Web Page. At the Save As dialog box, key a name for the document in the File name text box. The file extension for the file name should be either .htm or .html. If you want the worksheet to be interactive, click the Selection: Sheet radio button and then click the Add interactivity check box. You can interact with only one worksheet at a time in a Web browser. Click the Save button. After the workbook has been saved as a Web page you can open it in a Web browser. The document displayed in the browser looks exactly like the original document created in Excel. All the formatting and functionality remain intact. If the Add interactivity option was selected, then the worksheet can be edited in the Web browser. Once the worksheet has been edited in the Web browser, it can be imported to Excel using any of the methods discussed in the previous section. The worksheet will survive the "round trip"—from Excel to a Web browser and back to Excel—without losing any formatting or functionality.

exercise 6

Importing Data from a Web Page into Excel

1. Complete the following steps to use the copy and paste method to import data from a Web page into Excel:
   a. Open Internet Explorer (or Netscape). You do not have to be online.
   b. Click the File menu in Internet Explorer and then click Open.
   c. The Open dialog box appears. Locate the sales_reps.html file on your data disk and open it.
   d. Open a new workbook in Excel. Arrange the windows so that you can see both the entire width of the table in the Web browser and at least cell A1 in Excel.
   e. The Web page lists the phone numbers of the sales representatives for Case 'N Crate. Click the First Name box in the upper left corner of the table and drag to the last telephone number in order to select the entire table.
   f. Click on the selected table in the Web browser and drag the mouse pointer to cell A1 in the Excel worksheet.
   g. Click the Minimize button to place Internet Explorer on the taskbar.
   h. Switch to the Excel worksheet and maximize it.
   i. Widen columns C and D so that the data in these columns is displayed on one line.
   j. Save the worksheet using the file name Excel E8, Ex 06a.
   k. Create a custom header for the worksheet that displays your name at the left margin and the file name at the right margin.
   l. Print the worksheet and then close it.
2. Complete the following steps to use the Open command to import data from a Web page into Excel:
   a. Click File and then click Open.
   b. Locate the sales_reps.html file and open it.
   c. If the Case 'N Crate logo is covering the title *Sales Representatives*, click the logo to select it and drag it to the right so that it is no longer covering the title.
   d. Save the worksheet as an Excel workbook using the file name Excel E8, Ex 06b.
   e. Create a custom header for the worksheet that displays your name at the left margin and the file name at the right margin.
   f. Save the worksheet using the same file name.
   g. Print the worksheet and then close it.
3. To take an Excel worksheet on a "round trip," complete the following steps:
   a. Open Excel E8, Ex 03. You created this file in exercise 3.
   b. Click File and then click Save as Web Page.

c. The Save As dialog box is displayed. Click the Se̲lection: Sheet radio button to select it.
d. Click the A̲dd interactivity check box to select it.
e. Key **CNCFirstQtr.htm** in the File n̲ame box.

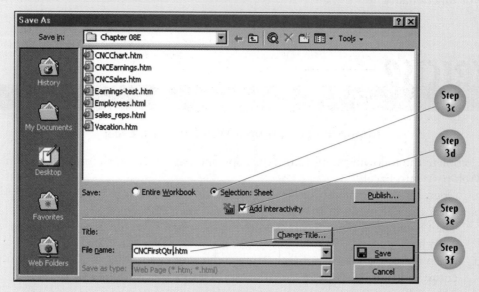

f. Click the S̲ave button.
g. Close the Excel E8, Ex 03 workbook. You do not need to save any changes.
h. Open Internet Explorer. You do not have to be online.
i. Click the F̲ile menu in Internet Explorer and then click O̲pen.
j. The Open dialog box appears. Locate the CNCFirstQtr.htm file on your data disk and open it.
k. Make the following changes to the CNCFirstQtr.htm file in Internet Explorer:
    1) Key **TOTAL** in cell E3.
    2) Right-click cell E3. Click Property Toolbo̲x on the shortcut menu that appears.
    3) The Spreadsheet Property Toolbox appears. Click the Bold button.
    4) Click the down arrow to the right of the Horizontal alignment box and then click *Center*.

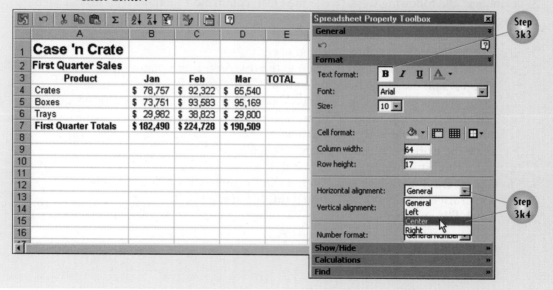

        5) Close the Spreadsheet Property Toolbox.

        6) Key **=SUM(B4:D4)** in cell E4.

        7) Key **=SUM(B5:D5)** in cell E5.

        8) Key **=SUM(B6:D6)** in cell E6.

  l. Select cells A1 through E7.

  m. Right-click the selected cells and click <u>C</u>opy on the shortcut menu that appears.

  n. Close Internet Explorer.

  o. Switch to Excel and open a new workbook if necessary. Click cell A1 to select it and click the Paste button on the Standard toolbar.

  p. Optimize the widths of columns A through E. Notice that the formatting and formulas you entered using Internet Explorer remained intact.

  q. Save the workbook using the file name Excel E8, Ex 06c.

  r. Create a custom header for the worksheet that displays your name at the left margin and the file name at the right margin.

  s. Print the worksheet.

4. Save the file using the same file name (Excel E8, Ex 06c) and close it.

exercise 7

Running a Web Query

(Note: To complete this exercise you need to be connected to the Internet. Connect to your Internet Service Provider if you do not have a direct Internet connection.)

1. If necessary, open a new workbook in Excel and click cell A1.

2. Complete the following steps to run a Web Query:

  a. Click <u>D</u>ata, point to Get External <u>D</u>ata, and click Run Save<u>d</u> Query.

  b. The Run Query dialog box is displayed. Click Microsoft Investor Currency Rates.iqy.

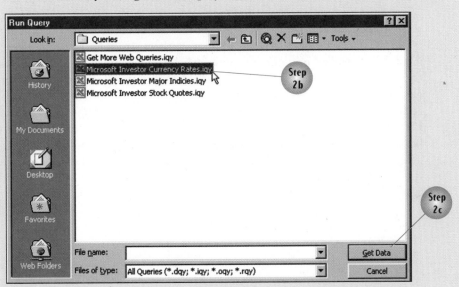

  c. Click <u>G</u>et Data.

d. The Returning External Data to Microsoft Excel dialog box is displayed. You want to put the data in cell A1 of the existing worksheet, which is the default setting. Click OK.

e. You may have to wait few moments, but the data eventually will display in the worksheet. Save the file on your data disk using the file name Excel E8, Ex 07.

f. If necessary, adjust the column widths so that the headers are all displayed.

g. Create a custom header for the worksheet that displays your name at the left margin and the file name at the right margin.

h. Change the orientation of the page to landscape.

i. Print the worksheet so that it fits on one page. Save the workbook and then close it.

3. If necessary, disconnect from your Internet Service Provider.

Using Microsoft Query

Another way to retrieve external data into Excel is by using Microsoft Query. Microsoft Query is a program that enables you to access databases, such as Microsoft Access, in order to retrieve data into a worksheet where it then can be analyzed in Excel. Whenever the database is updated with new information, Excel reports or summaries based on that data are automatically updated.

In order to retrieve data from a database into Excel, you create a query or question based on the data. For example, you might want to know last year's sales figures for a particular product. When creating the query, you select only the specific data you want to retrieve. There are three steps to using Query to retrieve data. First, you establish the data source of the data to be retrieved; second, you use the Query Wizard to select the specific data to be retrieved; and third, you return the data to Excel where it can be formatted, summarized, and used for creating reports.

Although you can work directly in Query, the easiest way to retrieve data using Microsoft Query is by using the Query Wizard. With the Query Wizard you can select the tables and fields to be included, sort the data, and do simple filtering before the data is returned to an Excel worksheet. In order to use Microsoft Query, it must be installed on your computer. Click the cell on the Excel worksheet where the external data range is to start. Click Data, point to Get External Data, and then click New Database Query. The Choose Data Source dialog box shown in figure 8.5 is displayed. This dialog box is used for establishing the data source. On the Databases tab, make sure the Use the Query Wizard to create/edit queries check box is selected. Double-click the database from which the data is to be retrieved. The Select Database dialog box is displayed. Double-click the database file where the data is located. From this point you can follow the directions provided by the Query Wizard.

figure
8.5

The Choose Data Source Dialog Box

Double-click the database from which the data is to be retrieved.

To get external data by using the Query Wizard, the Use the Query Wizard to create/edit queries check box must be selected.

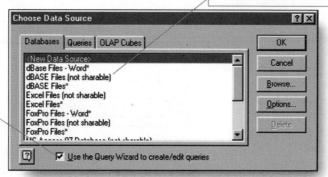

exercise 8

Using Microsoft Query to Query a Database

(Note: In order to complete this exercise, Microsoft Query must be installed on the computer and the CD-ROM that accompanies this book must be in the CD-ROM drive.)

1. If necessary, open a new workbook in Excel and click cell A1. Make sure the CD-ROM that accompanies this book is in the CD-ROM drive.
2. There is a Microsoft Access database file on the CD-ROM called Payroll.mdb. Retrieve data from this database from the *Excel Expert Student Files* folder using Microsoft Query by completing the following steps:

   a. Click Data, point to Get External Data, and then click New Database Query.
   b. If necessary, click the Databases tab.
   c. Make sure the Use the Query Wizard to create/edit queries check box is selected.
   d. Double-click the *MS Access Database** option.
   e. The Select Database dialog box is displayed. From the drop-down menu for the Drives box, select the CD-ROM drive. Usually, this is drive E. If your CD-ROM drive is a drive other than E, ask your instructor for help.
   f. Double-click the *payroll.mdb* option from the Database Name list.

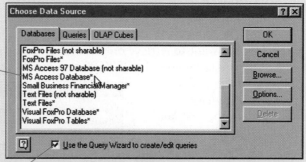

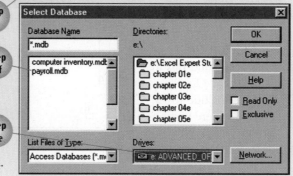

Step 2d

Step 2c

Step 2e

Step 2f

g. The Query Wizard – Choose Columns dialog box is displayed. Click the plus sign next to *Employee Information*.

h. A list of all the fields in the Employee Information table is displayed. Click the *Firstname* option in the <u>A</u>vailable tables and columns list.

i. Click the top arrow button. The *Firstname* option has now moved from the <u>A</u>vailable tables and columns list to the <u>C</u>olumns in your query list.

j. Click the *Surname* option in the <u>A</u>vailable tables and columns list. Click the top arrow button.

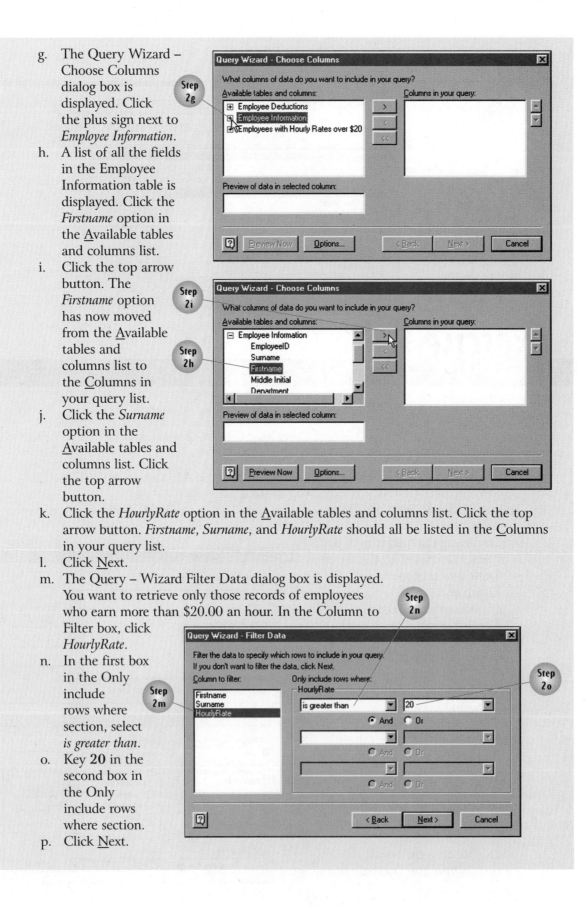

k. Click the *HourlyRate* option in the <u>A</u>vailable tables and columns list. Click the top arrow button. *Firstname*, *Surname*, and *HourlyRate* should all be listed in the <u>C</u>olumns in your query list.

l. Click <u>N</u>ext.

m. The Query – Wizard Filter Data dialog box is displayed. You want to retrieve only those records of employees who earn more than $20.00 an hour. In the Column to Filter box, click *HourlyRate*.

n. In the first box in the Only include rows where section, select *is greater than*.

o. Key **20** in the second box in the Only include rows where section.

p. Click <u>N</u>ext.

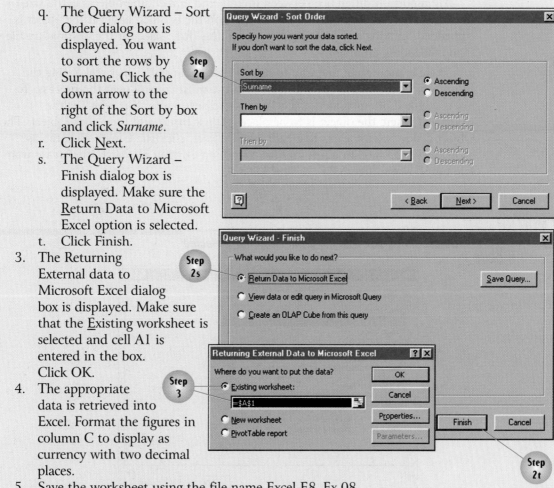

q. The Query Wizard – Sort Order dialog box is displayed. You want to sort the rows by Surname. Click the down arrow to the right of the Sort by box and click *Surname*. **Step 2q**

r. Click Next.

s. The Query Wizard – Finish dialog box is displayed. Make sure the Return Data to Microsoft Excel option is selected. **Step 2s**

t. Click Finish.

3. The Returning External data to Microsoft Excel dialog box is displayed. Make sure that the Existing worksheet is selected and cell A1 is entered in the box. Click OK. **Step 3**

4. The appropriate data is retrieved into Excel. Format the figures in column C to display as currency with two decimal places. **Step 2t**

5. Save the worksheet using the file name Excel E8, Ex 08.

6. Create a custom header for the worksheet that displays your name at the left margin and the file name at the right margin.

7. Print the worksheet.

8. Save the workbook using the same file name (Excel E8, Ex 08) and close it.

Linking and Embedding Objects

Another way of sharing Excel data with other applications is by copying the information as either a linked object or an embedded object. The information that is being copied is called the object. The file from which the object comes is called the source file. The file into which the object is being copied is called the destination file.

A linked object is stored with the source file. Any changes made to the object in the source file are automatically reflected in the destination file. An embedded object is stored with the destination file. If an object is embedded, there is no link to the source file. Therefore any changes made to the object in the source file are not reflected in the destination file. Since an embedded object is stored with the destination file, it only can be edited in the destination file.

> Be sure to make a backup copy of the source and destination files before linking and embedding data.

> In order to edit an embedded object, the application that created the object must be stored on the computer.

An important difference between linking and embedding objects is the size of the destination file. The size of the destination file is much larger if the object is embedded. Linking an object requires much less disk space for the destination file than embedding an object.

There is more than one way to link or embed an object in Excel. Using the Insert Object command provides you with the most control over the process. To insert a linked or embedded object, access the destination file, which is the worksheet where the object is to be placed. Click Insert and then click Object. The Object dialog box appears. To create a new object, click the Create New tab as shown in figure 8.6. To insert an object from an existing file, click the Create from File tab shown in figure 8.7.

figure
8.6

Object Dialog Box with the Create New Tab Selected

figure
8.7

Object Dialog Box with the Create from File Tab Selected

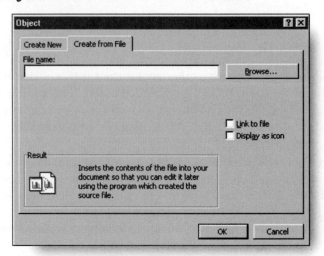

If you are creating a new embedded object, select the type of object you want to create from the Object type box. If you plan to put the workbook online, clicking the Display as icon check box will display the object as an icon that viewers can double-click to display the object. If you are inserting a linked or embedded object from an existing file, enter the name of the file in the File name box. If the Link to file check box is not selected, the object will be embedded. If it is selected, the object will be linked. Clicking the Display as icon check box will display the object as an icon to those viewing the workbook online.

In addition to inserting a linked object or embedded object from an existing file, you can copy information from an existing file as a linked or embedded object. First, select the information to be copied. Right-click the selected information and click Copy on the shortcut menu. Switch to the worksheet that is to be the destination file. Click Edit and then click Paste Special. The Paste Special dialog box shown in figure 8.8 is displayed. Selecting the Paste option from this dialog box copies the information as an embedded object. Selecting the Paste link option copies the information as a linked object. In the As box, make sure the option that has the word Object in its name is selected.

When data that has been copied as a linked or embedded object is pasted into the destination file, make sure that no data in the destination file is overwritten. *Hint*

figure
8.8

Paste Special Dialog Box

The Paste option copies the information as an embedded object.

The Paste link option copies the information as a linked object.

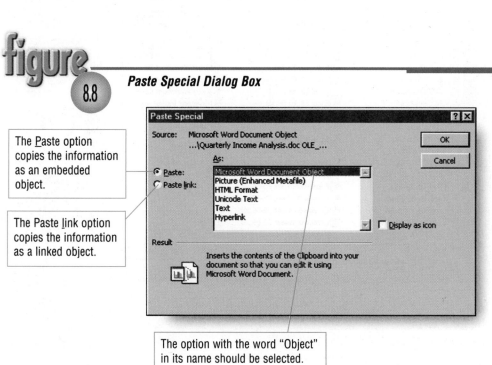

The option with the word "Object" in its name should be selected.

exercise 9

Linking Objects

1. Open Excel Worksheet E8-06.
2. Save the worksheet using the Save <u>A</u>s command and name it Excel E8, Ex 09.
3. Create a custom header that displays your name at the left margin and the file name at the right margin.
4. The logo for Linda Taylor's custom-made clothing store, Taylor Made, is stored in the Paint application that comes with Windows. Complete the following steps to insert the logo as a linked object:
   a. Click <u>I</u>nsert and then click <u>O</u>bject.
   b. The Object dialog box is displayed. Click the Create from File tab.
   c. Click the <u>B</u>rowse button.
   d. From the Browse dialog box, select *Taylor.bmp* from your data disk.

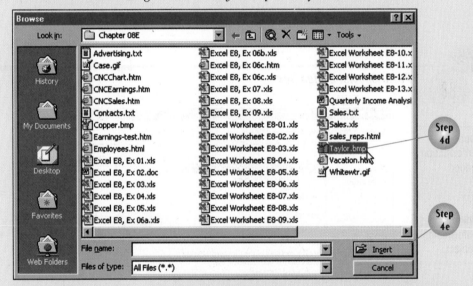

   e. Click In<u>s</u>ert.
   f. Click the <u>L</u>ink to file check box to select it.
   g. Click OK.
5. The logo is linked to the worksheet, but it is much too large. If necessary, click and drag the logo to move it to the upper left corner of the worksheet. Click the logo to select it. Click and drag on the handle in the lower right corner until the logo fits in the range of cells A1 through C8.

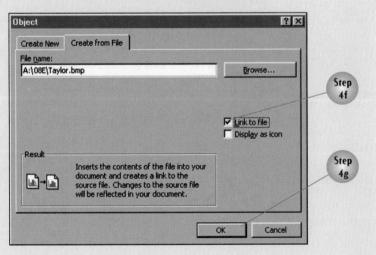

6. The figure for the proposed budget increase that needs to be entered into cell B10 can be found in the Budget.doc file. To insert text from the Budget.doc file into the Excel E8, Ex 09 file, complete the following steps:
    a. Click cell A19.
    b. Click Insert and then click Object.
    c. The Object dialog box is displayed. Click the Create from file tab.
    d. Click the Browse button.
    d. From the Browse dialog box, select Budget.doc from your data disk.
    e. Click Insert.
    f. Click the Link to file check box to select it.
    g. Click OK.
7. The linked object is inserted in the worksheet. Read the information that is displayed. Key **10** in cell B10. Save the workbook using the same file name (Excel E8, Ex 09) and print it.
8. Start Word and open the Budget.doc file. Delete *10* and in its place key **08**. Save the file. Exit from Word.
9. To update the link in the Excel E8, Ex 09 file, complete the following steps:
    a. If necessary, switch to the Excel E8, Ex 09 workbook in Excel.
    b. Click Edit. Expand the menu if necessary and click Links.
    c. The Links dialog box is displayed. For the source file of the link, select *Budget.doc*.
    d. Click the Update Now button.
    e. Click OK.

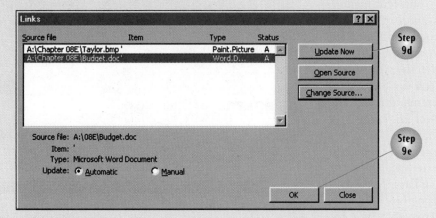

10. The text in the linked object automatically changed from *10* to *08*. Key **08** in cell B10. Save the workbook using the same file name (Excel E8, Ex 09) and print it.
11. Close the workbook.

exercise 10

Embedding an Object

1. Open the Windows Paint application. On some systems the application is opened by clicking the Start button, selecting Programs, selecting Accessories, and clicking Paint.
2. Click the File menu in Paint and then click Open.
3. Open the Taylor.bmp file on your data disk.
4. Linda Taylor wants to embed the logo in a worksheet so that it can be edited from the destination file. Complete the following steps to copy the logo:
   a. Click Edit and then click Select All.
   b. Right-click the selected logo.
   c. Click Copy on the shortcut menu.

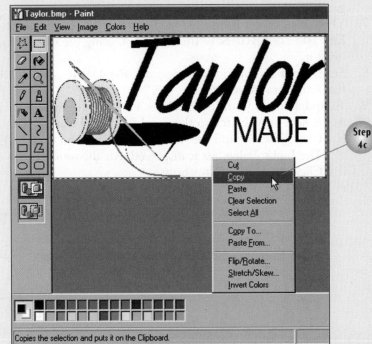

5. Switch to the Excel program. Open Excel Worksheet E8-07.
6. Save the worksheet using the Save As command and name it Excel E8, Ex 10.
7. Click the Edit menu in Excel and then click Paste Special.
8. The Paste Special dialog box is displayed. Check to make sure that Bitmap Image Object is selected in the As box and that the Paste option is selected. Click OK.

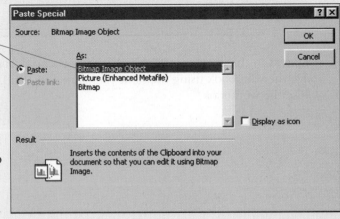

9. The logo is embedded in the worksheet, but it is much too large. Click the logo to select it. If necessary, drag the image to the upper left corner of the worksheet.
   Click and drag on the handle in the lower right corner until the logo fits in the range of cells A1 through D8.

10. Complete the following steps to edit the logo in the destination file so that it is in black and white instead of color:

   a. Double-click on the logo. The menu options from Paint are now available to you in Excel.

   b. Click Image and then click Attributes.

   c. Click the Black and white option to select it.

   d. Click OK.

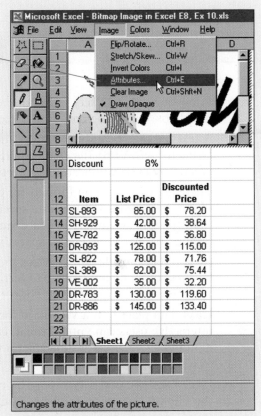

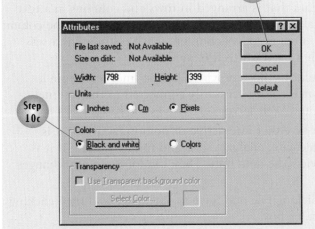

   e. A dialog box appears warning you that converting to black and white cannot be undone. Click Yes.

   f. Click anywhere outside the logo to exit Paint Editor.

11. Create a custom header that displays your name at the left margin and the file name at the right margin.

12. Save the workbook using the same file name (Excel E8, Ex 10) and print it.

13. Close the workbook. Close Paint.

chapter summary

➤ Importing data to Excel refers to sending data from another application to an Excel workbook. Exporting data from Excel refers to sending Excel data to another application.

➤ A text file only contains printable letters, numbers, and symbols, usually from the ASCII character set. A text file contains no formatting codes. A text file is supported by practically every application on every computer platform.

➤ There are two common formats for data that is arranged in rows and columns in a text file. A delimited text file uses a special character called a delimiter to separate one column from the next. Commas and tabs are often used as delimiters. Each column has a set number of characters and/or spaces in a fixed width text file.

➤ An intranet provides the services similar to those provided by the Internet within a business or an organization. An intranet is not necessarily connected to the Internet. Intranets use the same Web browser and Web server software as the Internet.

➤ Excel data placed on a Web page can be either interactive or noninteractive. If it is interactive users can enter, format, calculate, analyze, sort, and filter the data. If it is noninteractive, users will be able to view the data only. They cannot make any changes to it.

➤ Place Excel data on a Web page by clicking File and Save as Web page and then clicking the Publish button on the Save As dialog box.

➤ You can import data from a Web page into Excel by copying and pasting, by using the Export to Excel button in the Web browser, by using a Web Query, or by using the Open command on the File menu in Excel.

➤ During the linking and embedding process, the information being copied is called the object. The file from which the object originates is called the source file. The file into which the object will be placed is called the destination file.

➤ A linked object is stored with the source file. Changes made to the object in the source file are automatically reflected in the destination file.

➤ An embedded object is stored with the destination file. Any changes made to the source file are not reflected in the destination file. Changes can be made to an embedded object in the destination file only.

➤ If an object is embedded in the destination file, the destination file will be significantly larger than if the object is linked to the destination file.

➤ Objects can be linked or embedded by using the Copy and Paste Special commands.

commands review

	Mouse/Keyboard
Importing from a text file	Click File, Open, select *Text Files* from the Files of type list box
Exporting to a text file	Click File, Save As
Exporting Excel data to a Web page	Click File, Save As Web Page, Publish
Importing Excel data from a Web page	Right-click the data to be imported, click Copy, click a cell on the worksheet, click the Paste button
Running a Web Query	Click Data, Get External Data, New Web Query
Query a database	Click Data, Get External Data, New Database Query
Open an .html file in Excel	Click File, Open
Insert a linked or embedded object	Click Insert, Object
Copy a linked or embedded object	In the source file, right-click the object to be copied, click Copy In the destination file click Edit, Paste Special.

thinking offline

Completion: In the space provided at the right, indicate the correct term or command.

1. This term refers to sending data from Excel to another application.

2. The characters from a text file usually come from this character set.

3. This term refers to a text file that uses commas or another special character to separate the columns.

4. Text files usually end with this extension.

5. This term refers to a local area or wide area network that provides a business or organization with services similar to those provided by the Internet without necessarily being connected to the Internet.

6. This is the name of the markup language used to create Web pages.

7. This is the only software users need to access Excel data that has been placed on the Web.

8. This term describes Excel data on the Web that can be entered, formatted, calculated, analyzed, sorted, and filtered.

9. One way to import data from a Web page into Excel is to click this button from the Web page displaying the data to be imported.

10. This type of object is stored with the source file. _____

11. This type of object has to be edited in the destination file. _____

12. If you are linking an object by copying it, you have to click this option from the <u>E</u>dit menu in the destination file. _____

13. List the reasons why you might need to import a text file to Excel.

_____

_____

_____

14. List the advantages of using a company intranet for distributing information.

_____

_____

_____

15. You need to share Excel data with other applications, but the available storage space is limited. Explain whether you would choose to link or embed the data and why.

_____

_____

_____

working hands-on

(Note: In order to have room on your disk to save all the files you will be creating in the following Assessments you may need to delete some files from your disk. You may delete the following files: Excel E8, Ex 01; Excel E8, Ex 02; Excel E8, Ex 03; Excel E8, Ex 04; Excel E8, Ex 05; Excel E8, Ex 06a; Excel E8, Ex 06b, Excel E8, Ex 06c, Excel E8, Ex 07, Excel E8, Ex 08, Excel E8, Ex 09, and Excel E3, Ex 10. Check with your instructor to make sure it is all right to delete these files.)

Assessment 1

1. Someone has sent you some advertising figures as a text file. You need to import them into Excel. Open the Advertising.txt file. Advertising.txt is a fixed width file. The data in the first column is text. The remaining columns should be formatted as General.
2. Save the workbook as a Microsoft Excel workbook file using the Save <u>A</u>s command. Name the file Excel E8, SA 01.
3. Create a custom header that displays your name at the left margin and the file name at the right margin.
4. Print the worksheet.
5. Save the workbook using the same file name (Excel E8, SA 01) and close it.

Assessment 2

1. Open Excel Worksheet E8-08.
2. This worksheet contains pricing information on some fabrics. Save this file as a Text (Tab delimited) file. Name the saved file Excel E8, SA 02.txt.
3. Close the Excel E8, SA 02.txt file.
4. Start Word and open the Excel E8, SA 02.txt file.
5. Select all the text in the document and set left tab stops using the ruler at 2.25", 3", 3.75", 4.75", and 5.75".
6. Save the file as a Word document using the file name Excel E8, SA 02.doc.
7. Create a custom header for the Word document that prints your name at the left margin and the file name at the right margin.
8. Save the document again using the same file name (Excel E8, SA 02) and close it.

Assessment 3

1. Open Excel Worksheet E8-09.
2. Save the workbook using the Save <u>A</u>s command and name it Excel E8, SA 03.
3. Save cells A5 through E24 as a noninteractive Web page. The data should be published using the file name Addresses.
4. Print the Web page from Internet Explorer (or Netscape Navigator).
5. Close Internet Explorer.
6. Save the workbook again using the same file name (Excel E8, SA 03) and close it.

Assessment 4

1. Open Excel Worksheet E8-10.
2. Save the workbook using the Save <u>A</u>s command and name it Excel E8, SA 04a.
3. Designers who help design clothes for Linda Taylor's company, Taylor Made, often need to calculate how much the fabric for their designs will cost. Linda Taylor wants this worksheet published on the company intranet so the designers can use it when needed. Select cells A3 through E15. Save this worksheet as interactive data on the Web. When the Save As dialog box displays, click the option for saving only the selected range of cells. Set the title for the published data as Fabric Cost Calculations. The data should be published using the file name Fabric Cost.
4. When the Web page is displayed in Internet Explorer, delete the values in cells D2, D5, D9, and D10.
5. Key the following values in the cells indicated.

Cell	Value
D3	35
D5	18
D9	42
D11	20

6. Print the Web page.
7. Delete the values in cells D3, D5, D9, and D11.
8. Sort the data in the 01-24 yards column from the most expensive fabric to the least expensive fabric.
9. Filter the data so that only the fabrics that cost less than $100 a yard for 24 or fewer yards is displayed.

10. Key the following values in the cells indicated.

Cell	Value
D5	12
D8	26
D11	8

11. Print the Web page.
12. Change the filter so that all the fabrics are displayed.
13. Click the Export to Excel button.
14. The worksheet is displayed in Excel. Save the workbook on your data disk. Change the file type to Microsoft Excel workbook. Use the file name Excel E8, SA 04b. Print the worksheet and close it. Close worksheet Excel E8, SA 04a.
15. Close Internet Explorer.

Assessment 5

1. Open Excel Worksheet E8-11.
2. Save the workbook using the Save As command and name it Excel E8, SA 05.
3. This file can be used by designers and the office management at Taylor Made to break down the design costs of individual designs. Linda Taylor would like it placed on the company's intranet. Save this chart as interactive data on the Web. Set the title for the published data as Calculating Design Costs. The data should be published using the file name Design Cost.
4. When the Web page is displayed in Internet Explorer, key the following values in the cells indicated.

Cell	Value
B1	300
B2	175
B3	2560
B4	782
B5	679

5. Print the Web page.
6. Close Internet Explorer.
7. Save the Excel workbook using the same file name (Excel E8, SA 05) and close it.

Assessment 6

1. Open Internet Explorer (or Netscape). You do not have to be online.
2. Open the Employees.html file. This is a list of the employees who work at Whitewater Canoe and Kayak Corporation along with their titles and the number of years they have been employed there.
3. Open a new workbook in Excel. Arrange the windows so that you can see both the entire width of the table in Internet Explorer and at least cell A1 in Excel.
4. Select the entire table in Internet Explorer. Click on the selected table and drag it to cell A1 in Excel.
5. Close Internet Explorer. Maximize the Excel window.
6. Widen the columns as necessary so that all the data is displayed.
7. Adjust the row height of all the rows in the table to 12.75. Save the worksheet using the file name Excel E8, SA 06a.

8. Create a custom header for the worksheet that displays your name at the left margin and the name of the file at the right margin.
9. Print the worksheet. Save and close it.
10. From Excel, open the employees.html file.
11. Adjust the height of row 1 so the company logo fits in it.
12. Save the worksheet as an Excel Workbook using the file name Excel E8, SA 06b.
13. Create a custom header for the worksheet that displays your name at the left margin and the name of the file at the right margin.
14. Print the worksheet. Save and close it.
15. Open Internet Explorer.
16. Open the Vacation.htm file in Internet Explorer.
17. This interactive worksheet calculates the number of vacation days for which employees are eligible. Key **15** in cell B3 to see how it works.
18. Export the table to Excel using the Export to Excel button.
19. Save the data on your data disk as an Excel workbook using the file name Excel E8, SA 06c.
20. Create a custom header for the worksheet that displays your name at the left margin and the name of the file at the right margin.
21. Print the worksheet. Save and close it.
22. Close Internet Explorer.

Assessment 7

(Note: To complete this exercise you need to be online. Make a connection to the Internet.)

1. Open a new workbook in Excel.
2. Run the saved Query named Microsoft Investor Major Indicies.iqy. Save the workbook using the file name Excel E8, SA 07.
3. Create a custom header for the worksheet that displays your name at the left margin and the name of the file at the right margin.
4. Adjust the scaling so that the worksheet will print on one page.
5. Save the workbook using the same file name (Excel E8, SA 07) and print it.
6. Close the workbook.
7. Disconnect from your Internet service provider.

Assessment 8

(Note: In order to complete this exercise, Microsoft Query must be installed on the computer and the CD-ROM that accompanies this book must be in the CD-ROM drive.)

1. There is a Microsoft Access database file on the CD-ROM called Computer Inventory.mdb. Retrieve data from this database using Microsoft Query. From the Product List table include the *PartName, SupplierNo,* and *ListPrice* columns. From the Suppliers Table include the *SupplierName* column.
2. Filter the data that is retrieved so that only those records are retrieved where the supplier name equals ComputerWay or Jorge Computers.
3. Sort the data by SupplierName and then by PartName.
4. Return the data to Microsoft Excel.
5. Format the figures in column C as currency with two decimal places.
6. Save the worksheet using the file name Excel E8, SA 08.
7. Create a custom header for the worksheet that displays your name at the left margin and the name of the file at the right margin.
8. Save the worksheet again using the same file name (Excel E8, SA 08) and print it.
9. Close the worksheet.

Assessment 9

1. Open Excel Worksheet E8-12.
2. Save the worksheet using the Save As command and name it Excel E8, SA 09.
3. Create a custom header that displays your name at the left margin and the file name at the right margin.
4. The logo for Copper Clad Incorporated can be opened through the Paint application that comes with Windows. Insert Copper.bmp as a linked file.
5. Adjust the size of the logo so that it fits in rows 1 through 8.
6. Save the file using the same file name (Excel E8, SA 09) and print it.
7. Close the workbook.

Assessment 10

1. Start Windows' Paint application.
2. In Paint, open the Copper.bmp file.
3. You want to embed the logo in a worksheet. Copy the logo and use the Paste Special to paste it into the Excel Worksheet E8-13.
4. Save the worksheet using the Save As command and name it Excel E8, SA 10.
5. Adjust the size of the logo so that it fits in rows 1 through 7.
6. Double-click the logo to edit it.
7. Click Image and then click Invert Colors.
8. Click anywhere outside the logo.
9. Create a custom header that displays your name at the left margin and the file name at the right margin.
10. Save the file using the same file name (Excel E8, SA 10) and print it.
11. Close the workbook.

Performance Assessments

Excel EPA

EXCEL

ASSESSING PROFICIENCIES

In this unit, you have learned to create, apply, and edit custom formats, styles, conditional formatting, and templates. You also learned how to copy worksheets into a workbook, consolidate data into a list, and link workbooks. You learned how to use the PMT, PV, ROUND RAND, SUMIF, COUNTIF, VLOOKUP, and IF functions. You learned how to enter, edit, and delete data using the Data Form, use data validation, filter a list, use PivotTables, PivotCharts, Goal Seek, Solver, Scenarios, and Report Manager. You learned how to record, run, and edit macros; assign macros to command buttons; create custom toolbars; and use the auditing toolbar. You learned how to share workbooks; change workbook properties; apply and remove passwords, workbook protection, and worksheet protection; merge workbooks; import and export data from text files; place a noninteractive and an interactive worksheet on the Web; import data from an Access database and a Web page; use Web query; and link and embed objects.

Assessment 1 **one**

1. Open Excel Worksheet 01.
2. Save the workbook using the Save As command and name it Excel, EPA 01.
3. Create a custom header that has your name left-aligned and the file name right-aligned.
4. This workbook is an invoice used by the EastWest Crossroads Company which is a company that sells imported and unique gifts through the mail. The form is used for taking orders. Add a bottom border for filling in information to the following cells: C4, C5, C6, C7, C8, C9, F7, H7, K8, K9, C12, C13, C14, C15, F15, and H15.
5. Place an outline border around cells K4, K5, and K6.
6. Create a style called Header 1 that includes the following formatting:

Font:	Arial
Font style:	Bold
Font size:	10
Color:	Brown

7. Apply the Header 1 style to the following cells: A4, A5, A7, A8, A9, E7, G7, A12, A13, A15, E15, and G15.

8. Create a style that is based on Header 1 and name it Header 2. Header 2 should include the following formatting:

Font:	Arial
Font style:	Bold
Font size:	10
Color:	Brown
Horizontal alignment:	Right

9. Apply the Header 2 style to the following cells: I4, I5, I6, I8, I9, I26, I27, I28, I29, and I30.

10. Create a style that is based on Header 1 and name it Header 3. Header 3 should include the following formatting:

Horizontal alignment:	Center
Font:	Arial
Font style:	Bold
Font size:	10
Color:	White
Cell shading:	Brown

11. Apply the Header 3 style to the following cells: A18 through K18 and I31.
12. Format the worksheet so that zero values are not displayed.
13. Place an outline border around the following ranges of cells:

A19:A25, B19:B25, C19:C25, D19:D25, E19:E25, I19:I25, J19:J25, J26:J30, J31.

14. Enter the following data in the cells indicated:

Cell	Data
C4	Jo Ellen Gammon
C5	348 West End Road
C7	Arcata
F7	CA
H7	95521
K5	X
C8	(707) 555-0922
K8	9999 8955 1221 0032
K9	09/09/07

15. Save the worksheet again with the same name (Excel, EPA 01).
16. Print and then close Excel, EPA 01.

Assessment two

1. Open Excel Worksheet 02.
2. Save the workbook using the Save As command and name it Excel, EPA 02.
3. Create a custom header that has your name left-aligned and the file name right-aligned.
4. This worksheet keeps track of the number of hours of music lessons given for each instrument. Create a custom number format that will insert the text "hrs" (for *hours*) after a value. Format all the values on the worksheet using the custom format you create.
5. Use conditional formatting to display all the values in cells B4 through M20

that are under 200 in red and all the values that are greater than or equal to 450 as blue.

6. Set the left and right margins to 0.5". Change the orientation of the page to Landscape.
7. Use the <u>A</u>utoFit Selection command to automatically adjust the width of all the columns.
8. Format the worksheet using the Classic 2 AutoFormat.
9. Save the worksheet again with the same name (Excel, EPA 02).
10. Print and then close Excel, EPA 02.

Assessment three 3

1. Open Excel, EPA 01.
2. Save the workbook using the Save <u>A</u>s command and name it Excel, EPA 03.
3. Create a custom header that has your name left-aligned and the file name right-aligned.
4. Delete the contents of the following cells: C4, C5, C7, C8, F7, H7, K5, K8, K9, A19, A20, B19, B20, C19, C20, E19, E20, I19, and I20.
5. Save the file as a template using the file name EastWest Invoice.xlt.
6. Close the template.
7. Open the EastWest Invoice template.
8. Enter the following data in the cells indicated:

Cell	Data
C4	Gary Simpson
C5	467 Filbert Ave.
C7	Chelsea Heights
F7	NJ
H7	08401
C8	(732) 555-0933
C9	(732) 555-0805
K4	X
K8	7777 3471 1144 0008
K9	05/01/06
A19	35
B19	1
C19	XD489Z
E19	Bamboo Tea Pot
I19	32

9. Save the invoice as an Excel workbook using the file name Excel, EPA 03-a.
10. Print the Excel, EPA 03-a workbook and then close it.
11. Open the EastWest Invoice template.
12. Change the standard delivery charge in cell J27 to $7.50.
13. Save the edited EastWest Invoice template. You want to replace the original template.
14. Close the template.

15. Open the EastWest Invoice template.
16. Enter the following data in the cells indicated:

Cell	Data
C4	Sue Clanton
C5	4402 Feather Sound Dr.
C7	Clearwater
F7	FL
H7	33515
C8	(727) 555-6688
C9	(732) 555-5832
K4	X
K8	3333 4562 4578 9977
K9	06/01/07
A19	28
B19	1
C19	XD985R
E19	Russian Enamel Egg
I19	120

17. Save the invoice as an Excel workbook using the file name Excel, EPA 03-b.
18. Print the Excel, EPA 03-b workbook.
19. Delete the EastWest Invoice template.
20. Close the Excel, EPA 03-b workbook.

Assessment four 4

1. Open Excel Worksheet 03.
2. Save the workbook using the Save As command and name it Excel, EPA 04.
3. Create a custom header that has your name left-aligned and the file name right-aligned.
4. The EastWest Crossroads Company uses this workbook to calculate, in US dollars, the orders they placed in March. Since exchange rates are constantly changing, the exchange rate for the countries with which the EastWest Crossroads Company does business are kept in a separate workbook. You need to link the Excel, EPA 04 workbook with the Exchange Rates workbook. Open the Exchange Rates workbook.
5. Switch back to the Excel, EPA 04 workbook. Enter the following data in the cells indicated:

Cell	Data
C4	24,568
C6	48,952
C10	95,670
C16	205,678
C21	108,952
C25	3,467,890

6. Click cell D4. Enter a formula that multiplies cell C4 on the March Orders worksheet in the Excel, EPA 04 workbook by cell C4 on the Current Exchange Rates worksheet in the Exchange Rates workbook. The reference to cell C4 in the Current Exchange Rates workbook cannot be absolute. If it is, delete the dollar signs in front of the C and in front of the 4.

7. Copy the formula in cell D4 on the March Orders worksheet in the Excel, EPA 04 workbook to cells D5 through D25.

8. Print the March Orders worksheet.

9. The exchange rate for Indian Rupees has changed. Key **0.02387** in cell C16 on the Current Exchange Rates worksheet in the Exchange Rates workbook. Save the workbook using the file name Updated Rates.

10. Switch to the Excel, EPA 04 worksheet and print it again.

11. Save the workbook.

12. Close the Exchange Rates workbook.

Assessment 5

1. Open Excel Worksheet 04.

2. Save the workbook using the Save <u>A</u>s command and name it Excel, EPA 05.

3. Create a custom header that has your name left-aligned and the file name right-aligned.

4. This worksheet contains the instruments sold at the Little Music Shop. The selling price of each instrument is based on a percentage markup. The percentage markup is found in the markup table. For example, if the cost of an instrument is between $0 and $400, the markup is 14%; if the cost of an instrument is between $400 and $500, the markup is 10%; and so on. Enter a formula in cell C4 that uses the VLOOKUP function to calculate the selling price of a bass. The selling price is calculated by multiplying the cost by the markup percentage and then adding that total to the original cost.

5. Copy the formula in cell C4 to cells C5 through C20.

6. Print the Instruments worksheet.

7. Save the workbook using the same name (Excel, EPA 05) and print it.

8. Close the Excel, EPA 05 workbook.

Assessment 6

1. Open Excel Worksheet 05.

2. Save the workbook using the Save <u>A</u>s command and name it Excel, EPA 06.

3. Create a custom header that has your name left-aligned and the file name right-aligned.

4. Linda Taylor wants to use this worksheet to calculate what the budget for May expenses should be. Format the worksheet using conditional formatting so that any value that is less than zero is displayed as red.

5. May's budget is going to be based on the differences between what was budgeted in April and what was actually spent. If the difference between the budgeted amount and what was actually spent is greater than or equal to zero, then the budget for May is going to be the same as the budget for April. If the difference between the budgeted amount and what was actually spent is less than zero, then the budgeted amount for May is going to be 8% greater than the budgeted amount for April. Enter an IF function in cell E10 that calculates May's budget for insurance.

6. Copy the IF function in cell E10 to cells E11 through E19.

7. Linda Taylor wants to know the total amount of money that was spent in April that was over the budgeted amounts. Enter a SUMIF function in cell D21 that adds together any number in cells D10 through D19 that is less than zero.

8. Save the workbook using the same name (Excel, EPA 06) and print it.

9. Close the Excel, EPA 06 workbook.

Assessment 7 *seven*

(Note: You may need to delete some files from your disk in order to have room for the following exercises. You may delete the following files: Excel Worksheet 01; Excel Worksheet 02; Excel Worksheet 03; Excel Worksheet 04; Excel Worksheet 05; Excel, EPA 01; Excel, EPA 02; Excel, EPA 03; Excel, EPA 03-a; Excel, EPA 03-b; Excel, EPA 04; Excel, EPA 05; and Excel, EPA 06. Check with your instructor to make sure it is all right to delete these files.)

1. Open Excel Worksheet 06.

2. Save the workbook using the Save As command and name it Excel, EPA 07.

3. Create a custom header that has your name left-aligned and the file name right-aligned.

4. The Little Music Shop uses this list to keep track of students taking music lessons. Use data validation to make it easier to enter more data into the list. The ID numbers are all exactly seven characters long. Use the Data Validation command to allow a text length equal to 7 for column A. Include an input message that has *ID #* for a title. The message should read *Enter 7-character ID number*. Include an error message that has *Error* for a title. The message should read, *The ID number must be exactly seven characters long*.

5. Use the Data Validation command to allow a text length equal to 2 for column F. Include an input message that has *State* for a title. The message should read *Enter the two-letter abbreviation for the state*. Include an error message that has *Error* for a title. The message should read *You must use the two-letter abbreviation for the state*.

6. Create a drop-down list for the data in column I. Create the list from the age groups listed in cells N4 through N8. Include an input message that has *Age Groups* for a title. The message should read *Select the age group from the drop-down list*. Include an error message that has *Error* for a title. The message should read *The age group must be selected from the drop-down list*.

7. Create a drop-down list for the data in column J. Create the list from the instruments listed in cells O4 through O19. Include an input message that has *Instrument* for a title. The message should read *Select the instrument from the drop-down list*. Include an error message that has *Error* for a title. The message should read *Instrument must be selected from the drop-down list*.

8. Use the Data Validation command to allow any whole number between 1 and 12 for column K. Include an input message that has *Level* for a title. The message should read *Enter the student's level, from 1 to 12*. Include an error message that has *Error* for a title. The message should read *The class level must be a whole number between 1 and 12*.

9. Starting in row 7, enter the following records into the list:

ID#	OA-3698
Last Name	O'Neill
First Name	Andrew
Address	35 Ridgewood Cir.
City	Parkfairfax
State	VA
Zip	22302
Phone	(703) 555-0980
Age	5-9
Instrument	Drums
Level	2

ID#	FC-3873
Last Name	Finn
First Name	Carol
Address	1909 Park Place Blvd.
City	Franconia
State	VA
Zip	22310
Phone	(703) 555-4498
Age	Over 25
Instrument	Flute
Level	9

ID#	CB-3698
Last Name	Corley
First Name	Betsy
Address	602 Mitchell St.
City	Wellington
State	VA
Zip	22308
Phone	(703) 555-6642
Age	15-19
Instrument	Oboe
Level	10

10. Change the orientation of the page to landscape.
11. Save the workbook using the same name (Excel, EPA 07) and print it.
12. Close the Excel, EPA 07 workbook.

Assessment 8 eight

1. Open Excel, EPA 07.
2. Save the workbook using the Save <u>A</u>s command and name it Excel, EPA 08.
3. Create a custom header that has your name left-aligned and the file name right-aligned.

4. Import the text file Students.txt, which is a delimited file that uses a tab as the delimiters. The data format for all the columns, except the column that lists the level of the student, is text. The column that lists the levels is *General*. The data should be entered into the existing worksheet starting at cell A10. *(Hint: Click* <u>D</u>*ata, point to Get External* <u>D</u>*ata, and then click Import Text File.)*
5. Adjust the width of the columns as needed so that all of the data is displayed.
6. Sort the data in alphabetical order by last name first and then by first name.
7. Maria Serrato has moved. Use a Data Form to find her record and edit the address to the following:

359 Rosewood Ct.

8. Create an AutoFilter to find everyone whose instrument is piano and whose level is 3. Change the left and right margins to 0.5ɬ. If necessary, change the page break so that columns *A* through *K* print on page 1. Print page 1 of the worksheet. Display all the records.
9. Create a custom AutoFilter to find everyone who is in a level above level 9. Print page 1 of the worksheet. Display all the records.
10. Create a custom AutoFilter to find everyone who plays either the violin or the cello. Print page 1 of the worksheet. Display all the records.
11. Turn the AutoFilter feature off.
12. Insert four blank rows above row 3. Adjust their height to 12.75.
13. Copy cells A7 through K7 to cells A2 through K2.
14. Name the range of cells A2 through K4 *Criteria*.
15. Use Advanced Filter to find the records of students who are either over 25 or who are in level 12. Print the first page of the worksheet.
16. Show all the records.
17. Use Advanced Filter to find all the records of students who are both level 12 and piano students. Print the first page of the worksheet.
18. Show all the records.
19. Save the workbook using the same name (Excel, EPA 08) and close it.

Assessment 9

1. Open Excel Worksheet 07.
2. Save the workbook using the Save <u>A</u>s command and name it Excel, EPA 09.
3. Create a PivotTable Report that uses the data in cells A3 through G30. Place the PivotTable on a new worksheet. Rename the new worksheet PivotTable Report.
4. Create a custom header for the PivotTable Report worksheet that has your name left-aligned and the file name right-aligned.
5. Drag the Country button into the Drop Row Fields Here area.
6. Drag the Item button to the Drop Row Fields Here area, under the Country button. When the PivotTable is displayed, the Item field should be to the right of the Country field.
7. Drag the Profit button to the Drop Data Items Here area.
8. Format the values in the Total column as currency with no decimal places.
9. Display only China and Saudi Arabia. Print the PivotTable Report worksheet.
10. Display all the countries. Print the PivotTable Report worksheet.

1. Open Excel Worksheet 08.
2. Save the workbook using the Save <u>A</u>s command and name it Excel, EPA 10.
3. There are three different work schedules for the employees of the bookstore, Books Galore. Each employee gets two days off in a row. At the top of the Employee Schedule worksheet are the three schedules. The zeros represent the days off for that schedule and the ones represent the days worked. Cells C7 through I7 will display the total staff needed for that day. Cells C8 through I8 display the average number of customers who come into the store on a particular day. Cells C9 through I9 display the number of employees needed for each day based on a staff to customer ratio of one employee for every 80 customers who come into the store in a day. Cell B11 displays that ratio. The owner of the bookstore wants a comparison of two staff to customer ratios. Her goal is to find the lowest total payroll cost while adequately staffing the bookstore. Click cell B13 and enter the daily salary amount for one employee, which would be the average hourly salary times the average hours worked in a day. The average hourly salary is $10.00 and the average hours worked in a day is 8.
4. Click cell A16. Enter the total payroll amount. The total payroll amount would be the total staff needed, which is found in cell B7, times the daily salary, which is found in cell B13.
5. Use Solver to find the minimum payroll amount. The target cell is the total payroll, which is found in cell A16. You want the target cell to be equal to the minimum value. The cells that can be changed are cells B3 through B5. The following constraints must be applied:

    The cells that can change (B3:B5) must be an integer.

    The cells that can change (B3:B5) must be greater than or equal to 0.

    The total staff (C7:I7) must be greater than or equal to the staffing demand (C9:I9).

    When Solver finds a solution, save it as a Scenario. Name the scenario *Staff/Customer ratio of 80 to 1*. Be sure to click the Restore <u>O</u>riginal Values option before leaving the Solver Results dialog box.
6. Change the Staff/Customer ratio to 100.
7. Use Solver to find the schedule that finds the minimum payroll amount at this new higher ratio. The constraints all stay the same from step 6. Save the results as a scenario. Name this scenario *Staff/Customer ratio of 100 to 1*. Be sure to click the Restore <u>O</u>riginal Values option before leaving the Solver Results dialog box.
8. Use the Scenarios command to print a summary of each saved scenario. In the Scenario Manager dialog box click *Staff/Customer Ratio of 80 to 1* and then click Summary. The report type you want is Scenario summary and the result cell is A16.

9. Create a custom header that has your name left-aligned and the file name right-aligned for the Scenario Summary worksheet. Change the orientation of the page to landscape.
10. Save the workbook using the same name (Excel, EPA 10) and print it.
11. Close the Excel, EPA 10 workbook.

Assessment 11 eleven

1. Open Excel Worksheet 09.
2. Save the workbook using the Save As command and name it Excel, EPA 11.
3. Create a custom header that has your name left-aligned and the file name right-aligned.
4. This worksheet lists some basic information on many of the cruises offered by the travel agency Travel Advantage. You want to create two filters for the list, save them as macros, and create a third macro that displays all the records. Then you will customize a toolbar by creating three buttons to run each of the macros. Click anywhere in the list. Display the Visual Basic toolbar and click the Record Macro button. When the Record Macro dialog box is displayed, name the macro Under_1500. Enter the letter **u** in the Shortcut key box. Click OK.
5. Use AutoFilter to display cruises on which the average price is less than $1,500.
6. Click the Stop Recording button.
7. Follow steps 4 through 6 to create a second macro that turns off the AutoFilter feature. Name the macro Display_all and enter **d** as a shortcut key.
8. Follow steps 4 through 6 to create a third macro that displays all the cruises that provide children's activities. Name the macro Children and enter **c** as a shortcut key.
9. Press Ctrl + d to display all the records.
10. Display the Forms toolbar. Click the Button button on the toolbar. When the mouse pointer turns into a crosshair, click and drag in the shaded blue area at the top of the worksheet to place the button. Assign the Under_1500 macro to this button. The button should be .40 inches high and .85 inches wide. Change the name on the button to Cruises Under $1500.
11. Create a second button and place it in the blue shaded area next to the first button. Assign the Children macro to this button. The button should be .40 inches high and .85 inches wide. Change the name on the button to Activities for Children.
12. Create a third button and place it in the blue shaded area next to the second button. Assign the Display_all macro to this button. The button should be .40 inches high and .85 inches wide. Change the name on the button to Display All.
13. Click the Activities for Children button. Print the Cruises worksheet.
14. Click the Display All button.
15. Click the Cruises Under $1500 button. Print the Cruises worksheet.
16. Click the Display All button.
17. Save the workbook using the same name (Excel, EPA 11) and close it.

Assessment twelve

1. Open Excel Worksheet 10.
2. Save the workbook using the Save <u>A</u>s command and name it Excel, EPA 12.
3. Create a custom header that has your name left-aligned and the file name right-aligned.
4. Redwood Community College offers some computer classes at two extensions. The head of the Computer Science department on the main campus wants the enrollment figures for both extensions. Two different instructors are in charge of each extension. You want to set up this worksheet as a shared worksheet so that each instructor can enter the appropriate enrollment figures. Then you will merge the two worksheets. Before you do that, however, you want to enter a comment. Attach the following comment to cell C10:

   Since this is the first semester this course is being offered at the extensions, enrollment figures are expected to be low.

   Resize the comment box so that all the text is displayed.
5. Set up the Excel, EPA 12 workbook as a shared workbook.
6. Start a second copy of Excel and open the Excel, EPA 12 workbook. Save this copy of the workbook using the Save <u>A</u>s command and name it North Branch.
7. Key the following values in the cells indicated:

Cell	Value
B5	185
B6	78
B7	123
B8	118
B9	69
B10	35

8. Save the workbook using the same name (North Branch). Exit from the second copy of Excel.
9. Switch to the Excel, EPA 12 workbook.
10. Save this copy of the workbook using the Save <u>A</u>s command and name it West Branch.
11. Key the following values in the cells indicated:

Cell	Value
C5	210
C6	96
C7	162
C8	149
C9	112
C10	58

12. Save the workbook using the same name (West Branch) and close it.

EXPERT

13. Open Excel, EPA 12. Merge the North Branch and West Branch workbooks into the Excel, EPA 12 workbook.
14. Remove the workbook from shared use.
15. Save the workbook using the same name (Excel, EPA 12) and print it.
16. Close the workbook.

WRITING ACTIVITIES

The following activities give you the opportunity to practice your writing skills along with demonstrating an understanding of some of the important Word and Excel features you have mastered in this and previous units. Use correct grammar, appropriate word choices, and clear sentence constructions.

Activity 1 one

The Oak Springs Animal Care Clinic needs a form that will be used to keep the records of each animal seen at the clinic. Create a template that includes spaces for entering the following information:

- Owner's name, address, city, state, Zip Code, home and work telephone numbers
- Pet's name, birth date, breed, and sex

If you want, insert the clinic's logo onto the form. The Oaksp.tif file contains the logo. In the space below this general information, include a chart that looks similar to the following:

Age	Date	CANINE						FELINE		
		Distemper	Hepatitis	Leptospirosis	Rabies	Parvovirus	Canine Cough	Distemper	Upper Res.	Rabies

Save the worksheet as a template using the file name Clinic.xlt. Use the template to complete a form for one animal. If you own a pet, use that information for completing the form. If not, use your name and address, but make up information on the pet. After the form has been filled out, save it and name it Excel, Act E1. Print and then close Excel, Act E1.

Activity 2 two

Georgia and Paul Sorenson, owners of the decorating business Primrose Decorators, offer discounts on large contracts they receive. Rename the *Sheet1* worksheet tab, Contract Discounts. Create a header that prints your name at the left margin and the file name at the right margin. On the Contract Discounts worksheet, include an appropriate title for the worksheet and key the following data:

Contract #	Contract Amount	Discount	Total after Discount
PD-7843	$15,000		
PD-7931	$4,000		
PD-7935	$60,000		
PD-7943	$72,000		
PD-7948	$8,000		
PD-7950	$68,000		
PD-7956	$12,000		
PD-6004	$45,000		
PD-6010	$82,000		
PD-6012	$35,000		

Rename the *Sheet2* worksheet tab, Lookup Table. For contracts under $10,000 there are no discounts, for contracts between $10,000 and $20,000 there is a 1% discount, for contracts between $20,000 and $40,000 there is a 2% discount, for contracts between $40,000 and $80,000 there is a 3% discount, and for contracts over $80,000, there is a 5% discount. On the Lookup Table worksheet, enter a lookup table that reflects these discounts.

Switch to the Contract Discounts worksheet. In the first cell in the Discount column, enter a VLOOKUP function that uses the table on the Lookup Table worksheet to look up the contract amount. The function should return the discount given for that amount. Copy the formula to find the discount for all the contracts.

In the first cell in the Total after Discount column, enter a formula that subtracts the appropriate discount percentage from the contract amount. Copy the formula to find the total after discount for all the contracts.

After the Contract Discounts worksheet is completed, save it and name it Excel, Act E2. Print and then close Excel, Act E2.

Activity 3 three

The owner of the restaurant the Waterfront Cafe wants to be able to project the amount of money the restaurant might make on any one night depending on how many people are seated during the night and the average price each person spends on his or her meal. Prepare a worksheet that includes an appropriate title and a header with your name at the left margin and the file name at the right margin. Save the workbook using the file name Excel, Act E3. Use the Scenarios command to set up a scenario for holidays (which is when the restaurant tends to do very well), average nights, and slow nights. Use the following information for setting up the scenarios.

EXPERT
E-317

The operating expense is $2,800, which is what it costs per evening to operate the restaurant.

- On holidays, the restaurant typically seats 725 people in an evening and the average cost of each meal is $14.00
- On an average night, the restaurant typically seats 600 people and the average cost of each meal is $10.00
- On a slow night, the restaurant typically seats 475 people and the average cost of each meal is $8.00.

Each scenario should include the income for the evening which would be the total amount of money taken in (the cost of each meal times the number of people seated) minus the operating expense for the evening.

Display and print each one of the scenarios (holidays, average nights, slow nights). Create a scenario summary. On the Scenario Summary worksheet, create a custom header that prints your name at the left margin and the file name at the right margin. Print the Scenario Summary worksheet. Save the workbook again using the same file name (Excel, Act E3) and close it.

Activity four

Import the text file Sheet Music.txt into an Excel worksheet starting in cell A1. The data in the Sheet Music.txt file is Delimited. Tabs were used as the delimiters. The data format for all of the columns is text, except for the last column, *Price*, which is General. Save the file as an Excel workbook using the file name Excel, Act E4. This is a partial list of the Little Music Shop's sheet music inventory. Format the headings *Song Title*, *Artist*, *Instrument*, *Level*, and *Price* as bold. Sheet music by the Beatles has become quite popular. Adjust the width of the columns as needed. Use conditional formatting so that every "Beatles" entry is displayed as bold and red. Since you will be adding more records to this list, make sure the conditional formatting applies to the entire worksheet.

Create three drop-down lists for entering data into the list. One drop-down list is for the Instrument column, one for the Level column and one for the Price column. There should be two items on the drop-down list for the Instrument column: *Piano* and *Guitar*. There should be three items on the drop-down list for the Level column: *Easy*, *Intermediate*, and *Hard*. There should be four items on the drop-down list for the Price column: *$1.95*, *$2.50*, *$3.25*, and *$3.95*. Include appropriate Input and Error messages for each drop-down list.

Add the following records to the list:

Song Title	Artist	Instrument	Level	Price
Can You Feel The Love Tonight	John, Elton	Piano	Easy	$1.95
Can You Feel The Love Tonight	John, Elton	Piano	Intermediate	$2.50
Can You Feel The Love Tonight	John, Elton	Guitar	Easy	$2.50
Can You Feel The Love Tonight	John, Elton	Guitar	Intermediate	$3.25
Can't Buy Me Love	Beatles	Guitar	Intermediate	$2.50
Can't Buy Me Love	Beatles	Piano	Intermediate	$2.50

Sort this list first by Song Title, next by Instrument, and finally by Level. Create a custom header that includes your name at the left margin and the file name at the right margin. Save the workbook again using the same file name (Excel, Act E4) and print it. Close the workbook.

Activity five

Open workbook Excel, Act E4. Using the Save As command, name the workbook Excel, Act E5. Insert 4 rows above the list for a criteria range. Copy the labels for the list to the first blank row. Name the range of cells that includes the labels and the first blank row under them (A1:E2) *Criteria*. Create a macro that uses Advanced Filter to filter the list to a new location, starting in G5. Extract from the records all the songs by the Beatles written for the guitar. Include as part of the macro optimizing the column widths for the extracted records and deleting the words *Beatles* and *Guitar* from the criteria range. Create a second macro that deletes anything entered in the range of cells G5 through K100. Create a third macro that uses Advanced Filter to filter the list to a new location, starting in G5. Extract from the records all the songs written for the piano that are easy. Include as part of the macro optimizing the column widths for the extracted records and deleting the words *Piano* and *Easy* from the criteria range.

Create a command button on the worksheet for each macro. Give each button an appropriate name. Filter the list using the command button that displays all the songs by the Beatles for the guitar. Print the list. Delete the extracted records using the appropriate command button. Filter the list using the command button that displays all the songs for the piano that are easy. Print the list. Delete the extracted records using the appropriate command button.

A music teacher has requested a list of sheet music that is for guitar and by the Beatles. Filter the list again using the appropriate command button. Start Word. Write a business letter to the instructor thanking him for his inquiry. The address for The Little Music Shop is 459 Sundance Square, Boulder, Colorado 80301. If you want, you can use The Little Music Shop's logo, which is the file Lilmusic.tif, as part of the letterhead. The name and address of the teacher requesting the information is Rodman Bates, 2285 10th Street, Boulder, Colorado 80301. Copy the filtered list from Excel into the business letter. Save the completed letter and name it Word, Act E5. Print and then close Word, Act E5. Display all the records in Excel using the appropriate command button. Save the list again using the same file name (Excel, Act E5) and close it.

INTERNET ACTIVITY

The Bookstore Books Galore is starting a special reading group for mothers and their daughters who are ages 9–12. Make sure you are connected to the Internet and then explore the following two sites:

- www.amazon.com
- www.barnesandnoble.com

Each of these sites provides a special section for "Kids." In each of these sections you can search for books that are of particular interest to children ages 9 to 12. The reading group is going to focus on historical adventure books. Use the keywords **adventure and history** to search these web sites for books that would appeal to girls ages 9 to 12. Select at least five books you think the mothers and daughters would enjoy reading. Take notes on the name of the book, the author, a brief description of what the book is about, and the price.

In Word prepare an announcement for the reading group. The announcement should include the name of each book and a brief description of what the book is about. If you want you can use the Books Galore logo, which is the file Booksgal.tif, as part of the announcement. The reading group is going to meet from 7:00 to 8:30 the first Monday of the month from October through February and is open to mothers and their daughters ages 9 to 12. The reading group will meet at Books Galore. The address of Books Galore is 138 Waterhouse Street, Cambridge, Massachusetts. The telephone number is (607) 555-1221. Print the announcement.

In Excel prepare a worksheet that lists each book's title, author, and price. Books Galore wants to put this worksheet on their web site. Publish this worksheet on the Web as a noninteractive worksheet. Provide it with an appropriate title. Print the web page.

Index